An Introduction to Anthropology

Gretel H. Pelto and Pertti J. Pelto

Department of Biocultural Anthropology / University of Connecticut

Macmillan Publishing Co., Inc.
New York

Collier Macmillan Publishers
London

For Deana and Isaac, Jenny and Jacob
Our first teachers of anthropological ideas

Macmillan Publishing Co., Inc.
866 Third Avenue, New York, New York 10022

Collier Macmillan Canada, Ltd.

Library of Congress Cataloging in Publication Data

Pelto, Gretel H.
    The human adventure.

    Bibliography: p.
    Includes index.
    1. Anthropology.   I. Pelto, Pertti J., joint author.
II. Title.
GN24.P36 1976   301.2   74-7710
ISBN 0-02-393550-2

Printing: 2345678   Year: 67890

Sacred and Secular Realms of Adaptation

Preface

An introductory text in anthropology needs to accomplish several objectives that include the presentation of the major current lines of theory and research and an overview of the background information—the basic evidence from which anthropologists generalize about human biocultural evolution and contemporary human behavior. It should also give the reader a sense of the contemporary scene of anthropologists at work, including recent breakthroughs, problems, and debates. Finally, anthropology as a scholarly community has a certain philosophy, a cross-cultural, comparative perspective, which we try to express in books such as this as a contribution to general education.

As a discipline, anthropology is presently undergoing a complicated revolution. Some of the force for this revolution arose from powerful social currents, including events of the Vietnam war period and the growing concern about "the limits of growth," environmental pollution, and energy shortages. The shift of research from isolated "tribal" peoples to include the study of urban, industrializing communities is also having a powerful impact on anthropological method and theory. A third factor is the increased conflict between the older, humanistic style of anthropological research and the ideas of a more mature science, involving careful research design, the use of statistics, and computerized data analysis.

From a perspective somewhere in the middle of this transformation in anthropology, it is hard to be confident about predicting trends—"when you're up to your ears in alligators it's hard to remember that you came out there to drain the swamp." It seems likely, however, that we have learned some lessons from the past. One of these is that the outcome of struggles between antithetical extremes very often results in a compromise—a synthesis made up of ideas and propositions from each of the main competing positions. Thus, for example, we foresee the development of a synthesis between the humanistic and the quantitative, scientific side of anthropology in which the strengths of the more intuitive style of fieldwork will be wedded to the discipline of an objective, hypothesis-testing science.

A main trend of great importance is the expanded

v

interest in human-environment relationships that has promoted a steady growth of the study of "human ecology" or "cultural ecology." This interest is especially evident in the "new archaeology," in which researchers are much more concerned than formerly with *systems* of ecological relationships among people, plants, animals, climates, and other social-cultural environmental features. In social-cultural anthropology the concern with ecological relationships has led to exciting new studies of social organization and has generated creative and innovative theories about the adaptive nature of human sociocultural systems.

Developments in physical anthropology have added to a pattern of scientific convergence—the growth of the biocultural approach. Physical anthropologists today focus much of their attention on the interaction of environmental, cultural, and genetic factors in systems of human adaptations to arctic cold, high altitude, the tropics, and other habitats. In medical anthropology, biological and cultural anthropologists often work together to analyze problems of disease, nutrition, and health care.

Another significant trend is the growing concern with the study of social inequalities. Before the mid-1960s anthropological research and theory were relatively little concerned with questions of power, differential access to resources, social stratification, and the effects of colonialist expansion of the major Western powers. Now much more attention is directed to social and political conflict, rapid social change, the spread of "Westernization" and worldwide commercial and political influences into isolated regions, and human reactions to oppression and subordination.

Related to this change is the declining interest in "customs," "stable norms," and other abstracted constructs that fail to note the roles of individuals in shaping their own social patterns—by active processes of cultural selection, innovation, and experimentation. New theoretical concepts built up around ideas of individual-centered social networks, intracultural diversity, social pluralism, and other actor-oriented research have come to the fore as older ideas of static cultures and societies in equilibrium are abandoned.

In this introduction to anthropology we have tried to present the materials of the field and a view of the discipline that is congruent with these contemporary trends. Throughout the text we have taken a biocultural point of view wherever theoretical relevance and available materials permitted it. Some chapters are mainly biological, others mainly cultural, but each major section includes some interrelating of the two perspectives. For example, the discussion of language includes attention to the biocultural evolution of human language capacity and considers the implications of chimpanzee language capabilities. Part Five, on social organization, includes a chapter on female and male role behavior, with an examination of biological theories on this topic. In Part Six, after discussing ideational and symbolic realms of human behavior, we return to a biocultural perspective in "Disease, Diet, and Medical Practice."

A biocultural approach is also implicit in much of the final section, and our effort to prepare a textbook attuned to contemporary anthropology is perhaps most visible in our treatment of the major problems of population, energy, and pollution, as well as in our concern with changing styles and strategies of social movements and revolutions. Since the study of these phenomena is not well advanced in our discipline, we can only present some general ideas on these topics, urging the newer generation of anthropologists to take up the scientific exploration of these as social-ecological problems.

In recent years there have been rapid changes in peoples' perspectives and self attitudes, reflected in changes in language and labels. We feel that anthropologists should be sensitive to the social implications of these word-use issues and therefore we have tried to shape the language of this text to fit with the social realities of the 1970s. In this book we will try to describe human culture and history without the constant irritating presence of expressions like "man and his works," "mankind," and other markers of male dominance. We have also taken a few small steps toward using names for ethnic groups which reflect their social identity. In some areas groups seeking to reaffirm their identity and social worth have sought to discard the Euro-American-originated labels, labels that carry, however subtly, pejorative connotations. Thus we will use the term *Inuit* to refer to the peoples known widely as the *Eskimo.* (In Quebec the association Inuksiutiit Katimajiit, Inc., is working actively to bring the name *Inuit* into wider usage and to discourage the use of the term *Eskimo.*) Similarly, we will refer to the

Same, rather than to the *Lapps* (of northern Europe), as these peoples, too, are now quite clear about their preference. In coming years there will, no doubt, be many other changes in cultural labels, and we hope that these will come to be reflected not only in anthropological usage but also in general public media.

Often introductory texts present a picture of an already fully studied world. Our intent here is to raise awareness of the many, many unresolved questions. Some of these questions can be pursued by undergraduates, and we strongly urge teachers of undergraduates to direct their students into research projects—not just in the library, but in the "real world." In our experience, freshmen and sophomores are often keen observers of their social worlds and enter college study with many questions and much insight. They are often sensitive to problems of scientific evidence and suspicious of the superficiality of one-shot questionnaires and description based on two or three key informants. The experience of seeking information that goes beyond the immediate and obvious and of matching one's own data against the arguments and concepts of others in the classroom can be the first step toward a productive career in the social sciences.

Like everyone who tries to present an overview of his or her field in an introductory textbook, we owe the largest debt to fellow members of our discipline—the anthropologists past and present who have generated the data, developed and tested the theories that collectively make up the body of knowledge of contemporary anthropology. But we also have specific debts, and we wish to thank Paul Doughty, John Gumperz, Edward Hunt, Jr., J.

Anthony Paredes, Ronald P. Rohner, Willis Sibley, and Stephen Zegura for their thoughtful comments, criticisms, and suggestions. (We hasten to exempt them from whatever errors or omissions we have committed despite their suggestions.) For the use of their photographs, we wish to acknowledge Stuart Berde, Gerald Berreman, Frank Cancian, Paul Doughty, Gerald Gold, Deana Hoffman, William S. Laughlin, Lyn Miles, Ludger Müller-Wille, Gary Palmer, J. Anthony Paredes, Andrei Simič, and Geza Teleki. We acknowledge special thanks to Ken Scott of Macmillan who not only spent many hours in search of photographs, but encouraged, exhorted, and otherwise helped to see the long task of writing this book through to completion.

Karen Singer and Laurine Ford worked intelligently and for many hours helping us put together illustrations and bibliography, and we appreciate their excellent work.

Authors often acknowledge the help of someone "without whom this book could never have been written." In that vein, our debt to Frances Hayward is very great. Without her keen intelligence, sharp criticisms, and warm support, not to mention her great skill in transcribing tapes and manuscripts into intelligible English, we would indeed have had difficulty in completing this book.

Finally, we want to thank our sons, Jonathan and Ari, who patiently (and sometimes not so patiently) lived with several years of "The Book," developing in the course of it a serious interest in "the way things work" in human behavior and society.

G. H. P.
P. J. P.

Contents

x

Contents

Part
One

The aim of anthropology is to understand the human animal and its place in the natural order of things. The information that we need to accomplish this goal comes from many different sources, including the accumulated data about the human past (evidenced in fossil remains and archaeological excavations) and comparative studies of our closest animal relatives. The evidence of bygone humanity must be interpreted in relation to the living present. All the varieties of human societies and lifeways that are found in the world today can be related to the evolution of human biological characteristics and behavioral (cultural) systems. If we can put these two parts together in a coherent, unified theory we will be able to explain and understand the varieties of human activity, and we will have the keys for predicting at least portions of our future.

At the present time, however, we are very far from achieving these grand goals. We still have a great deal to learn about the details of past history. Furthermore, the description and analysis of contemporary sociocultural systems are, as yet, rather unsystematic.

On the other hand, because of the large amount of research and information gathering that has been carried out in the social and biological sciences during the past hundred years, we have enough general information about the varieties of human behavior and biological characteristics to provide us with a frame of reference and a theoretical strategy for developing a unified anthropological science. Nevertheless, some aspects of research in anthropology will require a good deal of refinement, and portions may have to be discarded altogether. In all sciences, the general frame of reference within which scientists operate is a provisional one, subject to possibly drastic revision with new discoveries and theoretical breakthroughs.

The Idea of Evolution

Over the centuries many naturalists have suggested that there has been a general EVOLUTION of living things from single-celled organisms to complex multicelled animals. The Greek Anaximander (611–547 B.C.) was one of the first theoreticians to suggest a sequence of forms—beginning with the first life that arose from the mud as it was warmed by the sun's rays, followed by plants, then animals,

Human Evolution and Adaptation: Basic Principles

1.1 In 1859 Charles Darwin made public his theory that all living forms have evolved from simple, one-celled life forms. (Courtesy of the American Museum of Natural History)

1.2 *H.M.S. Beagle* was Darwin's home for five years (1831–36) in one of the most rewarding scientific expeditions ever undertaken. (Courtesy of the American Museum of Natural History)

and climaxed by the development of humans. In Anaximander's scheme of things, as in all evolutionary systems since that time, we find the proposal that humans are relative newcomers on earth.

Although the general idea of the evolution of living forms is an old one, it was not until the nineteenth century that a workable explanation for the processes of evolution was developed. In 1859 Charles Darwin made public his theory that all living forms have evolved from simple, one-celled life forms through processes of NATURAL SELECTION.[1]

[1] The idea of evolution made famous by Darwin was developed independently by Alfred Russel Wallace at approximately the same time. In *The Death of Adam*, John Greene has a fascinating account of the history of this parallel invention.

The theory is based on the well-founded assumption that there is a good deal of individual variation *within* any plant or animal species. In an animal species the variations may take the form of differences in size, strength, acuteness of vision, coloration, resistance to diseases, preferences for particular foods, and a nearly endless list of other characteristics. Darwin reasoned that within this range of variation in any species *some* characteristics increase an individual animal's likelihood of surviving to maturity and having offspring. As a simple illustration, the rabbit that can run faster than its brothers, sisters, and cousins is more likely to escape its enemies and thus is more likely to live long enough to have offspring and to transmit its biological characteristics to ensuing generations.

A second essential element in Darwin's great theory is that the environments within which animals must survive are themselves quite varied. The SURVIVAL ADVANTAGE of any given characteristic depends upon the specific environment within which

Introduction to Anthropology: The Fieldwork Enterprise

the animal is living. In a very dry environment, individuals that are capable of maintaining themselves on relatively infrequent water supplies are likely to have a selective advantage over thirstier members of their species. We must keep in mind, by the way, that the focus of attention in this matter of natural selection is on differences in survival *within* a species rather than on the competition among *different* species. Although Darwin himself used some confusing language that seemed to emphasize "the survival of the fittest" among different kinds of animals within a particular locale, the focus of his theory of natural selection was primarily on the ways in which small differences *within* a single species can, through successive generations of small changes, be enhanced and expanded to produce new types or species.

The case of Darwin's finches of the Galapagos Islands provides an excellent illustration of this idea.

The Finches of the Galapagos

As a young naturalist Darwin visited the Galapagos Islands in 1835. These islands, located about six hundred miles off the west coast of South Amer-

ica, have a unique constellation of flora and fauna, although some of the birds and other animals found there are related to types of animals on the mainland of South America. Among the most interesting of these animals are the finches, for on the islands there are several different kinds that are similar to one another except for the shapes of their beaks. Some of them have beaks that are adapted to feeding on large seeds, others have strong, woodpeckerlike beaks for feeding on larvae, still another species has a parrotlike beak for feeding on buds and fruits, and there are several other types as well.

Another essential fact that Darwin noted was that there were very few other kinds of birds in the Galapagos competing with the finches for the available food supplies. He reasoned that at some point finches from the mainland of South America had strayed to the Galapagos, perhaps carried by high winds, and there they found few natural competitors. As the finches multiplied and "took over" the island, variations among individual finches offered the birds different degrees of selective advantage in the different MICROENVIRONMENTAL NICHES in the islands. For example, finches that had somewhat longer and stronger beaks tended to have a selective

Warbler finch
Certhidea olivacea

A cactus-eating finch
Geospiza scandens

Woodpecker finch
Camarhynchus pallidus

An insect-eating finch
Camarhynchus psittacula

Geospiza magnirostris
A seed-eating finch

Cocos Island finch
Pinaroloxias inornata

1.3 The finches on the Galapagos Islands evolved into several different species as they adapted to various environmental niches. The different shapes of beaks are specializations for varied food-getting styles.

Human Evolution and Adaptation: Basic Principles

advantage in locations where insect larvae were particularly plentiful. We can say that the great availability of the insect larvae offered a selective force for a particular type of bird beak. In time, through the continued intermating of those finches that had the special selective advantages within a particular microenvironment, these (at first) minor variations among the birds became fixed. A number of species developed, all of them descended from a single ancestral species from the mainland.

In the example of the finches the major event that set off the accumulation of changes leading to the development of different species was that some birds strayed into a new and very open environment.

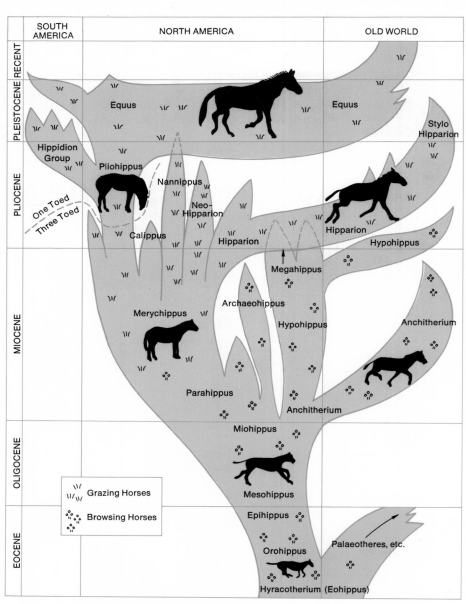

1.4 During the past 50 million years the ancestors of the modern horse evolved from a small, multitoed leaf-eater into a larger, grass-eating animal adapted to swift running in open country.

Gradual change in climate is another probable cause of evolutionary changes in plants and animals. The evolution of the horse provides an interesting illustration. Several million years ago, during the geological epoch called the MIOCENE, the ancestors of the modern horse changed their way of life from browsing on leaves and shoots to grazing on grasslands. As the famous geneticist Dobzhansky stated it:

It was not a fortuitous chance that the switch from browsing to grazing took place in horse evolution during the Miocene. [Earlier] most of the earth enjoyed warm and humid climates. Tropical evergreen and temperate broad-leaved forests were the widespread types of vegetation, and they offered ample food to browsing horses. But as time went on, the climates tended to become cooler, and in many parts of the world also drier. Grassy steppes, prairies, and savannas were becoming more and more widespread. And yet, during Miocene, few animals, or at least few mammals, were adapted to utilize grass as their main diet. Grass is very harsh food, and the low-crowned teeth of the browsing horses would have been worn down to the gums by tough grass. Merychippus [one of these ancient horses] evolved teeth which enabled it to feed on grass, and its descendants "inherited the earth," or at least the grass-covered part of it. But the new way of life necessitated also qualities other than high-crowned teeth. On grassy plains animals can be seen from greater distances than in forests. Accordingly, natural selection favored larger, stronger, and faster grazing horses, which could defend themselves or could escape from their enemies. (DOBZHANSKY, 1955:304)

This illustration shows another important aspect of the concept of natural selection and evolution. It is the commonsensical notion that "one thing leads to another." The ancestors of the horse were quite small animals—no more than a couple of feet high. The change, through natural selection, that brought about grass eating also set in motion a chain of further changes, including the very slow and gradual development of the special hoof form so important to the speed of the modern race horse. Almost any alterations in environmental circumstances, even rather small ones, can produce conditions that lead to new modifications of existing plant and animal species. Of course, these changes do not automatically *cause* the evolution of new species, and if new types of living things do come about because of altered environmental conditions, the process is a very slow one requiring many generations to complete. The idea of evolution through natural selection requires thinking in terms of very long periods of time to account for the evolution of distinctly different animal forms. This is especially true among larger animals, which usually require many years for each new generation.

Many refinements have been made in evolutionary theory since the time of Darwin, especially in the development of knowledge about the specific genetic processes by means of which changes occur. Biologists in recent decades have tended more and more to discard the imagery of "nature red in tooth and claw" in explaining natural selection, especially the idea that inferior species are eliminated totally by superior species of animals. Some species of animals and plants have been eliminated from the face of the earth by unusual concatenations of environmental events, but the more important aspect of evolution through natural selection is the constant tendency for environmental factors to eliminate *individuals* with less "favorable" characteristics in favor of those that carry traits that are better adapted to their particular environment.

Adaptation

The concept of ADAPTATION is one of the most important elements in the general idea of evolution. Because it is used extensively by people in both the biological and the social sciences, the term *adaptation* has come to assume a number of different meanings. The core of this concept rests on two assumptions: (1) all living things are in dynamic interaction with their environments and (2) the processes of change brought about through natural selection have survival value. In the example of the changes in tooth patterns among ancient horses we can talk about the general process by which the horses developed these new biological features as a gradual *adaptation* to a new environmental situation. We can say that the animals became adapted to a new way of life based on grazing. At the same time, the term can be used to refer to the biological feature that developed through the change process, so we can say that "The size and shape of the teeth in horses are *adaptations* to grazing."

In this example the mechanism of change was GENETIC; the evolution of new biological charac-

7

1.5 Humans have adjusted to a very wide range of environments, from the rush and stress of urban life to the cold and loneliness of the Far North. (Matthew Klein, Magnum)

(Courtesy of the American Museum of Natural History)

8

teristics took place through the operation of natural selection acting on the hereditary characteristics of the animals. In anthropology we use the term *adaptation* in two main ways. One primary meaning of the term refers to genetic mechanisms of change, as in the case of the horses' teeth. To help keep our meaning clear, we will call this *adaptation₁*, defined as follows:

> *adaptation₁*: the process of genetic (heritable) modification in some feature of an organism— morphological, physiological, or behavioral— that serves some end (food getting, escape, and so on) and that contributes in some way to the increased likelihood of survival, and hence the reproduction of individuals carrying this particular biological feature.

The second meaning of adaptation (which we will label *adaptation₂*) refers to modifications of behavior or physical characteristics that are brought about through nongenetic mechanisms. We can say that individuals *adapt* physiologically to aspects of environment (such as heat, cold, and altitude), disease, and diet, and we can also talk about the vast complex of learned behavior of humans in terms of its adaptive value. This meaning of *adaptation₂* can be defined as:

> *adaptation₂*: the process of nongenetic modification of behavior or physiological and morphological functioning that serves some end and that contributes to the likelihood of survival (or more effective functioning) of the individual (or group) that develops the modification.

The following list provides some examples of the many types of situations involving adaptation₂:

1. Humans generally adapt to cold climates by means of warm clothing and heated shelters.
2. People who live at very high altitudes (e.g., in the Andes of South America) develop large lung capacities as an adaptation to the lack of oxygen.
3. Goats can adapt themselves to a variety of different food sources.
4. John adapted to the loss of his job by going to live with relatives.
5. The dog adapted well to living in the same house with a cat.

6. City dwellers must become adapted to increasing amounts of noise and air pollution.
7. When the American pioneers left their homes to go west they had to develop new ways of adapting to conditions on the prairies.
8. The bilateral, flexible social organization of the Bushmen of the Kalahari is an adaptation to the variable and uncertain food sources of their desert environment.

These examples of behavioral and physiological adaptation all have one thing in common: the modifications are *not* transmitted to future generations through the sex cells. In the nineteenth century some theorists of evolution, including Darwin himself, believed that some acquired physical adaptations could be transmitted to the next generation. This is the well-known idea of LAMARCKIAN INHERITANCE.[2] More recently, some Russian geneticists, led by Trofim Denisovich Lysenko, revived this discredited idea for a time; however, modern evolutionary evidence is practically all on the side of natural selection.

We note that these nongenetic adaptations include at least two distinct types: (1) physical characteristics (e.g., calluses, well-developed muscles) that develop during the life of an individual in response to environmental conditions and (2) behavioral modifications, learned as habits or techniques and that may be taught by one generation to the next. It is especially this second type of nongenetic adaptation that is the basis of the complicated history of CULTURAL EVOLUTION, which makes up one major aspect of anthropological study. Anthropologists are interested in learning about the past adaptations of people that have led to the present patterns of human culture and society. At the same time, they want to use this information from the past for understanding the present, and they want to understand the principles of human (nongenetic) adaptation as they are expressed in contemporary living populations. Different human lifeways—the subject matter of cultural anthropology—present a bewild-

[2]Named for the nineteenth-century French naturalist Jean Baptiste de Monet Lamarck, who believed in the inheritance of acquired characteristics. According to this view, the lifelong neck-stretching of a giraffe browsing for tree leaves can result in physiological changes that are passed on to the individual's offspring.

Human Evolution and Adaptation: Basic Principles

ering variety of customs and traditions, but underlying this diversity are general principles of human adaptation that help make sense and order of both human history and the present sociocultural world map.

Unfortunately most research and writing about "human nature" have tended to concentrate on either biological evolution and adaptation or cultural, nongenetic qualities of *Homo sapiens,* as if these are quite separate realms. We feel that the two sides—the biological and the behavioral—are two aspects of a single whole: the totality of human BIOCULTURAL EVOLUTION. In the following chapters we will focus alternately on the biological facts and on sociocultural patterns, but these two bodies of information should be understood and studied together for a fuller understanding of ourselves, *Homo sapiens.*

Nongenetic Adaptations Can Be Both Evolutionary and (R)evolutionary

Until recent decades biologists have disagreed on the question of whether the evolution of new species of animals might occur in the form of rare, but striking, "leaps" of genetic mutation. Subscribers to the SALTATION theory (now largely discredited) held that the development of new species in biologi-

1.6 "Dropping out of the rat race" and taking up a communal life style represents an adaptive alternative for some young North Americans. (Dennis Stock, Magnum)

10

cal evolution took place through large, qualitative changes in genetic patterns. The more accepted view today is that nearly all biological evolutionary developments among the animals have occurred through the accumulation of small, step-by-step changes.

However, the emphasis on gradual change should not be taken to mean that all change is uniformly slow. The fossil record indicates that rates of change in different organisms vary widely. During the geological epoch known as the PLEISTOCENE (see Table 3.1), rates of evolutionary change in mammals varied tenfold (KURTEN, 1968). Some forms of reptiles (e.g., some lizards) have become so established in their particular environmental niches that they have shown very little evolutionary modification for millions of years. On the other hand, many animals have experienced extensive changes in a scant million years or less.

One of the main factors in explaining the relatively slow pace of evolutionary change is that most GENETIC MUTATIONS[3] are harmful to the organisms that experience them, and the larger the degree of genetic change the more likely that the modification will lead to the death of the individual bearer of the new physical trait.

Nongenetic adaptations, particularly in learned behaviors, are much less likely to have lethal consequences. New, learned adaptations are less threatening for a rather simple reason—the individual who tries them can stop and change its behavior back to the original if the actions prove to have dangerously negative consequences. No such back-to-the-original is possible in the case of genetic mutations. Therefore nongenetic adaptation is much more flexible than genetic mutation, as long as the animal experiencing it has the brain power to learn and assimilate new behavior patterns.

It follows that human adaptation through learned behavior can sometimes be quite revolutionary. Our definition (adaptation₂) applies to *any* modification of behavior, large or small. By this definition, a slight variation in a person's day-to-day routine may count as an instance of adaptive behavior, but so does the decision to "drop out of the rat race" and take on a totally different life style, such as subsistence farming. Each is adaptive behavior for the individual

if the consequences are experienced as furthering well-being and survival. Groups may adapt through small adjustments of behavior, perhaps by expanding their territory into previously unexploited lands. On the other hand, the Russian Revolution—and other similar massive upheavals and transformations of social systems—can also be seen as adaptations, however MALADAPTIVE they may be for the losers in the political-social struggle!

Adaptation in human biocultural evolution is neither inherently conservative nor markedly radical. It is neither active nor passive. Rather, it is the entire gamut of modifications and transformations, great and small, that over centuries and millennia have so profoundly transformed human lifeways and the physical-biological nature of *Homo sapiens*.

The Evolutionary Frame of Reference

Ideas of biological and cultural evolution have become more and more accepted as the general frame of reference for all of anthropology and the related social sciences. Theoretical developments and research results of the past decade have led to the greatly increased acceptance of this perspective. Since this is the frame of reference we are using here, the terms *adaptation* and *adapted*, and occasionally, *maladaptive* or *maladapted*, will occur frequently in this book. (The context will usually make clear which of the two general meanings is intended.)

Much of our discussion about the varieties of human behavior will be based on the assumption that humans are rational animals who modify their behavior in a constant search for more rewarding and successful adjustment to their environments. However, we do not assume that all individuals and groups are successful and well adapted. Furthermore, it is frequently true that actions which are adaptive for some people within a society (or for some nations) are seriously maladaptive in terms of their consequences for other members of the society (or other nations.) In this book we will be looking not only at some of the ways in which people organize to exploit their environments but also at the ways in which they organize to exploit each other.

It has been a step forward for anthropological theory that, to an increasing extent, researchers look

[3] A mutation is a change in the genetic message (within the genes and chromosomes), which results in a variation or change in a genetically controlled characteristic.

Human Evolution and Adaptation: Basic Principles

at various parts of behavioral systems in terms of their fit into total adaptation systems. On the other hand, we have to be careful not to assume that every behavior or "custom" has a positive adaptive function. Often we do not know the adaptive significance, if any, of particular traits or characteristics. At all levels, from individual biological functioning to international relations, the systems researchers are trying to understand are overwhelmingly complex, and, at the present time, knowledge is frustratingly limited.

The nature and degree of adaptational significance of any particular human behavior cannot be judged simply through armchair, logical exercise. A behavioral system has to be studied in relation to environmental conditions and other behavioral systems. All of this requires painstaking firsthand research.

The study of human behavioral systems usually takes the anthropologist into intensive fieldwork. More than any other human science, anthropology has developed as a study involving interaction with people in their natural habitats. Fieldwork is not the only type of anthropological research, and many of the best studies include a good deal of historical, archival, and other nonpersonalized information-gathering. Some research is based on comparative analysis of already published studies. But the idea of fieldwork is the hallmark of anthropology, and it makes good sense for us to begin, in the next chapter, with an overview of how anthropologists go about their research activities.

Introduction to Anthropology: The Fieldwork Enterprise

Anthropology, the study of *Homo sapiens,* is particularly characterized by the importance of fieldwork as a basic research activity. Each science has its own typical styles of collecting information: psychologists tend to do much of their research in laboratory settings, using experimental subjects. Historians often gather information of the past from the old letters, documents, and manuscripts of archives and libraries. Sociologists frequently conduct research using census records and other bodies of social data collected from samples of people in various communities, especially in North American society. And the image of the anthropologist is of a person who packs up clothing, tape recorders, notebooks, and cameras and goes to live for a period of time in some society or community different and distant from his or her familiar home base. Cultural anthropologists, much more than other types of social and biological researchers, travel to Africa, South America, the islands of the South Seas, and other supposedly exotic places to study the lifeways and characteristics of people whose cultural behaviors and technologies are very different from those familiar to us in urban, industrialized settings.

Fieldwork is also the principal research style of archaeologists. They, too, generally travel to distant places, instead of to the library or nearby laboratory, when they are engaged in primary information-gathering. Anthropological linguists, interested in describing and analyzing the intricacies of language systems different from our own, also do much of their data collecting in fieldwork settings. Physical anthropologists, who represent the biological side of anthropology, go to field locations to search for fossil materials as well as to gather information about the biological characteristics of living populations.

No wonder, then, that anthropology is sometimes labeled "the fieldwork profession," and those few anthropologists who have not gone out to do fieldwork are somewhat looked down on as having failed to undergo the "initiation rites" into anthropology.

During the 1960s and 1970s there has been a rapid growth of anthropological study in contemporary urban settings, aimed at gaining greater understanding of cultural institutions and social organization of modern, industrialized society. The places where anthropologists do fieldwork now include inner-city slums, hospitals, factories, and even middle-class suburbs. Of course, when anthropolo-

Fieldwork: The Hallmark of Anthropology

2.1 The fieldworker's notebook and pencil are primary working tools. Anthropologist John Lozier in a Mexican rural community. (P. J. Pelto)

2.2 H. Russell Bernard shares a bowl of *pulque* (fermented drink made from the sap of the maguey plant) with his informants. (P. J. Pelto)

gists direct their attention to studying social and cultural institutions close to home, they are more likely to encounter sociologists and other types of social scientists engaged in closely related research. Some examples of anthropological research in North American and European cultural systems include studies of "kinship and social networks among families in London," "street-corner men in Washington's inner city," "the psychiatric hospital as a small society," "a French suburb," and a growing number of works on American school classrooms.

A primary means of information-gathering in anthropology is through direct interaction with people. Much fieldwork, in fact, takes the form of extensive participation in the day-to-day scenes of other people's communities, so that much of anthropological information is derived from direct observation of behavior, along with informal conversations. Often this mode of research requires that the anthropologist learn the language of the people he studies—which usually is a good deal different from the "book version."

In order to carry out this face-to-face style of research successfully, the fieldworker must become well known and liked, or at least accepted, by the people he studies. The fieldworker tries to become so much a part of the society that the people will regard him (or her) as a kind of "insider," whom they can trust and with whom they will behave in a natural manner.

As the cultural anthropologist Morris Freilich has expressed it, the anthropologist attempts to become a "marginal native"—not absolutely integrated into the community in every sense, but temporarily accepted. Immersion in the daily life of a community takes many forms, as in the following statements by fieldworkers:

1. Hortense Powdermaker (research in Lesu, Melanesia):

Although my competence in the language increased, I never became expert in it. But my friends were so pleased at my trying to learn their language that they exaggerated my ability to use it. (POWDERMAKER, 1966:66)

2. Morris Freilich (research in Trinidad):

My rapport-getting was much facilitated by my ability to play an adequate game of cricket. The British had introduced cricket to Trinidad, and the sport was popular with young and old. My knowledge of the game soon brought me into contact with Mr. Ed . . . [whose] house was a hangout for many of the Creole peasants. (FREILICH, 1970:214)

14

Introduction to Anthropology: The Fieldwork Enterprise

3. John J. Honigmann (research in northwestern Canada):

My field work among the Kaska was the most personally satisfying and ethnographically productive I have ever conducted. Both my wife and I were caught up in another culture as we never have been again. In terms of the larger Canadian society's social norms it happened to be a "delinquent culture" (by which I mean that the young people zestfully pursued activities that they knew were contrary to the larger society's norms and laws . . .), but this hardly detracted from our ability to identify with many of its values; perhaps it even added to the flavor of the life we enjoyed. (HONIGMANN, 1970:45)

4. Norman E. Whitten, Jr. (research among Blacks in Ecuador):

I relaxed with the people, too, visiting homes, saloons, cantinas, and taking part in every group activity that I could, always being careful, however, to participate as much as possible as a Negro of my approximate age would, not as a "community leader" such as a priest or political official. I learned to dance folk and national dances in the *costeño* style, and I learned the rudiments of drumming and marimba playing. (WHITTEN, 1970:352–353)

5. Aram Yengoyan (research in the Philippines):

At first, I established rapport primarily through the male elders in Pagpawan, who introduced me to different household members and explained why I was there. . . . I always inquired about crops, cropping activities, and techniques utilized, for I found these topics provided the best means to start my work. . . . The Mandaya are very detail conscious and always asked me if I had recorded all details correctly. (YENGOYAN, 1970:410)

6. Gloria Marshall (fieldwork among the Yoruba in Nigeria):

A relatively small group of women, ranging in age from about twenty-five to forty, became my friends. We used the term "ore" (literally, "friend") as one would use a personal name. Each of them referred to me, and addressed me, by that name, and I used the same name for each of them. When I wanted to distinguish among them, I spoke of *ore* from such and such a compound. This was the group of women for whom I did special favors (such as driving them to distant towns or lending them money), with whom I gossiped, to whom I went for advice, and who gave me all kinds of assistance and information relating to my research. (MARSHALL, 1970:179)

7. Ann Fischer (fieldwork among the Trukese in Micronesia):

2.3 Participant observation in the field. Ethnological fieldworkers try their hand at many different activities in the process of learning about peoples' cultural ways. (Gary Palmer)

During my stay in Mwan I was pregnant. This condition was very useful in terms of my field work—the subject of which was the Trukese mother—since the physiological experience of pregnancy was explained and commented upon by the Trukese about me. The physiological process also brought to mind many questions that I might not otherwise have thought to ask. My husband and I were given much advice about how we should behave under the circumstances. (FISCHER, 1970:267)

2.4 **The tape recorder is invaluable in gathering extensive interview material. J. Anthony Paredes with Creek informant in Mississippi.** (Roger Ball)

16

Collecting Information: Some Techniques of Fieldwork

Anthropologists generally explain their research intentions to the local people, who are usually well aware of the fact that the researchers are collecting information that will be used to write books and to teach students in the anthropologists' home communities. Most people, in most parts of the world, have been fairly cooperative and have generally approved of the idea that their particular community became the subject of this kind of attention. In recent times, however, especially among people who have been repeatedly revisited by many different anthropologists and other researchers (e.g., some of the American Indian reservations), negative attitudes have developed as the feeling has grown that they are being exploited, as little of benefit to them seems to be forthcoming from the research efforts. Also, fears have grown that the information collected by anthropologists might be used by government agents and others in ways to cause harm.

In addition to data from direct observation, fieldworkers rely on the hundreds of conversations they engage in with local people. Sometimes these conversations are completely open and undirected, while at other times the fieldworker systematically explores some particular area of information, especially with KEY INFORMANTS.[1] Because the key informants are never a fully representative sample of a local population, the anthropologist must be very careful to avoid distortions of information, as informants present their own personalized and subjective versions of the complexities of local behavior.

To guard against biases, the fieldworker often collects information from *samples* of people by means of *structured interviews*. These structured interviews are often used to gather data on household and family composition, occupations, types of landholdings, participation in various types of activities, and a host of other details. In cases in which the research communities are quite small, fieldworkers sometimes collect structured data from every house-

[1] Most anthropologists develop special relationships with a number of different, well-informed persons in the research community, who take on the role of information givers and information seekers for the anthropologist. These key informants are often the main sources of information beyond the direct observations made by the anthropologist.

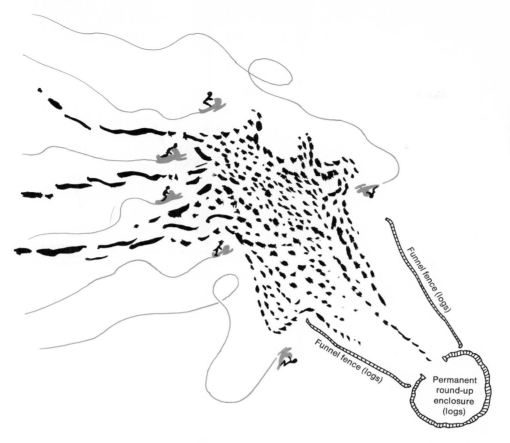

2.5 This schematic drawing depicts reindeer herder Arto Sverloff's view of the organization of a reindeer drive utilizing snowmobiles. Fieldworkers often ask key informants to draw maps, keep records, and construct diagrams to explain or amplify their verbal reports.

Funnel fence (logs)

Funnel fence (logs)

Permanent round-up enclosure (logs)

hold. This is a time-consuming process, and local research assistants are usually hired to help with the work.

Concerning this point the British anthropologist John Beattie (in his book, *Understanding an African Kingdom: Bunyoro*) reported that:

During 1953 I used these forms, each of which took about an hour to complete, in carrying out house-to-house surveys in Kihoko (nearly two years after I had first settled there), in Kasingo, and Kisindizi, in the north of the district. In 1955 I carried out a further smaller survey in the village of Tonya on the Lake Albert shore. I received a good deal of help from my assistants, but I did most of the interviewing and recording myself. We covered, fairly completely, all the households in the three upland villages, forty-three in Kihoko, fifty-eight in Kasingo and fourteen in Kisindizi. Only in one household, significantly that of a member of the aristocratic Bito clan, whose members have a not altogether merited reputation for haughti-ness and arrogance, did I meet with outright refusal to cooperate, though in several other cases my powers of persuasion were severely extended. To compensate for taking up people's time and to enhance good will I paid an honorarium of one shilling to the head of every household interviewed. (BEATTIE, 1965:40)

In most cases, by one method or another, anthropological fieldworkers try to obtain a complete census of the population and extensive household and economic data from at least a fully representative sample. In many parts of the world a great deal of information is also available from public records, such as census data, tax records, church books, and other written sources.

The physical description of people's geographic and social environments requires extensive mapping and photographing. Drawing a map that includes social data about who lives where is often one of the first tasks the fieldworker undertakes. Naturally,

17

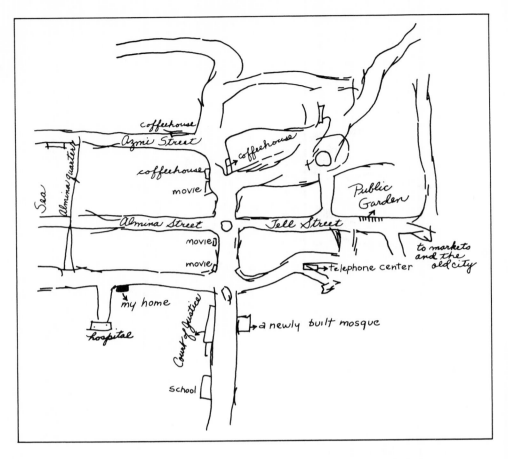

detailed mapping of fields or other economic possessions is an ill-advised opening move if local people are suspicious that the anthropologist is actually a tax agent, a government official, or CIA agent.

Many other methods of research are employed by field anthropologists to get the kinds of information discussed in this book. Some fieldworkers are more thorough than others in their style of research; some rely perhaps too heavily on the opinions of their few key informants; others depend much more on personal observations of day-to-day activities and informal contacts with all parts of the research community; still other researchers put much emphasis on the collection of carefully sampled interviews, questionnaires, and other structured data that can be analyzed statistically. Some of the best field research is that which has a mixture of quantified and nonquantified information-gathering. Quite often

personal impressions of the fieldworker, as well as the impressions of key informants, may be distorted or incomplete, unless they are supplemented with more carefully structured, quantifiable materials. Writing about her research in Southeast Africa, Elizabeth Colson emphasized the importance of checking informants' statements against more objective survey data:

I originally assumed that the period of seclusion for girls at puberty had been progressively diminished by mission and school influence. When I compiled material on the length of seclusion, classifying the material according to the decade in which the woman had been born, I found that there had actually been a progressive increase in the length of time. . . . Today I find that when I make a statement about the Tonga, I am inclined first to check it against the material drawn from the census to see whether or not I am coming any-

18

where near the facts of the case. Impressions can be thoroughly wrong; so can the statements of informants. (COLSON, 1954:57–58)

William Schwab, who carried out several field studies in West African urban settings, has commented on the importance of a mixture of quantitative and qualitative data:

Our emphasis on quantifying devices was not an attempt to reduce social relations to mere statistics, but rather a recognition of the fact that statistics and other quantifying mechanisms when used properly can be excellent scientific tools. Statistical data in itself does not usually provide the theory or conceptual framework, but it can add the substantive flesh to the theoretical skeleton. By this I mean that statistical data when properly collected and analyzed will reinforce or substantiate the researcher's hypothesis or theory. . . . At the same time, I wanted information and insights that are not ordinarily amenable to survey and statistical methods. . . . The two methods are not incompatible; in principal each should support the other. (SCHWAB, 1970:79–80)

Fieldwork in Linguistics

Anthropological linguists frequently carry out fieldwork in much the same manner as cultural anthropologists. They, too, often seek to become part of the local community, at least to the extent that they can find key informants who will assist them in details of the local language. When the goal of research is the formal analysis of a language, the linguist does not concentrate on information about people's daily activities, although he or she may participate actively in the life of the local people to help gain mastery of the language. The fieldwork of the linguist often takes the form of long hours of careful interviewing with a few skilled linguistic informants. These informants, after a time, learn the needs of the linguist and become quick to provide words and phrases in response to the endless questioning of the researcher.

In some unusual cases—especially when a language is dying out and few expert speakers remain—the field linguist may have to be content to work with only one or two informants. Such restricted interviewing is, of course, very fatiguing for both the informants and the researcher. More often,

however, the fieldworker collects language information from a number of persons. William J. Samarin, in his guide to linguistic fieldwork, said that:

The more one expects diversity in the language at some point or another, the more he needs to have a plurality of informants. It would have been foolish for me, for example, to have based my description of Sango on one or even half a dozen speakers of this Central African language. Since it is a lingua franca* used by about a million speakers, mostly as a second language (although many children learn it along with the language of their parents), it was necessary to determine to what extent there were variations correlated with geography, language background, amount of acculturation to European culture, age, sex, and religion. The final corpus of about 37,000 words represents the speech of fifty-six informants. (SAMARIN, 1967:28)

The basic work tools of the field linguist are notebook, pencil, tape recorder, and an extremely refined ear for detecting small differences in speech sounds. Texts of tales, riddles, and other folklore are often collected on magnetic tapes, which have totally replaced the older and cumbersome phonograph recordings. The excellent fidelity of some of the more expensive tape-recording apparatus enables the field linguist to collect masses of text that can be listened to and analyzed at a later time. However, linguists usually process and transcribe as much as possible of the collected text while they are still in the field, for the word-by-word transcription should be done with assistance from a native speaker of the language. Samarin notes that "even the original speaker can fail to understand his own recordings. This is presumably the reason why experienced field workers emphasize the importance of transcribing soon after the recording while the material is still 'warm'" (Samarin, 1967:104).

Quite a number of anthropological linguists today are more interested in the social aspects of *speaking* rather than in simply analyzing formal language structure. Such researchers in the field of SOCIO-LINGUISTICS, or "the ethnography of speaking," must do extensive observation and recording in many social settings, as well as interviewing key informants. To learn about the ways in which people

*Any language that is used in communications among people of differing native languages, e.g., Swahili in East Africa.

use their language in different kinds of situations and with different kinds of people, the sociolinguist must do a great deal of participant observation similar to the kind of work that a cultural anthropologist does, and must keep careful notes on the verbal behavior that takes place in these many kinds of activities.

Gathering Data in Physical Anthropology

In earlier times the fieldwork of the physical anthropologist consisted mainly of measuring people's bodily dimensions and checking the color of their skin, hair, and eyes. Today, however, physical anthropologists are concerned with many different types of problems and, depending on their theoretical interests, they choose from a variety of tools and techniques when they go out to do fieldwork. Some physical anthropologists carry out extensive dental examinations; others use X-ray equipment to gather their data. Anthropologists whose work is in the area of molecular biology do many of their studies with blood samples and other bodily fluids and have to cope with the problems of collecting and storing these materials under less than ideal conditions. (Often they have some difficulties in convincing people that their procedures are harmless, especially in those societies in which bodily products—such as hair, nails, blood, or excrement—are used in the practice of witchcraft.) Along with collecting various types of samples, physical anthropologists interested in genetics usually do extensive interviewing concerning kinship and marriage so that they can figure out who is related to whom.

Anthropologists concerned with the study of growth and development must make standardized observations of height, weight, and other more complex measurements designed to estimate body fat, bone growth, and other features related to nutrition and health. Just as the geneticist needs social data about kinship, the fieldworker needs information about the food habits and health characteristics of the different individuals and families in his samples. Thus many of the procedures of physical anthropologists involve a combination of physical and medical observations *plus* the gathering of social, cultural, and economic information. The different types of observations (which we have only barely touched on here) require a great deal more technical field equipment than is usual for cultural and linguistic anthropologists.

During the past two decades a relatively new field of study has grown to prominence among physical anthropologists. The interrelationships between physical and behavioral characteristics among other primates (especially monkeys and apes) have come to be seen as vitally important information concerning the processes of evolution leading to *Homo sapiens*. Therefore the study of PRIMATOLOGY has assumed an increasingly important role in physical anthropology. A fascinating part of this research takes the form of field observations of chimpanzees, gorillas, baboons, and other species under natural, free-living conditions. The long-term research by Jane Van Lawick-Goodall among wild chimpanzees is a well-known example of this type of work.

There is another branch of physical anthropology that has relatively little contact with living populations. Those researchers whose main concern is the study of the fossilized skeletal evidence of human evolution are like archaeologists in that their field

2.7 The late Professor L. S. B. Leakey, discoverer of ancient human fossils in East Africa. (Ian Borry, Magnum)

20

research consists of careful searching and digging for physical remains. The fieldwork of that famous physical anthropological family, the Leakeys, has become widely known as a prototype of this kind of research. John Pfeiffer has described the lifelong dedication of the Leakeys in these words:

Leakey returned again and again [to Olduvai Gorge in what is now Tanzania] over the years, accompanied by his wife Mary. Season after season, they camped not far from the edge of the gorge, walked down into canyons to explore areas as much as ten miles away, and shared a water hole with rhinoceroses and other big game. ("We could never get rid of the taste of rhino urine," Leakey recalls, "even after filtering the water through charcoal and boiling it and using it in tea with lemon.")
They found many concentrations of tools and animal bones, sites to be excavated sometime in the future if sufficient funds and help became available, but few hominid fossils until one July morning in 1959, when the Leakeys were digging on borrowed time, having exhausted current research funds and drawn on the next year's budget. Prehistorians in the field never stop looking, and Mary happened to be walking along the same slope where her husband had first found tools nearly three decades before. Only this time a recent rock slide had exposed previously buried deposits. Mary noticed a bit of skull and, stuck firmly in the face of a nearby cliff, two very large and shining brown-black premolar teeth whose size and cusp pattern indicated a primate more advanced than the monkey or ape. It took the Leakeys nineteen days to free the teeth and parts of a fossil palate from the soft rock, sift tons of rubble and dirt, and gather a total of more than 400 bone fragments. (PFEIFFER, 1969:74–75)

While researchers like the Leakeys search for ancient fossil materials in locations where stream beds (or perhaps winds and rains) might have uncovered living sites or other remains of ancient peoples, other physical anthropologists may team up with the archaeologists for joint research in the ruins of old cities and prehistoric religious sites, such as those of the Maya of the Yucatán and Guatemala.

Archaeological Fieldwork

Archaeologists and researchers interested in human fossil remains are similar in that they go to the field to find physical remains rather than to

2.8 Archaeologists in their fieldwork dig up the evidence of bygone human activity—the monuments, the tools, and the garbage—to piece together information about the evolution of human adaptive systems. William S. Laughlin with field crew in the Aleutians. (Courtesy of W. S. Laughlin)

observe living populations. Of course, the present activities, settlement patterns, and other characteristics of living inhabitants who may be the descendants of "archaeological" populations are often quite important to their research, but their main focus is on the physical traces left by ancient inhabitants. There is much romance attached to archaeological research, especially in the excavations of famous old cities of the Near East, the Egyptian tombs, and the religious centers of the Maya, the Aztecs, and other bygone peoples of Middle America. The excitement and mystery of those excavations are sometimes heightened by the finding of valuable treasures of gold, silver, and precious jewels buried along with the more mundane remains. (We hasten to add here that most archaeological fieldwork, however exciting and interesting, is much different from the impressions of romantic treasure-hunting sometimes given in television productions.)

21

A major difference between fantasy and reality in archaeological fieldwork is that the digging must be extremely slow and painstaking in order to preserve all of the different fragments of materials that make up the most important kinds of evidence the archaeologist uses. The modern archaeologist is extremely concerned with qualities of soil; the minute grains of pollen at different levels in the research site; fragments of bone, seeds, and other remnants that testify to the food habits of the people who once inhabited the place; and a long list of other materials that would be discarded by the amateur digger as so much dirt. In larger and more complex living sites, archaeologists may occasionally find centuries-old unbroken pottery vessels, but these "glamor finds" are usually much less important for research than the thousands and thousands of broken potsherds that the archaeologists catalog and preserve. What is even more time consuming is the necessity that every item be identified exactly with respect to its location within the dig—how deep from the surface and in what sector within the general excavation plan. Of all anthropologists, archaeologists are, in fact, the most thorough in mapping, recording, and photographing their data. They have to be, because all they have to go on are the material remains from the lives and cultural behavior of bygone populations—they have no chance to interview informants or observe ritual behaviors. They must base their scientific results on careful inferences from the material stuff that remains in locations humans have used in their economic, ritual, and other activities.

Imagine an American Indian village five hundred years ago. Picture that there are some 150 or more semisubterranean houses constructed of poles and wooden frame covered over partly with dirt and partly with animal skins. Let your imagination run further and picture the Indians busy in their day-to-day activities—some scraping animal hides, some cooking food, others out in the fields of maize, a fair distance from the village, cultivating the crops. An anthropologist fieldworker entering this scene could, in a few hours, know a great deal about these people—their means of livelihood, the size of the community, their material possessions, and many other significant items of information. But now, five hundred years later, an archaeologist excavating the site where once this village stood must spend weeks of digging to locate the house pits and discover their shape and arrangement. After months of analyzing the evidences left in the soil these many years, our archaeologist would be able to reconstruct the approximate size of the community, the nutritional system, the locations of fields, and many other features. But it all takes time, and the techniques of fieldwork essential for getting this information have been developed only rather recently.

Many archaeologists of an earlier era, especially the romance-inspired amateurs (sometimes well meaning, sometimes crassly profit-seeking), despoiled—and in some cases ruined—significant archaeological sites. They generally worked quickly with spade and pick looking for the occasional art objects and other items that would look good in museum cases. They had few techniques and less motivation for the tedious uncovering, layer by layer, of the story archaeological sites can tell. Many archaeological locations of great theoretical importance to anthropology have held little of interest for the amateur diggers.

At times, however, amateur archaeologists have sensed the point at which they needed to turn to the professionals in order that significant nonmovable features could be carefully studied and perhaps preserved. One of the happier instances of such collaboration between amateurs and professionals is the case of the Sutton Hoo ship, found about one hundred miles northeast of London. In the late 1930s a series of mounds had been excavated in the region, some of which contained boats. An amateur archaeologist, digging in the largest of these mounds, recognized that this earthen hillock contained a ship of considerable size, and government archaeologists from the British Museum were called in to work on this difficult excavation:

It soon became apparent that the ship belonged to the Anglo-Saxon age. In the burial chamber in mid-ship were found gold jewelry, silverplate, weapons and bowls, the remains of cauldrons, buckets, and many other objects. . . . One of the most difficult and suspenseful tasks of the archaeologists was the exposure and recording of the large buried boat. The moist sand did not preserve wood and other perishable objects except in the form of a discoloration or stain. The wooden planks of the boat were gone; even the iron nails of the ship were badly rusted and although in their proper relative positions lay loose in the sand. The excavation had to be done from the inside working out until the stained layer was reached. This was exposed carefully, leaving the rusted nails in position, and from this painstaking task it was possible to reconstruct the whole boat with considerable accuracy and detail. The patience of the archaeologists was rewarded by seeing more and more detail of the construction as the excavation proceeded, until at the conclusion of the work the entire boat lay revealed. (MEIGHAN, 1966:124)

The research activities of archaeologists sometimes coordinate closely with the work of historians, for many archaeological sites are contemporary with early written records. For example, in the case of the Sutton Hoo ship, there were sufficient written materials available from the period so that analysis of documents supports the conclusion that the ship burial was for the East Anglian king, Aethelhere, who was known to have been killed in the battle of Winwaed (Yorkshire) in 655 A.D.

In any but the simplest archaeological fieldwork, the researcher must have the aid of a number of specialists from other fields. Often a geologist takes on the task of deciphering and interpreting the successions of soils, rocks, and other geological deposits that provide a time frame for the archaeological site. Other specialists analyze the pollen remains to reconstruct the past history of the vegetation; soil specialists study the productive capacities of the surrounding area, looking for evidence of previous food growing; paleontologists study the fragments of bone found in an archaeological site to find out what animals were utilized by the bygone inhabitants. In addition, there are now several specialized methods for dating radioactive materials that can be used to establish more accurate dates for archaeological sites. Dating radioactive materials calls for the expertise of physicists, and the analysis of all the different types of evidence from archaeological sites frequently necessitates complex computerized information storage and analysis.

Fieldwork in any branch of contemporary anthropology can require the collaboration of experts from a number of fields. To an increasing extent, research involves the joint work of archaeologists, cultural anthropologists, and biologically oriented researchers. For example, large-scale fieldwork has been carried out for a number of years in the Aleutian Islands in order to study, in detail, the past history and biocultural evolution of the Aleut peoples from their earliest origins to the present day. Extensive archaeological excavations have been carried out, a variety of physical measurements have been made on the surviving populations of Aleuts, and their language and other aspects of their culture continue to be studied in detail by cultural anthropologists and linguists. Other specialists in this complex and many-faceted research project include medical doctors, geologists, and geneticists.

Many anthropologists have come to feel that a fuller understanding of human biocultural evolution requires large-scale, multiexpert research. On the other hand, anthropological knowledge also depends heavily on the work of individual fieldworkers carrying out their more localized and focused projects. Thus anthropological field research, the hallmark of the entire profession, presents a range of variation itself, from simple to highly complex, from one-person-with-a-notebook to multidisciplinary team projects with much technical equipment.

From Field Research to Anthropological Theory

The main goal of the many different activities of anthropological fieldworkers is gathering valid and useful information concerning the human animal—its history and evolution and its contemporary behavior. Because the histories and present activities of different human groups are so diverse and complex, the information gathered by fieldworkers is itself an enormous mass of patterns and developments, bewildering and seemingly disordered.

Earlier, anthropology often consisted of endless listing and cataloging of the supposedly "quaint" and "exotic" customs and behaviors of different kinds of people around the world. The variety of human cultures is a fascinating body of information that, for some people, presents the same kind of entertainment as does the museum—a chance to encounter all kinds of strange and fascinating things outside one's daily experience. Anthropologists, however, study all of these materials about human diversity in order to increase our understanding and explanation of the human condition. They seek patterns and similarities in human behavioral systems in order to establish general principles and systematic relationships for explaining and predicting both the biological and the sociocultural features of *Homo sapiens*.

One unusual feature of the anthropologist's scientific work is that the raw data of human behavior involve so many different things, including economics, SOCIAL ORGANIZATION, and arts, as well as medical, physiological, and psychological elements. Compared to other social and biological scientists, anthropologists tend to be extremely general and HOLISTIC, trying to organize information from diverse sources with a great variety of methods and research techniques.

The Era of Armchair Theorizing

Protoanthropologists[2] of earlier centuries usually gathered their materials in order to build up a general theory of humankind, based on some kind of framework for *classifying* or *categorizing* human populations and cultural behaviors. In the physical anthropology of an earlier day, for example, much effort was devoted to compiling more and more complex lists and descriptions of the "races." These classifications and theories about human populations were not, however, based on firsthand field research. Usually they were developed by "armchair theorists" who perused reports by explorers, missionaries, colonial administrators, and other travelers about the kinds of people they encountered in their travels. The French scholar Georges Louis Leclerc Buffon (1707–1788) was one of these early categorizers, and he also developed some theories concerning the supposed causes of physical differences among human populations. His theories include the following:

The climate may be regarded as the chief cause of the different colours of men. But food, though it has less influence upon colour, greatly affects the form of our bodies. Coarse, unwholesome, and ill-prepared food, makes the human species degenerate. All those people who live miserably, are ugly and ill-made. . . . The air

and the soil have great influence upon the figure of men, beasts, and plants. In the same province, the inhabitants of the elevated and hilly parts are more active, nimble, handsome, ingenious, and beautiful, than those who live in the plains, where the air is thick and less pure. . . . Hence those marks which distinguish men who inhabit different regions of the earth, are not original, but purely superficial. It is the same identical being who is varnished with black under the Torrid Zone, and tawned and contracted by extreme cold under the Polar Circle. . . . The earth is divided into two great continents. The antiquity of this division exceeds that of all human monuments; and yet man is more ancient, for he is the same in both worlds. The Asiatic, the European, and the Negro, produce equally with the American. Nothing can be a stronger proof that they belong to the same family, than the facility with which they unite to the common stock. The blood is different, but the germ is the same. The skin, the hair, the features, and the stature, have varied, without any change in internal structure. (BUFFON, 1791, quoted in SLOTKIN, 1965:185)

When we examine the writings of the philosophers and protoanthropologists of past centuries, we find that almost all of them had theories about the causes and characteristics of the varieties of humans. To some extent everyone is an anthropologist. The novelist Tyssot de Patot, in a book about the voyages and adventures of "Jacques Masse," has a physician in his story saying:

Other Creatures having Organs like to ours, have no doubt the same Perceptions, and 'tis only the Degree of more or less, that can constitute the Difference. The Beasts therefore have Reason; and tho' they don't shew it, 'tis only for want, perhaps, of Speech to give Names, as we do, to things which affect them by being put in Motion; for, in other Matters, they are very capable of distinguishing. (quoted in SLOTKIN, 1965:191–192)

The earlier scholars were also much concerned with the origins and histories of different human cultural features. During the eighteenth century, for example, a number of people studied the characteristics of different languages of the world and tried to develop explanations about the origins of language. Many of the theories of humankind current in the eighteenth century were derived from interpretations of the Bible, and according to the Bible, all languages (like all varieties of humans) must be descended from a single source. Thus, many eighteenth-century scholars felt that Hebrew had to

[2] Anthropology became a recognized branch of science only in the latter part of the nineteenth century. Before that time the people who contributed to the study of humankind identified themselves as historians, philosophers, biologists, or physicians, and many of them carried out anthropological studies as an avocation. Hence, the term *protoanthropologists* can be used to refer to those people who earlier wrote about "races," "customs," "classification of language," and other topics now identified with anthropology.

be the parent of all languages—at which an irreverent poet poked fun:

Those learned philologists, who chase
A panting syllable through time and space,
Start it at home, and hunt it in the dark
To Gaul, to Greece, and into Noah's Ark.
    (WILLIAM COWPER, *Retirement*)

While many early linguists accepted as beyond debate the biblical theory of languages, others were more concerned with studying actual family resemblances and relations among the different languages. James Bernett, Lord Monboddo (1714–1799), believed that he could demonstrate the single origin of all the languages of the Old World:

The Greek, Latin, Teutonic or Gothic, Hebrew or Phoenician, were originally the same language.
    As to the Oriental languages, it is certain that the Hebrew, Phoenician, Syriac, Chaldaic, and Arabic, have all such an affinity, that either one of them must be the parent language of the rest, or they must all be children of some common parent.

He went on to state that there is a

probability . . . of a resemblance . . . betwixt the Bramin and Greek languages, which I think the more likely that I am persuaded both Indians and Greeks got their language, and all their other arts, from the same parent-country, viz. Egypt. (quoted in SLOTKIN, 1965:239)

This theory of relationships between the languages of India and those of Europe was given strong support in 1786 when William Jones demonstrated, through careful linguistic comparisons, that Sanskrit did, indeed, have strong internal grammatical resemblances to Greek, Latin, and the other Indo-European tongues.

While some anthropologists were engaged in categorizing and explaining the physical types of humans, and others, the languages, still others—the forerunners of modern-day cultural-social anthropologists—were more concerned with theories of "human nature" and the development of complex societies. The more theologically inclined scholars based their theories on the idea that the different cultures of the world had reached their present state as a result of degradations from the original paradise and perfection; other theorists argued quite the opposite: that humans had evolved complex social and cultural systems from much simpler, animal-like beginnings. Anne Robert Jacques Turgot (1717–1781) developed a comprehensive theory of cultural evolution, focusing on the development of economic stratification:

No doubt the mind of man everywhere contains within itself the seeds of the same achievements; but nature, not impartial in the bestowal of her gifts, has given to certain minds a fullness of talent that she has refused to others; circumstances develop these talents or leave them buried in obscurity; and from the infinite variety of such circumstances springs the inequality that marks the progress of nations.
    Barbarism makes all men equal; and in the earliest times, all those who are born with genius find almost the same obstacles and the same resources. Time passes, and societies are formed and grow: The hates of nations, and ambition—or rather avarice, the sole ambition of barbaric peoples—multiply wars and devastation. Conquests and revolutions commingle in a thousand ways, peoples, tongues, and manners. . . . The tillage of fields made habitations more permanent. It nourished more men than it kept busy, and thenceforth imposed upon those it left unoccupied the necessity of becoming useful or redoubtable to those who worked the soil. Hence cities, commerce, the arts of use and those of elegance, diversity of occupations, differences of education, greater inequality of conditions; hence, the leisure that allows genius, freed from the burden of elemental needs, to leave the narrow sphere in which they hold it and direct all its forces to the culture of the arts; . . .
    In a time when there was still a large quantity of uncultivated lands which belonged to no one, one might possess cattle without being a Proprietor of lands. It is even probable that mankind has almost everywhere begun to collect flocks and live on their produce before it gave itself up to the more toilsome labour of agriculture. It would seem that the Nations which cultivated the earth in the most ancient times are those which have found in their Country kinds of animals more susceptible of being tamed, and that have been led in this way from the wandering and restless life of the Peoples who live by the chase and fishing to the more tranquil life of Pastoral Peoples. Pastoral life necessitates dwelling for a longer time in the same place; it affords more leisure; more opportunities to study the differences of soils, to observe the march of nature in the production of those plants which serve for the support of cattle. Perhaps it is for this reason that the Asiatic Nations have been the first to cultivate the earth, and that the Peoples of America have remained so long in the state of Savages.

Fieldwork: The Hallmark of Anthropology

Table 2.1: Morgan's Stages of Evolution

(READ FROM BOTTOM UP)

Stages	Cultural Example	Differentiating Characteristics
Civilization	Europeans, Americans	begins after the alphabet was invented
Higher Barbarism	Greeks of ancient time	begins with use of iron
Middle Barbarism	Zuñi, Hopi Indians	begins with domestication of animals and plants
Lower Barbarism	Iroquois Indians	begins with invention of pottery
Higher Savagery	Polynesians	begins with use of bow and arrow
Middle Savagery	Australian aborigines	begins with fish diet, use of fire and speech
Lower Savagery	no known examples	before fire and speech were invented

Source: Taken from PELTO, 1966:20.

In the times bordering on the beginning of the societies, it was almost impossible to find men who were ready to cultivate the soil which belonged to others; since, as all the grounds were not yet occupied, those who wished to labour preferred to clear new lands and cultivate them on their own account. This is pretty much the position in which people find themselves in all the new colonies.

Violent men have therefore conceived the idea of obligating other men by force to labour for them; and they have had slaves. (quoted in SLOTKIN, 1965:360–362)

By the end of the nineteenth century, most anthropologists in Europe and America accepted as established fact a general scheme of cultural evolution much like the stages of human "progress" outlined by Turgot and his French Enlightenment contemporaries. Table 2.1 shows the stages of "man's progress" as set forth by Lewis Henry Morgan in his famous book *Ancient Society* (1877). Morgan was the foremost American anthropologist in the latter part of the nineteenth century, and his ideas of cultural evolution were widely accepted. Although Morgan had done some fieldwork among the Seneca Indians and had traveled widely among other Indian groups, his general theory, like that of his predecessors, was built up from a hodgepodge of information and misinformation, gleaned mainly from various secondhand sources.

There were two serious problems in nine-

Some of the modern anthropological emphasis on field research developed rather accidentally. A major proponent of full immersion in local lifeways as *the* fieldwork method was Bronislaw Malinowski, a Polish-born cultural anthropologist who received his training in London just before the outbreak of World War I. He had gone to the South Seas as part of a research expedition to the New Guinea region, and when the war broke out, he was interned as an "enemy alien" because his birthplace was in the old Austro-Hungarian Empire. Forced to stay in the South Seas for the duration of the war, he converted this necessity into a virtue, spending most of the time living in the Trobriand Islands, where he learned the local language and participated in all aspects of the local cultural scene. Although he was not actually the first anthropologist to become fully immersed in the daily lives of the people he studied, the Trobriand experience, along with the several best-selling books that he wrote about this fieldwork, set a model and prescribed methods that have had wide-ranging effects on both European and American anthropological research.

teenth-century anthropological theorizing. In the first place, the theorizers usually did not use fieldwork to check the accuracy of their armchair conjectures, so they lacked a "feel" for the realities of non-European ways of living. The other weakness, of serious consequence, was that these European and American scholars assumed, without question, that their own cultural ways represented the best, the most progressive, the most logical, rational, and scientific way of life, compared to the supposed superstition, irrationality, and cultural rigidity of all other peoples. They assumed that European-style monogamy, Christian monotheism, and liberal capitalism represented the highpoints of human achievement—an ideal of progress toward which all people were marching. This ETHNOCENTRISM also included some overt racism, although a number of leading anthropologists at the end of the nineteenth century were assuming antiracist attitudes. These theorists believed that all populations of humans were equally endowed with mental and physical capabilities. Differences in culture histories and environmental circumstances were invoked to explain the divergence between "higher" and "lower" cultures in their grand plans of evolution.

The Rise of Empirical Anthropology in the Twentieth Century

With the dawn of the twentieth century, anthropology, which had become recognized as a distinct scholarly discipline, took a sharply different direction as a group of American anthropologists, led by Franz Boas, reacted strongly to the nonempirical, ethnocentric biases of nineteenth-century theory. During the period from 1900 to 1930 a strong fieldwork orientation in anthropology was established. Researchers realized that much valuable information about the cultural systems of Indian groups was disappearing rapidly in the enforced misery and poverty of reservation life. In that first phase of twentieth-century anthropology much effort was devoted to lengthy interviewing of key informants concerning their prereservation life styles. Anthropologists felt that invaluable information would disappear forever unless researchers devoted all their energies to fieldwork—theory building could come later. In this way, especially among North American

anthropologists, the pendulum of scholarly focus swung all the way from armchair theorizing to an antitheoretical descriptive style of research. More recently, anthropologists have criticized the lack of theory in that phase of anthropology, but a great deal of basic field material was accumulated for later analysis.

At the same time, the extensive firsthand contact with Indian peoples and other non-Western, non-White groups had profound effects on the attitudes of anthropologists. Researchers who live in Indian communities or with "nonmodern" peoples for months at a time get a much different view of them than do scholars whose contacts are through the writings of missionaries, traders, and colonial administrators. The ethnocentric tendencies of anthropology were sharply reversed, and much of the recent literature of fieldwork shows signs that researchers become emotionally identified with the people they study, regarding them as in many ways superior in life style to the city dwellers of modern society.

The fieldwork orientation of twentieth-century anthropology gradually became imbued with a new version of the romantic "noble savage." North American Indians were portrayed as noble in warfare, kind to their children, honest in all dealings with the "treacherous White man," and conservers of nature's resources. A major theme in this orientation was that before the Industrial Revolution and before the rise of urbanized ways of life, human communities had lived in sensitive and balanced relationships with their environments, avoiding large-scale decimation of plants and animals and always seeking religious harmony between humans and other creatures. Field anthropologists found that the communities they studied often included persons with complex philosophies about themselves and the universe, as described, for example, by Paul Radin in his well-known book *Primitive Man as a Philosopher*. Even the word *primitive* denoted a number of positive characteristics in early twentieth-century anthropology. *Primitive* came to mean "non-European," "living naturally instead of artificially," "honest instead of corrupted," and "attuned to one's natural landscape instead of despoiling and polluting the environment."

Most anthropologists of that period tended perhaps to overromanticize the lifeways and positive features of non-Western peoples, especially the In-

27

2.9 Anthropologists have often idealized nonmodern peoples as attuned to the natural landscape instead of despoiling and polluting the environment. Hunter near Pulykara, Australia. (Courtesy of the American Museum of Natural History)

dians. This romanticizing tendency may even have been a factor in anthropologists' seeming indifference (at times) to the desperate economic poverty of many reservation Indian groups. That modern employment opportunities and economic advantages were so slow in coming to Indian communities was often looked upon by ethnographic fieldworkers as a positive feature: the corrupting influences of "civilization," with an eight-hour workday, had not yet totally replaced the less-scheduled and supposedly more carefree life style based on hunting, fishing, and trapping.

In every period the research activities of anthropologists have been strongly affected by their theoretical biases and concerns, and some of these theoretical directions have come into anthropology from the wider circles of contemporary social and political thought. To a certain extent, though, anthropologists, in their research and theorizing, have seen themselves as swimming against the tide of public opinion, and sometimes even against the tide of opinion current in other biological and social sciences. In the nineteenth century anthropologists were among the early leaders in arguing for Darwinian ideas of biological evolution, as well as for the related theory of cultural evolution. These evolutionary ideas were not completely new, but they were in opposition to a large body of theological

opinions supported by most educated people of the time.

In the late nineteenth and early twentieth centuries, the idea of biological evolution won increasing acceptance, and during this same period the notion of social evolution (often phrased in terms of "survival of the fittest") also became widely recognized. The application of Darwin's ideas to social history often took the form of justifying the expansionist, colonialist, supremacist policies of Euro-American society. European and North American domination of the non-Western world was simply the result of evolutionary forces toward "better and better" social forms, it was argued.

Early in the twentieth century anthropologists began to be aware of the serious scientific and ethical problems of SOCIAL DARWINISM, as the evolutionist argument came to be labeled. When they went out to do fieldwork, many researchers learned of the complexity and adaptiveness of non-Western life styles and came to realize the extent to which ethnocentric biases contaminated the scientific theories of the day. Also, in part as a result of their field experiences, they came to appreciate the difficulties of getting enough empirical evidence to support evolutionist (or any other kind of) theory. Thus, anthropologists of this period sharply counteracted the popularized and moralistic ideas of cul-

Introduction to Anthropology: The Fieldwork Enterprise

tural evolution, and the tone of theory and research became strongly *anti*evolutionary. Although they did not deny *biological* evolution or the evidence of the growth of technological complexity in human societies, many anthropologists expressed strong doubt concerning the ideas of evolution (and particularly of "progress") as applied to various aspects of culture.

In place of evolutionary theory, anthropologists sought to describe each cultural group in terms of its unique attributes, rather than seeking for similarities and uniform characteristics that could permit refinement of classifications of "types of cultures." Their chief message to the public during the early twentieth century was basically that each cultural system must be accepted and evaluated on its own terms, in relation to its unique past history and circumstances, rather than in terms of some pan-human measure of morality and cultural progress. This point of view has been labeled CULTURAL RELATIVISM, a term that calls attention to the idea that cultures or societies cannot be compared to one another in terms of any set of absolute judgmental criteria.

Now, in the latter part of the twentieth century, as the message of cultural relativism has become widely accepted, anthropologists once again are re-evaluating the concept of evolution. The ideas of moral progress and European cultural superiority that were such an integral part of earlier evolutionary theorizing have been dropped. It is likely that the savagery of World War I and World War II did much to demolish the idea of European moral and cultural supremacy. At the same time the great amount of empirical research, especially the information on culture history established through archaeological fieldwork, is providing a firmer basis on which to build a new type of evolutionary theory based on an ecological perspective which focuses on humans adapting to their total environments.

Description, Classification, and Theory Building: The Work of Science

In all branches of science a series of general axioms are accepted by most researchers as a basis for their continued scientific work. Among the important points are these:

1. Theoretical speculations, however interesting, are scientifically useless unless they can ultimately be tested by means of empirical observations.

2. "Mere description" or the undirected collection of miscellaneous information is, at best, a very low-level, prescientific exercise. (Realistically, "mere description" is logically impossible, for information-gathering is always guided by some preconceptions, even though the researcher may not be aware of them.)

3. The early stages of scientific progress often involve ordering and classifying available descriptive information; hence the preoccupations, for example, with animal species, genera, and so on. (Often theoretical progress in a science takes place only after a considerable amount of the tedium of classification has been carried out.)

4. DEDUCTIVE research, in which specific hypotheses derived from more general theoretical systems are systematically tested, and INDUCTIVE research processes, in which empirical data are sorted out and put together in a search for patterns and generalizations, are both valid means of scientific work at various stages of research. Usually an individual scientist's work is a mixture of inductive and deductive procedures.

5. Scientists do not generally believe it is possible to *prove* theoretical propositions or laws beyond all doubt. Rather, the work of science is to eliminate false ideas and mistaken hypotheses until the ideas that are accepted as the current theory are thought of as the "most probable" or "supported by all present data," although new and more sophisticated theoretical formulations may cause currently accepted theoretical positions to become obsolete.

6. Progress, in the form of accumulated knowledge, takes the form of more refined and accurate theoretical propositions, which are made possible by improved (more standardized and reliable) means of observation. Improved means of observation and better theory are mutually interdependent—they go hand in hand because more sophisticated theoretical insights often lead to new means of observation. On the other hand, technological breakthroughs in instruments and other means of observation can lead to bursts of creative theory building.

29

Although the *basic principles* of scientific method apply to all branches of science, specific laboratory and field techniques of observation are very different among the various scientific disciplines. Some sciences are closely associated with laboratory research procedures; for example, chemistry, physiology, and many aspects of biology. On the other hand, some branches of biology, including paleontology, ethology, and plant ecology, are as much fieldwork-oriented as the branches of anthropology. Psychology has its strong laboratory side, but some psychologists are clinically oriented, and still others have increasingly moved into field study in community contexts. Medical science is, of course, a mixture of laboratory work and clinical study, with considerable emphasis on fieldwork as well. Many economists carry out research in the form of analysis of numerical information concerning prices, work hours, costs of production, amounts of goods produced, and other data from publicly available record keeping.

The various techniques of information-gathering and analysis in scientific domains require different vocabularies of categories, concepts, and units of analysis appropriate to the subject being studied. In addition to the different basic vocabularies of the sciences, different kinds of numerical or statistical analysis, plus qualitative, descriptive styles of analysis, are necessary for working with various kinds of materials. For example, sciences such as geology, paleontology, and a portion of human biology are strongly historical in their theoretical concerns. That is, many of their goals of research involve time sequences or chronologies of past events. Chemistry and physics, on the other hand, are "timeless" in their theory structures. Anthropology is a thorough mixture of historical and nonhistorical theory; in fact anthropology is an eclectic mixture of scientific styles.

Anthropology and Science

As we have just suggested, the strong fieldwork orientation in anthropology grew up during the twentieth century, in part as a reaction to the weaknesses of too much armchair theorizing. The haphazard and often completely erroneous observations of amateurs were very inadequate as a base of information for building anthropological theory. The

science of humanity took very large steps forward when professional anthropologists made field research the focus of anthropological effort. Throughout the twentieth century there has been a continuing concern among anthropologists to improve the objectivity and thoroughness of their methods. New theoretical perspectives in cultural anthropology have strongly influenced some fieldwork methods by redirecting attention to aspects of behavior that earlier were neglected. For example, the growth of ecological interest among anthropologists has led to increased sophistication concerning the description of physical environments and the behaviors of plants and animals crucial for human food-getting systems. At the same time, greatly increased attention is now being paid to the ways in which human communities affect their physical and biological environments in the course of food production and other technological activities.

The careful reader of anthropological literature must always be wary of the sources used to generalize about human cultural behavior. We have long since learned to ignore stories about human societies that have no language system or supposedly totally lack religious beliefs and practices. We know that there are no such human societies. Similarly, we know that there are no tribes at the Antipodes that have mouths in the middle of their stomachs. But wild tales are still common in serious literature. A recent (1972) book concerned with male and female roles refers to "Amazon societies" in which females fought the wars, hunted the food, and totally dominated the hapless males of the local population. No such societies are known to have existed except in the imaginations of travelers and the anonymous creators of ancient mythologies!

Many theorizers about human aggression, human territoriality, and other supposedly "instinctive drives" of *Homo sapiens* have similarly presented distorted or downright fanciful information to support their theories. The psychoanalyst Sigmund Freud developed part of his theory of human history and culture based on imagined past events in human history: the killing of the father figure in the "primal scene," the guilt and shame of the sons leading to renunciation of sexual intercourse with sisters and mothers, and the emergence, full-blown, of the "Oedipus complex." Such theory building on the basis of false information ultimately leads nowhere.

Unfortunately anthropological standards of fieldwork description and analysis have not always been rigorous enough to provide solid information for theory building. Some researchers have been almost as carefree as nonprofessional travelers and missionaries in generalizing about the supposed personalities, "national character," and general "ethos" of individual societies. During World War II, for example, anthropologists developed a caricature of the Japanese national character that supposedly derived from their rigid toilet-training practices—a weak and tragicomical application of Freudian theory. In a similar vein descriptions of the national character of Russians were built up invoking the supposedly powerful psychological effects of swaddling, the practice of wrapping up babies tightly in swaddling cloths during their first few months of life. The point is that these theoretical conjectures were created with very little regard for basic supportive evidence. Although most anthropological research and description is much more modest in its theoretical claims and more careful in presenting evidence, people who read and use anthropological works are well advised to insist on objective data for generalizations and explanatory statements.

In this introduction to anthropology we have so much ground to cover, so many topics to touch on, that we will not be able, in every case, to present systematic evidence and information for the generalizations we make. Nonetheless, we will attempt to be as "evidence-oriented" and methodologically sys-

tematic as possible, given our limitations of space. Many of our generalizations about human biocultural evolution and ways of behavior will be supported with case illustrations. Our illustrative examples in the following chapters have been selected mainly from relatively recent field research, studies in which the field anthropologist was careful and thorough about recording the basic data.

Real understanding of the nature and complexities of human cultural systems is best achieved through participation in the activities of fieldwork. Research in anthropology is not basically a library activity; in cultural anthropology and linguistics, for example, it is fundamentally a social act involving communication with living people.

We feel that every student of anthropology who wants to "get the feel" of the subject should be exposed directly to the research process. Naturally, it is not always possible for students to get a chance to participate directly in archaeological digs or to work firsthand with prehistoric fossils. Some people might object that it is also difficult for most North American anthropology students to get in touch with people of cultures that are sharply different from their own culture. However, it is our feeling that anthropological "lab work" can profitably begin with the study of contemporary North American cultures. The process of learning about the nature of human cultural behavior can very well begin right at home.

Fieldwork: The Hallmark of Anthropology

Part
Two

Homo sapiens in Biological Perspective

If we are to understand human nature in all its complexity, we must start from a comparative perspective in which we examine the place of *Homo sapiens* in the animal world. It has become increasingly popular in both scientific and lay circles to present information about other animals in theorizing about human nature. Many contemporary writers on human AGGRESSION and warfare, sex and family, and other aspects of behavior comment about analogous characteristics in other animals. It is sometimes claimed, for example, that "man is the only animal that murders members of its own kind," (a false statement). In another vein, human monogamous sexual unions have been compared with the family behavior of the greylag goose, one of the more notable paragons of monogamic virtue.

Many comparisons and contrasts of humans with other animals focus on our similarities to the great apes, thought to be the closest relatives to *Homo sapiens*. Fortunately the primates in general have been relatively successful species, so that a great many different monkeys and apes are found throughout the world, providing a wide range of physiological and behavioral examples suitable for comparison.

Among the Animals: The World of the Primates

The Mammalian Class

Many millions of years ago, during the MESOZOIC era of geological history (see Table 3.1 for geological eras), the class of animals we refer to as mammals began to evolve from their reptilian ancestors. A basic feature of mammalian biology is the characteristic we call warm-bloodedness, which gives mammals much flexibility of behavior and adaptational capability compared with the cold-blooded animals (e.g., reptiles). Most mammals also developed physiological systems for reproduction through live birth (as contrasted with laying eggs), and they also evolved strong limb bones for carrying the body well clear of the ground (except for those mammals that took to the sea, like whales and walruses). With live birth these animals also developed the important feature of nourishing their babies with mothers' milk. As one writer exuberantly put it, "the provision of nourishment in the form of milk is superb." Babies of mammals generally don't have to be pushed out of their nests into the hostile world to

Table 3.1: The Geological Time Chart (Read from the bottom upward)

Era	Period	Epoch	Began Millions of Years ago	Duration in Millions of Years	Evolution of Living Things
CENOZOIC		Recent	.01	.01	Modern genera of animals with humans dominant.
CENOZOIC	Quaternary	Pleistocene	3(2.5–3.0)	3	Early humans. Giant mammals now extinct
CENOZOIC	Tertiary	Pliocene	10	7	Anthropoid radiation; mammalian specialization.
CENOZOIC	Tertiary	Miocene	25	15	Anthropoid radiation; mammalian specialization.
CENOZOIC	Tertiary	Oligocene	34	9	Modernization of mammals (and more species)
CENOZOIC	Tertiary	Eocene	55	20–21	Modernization of mammals (and more species)
CENOZOIC	Tertiary	Paleocene	65	10	Modernization of mammals (and more species)
MESOZOIC	Cretaceous		135	65	Dinosaurs dominant; marsupial and placental mammals appear; first flowering plants appear.
MESOZOIC	Jurassic		180	45	Dominance of dinosaurs; first mammals and birds, insects abundant.
MESOZOIC	Triassic		225	45	First dinosaurs and mammal-like reptiles.
PALEOZOIC	Permian		270	45	Reptiles displace amphibians as dominant group.
PALEOZOIC	Carboniferous		350	80	Amphibians dominant in luxurious coal forests; first reptiles appear.
PALEOZOIC	Devonian		400	50	Many fishes; first amphibians.
PALEOZOIC	Silurian		440	40	Sea scorpions and primitive fish; plants and arthropods invade the land.
PALEOZOIC	Ordovician		500	60	First vertebrates, the jawless fish.
PALEOZOIC	Cambrian		600(±20)	100	All *invertebrate* phyla appear.
PRE-CAMBRIAN			Back to Earth origins 4.5–4.9 billion years ago		First known fossils perhaps 3.3 billion years ago. A few soft multicellular invertebrates.

Homo sapiens in Biological Perspective

seek their own living, and they can be taken care of very nicely without the parents' having to frequently come back to the nest with food, since the nourishment in milk is relatively long-lasting. Furthermore, there is evidence that milk can carry antibodies developed by the mother that help protect the baby against disease.

Many other important physiological features, including the development of a highly effective and complex nervous system, have contributed to the tendency for mammalian species to be very adaptable in behavior and sociable in general living arrangements. Throughout the millions of years of successful evolutionary adaptation during the CENOZOIC era (the "Age of Mammals"), different branches of the mammalian stock became special-

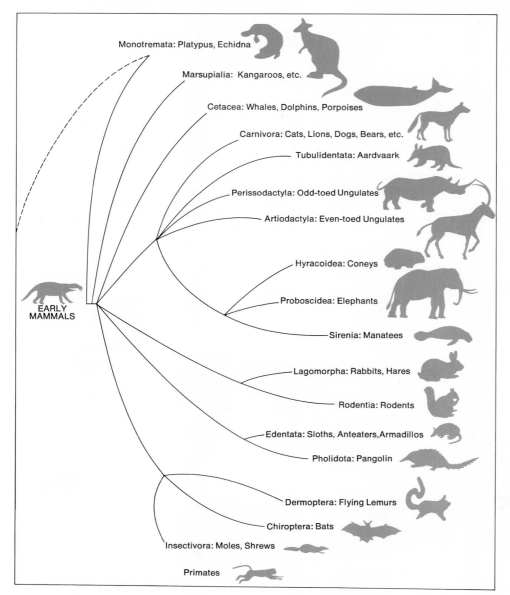

3.1 **The major orders of mammals.**

Monotremata: Platypus, Echidna

Marsupialia: Kangaroos, etc.

Cetacea: Whales, Dolphins, Porpoises

Carnivora: Cats, Lions, Dogs, Bears, etc.

Tubulidentata: Aardvaark

Perissodactyla: Odd-toed Ungulates

Artiodactyla: Even-toed Ungulates

Hyracoidea: Coneys

Proboscidea: Elephants

Sirenia: Manatees

Lagomorpha: Rabbits, Hares

Rodentia: Rodents

Edentata: Sloths, Anteaters, Armadillos

Pholidota: Pangolin

Dermoptera: Flying Lemurs

Chiroptera: Bats

Insectivora: Moles, Shrews

Primates

EARLY MAMMALS

Among the Animals: The World of the Primates

ized to different kinds of environmental situations, developing preferences for particular food and specialized defenses against predators.

Adaptive Radiation

The fossil records of past animal life, plus the interrelations and comparative physical characteristics of living animal species, suggest that there is much variation in the speed and patterning of biological evolution in different periods. Some animals become adapted to specialized ecological niches and remain relatively unchanged in basic form over millions of years. In other instances, however, as in the case of the finches of the Galapagos mentioned earlier, some species find open environments with few natural competitors or predators and "blossom out" fairly rapidly into a variety of different subspecies, ultimately leading to different species adapted to different subenvironments. This type of evolutionary pattern is called ADAPTIVE RADIATION.

The history of the successful expansion of mammals around the world throughout the Cenozoic era is a particularly massive adaptive radiation. As we will see below, the early primates, the forebears of monkeys, apes, and humans, apparently had an epoch of great success—expansion of habitats and development of different species and genera—early in the Cenozoic. Another famous example of adaptive radiation is that of the MARSUPIAL mammals that somehow "inherited" the island continent of Australia. In the absence of placental mammals, the marsupials (mammals that care for their newborn young in special pouches on the mother's belly) radiated into a number of different adaptive forms, many of them analogous in appearance and life style to corresponding placental mammals on other continents. There is a marsupial "wolf," a "mouse," a woodchuck sort of "rodent," a "mole," the squirrel-like phalanger, and a number of other species and genera.

The Evolution of the Primates

The earliest fossils regarded as belonging to the *primate* order date from the late Mesozoic and early Cenozoic eras. The "Age of Reptiles," was ending, and our favorite ancient animals, the dinosaurs,

3.2 The marsupial mammals of Australia have differentiated through adaptive radiation into a variety of species, some of them resembling the placental mammals occupying corresponding habitats on other continents.

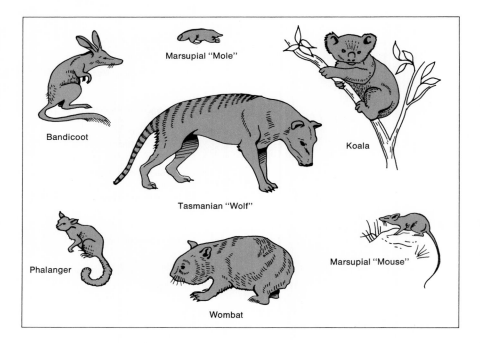

Marsupial "Mole"

Bandicoot

Koala

Tasmanian "Wolf"

Phalanger

Marsupial "Mouse"

Wombat

38

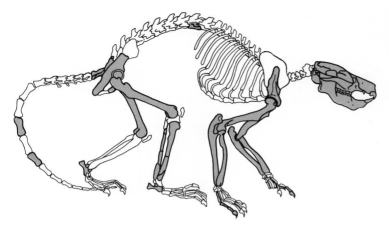

were already on the wane, leaving the modern-day reptiles (snakes, crocodiles, and so on) and the more efficient and versatile warm-blooded mammals. Plant life was also changing. Many of the flowering plants (angiosperms), which can be traced to late Mesozoic times, increased greatly in number of species and, in some cases, replaced the more primitive plants, such as the ferns.

Our oldest primate ancestors were very different from the living primates today. Fossils from France, Wyoming, Colorado, and other places in the Northern Hemisphere show that there were a number of different kinds of small, mouselike animals to which paleontologists have given names such as *Plesiadapis*, *Berruvius*, and *Navajovius*. Possibly the oldest known *proto*primate, found fairly recently, has been given the charming name of *Purgatorius* and dates from the Mesozoic era. Although the ancient primates, like *Purgatorius*, were contemporaries of the giant dinosaurs, it is doubtful that they had much to worry about from those awesome giants; the tiny, mouselike primates were insignificant among the animals that roamed those ancient landscapes.

Apparently the early primates had a number of adaptive advantages over their cold-blooded reptile contemporaries, so that, like many other branches of mammals, they evolved rather rapidly to occupy different environmental niches. Much of this early adaptive radiation was directed to life in the trees, which resulted in strong selection pressures for eyesight and motor coordination. The tree-dwelling adaptation of the primates also tended toward increased intelligence as a basic survival mechanism. Through a complex of other selection pressures, our

ARBOREAL ancestors developed a reproductive pattern involving the birth of very small numbers of offspring at one time. The biological rule of "only one offspring at a time" was in part necessitated by the fact that primates do not usually have permanent nesting locations. The adults must carry their offspring with them as they feed and explore. The one-at-a-time adaptive strategy, in turn, put a premium on longer life spans, so that the progenitors could replace their numbers. Longer life spans provided these animals with greater chances to maximize learning from experience as a significant adaptive feature.

Most of us have great difficulty believing that the small tree-shrew-like creatures from fossil beds of sixty to seventy million years ago are truly ancestral to modern primates. However, this part of the evolutionary picture becomes more credible when we note that there is a series of living primate forms today that show a range of diversity in size and living styles—from the apes and humans at one end of the spectrum, through monkeys, to still smaller animals.

The ancient primate shown in Figure 3.3 may have resembled the modern gray squirrel in some respects and is notable for the extreme versatility of its forelimbs, which were probably well suited to all kinds of clinging and leaping as well as other scrambling for a living. The early primates were not, however, completely tree-living. Very important for the later adaptations of primates was the tendency for those early forms to be quite generalized, exploiting food supplies from the ground at times and scrambling into the trees when the need arose. The

39

Among the Animals: The World of the Primates

great adaptive versatility of our ancient ancestors is best evidenced in the fossil remains found in a number of different locations in the New and Old Worlds.

During the EOCENE epoch, from about 55 million down to 35 million years ago, different *monkeylike species* apparently branched off from the basic primate stock. Some portion of the prosimian range of animal variation produced, through successive adaptations, creatures of increased size and with the other specialized features of monkeys, including greater differentiation of forelimbs for grasping and manipulating, tendencies toward semiupright posture, and larger brains.

The OLIGOCENE epoch (about 34 million to 25 million years ago) is rich in numbers of primate fossils that document the rapid, continued differentiation foreshadowing the present wide divergences of various monkeylike creatures. The New World monkeys (*platyrrhini*), with their amazingly versatile tails that make monkey watching such fun in the zoo, were apparently already a separate evolutionary line from the Old World monkeys (*catarrhini*) in this epoch. Only a few fossils of New World monkeys have been found, however. The first Oligocene monkey fossil was found in Egypt, hence it was named *Apidium*, for Apis, the sacred bull of ancient Egypt. Another famous fossil from Oligocene times in Egypt is that of *Parapithecus*, of which there are a number of different specimens. These and other fossils from North Africa demonstrate that several different branches of monkeylike creatures had evolved at least 25 million years ago. The *Parapithecus* fossil monkeys appear to have been about the size of the smallest of modern African monkeys. They are quite similar to the modern swamp monkey in tooth pattern and jaw size (Simons, 1972).

The earliest fossils indicating the differentiation of apelike animals also occur in the Oligocene. The fossil *Oligopithecus* from the Fayum area in Egypt is a form that appears to be borderline between apelike and monkeylike. Although some very primitive apes were beginning to evolve from the general primate stock 25 million years ago, they were only slightly different from their close cousins, the ancient monkeys.

The following geological epoch, the Miocene, was a time of important evolutionary diversification for the higher primates. Various kinds of grazing mammals also evolved during this period, as there was a gradual expansion of grasslands. As Elwyn Simons has put it:

About the middle Miocene there was also increased faunal interchange between North America and Asia across an Alaskan-Siberian land bridge. In North America a variety of camels and rhinoceroses existed together with primitive foxes, bears, dogs, peccaries, rodents, and hosts of other forms including primitive pronghorn antilocaprids and a variety of equids. In Eurasia the first giraffids, hyenas, deer, and bovids appeared. Mastodons and their relatives . . . spread out of Africa, and eventually . . . reached nearly all parts of the world except Australia. In the Old World, the families represented by pigs, cats, civets, dogs, and tapirs were diversified. In East Africa, great apes, *Dryopithecus*, and lesser apes . . . were common, and monkeys and bushbabies were present but rare. (SIMONS, 1972:14)

By the middle of the Miocene, about 15 million years ago, there was quite a variety of apes in Africa and Asia, as well as a few in Europe. The best-known Miocene ape fossil, *Dryopithecus*, is thought to be a direct ancestor of modern apes and perhaps of humans as well. Some of the vertebrae of the *Dryopithecus* fossils give evidence of an animal at least as large as modern adult male chimpanzees. In other respects, these fossils resemble modern gorillas in skeletal features. The *Dryopithecus* creatures that lived in East Africa during Miocene times appear to have enjoyed an environment that was not much different from the environment today, except that it was perhaps a little wetter. There were tropical rain forests and highlands surrounded by savanna-like terrain at lower elevations. The places in East Africa where *Dryopithecus* remains have been found suggest that early apes were already becoming adapted to ways of life similar to those of modern chimpanzees and gorillas. That is to say, they were adapted to the forest environment with a food regimen based mostly on a vegetarian diet.

Early in the twentieth century a few fragmentary apelike fossils were found in India. They were given the name *Ramapithecus*. Similar fossil materials have been found in East Africa. We will take up the story of *Ramapithecus* and the evolution of *Homo sapiens* in the next chapter.

40

Living Primates

The fossil materials of bygone ages would be quite difficult to interpret if it were not for the fact that some of those ancient bones resemble living species of animals. The present-day species that we list under the order primates are generally divided into two basic groups: the suborder Prosimii, or supposedly more "primitive" parts of the order; and the suborder Anthropoidea, the monkeys and apes. (See Table 3.2.)

The Prosimians

Throughout the Cenozoic era, after the original explosive evolution of prosimian forms, the number of these "primitive" primate species declined somewhat, perhaps pushed aside by the more successful primate forms. Today the prosimians—lemurs, tar-

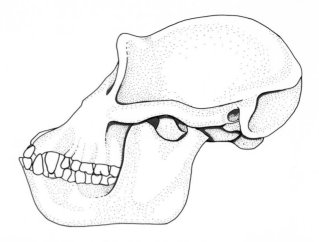

3.4 Skull of *Dryopithecus* (partly reconstructed).

3.5 Geographic locations of some important primate fossils.

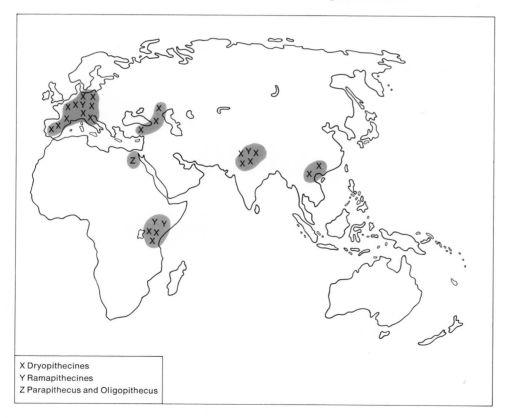

X Dryopithecines
Y Ramapithecines
Z Parapithecus and Oligopithecus

41

Among the Animals: The World of the Primates

Table 3.2: Classification of Modern Primates

Order	Suborder	Superfamily	Family	Living Representatives
Primates	*Prosimii*	Lemuroidea	Lemuridae	Lemur Indri
			Lorisidae	Loris Galago
		Tarsioidea		Tarsier
	Anthropoidea (Platyrrhine)	Ceboidea (New World Monkeys)	Callithricidae	Marmoset
			Cebidae	Cebus Monkey Spider Monkey Howler Monkey
	Anthropoidea (Catarrhine)	Cercopithecoidae (Old World Monkeys)	Cercopithecoidae	Macaque Baboon
				Leaf-eating Monkeys
		Apes	Hylobatidae	Gibbon
			Pongidae	Orangutan Chimpanzee Gorilla
			Hominidae	Humans

siers, and their relatives—are found mainly in the tropical forests of Africa, Madagascar, and Southeast Asia (especially Borneo and the Philippines). If it weren't for the long-term hospitality of Madagascar as a special homeland for lemurs, there would not be many left of the larger prosimian species. Once some ancestral lemur accidentally reached the shores of that great island, there were practically no natural enemies to contend with until the arrival of *Homo sapiens* much later. Meanwhile, the adaptive radiation of lemurs into different habitats had resulted in at least twenty-one species, ranging from little mouse-sized creatures to the recently extinct giant lemur, *Megaladapis*, bigger than a gorilla. The adaptive radiation of the prosimians on Madagascar was similar to the evolution of the finches on the Galapagos Islands that captured Darwin's attention.

Many of the prosimians are vertical clingers and leapers. Bushbabies and tarsiers, for example, have extremely powerful hindquarters and are able to make prodigious jumps. Alison Jolly (1972) refers to a Senegal bushbaby's achieving an upward vertical leap of 7 feet $4\frac{3}{4}$ inches. Prosimians achieve very precise targeting through their well-developed eye-hand coordination, and their flexible fingers are well designed for grabbing onto the twigs and branches they leap toward. The sifaka "measures its leap visually, pausing and weaving its head from side to side before launching itself across a 20-foot gap to a neighboring trunk. It springs away from its perch

Homo sapiens in Biological Perspective

3.6 This bushbaby, along with the pottos, the lorises, and other prosimians, are among the more distant primate relatives of *Homo sapiens*. (F. D. Schmidt, San Diego Zoo photo)

3.7 Tarsiers, like most other primate species, have extremely versatile hands for grasping and manipulating things. (Ron Garrison, San Diego Zoo photo)

3.8 Macaque family. (Ron Garrison, San Diego Zoo photo)

with body almost in a straight line, then twists in midair to land feet first" (Jolly, 1972:37). Another significant feature of the sifaka's locomotion is that it sometimes walks erect on its hind legs. Some of these prosimians, including the sifaka, are exclusively vegetarian, whereas bushbabies, lorises, and tarsiers rely on insects as an important food source. Tarsiers also kill and eat mice.

The prosimians are interesting to us chiefly because they testify to some of the basic primate characteristics on the basis of which the monkeys, apes, and humans have evolved. The prosimians have

43

tree-adapted, upright posture, which assumed special importance for our ancient ancestors when they came down from the trees and started spending time on the ground. Along with upright body posture most of the prosimians have well-developed hands with fingernails, and their forelimbs are extremely flexible and versatile for swinging, climbing, grasping, and other activities. Eating, for example, often involves manipulating and grasping food tidbits. Their activities generally require excellent vision— more so than is true for most other mammals, among whom the sense of smell is usually more important than sight.

Many of the little nocturnal primates are relatively solitary in social behavior, but the beginnings of more social organization are found among some of them. With bushbabies, pottos, and some of the small lemurs, it appears that each male controls a territory, which overlaps the territories of one or more females. Although these solitary males defend their territories from other males through vociferous shouting matches, they are more sociable toward their coterritorial members of the opposite sex. In some cases, females are more sociable than their male counterparts; for example, mouse lemur females sleep rolled up together in groups.

A few of the lemurs of Madagascar are daytime creatures that live in troops of socially interacting animals occupying demarcated territories. Thus

even among the prosimians there are some rudimentary forms of social organization and communication that become more highly developed as we go up the line of evolution toward the so-called higher primates.

New World Monkeys

As noted above, the New World monkeys, *platyrrhini*, have been a separate line of evolution for several tens of millions of years. They have evolved specialized physical characteristics—notably the prehensile tail—as well as many behavioral habits specialized to a tropical rain forest environment. Many of these animals, such as the spider monkeys and their relatives, are fruit eaters that live in social groups consisting of twenty or more individuals. They have highly versatile hands for climbing and swinging, but their thumbs are more or less aligned with the rest of their fingers instead of opposed, as in many Old World primates. Some of the New World monkeys have lost their thumbs altogether and hang on with their hooklike second and fifth digits. Thus, these platyrrhine monkeys are anatomically specialized in a direction away from the all-purpose manipulation characteristic of apes and humans.

In general, the New World monkeys feed mainly on fruits and insects, with less attention to leaves

3.9 Geographic locations of living monkey and ape species.

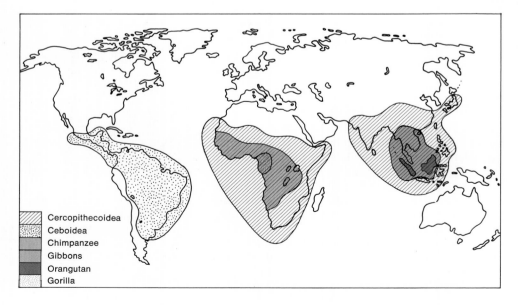

Cercopithecoidea
Ceboidea
Chimpanzee
Gibbons
Orangutan
Gorilla

44

Homo sapiens in Biological Perspective

and other green vegetable matter. Apparently they do rather well in this adaptation, for they can afford to waste a good deal of food. It has been observed that they drop more than half of their food to the forest floor, where it is picked up by birds and other animals. Of the most common South American monkeys only the *Cebus* species appear occasionally to eat small animals other than insects.

Old World Monkeys

There is considerable variation in physical characteristics and behavior patterns among the Old World monkeys. Some of them, such as the colobus and the langurs, are primarily leaf eaters, a characteristic that is reflected in their digestive tract anatomy. Others, including most members of the genus *Cercopithecus*, are fruit eaters. Still others, most notably the several baboon species, are adapted to a diet of shoots and roots, supplemented by insects and on special occasions by small animals.

As with the New World monkeys, most of the Old World species are arboreal (tree-living), although some of them make use of the forest floor and, when the opportunity presents itself, the treasures of farmers' fields. However, a few groups—baboons, macaques, and patas—are ground-dwelling, and because of their terrestrial habits they are particularly interesting for comparisons with the great apes and humans.

There have been a number of important field studies of baboons and macaques, and we know a good deal now about their adaptive styles, including their considerable capabilities for learned behavior. For example, Japanese researchers working with troops of macaques found that there were variations in child-rearing techniques and food preferences that were *not* clearly related to differences in habitat (or other easily specifiable environmental factors) but that seemed to reflect differences in "customs," socially learned ways of carrying out certain tasks. (We will return to the matter of primate learning in Chapter 7.)

Extensive observations of baboons in their natural habitats have provided much data about how they manage the basic issues of defense, food getting, and mating. On the open grasslands of East Africa they usually live in groups composed of adult males and females, adolescents, children, and infants. These groups, which have variable composition (in terms of numbers of children and adults and proportion of males to females), seem to be fairly tightly structured organizations with a central HIERARCHY and a rigid order of dominance among the males, together with clear dominance of males over the females.

At least part of the rigidity and "authoritarian" social organization seems to be related to defense against the dangerous predators in their environment. When danger threatens, the dominant males move forward as a group to confront the predator (cheetah, lion, or other dangerous carnivore), while the females fall behind with the children and infants. This pattern has been observed many times and demonstrates the stability and effectiveness of baboon defensive strategy. The tight organization also works to keep young members of the troop from straying too far, where they might be beyond the protection of the male guard.

Some primatologists have suggested that the marked SEXUAL DIMORPHISM of baboons (males are much larger and more aggressive then females and have prominent canines that females lack) is due to in-group fighting and aggression. Social theorists who refer to the aggressive in-group social patterns of primates, such as the baboons, would do well to keep in mind the fact that *Homo sapiens* lack precisely those physical specializations thought to be the result of in-group aggressive characteristics: the large and offensively dangerous canine teeth.

Anthropoid Apes

The apes, especially the chimpanzees, are generally considered our closest animal relatives. This is because, of all the primates, the apes probably diverged from our own direct line of ancestry no more than 15 million years ago. Some of the evidence for our genetic relationships with the apes include similarities in blood groups and the fact that the apes are plagued by many of the same diseases (including measles, influenza, and syphilis) and play host to many of the same parasites. Today the apes are found mostly in tropical Africa (chimpanzees and gorillas) and in Southeast Asia (orangutans, gibbons, and siamangs), and their habitats are shrinking with the continued encroachment of human populations.

Gorillas (*Gorilla gorilla*) are the largest of the apes. In the wild, males average 300 to 400 pounds, and they can get very obese in captivity—up to 600 pounds. They are ground-living vegetarians; their

45

3.10 Young chimp using standard open-handed gesture to request food from his mother. (Geza Teleki)

3.11 Siamangs, like their near cousins, the gibbons, are true brachiators. Their main means of locomotion is by swinging from branch to branch with their long, powerful arms. (San Diego Zoo photo)

foods are principally leaves, shoots, and other vegetable matter—seldom fruits. They live in relatively stable groups of six to eighteen members, usually dominated by an older, silver-backed male. Often the smaller groups have only one fully adult male, and it is common to find lone males who occasionally join a group.

Chimpanzees (*Pan*) are smaller than gorillas; the average adult male weighs about 110 pounds, and the average adult female weighs about 88 pounds. Their sexual dimorphism is very much less than that of the gorillas, whose males usually weigh twice as much as females.

Chimpanzee diets are quite varied, although fruit is a main element. In at least one area in Tanzania, where they have been intensively observed in the wild, it appears that animal protein is a regular part of the diet. Gombe Park chimpanzees eat insects, birds' eggs, fledgling birds, reptiles, and the young of monkeys, baboons, bush pigs, and bush buck. They also engage in "hunting expeditions," in which there is clear evidence of cooperation in stalking and surrounding the game.

In addition to occasional cooperation in food getting, there are also reports that chimpanzees engage in food sharing. In the Gombe stream reserve the primatologist Geza Teleki witnessed 395 instances of individuals requesting food from animals possessing fresh meat. In 114 cases the request was successful, and "occasionally the possessor will detach a considerable portion of meat and with outstretched hand offer it to the requester" (Teleki, 1973:41). The food sharing among chimps is significant, for vegetarian animals seldom share food with one another.

Orangutans, gibbons, and siamangs are less familiar to North American zoo goers and movie watchers than gorillas and chimps. Orangutans and gibbons are found only in Southeast Asia and tend to be less sociable and less amenable to intensive observation. Gibbons, small animals that often weigh less than twenty pounds, have developed to an extreme the capability of swinging arm-over-arm in a form of movement called BRACHIATION. (The large apes brachiate occasionally, especially in childhood, as a heritage from their arboreal past, but adult gorillas and orangutans are too heavy to indulge in such gymnastics as a regular activity.) Gibbons are primarily vegetarians, although they do eat birds' eggs and insects. They have a social system consisting of separate adult pairs (mated for life) and their dependent offspring, all of whom occupy a small territory that they defend primarily through vocal threatening, males and females being equally vociferous in defense of home and hearth.

The orangutans live in trees more than do the other great apes. Their diet consists of wild fruit, leaves, and shoots. Typically adults reach weights of 165 pounds (male) and 81 pounds (female). In a seven-month field trip Richard Davenport of the Yerkes Primate Center was able to observe only sixteen members of their vanishing species. In only one instance did he see a group of orangs—a family consisting of male, female, and infant. Most of the orangs he encountered were lonely, solitary figures whose social style differed considerably from that of other primates. Recent observations show that the basic social unit of the orangs is the mother-child combination, which is augmented by the usually solitary male only at times of mating. Unfortunately

orangs are easily caught by humans (hence their near extinction) because they are very slow-moving compared to other apes; they are too large to travel rapidly through the treetops and cannot move on the ground as nimbly as the chimps and gorillas. As Vernon Reynolds puts it, they are "too big for their arboreal habits, too arboreal for their size" (Reynolds, 1967:157).

Do Monkeys and Apes Have Families? The Case of the Hamadryas Baboons

During the past decade studies of primate groups in the wild have produced many surprises for behavioral scientists, for monkeys and apes in nature display behavior that is much different from what we see in the zoo. Until these recent studies, a considerable part of the picture concerning primate behavior was based on meticulous observations of captive animals, although there had been some pioneering observations under wild conditions even in earlier times. Generalizing about monkeys and apes from behavior in the zoo is like generalizing about

3.12 Social organization of baboon troop, with infants and mothers in the middle protected by the largest males.

Among the Animals: The World of the Primates

human behavior from observing people in prisons and other closed institutions: the people in these captive conditions show a good deal of aggressive behavior, their actions often seem "neurotic," and social life is relatively uncomplicated (particularly if individuals are confined to separate cells or in rather small groups with little space to move around in). No wonder we have had a very distorted view of the adaptive styles and intellectual capabilities of our primate cousins!

When we began to accumulate studies of the more sociable monkeys like the macaques and baboons, the picture that emerged was one of cohesive "troops"—groups of monkeys in close and continu-ous social interaction, consisting of several adult males and females, juveniles, and infants, all inter-dependent. Although the familylike organization of the gibbons had been known for some time, it was generally felt that the primates organized themselves into "promiscuous hordes" in which sexually re-ceptive females mated with many different adult males and the offspring were cared for by the entire multiadult troop. (Figure 3.12 shows the social orga-nization of the baboons as reported from observa-tions in East and South Africa.)

In 1960 the Swiss ethologist Hans Kummer discov-ered that the hamadryas baboons in the arid grass-lands of Ethiopia have a social organization signifi-

3.13 Sociogram of Hama-dryas baboon one-male group. (Adapted from Kum-mer, 1971)

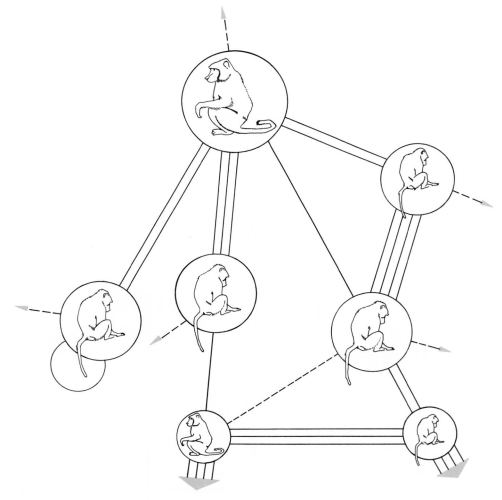

48

Homo sapiens in Biological Perspective

cantly different from that of most of the other baboon groups studied thus far. Like the olive baboons in Tanzania and elsewhere, the hamadryas maintain troops of several scores of members. Superficially their social system does not appear to be very different from the social systems of other baboons, as there are a number of adult males and females, juveniles, and infants. But the striking difference about these baboons of the Ethiopian drylands is the subdivision of the troop into smaller units, each consisting of one male and several females with their immature offspring. Often these little groups have subadult males attached to them, but each group has only one sexually active "father" with one, two, or three females. (Figure 3.13 shows a sociogram of the typical hamadryas family.)

Professor Kummer suggests that the one-male group form of organization is closely adapted to the available food supply. The basic food resources are scattered and consist mainly of the flowers and beans of acacia trees. Each tree provides food for only a few animals, and because these trees tend to be spaced out over the landscape, the special family-like organization of the hamadryas seems well suited to the food supply. As Professor Kummer puts it; "The one-male group thus appears as the 'single-tree-foraging unit.' The groves of ten or more large acacias on the larger riverbeds are usually occupied by one band at a time" (Kummer, 1971:44).

When night falls the little groups of baboons head for the rugged cliffs that are a prominent feature of the Ethiopian landscape. They turn in for the night clinging to ledges in the cliffs, forming multifamily gatherings of as many as seven hundred animals. The rocky cliffs are optimal sleeping places because they provide the best safety from predators in the area. (Baboons in most other areas of Africa sleep in trees.) The gathering for the night increases the protection, for it brings together a number of the powerful males, whose sharp canine teeth are an effective threat to predators, especially when several of the males put up a united front.

The one-male family group of the hamadryas baboons *appears* to be a social adaptation to a particular kind of environment. It is interesting to note that some other monkey groups also have somewhat similar social organizations, including the patas monkey, the gelada baboon, and some of the langurs in India. The maintenance of these one-male groups appears to require some kind of "respect system"

among the males, in which there is little conflict about sexual access to the females. Thus each female is attached to a particular male during most of her adult life. Not only will the male fight with any other baboon male that approaches his females, he will also fight ferociously to defend his females from predators. Kummer notes that "A male hamadryas would allow himself to lose his band rather than abandon his female when she is unable to follow because of wounds or disease; in contrast, anubis baboons, at least in Nairobi Park, do not wait for sick group members" (Kummer, 1971:69). The apparent possessiveness of hamadryas males is closely related to their protectiveness of the physically weaker and more vulnerable female members of the troop.

One lesson to be learned in the study of primate behavior is that "primate nature" has evolved as a system of behavior patterns closely adapted to two basic needs: (1) food getting and (2) protection from predators. For different types of monkeys and apes the need for food getting poses different problems of organization, and the various environments—in Africa and elsewhere—have varied degrees and types of predatory threats. The organization of the social group and the nature of mating relationships appear to be closely related to these environmental factors. Concerning "family organization," the important point to consider is not the specific features of mating arrangements but rather the subdivision of the larger bands or troops into a number of subunits with relatively exclusive sexual arrangements within each subgroup.

Territoriality Among the Primates

It has been repeatedly observed that among primate groups, as among many other mammals, the socially coherent groups of animals (often troops ranging from twenty to well over one-hundred individuals) attach themselves to particular geographical areas in which there may be a core area of most intense utilization and a wider expanse of occasionally used home range. The monkeys and apes are quite variable in the extent to which they will fight to defend these home territories. Figure 3.14 shows the relationships among four groups of gibbon families, in which we see that the groups are fairly

49

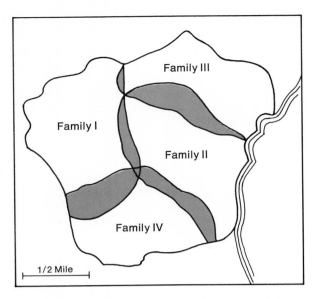

3.14 Relationships among four gibbon families. (Adapted from Jolly, 1972:104)

exclusive in their territorial behavior and defend the boundaries of their territories against other neighboring groups. Among gorillas, on the other hand, there is a much more flexible kind of territorial behavior, for they are not nearly so exclusive about their real estate. Small bands of gorillas may avoid one another—or threaten each other when they meet—but they do not pay much attention to territorial boundaries as such.

Chimpanzees are especially flexible and casual about geographic relationships. Vernon and Frances Reynolds observed chimpanzees in the Budongo Forest of Uganda for a total of 170 days in 1962. With respect to territorial behavior, the Reynolds found it very difficult to observe any clear regularities in the relationships of the chimpanzee groups to particular locations. This was because the groups themselves were so unstable. In a region of perhaps six to eight square miles there was a total of seventy to eighty animals, but they wandered about in very flexible bands containing anywhere from five or six individuals to as many as thirty in one group. These groups were of several types:

(1) adult bands, containing adults of both sexes, and occasionally adolescents, but not including any mothers with dependent young; (2) male bands, con-taining only adult males; (3) mother bands, containing only mothers with young, and occasionally other females; (4) mixed bands, containing mothers with young, other females, adolescents, and adult males. (REYNOLDS and REYNOLDS, 1965:398)

The memberships of the chimpanzee subbands changed frequently. The larger groupings that the Reynolds observed often consisted of a number of the smaller bands that had happened to come together temporarily because of the availability of fruit trees in a particular region. Apparently the chimpanzees communicated a good deal from one group to another about the availability of food, so that whichever groups happened to be near one another might "collaborate" in exploiting the food resources, after which they again moved off in their separate directions in the quest for food.

Dominance Hierarchies

In many monkey groups, notably the olive baboons of East Africa and some of the New World monkeys, there appear to be fairly distinct patterns

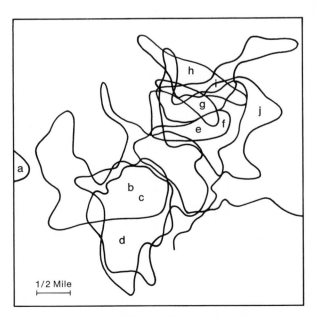

3.15 Overlapping home ranges of ten gorilla troops. (Adapted from Jolly, 1972:104)

50

Homo sapiens in Biological Perspective

3.16 **Pygmy chimpanzee mother with infant.** (San Diego Zoo photo)

of dominance and submissiveness among the animals within a troop or band. Over a period of weeks some observers have noted that almost all the animals in the troop deferred to the most dominant males. However, some of the members who were submissive to the dominant males, in turn, dominated over the rest of the members of the troop, and so on down the hierarchy of individuals until one reaches the bottom of the ladder—members who defer to every other member of the group. This pattern of dominance and submission is particularly evident in situations of conflict over desirable food items and sleeping places.

With chimpanzees, observers have noted that there are differences in "status" among individuals, but clear dominance of one animal over another is not a frequent feature in social interaction. It appears that chimpanzees can interact with one another a good deal without concern about status. Furthermore, the Reynolds found that "there was no evidence of a linear hierarchy of dominance among males or females; there were no observations of exclusive rights to receptive females; and there were no permanent leaders of groups" (Reynolds and Reynolds, 1965:415). Among the chimpanzees in Gombe Park, Teleki reported that one adult male occupied a position of social dominance over all of the 150-odd members of the population. However, in food-sharing behavior this dominant male, Mike, readily shared food with others, both males and females. What is more striking is that he was often refused when he requested food (Teleki, 1973).

Quarreling, including fairly aggressive fighting, does take place among chimpanzees in the wild. However, the Reynolds reported that during three-hundred hours of observation in the Budongo Forest they saw only seventeen quarrels in which there was actual fighting or at least displays of anger. These generally lasted only a few seconds.

Because sexual access to females is one of the situations that supposedly evokes differences of male status most clearly, the relatively "egalitarian" nature of chimpanzee social organization is evidenced by the rather undramatic and uncompetitive sexual activity. The Reynolds reported that there were very few signs of jealousy or aggression among males in groups that were traveling with sexually receptive females. Jane Van Lawick-Goodall observed occasions on which several males copulated with the same female, one after another. On one occasion a receptive female was entertained by seven "suitors" in succession. This kind of relaxed and noncompetitive attitude among males would be quite unusual among many other primates.

Chimpanzee individuals and groups do a good deal of social communicating through both vocal calls and a great variety of physical gestures and body movements. They groom one another, they touch, and they call from one group to another. Perhaps one of the reasons for their more amiable and open social system is their relative safety from dangerous predators. In addition to being highly intelligent and versatile, chimpanzees are strong and effective fighters.

The description of a "dominance hierarchy" in a monkey or ape troop is constructed by an observer

51

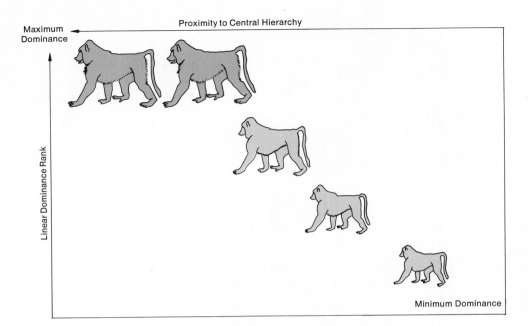

3.17 Schematic view of olive baboon dominance hierarchy.

from an analysis of hundreds of individual instances of dominance versus deference behavior. The hierarchy may turn out somewhat differently depending on what type of behavior the observer notes. Dominance patterns in sexual behavior are not the same as the interactions in selecting nesting locations, and competition in food getting encompasses yet a different system of interrelationships. As the primatologist Thelma Rowell has pointed out, the different components of dominance-deference interactions are not completely correlated with each other, so the abstract dominance hierarchies reported from field research are only rough approximations from diverse sets of behaviors that may be modified a good deal in new situations.

Tool Using Among Chimpanzees

Many observers have seen chimpanzees pick up branches, stones, sticks, and other objects and make use of them for various purposes. Jane Van Lawick-Goodall has reported clear instances of actual tool preparation and use among the chimpanzees in Tanzania. She saw the chimps take small sticks and prepare them in a standardized shape for poking into termite hills to get an especially delectable food:

When a chimpanzee sees a sealed-up termite hole, it scrapes away the thin layer of soil with index finger or thumb, picks up a grass stalk, thin twig, or piece of vine, and pokes this carefully down the hole. It waits for a moment and then withdraws the tool, the end of which is coated with termites, hanging on with their mandibles, and these the chimpanzee picks off with the lips. (GOODALL, 1965:442)

Table 3.3: Brain Sizes of Various Primates

Name of Primate	Range of Sizes	Average Brain Size
Baboon (*Papio*)	(no range given)	200 cc
Gibbon (*Hylobates*)	82–125	103 cc
Chimpanzee (*Pan*)	282–500	383 cc
Gorilla (*Gorilla*)	340–752	505 cc
Orangutan (*Pongo*)	276–540	405 cc
Homo sapiens (modern)	1000–2000	1330 cc

Source: Adapted from CAMPBELL, 1974:272.

52

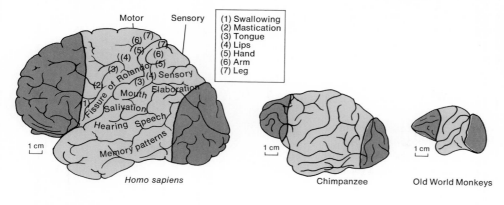

Motor   Sensory

(1) Swallowing
(2) Mastication
(3) Tongue
(4) Lips
(5) Hand
(6) Arm
(7) Leg

Homo sapiens   Chimpanzee   Old World Monkeys

3.18 **Comparisons of size and features of primate brains. The temporal lobe (in color) is relatively larger and more complex in *Homo sapiens*.**

Chimpanzee tool-using behavior is extremely simple compared to the complex technologies that humans use in their food quests and other adaptive behaviors. Nonetheless, they qualify both as tool making and as instances of adaptive cultural "traditions."

The research data that have so far been collected on chimpanzees under wild conditions seem to show quite a range of *variations* in the adaptive behavior of these extremely intelligent animals. Their brain size, although smaller than that of *Homo sapiens*, is relatively large, occasionally as much as 400 cubic centimeters (somewhat less than one third the human average). (See Tables 3.3 and 3.4.) The construction of their brains is rich in convolutions, and the frontal lobe, which is involved with higher association functions, is fairly well developed.

Some researchers use an index of cephalization (Table 3.4), computed as the amount of brain weight as a percentage of body weight.

Chimpanzees and Humans: The Important Similarities

With each new report from research teams observing chimpanzees in their natural settings, the evidence accumulates that they are indeed more humanlike than other higher primates. Although humans and chimpanzees differ greatly with respect to the features listed below, the similarities between *Pan* and *Homo* contrast, often markedly, with the other apes and monkeys:

1. Use of tools.
2. Flexible social organization.
3. Sexual dimorphism is not pronounced.

Table 3.4: Index of Cephalization

Animal Group	Index
Mammals in general (excluding primates)	.06
Three great apes	.29
Monkeys	.41
Modern humans	.92

Source: From CAMPBELL, 1974:272.

4. Omnivorous diet.
5. Active hunting, including group cooperation.
6. Food sharing in connection with hunting.
7. Susceptibility to many of the same diseases.
8. Complex social gestures and facial expressions.
9. Capability for symbolic communication (see Chapter 8).

As we learn more about the behavioral repertoires of chimpanzees it is likely that this list of similarities will be extended. This does not mean, of course, that we are biological descendants of chimpanzees. It does suggest that we can learn much about our basic primate heritage from fuller knowledge of both the physiology and the behavioral characteristics of chimpanzees.

Inferences from Animal Studies: *On Aggression* and *The Territorial Imperative*

Many writers have used comparisons from animal studies in order to produce theories about important

53

features of human behavior. One school of thought that has become popular, at least on the best-seller lists, argues that "human nature" can be understood if we study the "basic instincts" that supposedly still operate strongly in human behavior. Details of these "instincts" are thought to be discoverable from meticulous study of the aggressive and territorial behavior of fish, wolves, deer, rats, and other animals. According to one writer, we can understand much of human behavior if we consider *Homo sapiens* to be a "naked ape" that adapts and behaves in response to many of the same drives and biological instincts of the lower animals.

The biological, instinct-oriented explanations of human behavior that have gained much recent attention are extremely valuable studies in many respects, and the works of Konrad Lorenz, Robert Ardrey, and others deserve careful reading—not only because of their engaging literary style but also because they analyze in great detail some important features of animal behavior. However, we must look at these instinct theorists with a good deal of analytical caution. They are at their best when they describe in beautiful detail the courtship and aggression of stickleback fish and the greylag goose, but the logical connection between these examples and modern human behavior involves some very large and difficult steps of inference, in which conclusions can be led astray by superficially colorful argument.

One of the important points of the ethologist Konrad Lorenz in his book *On Aggression* (1963) is that aggressive behavior in animals serves a number of important positive functions. He says:

we find that aggression, far from being the diabolical, destructive principal that classical psychoanalysis makes it out to be, is really an essential part of the life-preserving organization of instincts. . . . Moreover . . . mutation and selection, the great "constructors" which make genealogical trees grow upward, have chosen, of all unlikely things, the rough and spiny shoot of intra-specific aggression to bear the blossoms of personal friendship and love. (LORENZ, 1963:48)

In a similar vein, Robert Ardrey in his *Territorial Imperative* notes the important survival functions of territoriality, defense of territories, and related animal behavior, but he then goes on to argue that

3.19　**Male chimpanzees sharing meat of a freshly killed monkey. (Geza Teleki)**

3.20　**Mandrill displays his sharp canines in threat gesture. (Ron Garrison, San Diego Zoo photo)**

an instinct-based, innate "territorial imperative" is at the base of much that is destructive and aggressive in the behavior of modern humans.

How can we interpret these instinct-based arguments about "human nature," and how can we unite into a single theoretical perspective the biological facts about the human animal and the complex, learned, culturally shaped behavior patterns that appear to make human behavior so vastly different from that of other animals? Even though there is considerable evidence that the human animal is not *completely* different from other animals, does it necessarily follow that biological instincts as described by Lorenz, Ardrey, and others are the most important baselines for our understanding of ourselves?

One of the most interesting clues to interpreting those instinct theories is that they *are inadequate for understanding the behavior of the nonhuman*

3.21 **Primate social behavior is very complex and involves a great deal of individual learning. Grooming behavior is one of the important bonds among many primate species, as with these baboons. (Ron Garrison, San Diego Zoo photo)**

primates, as well as other animals. The instinct theorists generally ignore the very great range of variation of aggressive and territorial behavior that we find among chimpanzees, baboons, and other primate societies. It is not just *Homo sapiens* that displays great flexibility of learned social behavior. In territoriality, for example, the more carefully the researchers observe the baboons, macaques, chimpanzees, and other primates, the more difficult it is to use simple ideas of instincts to account for the *divergences* of behaviors in different environmental situations. The versatile baboons, for example, behave more or less aggressively and more or less territorially depending on the nature of the local terrain, the availability of food supplies, and the amount of predatory threats. Like chimpanzees and other animals, they behave quite differently when they are caged and confined than they do in the wild state. Furthermore, many of these animals fail to develop important segments of appropriate behavior unless they have a chance to see the behavior performed by fellow members of their species. Chimpanzees as well as other primates are relatively incompetent sexually, for example, unless they have had a chance both to observe other animals' sexual behavior and to experiment with these activities themselves.

Japanese researchers working with macaque monkeys have noted that, contrary to earlier belief, the monkeys have few instinctive food preferences. They readily pick up tastes for new kinds of foods (including those introduced by the researchers themselves), and neighboring bands of monkeys differ from one another in the foods they eat even though their environments are closely similar. The main point is that among monkey and ape social groups behavior is much more variable and environmentally adjustable than one would suspect from the descriptions that focus on supposed instinctive behavior patterns.

The behavior patterns of more complex mammals, especially primates, are the end results of very complex interactions between biological heredity and environmental experience. Both the instinct theory and the exclusive focus on nongenetic learning theories of animal behavior are deficient and incomplete as models of explanation. This is the problem with books like *On Aggression* and *The Territorial Imperative.* It is not that animal behavior can't be extrapolated to human beings but rather that simplified instinct explanations are very inadequate even in dealing with the nonhuman animal world. The following are some of the basic elements needed for an adequate understanding of both nonhuman and human animal behavior:

1. Among animals with complex brains such as the primates, there are certainly important biological mechanisms underlying *all* behavior patterns, but these do not generally take the form of spontaneous tendencies toward particular actions as implied by the general idea of instincts. Certain basic needs and reactions to fulfill these needs are fundamental. All animals need to ingest food; they must protect themselves from extremes of temperature and other environmental features; they must breathe air to obtain oxygen; they must protect themselves from predators; and if they are to survive as species they must reproduce themselves. In addition to these basic drives, there are other biologically based features, but one of the most important biological mechanisms is that governing the patterns of learning—modifying behavior in the light of experience.

2. In every species, especially among the more complex social animals such as the primates, there is a great deal of intraspecific diversity of genetic characteristics. Among baboons, chimpanzees, and all other animals, there are some individuals with exceptional mental capabilities compared with other individuals; some individuals are larger and stronger than most of their fellows; and some individuals are born with serious hereditary defects, including inherited diseases. Coloring, facial contours, general body build, and other features vary from one individual to another, and in many other ways genetic *diversity* is an essential feature of the biobehavioral characteristics of species. Such genetic diversity is essential if natural selection according to the Darwinian model of evolution is to take place (see Chapter 5).

3. Because adaptation in both the short run of individual animals and the long run of species survival is dependent on relationships to given environments, in the more complex animals almost all aspects of behavior are inherently plastic and modifiable in relation to specific features of an environment. The full extent of this modifiability is not yet fully explored, but the behavioral repertoire of relatively wise animals, such as the monkeys and the apes, appears to be significantly more variable than was earlier thought. This makes sense when we consider that most of these animals have in the course of their species evolution experienced very considerable modifications in their physical environments, densities of population, and other living conditions.

4. Behavior patterns among different animals, groups, or species may often appear to be similar yet be derived from quite different mechanisms, including different components of inherited and environmental effects. For some kinds of animals (among a number of bird species, for example), certain patterns of territorial and courtship behavior may be determined largely by genetically inherited mechanisms with rather narrow modifiability; yet very similar behavior in other species can result from specific, learned patterns with little direct genetic programming. Geneticist Benson Ginzburg and his associates have demonstrated, for example, that they can raise strains of mice and dogs that are very aggressive toward other members of their species, and very little change can be induced in them through environmental learning. On the other hand, they have produced varieties within the *same species* of animals that appear very aggressive but are modifiable through training, and yet other strains are produced that appear to be unaggressive regardless of the amount of hostility learning to which they are exposed.

5. Whereas the instinct theories of Lorenz, Ardrey, and others assume some kind of pool or reservoir of spontaneous tendencies toward particular kinds of action (e.g., pent-up aggression that *must* be released sooner or later in some form), studies of aggressive behavior in human and nonhuman animals thus far indicate that individuals can have "pent-up" tendencies toward "spontaneous" aggression for the most part only as a result of complex interactions between their biological makeup and their environmental experiences. This is especially true of human beings. Although certain kinds of experience may dispose individuals toward aggression and tendencies toward hostile reactions may in some sense be stored up, such behavioral tendencies are only one of a number of *different* possible reactions to similar stimuli. Different individuals can react to the same stimulus situation with different behavioral patterns. A simple example of this is that certain baboons, especially larger, more dominant ones, may react with a confident, hostile attack

Homo sapiens in Biological Perspective

when confronted by danger, whereas less dominant, weaker members of the species may in the same context retreat.

6. General behavior patterns such as territoriality are theoretical constructs developed by observers as *abstractions* from various animal behaviors, and the specific details of such territoriality may be quite varied. They may involve a large number of different kinds of individual actions. The same holds for the general idea of dominance. There are no such things as dominance hierarchies as *real* entities among baboons or other animals who have been thus described. What one finds instead are complex constellations of behavior, often very flexible from one situation to another with regard to the degree of deference or submissiveness that some animals display toward other animals within their primary groups. The same goes for behavior with regard to territories.

Among the Animals: The World of the Primates

4

The Evolution of *Homo sapiens*: The Big-Brained Primate

To continue with the story of human evolution we have to establish a time perspective and lay out the main kinds of time markers used by geologists, anthropologists, and others.

Until the nineteenth century most scholars generally accepted the biblical idea that the earth was only a few thousand years old. Even quite radical scientists like the French paleontologist Buffon allowed only seventy-five thousand years for the age of the planet earth. The biblical time chart was shaken somewhat as people kept finding fossils in unusual places—like marine fossils high up in the mountains—but these finds were generally explained as caused by "The Flood." Some people argued that there were a series of floods, a set of catastrophes that resulted in special features of the earth's crust and accounted for all the fossil plant and animal materials in various geological deposits.

Modern scientists now believe that the earth is perhaps 5 to 6 billion years old and that the first signs of life began at least 3 to 4 billion years ago. The development of more and more complex forms of life—from the earliest one-celled creatures to multicelled organisms capable of complex behavior—went on for billions of years, and it is "only" during the last 500 million years that the rich varieties of green plants and vertebrate animals began to spread around the dry land areas of the globe.

From that perspective, the total evolutionary life history of *Homo sapiens* is short indeed, for our ancestors diverged from our apelike primate relatives only a few million years ago. Humans as tool-using, upright-walking culture bearers are among the most recent products of the evolutionary process.

The Geological Timetable

In the previous chapter, Table 3.1 shows the sequence of geological time periods. The most recent era, the CENOZOIC, is of greatest interest to us in unraveling the story of primate and human evolution. In the preceding chapter we mentioned the names of the earlier epochs of this era, the Paleocene, the Eocene, the Oligocene, and the Miocene epochs. In this chapter we will be concerned mainly with the Pliocene, the Pleistocene, and the Holocene (relatively recent) epochs, especially the PLEISTOCENE, the epoch in which much of the *human* evolutionary story occurred.

Table 4.1: Glacial Periods During the Pleistocene Epoch

Geochronology	Glaciations (Europe)	Estimated Age (years B.C.)
Upper Pleistocene	Postglacial	
	Würm glacial	10,000
	Interglacial	70,000
		100,000
Middle Pleistocene	Riss glacial	
	Interglacial	200,000
	Mindel glacial	400,000
	Interglacial	500,000
Lower Pleistocene	Günz glacial	
	Interglacial	1,000,000
	Donau glacial	
		3,000,000

During the Pleistocene a series of great Ice Ages came and went, changing the face of the earth, causing large-scale climatic swings, and transforming plant and animal life (see Table 4.1). The first great period of glacial ice has been called the Donau GLACIATION, named after a locale in Eastern Europe where the physical evidences of this Ice Age were first discovered. The Donau glacial period is believed by geologists to have occurred about 2 million years ago, followed by a long warm period (warmer than our present world climate). Then, perhaps slightly more than a million years ago, came a new Ice Age, conventionally labeled the Günz glacial period. From that time until the present there have been alternating periods of arctic cold, in which great sheets of ice covered large parts of the Northern Hemisphere, and interglacial warm periods. Some geologists argue that our present climate is simply an interglacial time and that in a few thousand years the inhospitable cold will return again.

In North America the Ice Ages are named for the states in which their moraines (ridges of rock and debris left by glaciers) have been found. In chronological sequence they are the Nebraska, which cor-responds with the Günz, the Kansas (Mindel), the Illinois (Riss), and the Wisconsin (Würm) glaciations. Nothing corresponding to the Donau glaciation is clearly indicated in North American geology.

The advance and retreat of the great Ice Age geological events provide a handy time frame within which the different fossil and archaeological remains of human evolution can be organized. Thus the earliest known humanlike fossils from East Africa appear to be older than the first (Donau) glacial time period. All of the authenticated evidences of early humans in Europe fit into geological time slots *after* the Günz glaciation and are therefore less than a million years old. Finally, as can be seen in Figure 4.1, all of recorded history, all of plant and animal domestication, and all of the settlement of people into sedentary village and town life—all of these striking developments in human cultural growth—came after the last glaciation (Würm), within the past ten thousand to fifteen thousand years.

The Divergence of the Hominids from Ancestral Primates[1]

The best evidence we have now indicates that the human line of evolution diverged from that of our cousins, the apes, no more than 15 million years ago during the Miocene epoch. There are two kinds of evidence for this idea: fossil finds and chemical analysis. Fossil evidence shows that as we go back in time to older and older precursors of humans, the forms look more and more like fossils that could also be ancestral to the modern apes. There are, of course, some fossils that are clearly ancestral in the ape line, and they indicate something of the ways in which the chimpanzees, gorillas, orangutans, and, much earlier in time, the gibbons gradually diverged from a common primate ancestor.

One thing that should be plainly stated is that we are not descended from a creature that was just like the living apes of today. No living ape resembles the ancestor of *Homo sapiens*. The apes that we see in

[1]The members of the family Hominidae include all of the fossil and living humans—from somewhat humanlike apes to present-day *Homo sapiens*—that make up the distinctly human line, separate from the apes.

The Evolution of Homo sapiens: The Big-Brained Primate

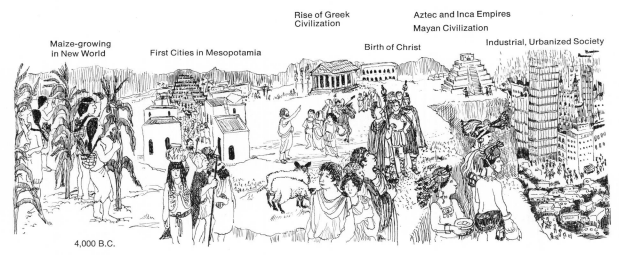

First Arrivals in New World (via Alaska)

Java and Peking Fossils

Human-like Fossils from East Africa

Western European Cave Art

Many Stone Tools

Grain-growing in Near East

New Forms of Stone Tools

Australopithecus and *Homo habilis*

Neanderthal Fossils

Crude Pebble Tools at Olduvai Gorge

Handaxes in Old World

2.5 Million B.C.   1.7 Million B.C.   600,000·500,000 B.C. 100,000 B.C.   15,000 B.C.   6,000 B.C.

Rise of Greek Civilization

Aztec and Inca Empires

Mayan Civilization

Maize-growing in New World

First Cities in Mesopotamia

Birth of Christ

Industrial, Urbanized Society

4,000 B.C.

4.1 The human trek, as read from the archaeological evidence.

the zoos and in the wild have themselves evolved over a long trail of evolution into the specialized creatures they are today.

Biochemical analyses of blood (e.g., the ABO blood-type series) and related information lead to somewhat the same picture as the fossil record. Figure 4.2 compares the "family tree" of primate evolu-

tion based on the fossil evidence with one constructed in terms of biochemical analyses. Computations based on the biochemical data suggest a more recent separation of human and ape evolution.

We have very little fossil evidence concerning those earliest ancestors whose evolution marked the separation of a HOMINID line from the great apes. There are two types of fossils that are of great interest in

Homo sapiens in Biological Perspective

this respect and several schools of thought concerning their interpretation. These ancient candidates for hominid ancestry are called *Ramapithecus* and *Gigantopithecus*.

In the 1930s researchers discovered some fossil remains of very great antiquity in the Siwalik Hills of north India. The new fossil was given the name *Ramapithecus*. More and more *Ramapithecus* fossils have been found in ensuing years, and it now appears that in the period from about 14 million to 10 million years ago there existed quite a number of these little "apes" in north India. The original discoverer, G. Edward Lewis, felt that the *Ramapithecus* fossils he had found should be considered hominids, directly ancestral to later, more human-like animals. Unfortunately the fossils he was working with consisted of only a few jaw fragments and some teeth. Nonetheless, the size and shape of teeth in fossils are among the most important kinds of evidence that scientists use in sorting out evolutionary lines and making inferences about the diet and other characteristics of ancient animals. The teeth of *Ramapithecus* were very unlike those of modern apes. The difference lay especially in the size of the

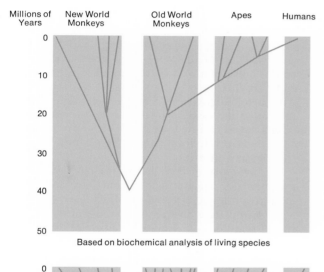

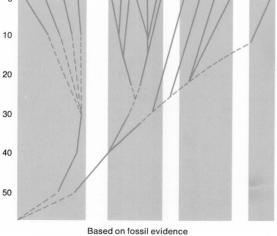

4.2 **Evolutionary differentiation of higher primates, based on two different kinds of evidence.**

The Evolution of Homo sapiens: The Big-Brained Primate

canine teeth, which were not as large and protruding as those of chimps and gorillas. The physical anthropologist David Pilbeam has commented that *Ramapithecus* ''was, or was becoming, a ground feeder eating a diet including numerous small, tough morsels,'' and that ''Taken as a whole, the evidence to be obtained from the *Ramapithecus* material points to an animal with a facial-dental complex of characteristics similar to or foreshadowing those of later hominids, both morphologically and functionally'' (Pilbeam, 1972:94).

The teeth and fragments of jawbone from north India are not very convincing by themselves, but they assume greater importance in the light of related fossil finds in East Africa. Africa, in fact, has become more and more significant in the past decade as a region full of important fossil evidence about the origins of *Homo sapiens*. In 1961 the famous anthropologist Louis B. Leakey announced a new find in Kenya which was assigned an age of 14 million years (radiometric dating) and to which he gave the name *Kenyapithecus*. Later studies have suggested that *Kenyapithecus* was very much like *Ramapithecus* in many particulars. It is significant to note that at that time the general climate and fauna of East Africa were fairly similar to those of north India, where *Ramapithecus* was found.

While many physical anthropologists tend to agree with Lewis's view that *Ramapithecus* is an ancestral hominid, other scientists strongly disagree. These scholars argue that there is considerable justification for classifying *Ramapithecus* as a pongid. That is, they suggest that this animal was already too much like modern apes to be directly ancestral to humans. Some, though not all, of the anthropologists who take the latter view feel that the fossil form known as *Gigantopithecus* is a more significant candidate for human ancestry.

The first evidence of *Gigantopithecus* came to light not at an anthropologist's research site but in a Chinese apothecary shop. Since fossil bones and teeth have been commonly used in Chinese medical preparations, the paleontologist G. H. R. von Koenigswald occasionally visited chemists' shops to see what treasures he might find. One day (in the 1930s) he discovered an enormous tooth, badly worn but still recognizably primate.

Von Koenigswald suggested that the fossil tooth represented a newly discovered form, which he named *Gigantopithecus*. However, another anthropologist, Franz Weidenreich, suggested that the tooth had belonged not to a giant ape but to a giant man and that this form was ancestral to early humans. Although many scholars feel that the original name, indicating the fossil's pongid status, is appropriate, others have supported Weidenreich's claim that the creature might, indeed, have been a hominid rather than an ape ancestor.

The evidence of both *Ramapithecus* and *Gigantopithecus* is frustratingly incomplete, and more definitive interpretation of these fossils will have to wait. Fortunately the physical remains of a later fossil hominid—*Australopithecus*—are relatively extensive, and anthropologists are beginning to put together a fairly extensive picture of this early ancestor of ours.

Species: The Problems of Classification

Throughout this book we will be wrestling with problems of classifying things—including physical creatures and cultural patterns. In the real world there are usually many cases that do not fit neatly into categories, a fact of life that makes procedures for classifying difficult. Because we have words for putting all those individual things into some sort of order, our language leads us to think in terms of "types" or "kinds" or "species," often ignoring the presence of intermediate or ambiguous cases. The problem is made more complex by the bewildering variations within any individual category of things that we want to study.

In the eighteenth century the great naturalist Carolus Linnaeus worked out a comprehensive system for classifying all living things into a hierarchical system of categories from subspecies and species up to phylum and kingdom. According to the Linnaean system, we humans belong to the species *sapiens* of the genus *Homo*. The rest of the Linnaean system of classification, from the viewpoint of where *Homo sapiens* fits in, is as follows:

62

Homo sapiens in Biological Perspective

Kingdom:	**Animalia (as contrasted with plants)**
Phylum:	**Chordata (because we have backbones instead of, for example, exoskeletons like bees)**
Class:	**Mammalia (as contrasted, for example, with the reptiles)**
Infraclass:	**Eutheria (the placental mammals)**
Order:	**Primates (as contrasted with the carnivores, for example)**
Suborder:	**Anthropoidea (monkeys, apes, and humans)**
Superfamily:	**Hominoidea (the largest anthropoids, including the apes and humans)**
Family:	**Hominidae (humans and their ancestors)**
Genus:	***Homo* (includes "Java Man," "Peking Man," "Neanderthal Man," and modern humans)**
Species:	***sapiens* (includes Neanderthal as well as modern humans)**

The foundation of the Linnaean system of classification is the concept of SPECIES. Biologically, a species is an interbreeding population of animals that is reproductively isolated from other animals. Interspecies mating either does not occur or else the progeny of the union is reproductively impotent. Mating between a horse and a donkey, for example, produces a living off-spring (a mule), but mules cannot reproduce. Horses and donkeys are both members of the GENUS *Equus*, but they are different species. It is generally assumed that two different species that still mate (like horses and donkeys) were once a single, intermating population, but they become reproductively isolated from each other because of geographical separation or divergence in sexual behavior. Subspecies, on the other hand, are not reproductively isolated, even though they may "look different." The various breeds of dogs are examples of subspecies.

There are a great many problems with the precise definition of the individual species, not the least of which is the lack of clear experimental evidence to show whether two closely related species can or cannot mate and produce fully potent offspring. Some different species of monkeys, for example, may turn out to be geographically isolated subspecies.

If we look at the Linnaean chart we note that some extinct fossil populations, such as Neanderthal and "Java Man," are included within the same genus as *Homo sapiens*. Most anthropologists consider Neanderthal to be of the same species as modern humans, so they refer to *Homo sapiens neanderthalensis*, suggesting a subspecies difference. Java Man, on the other hand, is considered to be *Homo erectus*, a different species. We can refer to *erectus* as a PALEOSPECIES, noting that *erectus* is distinct from modern humans mainly because we do not have a complete, unbroken sequence of fossil evidence stretching back to Ice Age times, half a million years ago. If we did have the entire continuous series of data about the evolution of *Homo* from *erectus* to modern *sapiens*, we would be hard pressed to designate any particular point for separating these populations into different species. In one sense, *Homo* might be considered a single *evolutionary species* that changed its form over time, during several hundreds of thousands of years of biological evolution.

The Evolution of Homo sapiens: The Big-Brained Primate

Naming the Fossils: "Lumpers" and "Splitters"

One of the joys of finding fossils is that the discoverer has the honor of naming the fossil with a species and genus designation. This exercise in science and imagination has occasionally led to some egocentricity, when the discoverer decided to name the fossil after himself. More often the honor is bestowed on some other individual. In that spirit the paleontologist Von Koenigswald gave the name *Gigantopithecus blacki* to the fossil tooth found in the Chinese drugstore, in honor of the late Davidson Black.

In earlier days nearly every newly excavated hominid fossil received a unique name, as if every one of them belonged to a different genus and species. The list of fossil names grew and grew, to the frustration of college students and others who had to memorize all those different latinized words. As more fossils have accumulated, and theories of human evolution have become more refined, fossils with similar characteristics have been classified as belonging together and the names have had to be changed accordingly. The Peking fossils (once known as *Sinanthropus pekinensis*) and the Java materials (formerly *Pithecanthropus palaeojavanicus*) are now grouped as *Homo erectus*, suggesting that they belong to the same species and are our direct ancestors.

Some anthropologists take the position that there have been only a small number of different genetic lines of hominid evolution, so that most of the fossils should be lumped together under a few species and genus labels. Other theorists, though, emphasize the differences among the fossils, preferring to split them into a wide variety of categories, at least until more specimens are found. Obviously the problems of dating fossils add to the arguments between the "lumpers" and the "splitters."

The Evidence from Olduvai Gorge

Our knowledge of our ancient ancestors took several steps forward beginning about 1959, when Louis B. Leakey, his wife, Mary, and their incredibly persistent and hardworking research crew found some important new fossil remains in a remarkable canyon in Tanzania. Some hundreds of thousands of years ago a newly formed river began to cut through the Serengeti Plain of Tanzania, exposing more and more prehistoric geological deposits as it formed a canyon. The walls of that canyon portray a geological sequence that extends back nearly 2 million years. For much of its history there was a lake in the vicinity, and the plain was full of animals, among them, apparently, quite a number of our ancestors. For a long time, the habitat was open woodland and parkland with grasses around the lakeside. To make matters even more interesting, there were a series of volcanic eruptions in the area nearly 2 million years ago, and the materials spewed out by the volcanos provide us with geological markers which physicists can date with considerable accuracy.

The excitement of Olduvai Gorge consists not only in the way in which years and years of human evolution have been exposed on the face of the cliff but also in the discovery of some of the oldest evidence of stone tools. These forerunners of our modern technological complexity consist of simple pebbles chipped to form an edge or blade for greater cutting power. Some of these stone tools, it appears, had been used for pounding or scraping or crushing. Any one of them would probably pass unnoticed and unrecognized in a gravel pit or stream bed, but they are recognizable as tools mainly because many of them have been found grouped in small areas that must have been the day-to-day living floors of those ancient hominids who made and used them. The same living floors also have fragments of bones that are the remains of butchered animals, and evidence of vegetable food, including seeds and nuts. These living areas were buried under the earth's surface until the river cut through and exposed them.

Homo sapiens in Biological Perspective

How Old Are the Olduvai Gorge Materials?

The volcanic layers near the bottom of the canyon at Olduvai enable physicists to give a fairly precise estimate of the age of these fossils and related mate-rials. The method now used for this type of chrono-logical estimating is called potassium-argon dating. It is based on the fact that volcanic deposits contain a form of potassium (K^{40}) which decays, through radiation, at a constant rate. As electrons are thrown off in the radiation process, the potassium converts to argon (Ar^{40}). The decay rate is such that half of

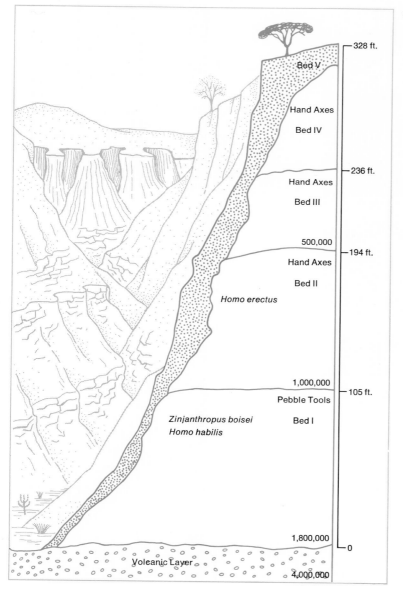

4.3 Schematic diagram of the geological strata in Olduvai Gorge, showing approximate levels at which fossils and stone tools were found.

The Evolution of Homo sapiens: The Big-Brained Primate

4.4 **Professor Leakey at Olduvai Gorge. (Ian Berry, Magnum)**

take place? The bottom of the gorge, "Bed One," has been dated at about 2 million years, and some of the fossil evidence of hominid life is very close to this 2-million-year baseline. It seems fairly likely that the fossils and stone tools at the bottom of the gorge are somewhere around 1.75 million years old.

There are other geological markers farther up which range in age from a million years to a half million years. Contemporaneous with the hominids and their stone tools were some interesting animals, now extinct, including giant pigs, the elephant like *Dinotherium*, and a huge deerlike animal, *Siwatherium*, an ancestor of modern giraffes. The now-extinct saber-toothed tiger and other carnivorous cats prowled the area. The fossilized remains of these extinct species add strength to the chronological estimates made by the physicists. A point of further interest is the progression in the evolution of different animals which is evident as one moves upward on the face of the Olduvai cliff: as one gets closer and closer to the surface, the structure of animal bones becomes more and more like that of the creatures now inhabiting that part of east Africa.

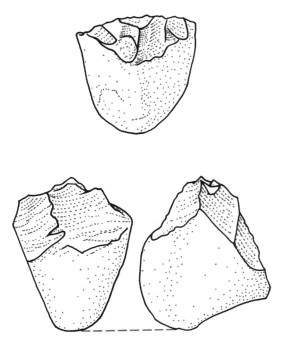

4.5 **Items in the *Homo habilis* tool kit.**

the radioactive potassium is dissipated after 1.3 billion years. The constant rate of decay gives physicists a method for determining the age of specific geological specimens by measuring the amount of argon that has developed in volcanic materials.

Some of the living sites and ancient creatures in Olduvai Gorge were enclosed or sandwiched between two layers of volcanic deposits. Clearly these hominids had lived *after* the first volcanic eruption and *before* the second volcanic event. When did this

Homo sapiens in Biological Perspective

Hunters and Vegetarians: The Rise of the *Australopithecinae*

From the many fragments of fossil evidence painstakingly accumulated by Louis and Mary Leakey in the Olduvai Gorge region, together with a number of fossil finds from other parts of Africa, it appears that about 2 million years ago there were at least two different kinds of hominids in East Africa. Fortunately the evidence is not simply a few teeth and fragments of jaw, as in the case of *Ramapithecus*, for our fossil ancestors, now generally labeled *Australopithecus*, are evidenced by a large number of parts of the jaws, hands, pelves, legs, and feet. Thus a good deal is now known about the physical structure of these hominids.

The name *Australopithecus* (literal translation: "southern ape") was given to a fossil from South Africa back in 1924. The first evidence of the southern ape was a nearly complete child's skull discovered in a limestone mine at Taung in Cape Province, South Africa. Since the discovery, a number of other fossils have been found at Sterkfontein, Kromdraai,

and Swartkrans. During the past fifty years the physical remains of these early hominids have gradually accumulated as fossil hunters have continued their searches. The great majority of the finds are from South and East Africa, although some specimens from Asia are now also considered Australopithecines.

Many researchers suggest that there were two different forms of *Australopithecus*. One form, called *Australopethicus robustus*, was husky, with heavy bones (weighed over 100 pounds), rugged facial features, heavy brow ridges, and massive jaws. It had large molars with especially well-developed grinding areas, indicating that possibly it was a vegetarian living mainly on roots, bulbs, and tough shoots and leaves.

The other form, including the baby from Taung, was a smaller animal (under a hundred pounds) with less rugged facial features, finer bones, a near-human dentition, suggesting that its diet differed from that of *A. robustus*. Many physical anthropologists agree with the Leakeys that this hominid, *Australopithecus africanus*, may well have been more of a meat eater. It had a somewhat larger brain (for its size) than its bigger, vegetable-preferring cousin.

It has frequently been suggested by physical anthropologists that the teeth and other physical features of the smaller, more carnivorous animal (*A. africanus*) have more resemblance to modern *Homo sapiens* (and the intermediate fossil types) than do those of *A. robustus*. The theory most accepted at this time is that *A. robustus* died out in evolutionary competition and that the hominid that came to dominate Africa and adjacent areas some hundreds of thousands of years ago was the smaller, relatively bigger-brained form believed to be the maker of those earliest stone tools discovered at Olduvai.

There is always the possibility that both forms are side branches rather than direct human ancestors, and there is still difference of opinion about the interpretation of all the early hominid fossil remains. Some researchers have argued that the smaller, more lightly built *A. africanus* was simply the female, or perhaps some smaller subvariety of a single species. According to this view the various *Australopithecus* fossils are no more different from each other than is the range of sizes and shapes of *Homo sapiens* today. A fair amount of evidence has accumulated, however, to indicate that the hypoth-

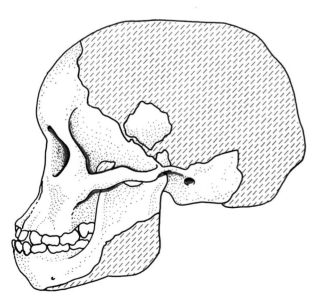

4.6 Reconstruction of skull of *Australopithecus africanus* from Taung.

67

esis of two separate species, one large and husky and the other small and slender, is quite plausible.

There is evidence of still other types of *Australopithecus*. In 1959, a complete skull and a leg bone of an extremely massive and robust creature was excavated at Olduvai, and was given the name *Zinjanthropus boisei*, suggesting that it was a different genus and species from the *Australopithecus*. Many researchers considered "Zinj" to be a member of the *Australopithecus* "family" but perhaps of a yet different species, even huskier than *A. robustus*. Those people who have spent the most time studying the Zinj remains now think it is possible that

this remarkable specimen is one of the later specimens of the *A. robustus* form instead of a separate evolutionary line. Therefore "splitters" call it *Australopithecus boisei* and "lumpers" use the term *A. robustus*.

In 1964 the Leakeys and their associates identified another type of hominid at Olduvai which they named *Homo habilis*. They regarded it as essentially contemporaneous with *A. boisei*. *H. habilis* included the jawbone with teeth of a fairly young person, some parts of the skull, and a few bones from the hand. They resemble *A. africanus*. The reason the Leakeys and some other researchers con-

4.7 *Australopithecus africanus* **fossil materials from South Africa.**

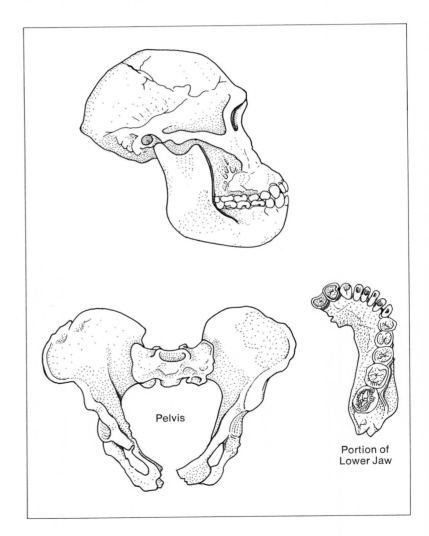

Pelvis

Portion of
Lower Jaw

68

Homo sapiens in Biological Perspective

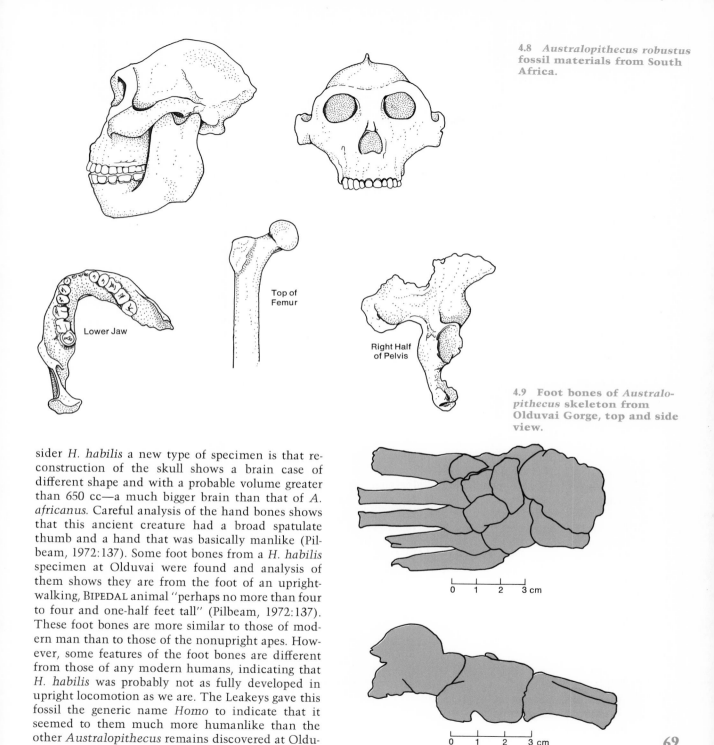

Top of Femur

Lower Jaw

Right Half of Pelvis

sider *H. habilis* a new type of specimen is that reconstruction of the skull shows a brain case of different shape and with a probable volume greater than 650 cc—a much bigger brain than that of *A. africanus*. Careful analysis of the hand bones shows that this ancient creature had a broad spatulate thumb and a hand that was basically manlike (Pilbeam, 1972:137). Some foot bones from a *H. habilis* specimen at Olduvai were found and analysis of them shows they are from the foot of an upright-walking, BIPEDAL animal "perhaps no more than four to four and one-half feet tall" (Pilbeam, 1972:137). These foot bones are more similar to those of modern man than to those of the nonupright apes. However, some features of the foot bones are different from those of any modern humans, indicating that *H. habilis* was probably not as fully developed in upright locomotion as we are. The Leakeys gave this fossil the generic name *Homo* to indicate that it seemed to them much more humanlike than the other *Australopithecus* remains discovered at Oldu-

0   1   2   3 cm

0   1   2   3 cm

69

The Evolution of Homo sapiens: The Big-Brained Primate

vai. However, "lumpers" prefer to call it *A. Africanus* because it resembles that specimen, and "splitters" prefer to call it *Australopithecus habilis* because they consider it a later development from *Australopithecus africanus*.

In 1973 Richard Leakey (son of Louis Leakey) announced a discovery that adds some support to the theory that *H. habilis* may be a separate, more human developmental line. At Lake Rudolf in Kenya, Leakey found some fossil materials that are generally similar to *Australopithecus* but larger-brained (a cranial capacity of 800 cc) and dating back to nearly 3 million years ago. He has suggested that this form, which he classifies in the genus *Homo*, may be ancesteral to *H. habilis*. Thus it is possible that a couple of million years ago there were at least *three* lines of hominid development in East Africa, one of which probably led to *Homo sapiens*.

Homo habilis—Our Ancient Ancestor?

If the East African fossil *H. habilis* is our ancestor, we are naturally curious about what he and she looked like. *H. habilis* had a bigger brain than the other *Australopithecus* creatures in East Africa at that time, although it lacked the high forehead and flattened face that seem to us a major mark of humanness. The collarbone was not much different from that of modern people, indicating that the suspension of the arms and the structure of the shoulders permitted movements and activities like those of *Homo sapiens*. The structure of the pelvis shows more similarities to that of modern humans than to the pelvis of apes, suggesting that *H. habilis* and other *Australopithecus* creatures were capable of upright posture and bipedal movement.

If, as the skeletal materials suggest, this creature weighed less than a hundred pounds and its teeth resemble those of modern *Homo sapiens*, then we are confronted with some very interesting questions about the lifeways and adaptive behavior of this, our ancient ancestor. Of course, all reconstructions of cultural behavior and social organization of the *Australopithecus* specimens are based on a series of assumptions and inferences. Nonetheless, these projections are valuable because they serve as guidelines for assumptions about human origins. They are

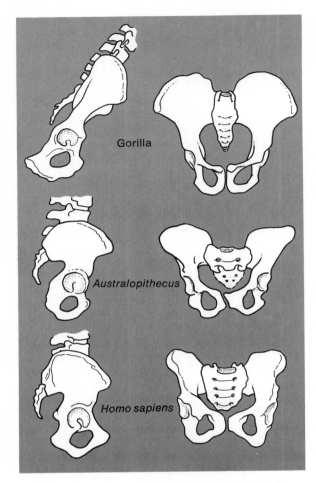

4.10 **Comparison of pelvis of gorilla, *Australopithecus*, and *Homo sapiens*, front and side view.**

more reliable than pure speculation. Interpretations from the current fossil materials will, in time, be supplemented and corrected by further research materials as researchers continue to dig in the as yet unexplored back regions of East Africa, north India, and other promising areas. It should be noted that there is a large stretch of area between Africa and India that might yet reveal further important fossil data.

The early evolution of hominids seems to have taken place on the fringes of forested areas, near bodies of water, in habitats that provided an abun-

Homo sapiens in Biological Perspective

dance, and a rich variety, of food. As the evolution of our ancestors continued, these hominids probably became more and more adapted to life in open grasslands as their upright posture and other physical developments gradually enhanced their food-getting abilities as well as their defenses against predators. Judging from the evidence at Olduvai Gorge, a mixed food-getting strategy of hunting and gathering was developed at least 2 million years ago, perhaps even earlier, by one of the hominid species.

Increased dependence on hunting would have had important consequences for the social behavior of those ancient ancestors of ours. An omnivorous diet generally requires a much larger home range than does a strictly vegetarian diet, since animal food is spread out more thinly and more traveling is required to find and catch the available game. Partial dependence on hunting may have brought about a division of labor between males and females along the lines of some present-day hunting-gathering societies. Males may have *tended* toward hunting activities, whereas the females, partly because of their infant care responsibilities, may have stayed closer to home bases—keeping the children safe from predators and gathering vegetable foods for much of their sustenance. At the same time, hunting activities among primates, the big cats, and other species tend to result in food sharing and cooperation, as the hunters regularly bring back some of their kills to those who have stayed close to home base. That is the pattern among wolves and among hunting and gathering human societies such as the Inuit, Bushmen, and the Australian Aborigines.[2]

The increased division of labor that tends to occur in hunting and gathering as compared to the "indi-

[2]See Preface, p. vi.

vidualism" of strictly vegetarian living apparently put a premium on the development of effective social communication as well. That is, if the *Australopithecus* groups regularly split up to carry out different specialized activities, coming together again after the day's tasks, this increased complexity of behavior would be facilitated by more complex communications and signal systems. The complex social communication of chimpanzees, coupled with their hunting and food sharing, illustrates this general idea. Social communication and division of labor would have required a growth of cooperative social attitudes, so that they would agree to share their food, cooperate in hunting activities, and refrain from tearing one another to pieces if food was scarce or if there wasn't a sufficient balance of the sexes in mating. As Professor Pilbeam has put it:

Planning and forethought, cooperation, and memory are all hominid behavioral characteristics essential to our success, and it seems highly likely that it was the transition to the hunting-gathering way of life in relatively open country that produced these changes. Certainly the hunting aspects of this new way of life would have required all these traits, but the gathering part should not be forgotten. Gathering enough plant food in savannah or savannah woodland subject to a seasonal climate would also require skill, knowledge of the terrain, planning, and memory.

It is possible that during this period male-female permanent bonds were evolved. (PILBEAM, 1972:154)

Of course, we must be very cautious and skeptical when trying to reconstruct aspects of the social life of our early ancestors. We have to put together the scraps of evidence from fossils and stone tools, plus careful inferences from the behavior of our nearest primate kin like the chimpanzees and gorillas. In

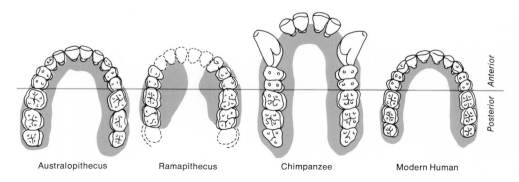

Australopithecus   Ramapithecus   Chimpanzee   Modern Human

Posterior   Anterior

4.11 **Modern humans, as well as our fossil ancestors, have a dental arch in the form of a parabola, compared with the nearly straight rows of teeth in the chimpanzee. Also note the large canine teeth and the tooth gap (diastema) in chimpanzees, which are entirely absent in the human evolutionary line.**

The Evolution of Homo sapiens: The Big-Brained Primate

addition data from historically recent hunting societies are also helpful. Part of the logic of all this depends, of course, on the evidences of continuities from *Australopithecus* down to modern times.

The Significance of Brain Size, Tools, and Upright Posture

As we examine the fossil evidence of the early hominids, three features clearly stand out: their large brains, their upright posture, and their tools. All advanced primates have relatively large brains, many of them are capable of some rudimentary tool use, and, on rare occasions, some primates can manage temporary bipedalism, so that these traits are not strictly unique to hominids. However, they are strikingly important among hominids, and the interrelationships among them become increasingly clear as we examine further developments in the human family history.

Upright posture, which was well developed in the Australopithecines, freed the hands for tool use. The use of tools requires good eye-hand coordination, a trait that calls for a well-developed brain. A more well-developed brain (that is, greater intelligence) in turn increases the possibility of more effective use of tools. Thus through generations of selective pressure our earliest ancestors developed larger brains, became progressively more efficient at using tools, and developed social organizations that facilitated exploitation of their nonarboreal habitats.

In our discussion of the significance of brain size in human evolution we assume that there is a relationship between brain size and intelligence. When we compare the mental capabilities of different animals we find that mental performance in learning and remembering information seems to be approximately related to overall brain size. (Dobzhansky, 1962). However, the size of the brain of modern people varies widely, without necessarily indicating anything about wisdom. The mental capabilities of people with brain sizes of 1000–1100 cc are equal to those of others with brain sizes of 2000 cc or more. The Russian author Ivan Turgenev had a cranial capacity of 2012 cc, almost matched by the German militarist Otto von Bismarck, with a brain size estimated at 1965 cc. Anatole France, the distinguished French author, kindly donated his brain for the

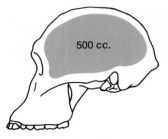

Australopithicus

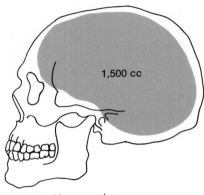

Homo sapiens

4.12 Relationships of brain and face in *Australopithecus* and *Homo sapiens*.

inspection of scientists, who found that his gray matter barely reached 1000 cc—less than half the brain size of his contemporary, Turgenev; yet their literary achievements are regarded as being fairly equal.

Human females have brain sizes that are, on the average, 100–150 cc smaller than those of males, without any diminution of intelligence. The difference, of course, is related to differences in overall body size. In proportion to total body size, the human female's brain is as large as the male's, if not larger. When we talk about a correlation between brain size and mental capability we must allow for differences in total body size. Even so, the relationship of relative brain size and intelligence is only approximate. On the whole, though, there is a relationship between the gradual growth of brain size and complexity over the millennia and the development of more complicated information-processing and storage capabilities.

Homo sapiens in Biological Perspective

Homo erectus—Grandchild of Australopithecus

The so-called Java Man—a hominid fossil from the middle Pleistocene—was discovered in the 1890s by the Dutch physician Eugene Dubois. He had gone to Java with the express objective of finding evidence of ancient remains, and in 1891 he announced that he had found a portion of skull very different in shape from that of modern *Homo sapiens*. This famous fossil was at first given the name *Pithecanthropus erectus* ("upright ape man"). A femur (thighbone) found near the skull was the basis for the inference that *P. erectus* did indeed have upright posture much like modern humankind, since the shape of this thighbone was remarkably similar to that of *Homo sapiens*. In the decades since the discovery by Dubois, a number of other fossils have been found in Java, giving further testimony to hominid biological evolution in the period perhaps a million years after the age of *Australopithecus*. In the 1930s the physical anthropologist Von Koenigswald found some skulls and jawbones in Java that had features similar to those of the earlier Java specimen discovered by Dubois. Some of the fossils from Java have shown similarities to *Australopithecus* of East Africa, suggesting that early hominids had probably spread as far as Southeast Asia nearly 2 million years ago.

The Java fossils that were long known as *Pithecanthropus* have been reevaluated and most anthropologists feel that they are similar enough to modern *Homo sapiens* to be labeled Homo *erectus*, indicating their direct relationship to us. *Homo erectus* skulls are larger than those of *H. habilis* of East Africa, for their average cranial capacity appears to be over 800 cc, compared to about 600 cc for *H. habilis*. The skulls are longer and broader than those of *Australopithecus*, but not much higher. *Homo erectus* was a rather strange-looking creature from a modern point of view, for the skull sloped sharply back from the brow ridges with practically no forehead. The Java skulls are much thicker than those of *Australopithecus* (especially *H. habilis*). *H. erectus*, averaging five feet, was probably a foot taller than its probable East African ancestors, the Australopithecines. Judging from the leg bones, *Homo erectus* was more fully adapted to permanent upright posture and probably could walk and run better than *Australopithecus* (Pilbeam, 1972).

Peking: *Homo erectus* in China

An even better selection of fossil skulls and other bones of *Homo erectus* was discovered during the 1930s in China at Choukoutien cave near Peking. These fossils, which disappeared mysteriously during World War II and have never been recovered, were much like the Java specimens but with somewhat larger brains. The brain sizes from Choukoutien vary from about 850 to 1300 cc (average: 1060 cc), and the skull vaults are slightly higher and more rounded than those of the Java specimens. Fortunately for modern science, the researchers who had worked with the Choukouien materials before the war had already published good descriptions, and plaster casts had been made of the specimens

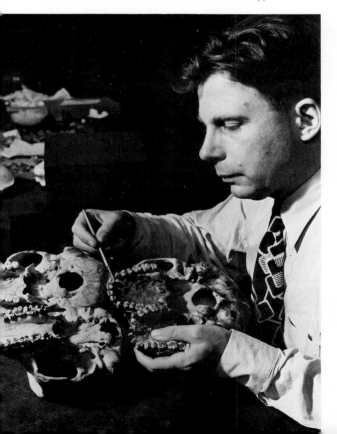

4.13 Dr. von Koenigswald holding skull of *Homo erectus* fossil from Java. For comparison, skulls of modern *Homo sapiens* (upper left) and gorilla (lower left) are also shown. (Courtesy of the American Museum of Natural History)

before the originals disappeared. Also, since 1949 Chinese paleontologists have uncovered several other fossils from the same area. The age of these specimens is thought to be between 500,000 and 800,000 years, somewhat younger than the estimates for the Java *Homo erectus* creatures. (The dates of the Chinese and Javanese *Homo erectus* fossils have been estimated from geological data plus evidence from the associated flora and fauna.)

Unlike the Java specimens, *Homo erectus* at Choukoutien cave had a rich variety of stone tools associated with the bone remains. Even more important, remains of fire at Choukoutien give us one of the oldest positive indications of an important technological development. Our ancestors at Choukoutien evidently cooked their food and kept themselves warm in their caves by using fire. Around the several fireplaces at Choukoutien are bones of fairly large animals, including two species of deer. Some seeds near these same hearths give evidence that vegetables were part of their diet.

The most notorious piece of information from the Choukoutien caves is that some of the skulls appear to have been split open, suggesting that these hominids had practiced cannibalism. Similar indirect evidence of cannibalism has also been found in some fossil sites of more recent vintage in Europe.

The hominid creatures who inhabited Choukoutien were there when the advance of the great glaciers of the north had brought on bitter cold. It is hard to believe that these hominids would have been in the area if they had not had the caves and the use of fire to protect themselves against the weather. They had other problems as well. Sabertoothed tigers and huge hyenas (of a type now extinct) competed with them for occupancy of the caves. There were apparently periods when the "owners" of the caves were the carnivores; at other times, *Homo erectus* took over. All this information and a great deal more was contained in accumulated deposits of earth totaling about 160 feet of fossil-bearing debris. These deposits are a mixture of limestone, windblown soil, garbage left by *Homo erectus* and the other tenants, and rocks that had fallen from the ceilings of the caves. The evidence of the hominids' dietary habits suggests they exploited approximately sixty different species of animals ranging from small rodents to horses, camels, and even elephants (Howell, 1970).

Homo erectus was evidently a much more effec-

4.14 Items from the tool kit of *Homo erectus* (Choukoutien).

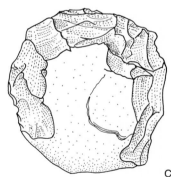

Chopping Tools

Quartz Flakes

Homo sapiens in Biological Perspective

tive hunter than was *Australopithecus.* When we consider the cold climate in which they were living, these people had to be effective hunters. For a number of months each year they must have had to depend to a large extent on animal foods, just as do modern Inuit in the arctic north. *Homo erectus* may therefore be regarded as much more versatile in its adaptations than was the tropic-dwelling *Australopithecus.* Until hominids had developed the tool-using techniques and social organization that ensured effective big game hunting, movement into temperate and subarctic regions was impossible.

Meanwhile, Back at Olduvai Gorge . . .

We mentioned earlier that one of the most exciting features of Olduvai Gorge is the continuous record of evolution from ancient times to more recent periods. Evidence for the likely relationships between *Australopithecus* and the later *Homo erectus* comes in part from fossils found in deposits that lie directly above the *Australopithecus* specimens. The ages of the *Homo erectus* materials at Olduvai are about the same as the ages estimated for the Peking and Java specimens. The oldest Olduvai *Homo erectus* materials are perhaps three-fourths of a million years old. The skulls of the East African *Homo erectus* differ in some details from those of their Asiatic kinsman: they are heavier and the brow ridges more robust. The brain size of about 1000 cc fits well with estimates from Java and China and further supports the general impression of extensive brain development from *Australopithecus* to more recent *Homo.* There are many stone tools associated with the *Homo erectus* finds at Olduvai, and they are much more refined and complex than the crude pebbles shaped by ancient *Australopithecus.*

Of course the fact that the *Homo erectus* fossils are in the same location but geologically more recent than *Australopithecus* does not *prove* that they are direct descendants of those older hominids. It could be argued that the *Homo erectus* creatures were descended from some other line of hominids and migrated into the East African area, replacing *Australopithecus* or simply occupying areas in which *Australopithecus* had already become extinct. Resolving these questions will have to await further fossil evidence.

Homo erectus in Europe

There are very few fossil remains from Europe that indicate the presence of *Homo erectus* or any other hominid of comparable age. In 1907 a very husky *Homo erectus*-like jawbone was found near Heidelberg in Germany, and its age has been estimated at somewhere between 250,000 and 500,000 years. Like other ancient hominids, the Heidelberg creature had no chin, but it is not easy to say much

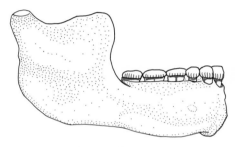

4.15 The Heidelberg jaw fossil.

else about this individual specimen. Near Budapest in Hungary researchers have recently uncovered some fragments of bone and teeth that appear to be *Homo erectus* materials, associated with pebble tools and several hearths. They may be about as old as the Heidelberg jaw but not much information is available. These scraps of evidence concerning the spread of *Homo erectus* into Europe would be fairly unconvincing if it were not for the fact that a number of fossils of somewhat more recent geological vintage have come to light, and there is a rich variety of stone tools from *Homo erectus* times in a number of European archaeological sites.

One of the more interesting sites in Europe is in the Ambrona Valley in Spain, excavated by Clark Howell of the University of Chicago. This locality was known as a good place to find animal bones and stone tools before the turn of the century. A Spanish amateur archaeologist had dug up materials and published notes about them early in the twentieth century, and Professor Howell used that clue to go back into the area in 1961 for serious excavations. Although fossil hominid remains have not been found in Ambrona, tools, fireplaces, and the bones of game animals are plentiful. Most of the bones

75

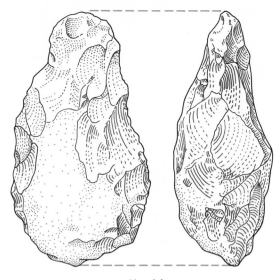

Hand Axe

4.16 Hand axe from the tool kit of *Homo erectus* (Europe and parts of Africa).

belong to the huge, now-extinct, straight-tusked elephant (*Elephas antiquus*). This massive animal roamed southern Europe throughout most of the Ice Ages and may have become extinct because of the

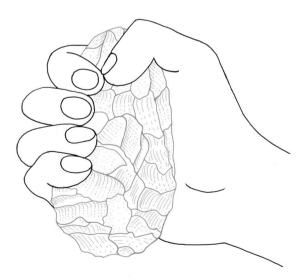

4.17 More refined model in *Homo erectus* tool kit.

efficient game-killing capacities of our hominid ancestors. In addition to the elephants, the hunters at Ambrona also killed deer, horses, and a number of other creatures. Like their distant cousins in China, they had to be very effective hunters of animal food throughout the long winters, when nuts, berries, and other vegetable food materials were not available.

Detailed geological study of the Spanish sites excavated by Howell, including analysis of fossil pollen materials, gives an age of perhaps 300,000 years for those big game hunters at Ambrona and a nearby site, Torralba. The inference that the hominid hunters at these sites may have been *Homo erectus* is based on the observation that their stone tools show many resemblances to the tools found with *Homo erectus* at Olduvai Gorge and other sites in Africa.

Hunting big game such as elephants, rhinoceros, and the other large animals required a highly developed technology as well as a complex social system—complex compared to the social organization of our cousins, the great apes. One man alone could hardly kill an elephant or any other large animal, given the weapons available to *Homo erectus*. They must have had some cooperative systems of surrounding and driving animals, luring them into traps, frightening them into stampedes over cliffs, or tricking them into swamps and quagmires where the animals would be helpless—easy victims of the hand-held stone and wooden weapons carried by their hominid pursuers. The Ambrona site, indeed, appears to have been an ancient bog into which elephants and other animals were driven, perhaps partly through use of that powerful technological item, fire (Howell, 1970).

One of the more intriguing bits of evidence concerning the presence of *Homo erectus* at Ambrona is a row of bones:

a tusk, two disjointed femurs, and two tibias belonging to a single large elephant. . . . It seems unlikely that the bones were laid thus as part of a ceremony since no evidence of such behavior by *Homo erectus* exists from other sites. One possible explanation is suggested by the deep mud in which the elephants were mired. Such terrain would be nearly impossible for a burdened man to cross. The leg joints, then, after having been cut from the carcass, might well have served as a causeway to firmer ground. (HOWELL, 1970:97)

Anyone who has ever tried to butcher even a small animal such as a rabbit or deer has experi-

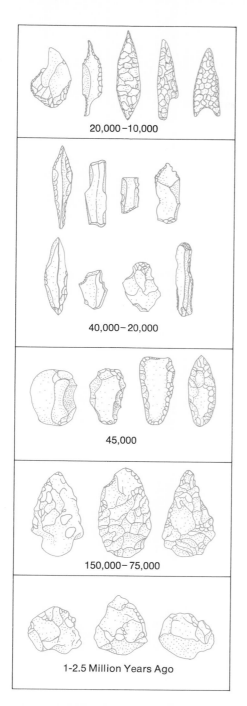

20,000–10,000

40,000–20,000

45,000

150,000–75,000

1–2.5 Million Years Ago

4.18 **The evolution of stone tools, from** *Austra-lopithecus* **to** *Homo sapiens sapiens.*

enced the difficulties of chopping through the hide and then the tough sinewy flesh. L. S. B. Leakey has shown that the largest animal he could skin with hands and teeth alone was a rabbit. Chimpanzees can skin animals up to nearly twice their own body size without tools, but the weaker teeth of hominids were probably never up to this task. Instead, early humans must have used tools to cut up their game. Leakey once skinned and butchered a large animal using an Olduvai hand ax as fast as his assistant could do it with a steel knife.

By the time our hominid ancestors had reached the *Homo erectus* stage of biological and cultural development, they were not satisfied with a simple pebble chipped to form a cutting edge. Special deposits of excellent stone, such as a variety of types of flint, provided them with raw materials from which they carefully chipped and shaped a number of different tools. Some of these ancient implements are labeled "HAND AXES," others are "cleavers," and the variety of tools that were probably used to work on hides are called "scrapers." Figure 4.18 illustrates some of the different types of stone tools, from the earliest "pebble tools" of Olduvai up to developed Late Stone Age implements.

Neanderthal: Victim of a Bad Press

As we move closer to modern times in our tracing of the record of biological evolution, we naturally find larger numbers of specimens and a greater variety of secondary information to fill in the picture of human development. We know a good deal about the life styles of "cave dwellers" of the late Ice Age, and more information becomes available year by year as archaeological investigations continue to turn up further traces of their activities.

The famed skull of Neanderthal was discovered in 1856 in the Neander Valley, Germany. The heavy brow ridges, thick skull walls, and heavy protrusion at the back of the skull (the OCCIPITAL region) gave an impression of a specimen different enough from modern humans so that it was labeled *Homo nean-derthalensis.* After the discovery there was a good deal of argument over whether this was evidence of "an ancient race" or simply some rather pathological and unique specimen of a person, perhaps an imbecile who had accidentally wandered into the cave

The Evolution of Homo sapiens: The Big-Brained Primate

and died. Throughout the latter part of the nineteenth century a number of other fossils were found that resembled the Neanderthal specimen, so it became apparent that its special physical features were not a pathological accident but the characteristics of a hominid population that must have lived all over Europe in the time period from about 100,000 years to perhaps 50,000 years ago. Furthermore, similar fossils have been found as far east as Java, as well as in South Africa. A South African fossil, called "Broken Hill Man" after its location in Rhodesia, is especially interesting because it is extremely rugged, almost super-Neanderthal—yet probably lived less than 30,000 years ago.

Nowadays, Neanderthal specimens are usually given the scientific name *Homo sapiens neanderthalensis*. The main reason for regarding them as members of the *sapiens* species is that they possessed very large brains; in fact, on the average their cranial capacities (1540 cc) may have been greater than those of modern Europeans. In other respects, however, the physical characteristics of Neanderthals, especially the fossils from Europe, are quite different from those of modern humans. They were short and very heavy-boned, and they had large faces with big teeth, as well as the more famous characteristics described above.

All of the hominids of this general time period did not, however, look alike. Excavations at Mount Carmel in Israel revealed caves in which some of the former inhabitants looked like the so-called Classic Neanderthals, while others of the same time period looked remarkably "modern." In another cave with a number of skeletons (a whole cemetery of at least ten people) there were stone tools of the type usually associated with Neanderthal peoples. The puzzling thing about the skeletons is that some of them are like Classic Neanderthals, while others are much less rugged and more like modern *H. sapiens.*

In another location in the Middle East, at a cave in the mountains of northern Iraq, a number of skeletons were found in the late 1950s that seem somewhat like the Mount Carmel people because some are Neanderthal, others "modern." All of these Near Eastern skeletons are about 40,000 to 50,000 years old. There is at least one other set of hominid fossils that also shows physical features midway between Classic Neanderthals and modern *H. Sapiens.* They were found in a rock shelter at Krapina in Yugoslavia, with over a thousand flint tools and other materials. The dating of these materials is in some doubt, for some researchers feel that the fossils may be as old as the third interglacial period, more than 100,000 years old.

All of these fossils give us the impression that 40,000 to 50,000 years ago our ancestors on earth consisted of a range of variation from those rugged "cavemen" of Western Europe (and parts of Asia and Africa) to the "modern-looking" types with higher skull vaults, no heavy brow ridges, and features that would hardly attract much attention if you happened to meet one of them on the street.

Regardless of their physical appearances, the mate-

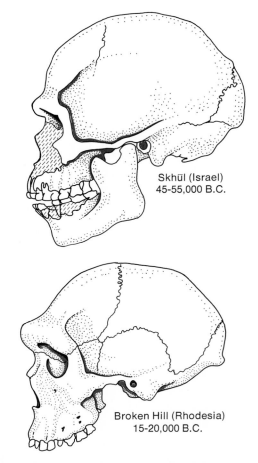

Skhūl (Israel)
45–55,000 B.C.

Broken Hill (Rhodesia)
15–20,000 B.C.

4.19   Comparison of Classic (Broken Hill) and Progressive (Skhūl) Neanderthal skulls.

Homo sapiens in Biological Perspective

rial remains of Neanderthal peoples show that they were capable of a great deal more than bashing each other over the head with huge clubs, as they are so frequently portrayed in popular literature.

Technology and Social Change in Neanderthal Times

There is much evidence to indicate that Neanderthal peoples had more complex technological equipment and a richer cultural life than their predecessors. Of course, these ideas are based on inferences from a variety of archaeological remains —but the remains are much richer and more complicated than those from earlier periods. The time we are talking about is from perhaps 100,000 to 130,000 years ago, down to the relatively recent days of just 30,000 years ago.

Compared with the fairly simple "tool kit" of *Homo erectus*, the tools manufactured by the Neanderthals are much more interesting. From one area in Germany, near Weimar, there are collections of implements that include stone points probably used on the ends of sticks as spearheads. From various Neanderthal sites there are borers and engravers,

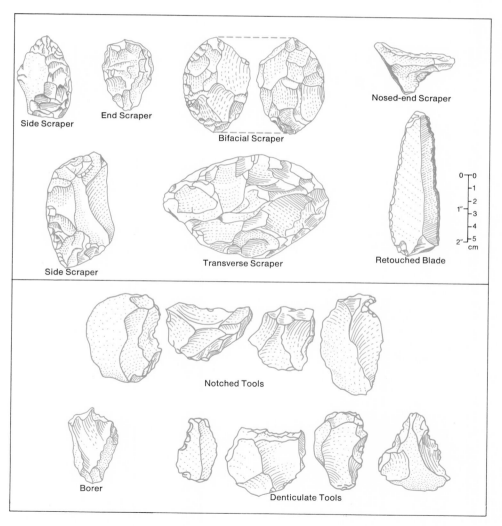

4.20 The tool kit of Neanderthal peoples was much more varied than that of *Homo erectus*.

Side Scraper

End Scraper

Bifacial Scraper

Nosed-end Scraper

Side Scraper

Transverse Scraper

Retouched Blade

Notched Tools

Borer

Denticulate Tools

The Evolution of Homo sapiens: The Big-Brained Primate

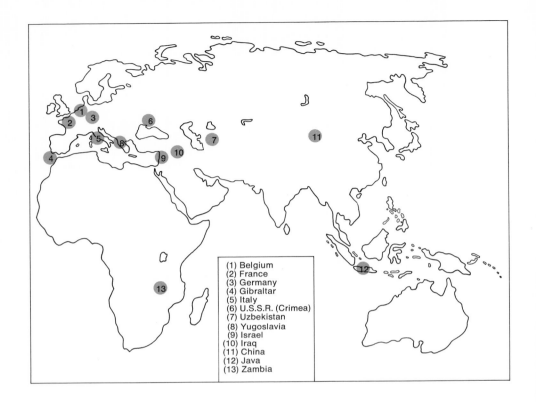

(1) Belgium
(2) France
(3) Germany
(4) Gibraltar
(5) Italy
(6) U.S.S.R. (Crimea)
(7) Uzbekistan
(8) Yugoslavia
(9) Israel
(10) Iraq
(11) China
(12) Java
(13) Zambia

which were very likely used as woodworking implements, and tools for scraping and shredding, as well
as various types of knives for cutting. During the
time of Neanderthal new techniques of toolmaking
were invented, techniques that required a great deal
of dexterity and practice to perfect.

One of the major developments during the Neanderthal phase was the spread of hunting and gathering peoples widely throughout the cold areas of
Eurasia. These were arctic or subarctic tundra and
steppe environments that supported a large number
of game animals, but that required a high level of
technology to exploit successfully. The glaciation
known geologically as the Würm was spreading glacial ice and frigid climate widely across the face of
Europe while other parts of the world experienced
similarly large changes in climatic conditions. With
Neanderthal populations and their contemporaries,
we find a spread of hominid populations over very
much wider areas of the world than had been true
of *Homo erectus* half a million years earlier.

Neanderthal peoples are the first hominids for

whom we have clear evidence of ceremonial burial
of the dead. Although some of the skeletons at
Krapina (Yugoslavia) appear to have been dumped
unceremoniously with the remains of other animals,
evidence at Shanidar cave in Iraq shows a careful
burial with pine boughs and flowers. The fossil pollen from the burial site gives evidence of grape hya-
cinths, bachelor's buttons, hollyhocks, and yellow-
flowering groundsels (cf. Pfeiffer, 1969). In France
at the Neanderthal site of LaFerrassie, "Anthropologists discovered what appears to be a 40-thousand
year old family cemetery containing the skeletons
of two adults and four children. The presumed parents were buried head to head; two skeletons . . .
possibly those of their children, each about five
years old, were neatly interred near their mother's
feet" (Howell, 1970:128). One of the children in this
family grave site was so tiny that it may have been
a just-born infant. Some of the skeletons had flint
objects buried with them, perhaps as offerings to the
spirits.

The Neanderthal site at LeMoustier in southern

Homo sapiens in Biological Perspective

France has a grave in which the dead man was buried with his head on a "pillow" of flints, with several other stone implements and some animal bones placed around it. Another interesting ceremonial burial is that of a child in Uzbekistan in the Soviet Union. The Neanderthal child's skull is surrounded with a circle of ibex horns. The ibex, with its spiral antlers, was an important game animal for Neanderthal and later peoples.

There is other evidence of the ceremonial and ritual tendencies of Neanderthal. At Drachenloch in Switzerland there is a stone pit with a stack of bear skulls. Also in the same place was a bear skull with a leg bone neatly placed through the cheek, with other bones set in a manner suggesting some sort of ritualistic activity. A number of other places in Europe of somewhat more recent vintage also have some kind of special ceremonial disposition of cave bear remains. This is from a period of time when Neanderthals hunted cave bears—their competitors for the warm and protected shelters from arctic cold. These bears must have been fearsome creatures— much bigger than any bears living today—and tackling them in the dark recesses of their caves was heady sport not meant for cowards. (Of course, if the Neanderthals attacked the bears only during their winter sleep, they might have been easy prey.) As we get more and more evidence of the cultural and technical accomplishments of the Neanderthal, we have to reconsider the stereotype of the "brutish" and "dull-witted" cavepeople.

Neanderthal people not only buried their dead ceremonially, but they must at least occasionally have taken good, humane care of their living members. One of the Neanderthals at Shanidar Cave in Iraq was a cripple, who probably had been cared for by his contemporaries for many years, perhaps from childhood, until at about the age of forty the roof of a cave fell in and killed him. Similarly, a man whose remains were found at LaChapelle in France was severely arthritic and was probably supported by his more able-bodied kin during his last years.

Neanderthal peoples used fire regularly and dug little fireplaces in their caves. Some people have suggested that the use of fire by those ancient hominids at Choukoutien nearly half a million years ago may have represented fire "captured" accidentally by *Homo erectus*, which they could not themselves produce. The regularity of use of fire among Neanderthal people certainly suggests that they were fire producers as well as fire users, although that may have been true as well among much earlier *Homo erectus* populations.

Was Neanderthal an artist? At some sites a few pieces of bone and other material show scratches or markings, and red ocher was used in some way— conceivably as personal adornment. However, there is very little evidence of artistic creativity resembling the monumental works of art developed by *Homo sapiens sapiens* in Western European caves some thousands of years later. With respect to clothing, it is hard to believe that Neanderthals would not have developed fairly effective skin clothing. However, no evidence of needles, awls, or other tailoring implements has been found. It may be that real sewing skills were not developed until after the Neanderthal period.

Homo sapiens sapiens: Evolutionary Newcomers or Were They Around All the Time?

There are many fossils from between thirty thousand and forty thousand years ago that are considered *Homo sapiens sapiens* in all their features. The skulls do not have massive brow ridges; they do not have the protruding "bun" at the back of the head as Neanderthal skulls have; the walls of the brain case are not as thick as those of Neanderthal; and they have a well-developed chin. The fossil name that has been associated with the earliest unequivocally "modern" human skeletons is that of Cro-

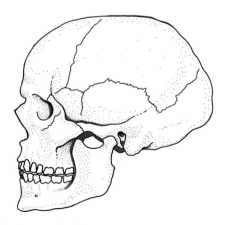

4.22 **Skull of Cro-Magnon fossil.**

The Evolution of Homo sapiens: The Big-Brained Primate

Magnon. (Cro-Magnon is a rock shelter in southern France from which some of these modern skeletons and their stone implements were excavated in 1868.) From the period thirty-five thousand years ago to modern times there are a large number of fossil sites in Europe, Africa, and Asia containing these hominid specimens.

One of the most puzzling and interesting problems about human evolution for which we do not yet have good answers is the question of the origins of *Homo sapiens.* Complicating the picture further is the mysterious "disappearance" of the Neanderthal people. We are not certain what happened to that large-brained, apparently highly capable hominid. Some anthropologists have theorized that Neanderthal types interbred with more progressive, modern *Homo sapiens* and simply evolved into (or were absorbed into) the modern populations. This line of argument includes the possibility that powerful selective forces favored the most *"sapiens"* of the Neanderthal types and brought about rapid genetic

changes in the direction of *H. sapiens sapiens.* Other anthropologists, however, feel that Neanderthal people became extinct as they lost in competition with *H. sapiens sapiens.* Still other scholars have taken a middle road, suggesting that both the extinction of large numbers of *H. neanderthalensis* and some interbreeding were involved.

We do know that in some European sites there is a break in the types of tools, beginning about forty-thousand years ago. Instead of the stone implements that are often associated with Neanderthal remains, the new tools, which are often highly refined, are the types that are found more usually with Cro-Magnon specimens. There are, naturally, many more places where stone materials have been found than there are remains of their human makers, since stone is much more durable than bone. Many anthropologists argue that when they find tools that are like the types that have been found in sites with Neanderthal bones they were probably made by Neanderthals and that the new types of tools ap-

4.23 Tools from the later Ice Ages in Europe (40,000 to 20,000 years ago).

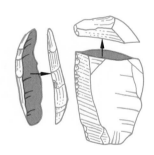
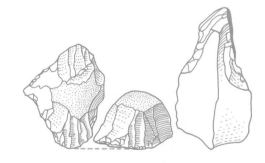
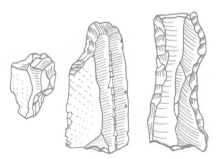

82

Homo sapiens in Biological Perspective

pearing in Europe at the close of the last glaciation can be interpreted as evidence that different (non-Neanderthal) people made them. On the other hand, there are many sites (e.g., in the Middle East) where no distinctive break in tool types appears, so the hypothesis that the Neanderthals were simply replaced by modern *Homo sapiens* is undoubtedly an oversimplification of a complex process of biological and cultural change.

Who were the newcomers and where did they come from? Again, there is disagreement among the experts. Some anthropologists (a definite minority nowadays) have argued that *Homo sapiens sapiens* was there all along, but perhaps in small numbers. Among the pieces of evidence that are used to support this point of view are a couple of very old fossils—one from Steinheim in Germany, the other from Swanscombe in England—which date back to perhaps 150,000 to 200,000 years ago. They are not complete skeletons, but on the basis of the remains that exist they appear to be "more modern" than the Neanderthals, and some researchers have suggested that they are direct precursors of the Cro-Magnon people. However, from the complicated measurements and the application of statistical techniques, it seems that they are really very similar to the Neanderthals and probably their ancestors.

Other fossils from a somewhat later time period (70,000 to 100,000 years ago) have also been interpreted as evidence of an ancient appearance of *Homo sapiens sapiens*. A hominid skull from Omo in Ethiopia (where some very early Australopithecines were found) is probably at least 100,000 years old, but the brain case is high, there is no bulge in the occipital region, and the brow ridges jut out somewhat, though not nearly as heavily as Neanderthal brows. Trying to make judgments about the degree of similarity between those hominids and modern humans is extremely difficult, particularly because the evidence is so sparse. There have been heated debates about these fossils, and many scholars feel that it is totally unjustified to conclude on the basis of these finds that *Homo sapiens sapiens* lived for 100,000 years or more before they strewed their finely made tools around the European scene. David Pilbeam, for example says, "The evidence does not support the view that there were two distinct lineages throughout the middle and late Pleistocene, one leading to Neanderthal man and the other to modern man" (Pilbeam, 1972:178).

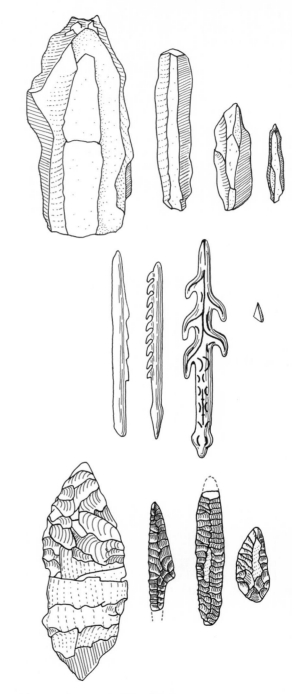

4.24 **Tools from 20,000 to 10,000 years ago (Europe).**

The Evolution of Homo sapiens: The Big-Brained Primate

Technology in the Late Ice Age

A major technological change, already beginning to develop in the time of the Neanderthals but becoming much more important about thirty thousand years ago, was the use of small, finely worked tools of a great variety of types. Some of the smaller flint chips and points were fitted into clubs and hacking equipment, and many kinds of stone chips were developed for working in wood and bone. A small stone tool called a burin was created that maximized the strength of stone for use in engraving. In addition to the direct, "practical" uses of these tools, burins were also used for stone carving—sometimes for the preparation of complex art objects.

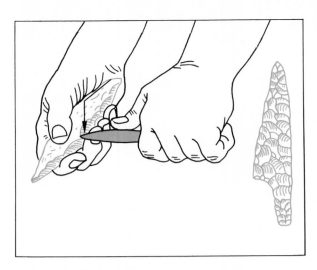

4.26 Pressure flaking—a method for producing finely worked projectile points and other tools. The craftsman chips off small flakes using a wooden or bone implement.

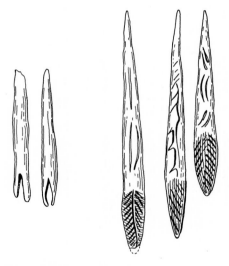

4.25 Bone tools from the late Ice Ages.

The perfecting of spear points and other projectile tips was an important development of the last part of the Ice Ages. During this time the spear thrower was also invented. Spear throwers are simply shafts or sticks that, when gripped in the throwing hand, increase the length and leverage of the person's arm, as the end of the thrower engages a notch at the end of the spear itself. Many contemporary hunting and gathering groups use the spear thrower with good effect (it is also a well-known toy among children in modern societies). The hunger-gatherers of terminal Ice Age times made use of a large variety of bone, antler, wood, and stone implements.

Migrants to the New World: Hunter-Gatherers in America

As archaeological research continues there are increasing reasons to believe that *some* human populations migrated to the New World perhaps fifty thousand to sixty thousand years ago, although the evidence is still debatable. What is clear, however, is that between the time period of roughly twenty-eight thousand to ten thousand years ago, free movement of hunters from Siberia to Alaska (and perhaps vice versa) was possible over a land bridge which linked Asia and North America. During that time sea levels were much lower than they are today. The extremely adaptable technical and social skills of *Homo sapiens sapiens* made long-range migration along this arctic and subarctic "bridge" relatively easy, and there appears to have been abundant game on both sides, motivating these human groups in their migration toward the New World. In any case the archaeological record shows that there were humans as far south as Mexico over twenty thousand years ago (Chard, 1969).

Homo sapiens in Biological Perspective

Only a few decades ago, many archaeologists and other scholars claimed that human populations had been in the Americas for perhaps only a few thousand years. However, we must note that cultural inventories and the physical features of Indians in the New World had developed a great many variations and complexities before the coming of White people in the fifteenth century, so it is credible that hunting peoples had at least twenty thousand years in which to develop their various different adaptations to the flora and fauna and other environmental characteristics of the Americas.

4.27 Some important archaeological sites in the Americas that testify to the antiquity of humans in the New World.

(1) Cape Denbigh, Alaska
(2) Flint Creek, Alaska
(3) Wilson Butte Cave, Idaho
(4) Lindenmeier, Colorado
(5) Dent, Colorado
(6) Clovis, New Mexico
(7) Folsom, New Mexico
(8) Domebo Canyon, Oklahoma
(9) Ventana Cave, Arizona
(10) Borax Lake, California
(11) Durango, Mexico
(12) Tepexpan, Mexico
(13) San Raphael, Mexico
(14) El Jobo, Venezuela
(15) Muaco, Venezuela
(16) El Inga, Ecuador
(17) Ayacucho, Chile
(18) Tagna Tagna, Chile
(19) Lagoa Santa, Brazil
(20) Confins Cave, Brazil
(21) Fells Cave, Chile
(22) Palli Aike, Chile

The Evolution of Homo sapiens: The Big-Brained Primate

Art and Culture of the Late Ice Age in Europe

The late Ice Age period of human prehistory is best known from remains in Western Europe and adjacent areas. This is true mainly because the prehistorians and physical anthropologists who have had the time and the financial backing to do the research have been mostly from Western Europe, especially England and France, and more recently from North America. Other parts of the world are archaeologically less well known in part because they have not had nearly the number of labor-hours and amount of excavation finances expended on them. There is an additional factor, though. Late Ice Age times in Europe saw the development of a refined and highly complex hunting-fishing-gathering technology, accompanied by an art style of great aesthetic excellence. In fact, it is hard to claim that the artistic achievements of late Pleistocene painters have been surpassed by any of the schools of art of recent times. It is a matter of geological accident and fortuitous cultural circumstances that Western Europe happens to have a considerable number of limestone caves suitable for the decorative effects those "cave people" developed. The limestone caves are full of underground rivers and pools, mysterious side galleries and passages. The people who produced those cave paintings did not live in those cold and forbidding caverns. Some of them may have lived out in open dwelling places, others in rock shelters or shallow caves much more open to daylight and fresh air.

Most people who have studied the underground cave art at places like Lascaux in France and Altamira in Spain have theorized that the cave paintings were created for magical purposes. So much of this art represents the hunt, often with spears painted as hitting the target, or scenes that show traps or pitfalls with animals caught in them, that it suggests a practice found among many living hunting peoples—a portrayal of successful hunting activities intended to aid magically in their own real-life activities. Here is Clark Howell's interpretation of the purposes of the art:

Cro-Magnon man was a hunter, perhaps as good as any the world has ever seen. He was strong, intelligent, well equipped with all kinds of weapons from spears and knives to slings. He knew how to make traps for small animals and pitfalls for large ones. He could ambush and stampede. And he has left impressive records of his skill behind him. In Predmost, Czechoslovakia, there are skeletons of 1,000 mammoths, and below the great cliff at Solutre the remains of more than 100,000 wild horses. Nevertheless, despite his formidable powers, he knew, as all primitive men do, that he walked always in the shadow of unpredictable and incomprehensible events, of malign forces. Doubtless he felt it necessary to try to forestall misfortune, injury and sometimes death—for some of the prey he hunted was extremely dangerous, notably the cave bear.

It was not enough merely to dodge misfortune. The hunter had to be positively fortunate too; he had to find an animal and he had to kill it. He improved his chances by painting a picture of the animal he wished to kill and then performing certain religious or magical

4.28 Cave painting of a deer hunt from Castellon, Spain. (Courtesy of the American Museum of Natural History)

4.29 Scene from a wall of the famous caves in Lascaux, France. (René Burri, Magnum)

rituals before the hunt to strengthen the power of his wish picture. (HOWELL, 1970:148)

The paintings of bison, horses, mammoths, reindeer, and other animals are often superimposed, perhaps because one set of pictures served for a particular magical ceremony and was superseded by new art on the next occasion. These early artists also included paintings of traced outlines of hands, some of them with a few finger joints missing, and there is a famous picture of what would appear to be a sorcerer with the ears and antlers of a deer, the tail of a wolf and humanlike features. Occasionally there are human figures in these paintings, but by far the most common themes are animals of the hunt.

The colors are striking even today. Much of the work is in red and yellow ochre, and black charcoal, all of which have been kept in an excellent state of preservation because of the total lack of light in the caverns. Moreover, winds, rains, and other environmental effects, including the polluting effects of human activity, have not reached these places until recent times.

4.30 The famous cave painting at Les Trois Frères in France is generally thought to represent either a shaman or a diety because it combines human and animal features.

87

The Evolution of Homo sapiens: The Big-Brained Primate

4.31 The "Venus of Willendorf"—one of the earliest evidences of human artistic creativity. (Courtesy of the American Museum of Natural History)

In addition to mural arts, the Cro-Magnon people used red ochre to paint their bodies, and they decorated themselves with bracelets and other body adornments. Pierced teeth and colored beads were used for necklaces. A variety of small sculpted objects have been found, ranging from female figurines to small, polychrome painted pebbles that some regard as Stone Age artists' practice materials. The best known of the female figurines (regarded as a tiny "earth goddess," "fertility figure," or perhaps a "household good luck charm") is the humorously charming "Venus of Willendorf," a limestone figure (about four inches high) with a wavy hairdo, huge breasts, and fat buttocks.

Hunting Magic and Modern Magic

Returning to the matter of the possible use of the cave art as a magic aid in hunting, perhaps the best analogy for understanding its motive and inspiration is the magical ritual that has, at least until recently, played a major role in the rituals surrounding college football and other sports. All of us are familiar with the magical ceremonials that take place on college campuses on the eve of important games. Very often these enactments require the building of elaborate artistic structures of TOTEM animals. The totem animals take the form of bears, wolverines, huskies, gophers, badgers, and some anthropomorphic figures such as "Trojans," "Indians," and others. Often these works of art portray one of the totem figures attacking and destroying its antagonist. The figure of a gopher is seen viciously attacking the wolverine and vice versa, and on one far western college campus it is not unusual to see totemic displays which show the "Indian" scalping its totemic opponent.

Just as in those cave paintings of the ancient past, the intended quarry is often portrayed with a spear or knife or ax or some other weapon endangering its life, perhaps with blood already flowing. These works of art are often the central focus of ritual enactments, which are thought to have most magical force if they take place a night with flickering bonfires as the only illumination.

There are several significant features of the magical rituals enacted in the presence of these totemic art works:

1. The ceremonial events take place on the eve of important encounters with "the enemy," and the ceremonials are thought to generate psychological states in both the direct participants (the athletes or hunters) and the spectators. Proper emotional states—expectation of victory, as well as willingness to "fight to the death"—are seen as essential to the actual outcome of events the next day.

2. Elaborate artwork is used to call up the proper images both of the intended quarry or enemy, as well as to portray at least part of the intended outcome of the action—victory.

3. Although no one believes that the ceremonial rituals themselves are *sufficient* to bring about victory, failure to enact these rites can be anxiety-provoking, since the proper spirit in both partici-

88

Homo sapiens in Biological Perspective

pants and spectators may not be generated unless the rituals are performed.

4. The artistic productions that play an essential role in the ceremonies are very frequently quite temporary and may be discarded altogether after a single performance. Each new encounter requires, to some extent, a *new* portrayal of the totemic protagonists.

5. At least some of the major actors in the social drama we are describing are dressed in a manner to represent the totemic creatures. They may not be strictly analogous to that famous sorcerer figure from the cave at Les Trois Frères, but it is perfectly possible that somewhat similar roles are suggested. That is, the magical import of the ceremonials can be enhanced by the special costumes of the participants.

One of the major differences between the magical ceremonials prior to modern athletic events and the cave art portrayals lies in the fact that the ancient Cro-Magnon people apparently did not have much interest in artistic portrayals of themselves and their *own* totemic identities. Their focus was on the quarry, the game they intended to bring down in the hunt. Perhaps in the ceremonials in those Ice Age cave settings the roles of the hunters themselves were enacted by living persons and did not have to be portrayed with mural art.

Summary

In this chapter we have covered some of the high points of the remarkable biocultural evolution of the human animal—from the earliest upright-walking, East African, tool-using creature down to the magico-religious practices of modern college students in weekend game preparations. Naturally this is a very superficial coverage, and there are many exciting and readable books that describe in greater detail the fossil materials and the cultural remains of our ancestors.

In thinking about human evolution, several main points should be especially stressed:

1. During the past hundred years the evidence of human evolution has accumulated at an increasing rate and some of the most important information, notably the rich variety of materials from the East African sites, has become part of the picture only since about 1960. More striking fossil materials will undoubtedly be unearthed in coming decades, and new breakthroughs will be made in assigning chronological time sequences to the human fossil record. Some of the materials that will come to light in the next few years will force revisions of the evolutionary story, perhaps calling for large modifications in chapters like this one.

2. The unique path of evolution leading to modern human physiology and lifeways was produced by an *interaction* of cultural behavior and biological evolution. Neither aspect of our development can be treated separately as the main cause or chief factor in this complex chain of events. Certain biological developments triggered new forms of behavior (or made them possible), and the behavioral forms—e.g., tool using—affected the directions of further biological evolution, and so on, for millions of years.

3. Bipedal, fully upright locomotion was a major accomplishment that prepared our ancient ancestors for tool using and greater brain development.

4. Of the biological developments during Pleisto-

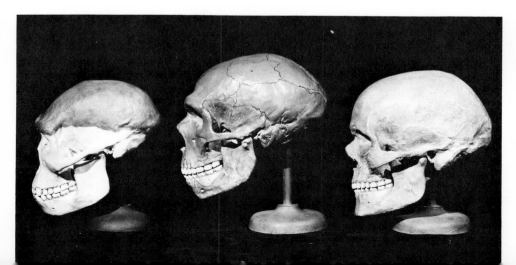

4.32 **Skulls of prehistoric hominids. Left to right:** *Homo erectus,* **Neanderthal, Cro-Magnon. (Courtesy of the American Museum of Natural History)**

cene times, the most important surely was the enlargement and increased complexity of the brain. The expanded information-processing capacities of *Homo sapiens* and their immediate predecessors facilitated more complex social organization, enlarged tool inventories, and perfected the eye-hand coordination for food getting and other activities.

5. The rate of cultural change during our first 2 or 3 million years was slow indeed. Some improvement in the design of tools came about; the use of fire was perfected; and gradually the hunting skills of Ice Age peoples reached a level of capability that permitted humans to move into quite difficult environments, including the chilly landscapes of Western Europe during the glaciations. Very few animals can boast of the wide range of hot and cold, wet and dry, forest and plain to which humans of the late Pleistocene were capable of adapting.

6. The considerable fluorescence of cultural complexity, including art, ritual, and "religion" (if we accept ritual burial as a sign of the human tendency), in the last ten thousand to thirty thousand years may represent the rapid development of new ideas that comes with fully developed language capability. Not that humans did not speak to one another earlier than that, but some new developments, both physiological and psychological, may have crossed a qualitative threshold. At any rate, late Ice Age times saw a splendid burst of human cultural energies, foreshadowing the "great leap forward" that came with the first domestication of plants and animals.

7. While the complexity of modern cultural evolution is bewildering in its speed and ramifications, we cannot assume that human *biological* evolution has ceased. In important ways our biological capacities and characteristics are still in the process of changing, though it is impossible to sort out the strictly genetic, biological changes from the massive input of social and cultural change.

Homo sapiens in Biological Perspective

Human Variations: The Genetic Basis

To understand the general processes of biological evolution that have produced modern *Homo sapiens*, we need to examine some basic information about the genetic mechanisms which lie at the heart of evolutionary changes. We should note, by the way, that Charles Darwin in his monumental exposition of natural selection as the key to evolution did not have knowledge of the specific mechanisms in individual animals that caused the evolutionary results. For this reason it was felt for a time that Darwin's theories were totally inadequate. When scientific genetics was developed during the first decades of the twentieth century, the geneticists found that they could fit the details of hereditary mechanisms with Darwin's general theory—some people refer to this new synthesis as "NEO-DARWINISM."

Some of the basic principles of genetics were first discovered many years ago by an Austrian monk, Gregor Mendel, who was experimenting with varieties of garden peas. Mendel announced his results to the world in a scientific paper published in 1865. However, the world wasn't listening, or didn't care, and the information that he produced was practically forgotten until the same genetic principles were rediscovered by researchers beginning in 1900.

The Law of Segregation: Mendel's First Law

Until the basic principles of genetics were carefully studied, it was generally believed that hereditary characteristics were transmitted from parents to offspring by "blood" and that a child is the result of a *blending* of more or less equal parts from the two parental sources of "blood." Even Charles Darwin accepted this view as fact. The most significant and startling discovery in Gregor Mendel's pea garden was his observation that heredity operates basically in terms of individual traits or characteristics and that these traits are transmitted by parents to their offspring as *discrete units* rather than as a generalized blending. Mendel's garden had some peas with purple flowers and others with white flowers. Some of these peas had yellow seeds, others green. Furthermore, they differed in another characteristic: round versus wrinkled seeds. If the idea of inheritance by "blood" and the blending of characteristics was correct, then when Mendel crossed his

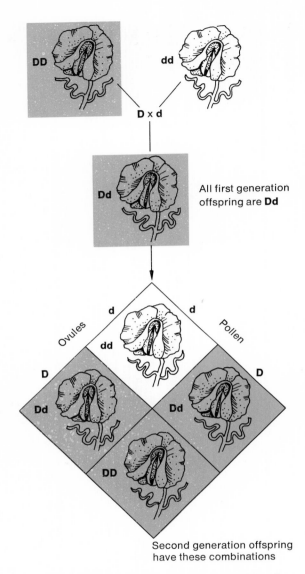

All first generation offspring are **Dd**

Ovules   Pollen

Second generation offspring have these combinations

5.1 The *law of segregation* is illustrated in the interbreeding between two varieties of sweet peas, one with purple flowers and the other with white flowers. *D* stands for the allele for purple color and *d* represents the allele for white. Note that purple is dominant over white, so that all plants with the *D* allele have purple flowers.

purple-flowered peas with white ones, he should have gotten some sort of light purple color, and the round and wrinkled seeds should have produced

"slightly wrinkled" seeds. When Mendel crossed (interfertilized) his varieties of peas, however, he found that purple crossed with white gave him purple flowers in the next generation. Yellow crossed with green seeds gave yellow; smooth with wrinkled seeds produced smooth seeds. These curious results reflected what we now know as the difference between dominant and recessive GENES. The characteristics of Mendel's peas, as well as our manifold human biological characteristics, are carried in tiny chemical messages to which the great geneticist Johanssen gave the name *genes*. The gene for purple flowers evidently masked or *dominated over* the gene for white color, yellow dominated over green in the genes for seed color, and round dominated over wrinkled in the genes for seed coat.

So far, so good. But Mendel's *second* generation of peas showed startlingly different results. Instead of all purple, he got about one fourth white flowers, and three fourths purple flowers. Similarly, the green seeds showed up again (in one fourth of the plants), and the wrinkled seeds also appeared in one fourth of the plants. These results can be understood and predicted mathematically if the units of heredity—the genes for purple flower color, white flower color, wrinkled seeds, and so on—are *independent units that do not blend with their opposite numbers*, and if the hereditary transmission from parents to offspring is in the form of a single gene from each of the parents, producing in the offspring *paired* genes for each characteristic.

Figure 5.1 shows Mendel's basic genetic discovery, which is often referred to as *the law of segregation*. We see in the diagram that in Mendel's first-generation hybrids (called the F_1 generation) all of the plants carried the dominant gene for purple flowers *plus* the recessive gene for white flowers. The dominant purple gene completely masked the presence of the white flower genetic potential. Since each parent transmits to its offspring only half of its genetic material, in the second generation each of the hybrid peas transmitted to the offspring (the F_2 generation) its purple gene approximately half of the time, and its white genetic message half of the time. The random crosses produced from these hybrids would result in the following gene pair combinations:

Purple + purple = one fourth of the time
Purple + white = one half of the time
White + white = one fourth of the time

Homo sapiens in Biological Perspective

Since the hybrid offspring (the purple + white) produce purple flowers, as does the purple + purple combination, only the white + white, occurring in one fourth of these second-generation offspring, would actually show only white flowers.

In our example, taken from Mendel's now-famous experiments, the purple + purple genetic types are HOMOZYGOUS for color since they have received the *same* genetic code messages from both parents for that particular characteristic. The same thing is true for the white + white combinations. The purple + white plants are HETEROZYGOUS since they have received two different genetic messages from their two different parents. When we focus on the *genetic* composition of these plants, we refer to them as GENOTYPES. When we refer to the *physical appearance* of the specimens, we call them PHENOTYPES. Thus, Mendel's F_1 generation, peas in Figure 5.1, were all genotypically heterozygous, but they were *phenotypically* purple.

The Principle of Independent Assortment: Mendel's Second Law

Mendel's second important discovery was that the genetic traits of flower color, seed color, and seed coat (and other characteristics) did not "stick together." Instead, they turned up in various different combinations in his F_2 generation and succeeding generations. Some of his purple flowers had round seeds, whereas others had wrinkled seeds. The random way in which each parent transmitted its color genes to its offspring was completely independent of its transmission of a gene for seed coat, which in turn was independent of its random transmission of yellow or green seed color, and so on through all of the individual genetic characteristics transmitted.

We now know that Mendel's second law of independent assortment is not always true. There are cases in which particular genetic characteristics do "hang together" in some ways. There are also many instances in which genetic characteristics are transmitted by combinations of several genes. Skin color in humans is one such characteristic that results from a kind of "blending," of several genes, which is one of the reasons for the earlier supposition that all inheritance resulted from a "blending" of the parental "blood." Furthermore, gene pairs are not always clearly dominant versus recessive. In some cases the two genes can combine to produce mixed phenotypic characteristics—that is, the genes are then CODOMINANT. Our familiar blood types A and B are codominant, so that a person who receives the gene for type B blood from his father and the gene for type A blood from his mother will have type AB blood (See Table 5.1).

A significant design feature of sexual reproduction is apparent in our discussion: since each individual receives two genes for each characteristic (sometimes more), there is a built-in safeguard against accidental loss of a genetic trait. The pairs of genes that affect the same traits (e.g., the gene for purple flowers and the gene for white flowers) are called allelic pairs. The genes for blood types A, B, and O are ALLELES of each other because they are the alternative genetic messages (about blood type) located at a particular spot in the human chromosome system.

Meiosis (see Fig. 5.4) operates in a way that randomizes the selection of genes from each chromosome pair in an individual. This means that each male sex cell, for example, receives *either* an X or a Y chromosome. It also receives randomly one or

Table 5.1: Human Blood Types (ABO Series)

Genes from Parents		Child's Genotype	Child's Phenotype (blood type)
MOTHER	FATHER		
A	B	AB	AB (universal recipient)
A	O	AO	A
A	A	AA	A
B	O	BO	B
B	B	BB	B
O	O	OO	O (universal donor)

93

Human Variations: The Genetic Basis

the other chromosome from each of the 22 pairs of autosomes. By the mechanism of *independent assortment* of chromosomes, we can see that every individual parent produces millions of *different* chromosome combinations. Independent assortment in meiosis, when combined with the further random variation in the actual "mating" of the male cell (sperm) and the female cell (ovum), accounts for the fact that no two human individuals are genetically alike, not even the offspring of the same parents (except in the special case of identical twins). The marvelous mechanism of sexual reproduction,

5.2 The *law of independent assortment* is illustrated in the interbreeding between two varieties of sweet peas, one with smooth, yellow seeds and the other with green, wrinkled seeds. *A* represents the allele for yellow, *a* the allele for green; the allele for smooth seeds is represented by *B* and that for wrinkled is shown here as *b*. The second generation shows all the possible combinations of these two traits.

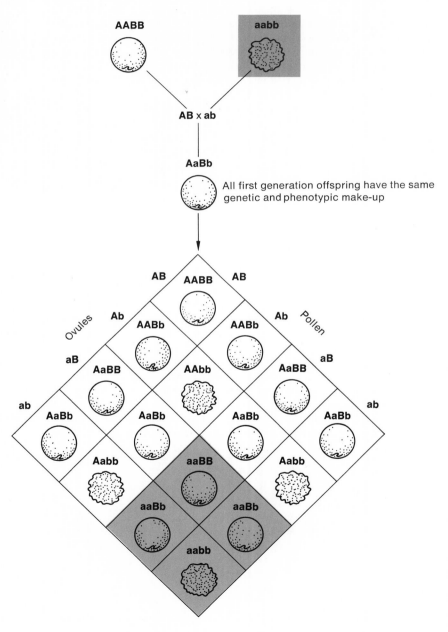

Homo sapiens in Biological Perspective

The explanation of hereditary transmission in Mendel's pea plants requires us to keep in mind that each parent transmits to its offspring only one half of its genetic potential. For any particular hereditary characteristic an individual receives a pair of genes, one from each parent. This means that the sex cells, in humans as in other sexually reproducing creatures, are the result of a splitting process within the reproductive system. In the human animal all of the reproductive code information is carried in 46 gene "packages" called CHROMOSOMES. Forty-four of these chromosomes are called AUTOSOMES or somatic chromosomes, and 2 of them are the SEX-DETERMINING chromosomes. These sex determiners are the X and Y chromosomes. Human males normally have one X and one Y chromosome; females normally have two X chromosomes.

Our bodies build millions of new cells every day through a process of cell splitting called MITOSIS. When the cells divide, each "daughter cell" is a carbon copy of the original in essential characteristics, including the 46 chromosomes. When sex cells are manufactured, on the other hand, only one of each pair of chromosomes ends up in the new cell. The results of this splitting process, MEIOSIS, are cells that contain only one half the number of chromosomes. Thus individual sperm and ova each contain only 22 autosomes plus a sex determinant. The 23 chromosomes carry an estimated total of somewhere between 10,000 and 100,000 individual genes.

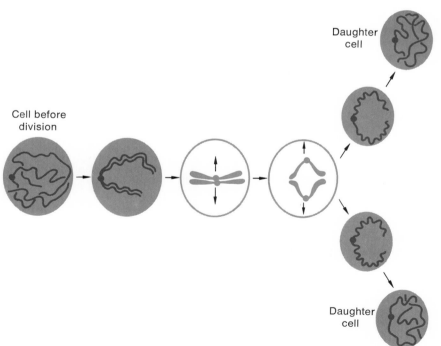

Daughter cell

Cell before division

Daughter cell

5.3 The body-building process of cell division, called *mitosis*. The drawings illustrate the process in a single chromosome as it divides into two identical "daughter" chromosomes. The resulting cells are normally exact replicas of the original in chromosome contents.

95

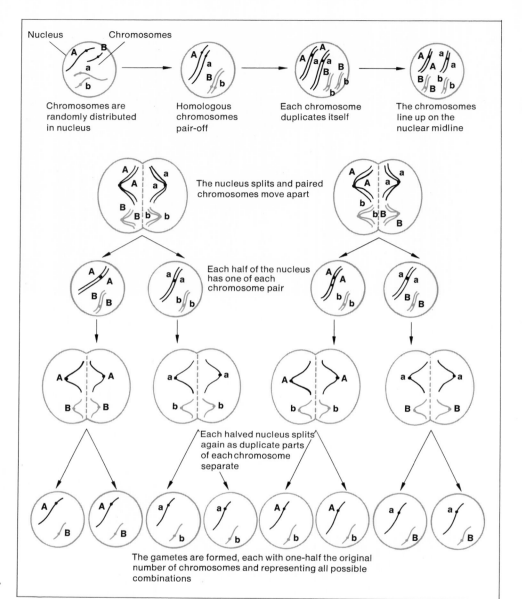

Nucleus Chromosomes

Chromosomes are randomly distributed in nucleus

Homologous chromosomes pair-off

Each chromosome duplicates itself

The chromosomes line up on the nuclear midline

The nucleus splits and paired chromosomes move apart

Each half of the nucleus has one of each chromosome pair

Each halved nucleus splits again as duplicate parts of each chromosome separate

The gametes are formed, each with one-half the original number of chromosomes and representing all possible combinations

5.4 The process by which sex cells are produced is *different* from normal cell division, because the chromosomes pair off and *only half* the chromosomes go to each cell. Each *gamete* thus formed in the process of *meiosis* is only a "half-cell" in its chromosomal genetic contents.

with genetic characteristics carried in individual little "packages" which sort themselves out randomly for each individual, ensures that human populations, like those of other animals and sexually reproducing plants, have a very wide range of genetic variability, an important source of adaptive flexibility.

Many refinements have been made in the original formulations set out by that Austrian monk more than a hundred years ago. Nonetheless, his "law of segregation" and "law of independent assortment" are basic principles of genetic processes that go a long way toward explaining what happens in hereditary transmission.

96

People often argue vociferously on the perennial question of heredity versus environment. "Is mental illness hereditary or is it caused by environmental experiences?" "Is intelligence inherited?"

These questions are meaningless and misleading from the point of view of modern genetics. *Every* human characteristic is an outcome of complex interactions between genetic potentials and environmental experiences. Even so-called hereditary diseases, such as diabetes and sickle-cell anemia, manifest themselves in a variety of different ways in people, depending on the individual's prenatal experiences, nutrition, illnesses, and countless other environmental influences. The medication given, for example, to a diabetic is simply one more environmental factor that affects the ways in which the inherited genetic potential is expressed.

The misleading heredity-versus-environment questions always have to be rephrased in terms of *how much* or *how flexible* the genetic "messages" are in their interaction with different environments. Stature, for example, is often thought to be largely hereditary, but we now know that factors such as the health of the mother, levels of infant nutrition, and disease history can make significant differences in individuals' adult heights. Modern Europeans and North Americans are, on the average, notably taller than their ancestors of past centuries, mainly because of environmental changes, though some genetic factors are also involved.

Phenotypes—the visible characteristics of individuals—are always affected directly or indirectly by genetically inherited biological messages, but these messages are translated, diverted, distorted, and sometimes completely suppressed by the environmental system.

The Genetic Code Information— Deoxyribonucleic Acid (DNA)

The tiny threads of genetic material (chromosomes) with their bits of individual genetic information units (genes) are composed primarily of nucleic acid. The usual form of nucleic acid is deoxyribonucleic acid, now widely known simply as DNA. DNA is a highly complex material made up of NUCLEOTIDES that are put together from three different kinds of molecules: a phosphate group (phosphoric acid), a sugar (deoxyribose), and organic bases (made up of various amounts of carbon, hydrogen, oxygen, and nitrogen atoms). It is in the combinations and patterns of the *organic bases* that genetic code information is carried. These bases are *adenine*, *guanine*, *cytosine*, and *thymine*.

Thousands of the subunits we call nucleotides go together to make up a single strand or chain of DNA. The fantastically complex DNA molecules are made up of complementary strands of nucleotides coiled together in the form of a *double helix*. The individual bases in one strand within the molecule are always linked together to the bases in the other strand of the double helix in quite specific combination: for example, guanine is always paired with cytosine, and adenine hooks together with thymine.

One of the most thought-provoking things about DNA is the fact that this basic chemical genetic message system is fundamentally the same in all living organisms, both plants and animals, above the level of viruses. Some of the simplest living things, such as viruses and bacteria, have a somewhat different kind of sugar (instead of deoxyribose) and somewhat different bases than the ones in the model here. However, even in those cases the basic system is not fundamentally different from the way DNA operates in humans.

In the process of cell replication (mitosis), in which living somatic cells endlessly reduplicate themselves, each DNA double helix goes through a process of unwinding and then rewinding with new complementary strands. Because of the specific ways in which the particular bases must combine with one another (adenine with thymine, and guanine with cytosine), when the double-stranded DNA splits in two, the newly formed strand that joins with each half is an exact complementary (mirror image) of the original strand.

Now, where does the genetic *coding* come in? The

97

detailed genetic information—which makes the difference, for example, between purple and white flowers—is in the *sequences* of those four bases, which we will refer to here by their letters A, G, C, and T. A, G, C, and T are thus the letters of the biological alphabet, and all genetic messages are written out using these four letters. The millions of different kinds of genetic messages are all different "words" put together from the four basic "letters."

It is a long, long way from the DNA molecules to complex creatures such as human beings. Fundamental to putting together a large, complex animal like a human is the production of a variety of different proteins. Not only are living cells made up to a considerable extent of proteins, but also the chemical messengers that affect various physiological processes are composed of proteins. ENZYMES, for example, are the chemical agents that break down the food we eat; they regulate the production of skin pigments; and so on. Still other types of proteins within living systems—HORMONES—are the regulators of processes, including growth, reproduction, and defensive and offensive arousal. Proteins themselves are built up from subunits called *amino acids.* There are about twenty different amino acids, and all proteins are made up of different sequences of these basic building blocks. Evidently the genetic code, built up from the four letters A, G, C, and T, carries instructions about the combining of amino acids into proteins.

In our simplified presentation of the basic idea of the genetic code, we are omitting some steps in the process of protein synthesis. This synthesis requires two intermediate substances we have not discussed: messenger RNA and transfer RNA. RNA is similar to DNA in its basic composition, although it appears to be a single strand instead of a double helix. Messenger RNA copies off the code from one strand of the DNA molecule and carries it to the site where protein is to be constructed. Transfer RNA picks up the free roaming amino acids and takes them to the construction site. These activated amino acids are then strung together in the correct order to form a particular protein by their contact with the genetic code carried by the messenger RNA.

A gene can be regarded as a segment of a DNA molecule. The *structure* of DNA, the *processes* of transfer of DNA through sex cells to new living organisms, and the *building up* of more and more

cells in a multicelled organism through further cell division and reduplication are processes that are infinitely more complex than our simplified discussion here. Many of the details of how DNA actually works in genes and chromosomes are yet to be worked out. The experimental evidence about these processes is hard to get from human subjects, partly because it takes a long time to move from one generation to the next. Geneticists, therefore, most often work with short-lived creatures, for which the specifics of genetic transmission can be worked out in generations that happen many times a year, as in fruit flies and other small creatures.

Incidentally, the geneticist H. J. Muller has calculated that there may be something like 4 billion nucleotide pairs (pairs of individual code letters) in the chromosomes of a single human sex cell. If one assumes that *any change in any single nucleotide pair* makes a *new* gene, and if one assumes also that any combination of nucleotides makes genetic sense, then the total possible number of different genetic endowments is something on the order of $10^{2.4 \text{ billion}}$. That is quite a few, when we consider that it is estimated that the total number of atomic particles in our universe is only 10^{76}!

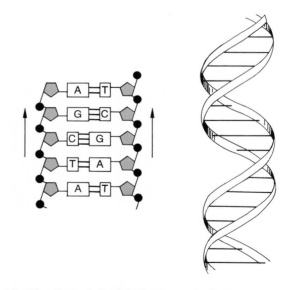

5.5 **The famed double helix (spiral) shape of the DNA molecule is made from four basic building blocks: the chemical bases adenine, guanine, cytosine, and thymine (A, G, C, and T in the diagram).**

Homo sapiens in Biological Perspective

Mechanisms of Change: Mutation and Natural Selection

In biological evolution the gene materials—the chemical messages in organic cells that set the limits of growth patterns and characteristics—do not change themselves because a specific environment "requires" a particular genetic development. Foxes, rabbits, and other creatures that moved farther and farther into arctic conditions did not develop white coats because the environment required that evolutionary change. Instead, those animals that came to be located in arcticlike conditions had, within their populations, a *range of variation* in their genetic potentials, including that of coat color. Since the whiter coat color provided greater protection from predators, the whiter animals tended to survive more of the time than did the darker animals. Over time there occurred a *natural selection* for the lighter coats from the existing *range of variation* of genetic raw materials.

The genetic materials are further changed from time to time through *mutations*. A *mutation* is any change in the genetic coding within living cells (most importantly in "sex cells" that are transmitted from parents to offspring) which results in genetic biological potentials in the offspring that differ in some significant way from the sex cell codes of the parents. These changes in genetic codes are known to be caused by such external agencies as radiation, certain chemicals, and heat. In humans, the mutagenic effects of radiation are probably the most significant. This is one of the reasons that people are warned to avoid excessive exposure to X rays (especially in the region of the sex organs). Probably there are other causes of mutations that we do not yet know about.

A most important point about mutations is that they have no direct relationships to the specific features of the environment to which animals must adapt. That is to say, if some individual animals, say, rabbits, had some mutations in sex cells that produced whiter fur color, that mutation for fur color was in no way *caused by* the specific environment (white snow and ice) the animals were living in. We must think of mutations as occurring in random fashion, so that in a population of rabbits living close to arctic conditions, random mutations

arise from time to time that produce individuals with darker fur, lighter fur, spotted fur, and a variety of other changes. Each of these mutations is completely accidental as far as its possible adaptational consequences are concerned. Most such individual mutations are by their nature harmful, since every animal is a finely tuned organism, well adapted to its environment, and internally adapted with regard to the interrelationships among the various organs and tissues. Any accidental mutation is most likely to upset this balance. In fact, many mutations that we know of are the causes of serious diseases in people and other animals.

Although individual mutations tend, on the average, to be harmful to individuals, the general effect of ongoing mutation is to maintain levels of genetic variation within populations. Of the many mutations that arise, some *small* fraction are potentially useful in the face of environmental changes, or perhaps in the development of new characteristics that increase the animal's potential in the present environment. These "successful" accidentally produced mutations tend to be preserved in the next generation through natural selection.

Natural Selection: The Salt-and-Pepper Moth

There is a well-known example from recent biological history that is frequently cited to illustrate the interactions of mutation and natural selection. In England during the Industrial Revolution coal was a main source of energy for running mills and factories. In time the vegetation became coated with the soot of modern industrial pollution. The dark coating on buildings, plants, and other features of the landscape represented a significant change in the environment for many creatures, especially insects.

One of these, a little moth, was in preindustrial times a speckled creature, with lots of gray on the upper wings mingled with some areas of black. Its salt-and-pepper appearance was well adapted as camouflage in the preindustrial environment of trees speckled with lichen. As the trees became darker, it was observed, around 1840, that a black form of this moth had appeared near Manchester. Apparently, each generation of moths from 1840 on included more and more of the black form, with a progressive diminution of the formerly well-adapted

99

speckled moths. By 1895 about 98 percent of the moth population in the Manchester area was of the black type. The black color in this moth was apparently produced by a single dominant gene, and the powerful effects of the sooty shift of environmental characteristics must have put enormous pressure for change on the population, since it took only about sixty generations to bring about this evolutionary transformation. Details of this example have been documented in much detail by the British naturalist H. B. D. Kettlewell (Birdsell, 1972:393).

Unlike some of his fellow naturalists who might have been content with simply observing this evolutionary shift of moth color, Kettlewell set out to see if he could demonstrate the operation of natural selection experimentally. He bred populations of speckled moths and black moths and turned them loose in unpolluted forest areas to see if it was true that the speckled moths would be favored by natural selection in the nonindustrial environment. He found that birds captured the black moths six times

as frequently as they did the more camouflaged moths. Thus the mixed population showing the effects of industrial pollution would have reverted to salt-and-pepper coloration in an unblackened environment.

Kettlewell must have been utterly fascinated by this clear demonstration of Darwinian evolution. He reversed his experiment, taking equal numbers of the two different types of moths and placing them in a polluted area. There he found that the speckled or gray-and-black moths were caught by the birds much more frequently than were the black moths. We must repeat here that the original mutation for a black moth in the industrial environment of Manchester did not come about *because* of the changed physical environment. That original mutation (or number of mutations) was a genetic accident, perhaps caused by ultraviolet radiation or some other totally neutral and nondirected agent.

For purposes of this discussion we have accepted the assumption that the black moth color developed

The Chemical Nature of Mutations

The changes in genetic messages that we refer to as mutations are, in some cases, simple substitutions of one "word" in the DNA code. For example, the difference between normal *hemoglobin* (the main protein in red blood cells) and the abnormal hemoglobin in sickle-cell anemia is in the substitution of the amino acid valine for glutamic acid at one point in one thread of the gene. The following illustrates this mutation-by-substitution (only part of the total molecule is shown).

Sequences of Amino Acid Code Units

Beta-chain of
normal
hemoglobin   Val-His-Leu-Thr-Pro-GLU-Glu-Lys-Ser-Ala-Val

Beta-chain of
sickle-cell
hemoglobin   Val-His-Leu-Thr-Pro-VAL-Glu-Lys-Ser-Ala-Val

Source: Adapted from Buettner-Janusch, 1973:443.

The minor "misspelling" in one gene affecting hemoglobin characteristics results in a serious weakness in the red blood cells' capacity to transport oxygen. This weakness can show up in individuals in a number of symptoms, including anemia, rheumatism, and enlarged spleen.

Mutations in genetic materials are not always simple, however. Sometimes the chromosomes in sex cells become entangled or break down, so that entire sections containing large numbers of genes become lost or reattached in a changed sequence. The chromosomal rearrangements may spell out extensive shifts in genetic coding. Even the simple inversion of a chromosome segment (see Figure 5.7) produces biochemical changes in individuals, for it turns out that the effects of a gene depend on its placement in relation to other individual genes in the chromosome.

100

Homo sapiens in Biological Perspective

from a mutation that occurred during the time of growing industrialization. In many instances of evolution through natural selection, it is not necessary to assume some *new* mutation. Usually the *existing range* of genetic materials already present in a varied population contains within it some fraction, however small, of the particular genetic code that will prove most adaptable to new environmental circumstances. With coat color, for example, we note that practically all mammalian species have a rather wide range of color combinations present in their populations. Such color variations are frequently quite evident in a large herd of wild animals such as caribou or elk. Although most individuals in the herd may appear to be "pretty much the same" in coloration, there are generally small numbers of variant colors of several different hues present within the group. This *existing* genetic variation in any population is extremely important for ensuring the adaptability of the group. If there is a considerable change of environment (and it does not have

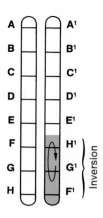

5.7 **New genetic forms can arise from breakage of chromosomes. In this illustration a mutation has occurred because of "chromosomal inversion": the "F-G-H" segment of one chromosome broke off and rehealed in an inverted position. Even though the original genetic messages are all present, the results in an individual may be different simply because of the change in *sequence* of the genetic code.**

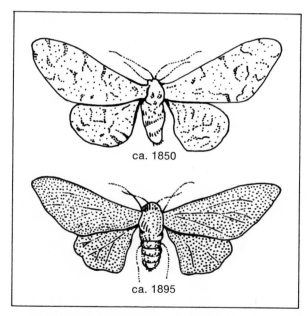

5.6 **The salt-and-pepper moth was well adapted to its environment in England until industrial pollution darkened the trunks of the trees and other vegetation. The dark moth evolved as a new adaptation to the industrial environment.**

to be nearly as drastic as the darkening of the landscape in industrial England), the animal species that is most likely to adapt successfully to the changed environment is one that (1) has a considerable range of intragroup genetic variation and (2) is not overly specialized into some particularly narrow environmental niche.

Rates of Mutations

Until recently it had been widely assumed that mutations are very rare events in human biological history, so that only an occasional genetic anomaly would be noticeable in human populations. All the rest of us are perfectly healthy and normal. This view had developed because genetic mutations in human populations were recognized mainly in particularly clear-cut and gross instances, such as those of albinos, hemophiliacs, and achondroplastic dwarfs. But mutations come in all shapes and sizes, and many of them affect "invisible" characteristics of individuals, such as endocrine functioning, composition of blood sera, and other not easily detect-

101

Table 5.2: Estimated Mutation Rates For Harmful Human Traits

	Mutation Rate
Autosomal Dominant Genes	
Muscular dystrophy	8 per 100,000
Retinal blastoma (tumor of eye)	2.3 per 100,000
Huntington's chorea (involuntary uncontrollable movements)	5.4 per 1,000,000
Aniridia (absence of iris of eye)	4 per 1,000,000
Achondroplasia (achondroplastic dwarfs)	4.2 per 100,000
Autosomal Recessive Genes	
Cystic fibrosis of pancreas	1 per 1,000
Epidermolysis bullosa	5 per 100,000
Albinism	2.8 per 100,000
Congenital total color blindness	2.8 per 100,000
Infantile amaurotic idiocy	1.1 per 100,000
Microcephaly	3 per 100,000
Sex-linked Recessive Genes	
Childhood progressive muscular dystrophy	3.2 per 100,000
Hemophilia (defective blood clotting mechanism)	4.5–6.5 per 100,000

able features. Geneticists working with various kinds of animals, ranging from the fruit fly *Drosophila* to larger animals, such as dogs and cats and primates, have estimated that mutation rates for a particular gene may be as high as 1 mutation per 10,000 sex cells in some species and 1 per 100,000 in others. One of the leading figures in human genetics, Theodosius Dobzhansky, has estimated that "close to 20 percent of all people, will carry one or more newly arisen mutant genes" (Dobzhansky, 1962:48–50).

Fortunately, most of these mutations carried around by us humans are relatively minor. The really serious genetic mutations that cause drastic illness or early death are rare. Table 5.2 lists some estimates of genetic mutation rates in humans.

These estimated rates of serious harmful mutations have been made from counting the number of cases in large populations. Some of these population estimates show that mutation rates are likely to be different for particular characteristics in different populations. On the whole, though, there is no reason to expect that the various populations of humans are likely to be very different in their overall rates of mutation. When we concentrate on the dramatically harmful mutation effects, we are likely to experience a feeling of fear at the idea that one in five of us carries from one to five mutant genes.

But most individual mutations are recessive and appear in individuals as harmless heterozygosis. As already noted, mutation is extremely important—in fact, essential—for maintaining genetic variability and hence the adaptability of individual populations. It is interesting to note that if the genetic transmission process were perfect, so that sex cells from parents were always exact copies transmitted to offspring, with no mutations or "accidents" in the genetic codes, populations would tend to become more and more homogeneous and lose adaptive flexibility.

Genetic Stability: The Hardy-Weinberg Principle

When geneticists first developed the idea of dominant and recessive genes, it was believed by many that, logically, the dominant genes would drive out the recessives, regardless of natural selection. The question is: What *does* happen to the proportions of various genes in a population over time? The answer to this question was given in 1908 by two men, G. H. Hardy (British) and W. Weinberg (German).

Hardy and Weinberg demonstrated mathematically that the percentages of the different alleles

Homo sapiens in Biological Perspective

for each gene in any population will tend to remain constant *to the degree* that the following conditions are met:

1. That mating is completely random, rather than clustered in terms of class strata, kinship groups, or other nonrandom patterns.
2. That the population is very large (infinitely large) so that accidental fluctuations in the production and survival of particular genetic combinations do not occur.
3. That each mated pair produce the same number of living offspring.
4. That no mutations and no natural selection take place.

Clearly these special conditions for genetic equilibrium are never found in living populations, but geneticists can compare actual populations with the hypothetical model in order to calculate the likelihood of genetic change and evolution. The Hardy-Weinberg equilibrium model provides a frame of reference for sorting out the different factors affecting any particular population.

Assuming random mating in an infinitely large population, what is the relationship between the frequencies of individual alleles of genes and the resulting phenotypic characteristics? The computations for answering this question are known as the HARDY-WEINBERG FORMULA. The formula begins from a simple binomial equation:

Frequency of allele A plus frequency of allele B = 1

If we let p stand for the frequency of one allele and q for the other, we can write the equation as:

$$(p)A + (q)B = 1$$

To calculate the actual genotypic combinations in a population, we must "mate" or pair every individual A gene with every possible B gene, which can be accomplished mathematically by simply squaring the basic equation:

$$(pA + qB) \times (pA + qB) = 1$$

The solution:

$$
\begin{array}{l}
pA + qB = 1 \\
pA + qB = 1 \\
\hline
p^2AA + \ pqAB \\
\qquad\quad pqAB + q^2BB \\
\hline
p^2AA + 2pqAB + q^2BB = 1
\end{array}
$$

Now let's try it out on Mendel's purple and white peas. Let us assume that there are only two alleles in the population and that the frequency of the purple gene alleles is one fourth (.25). The gene for white is therefore .75 of the total gene pool. Our equation now becomes:

(.25 purple + .75 white)
$$\times \ (.25 \ purple + .75 \ white) = 1$$

Solution:

$$
\begin{array}{l}
.25 \ purple + .75 \ white \\
.25 \ purple + .75 \ white \\
\hline
.25 \times .25 \ purple + .25 \times .75 \ purple\text{-}white \\
\quad .25 \times .75 \ purple\text{-}white + .75 \times .75 \ white
\end{array}
$$

Results:

$$
.0625 \ purple\text{-}purple + .375 \ purple\text{-}white \\
+ .5625 \ white\text{-}white = 1
$$

Since the genes for purple flowers are dominant over the white flower allele, we can calculate that the total percentage of purple flowers will be .0625 plus .375 or .4375. Thus, .5625 of the population will be phenotypically white.

Using the Hardy-Weinberg formula we can work backwards from the observed frequencies of genetic types in a population (provided we know the dominance-recessive relationships) to establish the frequencies of the individual alleles. All that is needed is an accurate count of the frequency of the AA (homozygous) or the AB (heterozygous) or the BB (homozygous) individuals in the population. Whenever calculations of expected frequencies of genes, or of genotypes in a population, fail to match this theoretical model and the discrepancy is in a consistent direction, the researcher knows that one or more mechanisms of evolutionary change are likely to be operating to cause the deviations.

Genetic Drift: Evolutionary Change Without Natural Selection

Discussions of biological evolution sometimes make it sound as if all evolutionary changes are due to the action of natural selection. This is not the case. The genetic characteristics (frequencies of various alleles) of populations can change over the generations because of "accidental events" in random mating that have nothing to do with natural selection. This evolutionary factor is called GENETIC DRIFT, and it is most likely to occur in small populations—that is, in groups that violate conditions of the Hardy-Weinberg model of large stable populations.

Genetic drift, as a factor in biological evolution, is something that most of us will recognize in terms of common-sense examples. Suppose that a population of hunting and gathering people has a total of about fifty adults and fifty children (actually quite large for a hunting and gathering band) and that within the group there are four or five adults whose genetic codes include curly hair, while all the rest of the group have straight hair. (For purposes of the hypothetical illustration, let's assume that the curly hair arises from a single dominant gene, so that all individuals who have any genetic coding for curly hair display this trait.) As long as this hunting and gathering band stays together in one group, a visiting physical anthropologist, or anyone else, would report that the group has approximately 10 percent curly-haired and 90 percent straight-haired genetic characteristics.

Now suppose that for some reason the group splits up, as has occurred countless times in the prehistory of human groups. Such a split would most likely occur along family lines—a cluster of three, four, or five families closely linked in kinship may decide

to set out on their own, leaving the rest of the group in their formerly common territory. With such small numbers of persons involved, it could very easily happen that *all* the curly-haired people *happened* to be in the group that left in search of better hunting in some new territory. If that small group of about fifteen adults just happened to include the five curly-haired people, then a full third of this new population would have curly hair while the group that was left behind now has zero genetic frequency of this trait, and 100 percent straight hair. In ensuing generations *if* no further changes take place our adventurous migrant group would tend to have progeny showing approximately one third curly hair, while the stay-at-homes in the former territory would continue through the generations to produce offspring with straight hair. We are assuming in this example that neither straight nor curly hair has any adaptive significance whatsoever.

One area of the world in which this type of genetic drift may have occurred is in the South Sea islands. The islands have been settled during the past two thousand years by successive waves of migrants with their sailing canoes—most of them descended from the same parent stock, Malayo-Polynesian–speaking people from somewhere in the Southeast Asian region. Patricia Gindhart has studied a series of genetic characteristics among five different island populations in wide-flung Polynesia.

5.8 One type of genetic drift, the "boatload effect," as imagined by our artist. In the example most of the light-haired people were in the migrant group, so their new colony is likely to look different from the parent population in hair color.

Homo sapiens in Biological Perspective

The genetic drift that has possibly occurred in connection with these traits is exactly the same, in principle, as in the case of our curly-haired hypothetical population. Table 5.3 shows the genetic variation among these five island groups.

If all five of these groups are descended from a single parent stock, as archaeological and linguistic evidence indicates, then these differences in genetic characteristics were very likely due to the kind of genetic drift discussed above. More specifically, these fairly wide variations in gene frequencies for particular blood types may have come about because the different "boatloads" of people who migrated to the various Polynesian islands represented different "sampling errors" from the original parent stock. This type of genetic drift is, in fact, sometimes referred to as "boatload drift." It is also referred to as the "FOUNDER EFFECT" or "founder principle." Under unusual circumstances this founder effect can produce dramatic shifts in gene frequencies in a population, but we should note that it is a "one-shot" effect.

A second type of genetic drift, perhaps less dramatic, is that which occurs within a population through sampling deviations *from one generation to the next*. As with the founder effect, a likely deviation in genetic sampling is that a relatively rare gene is accidentally eliminated. On the other hand, sampling errors can also produce increases in the frequencies of a previously rare genetic trait. This may be brought about because some individuals just happened to have a lot of children. Once again using our hypothetical hunting-gathering band with fifty adults, suppose that one of the curly-headed men was an exceptionally able hunter and was able to provide for three wives and that in addition he occasionally had sexual intercourse with three or four other females in the group. (This is not an uncommon situation in hunting and gathering bands, who frequently have relaxed views about extramarital sex.) The single curly-haired hunter with three wives might father nearly half the children of the next generation, bringing about a clear change in the gene frequency for curly hair. On the other hand, it is just as likely that our curly-haired males were out hunting one day and two of them fell through the ice and drowned. The effect could be the accidental reduction of the number of genes for curly hair in the next generation.

We have dwelled on the nature of genetic drift

Table 5.3: Genetic Variation Among Five Island Populations of Polynesia

(*Frequencies of four sample genes*)

POPULATION	GENETIC CHARACTERISTICS			
	A	B	C	D
Easter Island	.40	.65	.35	.15
Marquesas	.35	.65	.45	.42
Tonga	.25	.25	.55	.15
Kapingamarangi	.25	.25	.75	.45
Rarotonga	.45	.45	.55	.15

Source: Cited in JOHNSTON, 1973:55–56.

partly because it is this process, rather than natural selection, that probably accounts for many of the differences by which populations in different geographic regions have come to "look different" from one another. This is not to say that all such population differences were brought about by genetic drift. Mutation and natural selection have also been important mechanisms, but most likely genetic drift is responsible for differences that appear fairly rapidly among small populations.

Assortative Mating

The effects of genetic drift become minimal as populations grow larger. Statistical "accidents" in sampling from parental population to the next generation become rapidly smaller and smaller as breeding populations rise above a thousand persons. With many people intermating in a large population the accidental features of differential fertility, chance migrations of individuals, accidents that occur to particular families and individuals, and other random events *tend* to balance out, if the males and females in that population are mating with one another in a "mathematically random fashion"—that is, if mate choices are random with regard to genetic characteristics. In real life, though, human mating is frequently not random; people tend to select individuals like themselves as marriage partners. For example, in our own North American population, as well as in many other groups around the world, tall people tend to select tall mates. Conversely, very short individuals (especially males) tend to prefer correspondingly small-statured marital and sexual partners. To the extent that such nonrandom selection of mating partners occurs, the genetic characteristics within a population will be skewed instead of randomly distributed within that population. Such a deviation from randomness could, under some circumstances, have consequences for future generations. This nonrandomness in mating patterns is called ASSORTATIVE MATING. Assortative mating is the main strategy used by animal breeders in trying to develop superior show horses, breeds of sheep, excellent milk cows, and other specialized domestic animals. If assortative mating were developed to a high degree in a human population, it could, over the generations, lead to the establishment of specialized subgroups of very tall people, highly intelligent subgroups, or other physically and genetically distinguishable enclaves within the population. To what extent, then, does assortative mating take place?

Probably the clearest example of assortative mating within our own population is in terms of size. James Spuhler (1962) has studied a large number of married couples in Ann Arbor, Michigan, where he found that assortative mating did take place to a significant degree. However, he also found that assortative mating for height and size was far from 100 percent. Also, there was no clear evidence of differential fertility between the shorter and the taller couples in his sample. Therefore he concluded that this type of assortative mating in a modern North American population was not resulting in any *change* of gene frequencies for the next generation.

Assortative mating may occur to some degree in modern populations, but it is practically always much less than 100 percent, and its effects are very, very difficult to determine. Assortative mating, we should note, can be either *positive* or *negative*. Some inconclusive studies within our own North American population have indicated that there may be *negative* assortative mating among redheads. If this is true, it means that for some reason redheads tend to avoid marrying one another.

One exceptional example of possible assortative mating has been described by J. B. Birdsell concerning the royal families in several Polynesian island societies. Some of the kings, queens, and princes among the Polynesians have been people of very large size. They are "not infrequently six feet, six

inches tall and 300 or more pounds in weight. The women in these royal families are built on the same generous lines. . . . It seems evident that preferential mating has been practiced to breed up chiefly lineages characterized by impressive size" (Birdsell, 1972:376). Such assortative mating does not by itself change the total count of genetic characteristics in a population, but it does change the distribution of these genetic characteristics. Also, by the way, we do not have definite evidence even in the Polynesian island case, since it has not been studied in detail with this question in mind. In general, assortative mating may have been of some slight significance in human evolutionary history, but it does not appear to have had any major consequences.

Inbreeding in Human Populations

Whenever the man and the woman in a mated couple share a common grandparent or great-grandparent (more distant ancestors can be ignored for practical purposes), we can regard this union as INBREEDING to some degree. Since people share some common, ancestral, genetic materials in inbreeding, the effect is to increase the number of homozygous genotypes. Persistent inbreeding within a small population can result in an overall increase in homozygosity within the population, which can have seriously harmful effects *if* the population contains some *recessive* genes of a harmful nature. The greater the degree of inbreeding in a population, the more likely it is that an individual will receive the same harmful recessive gene from *both* parents and hence suffer from some serious defect (e.g., cystic fibrosis, muscular dystrophy, mental retardation, hemophilia, sickle-cell anemia, thalassemia or Mediterranean anemia, and so on). The specific nature of such harmful genetic results in inbreeding will differ, of course, depending upon what kinds of harmful recessive genes are present in the population.

An example of the occurrence of relatively rare diseases in a somewhat inbreeding population has been described by Victor McKusick and his colleagues from research among the Amish people of Pennsylvania. They found a somewhat greater than expected frequency of polydactyly (six fingers) as well as the Ellis van Creveld syndrome (a series of

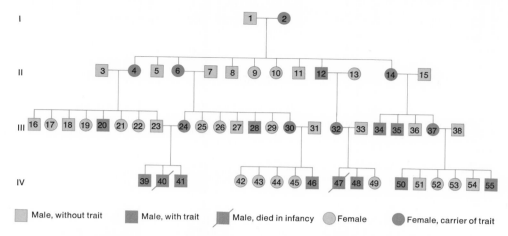

I

II

III

IV

| Male, without trait | Male, with trait | Male, died in infancy | Female | Female, carrier of trait |

5.9 "A royal pedigree of hemophilia. Part of the genealogy of royal families of Europe shows the pedigree of hemophilia, a rare X-linked recessive trait. It is presumed that Queen Victoria (2) was the original carrier of the trait in European royal houses. For those readers who are interested in royal lineages, the following individuals are in the pedigree: (1) Prince Albert, (2) Queen Victoria, (3) Frederic III of Germany, (4) Victoria, Princess Royal, (5) Edward VII, (6) Alice, Duchess of Hesse, (7) Louis IV (Ludwig) of Hesse, (8) Alfred, (9) Helena, (10) Louise, (11) Arthur, (12) Leopold, Duke of Albany, (13) Helena of Waldeck and Pyrmont, (14) Beatrice, (15) Henry Maurice of Battenberg, (16) Kaiser Wilhelm II, (17) Charlotte, (18) Sigismund, (19) Victoria, (20) Joachim, (21) Sophie, (22) Margaret, (23) Henry of Prussia, (24) Irene, (25) Victoria, Marchioness of Milford Haven, (26) Elizabeth Fedorovna, (27) Ernest Louis (Ludwig) of Hesse, (28) Frederick William, (29) Marie Victoria, (30) Alice Alexandra, (31) Czar Nicolas II, (32) Alice, Countess of Athlone, (33) Alexander of Teck, Earl of Athlone, (34) Leopold of Mountbatten, (35) Maurice of Battenberg, (36) Alexander of Carisbrooke, (37) Victoria Eugenie, (38) Alfonso XIII of Spain, (39) Sigismund, (40) Heinrich, (41) Waldemar, (42) Olga, (43) Tatiana, (44) Marie, (45) Anastasia, (46) Czarevitch Alexis, (47) Maurice, (48) Rupert, Viscount Trematon, (49) May Helen, (50) Alfonso Pio of Asturias, (51) Jaime, (52) Beatrice, (53) Maria, (54) Juan, (55) Gonzale. Many individuals in Victoria's lineage have been omitted from generations III and IV. For two of the males who died in infancy, (40) and (47), there is no evidence that they either had or did not have the trait." (From John Buettner-Janusch, *Physical Anthropology: A Perspective*, 1973:337, by permission of John Wiley & Sons, Inc.)

facial and dental abnormalities) among the Amish as compared with the general population of Pennsylvania. These two genetic patterns are known to result from the occurrence of a homozygous recessive genotype, so it would appear that their somewhat elevated rate among the Amish is due to inbreeding. Studies of the offspring from incestuous matings in modern North American populations have also shown a higher than expected incidence of genetic anomalies, including mental retardation, stillbirth, and other defects.

On the other hand, it should be noted that inbreeding, no matter how pronounced, will have no harmful effects if the inbreeding population contains no harmful recessive genetic materials. A great many semi-isolated populations have higher levels of homozygosity than do our large, urbanized, and "heterozygosized" populations; yet many of them do not show any serious effects from this degree of inbreeding. Geneticists have pointed out that Charles Darwin's own pedigree included a number of first-cousin marriages, and so did that of his wife, Emma Wedgewood. Charles and Emma were first cousins, and both "lineages" were highly inbred. Notwithstanding, their genetic "family line" included a number of persons with high artistic and

107

scientific eminence, and they did not exhibit much in the way of genetic defects. Many other such examples could be cited.

Perhaps the most famous instance of the genetically negative effects of inbreeding is that of the rare disease hemophilia among the royal families of Europe. As our history books make abundantly clear, the crowned heads of Europe had a strong tendency to marry off their children to other royal families, with the inevitable result of inbreeding. Among the European royalty it is thought that Queen Victoria was the carrier of the semilethal recessive gene for hemophilia. The effects usually appear only in males, but females are the usual carriers of the trait since many of the affected males die before reproducing. Figure 5.9 shows the royal pedigrees of Europe affected by Queen Victoria's dreadful secret. We see from the pedigree that Victoria's daughter Victoria married Frederick III of Germany, who had several normal sons and one son who was a hemophiliac. Another of Victoria's daughters, Alice, Duchess of Hesse, passed on the hemophilia gene to three offspring, two females and one male. One of the granddaughters married Henry of Prussia (Number 23 in the diagram) and we note that two of their three male children were hemophiliacs. The other son died in infancy.

The harmful effects of inbreeding must have been fairly evident to those crowned heads of Europe, but they nonetheless persisted in marrying their children to one another. Most situations of inbreeding are probably somewhat less striking than this instance of hemophilia, and most populations do not practice inbreeding to any large degree except under very unusual circumstances. In fact, many of the really clear instances of inbreeding have been within families of royalty. The extremes of such practice in times gone by were the brother-sister marriages of some of the pharaohs of Egypt, the divine royalty of the Incas of Peru, and similar practices among Hawaiian kingly lineages.

In many non-Western populations, ethnographers have reported a preference for marriage with particular types of first cousins. In the instance of first cousins, who share one pair of grandparents in common, their offspring will have approximately 6 per-

Table 5.4: Estimates of the Frequencies of First-cousin Marriages

Population	Time Period	Total Number of Marriages	Frequency of First-Cousin Marriages
Baltimore, Maryland	1935–1950	8,000	.0005
Watauga County, North Carolina	1830–1849	299	.0408
	1910–1929	439	.0091
France	1876–1888	1,410,889	.0103
Bavaria	1926–1933	474,268	.002
Alpine community, Switzerland	1880–1933	77	.039
Obermatt, Switzerland	1890–1932	52	.115
Londonderry County, Ireland	1954	717	.0139
Tyrone County, Ireland	1954	3,000	.002
Swedish Parish of Pajola	1890–1946	843	.0095
Swedish Parish of Munonionalusta	1890–1946	191	.0680
Denmark (sample of entire country)	1900–1920	498	.012
Nagasaki, Japan	1949–1950	16,681	.0503
Hiroshima, Japan	1948–1949	10,547	.0371
Bombay, India (Parsees)	1950	512	.129
Bombay, India (Marathas)	1950	137	.117
Fiji Islands	1850–1895	448	.297

Source: Adapted from BUETTNER-JANUSCH, 1973:347.

Homo sapiens in Biological Perspective

cent homozygous genotypes (homozygous for particular genes) based on this inbreeding. Cousin marriage would eventually lead to a considerable increase in homozygosity in a population if it were practiced consistently. However, in all societies that have maintained rules of preferential cousin marriage, the "cousins" who are the preferred marital partners are often fairly distant kin who are classified as "cousins" because of their membership in particular kin groups. Thus in most of these ethnographic cases, the actual rates of cousin marriage are rather low. Naturally, other things being equal, rates of inbreeding and the resulting homozygosity in a population are much affected by the population size as well as by the stated cultural norms of mate choices. In large urban populations in which any matings between consanguineous kin are discouraged (as in most North American and European populations, for example) the rates of cousin marriage and general inbreeding will be quite low. Table 5.4 shows some rates of first-cousin marriages in different populations.

Gene Flow: The Fruits of War, Migration, and Other Activities

In recent centuries improvements in transportation have brought about vastly increased contacts among different populations of the world. Great numbers of Europeans, Africans, and Asiatic peoples have come to the New World, and people from Europe have spread to practically every region of the world in connection with colonial expansion. In all parts of the world there is now much greater intensity of social contact between urban and rural populations, and cityward migration of rural people may be the greatest migration in history.

All of these movements of people bring about GENE FLOW from one breeding population to another. Thus, HYBRIDIZATION among different populations and subpopulations is extremely common today. Military activities are, of course, notorious for their effects on gene flow. Wars in Vietnam, Korea, and elsewhere have resulted in a sizable flow of North American genetic materials to populations of East and Southeast Asia, as well as into Europe. So-called "war babies" are the most publicized expression of such gene flow.

Since humans are all members of the same species, mating between individuals from two different genetic populations (no matter how different they may appear to be) results in normal offspring. Moreover, such "hybridization" often results in HETEROSIS or "hybrid vigor." The theory of hybrid vigor is based on the assumption that the highest adaptibility is associated with high levels of heterozygosity. Our complex makeup includes fairly considerable levels of "weak genes"—genetic materials that at least in some environments exhibit adaptive disadvantages. When mating takes place between individuals from different populations such "defective" genetic inheritance is minimized, as the (usually) recessive defective genes are masked by healthy dominant ones. The phenomenon of hybrid vigor is best demonstrated in controlled experiments, as with hybrid corn. It is difficult to sort out the effects of heterosis from environmental effects among human populations.

It is frequently noted that modern North Americans are taller, larger, and stronger than their nineteenth-century forebears. Much of the difference is the result of better nutrition and improved control of infectious diseases, but several studies have demonstrated that there is also a hybridization effect operating. The mixed Polynesian-European-Asian population of Hawaii is also frequently given as an example of the adaptive advantages of genetic mixture. The present inhabitants of tiny Pitcairn Island in the South Pacific are the descendants of the famous mutineers of *H. M. S. Bounty* and the Polynesian women they married. These hybrid progeny have been studied in detail by the anthropologist Harry Shapiro, who finds them to be a large, vigorous, and healthy population.

While there have been great opportunities for gene flow in recent times, we should not lose sight of the fact that there have been large-scale movements of peoples, hence gene flow between populations, throughout all recorded history. Archaeological records extend the evidence of genetic exchanges among populations far back in time. Thus the populations of the world have been affected by interpopulation gene flow for many thousands of years, although the worldwide intensity of such population contacts has been heightened in the past couple of hundred years.

109

Some Points to Keep in Mind

Our discussion in this chapter has included only certain main features of genetic mechanisms, the understanding of which seem essential for getting the picture of how biological evolution "works." When we look at human evolution, the highly complex biochemical events of the DNA genetic code system must be related to culturally patterned behavior in mating, migrating, and other genetically significant activities. Once we understand the ways in which the biological genetic system itself works, at least in broad outline, we can understand somewhat more clearly how natural selection and other evolutionary factors have brought humankind to this present complex stage of biocultural evolution. Some main points that should be kept in mind are these:

1. The major evolutionary significance of the sexual reproduction system in humans, as in other animals, is that a balanced range of variation in genetic traits is maintained within broad limits. That is, the transmission of genetic characteristics from parents to offspring produces individuals who resemble their senior generation in many respects, yet they are never exact copies.

2. The processes of natural selection and those of genetic drift are significant in changing the genetic composition of populations through a progressive "weeding out" of some characteristics, leaving intact certain genetic characteristics in individuals who have been successful in surviving and passing on their genetic characteristics to their offspring. Although sometimes people have, in careless fashion, thought of natural selection as being a kind of bloody conflict between different species, the focus of our attention should be on the selection going on *within* individual populations.

3. Since evolution is sometimes simply defined as "descent with modification," we need not assume that every single feature of every population has some kind of adaptive and selective significance. Some of the biological changes that have come about are the result of genetic drift, which, as pointed out, may have no adaptive significance. Probably many of the visible differences among various geographical populations have been the result of accidental genetic drift factors rather than natural selection.

Homo sapiens in Biological Perspective

Human Variations: The Problem of "Race"

From the raw materials of our discussion of genetic processes in human populations, we can begin to examine some of the data about biological similarities and differences in human populations. Some of the more visible and *socially* significant differences in human populations have come to be lumped under the concept of "races," and a great deal of heated argument can be found in recent literature on this sensitive topic. Philosophers and scholars of ancient times noted differences in the types of humans, particularly in relation to different geographical regions, and some of these human variations are mentioned in the Bible. However, it appears that Europeans did not attach tremendous significance to mere physical differences among populations until the eighteenth and nineteenth centuries.

The Age of Discovery, which sent European entrepreneurs, military units, and religious missionaries rushing to the far corners of the globe in search of wealth, fame, and other things, brought the relatively light-skinned Europeans into close, firsthand contact with many populations in Africa, Asia, and the Americas—populations that in skin color and other visible attributes appeared very different from the human features to which Europeans were accustomed. Another significant factor affecting the Europeans' perceptions and definitions of these other populations was that the non-European peoples had cultural systems and social behavior very different from those of the white-skinned intruders on the scene. Because Europeans had been used to thinking of cultural and social behavior as very likely biologically inherited, the different behaviors of the African peoples, the Asiatics, and the Indians of the Americas were taken as evidence of some kind of biological gulf between the Europeans and the rest of the world. Finally, when we add that the Europeans often conquered those other peoples and set about exploiting them economically, we can begin to understand (though certainly not to forgive) the strong tendency that developed among Europeans to regard their own relatively white-skinned populations as inherently superior and dominant biologically and socially as compared with the other peoples of the world.

Before we go on to discuss further the social and biological information on human population variations, it is well to inject at the very start a strong

6.1 An Israeli. (Erich Hartmann, Magnum)

6.2 **Blue-veiled Tuareg tribesmen. (Marc Riboud, Magnum)**

6.3 **Indian woman in Mexico. (P. J. Pelto)**

statement from some recent ideas about the concept of race as discussed by anthropologists. Ashley Montagu writes, in the introduction to *The Concept of Race:*

Most readers will be aware that the social (sometimes miscalled the ''sociological'') concept of race, the doctrine, to put it briefly, that there exists superior and inferior races, has long been unacceptable to anthropologists. What most readers may not be aware of is the fact that the biological concept of race has become unacceptable to a growing number of biologists on the one hand and to an increasing number of physical anthropologists on the other. (MONTAGU, 1964:xi)

With that caution light blinking in our consciousness, we can now proceed to examine some of the features and problems of the term ''race'' and the human variations to which, in various ways, the term supposedly refers.

Monogenists Versus Polygenists

Contrary to some current belief, white-skinned Europeans have not always been overwhelmingly racist in their views of the rest of the world. In fact, as long as much of the philosophical thought of Europe was dominated by biblical doctrine, there was wide acceptance of the Book of Genesis version of our human origins and the natural equality of all human groups. Thomas Aquinas (1225–1274?), one of the notable theological philosophers of the Middle Ages, set forth the orthodox Christian view when he argued that "all men born of Adam may be considered as one man, inasmuch as they have one common nature, which they received from their first parents." And furthermore, that "by nature, all men are equal" (quoted in Slotkin, 1965:25).

The biblical view of the fundamental equality of all human groups was reinforced by the interpretation of the Scriptures, according to which the creation of the earth, Adam and Eve, and everything else on the face of the earth supposedly occurred only about six thousand years ago. In fact, the learned Archbishop Ussher, a noted English clergyman of the eighteenth century, calculated the exact origins of the earth from chapters in the Bible and assigned the date of creation as 4004 B.C. Because, furthermore, this biblical view of man, woman, and creation assumed that the various types of animals and humans were all created as fixed types as God intended them, there was nothing from the Scriptures that would permit easy explanation for supposed racial inequalities. Now, actually, some theorists did suggest that the nonwhite, non-European populations of the world had sinned in the eyes of God more than others and were therefore in some sense inferior to white-skinned sinners, but the powerful dictates of the Catholic Church did not uphold this doctrine of essential inequality.

It is ironic that the orthodox theologians, who have often been among the more conservative and "antiliberal" in their social influence, on the matter of explanation of "the human races" took a position that we would now regard as the liberal, *egalitarian* view, whereas the supposedly more "scientific" and freethinking scholars had by the beginning of the nineteenth century taken a more and more antiegalitarian view. During the nineteenth century, per-

6.4 **Young girl in Nigeria on way to market.** (Marc Riboud, Magnum)

haps strongly influenced by white European exploitation of the rest of the world, many scholars theorized that the darker-skinned peoples of Africa and the widespread "Mongoloid" populations of Asia were not just different "races" but that they were actually different *species* from the white-skinned Europeans. This doctrine of POLYGENISM became more widespread toward the middle of the nineteenth century.

Among anthropologists of the nineteenth century, there were many who took the polygenist view that the different human populations on the face of the earth were different species. On the other hand, a number of leading anthropologists were also found on the monogenist side—arguing for the physical and natural unity of all humankind.

The beginnings of "Darwinism" and the growing strength of evolutionist thinking in the middle of the nineteenth century in some ways aided the argument of the polygenists, since Darwinian evolution provided a possible explanation of how the different human populations could have diverged and become separate species. Darwin himself felt

113

that the divergence of human populations and "race formation" were a process that occurred "at a very remote epoch," which helped to explain "the remarkable fact that at the most ancient period, of which we have as yet obtained any record, the races

6.5 Hill tribe woman of Nepal. (U.N.)

of man had already come to differ nearly or quite as much as they do at the present day." Thus, Darwin did not consider the different human populations to be separate species, but he was strongly impressed with what he felt to be their physical and mental differences.

A major problem for understanding human varia-

tions that persisted throughout the nineteenth century and well into the twentieth century was the inability of scholars, even some of the best biologists and other scientists, to understand the full implications of the fact that varieties of languages and cultures are *only very accidentally* related to variations in the physical appearance of humans. Many writers appear to have assumed that the type of culture or type of language spoken by people is in some way related to their biologically inherited physical appearance. The rise of anthropology, beginning about 1900, was to a considerable degree an attack on this lumping together of physical appearance and cultural and mental characteristics.

The "Major Races"—Some Problems in Classification

Both the polygenists and the monogenists of the nineteenth century were convinced that the populations of the world could be neatly divided into three or four (or perhaps five) major "races," even though it was quite evident, to at least some of the more perceptive scholars, that there was a lot of variation *within* each of these supposed racial groups. One of the mental blocks that affected practically all anthropological thinking of the nineteenth century, and that has persisted to modern times among some people (both scientists and the general public), is the pervasive habit of thinking in terms of "ideal types." This TYPOLOGICAL THINKING raises serious logical problems in connection not only with supposed racial types but also with theories of "cultural types," "types of psychiatric illnesses," "types of societies," and other aspects of the social sciences. The problem is that "types" are often developed from circular reasoning. In terms of human populations, it goes something like this:

1. Observer sees a group of people—e.g., Chinese people around Shanghai.

2. He or she assumes that they are a "type" or "race"—obviously different from European white "Caucasoid" types.

3. Having assumed the existence of the type, the observer feels that his classification is completely accurate and useful as he meets more Chinese, from Peking, from Hong Kong, and from other areas. (He has to make some adjustments in his type when he finds that the northern Chinese are considerably

Homo sapiens in Biological Perspective

taller than the southern populations, so the adjective *short* has to be dropped out of the type.)

4. The observer feels that his racial-type idea is still sound when he observes Japanese, although some of the characteristics now have to be stretched a bit more.

5. Traveling in Southeast Asia, in Indonesia, and in the Philippines, the observer finds that some of the populations he encounters no longer "fit the type." Still believing that the type is a useful idea, he assumes that he has crossed over into a different type, and in between there are some mixed types.

6. As our observer travels on to North America and encounters a variety of Indian populations, he has to decide whether to stretch his Mongoloid race type to include North American Indians—or should he assume that they are yet another type, a different "race"?

This "typologizing" process will lead an observer to a varying number of different types, depending on which groups he happened to start with in his classification and what route he followed in classifying all of the different populations in the world. It is not surprising, then, that some physical anthropologists have maintained stoutly that there are "at least three major races visible among the populations of mankind, which may be subdivided, however, into 'local races'" (Buettner-Janusch, 1973:491–493).

It is important to understand that there will never be agreement among physical anthropologists or anybody else on the correct number and designation of major races of *Homo sapiens*, because the lines dividing up the populations of the world can be drawn in a variety of different ways, depending on how many criteria one wishes to use to divide the populations. As Frederick Hulse has noted:

Most of the attempts to reconstruct racial history postulate an original threefold division of our species into Mongoloid, Negroid, and Caucasoid stock, each of which later divided into subraces. Minority opinions maintain that the original division was twofold, fourfold, or even sixfold. Some anthropologists have stressed the role of hybridization among the major stocks as well as divisions within each of them. As [we] have demonstrated, however, we cannot expect taxonomic neatness at the subspecific level, and there is really little evidence to support the notion that at one time there were just two or three or four distinct races of Homo sapiens. (HULSE, 1963:344–345)

The Same[1] and the Finns: Secret Mongoloids?

Some of the problems of attempted racial classifications can be highlighted if we glance for a moment at the history of race taxonomies (classifications) as they have touched on the Same and the Finns of Northern Europe. Early observers were perhaps especially impressed by skin color, hair color, and stature in establishing their racial types. At the same time, they also paid attention to sharp cultural and language distinctions. It happens that the Same and the Finns differ markedly from the rest of Northern Europe in language, as their Finno-Ugric language is not at all related to the Indo-European languages (spoken by practically all the people who developed the early racial classifications). As a result, physical anthropologists such as J. F. Blumenbach divided all humankind into five major races, of which "the Caucasian variety includes the inhabitants of Europe —except the Lapps [Same] and the remaining descendants of the Finns" (Blumenbach, 1865:265). Blumenbach then assigned the Same and the Finns to the Mongolian variety of humans. A number of other physical anthropologists throughout the nineteenth century, invoking various different kinds of criteria, tended to regard them as either Mongoloid or some kind of special northern "Hyperborean" race. Finally, in 1899 William Ripley published a new and widely cited racial classification in which he argued that Same and Finns are extremely different in physical appearance and could not possibly *both* be members of the Mongoloid "race."

In the early part of the twentieth century, the Finns had been completely accepted within the Caucasoid white "race," whereas the identity of the Same wavered somewhat. Physical anthropologists eventually defined the Same as a special, "unusual" branch of Caucasoid populations. The physical anthropologist Carleton Coon suggested that they represented some remnants of an ancient Mongoloid ancestry, "in modern times much mixed with Ladogan and Nordic [Caucasoid races]." (Coon, 1939:292).

In most recent times, physical anthropologists have made more use of blood group data (ABO series, Rh negative and positive, and other blood

[1]See Preface, p. vii.

115

6.6 Northern European Same were first classified as "Mongoloid" by anthropologists. (Lessing, Magnum)

constituents) in studying the relationships among different populations. In blood type the Same have turned out to be extremely "non-Mongoloid," especially in the very low frequencies of type B in the population. (Type B blood as a genetic characteristic tends to be high among populations of Central and East Asia, as compared with Western Europeans.) The lesson in all this shifting back and forth of the supposed racial classification of Same and Finns is that *it depends a good deal on what characteristics are used to identify the "type."* None of the nineteenth-century racial classifiers had blood type information available to them, so they used features of external physical appearance. Some of them made much of differences in head shape, claiming that round-headed populations are very different from long-headed populations in racial ancestry. The emphasis on head shape began to fall apart in the twentieth century as it was found that European populations that were supposedly distinct from one another actually contained grand mixtures of round-headed and long-headed individuals.

116

Genetic Variation and Clines

By this time the perceptive reader will have noticed that the nineteenth-century idea of "racial

6.7 A Finnish woman. Finns were also classified as "Mongoloid" by nineteenth-century anthropologists. (P. J. Pelto)

types" depended, to a considerable extent, on concepts of genetic heredity that were *disproved* by Gregor Mendel and later geneticists. In fact, if we take only the "law of independent assortment," we can expect that various physical characteristics will vary *independently*, so that any set of "racial types" will shift around a good deal, depending on which particular features are used for classification. It is no wonder, then, that racial classifications of the twentieth century, making use of blood type information and other "invisible characteristics," result in racial classifications that are different from those of the nineteenth century, based on skin color, hair form, and head shape.

To make this point about independent assortment clearer still, let us take just three different genetic traits and see how they look on the world map. First, we will take the matter of stature because it has been widely used in the past as an element in racial classification. Figure 6.8 shows the world distribution in terms of averages in populations. For our second genetic characteristic, let us take blood type A (Figure 6.9), and we note immediately that the distribution of blood types apparently has a much different genetic history than has the feature of stature.

For the third genetic feature, we will use skin color, as shown in Figure 6.10. If we look at skin color distribution alone, we note that there *seems* to be some way that we could divide the peoples of the world into, say, three or four major races, but if we did that, we should lump the Africans south of the Sahara with the Australian aborigines. Unfortunately none of the leading racial classifiers would agree with us on that point. If they wanted to use *our* three criteria for races, they could point to our map of blood group A and say that obviously the Africans are very different from the Australians. With a variety of tricky lumping and splitting, we could, in fact, come up with some sort of classification that resembles one or the other of the existing "races of mankind" systems. However, the more genetic traits we add to our selection criteria, the more complicated our classification becomes, and the more different "subpopulations" or "subraces" we will have to devise to make sense of the data. Barnicot has summarized the lesson very clearly:

Though order exists in the external world of nature, classifications do not. They are schemata devised by men to assist them in dealing with complex material and are in this sense artificial. Many kinds of scientific work, both pure and applied, would not be possible unless the vast array of organic variation were reduced to some manageable system of named categories for identification, reference, and contemplation. Although, as a student of variation, the taxonomist can

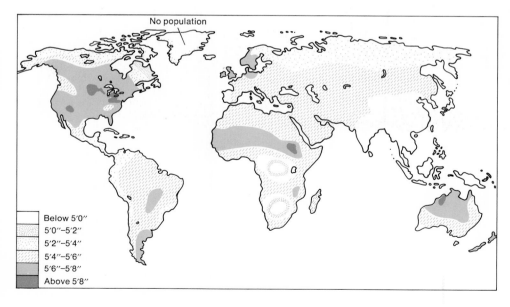

6.8 **Average male stature among different populations. (The figures for North and South America are those of the Indian inhabitants.)**

Below 5'0"
5'0"–5'2"
5'2"–5'4"
5'4"–5'6"
5'6"–5'8"
Above 5'8"

No population

Human Variations: The Problem of "Race"

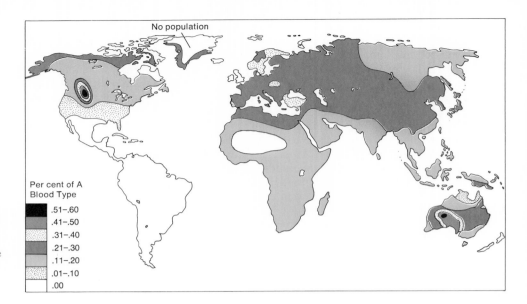

6.9 **Frequencies of blood type A in world populations (before 1492). Note the almost total absence of this genetic trait in most of the Indian peoples of the Americas.**

Per cent of A Blood Type

- .51–.60
- .41–.50
- .31–.40
- .21–.30
- .11–.20
- .01–.10
- .00

No population

hardly fail to be interested in the processes which give rise to biological diversity, much of his work is utilitarian and in constructing systems of classification he must often reach a compromise between theoretical ideals and practical needs. (BARNICOT, 1965:182)

The range of variation in the frequency of a particular genetic trait (e.g., blood type A in Figure 6.9)

is called a CLINE. Figures 6.8, 6.9, and 6.10 of genetic traits are world *clinal* maps. The cline of each genetic trait is uniquely different from that of every other physical trait, in accordance with the genetic principle of independent assortment. Some particular clines for genetic traits tend to have similar patterns, so that superficial external appearance based on skin, hair, and eye color plus hair texture makes

6.10 **Average skin color values in human populations. Darker skin color tends to be found in areas nearer the equator.**

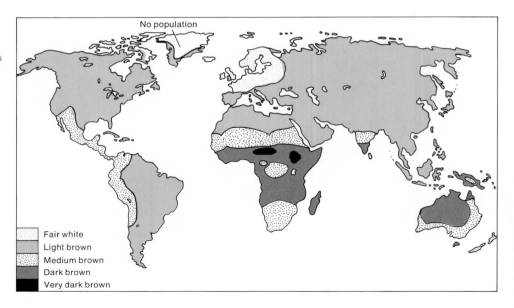

No population

- Fair white
- Light brown
- Medium brown
- Dark brown
- Very dark brown

118

Homo sapiens in Biological Perspective

possible some fairly pervasive social distinctions among major segments of world populations. That these are *social* distinctions rather than basic genetic distinctions is evident in the fact, for example, that the offspring of a "Caucasoid" male and a "Negroid" female will practically invariably be regarded as "Negro" in social identification; in North America practically *any* visible degree of purported "Negro blood" will lead to the classification of an individual as "Negro" in social race.

Since the development of very sophisticated genetic theory, based on understanding of genes and chromosomes and the DNA code system, much of the research on the genetic characteristics of human populations has focused on clinal variations and their meaning, along with analysis of possible adaptive significance of various individual genetic traits. This type of research has been carried out with units of study that do not depend on broad "racial classifications." Much of the best genetic research has been on intrapopulation diversity rather than on broad comparisons among two, three, or more "races."

The term "race" and the various racial classifications have more social significance than biological evolutionary significance. They are important for anthropological study because they are *social* constructs that have important influences on peoples' behavior. As long as people *believe* they can identify some physical differences on which to base their antagonisms and invidious distinctions, they are likely to continue to use these physical criteria as guides to action. Thus, various "folk classifications" are used in social encounters and have important social meaning, but as genetic, biological information a worldwide classifying of "the races" does not have much scientific usefulness.

The Significance of Skin Color as an Adaptive Mechanism

Skin color has been a highly salient factor in social interactions around the world and thus has undoubtedly more cultural significance than biological significance. On the other hand, there is considerable evidence that differences in skin color among world populations have developed in part as adaptations to environmental differences. The darkness or lightness of human skin is largely caused by the amounts of a dark pigment called MELANIN in some specialized cells of the skin. Dark-skinned people have many more granules of melanin in their skin than do light-skinned persons. Also, individuals vary in the extent to which they produce additional quantities of melanin when they expose their skin to sunshine. Some people "tan" to a very dark color, whereas other people never tan, but instead run the risk of serious sunburn.

The inheritance of the skin color characteristic in humans is not a "simple Mendelian trait" and appears to be based on the action of several genes, which probably have an additive effect. The additive effects of the genes for skin color usually result in offspring that are intermediate compared to the melanin characteristics of their parents. However, the actual genetic effects are more complex, as we note that the offspring of a dark-and a light-skinned parent can have a wide range of variation in skin color.

For a very long time—at least since the days of the Greeks—it has been suggested that skin color represents some kind of adaptation to sunlight. One clue to this adaptation is that light-skinned persons tend to be more subject to skin infections and skin cancer than are dark-skinned people when they are exposed to intense sunlight. It appears, for example, that the incidence of cancer in "white people" is seven or eight times higher than in "blacks" living at the same altitudes. The melanin particles of dark-skinned people apparently protect them from the damaging effects of ultraviolet radiation.

Since the fossil evidence indicates that the ancestors of present *Homo sapiens* evolved in the warmer regions of Africa and Asia close to the equator, it may be hypothesized (though the evidence is hard to come by) that the ancestors of modern humans developed dark skins a long time ago, at the same time that they lost that outer coat of hair that characterizes all the other primates. If this view is correct, why have some populations—especially in northwestern Europe—become so bleached out? The answer to this question may lie in the fact that our bodies require exposure to sunlight in order to produce vitamin D. Those of our ancestors who moved farther and farther north in their hunting and gathering activities ran increasing risks of serious illness from vitamin D deficiencies as long as they had dark skins. This was especially critical, perhaps, in West-

119

ern Europe, where the available sunlight is often cut down by pervasive cloudiness. Natural selection favored those persons with the lighter skins, who were less likely to suffer from vitamin D deficiency. Of course, the greatly increased sunlight of summertime posed the opposite kind of problem for these light-skinned individuals—hence selection pressures favored persons whose skin color was changeable from winter to summer. These selection pressures, especially the threats of sunlight to light-skinned persons, were somewhat lessened as these populations developed fully effective tailored clothing.

There are a number of factors that complicate the picture of skin color in the world's population. First of all, there is another element in skin color that is as yet little understood. *Carotene* produces a yellowish effect and accounts for some of the differences between European and East Asiatic populations. Furthermore, the color of skin is linked to hair color and eye color, and the environmental effects that might tend to select light-colored eyes (e.g., in Northern Europe) do not necessarily coincide directly with the natural selection for skin color. Also, the present distribution of world populations has come about to a considerable extent from quite recent migrations in response to population pressures, new modes of food production, and other factors. Thus, the skin color map (Fig. 6.10) does not display a neat, clear-cut correlation between tropical areas and dark skin. On the other hand, when we subtract out of this picture the effects of recent migrations as they are known from archaeological evidence and other data, the overall distribution of skin color in human populations tends to give strong support to the adaptation hypothesis. Most of the light-skinned populations that are anywhere close to the equator today, for example, have arrived there only recently, and they keep themselves well protected from the sun with pith helmets and clothing.

Some Summary Comments: Part I

1. The actions of genetic mutations, genetic drift, migrations, and natural selection have acted over time to maintain a very great range of genetic diversity in human populations. This diversity is extremely important as an adaptive potential in *Homo sapiens* as in all other animals and plants.

2. Individual traits, on the whole, are passed on to the next generation as discrete units since they are carried in individual *genes*. Characteristics such as blood type, hair color, skin color, head shape, and other features each has its separate genetic history and distribution—and every individual has his or her own unique combination of genetic characteristics.

3. Any classifications into "racial types" or other such categories are creations of the human mind, and do not refer to real, clear divisions among peoples. Classification of human populations into different races has been especially confusing because of the complex mixture of biological variations and cultural-social characteristics. Although categorizing and classifying is an essential operation for thinking about anything (that is what our language system is all about), classifications must be recognized as arbitrary, and some of them are useless, misleading, and evil: "Do not obtain your slaves from Britain because they are so stupid and so utterly incapable of being taught that they are not fit to form part of the household of Athens." (Cicero to Atticus, first century B.C.)

Race and Intelligence

The pervasive racism that is found in the social distinctions people make on the basis of skin color and other human features often includes assumptions concerning supposed inherited differences in intelligence. In recent times, with the advent of complex educational systems and their use of "intelligence tests," some people have tried out these academic tools to "test" theories of racial differences. The Stanford-Binet types of IQ tests were developed early in the twentieth century and came into wide use during World War I. American soldiers drafted for service in the "war to end all wars" were perhaps the first in history to be screened for "mental fitness."

Racists were quick to point out that White draftees had, on the average, higher scores in the IQ tests than did non-Whites. This, they claimed, proved that Whites were superior in hereditary intelligence.

Homo sapiens in Biological Perspective

Furthermore, it was noted that Anglo-Saxons did better than other Europeans in the Army's tests. The scores in these examinations were assigned letter grades from A to E, with the breakdowns shown in Table 6.1.

Although some racists may have gained some initial satisfaction from these statistics, it didn't take long for people to notice the discomforting fact that the Italian and Polish IQ scores were rather closer to the Black test performance than they were to other "Caucasoids," yet Italians are the descendants of the "noble Romans." Clearly there must have been some significant environmental (nonhereditary) effect operating in these tests. Sorting out the test scores by geographical region, as in Table 6.2,

gives us some additional evidence of this environmental effect.

The sharp differences between the IQ test performances of the northern versus southern Black soldiers are a clear indication of the effects of schooling and other social opportunities. Any lingering faith in these tests in the hearts and minds of dyed-in-the-wool racists had to suffer a severe shock when both Blacks and Whites are compared in terms of geographic regions, as in Table 6.3. That whisker of a difference in test performance between Alabama Whites and New York Blacks disappears completely when we compare the scores among the "illiterate" soldiers on the Army Beta I.Q. test, as in Table 6.4.

Table 6.1: Results of World War I Army Intelligence Test

| Group | Number Tested | PERCENTAGES | | |
		Below C	C	Above C
Englishmen	411	9	71	20
All White draftees	93,973	24	64	12
Italians	4,007	63	36	1
Polish	382	70	30	.5
Blacks	18,891	79	20	1

Table 6.2: Intelligence Test Scores by Region

| Group | Number Tested | PERCENTAGES | | |
		Below C	C	Above C
Blacks (5 northern states)	4.705	46	51	3
Blacks (4 southern states)	6,846	86	14	.3

Table 6.3: Results of Alpha Test for Literates

| Group | Number Tested | PERCENTAGES | | |
		Below C	C	Above C
All Whites	72,618	16	69	15
Alabama Whites	697	19	72	9
New York Blacks	1,021	21	72	7
Alabama Blacks	262	56	44	.4

Human Variations: The Problem of "Race"

Table 6.4: Results of Army Beta Test for Illiterates

		PERCENTAGES		
Group	Number Tested	Below C	C	Above C
All Whites	26,012	58	41	1
Italians	2,888	64	35	1
New York Blacks	440	72	28	0
Alabama Whites	384	80	20	0
Alabama Blacks	1,043	97	3	.1

Table 6.5: Klineberg's Tests of Harlem Children

Years in New York City	Average IQ
1 to 2	72
3 to 5	76
5 to 6	84
7 to 9	92
Born in the North	92

Source: KROEBER, 1948:197.

The *environmental* effects of schooling, social opportunities, income levels, and related factors of social stratification are clearly reflected in these statistics. Obviously the *major* cause of the differences in scores cannot be due to any supposed biological "racial" variations.

The psychologist Otto Klineberg added further demonstrations of these environmental effects in a classic study of twelve-year-old Black children in Harlem. To test for environmental factors he divided the children into groups according to the number of years they had lived in New York City (most of the children were born in southern states). He got the IQ test averages shown in Table 6.5.

The Meaning of IQ Tests

So far we have been looking at the statistics from the early "intelligence tests" simply to discover something about the factors that might be responsible for differences in the scores. The evidence shows quite clearly that there is a very large input of environmental influence on test performance. But what do the tests actually test? What is IQ?

The best definition of *intelligence* as deduced from the standard IQ tests is: "Whatever it is these tests measure." That is, the whole idea of "intelligence" is a very abstract concept about individual capabilities in literally millions of different activities. Most IQ tests select a small range of tasks (closely related to the things that children must do in standard North American and European classrooms), like reading, answering questions about the reading, identifying relationships among numbers, looking at geometric shapes and sorting them out, and so on. It has been fairly well demonstrated that IQ tests are pretty good predictors (although far from 100 percent accurate) concerning (1) how individuals will perform on *other similar tests* and (2) how individuals will perform on a lot of the other things that teachers make them do in classrooms. Beyond these narrow definitions of performance the tests are on much shakier ground.

The contents of all intelligence tests are quite *culture-bound* (that is, much influenced by social environment and cultural experience), since the very idea of a "test" in the usual paper-and-pencil format is the product of particular, school-oriented cultural system. For many people in the world, the test situation itself is a completely alien experience.

Now some people have argued that all those North American children, Black and White, who have been exposed to approximately the same duration of schooling are essentially "culturally comparable" in the IQ test situation. This argument ignores a major factor, however. What many educators (as well as racist interpreters of IQ tests) have ignored is the fact that any test is a *social interaction* between the tester and the tested. Generally the tester is White and "middle class" and speaks a version of "standard average English." For the average "middle-class" school pupil, the tester does not pose an extremely difficult psychological problem because the social distance between them is not very large. For children of immigrant parents or from poverty-stricken homes, often with nonstandard English as their spoken idiom, the social distance between pupil and teacher (between tester and tested) is great. The distance is further emphasized by the fact that the teacher usually conveys to the "nonstandard" pupil the unspoken sense of the pupil's cultural and intellectual inferiority. The social encounter in the IQ test, therefore, takes on some very different dimensions when the pupil being tested is non-middle-class, perhaps "nonstandard" in language use, and non-White.

IQ Tests and "Race": Round II

For a long time after World War II (in which the overt racism of the German Nazis was soundly de-

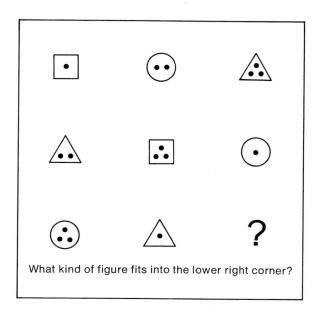

What kind of figure fits into the lower right corner?

6.11 A question from an IQ test.

feated) there was very little new in the "race and intelligence" controversy except for the far-out fulminations of a few extremists. Then, in the 1960s, "respectable racism" surfaced again, this time in some supposedly new, sophisticated statistics purporting to show that even though some of the differences among groups in IQ scores are clearly due to social environment, the effects of sociocultural factors are not enough to close the "gap" between Whites and Blacks in IQ test scores. The best-known author of this new material on intelligence testing is Arthur Jensen, a psychologist who achieved overnight notoriety with his "How Much Can We Boost I.Q. and Scholastic Achievement?" published in the *Harvard Educational Review* in 1969.

To start with, Jensen and all modern IQ testers admit that there is a good deal of intragroup variation in "intelligence," and they are also sophisticated enough to note the part sociocultural factors play in IQ test performance. We have indeed come a long way from the crude racist arguments of the 1920s. Thus the logic of argument starts with the assumption that the differences between groups in IQ performance (P) are the result of the *interaction* of "environmental influences" (E) *and* biological heredity (H). So far, so good:

$$E + H = P.$$

One of the ways to assess the effects of E (environment) and H (heredity) on individuals and groups is to test pairs of identical twins. (MONOZYGOTIC twins are the genetic results of the splitting of a single fertilized ovum, so they are thought to be *essentially identical* in all genes and chromosomes). If such identical twin pairs differ from each other in IQ (or anything else), that difference must be due to the effects of environment. The degree of such differences can then be calculated as an average, to show the *relative* percentages of effects due to E (environment) and H (heredity).

When identical twins are raised together in the same environment, their IQ test scores show an average correlation of .80. They are indeed very similar, although clearly not identical. When identical twins are raised in separate environments, the average correlation of their test scores is .75. This difference is a further demonstration of the effect of environment on IQ test scores.

From the information on White identical twins

Jensen derived a computation of (H)eritability of 80 percent. In general, this means that 80 percent of the variance *among the people in the test group* is due to inheritance, whereas 20 percent comes from sociocultural factors. Many reputable geneticists and other scholars accept this computation as useful —with one additional qualification: that the calculation is valid only for the *particular population studied* under the *particular environmental circumstances of that population.*

Now we come to the flaw in Jensen's argument. Jensen claims that the *average difference* between Black and White populations in IQ test scores is 15 points. He then argues that the mere .20 contribution of environmental factors to the variations in individual IQ performance is too narrow to make up the 15-point discrepancy, but the whole argument hinges on his claim for .80 H.

Let's take a simple nonhuman example. Suppose we planted a couple of rows of corn in a *completely uniform environment.* That is, the soil, moisture, sunlight, fertilizer—everything—is exactly the same for all the corn plants. In such a case, *by definition* all of the differences among the corn plants would be the reflection of genetic variations. We could, by controlling the environment fully, demonstrate, in this particular case, 100 percent H and 0 percent E effects.

If we begin with the same set of corn seeds and plant them in extremely varied environments— some without water, some with lots of fertilizer, some with no sunlight—you can be sure that there would be *plenty* of variation among the plants due to E. Why? Because we *introduced large environmental effects.* If we have learned anything in the last hundred years of biological and social study, it is that we can get big differences in living things (or even kill them off) by manipulating the environment.

We return now to Professor Jensen's .80 H. How much environmental "experimentation" was there in the .20 E for the identical White twins? First of all, we must note that because they are White, those twins had never experienced the powerful environmental effects of the racial segregation and oppression of our North American way of life. However much environmental variation the White twins may have experienced, there is no way they could be regarded as representing the full range of environmental experience that is the difference *between* the average life chances of a White child compared to those of a Black child in most of our North American cultural scenes. If Jensen's calculation of .20 E (environmental effects) was correct for all the White monozygotic twin pairs, then we can suggest that in a Black-White mixed population, the importance of E is likely to be at least 50 percent or even more. *This fact alone is enough to render the entire force of the Jensen argument invalid.*

If, as we argue, the full range of environmental differences in North America would cause environmental effects of *at least 50 percent of observed variations,* then the alleged IQ difference between Blacks and Whites can *easily* be totally erased if changes in the socioeconomic environmental situation could be instituted. But that is exactly the problem that haunts us in IQ tests, as in everything else in our racist North American cultural scene. It is, in fact, very difficult to get truly effective changes in environmental situations. It is hard to find unprejudiced teachers; it is hard to desegregate communities; it is hard to get any *real* changes in employment opportunities for large numbers of unemployed non-Whites in our society.

Race and Intelligence: The Case of the Jews

One of the founding fathers of the "IQ idea" was the famous British statistician Karl Pearson. As a patriotic Englishman, Pearson was concerned with the "quality of the racial stock immigrating into Great Britain." In the early part of the century there were a considerable number of Eastern European

Table 6.6: Effects of Kibbutz Environment on IQ Scores

	AVERAGE IQ	
	At Home	Kibbutz
Middle Eastern Jewish children	85	115
European Jewish children	105	115

Source: HIRSCH, 1972:29.

Homo sapiens in Biological Perspective

Jews coming to England as they sought escape from anti-Semitic terrorism in Poland and Russia. Pearson said that he had no special reason to criticize Jews, but "Let us admit . . . that the mind of man is for the most part a congenital product, and the factors which determine it are racial and familial; we are not dealing with a mutable characteristic capable of being moulded by the doctor, the teacher, the parent, or the home environment" (Pearson, quoted by Hirsch, 1972:12)

We should note, to begin with, that the Jews are not, a "race." There are, to be sure, stereotypes of "typical Jews," but genetically the cultural-religious population identifiable as Jewish is extremely diverse, since they have been spread around different parts of Europe, North Africa, the Near East, (and even India and China) for many centuries.

Recently there have been studies in Israel concerning the degree to which manipulation of the environment can affect IQ scores on standard tests. One of the significant Israeli social problems is mirrored in the fact that Middle Eastern Jewish children tend on the average to have IQ scores much lower than the children of European Jews. The difference between the two groups is nearly 20 IQ points for children raised in the ordinary home environment. The effect of the special experimental social environment of the KIBBUTZ is striking, as we see in the statistics in Table 6.6.

These statistics demonstrate clearly the main point that racists try to deny: the powerful effects of environmental conditions. Contrary to Jensen (and many others), an increase in average IQ scores of 15 to 20 points is not only possible, *it has been clearly demonstrated in a number of studies.*

Intelligence Tests and Social Background

Who are the people who use IQ test scores and other similar measures to proclaim their own racial superiority? Recently a study was made of eighty-two persons who have written articles and made studies concerning intelligence tests. Many of these were not racists—in fact, they were researchers who came to the conclusion that so-called racial differences did *not* account for differences in IQ test averages. Some of them, however, claimed to demonstrate that

Blacks are "innately inferior." Who are these, the more racist-oriented scholars? Sherwood and Nataupsky (1968) found that, *on the average,* "These researchers [who indicated Black inferiority in intelligence] . . . tended to be . . . first-born, with American-born grandparents, with parents who had

6.12 **Overt racism in South Africa. A park for Europeans, blind people, and non-European nurses accompanying European children. "The general European public is permitted in the park during 12 noon to 2 P.M. by Order." (Jerry Weisburd)**

many aggregate years of schooling, of rural backgrounds, and with high scholastic standing as undergraduates" (Alland, 1971:207). Translated in other social information, these data can be read to mean that the more racist researchers among those studied are from a wealthier social background and *not* born of recently immigrated families. Perhaps the people who have "made it" in the North American socioeconomic competition are the people who tend to develop research purporting to "prove" their supposed inherent superiority!

125

6.13 A lesson in biology. (Roger Malloch, Magnum)

Summary: Part II on Race, Intelligence, and Racism

1. Intelligence as measured in so-called IQ tests is an extremely elusive and vague concept, with no clearly agreed-on meaning. Different kinds of tests of "capability" measure different abilities of individuals, and all of them are very small and artificial slices from the vast complexity of human behavior.

2. Nowadays all serious investigators (even Jensen and company) agree that sociocultural environment does indeed affect test results. The argument is about how much. Although those people who argue in favor of important "racial differences" admit to *some* environmental effects, they claim that "most" of the differences in IQ are due to innate (genetically inherited) capabilities.

3. Available information about environmental effects on IQ performance (e.g., the study of kibbutz and nonkibbutz children in Israel) demonstrates very strong environmental effects, and these may have touched only the tip of the iceberg of *possible* environmental modification.

4. The racist arguments of people like Arthur Jensen are *statistically* and *genetically* invalid, as well as downright naïve in social terms, for Jensen's

Homo sapiens in Biological Perspective

specific arguments are based on a misapplication of the concept of "heritability." It is necessary to go into some detail on these things particularly because a great amount of public debate continues on the twin bogeymen, "race and intelligence," and much of the public discussion continues to be full of misconceptions about the nature of human population variations.

Part
Three

Adaptation Through Learning and Communication: *Homo sapiens sapiens*

Compared to other animals, the major adaptive strategy of *Homo sapiens* has been the continued development of behavioral flexibility and learning from experience. The behavior that we humans engage in to survive and to cope with our environments is not programmed into each of us as FIXED ACTION SEQUENCES, even though all features of human behavior depend on genetically transmitted, biological foundations. In older terminology, the human species exhibits very little "instinctive" behavior. Instead, each human comes into this world equipped with a complex brain for recording experience and for modifying behavior in the light of that experience. The ability to learn from experience is not unique to humans, of course, for all animals have that capability. Psychologists have demonstrated that earthworms can be taught to make their way through a maze, and almost every sentient animal has mechanisms for storing information from past encounters with the environment. The difference between us humans and other animals is in the much greater repertoire of behavior that can be learned and, secondly, in the extent to which successful adaptation depends on the transmission from generation to generation of large amounts of previously learned knowledge. Almost every other animal can learn enough from its own experience to "get by" and adapt to its environment, but the infant human, dropped off in the forest without human teachers, is incapable of surviving—except possibly for a few fantastically unusual cases of so-called feral children in Europe and Asia whose authenticity is still in doubt.

Reinforcement: The Basic Mechanism of Learning

The crucially important process of learning—of accumulating new knowledge and hence new adaptive behavior—has been studied in great detail by psychologists. We do not have to go into the intricacies of the general mechanisms involved in learning—in accumulating new knowledge and new adaptive behavior—except to note the fundamental elements of learning that appear to be general among all sorts of sentient creatures. In order for learning to take place in humans, apes, rats, or earthworms, the following must occur:

Learning, Science, and Culture

7

7.1 For complex tasks like spear making a combination of verbal instruction and imitation may be the best way to learn cultural information. Amazonian Indian father teaching his son. (Cornell Capa, Magnum)

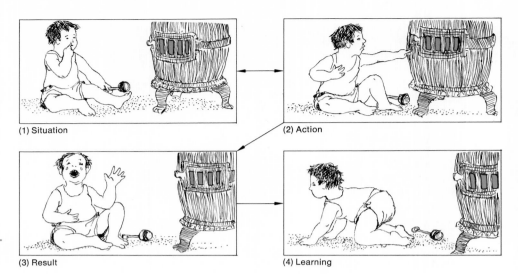

(1) Situation   (2) Action

(3) Result   (4) Learning

7.2 **Learning from experience, the basis of human adaptation.**

1. The animal must do something—engage in some action, move in a particular manner, vocalize something, or perhaps (among humans) only picture such actions or motions in mental imagery.
2. The "environment" (social, biological, and physical) responds to the animal's action by some change or response that affects the animal's needs, desires, and so on.
3. The animal in some way remembers the circumstances, situation, or context of its action *and* the positive or negative consequences of its action, so it can decide whether or not to repeat the action.

If a particular behavior has results that lead the animal to repeat the behavior, we can say that it was "positively reinforced." If, on the contrary, the environmental "response" to the animal's behavior tends to lessen the likelihood of a repetition of the behavior, we say that it was "negatively reinforced."

The simplest example of animal learning is the classic sequence of B. F. Skinner's famous pigeons: (1) pigeon pecks (accidentally) a bar; (2) pellet of food drops into food tray (environmental effect); (3) pigeon evidently likes to get the food pellet, for it "remembers" to peck the bar in order to repeat the sequence.

Figure 7.2 illustrates this basic learning sequence. In the diagram, the most important thing to remember is that learning is always a transaction between an animal and its environment. In some sense the environment is always there prior to the animal's action, but the most significant triggering mechanism for learning is the behavior of the animal itself. This fundamental idea—of learning by doing—is often lost sight of in school classrooms. Learning is, above all, a problem-solving activity. The sequence of actions in Figure 7.2 has meaning for an individual especially if the initial situation poses some sort of problem concerning food, health, entertainment, or other bodily or mental need. A basic point to remember is that each individual accumulates information and modifies its behavior because of information coming in *through all its senses*. Because of formal school systems in our modern society, we often equate learning with the materials acquired from books and lectures. Some people have even presumed that learning is practically always mediated by language among humans. It takes only a moment's reflection to realize, however, that we all learn a great deal through nonverbal channels and that there are many kinds of information and learning processes each of us experiences that "can't be expressed in words." Try, for example, to explain verbally the difference between the smell of roses and the fragrance of lilacs. Many people have experienced the frustration of trying to put into words the complex body motions that are involved in, say, driving an automobile, kneading bread, or acquiring skill in football, ballet, or gymnastics. We are not

132

Adaptations Through Learning and Communication: Homo sapiens sapiens

denying the power of language to evoke complex emotions and many-splendored events, especially in the hands of skillful storytellers and poets. We must note, though, that most of us experience all kinds of significant events and feelings without assigning words to them all, and we also must keep in mind that great poetic works do not accurately describe —they achieve their greatness through artfully *suggesting* what cannot be directly expressed.

Learning Through Imitation

A great amount of learning in every human group takes place through observation and imitation. The child watches the adult's dance performance and then imitates the steps; the shop apprentice watches a master machinist and follows the example; and young and old observe the behavior of famous people and imitate some of their walk and some of their talk. This kind of learning is not basically different from the learning through experience discussed above. The novice learner who watches and imitates partakes vicariously in the action of another, pictures himself engaged in the same action, and by

"proxy" absorbs the lessons of right and wrong. Learning by observation and imitation is another sector of human adaptation that has a great amount of nonverbal content. How often we are frustrated in trying to "explain" how to do something and turn to a demonstration, giving an example to make clear a style or technique that words cannot describe.

Learning as Probability Inference

During the course of a lifetime, or even in just making it through an ordinary day, a human being must make a fantastically large number of decisions. Because most of our behavior is not genetically programmed, we must decide (consciously or unconsciously) from moment to moment what we are going to do next. These decisions for action are made largely on the basis of our prior information about the environment and about the probable consequences of any particular act. The hunter walking through the forest in search of game turns left instead of right; the politician in the midst of a sentence decides to say "my friends" before completing the predicate clause; the quarterback, back to pass, suddenly tucks the ball under his arm and runs toward the sidelines instead; guests at a party decide

7.3 Cultural learning by imitation. (Elliott Erwitt, Magnum)

7.4 **Sex-role learning through imitation.**
(Leonard Freed, Magnum)

that the hour is late and it's time to say good night to the hosts. What do all of these situations have in common? In each of them individuals make rapid assessments of the situation, predict the possible results of different courses of action, and in a split second, often without any conscious thought, reach a conclusion concerning probable action. Charles Erasmus, in his book *Man Takes Control*, has discussed this decision-making process as follows:

Cognition as a causal factor in cultural behavior takes the form of probability prediction—frequency interpretations derived from inductive inference. Experience or observation is the raw material from which frequency interpretations are inductively derived. Tossing a coin, for example, provides experience or observation from which it can be inductively inferred that the frequency of occurrence of each face is the same. It can be predicted, then, that in repeated throws the coin will land heads up 50% of the time. Human knowledge, on which cognition builds, is made up of predictions which are simply tentative probability statements—never final truths. (ERASMUS, 1961:22)

Erasmus goes on to point out that FREQUENCY INTERPRETATION is not an exclusively human phenomenon:

Experiments have shown that birds have a number sense which enables them to select boxes with the same number of spots (never more than seven) as those presented on a cue card. Even in simple trial-and-error learning among animals, certain positive associations are built up when successful choices frequently lead to a reward. The experimental animal is clearly anticipatory in his actions; and as successful responses grow more strongly motivated, one might even consider the animal's behavior "predictive." (ERASMUS, 1961:22)

The PROBABILITY INFERENCES that Erasmus speaks of are accumulated by each individual during the course of day-to-day living, and we are all well aware of the fact that individual probability inferences are often wrong. Each of us has turned the wrong direction into one-way streets, and we have said the wrong thing at cocktail parties. We have guessed wrong about presidential elections, and we have made wrong predictions about the personalities and motives of people we have met for the first time.

134

If we did not experience these mistakes, the learning system would, in fact, be less effective; there's a lot of truth in the expression, "We learn more from our mistakes than from our successes."

Probability Inferences and Science

Discussions about the nature of science often draw a sharp contrast between the ways of thought and modes of investigation of the "scientific method" as contrasted with ordinary, "traditional" modes of problem solving. Some people argue that "real scientific method" was invented less than three hundred years ago. Although it is certainly true that modern scientists in their laboratories and field research carry out more extensive data-gathering in a much more formalized manner than is the daily practice of hunters or peasant plowmen, human beings have adapted throughout their history to the realities of their environments, accumulated new information, and corrected their mistakes in a manner that is *not basically different* from the kind of information processing that goes on under the heading of science. Rational, problem-solving behavior is characteristic of humans everywhere. Of course, some people are more "tradition-bound" than others; some people are kept from using their best information because they are under the control of demanding masters; and many people live in environments so unfruitful that they have little margin (of food supplies, safety, or cash resources) either for experimentation with new techniques or for the nonutilitarian joys of acquiring knowledge for knowledge's sake.

The institutionalization of the scientific method in our universities and laboratories does represent a degree of organization of learning that goes beyond the information-processing systems of nonindustrialized peoples, but the basic processes are not different and, to some degree, all people use the "scientific method" in learning from experience. As the physicist Marshall Walker puts it:

The scientific method is merely a formalization *of learning by experience*. Anything that learns by experience is using the scientific method in a primitive form . . . . consider a child who reacts to a first stimu-

lus of thirst by drinking from his glass of milk. One day the glass is filled with buttermilk, and the child receives an unexpected second stimulus. The next time he is thirsty he may refuse his milk until convinced that it is not buttermilk. . . . The child with the milk is obviously using the scientific method even though he can hardly talk. He has a model based on experience and predicts from his model that the glass of white stuff will taste good. For a large number of instances his predictions are correct. Then he encounters a glass of white stuff that does *not* taste good, alters his model accordingly, and predicts that the next glass of white stuff will taste bad. And he will retain this second model until further experience leads him to modify it. It is very unlikely that he has been consciously following the steps of the scientific method. Nevertheless, it seems a reasonable inference that the steps of the scientific method have been followed automatically. (WALKER, 1963:14–15)

Walker goes on to suggest:

The scientific method is a survival technique that developed during the biological evolution of living things. Any organism or device that includes a suitably connected memory unit can "learn by experience," and this learning by experience contains the basic elements of the scientific method. (WALKER, 1963:15)

The scientific method, as Walker presents it, involves the following steps:

1. The individual postulates a *model* based on existing observations (prior experience) of some aspect of "the real world."
2. On the basis of the model he or she makes a prediction (or series of predictions) and then checks these against further *observations* of the phenomena in question.
3. The model is then adjusted or replaced as required by the new observations or measurements. The third step leads back to the first step, and the process continues without end:

If the "scientific method" is found among people everywhere as a basic process of learning, then are there *any* processes of idea construction that are not in some sense "scientific"? The answer may seem obvious, but deserves careful attention. Logical theorizing, *devoid of empirical* checking and testing, is not scientific, however brilliantly executed. By our interpretation of commonly accepted definitions, free-

135

flowing speculation and logic do not become scientific until they are put to empirical probing. Construction of complex theologies, Christian, Jewish, Buddhist, or whatever, is not science. Programmatic ideologies of revolution, reaction, or meditative retreat are not "scientific" except in incidental ways, since they deal with hoped-for changes and future improvements in the human condition, rather than with empirical observation and explanations of the here-and-now. That doesn't make religious, ideological, and metaphysical ideas useless and invalid—far from it! They are constructs about value-laden intentions of people which have had profound effects on our cultural systems. We don't need (or want) to have everything "scientific." (WALKER, 1963:5)

Some people feel that we can define science as the *systematic application* of the scientific method. Before we do that, however, we should remember that many scientific achievements have come about in a variety of quite unsystematic ways. The verification of these serendipitous discoveries may have involved systematic procedures, but we should not ignore the less than systematic circumstances in which they were first made. Some important and renowned scientific discoveries came about by sheer accident; others arose in the dreams or fantasies of the scientists who gained fame from their moments of inspired dreaming. Friedrich Kekulé, a German chemist, developed the idea of the benzene ring in the course of a "dream" as he sat relaxing in front of the fireplace. He recalled how the atoms in the ring "flitted" before his eyes:

"Long rows, variously, more closely, united; all in movement wriggling and turning like snakes. And see, what was that? One of the snakes seized its own tail and the image whirled scornfully before my eyes. As though from a flash of lightning I awoke; I occupied the rest of the night in working out the consequences of the hypothesis. . . . Let us learn to dream, gentlemen." (Quoted in BEVERIDGE, 1957:76)

Another instance of a somewhat different type of serendipity is the discovery of penicillin by the British scientist Alexander Fleming, whose award-winning achievement apparently came about because there was penicillin in the dust and contamination in his inadequate laboratory. Many other examples of accidental scientific discoveries demonstrate that science is never a completely systematic, controlled process of experiments and observations.

All of this suggests a definition of science something like this: "Science is whatever it is that is happening when scientists (specialists in the discovery of new information) are productive." "Whatever it is that is happening" includes the systematic accumulation of empirical observations (the individual instances from which theoretical models can be built); the formulation of theoretical models that can be tested through more research; and the further steps in information gathering and checking. Of course, scientists' activities and theoretical systems have become very complicated in recent decades, especially with the aid of complex laboratory and computer technology. But we must not forget that the essence of the scientific process is different *only in degree* from the child with his glass of milk or the hunter who predicts the location of his wounded quarry and then tests his hypothesis through further action.

Furthermore, as Professor Walker says, there have been "scientists" on earth long before the specific label was invented. Among all peoples, now and in the past, there have been individuals who were more perceptive and curious about the "laws of nature" than their kin and neighbors. It is not hard to imagine unknown and unsung individuals of past centuries actually setting up experiments to test their ideas about the way animals behave, plants grow, and so on.

Unfortunately the context and details of most human inventions and advances in systematic knowledge of past centuries were not recorded for posterity. Some unknown individuals among the ancient Peruvians thousands of years ago discovered how to drill holes in the skull for medical purposes. The purpose of this surgery, apparently, was to remove bone splinters caused by a blow to the skull. Their medical science must have required considerable experimentation to perfect the techniques. Other unknown "protoscientists" played their anonymous roles in the invention of paper (probably in China), the gradual production of various domesticated plants and animals (including maize, beans, potatoes, and tomatoes in the Americas; the rice complex in Southeast Asia; and wheat, barley, pigs, and cattle in the Near East), and many other important "cultural breakthroughs." The major developments were not invented only once by some one culture hero; almost certainly they were the result of the gradual accumulation of more and

136

more knowledge. But this is not different from the situation of science and invention today. In spite of the tremendous publicity and acclaim given to a few individuals who get the credit for making the "breakthrough," significant inventions and discoveries are usually the result of long years of work by many people. Usually they depend on a large amount of prior information developed in previous generations. James Watson's candid account of the discovery of the structure of the DNA molecule makes very clear his indebtedness to literally hundreds of other researchers (WATSON, 1968).

On some rare occasions anthropologists have observed nonmodern peoples experimenting with new kinds of crops. Among the Lamet people of Laos, for example, it appears to be the practice for older men to try out different plants in small garden plots near their homes, seeking new varieties of food:

These gardens have to some extent the function of serving as "fields of experimentation." One old man in my village was extremely interested in new plants. He had obtained a number from Lamet boys who had been away in other parts, and when I came to Mokala Panghay and laid out a garden, he showed decided interest and begged seeds and plants of me which he immediately set in his own garden. There he had a number of experimental plants, and if these were successful, he intended to plant them on a larger scale down in his swidden. (IZIKOWITZ, 1951:259–260, cited in JOHNSON, 1972:155)

Here is another example from Brazil:

In Northeastern Brazil I was surprised to find several cases of experimentation among illiterate swidden farmers. One old man was experimenting with a new strain of manioc he had received from a friend living somewhat distant; he had set aside a small portion of a manioc field to test the new variety and when questioned about it said, "Whenever we hear of something new, we like to try it out." (JOHNSON, 1972:154)

Untold numbers of non-Western, nonindustrialized peoples have experimented from time to time with new forms of social organization as well as with new crops and other material things. One interesting example of "social science" comes from the Yombe people of Zambia. Traditionally the married men with more than one wife allotted separate fields to each woman. One man, however, decided that it might be more efficient to have his wives working together in the same fields—each with different rows but working near each other. His experiment proved productive and thus brought about a small-scale change in customary work organization.

Nonindustrial peoples have often been stereotyped in our popular thinking as creatures of habit, resistant to any changes in their daily routines and techniques. Anthropologists must be blamed for some of this stereotyping, for ethnographic descriptions of non-Western cultures have often been written in ways that present the people as quite homogeneous and unchanging. Such impressions seriously distort the facts about human life styles. In all societies there are individuals who "try new things out," sometimes with rudimentary controlled experiments. The chief differences between these nonmodern scientists and our own professionalized researchers lie in two significant features:

1. Modern societies have sufficient productive capacity to allow the scientific specialists *full time* for their research, experimentation, and training of others.
2. The presence of a complex writing system makes it possible to accumulate knowledge in books and other recorded forms, thus preserving and refining the results and methods of those who investigate the nature of things.

Culture: Our Major Adaptive Device

A considerable portion of the adaptive tactics and strategy of *Homo sapiens* is made up of learned and culturally transmitted patterns. Some of the fundamental patterns of learning among humans are based solidly on genetic foundations, and, however much we emphasize the cultural *variations* of behavior in different human communities, it would be foolish to ignore the biological foundations of cultural behavior. Throughout this book, in a number of different ways, we will examine the interrelationships of culturally learned adaptive patterns and the biological characteristics developed in the course of thousands of years of evolution.

We will use the terms CULTURE and *cultural behavior* in a variety of different contexts, and we must note at the outset that the idea of culture is considered by most anthropologists to be the core concept

137

around which we can build our understanding of human adaptive behavior. We must also point out that the concept of culture is defined in a number of different ways by different anthropologists, and the reader of anthropological works must be somewhat patient with these varieties of usage. Because we want to emphasize the importance of information and conceptualization in the idea of culture, our definition, following that of many other anthropologists, is as follows:

Culture: the systematic patterns of explicit and implicit concepts (ideas) for behavior and for behavior settings (environments) learned and used by individuals and groups in adapting to their environments.

Although this definition of culture is intended to focus attention on the *ideas* people carry around with them (somehow stored in the brains of individuals), we should not forget that very large inventories of information and ideas are preserved in some physical form, in the works humans have produced. Most obvious is the cultural information preserved in libraries of written materials. Also, physical objects—tools, containers, buildings, clothes, and other things—generally have inherent in them the "congealed" information about their uses, and how to duplicate or rebuild them. Whenever people move from their traditional areas to new locations, leaving their buildings and other physical items behind, there is an inevitable loss of cultural information.

By extension, we can also see that cultural information is "stored" in the motor habits and styles of individuals. The great dancer has learned a large amount of expressive information in the form of habitual body movements, which can be transmitted to others through demonstration. When a dancer (or hunter, artisan, or other skilled person) dies, the social group suffers a loss of cultural information thereby.

This definition of culture must be broken down into its main parts. In the first place, we think of culture as composed of "systematic patterns" in the sense that there are logical interrelationships among different sets of ideas. Consider the following example:

1. People with much social position, wealth, and prestige (e.g., kings and nobles) are considered

"higher" than persons of ordinary birth and occupation.
2. For a person of ordinary birth to be "higher" than a king or a noble would be presumptuous.
3. *Therefore*, when the king or noble approaches, ordinary people should fall to their knees or crouch so that they will be "lower" than the person of high rank.

This example, which applies to many different societies around the world, shows one way in which behavior is linked to belief—in this case, about social worth. Interconnectedness of this type can be found in all spheres of human activity. As we all

7.5 **Formal classroom instruction is one of the ways our cultural ideas are passed on to the younger generation. Educational TV in Niger. (Marc Riboud, Magnum)**

Adaptations Through Learning and Communication: Homo sapiens sapiens

know, however, consistency between belief and action or between one belief and another (or one action and another) is far from perfect. In fact, cultural inconsistency is a major source of social tension and interpersonal conflict.

A certain amount of predictability in human interaction is brought about because individuals have a fair degree of consistency in their private idea systems. A person who is extremely precise in keeping appointments and meticulous in dress is also likely to insist on neatness and order at home and in work habits. The fact that a person is a practicing Catholic (contrasted with an avowed atheist) is likely, on the average, to predict some other elements of his ideas and living style.

The idea that learned cultural patterns are both "explicit" and "implicit" is perhaps best illustrated in language use. Many of the rules or patterns of the English language, for example, are quite consciously known and apparent to many speakers. But there are many rules and regularities of English that the average speaker is entirely unaware of. Our gesture language, or body language, is even more unconscious or "implicit." Most people have "intuitive" expectations about how physically close people should be to one another in ordinary conversational settings. A violation of the expectations or rules of social spacing may cause discomfort and embarrassment (hence new learning), even though people may not be entirely aware of what caused the uneasiness. Some anthropologists refer to these implicit patterns of behavior as *covert culture. Overt culture*, on the other hand, refers to the myriad bits of information that are conscious and that people can talk about.

In our definition of culture, we are using the terms *concepts* or *ideas* to refer to a very wide range of meanings. Many ideas are coded in sequences of words. (Words themselves are symbols for ideas, of course.) Other ideas may have a verbal expression (i.e., a name), yet their "reality" is primarily apparent in physical forms. Thus a particular type of stone tool visually represents a set of ideas (about how to make it and use it). When we don't know the name of an object, as is usually the case with archaeological materials, we can still make inferences about the idea behind the tool. In middle-class, highly literate circles, people spend so much time talking about everything that some people believe that "It's not culture unless there are words for it." But that seems, to us, to be a limited view.

7.6 **Body movements, like bowing, signal important information about social status. (Inge Morath, Magnum)**

The last part of our definition focuses on the primary function of culture as a system of adaptive ideas used by people to cope with their environments. In other words, different cultures are not simply collections of quaint customs, superstitions, and other oddments somehow accumulated as "tradition," for they represent the distillations of generations of human adaptive learning experiences. Many cultural practices that seem strange and unnatural to Euro-Americans have practical significance in their special environmental circumstances. For example, the practice of wrapping babies tightly in cradle boards, as among many Indian peoples and elsewhere in the world, is an effective baby-sitting

139

device that prevents infants from falling into the fire or into nearby water while mothers and other caretakers are busy with their daily work. In the course of this book, we will examine many, many aspects of the adaptiveness of cultural ideas.

On the other hand, we would not want to argue for a moment that every cultural practice in the world is "good" or has some positive adaptive function simply because it exists. There are many behavior patterns among many people that are of questionable utility. For an example close to home, we could point to the habit of cigarette smoking, which was perhaps regarded as harmless in an earlier day but now appears to be fairly dangerous to health. That's a particularly good example of our point, by the way, for it amply illustrates that even when some cultural behavior is thought to be harmful, people do not stop it.

The cultural ideas in any community include rules about correct manners and etiquette, regulations about property rights and ownership, and ways of carrying out practical activities, such as planting, harvesting, buying, selling, borrowing, and many, many other activities. There are also cultural norms or ideas about how to act when drunk; what kinds of hallucinations to experience if one is psychotic; and how to commit suicide. Cultural patterning applies to so-called abnormal behavior as well as to socially approved acts. Among some Indian groups in Canada, psychotic breakdown frequently took the form of uncontrollable cannibalistic desires. These were related to beliefs about the Windigo, a cannibalistic supernatural spirit. Similarly, among those people who take peyote, mescaline, and other hallucinogenic drugs, there are generally some culturally patterned norms about what one expects to see when intoxicated. Thus cultural ideas refer to different levels of reality, and for some people reality includes ghosts, spirits, and other supernaturals.

The Units of Culture

Our definition of *culture* as consisting of a system of ideas or concepts should make clear that the basic building blocks of any individual culture must be recognized in those items that people think about, talk about, dream about, or in some way distinguish while solving daily their individual adaptive problems. They can be named and identifiable physical items (plow, rifle, computer, stone ax, snowmobile, horse). They may be subjective feelings (sadness, despair, love, fear, ambivalence). Cultural items or "traits" may be purely imaginary, to the best of our knowledge (the genii in the lamp, Santa Claus, mermaids, werewolves).

In we use our language as a set of clues to identify cultural units, we quickly find that almost any culture trait can be broken down into parts that are themselves culture units. A rifle has a trigger, a barrel, a stock, and sights; Santa Claus has a beard and special clothing and says, "Ho! Ho! Ho!"; and love can be "true" or "puppy love" or simply crude physiological lust.

The individual cultural units—traits, ideas, concepts—can be combined into larger and more general units that we can label culture *complexes*. For example, Santa Claus is part of the Christmas complex; love is part of the dating-and-marriage complex. And complexes put together with complexes become elaborate supercomplexes—and then maybe we should call them *institutions* (the monogamous family, the Christian religion, capitalism).

"A culture" (e.g., Same culture, the Ojibwa culture, Trukese culture) is the most difficult unit to define. Usually "a culture" refers to the PUBLIC CULTURE of a particular geographically localized people who have a common language. In fact, language boundaries are the most usual criteria for identifying cultural boundaries. This criterion is inadequate, however, in those many situations in which languages overlap so extensively that they cannot be used as sensible markers for differentiations among peoples. There are many communities in the world today where multiple languages are spoken. In the northwestern Amazon region of Brazil, for example, there are areas in which different languages are spoken by adjacent communities, and members of each language-local group *must* marry individuals from other communities—hence from a different language community. The result is a grand mixture of language in which everyone must be at least bilingual because each marriage pair is supposed to be bilingual.

Similar situations of language overlapping occur in many parts of the world, sometimes because of the fortunes of war between two inveterate competitors (e.g., the French and the Germans; or the Poles and Russians; or in the great confusion of languages that attended the breaking up of the old Austro-

Hungarian Empire). For that reason, a single community—a single cultural unit—may include two or more distinct languages as speech modes, and the "shared cultural system" may include rules about which languages will be spoken under what circumstances.

From what has been said, it should be apparent that the broader boundaries of cultural units are indeed blurred and probably serve no useful scientific function in most anthropological research. It is not particularly useful for researchers to try to define accurately and clearly the boundaries of "American culture," "Hopi culture," or other such broader cultural domains. But it is useful in a general way to use these labels as nonscientific signposts of the limits of ethnographic description. A particular study of "Finnish culture" may not include all the Finnish communities in the world—at least it is intended to tell us what the generalizations and descriptions are somewhere within that amorphous totality of Finnish-speaking peoples.

Interrelations of Culture and Biology

No controversy in science has been more pervasive and confusing than the interminable wrangling about "nature and nurture," "hereditary versus learned," and other versions of the same debate. If we use the biocultural view expressed in earlier chapters, perhaps the relationships between human cultural capabilities and "biological" qualities can be illustrated with some observations about food use.

In the first place humans *must* ingest a certain minimum of nutritive materials—including a variety of vitamins, trace minerals, and other items—to sustain life. Below certain levels of nutritional intake the individual will fall sick with beriberi, scurvy, pellagra, kwashiorkor, or other nutritional illness. Whatever their levels of food intake, individuals develop learned concepts (cultural ideas) about adequate food amounts and the *scheduling* of food intake. For some people the day is going badly if there isn't a large meal about 11:00 or 12:00 in the forenoon; others eat little until late afternoon. Some people feel it quite natural, almost physiologically necessary, to eat in the middle of the night. The scheduling of food intake is a *learned* cultural pattern, but once the individual has been on a particular schedule for a long time, a significant departure from the schedule will result in real physiological upset and perhaps even illness.

Furthermore, the definitions of proper food are culturally learned ideas, which vary from individual to individual. These are, in fact, some of the most emotion-laden and difficult to change idea systems of our entire cultural vocabulary.

Allan Holmberg described how he surreptitiously fed cooked snake meat to the Sirionó, who considered snake meat very obnoxious. When they found out what they had eaten, they rushed out and vomited up that culturally abhorrent lunch. There are very real, and significant, physiological reactions when individuals are forced to eat foods they have not learned to enjoy.

On the other hand, physiological factors play a role in affecting which foods people will come to define as edible and savory. The example of milk is particularly instructive. Many peoples around the world can't stand milk, apparently for clear physiological reasons, for, as adults, they lack the lactase

"When in Rome, do as the Romans do."

—Anon.

"Don't do unto others as you would have others do unto you; their tastes may be different."

—George Bernard Shaw

". . . if one were to offer men to choose out of all the customs in the world such as seemed to them best, they would examine the whole number, and end preferring their own; so convinced are they that their own usages far surpass those of all others."

—Herodotus

141

Learning, Science, and Culture

enzyme essential for digesting it. This physiological feature becomes transformed into a cultural statement, so that milk is regarded as food only for young children. The relationship between the milk intolerance and cultural beliefs about milk are a complex two-way interchange.

We have used food as our example here because the interaction of biological and learned cultural factors is especially clear in this vital aspect of behavior. It is our feeling that practically every aspect of culture shows a similar interaction or meshing of biological and learned components.

The Problem of Ethnocentrism

The ancient historian-anthropologist Herodotus was among the earliest known writers to comment about the human tendency we refer to as *ethnocentrism* (belief in the moral superiority and "naturalness" of one's own culture). The statement quoted above was an observation he made in connection with some "cultural experimentation" by the Persian king Darius, who had a keen sense of cultural differences as well as a cutting sense of humor. Darius, it appears, asked a certain group of Greeks, "What should I pay you to eat the bodies of your fathers when they die?" Their horrified answer was that they simply couldn't do it at any price. He then introduced the Greeks to some people (from India) who reportedly ate the bodies of their fathers. King Darius asked them "What should I give you to burn the bodies of your fathers at their decease?" (as was the Greek custom), at which they, in their turn, expressed great disgust.

Belief in the superiority of one's own cultural practices is so strong in many peoples that even fairly slight variations in practice are enough to arouse contempt and fear, or at least gossip and ridicule. Customary foods are a particularly good example: the favorite foods of some Europeans (e.g., bloodbread, grilled sheeps' tails, pigs' lungs, calves' ears, and snails) are thought disgusting and indigestible by other Europeans and North Americans. On the other hand, many Americans are fond of such bizarre foods as peanut butter, Twinkies, and Fruit Loops. Many Europeans consider American corn on the cob fit only for animals.

The phenomenon of ethnocentrism has been the subject of a good deal of research and theorizing by social scientists. Although it seems to occur in almost all human groups, and nearly all individuals show some ethnocentric behavior, there are great differences in the degree to which individuals and groups are ethnocentric. Exploring the possible causes for *differential* ethnocentrism, social scientists have come up with a number of theories. These include the possibility that enthnocentrism is related to authoritarianism, to levels of cultural evolution, to the need for strong in-group loyalties, and so on.

Two social scientists, anthropologist Robert LeVine and psychologist Donald T. Campbell, have been working on the study of ethnocentrism for a number of years. They have analyzed all the different theories about ethnocentrism and have designed extensive ways of measuring this characteristic as it appears in different kinds of societies. They have arrived at the following thoughts:

[The results] suggest a trend toward greater ethnocentrism as human society has developed over the last 10 thousand years, on the following grounds. The growth and expansion of human populations have increased conflicts of interest over resources for survival, particularly land and its products. . . . intergroup conflict has proved contagious, and its cognitive basis has been stabilized in cultural beliefs that exaggerate group differences. Groups with greater societal complexity have needed to engage in war more . . . and, as larger and more efficient organizations, have been more successful at it, thus spreading ethnocentrism through conquest, extermination, and provoked retaliation. Whatever the social and psychological mechanisms involved, on which theorists disagree, this directional, perhaps irreversible, tendency toward ethnocentrism in sociocultural evolution appears compatible with most theories [of ethnocentrism]. (LEVINE and CAMPBELL, 1971:223)

Culture Is the Property of Individuals and Groups

From the writings of some anthropologists one gets the impression that the concept of culture applies only to groups. There are references to "Pueblo Indian culture," "German national culture," or "Eskimo culture," but many anthropologists avoid using the term with reference to individuals. Yet

Adaptations Through Learning and Communication: Homo sapiens sapiens

following the definition of culture we have just discussed, we can say that every individual has his own unique store of learned and codified experience—his own private culture. This is to say that each individual farmer, gatherer, or fisherman has some unique and unshared ideas and information that he or she uses in food-getting activity. Each individual seller in a complex marketplace has a unique constellation of customers, ways of bargaining, and strategy for making a profit. In fact, most aspects of life would be fairly monotonous and unrewarding if it were not for the endless variety of people's individual concepts and patterns of behavior.

Most of us spend a good deal of time reminiscing and recalling past experiences to ourselves and to others. We often find that recounting the details of a particular action sequence—a trip, hunt, party, or business transaction—aids us in establishing certain points or sequences to be remembered. The endless storytelling concerning successful and unsuccessful hunting that goes on among hunters, and the reciting of fishing stories and bad weather episodes that occupies many fishermen's conversations, very likely are important mnemonic devices in the memory storage systems of hunting and fishing peoples. In these situations of reminiscence and recall, privately accumulated knowledge is shared with others, and private culture becomes part of a group tradition. Many of the past experiences of individuals and groups are felt to be so important in their learning implications that they are repeated over and over through the years and become part of the mythology and folklore of the community. Of course, apocryphal tales can always be invented to fill out an individual's or a group's repertoire of stored experi-

7.7 Even in seemingly uniform processes of cultural transmission, different individuals interpret "the message" in different ways. (Gordon Alexander, Magnum)

143

ence. Storytelling and experience-embellishing creativity of this sort is carried out for all kinds of reasons—for art's sake, for personality enhancement, for ridicule or enhancement of other people, and so on—but even the invented portions of any group's mythology and folklore contain a great amount of embedded learning experience or probability inferences that are handed on as useful knowledge to younger generations.

Cultural Homogeneity and Diversity

Along with the tendency to confine the use of the term *culture* to groups only, some anthropologists' descriptions imply a general homogeneity of behavior within social groups. When we read or hear about "Navajo characteristics" or the "customs of the Chippewa," the discussion is often presented in a manner that suggests uniformity of custom and behavior. Even in the descriptions of cultural behavior in complex societies, such as accounts of "child-rearing behavior among the Japanese" or "aspects of German national character" there is often an impression of homogeneity or uniformity that would be very difficult to demonstrate empirically.

Because our own personal experiences and common sense tell us daily that human behavior is extremely varied even within relatively small, homogeneous groups, the ethnographic portraits of the cultural behavior of non-Western peoples often give a rather unreal and distorted view—making them all sound like slaves and robots entrapped in their cultural traditions. Part of this distortion in descriptions of "those other people's" exotic lifeways is produced by the tendency among anthropologists and other people to report the *ideal* expected cultural patterns of various peoples as if they constituted a uniform code of practice and as if people actually behaved automatically in terms of these expectations in every society except our own. Marvin Harris has commented on this kind of ethnographic reporting as follows:

If permitted to develop unchecked, the tendency to write ethnographies [in this manner] will result in an unintentional parody of the human condition. Applied to our own culture it would conjure up a way of life in which men tip their hats to ladies; youths defer to old people in public conveyances; unwed mothers are a rarity; citizens go to the aid of law enforcement officers . . . television repairmen fix television sets. (HARRIS, 1968:590)

Personal Culture, Public Culture, and Culture Pool: The Organization of Diversity

Since each individual human has a unique set of biological characteristics and capabilities as well as a unique history of interaction with her or his own special niche in the world, it is useful and reasonable to speak of each individual's PERSONAL CULTURE. In fact, above the level of the individual, *culture* is an abstraction. But then how can individuals' different personal cultures form a basis for successful group interaction and performance? And what do we mean when we say "American culture," "Navajo culture," or "the subculture of professional football players"?

In the first place, people are able to interact with one another because they *learn* how to predict one another's actions and reactions. Part of everyone's personal culture includes a set of predictions or "hypotheses" about the behavior of the significant others in the social system. We learn to anticipate, for example, the culturally patterned behavior of teachers, storekeepers, dentists, and other social types of actors. Through continued interaction (and information about the interactions of others) the members of a social system reach some sort of ongoing accommodation of behavior, made up of the interrelated expectations and "cultural standards" in each different interactional setting. As Ward Goodenough has expressed it: "The standards they agree on for this purpose may be said to constitute their *public culture* for those activities. . . . In their mutual dealings, misunderstandings lead each individually to adjust his own version of the public culture to accord better with the expectations of his fellows" (Goodenough, 1971:38).

In keeping with the ideas just expressed, Goodenough has suggested that each society (community or subgroup) may be thought of as having a vast CULTURE POOL: "all the ideas, beliefs, values, recipes, and traditions that are known to one or more members of the society" (Goodenough, 1971:42). A very

144

large portion of the culture pool consists of items in individuals' *personal cultures* that are not part of the public culture at all. These "privately owned" portions of the culture pool are a rich source of variation and new innovations that may show up in the public culture when environmental conditions change and the people adapt their lifeways accordingly. In a fishing community, for example, there can be the situation in which one individual in the group has found an excellent fishing location "out there" beyond the usual fishing spots frequented by other members of the local group. He may keep this location a secret for some time, but in a time of shortages and poor fishing, some of the other people in the community may search out his secret, or he may be forced by public opinion to share the private knowledge with others. The same sort of process can occur in connection with many other kinds of technological and nonmaterial cultural information.

From what has been said, we can sum up by noting the following:

1. There is no sharp boundary between the learned knowledge of an individual and the traditions of the group.
2. The appearance of homogeneity and shared cultural tradition is often an illusion, a myth that may be perpetuated by some people (or by their enemies) as a considerable oversimplification about the habitual patterns of behavior within the group.
3. The sum of all the learned information in any group—their culture pool—includes considerable variation and informational heterogeneity, but group organization is maintained through the "arrived-at" modes of interaction built around their public culture.

In research among the Zuñi Indians of New Mexico John M. Roberts found an intriguing diversity of cognitive orientations and behavior, and he suggested that intracultural variation serves a number of functions. In the first place, if everyone had to conform to the same cultural patterns, there would be a great deal of frustration and hostility among those people whose personalities are not well suited to some single dominant cultural motif. In the second place, Roberts pointed out, intracultural diversity provides an effective information storage system. A cultural group is able to store and pass

on to its descendants a larger amount of information than can be kept in the head of a single individual. To this point we can add the observation that in every community there are divergences of opinion about cultural behavior that provide the younger generation with an object lesson in the value of empirically "finding out for oneself."

Intracultural Diversity Is Analogous to Genetic Diversity in Population

Intrapopulation diversity is considered by biologists to be an essential feature in the plasticity and biological adaptability of *Homo sapiens*. The same point can be made for intrapopulation or intrasocietal *cultural* diversity. In analogy to the facts of genetic variability, cultural variability provides the raw materials from which a population can adapt swiftly to changed circumstances. The problem of how small populations develop new ideas and new ways of doing things has long been a bone of contention among anthropologists. Because cultural systems have frequently been seen as made up of homogeneous, *shared* cultural ideas, theoreticians have had to speculate about the mechanisms that produce "innovators" in an otherwise conservative, stable, homogeneous society. With this overly static view of culture, "innovators" were often seen as disrupters or deviants, or marginal persons who were in some way psychologically aberrant or "out of step" with their society. If, on the other hand, we take into account the great amount of intracultural diversity in any population, it is easier to see that innovators are *always* present in any society, no matter how small, in the sense that there are always divergent points of view, some of which will come to the fore to meet the requirements of any changes in the situation.

The Human Brain and Culture

ALthough we define culture as a system of *learned* concepts and ideas, our great proliferation of cultural behavior is based on the biological structure of the human brain, evolved during the past several million years of culture-dependent adaptation. Compared to other animals, our brains have complex

145

speech and language centers, greatly expanded areas for associational thinking, and elaborated neural connections for the mediation of eye-hand coordination and other technical capabilities. Cultural behavior rests on firm biological foundations.

In recent years researchers have found fascinating new information concerning the separate functioning of the right and left hemispheres of the brain. Some of the discoveries have been made as the result of brain surgery on individuals with severe epilepsy. A new operation that has been quite successful in treating epilepsy is called *cerebral commissurotomy*—surgical separation of the two sides of the brain. The people who have had this surgical operation behave as if they have two separate, unconnected brains. More important, the two separate brains have different capabilities and qualities. The *left* hemisphere of the brain receives information from the *right* side of the body and controls the behavior of the right side. Also, the speech centers and language capabilities are controlled in the left brain. The *right* side of the brain controls the information input and motor coordination of the *left*

Left hemisphere	Right hemisphere
Verbal	Pre-verbal
Analytic	Synthetic
Abstract	Concrete
Rational	Emotional
Temporal	Spatial
Digital	Analogic
Objective	Subjective
Active	Passive
Tense	Relaxed
Euphoric	Depressed
Sympathetic	Parasympathetic
Propositional	Appositional

7.8 **The right and left hemispheres of the brain and the special functions thought to be especially associated with each.**

side of the body and appears to be especially important in understanding spatial relationships and a variety of other nonverbal information. The different characteristics of the two sides of the brain have something to do with the differences between the performances of our two hands (and feet). That is, practically all humans are *either* right-handed or left-handed. For the right-handed person, only that favored hand can carry out fine cutting, writing, and other technical skills, although the other hand is, in fact, better at certain kinds of tasks—including recognition of spatial relationships and design.

The people who have undergone cerebral commissurotomy show distinctive behavioral patterns that illustrate the differences in right and left brain functioning. The most important differences are based on the right brain's inability to use complex language. For example, if the person is given an apple into his *left* hand (but out of sight), he can recognize the object but he cannot name it or describe it. If we take the apple from him and place it with a bunch of other items, he can pick it out again. Furthermore, that *left* hand knows what to do with objects. Unlike normal humans, these "two-brained" people cannot identify an object with the right hand that was handled and recognized by the left hand. (Contrary to our popular folk saying, our right hand *does* know what the left hand is doing. That communication is cut off when right and left brains are separated surgically.) One of the things that "two-brained" individuals can do much better than "normal" people is simultaneous work with their right and left hands. Whereas most people have difficulty in keeping the work of right and left hands acting at the same time (try rubbing your belly and patting your head at the same time), these surgery patients could maintain the separate tasks of the two hands without cross-interference (Sperry, 1972).

From the relatively fragmentary information so far accumulated, we know that individuals can be very different in the extent to which they show clear separation of brain functions. The "styles of interaction" between our left and right brains can be quite varied. Also, it has been suggested for a long time that some people are more "left-brained" (verbal, language-dominated, analytic), while other individuals are more "right-brained" (synthesizing, nonverbal, spatial-relational, artistic).

Anthropologists Anthony Paredes and Marcus Hepburn have suggested that differences in right-left

Adaptations Through Learning and Communication: Homo sapiens sapiens

brain dominance and interrelationships may correspond to significant differences in cultures. The differences in mental styles between the right and left hemispheres correspond roughly with some of the differences that have been said to exist between, for example, cultural traditions with clear linear time orientation (like our own dominant Western thought styles) and cultures such as the Pueblo peoples of Arizona and New Mexico, whose language structure and cultural style emphasize nonlinear, nonsequential relationships. Many anthropologists have written about such overall differences in cultural orientations, but these ideas have not previously been linked to information about how human brains process and integrate information. Of course, these ideas are still very tentative and much research will have to be carried out before we understand more about their validity.

Do Other Animals Have Culture?

Most textbooks of anthropology, particularly before 1960, presented the concept of culture as a distinctly and uniquely human trait. Most people held the view that only humans have culture, and thus the development of the "culture-bearing capacity" was some sort of great leap in the course of evolution that made *Homo sapiens* qualitatively different from all the other animals. The tendency to consider human beings as utterly different from all other animals is a recurring theme in social thought—part of our egotistical and self-congratulatory human personality. This view of humanity was perhaps easier to maintain up to about 1955, before extensive studies of the behavior of other primates in their natural habitats had been made. Recent studies of the complexities of infrahuman primate behavior give us a more realistic picture and suggest that there are indeed clear continuities between the behavior of the other primates and the more complicated behavioral capabilities of humans.

One of the most interesting sources of documentation concerning cultural behavior among monkeys is from investigators at the Japanese Monkey Center of Kyoto University. Professors Junichiro Itani, Kinji Imanishi, and others found that among different troops of free-ranging macaque monkeys there were noticeable differences in food preferences, food handling, and other "customs." They found, for example, that only in the Takasakiyama and

147

Takahashi troops did male monkeys engage in baby-sitting activities while the mothers were feeding. Some of the troops would eat shellfish, others would not. One of these monkey troops was in the habit of making extensive predations on nearby rice fields, whereas their immediately adjoining neighbors apparently had no interest in eating rice shoots. There were a number of other localized variations in food use that could be best regarded as differences in local cultural customs.

The Japanese scientists began to introduce new foods to these macaque monkey troops in order to examine the processes of acculturation (the acquisition of new cultural traits through culture contact). They found that the adoption of some of the new foods (e.g., candy) often begins first with the marginal subadult males who are relatively distant from the center of influence and prestige in the troop. In some cases a new cultural item spread rapidly throughout a troop; in other cases only a portion of a monkey troop adopted a particular trait. In one case, a young female monkey was observed to wash a sweet potato before eating it. The cultural custom of washing sweet potatoes spread slowly throughout this particular troop. Several years later there were still some individuals in the group that did not wash their sweet potatoes before eating them.

Earlier (Chapter 3) we commented on tool use and other evidences of rudimentary culture among chimpanzees, especially in the field observations of Jane Van Lawick-Goodall. Another observer of wild chimpanzees, the Dutch primatologist Adrian Kortlandt, found that the animals will use a variety of weapons as clubs to attack an enemy. Kortlandt constructed a mock leopard with movable head and tail and placed this decoy in a spot where he knew the chimpanzees were sure to find it. The chimps broke off limbs from nearby trees and used a variety of other weapons to attack this "enemy" until they tore it to pieces.

Much more difficult to identify are the culturally learned social *behaviors* of the chimpanzees and other apes. Certainly the styles and regularities of interaction are quite complicated and depend on a large component of learning. Individuals learn their "place" in the patterning of dominance relations, and they also carry many other learned expectations about the behavior patterns of their fellows. Their styles of interaction with other species—e.g., chimpanzees interacting with baboons—undoubtedly also contain a cultural component.

Other animals besides monkeys and apes engage in some tool using and a variety of other behavior that involves socially learned actions. There are species of birds that have geographical differences in vocalizations that appear to be learned "dialects." Some of those Galapagos finches that put Charles Darwin on the trail of the idea of natural selection occasionally use small twigs to get at insects hidden in crevices of tree trunks. This technique, like a number of other instances of tool use among birds and mammals, appears to be learned through observation. Socially learned tool use (hence rudimentary culture) among these animals contrasts sharply with the nest building and other complex behaviors of bees, other insects, and those many birds whose specialized behavior is programmed genetically. One can elicit instinctive behavior patterns from animals by providing them with the appropriate circumstances or situation for the behavior, regardless of whether they have ever been exposed to that behavior before. Similarly, there are many birds whose songs are genetically programmed and will be sung by individuals whether or not they have ever heard the lyric at a previous time. Birds with socially *learned* repertoires show quite different patterns, for they sing whatever songs they hear during their youth.

With all this evidence of social learning, effective imitation, and occasional tool use among a variety of birds, insects, and mammals, the question arises: Why don't these animals develop complex language and accumulate a growing repertoire of tool-using technology? One answer is that those animals have generally been successfully adapted to their particular environments for considerable periods of time. The various bird species appear to be highly successful in their adaptations, and hence they don't "need" additional cultural proliferation. In the matter of tool use, the birds are fairly limited to objects they can grasp in their beaks, and most animals are able to grasp objects only very clumsily with their paws and forelimbs, which are usually needed for walking and running. Even the monkeys spend most of their time with all four limbs busy in locomotion. Apes and *Homo sapiens* are very unusual in that their bodies and organs are positioned for at least partially upright posture and their hands are rela-

Adaptations Through Learning and Communication: Homo sapiens sapiens

7.10 **Cultural information, including skills and techniques, are transmitted from one generation to the next. Here a young Same girl watches as her mother makes a pair of reindeer skin shoes. (P. J. Pelto)**

tively highly developed for grasping objects, compared to practically all other animals. The apes, especially the chimpanzees, are therefore physiologically adapted to the possibilities of extensive tool use but appear to have been quite successful in adapting to their various environments without the use of complex technology. They are, therefore, illustrative of the kind of "preadaptation" that made our ancestors likely candidates for the development of culture.

Somewhere in our past apelike ancestors gained some adaptive advantage through an increasing commitment to upright posture. This upright posture necessitated a series of other physiological changes in the animals but resulted in the freeing of the hands and arms for a much fuller commitment to tool use. At some point in this process of increased erect posture and hands available for tool use, these ancestors became *dependent* on tools, and further evolution in the direction of *Homo sapiens* was predicated on the use of hand-held weapons for defense and for food getting—a radically different way of making a living from that of the chimpanzees and other apes.

The accumulating evidence of various kinds of tool use and other simple cultural behavior among nonhuman primates and other animals demonstrates the essential continuity of all living forms, among whom only the human animal has developed a mode of adaptation that is completely dependent on complex, culturally learned tool use and other environmental modifications. If this makes us completely different from all other animals, so is every other animal different in some aspects of its unique adaptation to its environment.

A Perspective on Human Culture

We have defined *culture* as the mental, ideational aspect of human adaptive behavior because we feel that only with such an "ideal" definition can we go on to talk about explaining and understanding *behavior* as the resultant of complex interactions of biological, cultural, *and* environmental factors.

The ecological perspective throughout this book places much emphasis on environmental factors as contributing to the explanation of differences and similarities in human behavioral patterns around the world. Biological factors play their part in affecting differential adaptations to specifics of climate, altitude, and other environmental features. The ideas—mental inventions of people—objectified in their things, techniques, and social relations add another dimension to the multifactor, ecological perspective on human lifeways.

1. In spite of our view that other animals besides humans "have culture," we in no way intend to play down the obvious qualitative differences between the lifeways of humans and those of other primates. The prime differences are in the *numbers* of culturally patterned tools and other equipment in all human groups, plus the complex communications system (language) that greatly expands the adaptive capabilities of all human societies, and makes possible a very large body of "traditional heritage."

149

2. Cultural ideas are, on the whole, adaptive because they have been learned by individuals through trial-and-error processes of coping with their environments. Many cultural ideas come and go, with no real effect on long-term adaptations. Recently our college campuses were treated to the new fad of "streaking," in which students dashed buck-naked across the campus or through dining halls (usually at night) as a sort of fleeting defiance of social norms about nudity. Like the live goldfish-swallowing contests of earlier times, the adaptive value of "streaking" is probably nil from any long-term group point of view, but we should pause a moment to note its functional significance for individuals. On various college campuses students put together sums of twenty or thirty dollars in bets to see if individuals would dare to run around naked in public. The adaptive advantages for individual "streakers" included money and the peer-group prestige for the individual who successfully defied a cultural norm and controlled his or her cultural standards of modesty!

3. While fads and fashions, by definition, relate mainly to the adaptively neutral aspects of cultural systems, most cultural behavior has reference to the pragmatic problems of food getting, earning access to scarce economic resources, and other directly practical matters.

4. Many cultural ideas arise directly from positive physiological experience, and they may develop from short-term reinforcement that is not necessarily adaptive in long-term perspective. Thus the use of drugs, alcohol, and other substances that induce physiological effects may be quite understandable from a short-term learning perspective, even if it would appear that the overall consequences for individuals, as well as for their social groups, have quite negative features.

5. Much of the force of human culture as a factor accounting for behavioral features arises from the powerful information-processing capabilities of language. That very special human capability will be examined in detail in the next chapters.

Adaptations Through Learning and Communication: Homo sapiens sapiens

Language and Communication

The Nature of Human Language

Most of the higher primates, as well as other mammals, are highly sociable creatures who depend on interaction in the local group for health maintenance, survival, and reproduction. To maintain stable social systems, information must be passed about among group members, and, in general, the more dependent the group is on social interaction, the more complex the communication system. By COMMUNICATION we mean any act on the part of an individual, conscious or unconscious, that has an effect—that is, elicits a response from another individual. Here are some examples of various within-species and cross-species communication events:

1. Man pats dog—dog wags tail.
2. Baboon bares teeth—other baboon retreats.
3. Wolf urinates at various locations—other wolves respect territorial boundaries.
4. Bee, on returning to hive, "dances"—other bees set out in direction of pollen.
5. Skunk makes noxious stench—other animal retreats.
6. Male stickleback's belly turns red—female follows male.
7. Herring gull fledgling pecks at its mother's beak—the mother deposits food in the fledgling's mouth.
8. Baby cries—mother offers baby her breast.
9. Girl says, "Good-bye"—friend answers, "See you later."

These examples suggest that communication takes place in a great variety of forms and is not at all limited to sound produced by vocal mechanisms. The exceedingly complex communication systems of higher animals often depend on body motion—bristling, strutting, cowering, touching, licking, tail wagging, fluttering, and so on—though most animals also make a variety of vocal sounds that convey information to both friends and foes. Chimpanzees use a vocabulary of perhaps twenty-five to thirty different calls, shrieks, hoots, and other sounds. However, compared to human languages, the vocal call systems of all other animals are rather modest in the amount of information they transmit.

The linguist Charles Hockett has analyzed the human language system in comparison with the

8.1 Communication through reading from written texts is a major cornerstone of complex cultural systems. Children receiving Muslim religious lesson. (George Rodger, Magnum)

communication modes of a number of animals in order to sort out the principal DESIGN FEATURES of various communication systems. Figure 8.2 illustrates the thirteen design features Hockett has designated as characteristic of human verbal communication.

As you can see from the figure, many features of human verbal communication can be found in the communication systems of other living creatures. For example, the characteristic that Hockett refers to as TRADITIONAL TRANSMISSION (learned through social interaction) is a feature of communication in many animal species. (In the preceding chapter we mentioned that some birds have *socially* learned repertoires. An English sparrow raised with canaries will sing like a canary, not like a sparrow.)

Using Hockett's terms, the most important features of human verbal communication include the

VOCAL CHANNEL, which allows for the possibilities of DISCRETENESS and the development of DUALITY OF PATTERNING. These features, in turn, set conditions in which DISPLACEMENT becomes possible on a versatile and regular basis.

Discreteness is a design feature that contrasts with CONTINUOUSNESS in the structure of messages and signals. Consider the difference between the word *growl*, which is a discrete bounded message, and a dog's actual growl—*grrrr*—which is an indefinitely continued sound. If we take the sound-word *growl* and make a simple substitution of an *f* sound in place of *gr*, we have a *completely different* meaning—fowl. Since the word *growl* is complete in itself, we can modify it with other discrete words, such as *loud*, *threatening*, or even *friendly*. However, in the dog's system of communication, the *grrrr* is short or prolonged, louder or softer, inter-

152

mittent or steady, or otherwise modified into several different meanings without additional "words." Most physical gestures and body communication are continuous, whereas the human vocal language system gains part of its flexibility from the fact that the message units are discrete.

Duality of patterning in our human language system is perhaps the major factor that makes great

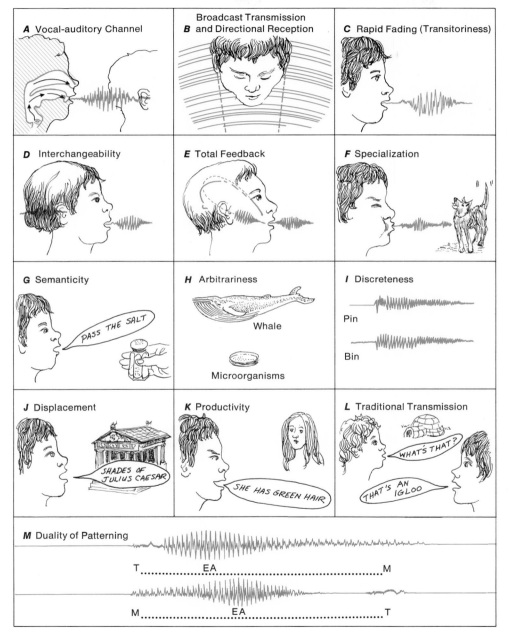

A Vocal-auditory Channel

B Broadcast Transmission and Directional Reception

C Rapid Fading (Transitoriness)

D Interchangeability

E Total Feedback

F Specialization

G Semanticity — PASS THE SALT

H Arbitrariness — Whale / Microorganisms

I Discreteness — Pin / Bin

J Displacement — SHADES OF JULIUS CAESAR

K Productivity — SHE HAS GREEN HAIR

L Traditional Transmission — WHAT'S THAT? / THAT'S AN IGLOO

M Duality of Patterning — T....EA....M / M....EA....T

153

Language and Communication

productivity possible. Human oral language systems are put together from basic units at two levels: the unit of sound (which we usually indicate in writing with single symbols such as *a, b, c,* and so on) and the basic meaning units (usually words), which we put together from the individual sound units. Note that exactly the same units of sound can be put together in different orders and combinations to produce completely different words. For example, the words *act, tac,* and *cat* are all composed of the same basic three sounds, but they are put together in different sequence. Human language systems generally employ only about twenty to forty basic sound units, so we must be able to use those sounds in many combinations if we are to produce very large numbers of different words. Actually many millions of words can be produced from all the possible combinations of a very small number of sounds; some languages do quite nicely with fewer than twenty different sounds. If a language had just sixteen basic sound units, and the units could be used in any order, there would be 2,092,278,988,800 different possible sequences of the sixteen sounds, more than 2 trillion different words. Of course, the fact that words differ in length makes the possible number of combinations still larger.

Displacement refers to the fact that the users of a human language can communicate information about the past or the future or about some other geographic locality. We humans can reminisce about our childhood, or even about evolutionary events of 10 million years ago. We can communicate about our mental images pertaining to possible future states. We can talk about life in New Guinea or life under the sea. Most animal communication systems cannot displace in this manner. The danger signal of a baboon refers to the here and now; this signal cannot be used by the baboon to talk about the cheetah that came prowling around last month.

Chimpanzees demonstrate displacement capabilities in some of their behavior. Although it is not clear that chimpanzee vocal calls in the wild refer to anything in the past or future, when the chimps select and fashion their termite "lollipop sticks" (see p. 52), they are clearly thinking about the future and at the same time recalling the past. The chimpanzee fashions his termite stick *before* he gets to the termite hill, and the way in which he sometimes discards unsatisfactory sticks and makes new ones seems to be a fairly good indication of his recalling past events. Many other animals give indications of conceptual recall of past events and anticipation of future events, but their communication systems provide little or no possibility for "talking about" them. The fact that human languages involve displacement is a primary factor in the accumulation of information that we call *cultural traditions.*

Generally speaking the main communicative forms in all animals are species-specific. The vocal repertoire of a Labrador retriever raised in Finland sounds much like that of a Labrador raised in New York, but an American child learns to describe the sounds as "bow-wow" or "woof-woof," whereas the Finnish child is taught "hau-hau" as an appropriate descriptive term. With humans the details of oral communication are culture-specific, varying from one group to another. The great diversity of human languages attests to the versatility and creativity of human speech capabilities. At the same time, however, we should recognize that the *capability* of using human vocal language is a species-specific trait, which evolved through time, along with other human characteristics and capabilities.

Language, Biology, and Evolution

There are several reasons to believe that human symbolic language capacity rests on a genetic biological basis. The linguist Eric Lenneberg has made the argument as follows:

Every language, without exception, is based on the same *universal principles* of semantics, syntax, and phonology. All languages have words for relations, objects, feelings, and qualities, and the semantic differences between the denotata are minimal from a biological point of view. . . . Phonologically, all languages are based on a common principle of phonemitization even though there are phonemic divergences.

Language universals are the more remarkable as speakers live in vastly different types of cultures ranging from an essentially Neolithic type to the highly complex cultural systems of western civilization. Further, language and its complexity is independent of facial variation. It is an axiom in linguistics that any human being can learn any language in the world. Thus, even though there are differences in physical structure, the basic skills for the acquisition of language are as universal as bipedal gait.

Owing to these considerations, it becomes plausible to hypothesize that language is a species-specific trait, based on a variety of biologically given mechanisms. (LENNEBERG, 1964:68–69)

On the Language Capabilities of Other Animals

From time to time people have tried to follow the marvelous example of Dr. Doolittle in exploring animal communications systems. The eighteenth-century philosopher James Burnett Monboddo felt quite sure that great apes like the orangutan could be taught human speech—it's just a matter of giving them the opportunity.

Perhaps the most famous serious attempt to teach apes to speak was made by the two psychologists who raised the chimpanzee Viki from infancy along with their own human infant. Viki appeared to learn most other things just about as fast as the human child (sometimes a good deal faster), but she learned only three or four words, and uttering these human-like sounds was extremely difficult for her. Although she displayed good memory capabilities, plenty of intelligence, and imitative skills, she couldn't talk. The vocal tract of chimpanzees is not built to make sounds of the sort that *Homo sapiens* make, so the attempt to teach them to speak is foredoomed to failure.

Based on Viki's failure, plus the long-standing assumptions of human uniqueness, most researchers continued to believe that animals did not have humanlike language capabilities until some new and startling developments of the 1960s. In the past decade or more, several chimpanzees have learned to communicate effectively using complex symbolic systems. Psychologists Beatrice and Allen Gardner (Gardner and Gardner, 1969) began teaching the now-famous Washoe the sign language that is used by deaf-and-mute people. Washoe has accumulated a vocabulary of well over 150 signs. She is capable of using the signs in a variety of ways to express ideas. For example, the command "open" is used with reference to doors as well as to closed containers such as the refrigerator, cupboards, drawers, briefcases, and jars. Several hundred different word combinations used by Washoe have been recorded. She can say, "You tickle Washoe"; she can ask for food or drink; and she can express many other

8.3 Some nonhuman primates, like this howler monkey, have special equipment for communications, but the expanded vocal sacs are mainly for volume rather than complex sound manipulation. (Ron Garrison, San Diego Zoo photo)

abstract ideas. The evidence is quite clear that she understands the concept "dog," for she makes the proper sign when she sees a dog and has also used it when she heard a dog barking. She has also used the proper sign to identify the cartoon of a dog. Washoe has also spontaneously invented new signs. Most impressive of all, she appears to generalize meanings, including use of the word "dirty" as a derogatory term for a monkey she didn't like (Miles, personal communication).

The language performance of Washoe and other chimpanzees now learning and using sign language; the equally impressive capabilities of the chimpanzee Sarah, who learned a system using small metal figures (circles, triangles, squares, and so on) of

Language and Communication

speech production. . . . Human speech is the result of a source, or sources, of acoustic energy being filtered into the supralaryngeal vocal tract. (LIEBERMAN, 1973:4)

The unique feature of humans is that we have a sharp bend in the vocal tract—a feature that Lieberman argues makes possible a number of the distinctive features of human speech. The "double-barreled" character of our vocal tracts permits a number of devices that make human speech far more versatile and communicative than the sound systems of the other primates or indeed other mammals.

8.4 The chimpanzee, Booee, gives the sign for *hat* to researcher Roger Fouts. (Courtesy of Lyn Miles)

different colors; and the virtuosity of a chimp named Lana, who communicates using a computer, indicate that chimpanzees are capable of fairly sophisticated use of a symbolic language system, even though they did not invent it themselves. Their lack of vocal symbolic complexity must be due to their relatively unversatile vocal tract, rather than lack of mental powers.

Most interesting recent developments in the investigation of human speech have been those of P. Lieberman and his associates working on analysis of the physical apparatus of speech. They have identified the features of the human vocal apparatus that are different from the comparable systems of chimpanzees, gorillas, and other primates.

Nonhuman primates have supralaryngeal vocal tracts in which the larynx exits directly into the oral cavity. In the adult human the larynx exits into the pharynx. The only function for which the adult human supralaryngeal vocal tract appears to be better adapted is

8.5 Booee made this painting and, in response to the researcher's question about what the picture portrayed, he named it "baby." (Courtesy of Lyn Miles)

Adaptation Through Learning and Communication: Homo sapiens sapiens

If these specialized features of the human vocal system are indeed the cue to our elaborate language capability, then are there any clues in the fossil skeletons that would tell us at what point in human evolution our line of hominids developed the "bent" vocal tract? (Lieberman notes that the peculiar shape of our vocal system has some distinct *disadvantages* for other aspects of survival. It creates increased possibility of choking on food, for example. Furthermore, the bend interferes somewhat with our breathing. Therefore the development of the specifically human shape of vocal tract must have had very large positive adaptive advantages in communication to overcome these negative features.) (Lieberman, 1975).

Although the vocal tract itself is part of the soft materials of human flesh, there are some clues to the shape of the vocal tract that can be read from the bones. Lieberman and his associates have noted that the specifically human shape of vocal tract is related to the forward-jutting *Homo sapiens* chin, the placement of some of the muscles in the lower jaw (attachment points on bony structures are identifiable from small bumps (tubercles) and depressions (fossae) that increase the strength of muscle-to-bone connections), as well as the contour of the base of the skull, to which the palate (roof of the mouth) connects. A combination of these features, Lieberman feels, provides fairly firm identification of the modern human vocal apparatus, as contrasted with more primitive, less effective vocal tracts. He notes that the human infant at birth comes equipped with a vocal tract that does *not* have the flexibility and special features, including that all-important bend, which develop after the age of two years.

In examining some of the better-preserved fossil materials, Lieberman found that the Cro-Magnon and other *Homo sapiens sapiens* fossils seem to have had modern vocal tracts; *Classic Neanderthal peoples seem to have had a much less well-developed vocal tract;* and one of the more modern-looking skulls from Mount Carmel (see p. 78) also had a modern vocal tract. Going back to earlier fossils, Lieberman and his associates feel that *Australopithecus* clearly did not have modern vocal capabilities; somewhere between *Australopithecus* and Cro-Magnon the first signs of modern vocal capabilities must have emerged in the course of human evolution.

The Structure of Language

The study of linguistics is an extremely complicated and demanding discipline with a technical vocabulary of its own. Comparative study of human languages requires the meticulous, painstaking attention to detail that we associate with mathematics, often in combination with abstract, philosophical logic concerned with the "meaning of meaning" and other aspects of the philosophy of science. Because of the complexity of language study, we can give only some glimpses here of how descriptive linguists go about their work. To begin with, there are those basic sound units that linguists call PHONEMES. A phoneme is the smallest basic unit in language and corresponds roughly to those individual sounds we try to indicate with the letters of the alphabet. The correspondence is not very close, however, especially in written English. The discrepancies between the phonemes of speech and our customs of writing were graphically illustrated by George Bernard Shaw when he pointed out that one could write *fish* as *g-h-o-t-i*. The *gh* is pronounced as in the word *tough;* the *o* as in *women,* and the *ti* as in *notion.*

When a linguist begins to study the system of sounds (the *phonological system*) of a language, his major aim is to discover or isolate all the sounds that "make a difference." As Charles Hockett puts it, "it must be remembered that sounds and differences between them have one and only one function in language: *to keep utterances apart*" (Hockett, 1958:15). The main strategy that linguists use to discover the phonemes of a language is to examine pairs of utterances to see how they differ. The critical test is with *minimal pairs*, words that differ in only one sound. For example, the differences between *pin* and *bin, bat* and *pat,* and *pie* and *buy* tell us that, in English, the difference between a *b* sound and a *p* sound makes a difference. By systematically examining hundreds of utterances and looking for the minimal pairs that confirm their hypotheses about the phonemic status of particular sounds, linguists are able to establish the phonological system of a language.

The concept of a *phoneme* and the idea of a *phonemic system* become clearer when we see how linguists use them in a language that we are all more or less intimately familiar with—English. Table 8.1 shows the phonemes of English as analyzed by Hockett.

Language and Communication

Table 8.1: The Phonemes of English

Consonants (as in)

[b] *buy*, ta*b*	[f] *feel*, *fie*
[p] *pie*, ta*p*	[θ] *ether*, *thigh*
[d] ta*d*, *die*	[s] *seal*, *sane*
[t] *tap*, *tie*	[š] *shy*, *Shane*
[g] *tag*, *guy*	[m] *tam*, *my*
[k] *key*, tac*k*	[n] *tan*, *no*
[ǰ] ri*dge*, *Jane*	[ŋ] *tang*, *ring*
[č] *rich*, *chain*	[r] *raid*, *rain*
[v] *veal*, *vain*	[l] *laid*, *lie*
[ð] *thine*, ei*ther*	[y] *yell*, *you*
[z] *zeal*, *zoo*	[w] *well*, *woe*
[ž] allu*s*ion, rou*ge*	[h] *hell*, *hoe*

Vowels (as in)

[ij] *bee*	[ɔ] *hall*
[ej] *bay*	[a] *bar*
[aj] *by*	[æ] *bat*
[oj] *boy*	[e] *bet*
[uw] *howl*	[ə] *but*
	[i] *bit*
	[u] *book*

Source: Adapted from HOCKETT, 1958:30–31.

English has more phonemes, especially more consonants, than many other languages in the world. Possibly this is because of the large amount of borrowing from other languages that has crept into English. Other languages that are quite complex, with large vocabularies, get by with a smaller list of basic units of sound. It is thought that Hawaiian (a Malayo-Polynesian language) has fewer basic phonemes than any other language. They do quite nicely with only thirteen different sound units. The largest number of phonemes in a language is recorded from one of the small language groups in the northern Caucasus, which supposedly has seventy-five phonemes. Hockett reports that "69 languages, selected at random, including Hawaiian and Chipewyan, show an average of slightly over 27 . . . phonemes" (Hockett, 1958:93). Of course, in all languages the speakers produce a great many more types of sounds than those designated by the list of phonemes. There are larger or smaller dialectical variations, which make it possible to recognize speakers from different localities or social groups. The list of *phonemes* is not a set of all the sounds used in a language but instead consists of the basic number of sounds that *make a difference* in the meanings of words.

The basic sound units of language are put together in longer or shorter clusters that we call words in common language, but a more technical way of looking at it is to refer to the smallest sound-meaning clusters as MORPHEMES. These are the basic *meaning* units in any language. Many "words" in the English language are morphemes, but many of our words contain more than one basic meaning unit. For example, the word *sexless* has two basic meaning units: *sex* and -*less*, "lack of." In some languages, such as those of the Inuit and many American Indian tongues, sentences often consist of numerous morphemes strung together almost as if they were one word. In fact, in some languages it is very difficult to distinguish between "words" and "sentences." In the English language, as in most other languages, there are large numbers of morphemes that cannot stand by themselves as words but are "bound morphemes" used to indicate past tense and other verb modifications, plural versus singular, and various other kinds of adverbial and adjectival ideas. Note the "bound morphemes" in the following: "talk*ed*," "furious*ly*," "rule*s*," "govern*ing*," "*dis*like," "*un*natural."

When we listen to a foreign language we do not know, at first we hear only jumbled sound, but fairly soon we begin to note certain patterns of sound clusters that "sound like words." As we continue to listen to the foreign language and start to learn about its structure, we begin to understand something about the rules by which the basic meaning units, the morphemes, are put together. If the language is Finnish, a non-Finnish speaker would be struck by the frequency of certain kinds of word endings, such as the following:

valkoinen	white
sininen	blue
vesinen	watery
kivinen	stony
hevonen	horse
ampiainen	bee
kärpänen	fly
poikanen	boy (diminutive)
menee	goes (third person singular)
tulee	comes (third person singular)
näkee	sees (third person singular)
kampaa	combs (third person singular)

158

Adaptation Through Learning and Communication: Homo sapiens sapiens

sataa	rains (third person singular)
makaa	lies (third person singular)

Finnish appears to be composed of a fairly regular alternating of vowel and consonant sounds in which the form *-nen* seems to be a widely recurring morpheme denoting "quality of." Another sound-meaning regularity that seems obvious is the appearance of a double vowel (which lengthens the vowel sound) in the third person singular verbs. If we were beginning to learn the Finnish language and were given a large list of verbs in Finnish, we would soon discover that the forms with *-ee* and *-aa* are extremely common but that other forms occur, including *-oo*, *-yy*, *-ii*, *-öö*, and *-uu*. Once we discover these regularities in the way phonemes are put together, we might look to see if they correspond to any general feature in our own language. Apparently the terminal double vowel in Finnish plays the same role as the *s/z* sound in English verbs. (rain*s*, eat*s*).

The next steps in our analysis of the Finnish language would require us to locate more and more "rules" about how to string phonemes together into morphemes, then the rules for putting morphemes together into more complex words, and then the rules for combining words into larger expressions. But how would we set about doing this if we were carrying out fieldwork among Finnish speakers, concentrating on the spoken language and ignoring written sources? If we found a bilingual person who was fluent in both English and Finnish we could ask that person to say a series of words and sentences (into a tape recorder) and to give the English equivalents of these utterances. To get greater naturalness of speech, we could ask the Finnish informant to tell stories or to give other connected discourse to get a large variety of speech forms. We could then listen to these tape-recorded materials over and over again, until we have identified all the different phonemes and developed a number of hunches about the rules by which the phonemes are combined. Then we would cross-check with our informant to find out if there are "exceptions" to the rules we have identified. But how do we write down the phonemes, especially if some of the sounds are quite different from those of the English language?

Linguists have developed complex notational systems for recording different kinds of consonant and vowel sounds. One of the first and extremely difficult tasks of a beginning linguist is to learn this phonetic alphabet system and to learn to distinguish the minor nuances of sound that make the differences in human languages and their dialects. Just as some people are "tone deaf" in musical terms, some people have great difficulty in distinguishing phonetic differences in human speech. Accomplished linguists can often amaze us by their ability to detect minor nuances of speech sounds that identify particular localized geographic dialects.

As the field linguist works to perfect his ear for detecting the special phonetic sounds of the language he is studying, he is also looking for patternings in the sound clusters that seem to apply to particular ideas or "words" in different positions in "sentences." He begins to look for grammatical patterns. Sarah Gudschinsky has described the field techniques of linguists, pointing out that there are basically two techniques for finding grammatical patterns:

1. Stretches of speech can be compared to find repetitions of the same unit with the same meaning; and
2. An informant can be asked to speak a series of utterances in which different forms are substituted for each other in the same position. (GUDSCHINSKY, 1967:10)

Gudschinsky offers the following exercise as a good opener to illustrate one of these methods:

Exercise One
Compare the following sentences and identify the unit meaning "person" or "people":

Mazatec language (Mexico)	English meaning
ha³'ai³ čo⁴ta⁴	people came
ha³'ai³ kao⁴ hnko³ čo⁴ta⁴ yo⁴ma⁴	they came with a sick person
ño³ čo⁴ta⁴ tsa³k'a³ nk'a³	four people carried him

[*Note:* In the Mazatec transcriptions here, the number one indicates high pitch; two, semi-high pitch; three, semi-low pitch; and four, low pitch. The illustration indicates that pitch is a significant feature in the Mazatec language.] (GUDSCHINSKY, 1967:11)

"Exercise One" gives the fieldworker a chance to look for the idea *people* or *persons* in several different positions in the statements. It seems clear that the morpheme that is repeated in these three sentences is *čo⁴ta⁴*. At this point we have a hunch this morpheme carries the meaning "people." When the lin-

159

guist has that information in hand, he may decide to ask his linguistic informant for a series of further sentences using the word in order to see how the other grammatical units change in relation to the morpheme in different uses. This might result in a series something like this:

English	Mazatec
people went	ki^{43} čo^{4}ta^4
people are sick	ti^{1}m e^3 čo^{4}ta^4
people dance	ti^{1}te^2 čo^{4}ta^4
one person	hnko^3 čo^{4}ta^4
two persons	hao^2 čo^{4}ta^4
three persons	ha^2 čo^{4}ta^4
four persons	ño^{3}čo^{4}ta^4

These exercises illustrate only one aspect of the meticulous work of linguistics. Examples like these are always deceptively simple—and, perhaps, deceptively boring. The discovery process in a field study of a language system can be as exciting as detective work—but it requires a particular kind of patience that perhaps is not characteristic of many North Americans these days.

Structural Linguistics and Transformational Grammar

We began our examination of descriptive linguistics at the level of discrete sounds (phonemes), building up to larger and larger units, because that sequence reflects something of the recent history of language study. Until very recently anthropological linguists have been very field-data–oriented, and their theories of language analysis came to be based on the idea that the researchers had first to master the *sound* units of a language, then the next level (*morphemes*), and then (if they ever got there) to deal with SYNTAX and meaning of whole sentences.

During the 1950s there was a sharp break in the development of language theory, much of it brought on by the work of Noam Chomsky and his ideas of TRANSFORMATIONAL GRAMMAR. Chomsky's approach turned the theory of language study upside down—by postulating universal structures or models of language, from which the linguist could "generate" different actual sentences by application of "transformational rules."

The system works something like this:

1. Any sentence (S) can be considered to have a universal structure consisting of NP (noun phrase) and VP (verb phrase), with the optional feature of ADV (adverb or adverbial phrase) tacked on.
2. Each of the parts (NP, VP, and ADV) usually consists of subunits, including auxiliary verbs or phrases (AUX), verbs, nouns, and so on.
3. The composition of a sentence, looking at these constituent parts, can be expressed as the outcome of the basic NP plus VP (plus ADV) structure, transformed into actual contents through a series of *rewrite rules*.

Example: The sentence "A girl cut the flower yesterday" is generated from the following set of instructions:

1. S_____NP plus VP plus ADV
2. VP_____V plus NP
3. NP_____Det (determiner) plus N
4. Det_____the, a
5. N_____girl, flower
6. V_____cut
7. ADV_____yesterday

Applying this set of rules, one at a time, we or a computer or anyone can re-create the sentence. The step-by-step procedure can be visualized as in Figure 8.6.

We note that we can describe a great many other sentences in the same fashion, simply by substituting words within the same structure:

A boy	cut	the flower	yesterday.
John	cut	the flower	yesterday.
John	bent	the flower.	
A boy	cut	John	yesterday.
Etc.			
Etc.			
Etc.			

Now, if we wish to move from that sentence to a related form, new translation rules must be introduced. For example,

The flower will be cut by John tomorrow.

This sentence is clearly a derivative of our earlier set of rules, but it requires some further trans-

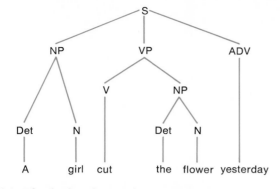

8.6 The logic of transformational grammar.

Noam Chomsky and others has been to free the study of linguistics from a confining and unimaginative research style that had threatened to lead the study of language into complete isolation, unrelated to the rest of anthropology. Some imaginative educators have made use of transformational grammar for rejuvenating the ofttimes dull business of language teaching in grade school classrooms.

formations (additional rules) to change the tense, introduce *by*, and transform the ADV to *tomorrow*.

The structure of any language, linguists feel, can be reduced to some finite set of instructions, which are the (usually) unconscious rules we apply in daily speech. As in the simple example above, a near-infinite number of new sentences can be generated from the basic model through the substitution of new vocabulary items. Further uncountable individual sentences are created (or creatable) if we introduce secondary transformations into the basic structure.

The importance of this new kind of linguistic analysis lies in the possibility that the logical steps as set forth in the example above are actually quite close to the ways in which humans organize their speaking and that the basic speech models are the same in all languages. Those basic models of language are often referred to as the DEEP STRUCTURE of language, as opposed to the SURFACE STRUCTURE of particular individual strings of words and sentences. Obviously the surface structures of languages are very different from each other, but there is increasing evidence about the inherent similarities in *deep structures* that apply not just to language as such but to other human symbolic systems related to language.

Transformational grammar is not the only structural linguistics, nor is it yet demonstrated that the transformationalists have the best system for developing fuller and "more natural" (or more useful) descriptions of how language systems work. However, the effect of these exciting developments from

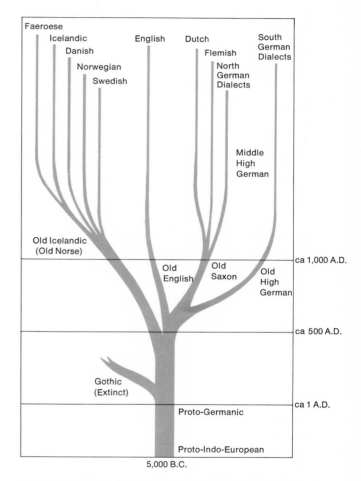

8.7 The family tree of Germanic languages as they have developed from the Indo-European ancestral language. The Scandinavian, German, and English branches began evolving into separate languages between 500 and 1000 A.D. See p. 163.

161

8.8 Major language families of Europe and Asia.
Key: **(A) Basque. (B) Indo-European. (C) Caucasian. (D) Finno-Ugric. (E) Altaic. (F) Semitic. (G) Dravidic. (H) Sino-Tibetan. (I) Mon-khmer. (J) Annamese. (K) Malayo-Polynesian. (L) Korean. (M) Japanese. (N) Ainu. (O) Yukaghir. (P) Chukchee-Koryak-Kam-chadal. (Q) Inuit. (Several small language families are not shown.)**

Linguistic Change and Language Families

The different forms of English now spoken in the world are the descendants or modifications of a common "parent tongue." Since the development of these various dialects has taken place within the last two or three hundred years, we can, if we wish, pinpoint quite accurately the times at which each of the different dialects of English branched out from

the point of common origin. For example, the special pronunciation of "Australian English" evolved after 1788, when the first British settlers landed there.

Although most speakers of English occasionally encounter subdialects of English that they do not understand, we generally recognize that all the different forms of English are variants of the same parent tongue. In an exactly parallel way English, German, French, Italian, Swedish, and most of the other languages of Europe as well as several languages of the Middle East and India (e.g., Sanskrit)

162

Adaptation Through Learning and Communication: Homo sapiens sapiens

are all "daughter tongues" of a single ancient ancestral language—Indo-European. Figure 8.7 (see p. 161) is a simplified family tree of these Indo-European languages, showing that the various subgroups—Slavic, Germanic, Celtic, and others—separated off from the proto–Indo-European main "stem" at different points in time.

Linguists have used a variety of methods in an attempt to give some kind of approximate dates to the various branchings of Indo-European languages. Charles Hockett (1960:6) has suggested that proto–Indo-European as a common language ancestor of European tongues goes back to approximately 5000 B.C. After several branches such as ancient Italic and proto-Celtic as well as the languages of India had broken off through migration, the general ancestor language of Germanic-speaking peoples may have continued to be a single proto-Germanic language until about twenty-seven hundred years ago. A sepa-

8.9   Major language families of Africa before the spread of Islamic and European peoples. (after Murdock, 1959)

Indo-European				Finno-Ugric
English	German	Swedish	Russian	Finnish
brother	bruder	broder	braht	veli
daughter	tochter	dotter	doch	tytär
door	tür	dörr	dvyer	ovi
father	vater	fader	ahtyets	isä
foot	fuss	fot	noga	jalka
hair	haar	hår	volosi	hiukset
heart	herz	hjärta	syerdtsa	sydän
knee	knie	knä	kalyeno	polvi
man	mann	man	chyelovyek	mies
mother	mutter	moder	mahtch	äiti
son	sohn	son	seehn	poika
one	ein	en, et	ahdyin	yksi
two	zwei	tvä	tva	kaksi

Reading across the four different Indo-European languages, we can easily recognize resemblances in the first three because they are all of the Germanic branch of Indo-European. The resemblances between Russian and the Germanic words are more difficult to distinguish, although most of the words are derived from the same common origin. The basic sound shifts in Russian have gone in a much different direction from the pronunciation drift that has occurred among Germanic speakers during the centuries the two languages have been diverging. Using information about the systematic sound shift patterns between Slavic and Germanic languages, we would be able to recognize the ways in which some of these Russian words are related to the Germanic forms. The column of Finnish words, on the other hand, seems totally different. Only the word for daughter (tytär) shows any resemblance at all to either the Germanic or the Russian vocabulary. This resemblance in the word for daughter suggests to us that very likely the word has been borrowed into the Finnish language from Indo-European neighbors.

163

Language and Communication

ration of English and German has been calculated in a variety of ways; Hockett suggests a date of about 400 A.D. for this (Hockett 1958:534). This would suggest that until about sixteen hundred years ago the linguistic ancestors of the English and of the Germans were the same or very closely related peoples, speaking a common language somewhere in the area of North Germany–Denmark. As the ancestors of modern English-speaking peoples (the Angles, the Saxons, and the Jutes) went west and began to take over territory from the ancient Britons, their language slowly diverged from the vocabulary and pronunciation of the Germanic speakers who remained in north central Europe. Because these

8.10 Language families of North and South America. *Key:* **1. Inuit. 2. Athabascan. 3. Algonkin. 4. Iroquoian. 5. Siouan. 6. Muskogean. 7. Uto-Aztecan. 8. Mayan. 9. Arawak. 10. Chibcha. 11. Carib. 12. Gê. 13. Tupi. 14. Araucanian. 15. Aymará. 16. Quechua. 17. Tucano. 18. Pano. 19. Diaguita. 20. Guaycurú. 21. Puelche. 22. Tehuelche.**

Adaptation Through Learning and Communication: Homo sapiens sapiens

groups were separated geographically, they were subject to differing influences from wars, migrations, and other forces tending toward linguistic change. Probably the single greatest influence causing English to be different from German was the powerful influence of the Norman French.

All of the other variations in languages and dialects found within the Indo-European language family have come about from processes basically similar to those just mentioned. Through geographical separation, migration, and ensuing differences in cultural history, the various Slavic languages separated out from each other in the past several centuries, and, similarly, Swedish, Norwegian, Danish, Icelandic, and the other Scandinavian languages branched out from their originally unitary Old Icelandic tongue.

Systematic Language Changes: Grimm's Law

When we examine lists of words in related languages, we are immediately struck by the fact that there seems to be some clear patterning in the ways that the words are different from one another in related languages. Consider the words in Table 8.2.

Table 8.2: Comparison of English/Latin Words

English	Latin
father	pater
full	plenus
for	pro
foot	pes
three	tres
thin	tenuis
mother	mater
thou	tu

Apparently in the long centuries of linguistic change, sounds that in Latin were rendered with a *p* have in English taken on the sound *f*. We note that both *f* and *p* are lip sounds. Similarly, in our second set of comparisons it appears that the Latin words have a *t* in a position where the English language has come to have a *th* sound. These sound correspondences in related words demonstrate that when pronunciations change in individual language systems, they change for whole classes of sounds (in particular positions), rather than word by word. Table 8.3 gives examples from English of this kind of systematic sound change.

Table 8.3: Comparison of Some Old English and Modern English Words

Old English[a]	Modern English
stān	stone
hāl	whole
bāt	boat
gāt	goat
gān	go
hūs	house
mūs	mouse
lūs	louse
hū	how

[a]The mark ¯ placed over the vowel indicates the length of vowel sound; thus *hūs* rhymes with *loose*; *stān* sounds like the proper name *Stan*.

These regular correspondences in sound patterning among related languages make possible the demonstration of relationships among the members of a language family, and they also permit us to reconstruct some features of the parent tongue. Thus, by systematic comparisons, linguists are able to put together something of the history of language patterning and are able to fill in evidence concerning the relative times of separation of the different languages. The systematic investigation of sound equivalences in related languages was begun by the German philologist Jacob Grimm, hence the name GRIMM'S LAW is sometimes applied to the set of regular sound correspondences identifiable through an analysis of English, Latin, and German words. If we modify the idea of Grimm's law to apply generally to all human languages, it would go something like this:

As languages change in their pronunciations over time (as they always do), the pronunciation shifts apply not to single words in isolation but to categories of sounds in particular locations within words or types of words (as in the examples on p. 163).

165

Changes in language affect not only pronunciation but vocabulary and other elements as well. Many changes are reflections of changes in technology and other aspects of culture; witness words like *snowmobile, polyunsaturated, microbus,* and *defoliant.*

Language and Cognition

The structure of many languages displays a complexity of inflexions, verb declensions, and other grammatical characteristics that is very different from English. For example, Finnish contains some fifteen case endings for nouns, and these case endings take the place of various prepositions as well as other morphemes common in English. The student of language who is totally unacquainted with this type of structure may experience some difficulty in perceiving that there are no such things in Finnish as words for *in, for,* or *from.* Anthropological linguists who study unwritten languages must begin by deliberately forgetting the typical structuring of Indo-European languages—they must forget about the progression of nouns, verbs, adjectives, and other parts of speech that most Europeans have come to regard as logically essential. For verb forms they must forget about time distinctions such as "present," "past," "past perfect" and future tenses.

A great many languages have verb morphemes that are much less concerned with time orientation than is the case with our Indo-European languages. As Benjamin Whorf pointed out several decades ago, languages like that of the Hopi Indians of the Southwest have no "tenses" of the form we expect in Indo-European. Instead, the Hopi Language has "validity forms," "aspects," and other refinements built into the verbs. The "validity forms" tell us what the speaker expects about a particular situation (roughly corresponding to our past and present) or that he expects it in the future. The Hopi verbs also have built-in "aspects" that denote different degrees of duration as well as different kinds of tendencies (Whorf, 1941:82).

This example from the Hopi is enough to warn us that there may be many other ways to modify verbs besides that of time. Among the Navajo people certain verb forms must be modified depending on the form of the objects involved. Thus whenever a Navajo is using verbs concerned with "handling" he must use an appropriate word stem that denotes whether the object to be handled is a rigid one such as a stick, a long and flexible one such as a string, a flat, flexible material such as paper or cloth, and so on. This set of distinctions is quite unfamiliar to speakers of Indo-European languages, so a field linguist who encounters this verb system must be prepared to forget about the basic structures of his own language in order to put together the clues that will solve the puzzle of a different kind of language system.

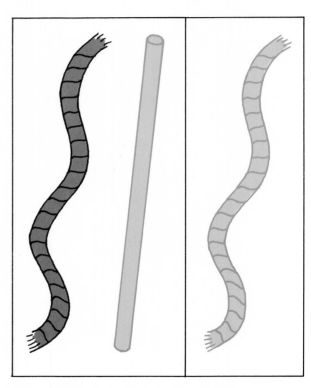

8.11 A test of the effects of language systems on cognition. Navajo children were shown the two objects on the left and then asked which one of them was "most like" the object (rope) on the right. If they said it was the rope, they were responding to *form,* whereas if they answered "the stick," they were giving more attention to color. As predicted from Navajo language structure, the children who spoke mainly Navajo tended to choose answers in terms of form. English-speaking Navajo tended to answer more in terms of color.

166

There are many, many ways in which non-European languages "cut up the pie of experience" in fashions that are quite different from those of Europeans. Some scholars have argued that people with radically different language systems must think in very different ways and solve their adaptational problems in very different ways, so that we cannot possibly understand non-European peoples unless we learn their language system.

Now, if people's systems of thought and reactions to reality were truly as different as language systems appear to be, then anthropological fieldworkers would *never* be able to get to first base in understanding other cultures and there would be no way to translate other languages into our own vernacular. It is extremely important for us to grasp fully the significance of the fact that anthropologists and linguists *have been able* to learn other languages, to transcribe them using cross-culturally standardized methods, and to "explain" other languages and thought systems in Indo-European language forms. Clearly *something* is equivalent about all of these systems, even though the differences in their details are certainly of great importance. The Hopi apparently conceptualize time (as expressed in their verbs) differently than English speakers do, and the Navajo deal with form (in their verbs) in a manner quite different from English speakers, but interaction among Navajo, Hopi, and Anglo-Americans is not obstructed by these differences. Both the Navajo and the Hopi have clearly demonstrated an understanding of the dominant English-speaking cultural system.

Basic Color Terms: Evolution in Language?

The language coding for colors has often been used by anthropologists to point out how differently various peoples in the world categorize experience. Many peoples do not have separate words for the colors "blue" and "green"—instead a single word appears to span these two color ideas. People like the Zuñi Indians, and many others, make no verbal distinction between orange and red, lumping together a considerable range of colors and shades that the English language and other major European languages differentiate quite specifically. (Some anthropologists have gone so far as to suggest that people who do not differentiate between green and blue or orange and red cannot "see" them as distinct colors. Careful research has demonstrated, however, that people like the Zuñi do, in fact, clearly distinguish between the color orange and something that is "red" in our terms, even though they lack terminology for the differences.)

Recently two anthropologists, Brent Berlin and Paul Kay, undertook a research project to test their hypothesis that, contrary to the prevailing opinion concerning cultural relativity in color terms, there are SEMANTIC UNIVERSALS in the domain of color vocabulary. During the course of their research they not only built up considerable evidence to support their view, but they also discovered that there seems to be a regular evolutionary progression of color terms.

As the first step in their research, Berlin and Kay selected twenty different languages and asked an informant from each of the different languages to list all of the color terms he or she could think of. Then each informant was given a standard set of Munsell color chips and was asked to indicate which of the chips corresponded to a particular color term. The researchers found there was a high degree of correspondence in the "center of gravity" of the color terms in the different languages.

Berlin and Kay then turned to a variety of sources to obtain the patterning of the color terminology in different languages. To qualify as a "basic color term" a word had to be applicable to all kinds of things (e.g., various colors for horses in the English language, such as *bay*, are not "basic" terms), and the term had to be a simple word, not a construct from an object (such as *lemon-colored* or *salmon-colored*). As the researchers found different languages with different numbers of basic color terms, they were able to develop the statement of a near-universal progression of color terminology in human languages. The sequence of development of color terminology in human languages looks like this:

$$\left.\begin{array}{l}\text{White}\\\text{Black}\end{array}\right\} \rightarrow \text{Red} \rightarrow \left\{\begin{array}{l}\text{Yellow}\\\text{Green}\end{array}\right\} \rightarrow \text{Blue} \rightarrow \text{Brown} \rightarrow \left\{\begin{array}{l}\text{Purple}\\\text{Pink}\\\text{Orange}\\\text{Gray}\end{array}\right.$$

167

All languages have words for black and white. Those that have more than the two basic terms go on to red, then yellow *or* green, then green *or* yellow, and so on.

It is not particularly surprising to learn that the languages with the simplest color terminologies tend to be relatively simple in technological development and lacking in complex bureaucratic and highly stratified social structure. Languages with complex color terminologies tend to occur in societies with great complexity of technology and related cultural features. Even though there are some apparent exceptions to the "evolutionary progression" of color terms discovered by Berlin and Kay, this is striking evidence of quite consistent patterning in the directions of increased complexity in taxonomic systems paralleling increased complexity in other aspects of social and technological organization. However, it is important to point out that when it comes to the matter of basic structure, "logicalness," and capability for expressing complex ideas, *all human languages appear to be approximately equivalent.* The languages of complex industrialized and urbanized nations have much larger vocabularies than the languages of societies with simpler technological inventories, but there is no evidence that the simpler unwritten languages are in any way inferior in their capabilities of adapting to sociocultural changes, technological growth, and other modifications in life styles. All languages appear to be capable of change, fast or slow, to accommodate and perhaps to facilitate economic and social adaptation.

Universals in Human Languages

The *design features* mentioned above (pp. 152–154) are general universals that permit us to examine human language systems in relation to the wider topic of animal communication systems. In addition to those basic design features there are a number of other aspects of language that appear to be universal in human societies, although there can be considerable disagreement on some of these topics. Anthropological linguists may be roughly divided into "relativists" and "universalists" in terms of their tendencies to look for either, on the one hand, the diversities and differences in human languages or, on the other hand, the universal, cross-culturally significant features. The following statements of universals are a very incomplete and very tentative listing:

I. Every human language has a system of "word substitutes" such as personal pronouns, demonstrative pronouns, and others. Among these "word substitutes" first and second person singular pronouns apparently occur in all languages.

II, Every human language has some "markers" that mean nothing in themselves, but which make a difference in the rest of the sentence. Such "markers" include the English forms "and" and "or."

III. Every human language has proper names.

IV. Every human language has "nouns" and "verbs," although in some languages these forms are not as clearly identifiable as they are in Indo-European languages.

V. Every human language appears to have a two-part structure as a basic clause type; one part which we can label "topic" and the second, "comment."

VI. In declarative sentences with subject and object, the dominant order in human languages *tends* to be one in which the subject precedes the object. Many language systems, including most Indo-European languages, have a dominant structure of subject-verb-object. Other languages, such as Berber in North Africa, Hebrew, and Maori, have a dominant structure in which the verb occurs *before* the subject. Another common type of dominant structure in declarative sentences takes the form subject-object-verb. Turkish, Japanese, Hindi, Burmese, and Quechua (Indian language in the highlands of Peru and Bolivia) are all examples of this third type of basic language structure. In spite of the fact that the ordering of object, verb, and subject is quite strikingly different in these different types of languages, the general rule still applies: subject precedes the object, no matter where the verb is. A further note should be added to this universal: In all languages there are secondary sentence forms that switch the ordering of subject, verb and object into different patterns for special purposes. For example, in Finnish one can ask the question: *Hevoselleko sinä annoit ne heinät?* Trans: To the horse (?) you did give the hay?

VII. Phonological redundancy tends to be about fifty percent in every language. (HOCKETT, 1963:24)

REDUNDANCY means extra or repetitious information that one doesn't really need. If we take a typical written English sentence and cut away some letters,

168

or substitute nonsense letters in their place, we find that most of the meaning can be gotten even though parts of the message have become scrambled. We have all had the experience of reading a letter that has ink or wine or perhaps mud splattered on it, and usually "we got the message." Consider the following slightly botched sentence:

> Go awax I donx wanx to taik wich you ant more todax.

Almost anyone reading this item gets the message immediately. Redundancy makes it possible for us to understand most of the messages we exchange, even though we frequently don't hear every word and even though speakers sometimes slur parts of their speech or omit grammatical elements.

VIII. Sound change and "linguistic drift" occur in all languages.

IX. When yes/no questions are differentiated by intonational cues from assertions, the distinctive intonational features are at the end of the sentence rather than in the beginning (GREENBERG, 1963:80).

X. In conditional statements, the conditional clause precedes the conclusion as a normal order in all languages.

XI. If either the subject or the object noun agrees with the verb in gender, then the adjective always agrees with the noun gender.

Summary

At the present time there is little doubt that the human *capacity* for language is a biologically inherited characteristic, but one with so much flexibility that a great diversity of language forms is possible. Because chimpanzees have been able to manipulate symbols when they are taught to do so, it is quite probable that they have sufficiently complex brains to have developed a symbolic language system. The apparent lack of complex symbolic vocal language among the apes is perhaps best explained by the relative inflexibility of their vocal tract.

Human languages exhibit certain universal features (though the study of these is only just well under way), including probably some pervasive features of "deep structure."

Clues from the historical study of languages have been used for a long time as a major aid to understanding the processes of culture history. More recently anthropological linguists have turned to analysis of the details of short-term "micro-events" of language behavior, seeking to gain greater knowledge of language manipulation in conversational encounters, in marking social differentiation, and in other ongoing processes. This developing area of study, with all its complex interrelating of linguistic and social data, will be the focus of the next chapter.

9

Speech, Body Language, and Writing

Language systems are so complex and diverse that specialists in language study have, until recently, spent most of their efforts developing systematic methods of language analysis, without much regard for the varied circumstances of actual speech behavior. The differences between language as a formal system and speech as a human activity have been obvious for a long time, particularly since the French linguist Ferdinand de Saussure wrote his famous distinction between *langue* (language) and *parole* (speech) (de Saussure, 1916).

One area of language study that led to research in actual speech behavior is the subfield of DIALECTOLOGY, which is concerned with the analysis of variations in pronunciation, grammar, and vocabulary among different subgroups within national speech communities. Dialectology became a significant branch of linguistics in the nineteenth century.

Studies in dialectology suggested a strong relationship between political systems and the patterning of dialectical variation. For example, it was noted that:

France, dominated for the last few centuries by a single center of political and economic power, shows few sharp dialect boundaries; transitions are gradual. . . . Germany, where political fragmentations and small states were the rule, shows many small dialect areas, separated by relatively large transition zones, reflecting the lack of political stability [of earlier centuries] and the many territorial changes in recent history. (GUMPERZ and HYMES, 1962:3)

Since 1960 there has been a rapid development of interest in the study of speech behavior under the heading of SOCIOLINGUISTICS and the "ethnography of communication". The aim of these studies is to examine how individuals and groups *use* language in day-to-day and long-term adaptation to their sociocultural environments. At the same time, there has been a development of a strong interest in the effects of so-called "substandard dialects" on the dilemmas of our public education system and other social contexts.

Forms of Address and Social Differences

One of the first linguistic lessons taught children in many societies is the proper address for important

9.1 **Like most primates, these titi monkeys enjoy close body contact. (Ron Garrison, San Diego Zoo photo)**

persons both in and outside the immediate family. Sometimes it is important to show the proper respect for father at an early age. More usually it is other relatives who should be greeted with "Sir," "Uncle," "Doña," or some clan or lineage title. In almost all societies the niceties of social relationships are at least fleetingly reflected in the forms and processes of greetings. In more complex and stratified societies the processes of deference and demeanor often go much further, so that many speech acts may be colored by the necessity for selecting the proper language to reflect appropriate relations between speakers.

Although most European languages force speakers to decide on the degree of familiarity and therefore also on the question of superordinate-subordinate status, the problem is nothing like the complexities of social and language stratification in Java as described by Clifford Geertz and other researchers. The Javanese have a very wide range of speech styles—with different vocabularies—that mark the levels and dyadic relationships in different social strata.

In the Javanese system, social relationships of higher and lower status are expressed whenever a speaker opens his mouth to communicate with another person. In Table 9.1 the top line is the most elegant and honorific, the bottom, the more common. The fact that the honorific levels for different words vary in different ways adds to the powerful impression of social status concern that pervades the entire Javanese language system.

It is not surprising that complexities of language forms, including especially the several options in pronouns, tend to be found in more complex, stratified societies. In some European contexts, for example, one can find "egalitarian" language usage in rural, peasant communities, while the same basic language in urban "high society" involves many more nuances of social status indicators. This is not to say that the "simpler," rural versions of the language are in any way inferior or logically lacking—it's just that they don't have to be eternally concerned about the signaling of social status. Anthropologist John Bregenzer has examined a wide variety of language systems around the world and finds that on a worldwide basis there is a rather high (though not absolute) correlation between complexity of society (stratification) and complexity in pronoun usage.

Social Identity and Language Change

We are quite aware of the fact that within some social groups—e.g., teen-agers, professors, and advertising people—there is rapid invention of new vocabulary and that in many groups some special marker words become obsolete relatively quickly. Today, to use the term *beatnik* marks one as peculiarly old-fashioned, but in the 1950s it was an acceptable, even interesting, expression. The social scientist who has been out of touch with the latest developments on a particular topic (e.g., structural analysis of kinship) or the fluent speaker of a European language who goes back to visit his native land after twenty years in America may each have occa-

Table 9.1: Javanese Linguistic Variants

Level	Are	You	Going	To Eat	Rice	And	Cassava	Now?
3a	menapa	pandjen-engan	badé	dahar	sekul	kālijan	kaspé	samenika
3	menapa	sampéjan	badé	dahar	sekul	kālijan	kaspé	samenika
2	napa	sampéjan	adjeng	neda	sekul	kālijan	kaspé	saniki
1a	apa	sampéjan	arep	neda	sega	lan	kaspé	saiki
1		kowé	arep	mangan	sega	lan	kaspé	saiki

Source: GEERTZ, 1960:250.

Table 9.2: Class Variations in Pronunciation of (oh)

	0 1 2	3 4 5	6 7 8	9
	Lower Class	*Working Class*	*Lower middle Class*	*Upper Middle Class*
Pronunciation of (oh) in casual speech	Low	High	High	Low
Degree of change in pronunciation from one speech context to another	None	Slight	Extreme	Moderate

Source: Adapted from LABOV, 1972:528.

sion to experience, rather painfully, the rapidity with which languages change. New ways of saying things are constantly developed, while the basic structure remains stable.

Some people invent new vocabulary because they must name new "things" and new "concepts" under conditions of general cultural change. This applies to most sectors of human societies today. But people also invent new vocabulary and modify their speech patterns in response to changing social alliances and identifications. The sudden strangeness in the college freshman's speech when he returns home for Christmas vacation has been a shock to many a parent, especially if they sent their beloved offspring to some school geographically or socially removed from thier own sociospatial location.

The linguist William Labov has studied some recent linguistic changes on Martha's Vineyard (Massachusetts) involving the centralization of the sound (aw) which occurs in words such as *out, house, about, mouth,* and so on. In examining the social factors affecting the pronunciation of (aw) among the Martha's Vineyard people, Labov found that differences in pronunciation were related to different degrees of "native status as a Vineyarder":

Thus to the extent that an individual felt able to claim and maintain status as a native Vineyarder he adopted increasing centralization of (aw). Sons who had tried to earn a living on the mainland, and afterwards re-

turned to the island, developed an even higher degree of centralization than their fathers had used. But to the extent that a Vineyarder abandoned his claim to stay on the island and earn his living there, he also abandoned centralization and returned to the standard, uncentralized forms. (LABOV, 1972:525–526)

In research among different groups in New York City, Labov found some curious differences in the pronunciation of the (oh) sound in words such as *law, talk, broad, caught, off, more, four, board.* He divided his sample of speakers into ten socioeconomic class steps (see Table 9.2) and found systematic differences among these social classes. Since he collected speech samples from people's reading of word lists, their casual speech, and their careful speech, he was able to note the degree to which people tried to "correct for" supposed deviations from "proper" pronunciation. He found that the pronunciation of the (oh) sound varied from a high sound such as the (u) in *sure* down to the level of (o) as in *cot.*

Labov's diagram (Table 9.2) shows a number of important things about this particular item of pronunciation. First of all, at the "lower class" end of the scale there tends to be relatively little difference in the pronunciation of the (oh) sound regardless of type of speaking. In other words, lower-class speakers do not consider distinctions in this sound to be of any significance. On the other hand, the

Adaptation Through Learning and Communication: Homo sapiens sapiens

middle-class speakers tend to use the high (oh) pronunciation in their casual speech, but they recognize it to be "improper," so they correct for it quite sharply in careful speech and even more sharply in the reading of word lists. Upper-middle-class people, on the other hand, were not as concerned about this distinction. Labov also found that ethnic group membership was quite relevant to New Yorkers' use of the (oh) sound. In all except the upper middle class, the Jewish group used higher levels of the (oh) sound than did, for example, the Italians.

From the study of a number of sound changes of the sort we have detailed here, Labov has developed a general theory of pronunciation change that may well be extended to vocabulary and also to other aspects of language. He notes that a particular kind of pronunciation may be distinctive of a subgroup within a community. If this subgroup is of low status, the unusual pronunciation pattern may become *stigmatized*; on the other hand, if the subgroup is of high status in the community, their pronunciation forms may become the *prestige model*. Although some segments of the community may shift their pronunciation closer to the prestige model, variations within the community will continue to exist because different social and ethnic groups do not all have the same degree of interest in the pronunciation pattern as a prestige marker.

Turning to a broader historical view of language changes, we can find many instances in which Labov's ideas concerning social identification and language uses are supported. In the history of the English language, for example, it seems clear that there was a time when the use of French vocabulary was identified with high prestige. This impact of French upon English dates from the Norman conquest of 1066, which brought the French-speaking Normandy knights, led by William the Conqueror, into power in England. The French speakers became the noblemen and landowners—an imposed upper class—resulting in clear linguistic stratification in England. At first these languages were quite separate and distinct, but the Norman conquerors gradually began to consider themselves at home in England and more and more of them became bilingual. The Norman-French language itself was modified, but Old English was modified much more decisively since it was "at the mercy" of the French conquerors. For a time the scribes were mostly Frenchmen, who didn't care very much about maintaining anything like "correct" Old English. The elaborate inflections of Old English were quickly broken down, leading to rapid changes in grammar, vocabulary, and pronunciation. Thousands of words were borrowed into English from French in subject areas from prestige foods (*beef, veal, mutton*) to matters military (*camp, war, chase, state,* and *file*). In some areas of speech, English gained a dual vocabulary from this process, with the French forms (plus Latin forms) generally fancier and more prestigious than the simpler Old English words. Consider the following pairs: *climb–ascend; live–reside; get–acquire; house–mansion.*

The histories of many other languages and language groups, in Europe and elsewhere, provide many illustrations of the ways in which social identities have shaped language change. There are, of course, other factors at work to bring about a constant modification of language systems. It makes a good deal of difference if a language has both written and spoken forms. If there are written forms, it makes a good deal of difference who the writers are. In many societies the writers have been specialists who imposed their own standards and preoccupations on the spoken language. Sometimes this has led to marked discrepancies between the written and the spoken forms of the language, as in Chinese.

When we consider all the forces for change and evolution, it is not surprising that languages often change rather rapidly. We need go back but a few hundred years (to Middle English) to find forms of English which most of us in North America today would have a great deal of difficulty in understanding. English was a rather unimportant language in the world, spoken by only a few million people until the late eighteenth and early nineteenth centuries. Then it spread rapidly around the world, and in a variety of environments and social contexts a number of strikingly different forms of English have emerged. The English of Jamaican and Trinidadian peasants cannot be understood by the average North American, nor can the average North American understand some forms of street cockney in England. During the last two hundred years distinctive forms of North American English have emerged, ranging from the "drawl" characteristic of the Deep South to the rapidly changing and rich-textured street language of inner-city Black populations that has recently been described in detail as

173

"Black English," or "NNE" Negro Nonstandard English) by William Labov and others (Labov, 1973).

"Standard" and "Nonstandard" Language Use

Wherever social systems have grown in complexity, so that many different dialects and languages are spoken within the same state, nation, or empire, there has been a strong tendency for *one* of these languages or dialects to become the "standard" speech while other dialects and languages are considered more or less "vulgar" or "substandard" or perhaps only "quaint." This process of invidious distinction in language, or "language imperialism," is not restricted to European instances by any means. In pre-Columbian Mexico the Aztecs extended their domination over many different peoples and became lords of a vast empire. Accordingly,

The [Aztec language] is considered the mother tongue, and that of Texcoco was thought the noblest and the purest. All the languages other than this were held to be coarse and vulgar . . . barbarous and strange. . . . [Aztec] is the richest and fullest language that is to be found. It is not only dignified but also soft and pleasing, lordly and of high nobility, succinct, easy, and flexible. (MUÑOZ CAMARGO DIEGO, *Historia de Tlaxcala, Mexico*, 1892:25, quoted in SOUSTELLE, 1964:233–234)

In European history the languages that came to dominate the various nations were generally standardized from the dialect spoken at the seats of political and economic power. Thus, the dialect around the London area set the tone for what became standardized English, while in France the dialect of Île de France (Paris) came to be regarded as "proper" French and the other dialects were gradually demoted in social status. In addition to their control of political and economic resources, the privileged classes in any society generally travel and communicate much more widely than do persons of lower social status. Their social contacts involve persons from different geographical areas, resulting in a gradual spreading and standardization of the "superior" dialect throughout the land. As writing systems become standardized, the one dialect among many comes to be accepted throughout most of the nation as "correct speech." People seeking upward social

mobility try to change their linguistic habits to conform more nearly with the pronunciation and vocabulary of the privileged classes.

As standardized languages become established, localized dialects do not automatically disappear, and they may be maintained as signs of local identifications even though most individuals are fluent in the "proper speech" of the national language. Thus, to a greater or lesser extent, large numbers of peoples in modern nations are "bidialectical," switching back and forth between their local dialect and the national standard dialect as occasion demands.

Speech variations in Norway are an interesting illustration of these processes. In earlier times the socially dominant dialect had been a form derived from Danish (from the days when Danish kings ruled Norway); later it was replaced by a supposedly more home-grown language called *landsmål* ("language of the country"). The older Danish-derived form (called *riksmål*) and *landsmål* have continued to compete side by side as official languages in Norway.

Since education is universal and the school system is quite effective, most rural Norwegians, no matter how isolated they may be from urban centers, receive education in one of the two "standard" languages. Jan-Petter Blom and John Gumperz have studied the interactions between standard Norwegian and local dialect in the small northern town of Hemnesberget in Ranafjord. Most of the residents speak the dialect Ranamål, which is one of the local dialects of northern Norway. But the school system and all official transactions, religious observances, and mass media in the town employ one of the standard Norwegian languages.

Blom and Gumperz found that most of the people in Hemnesberget were fluent in both the local dialect and the national "standard" Norwegian. There were considerable variations, though, in the contexts in which the two languages were employed by various speakers. In general, whenever the local dialect was employed, it served to emphasize local group identification and concern with local issues. Communication with outsiders and discourse about national issues were likely to involve switching to the standard Norwegian.

On one occasion, when we, as outsiders, stepped up to a group of locals engaged in conversation, our arrival caused a significant alteration in the casual posture of

174

the group. Hands were removed from pockets and looks exchanged. Predictably, our remarks elicited a code switch marked simultaneously by a change in channel cues (i.e., sentence speed, rhythm, more hesitation and pauses, etc.) and by a switch from [local dialect] to [standard] grammar. Similarly, teachers reported that while formal lectures—where interruptions are not encouraged—are delivered in [standard speech] the speakers will shift to [local dialect]when they want to encourage open and free discussion among students. (BLOM and GUMPERZ, 1972:424)

It was particularly interesting to note the speech habits of college students returned home for the summer. In interviews these students claimed that they spoke pure dialect and also claimed that they preferred to use the local dialect. However, in a social gathering the students' dialect switched back and forth between local and standard, depending upon conversational topics. It was particularly revealing that "when an argument required that the speaker validate his status as an intellectual, he would again tend to use standard forms" (Blom and Gumperz, 19:430).

Large numbers of people in every nation switch back and forth between "standard" and "local" speech as they play out various roles in different social contexts. Identification with the local group, whether it is a village, a valley settlement, a neighborhood in a city, or a particular ethnic minority, is signaled by the use of localized in-group language and social manners. However, in encounters with the wider world people "put their best foot forward" and show their sophistication by using "standard" language.

In the Norwegian example we are dealing with a case in which the people are not a deprived minority, so that serious, invidious distinctions are not made concerning their language use. When we turn to speech patterns in urban North America, however, we find quite a different situation, especially concerning the dialects of English spoken by Black people in inner-city situations. Although they are surrounded by speakers of so-called "standard" English, they are so socially and residentially segregated from White populations that they often have little occasion to develop fluency in standard English. Social segregation thus promotes language barriers, and the language barriers feed back to further reinforce the social distinctions. This vicious circle of segregation has tended to produce speech styles with

vocabulary, grammatical categories, and pronunciation markedly different from those of "mainstream" America. William Labov is one of several linguists who has studied "Black English" in great detail. In his discussion of "the logic of nonstandard English," Labov points out that the language spoken by Black people in the inner city in New York is *not* a substandard version of ordinary English, but is a fully developed, distinctive dialect, with clear grammatical rules and all the other features and developed vocabulary characteristic of all human languages (Labov, 1969:153–189).

The language spoken by many Black peoples is sufficiently different from the speech of most White persons, especially in positions of authority, so that serious communications difficulties often arise in such interlinguistic interaction. These problems of communication are a factor in many of the social problems of the inner city, but they are nowhere more evident than in the schools. Since the predominantly White teachers and administrators have difficulty in understanding much of Black English speech, they quickly label this language as "inferior" and regard it as a serious obstacle to learning. They feel it necessary to "stamp out" the (to them) "ungrammatical" aspects of Black English.

Of course, we are not claiming the language differences are a major *cause* of the many problems in inner-city school systems or in other contexts of interaction between Black and White populations. The point we are making here is that language differences are sensitive markers of social identifications and cleavages—and some panhuman tendencies with regard to social use of language come into play as factors in intergroup relations. The near-universal tendency to downgrade the intellectual competence of persons speaking other languages and dialects, and the strong tendency to assert moral and intellectual superiority for the dominant "standard" language of a society play a part in adding to misperceptions and misunderstandings, especially on the part of the dominant sector of the society, which has little opportunity to find out about the complex communication systems of the nondominant peoples.

Misunderstandings in the dominant sector of the society have been heightened in recent times by researchers who have claimed to demonstrate intellectual inferiorities in so-called "substandard" speech forms. One of these researchers, Basil Bern-

175

stein, has asserted that working-class and poor people speak in a "restricted code" or dialect compared to the "elaborated code" of standard middle-class speech. A restricted code is supposedly simple in grammatical construction, incapable of complex abstractions, and capable of dealing more with emotional and present-tense content than with logical, planned-out discourse involving future events or past circumstances. One problem with the work of Bernstein and a number of other similar researchers is their lack of understanding of the contexts of speech behavior. Frequently their evidences concerning language use are gathered in interview situations that are threatening and demoralizing to the people of lower social status whose language is being studied. The resulting interaction between researcher and research subject often involves a maddening exchange of evasive monosyllables or other simple answers to the researcher's questions, as the subject is motivated to end the interview as soon as possible rather than to demonstrate his speech style. Such encounters are hardly conducive to the study of language systems, yet they have been used as a basis for distorted generalizations concerning the supposed inferiorities of nonstandard English speech.

There have been experiments recently with the use of Black English as an auxiliary teaching language in inner-city schools. These experiments involve great complexities and problems, so their effects and possible usefulness remain to be assessed. In any case, the research of Labov and others makes it clear that so-called nonstandard dialects are not intellectually inferior to "standard" language systems, but they pose some serious social problems at points where the different dialects meet in crucial interaction.

Nonverbal Communication: Body Language

In spite of the fact that human communication involves a complex interrelating of vocal language and body motions, gestures, and other PARALINGUISTIC features, there is a serious lack of detailed study of nonverbal communication. Nonverbal components of the message are nearly always important in conveying meaning, and the more personalized and emotion-laden the message, the more likely it is that the vocal channel by itself is inadequate to do the job. We have to add caresses, eye motions, and other gestures to convey love or warmth, while anger and frustration require some contortion of facial features or other body changes before the message becomes really credible.

In 1872 Charles Darwin published a book, *The Expression of the Emotions in Man and Animals.* He had collected a large number of reports from zoos, from travelers in distant lands, and a number of other sources, including the following:

With respect to the natives of India, Mr. J. Scott has sent me a full description of their gestures and expression when enraged. Two low caste Bengalees disputed about a loan. At first they were calm, but soon grew furious and poured forth the grossest abuse on each other's relations and progenitors for many generations past. Their gestures were very different from those of Europeans; for though their chests were expanded and shoulders squared their arms remained rigidly suspended, with the elbows turned inwards and the hands alternately clenched and opened. Their shoulders were often raised high and then again lowered. They looked fiercely at each other from under their lowered and strongly wrinkled brows, and their protruded lips were firmly closed. They approached each other, with hands and neck stretched forward, and pushed, scratched, and grasped at each other. This protrusion of the head and body seems a common gesture with the enraged; and I have noticed it with degraded Englishmen while quarreling violently in the streets. In such cases it may be presumed that neither party expects to receive a blow from the other. (DARWIN, 1872 (republished 1965):246–247)

Darwin reviewed evidence that seemed to justify for him the conclusion that:

The chief expressive actions, exhibited by man and by the lower animals, are now innate or inherited—that is, have not been learned by the individual. (DARWIN, 1965:350)

On the other hand, he pointed out that:

Certain other gestures, which seem to us so natural that we might easily imagine that they were innate, apparently have been learnt like the words of a language. This seems to be the case with the joining of the uplifted hands, and the turning up of the eyes, in prayer. (DARWIN, 1965:352)

176

The Study of Kinesics

Darwin had to base his conclusions on fairly questionable types of information—mostly anecdotal reports. But we do not have very much more to go on today, partly because only a few scholars have undertaken serious study of this dimension of behavior and partly because the research is very difficult. The term KINESICS is often used to identify the study of human body motion (the root *kin-* pertains to motion, as in *kinetic*). Specific body motions that convey meaning can be listed and identified as *kines*. These include "salute," "pointing," "nodding," "shaking the head in negation," and so on. Ray Birdwhistell, professor of communications at the University of Pennsylvania, has been one of the pioneers in kinesic research. Earlier work was based on the analysis of filmed behavior, but more recently video tape has provided a much more flexible research tool. PROXEMICS, on the other hand, refers to the study of the use of space in interpersonal communication.

Birdwhistell's research demonstrates the fact that in most human conversational episodes several channels of communication are always operating at the same time, sometimes in a kind of "harmony" and often with somewhat different kinds of messages in the different channels. While the vocal tract (channel one) conveys the most complicated information, positioning of the body (channel two) lends further support and elaboration to the vocal presentation. Hand gestures (channel three) often present some specific further information, such as identifying particular persons as "he" or "she," while a sweep of the hand can tell us who is intended by the words "those people." Facial expressions (channel four), especially around the eyes and mouth, often directly underscore degrees of positive information, hostility or aggressiveness, or other emotional qualities. Baring of the teeth, for example, heightens the aggressive message carried in the vocal channel. Sometimes the feet (channel five) carry still further, perhaps conflicting, information, such as restlessness, uneasiness, or even preparation for departure. Kinesic study requires attention to all these different channels of body communication, and it generally makes no sense without fairly detailed analysis of voice patterns themselves. No wonder the research is so difficult.

Touching: The Primal Message

The helpless newborn human infant needs a great deal of direct contact with adults in order to secure food, warmth, and other life-preserving attentions. Patting, cuddling, and other body contacts are pleasurable and essential daily fare for the human infant. Humans are not much different from other mammals in this regard.

In addition to the importance of physical contact with parents, most young mammals experience a great deal of tactile stimulation in play activities with their litter mates and other age peers. Lion cubs and other carnivores play at fighting one another, mouthing, cuffing, racing, tumbling, biting, tail chasing, and other bodily communication. Juvenile baboons, chimpanzees, and other primates have this same pattern of endless play routines, involving all kinds of body contact. Much of this is "play-aggression," as the little primates learn more and more about the ways in which threats, counterthreats, and occasional bared-teeth fighting lead to the social relations of dominance and submission. But these semiaggressive play activities also include many "friendly" touching acts, reminding us that the cohesiveness of baboon troops and the sociability seen among chimpanzees in the wild are based on very powerful positive social attractions and not just sex and dominance.

Grooming behavior among primates (including humans) is the all-time favorite in "contact sports." Grooming an individual by removing lice and other objects from the fur is carried out by means of hands, lips, and teeth, and has important health-preserving functions in addition to the pleasurable communication of touching. There is a good deal of variation in grooming behavior among various primate species. Many New World monkeys groom mainly as mated pairs, in prelude to copulation. Among baboons, rhesus monkeys, and others grooming reflects social ranking—females groom males much more than vice versa, except when the female is in estrus, during which time males are much more attentive to them (Jolly, 1972:196). Evidence of the long-term evolutionary importance of body contact through grooming is seen in the special "tooth comb" of lemurs and lorises, which "is formed of their lower canines and incisors, flattened, forward pointing, arranged for fur scraping.

177

It is quite possible that the saltiness of our sweat is evolved to reward the diligent groomer with crumbs of salt!" (Jolly, 1972:196).

The importance of touching as a form of communication has been rediscovered in the rapidly expanding "encounter group" movement, beginning in the 1960s. Many proponents emphasize the positive values of touching as communication experience, claiming that in our modern society people have become alienated from each other and are afraid of body contact.

Handshakes and Other Greetings

One of the most widely employed communication gestures involving touching is the handshake. This gesture of greeting, friendship, and, sometimes, agreement is said to have developed, among Europeans, from the practices of medieval knights who displayed nonhostile intentions by offering their right hand, in which they would normally have been holding a weapon if their intentions had not been friendly. It is likely, though, that the handshake goes back to greeting forms much older than the practices of armored knights, since many peoples of the world use similar forms of touching as a greeting.

Although the handshake is a ubiquitous greeting throughout the length and breadth of Western culture, there are significant differences in the occasions and frequencies of handshakes among different subgroups. In general, Europeans recognize many more occasions for handshaking than do most North Americans. In some segments of European society (also in Latin America) adults shake hands nearly every time they meet, even if they have been in interaction fairly recently. In North America, on the other hand, adults (especially males) shake hands at first meeting and then again in encounters following a considerable lapse of time during which they have not seen each other.

Many peoples of the world use some form of touching as part of their greeting style. Here are some examples:

When such strangers appeared, a stereotyped routine followed. They entered hesitantly and self-consciously, bending down to rub their hands along the shoulders or the thighs of people they knew in the crowd. (READ, 1965:70)

Naked children swarmed around us, ignoring the angry shouts of men who began to push their way toward us from the edge of the crowd. In the excitement I did not hear Young-Whitforde ask for Makis, but I guessed who it was when I found myself confronted by his dark, smiling face. He spoke a few rapid words then took me into his arms and held me against him in the customary full embrace of greeting. (READ, 1965:20)

When men from another community or tribe arrive for ceremonies, they usually first perform a penis offering ritual with their hosts. Each visitor approaches each of the seated hosts in turn and lifts the latter's arm. He presses his penis against the host's hand, so that the sub-incised urethra is in full contact with the palm, and then draws the penis firmly along the hand.

9.2 Touching is another form of learning. (Burk Uzzle, Magnum)

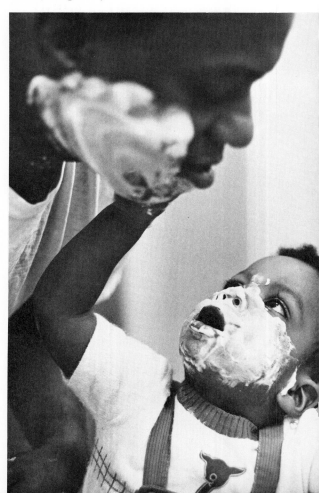

A man with a grievance against the visitor refuses to raise his hand for the ritual. . . . The Walbiri assert that they acquired this ritual of penis offering from the Pidjandjara to the south and in turn have taught it to the [peoples] . . . to the north. (MEGGITT, 1962:262–263)

One afternoon I saw two village girls arrive, followed by two servants who threw down loads of plantains and sweet bananas, and a sack of manioc flour. . . . The girls were Amina, daughter of an important Babira subchief, and her cousin. [Amina] obviously knew the Pygmies well, because without waiting to be asked she distributed the plantains. . . . Apparently she was well liked, because as soon as people heard of her presence they came over to shake her hand, in the manner of villagers, grasping each other's wrists. (TURNBULL, 1962:141–142)

Group Membership and Special Body Contact

Many groups, from the Boy Scouts to various secret societies, employ special forms of handshake to signal not simply amicable goodwill but membership in an in-group. Here is Lincoln Keiser's description of behavior among The Vice Lords, a Chicago street gang:

A form of behavior that is a part of on-going social interaction is handslapping. In handslapping a person puts his hand out with the palm up, and another

9.3 A Bedouin greeting. (Courtesy of the American Museum of Natural History)

9.4 A Japanese greeting. (René Burri, Magnum)

person touches the open palm with his own hand or arm. A handslapping exchange can begin in two ways. In some cases during the course of a social episode an individual puts his hand out with the palm raised. The proper response is to touch the raised palm with a hand or arm. Other times a handslapping exchange is initiated by the person raising his hand with the palm down. The proper response is to put out the hand with the palm raised. The first individual then slaps the outraised palm. In the first kind of handslapping exchange there are several kinds of responses to an outraised palm that are considered proper. Some, but not all, of these have different social significance. A person can respond to an outraised palm by slapping it with his own palm either up or down. This has no particular social significance. Touching the outraised palm with an arm or elbow is also a possible response. Further, an individual can vary in intensity of his slap. These last two differences—touching the palm with an arm or elbow rather than with the hand and varying the intensity of the slap—do have significance (KEISER, 1969:43–44)

Special forms of greeting involve fairly complicated messages of mutual esteem and social solidarity. Their use signals the presumption that the participating individuals consider themselves to be in some sense "on the same side" in the wider context of social encounters. Whereas a simple handshake can be exchanged between enemies in moments of truce or meetings under neutral circumstances, special in-group handshakes, handslaps, and similar communications are usually not exchanged across the boundaries of social conflict.

Writing Systems: Our Greatest Technological Invention?

Human speech and traditions of oral communication are very much more basic to human behavior than is a comparatively recent invention—writing, which has come to dominate so much of the communications process in complex, industrialized societies. Most of the languages of the world have no alphabets or other writing systems, and most human communication continues to take the form of oral expression, in spite of the fact that the development of writing systems has had profound effects on modern sociocultural systems.

The Invention of Writing

It is historical accident that some of the earliest human writing systems made use of very durable materials, so that important evidence concerning the history of writing has been preserved in the form of baked-clay tablets, inscriptions in stone, and other nonperishable forms. Many peoples of the world, at various times and places, have developed means of communication that involve putting some kinds of marks onto more or less flat surfaces. The Yukaghir of northern Siberia, like many North American

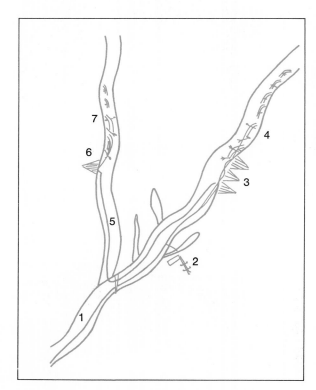

9.5 Picture writing by a Yukaghir in Siberia, telling about a fishing expedition. Lines in the middle of the river show the travel routes; the cross (2) shows that a man died; at 3 the tents show where the whole group camped; at 4 they had two boats and two canoes. One family group left and went up the other river (6); evidently they consisted of two families, judging from the number of boats and canoes (7). (From JOCHELSON, 1960:332)

180

Indian groups, traced figures and lines on the inner surfaces of birch bark with the points of their knives. A hunter, upon leaving his temporary camp site, sometimes left a letter on a nearby tree to inform passing kinsmen and others about where he had gone or what had happened. Figure 9.5 shows a figure that was found on a tree trunk in 1895 by the anthropologist Waldemar Jochelson and his Yukaghir traveling companions as they went up the Korkodon River. Jochelson's Yukaghir escorts learned from the letter "where their clansmen had been during the summer and what they had done. They guessed who had died and told [Jochelson] why two families had one tent on the Rassokha River" (Jochelson, 1960:331–332).

Picture writing among North American Indians often took the form of paintings on tipi covers. Clark Wissler reported finding a tipi in 1903 that had several hundred figures with sixty-six different "stories," most of them about activities of persons then living in the tipi.

Before the coming of the Whites, neither the Indians of the North American plains nor the Yukaghir developed anything like a full-blown writing system adequate for all kinds of different communications, despite the fact that they, like countless other peoples in the world, had taken the first steps toward a written symbolic system. Why didn't they go on to invent such a system? The best explanation, probably, is that they had no need for such refinements of communication, since everything they needed to know or communicate could be expressed and carried verbally within their limited circle of social contacts. A very large amount of information from the past can be carried in the form of "oral traditions" remembered by older persons of a tribe, and new information that must be carried from one group to another can usually be transmitted personally, even if the message involves considerable complexity.

Apparently, more complex writing systems have arisen in the world only among peoples whose social structures involved some kind of complex bureaucracy and economic functions, including taxation, that required notations and maintenance of records beyond the capacities of individual memories and oral traditions. That kind of social and cultural complexity arose in the Fertile Crescent region of Egypt-Mesopotamia in the period 4000–3000 B.C. As V. Gordon Childe noted:

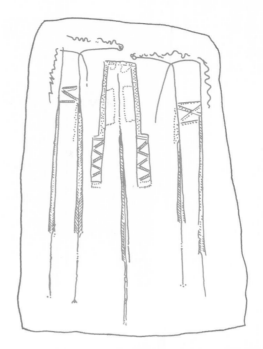

9.6   A Yukaghir love letter inscribed on birch bark. (From JOCHELSON, 1960:335)

The fortunate circumstance that the Sumerians adopted clay as their writing material and made their documents imperishable by baking the clay, allows us to follow the history of writing from its very beginning in Mesopotamia. It shows the development of writing and of city life advancing step by step. It is no accident that the oldest written documents in the world are accounts and dictionaries. They disclose a severely practical need that prompted the invention of the Sumerian script. (CHILDE, 1951:146)

Probably the first complex writing system in the world was that of the Egyptians, for the accounts, inventories, and other records from the Egyptian royal tombs dating from about 3000 B.C. show a system more developed than Sumerian documents of comparable age. At first, those Egyptian written messages were practically all PICTOGRAPHS, but soon symbols were added that represented ideas that were relatively nonpictorial (IDEOGRAPHS). Some signs were added to the message that represented sounds only. The Egyptian hieroglyphic system usually involved a considerable mixture of different kinds of symbols—some representing sounds and ideas but

181

The Advantages of Literacy (from Egyptian New Kingdom Documents)

Put writing in your heart that you may protect yourself from hard labor of any kind and be a magistrate of high repute. The scribe is released from manual tasks; it is he who commands. . . . Do you not hold a scribe's palette? That is what makes the difference between you and the man who handles an oar.

I have seen the metalworker at his task at the mouth of his furnace with fingers like a crocodile's. He stank worse than fish spawn. Every workman who holds a chisel suffers more than the men who hack the ground; wood is his field and the chisel his mattock. At night when he is free, he toils more than his arms can do (? at overtime work); even at night he lights (his lamp to work by). The stone cutter seeks work in every hard stone; when he has done the great part of his labor his arms are exhausted, he is tired out. . . . The weaver in a workshop is worse off than women; (he squats) with knees to his belly and does not taste (fresh) air. He must give loaves to the porters to see the light. (Childe, 1951:149)

As V. Gordon Childe notes, these documents might well be the sentiments of a farmer or a small shopkeeper writing to his son who has to choose between proceeding to higher education or entering industrial employment.

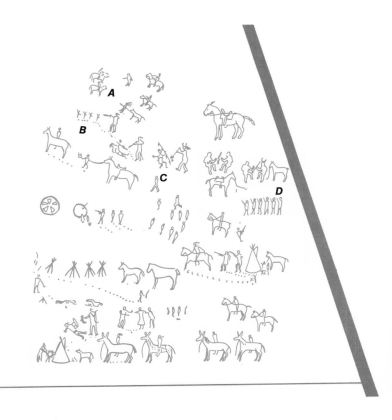

9.7 Picture writing on a Plains Indian tipi. At the top of the picture Bear Chief (A) is surprised by four Assiniboine Indians, but escapes. Double Runner (B) cuts loose four horses. Double Runner (C) and companion meet and kill two Gros Ventre warriors and take a lance from one of them. A series of adventures (D) with some Crow Indians, from whom Double Runner takes a gun. Several other stories are depicted also.

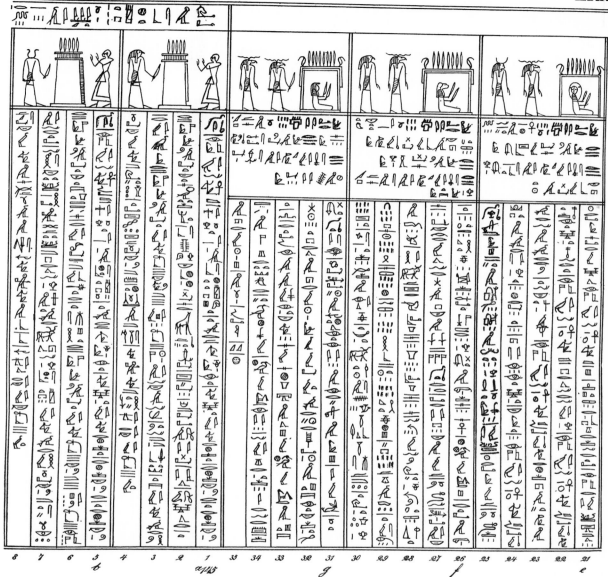

9.8 Egyptian hieroglyphics on the Turin papyrus. (Courtesy of the American Museum of Natural History)

with the addition of pictures for clarification. Such a system is, of course, very complex, and it required at least 460 different characters. The corresponding cuneiform Babylonian script had over 500 characters.

Writing systems of mixed pictographic and ideographic and phonetic characters were used for a very long time among the Egyptians, in the Sumerian-Babylonian cuneiform writings, and in the writing

183

Speech, Body Language, and Writing

systems of the Indus Valley farther east. The Chinese system of characters involved much the same principles, but was probably invented independently in the Far East.

The Alphabet—
A Unique Invention

Somewhere around 1500–1300 B.C. a group of Semitic-speaking peoples (probably Phoenicians) modified the mixed writing system with a dramatic and far-reaching innovation—probably the most significant technological achievement since the development of food growing. They dropped out the pictographs and other mixed symbols from their writing system and adopted a purely phonetic alphabet. This invention may have happened only once in all of human history. At least we can say that practically all of the alphabetic systems still in use are derived from that Phoenician prototype. Some of the evidence for this Semitic alphabet comes to us from the famous Moabite Stone, which King Mesha erected to commemorate his successful defense of Moab against the invading Hebrew kings of Judea and Israel in 860 B.C. Actually the origins of the alphabet go back several centuries before this date.

The next significant stage in the history of writing systems was the transmission of the Phoenician alphabet to the Greeks, whose language was wholly different from that of the Semitic peoples. Whereas the Semitic speakers had somehow managed with an alphabet that dealt only with consonants, ignoring

1.	ꔔꗋ.ꗵ ꔼꕬ.ꗵꙶꕬꗵꙶꗿꙶꗿꙶꕬꙶ.ꝋꙶꗿ.ꝋꞝꞝꔔ
2.	ꔔꝋꙶ.ꝋꙶꝋꙶꝋ.ꙶꙶ.ꙶꝋꙶꝋꙶꗵꗵꔔ.ꝋꙶꙶꙶ.ꝋꙶꔔꙶ
3.	ꞈNK·MSᴄ·BN·KMSMLD·MLK·ꞈB
4.	ꞈANᵒKⁱ MᵉSʰᵃᶜ BᵉN KᵃMᵒSʰMᵃLD MᵉLᵉK MᵒᵒAB
5.	I Meshaᶜ son-of Kamoshmald king-of Moab

9.9 **Some of the inscription on the Moabite Stone (860 B.C.): 1. The inscription, reading from right to left. 2. The same, reversed. 3. Translated into modern alphabet. 4. The unwritten vowels are included to show pronunciation. 5. Translated into English.**

vowels, the Greeks could not operate with simply a consonant alphabet. To eliminate the confusion, they had to develop letters for the vowels. Instead of inventing new letters, they used Semitic consonant signs they did not need. They simply changed some of these consonant marks into vowel symbols. For example, the first letter of the Semitic alphabet, the *aleph*, stood for the glottal stop, the closure at the back of the throat that English-speaking people make (soundlessly) *before* pronouncing vowels. The glottal stop is very important in Semitic languages but relatively superfluous for writing Greek. The Greeks therefore gave *aleph* a new meaning—the vowel *a*. The fact that the Greeks named this system the *alpha-bet* from the Semitic names for the first two letters underscores the fact that the Greeks got the system from their more easterly neighbors.

As the use of the alphabet spread around the Mediterranean, the Romans picked it up but modified it to suit the peculiarities of their language. It is this Roman alphabet that is most familiar to Euro-Americans and many other peoples in the world. On the other hand, the Greek alphabet was carried into Russia by the monk St. Cyril, with the result that the Cyrillic form of the alphabetical system came to be the distinctive feature of modern Russian writing. Many other modifications of the original alphabet were developed in different parts of the world: the complex Sanskrit alphabet in India and various specialized systems that grew up in Africa, Southeast Asia, and the Philippines, for example.

One other dramatic invention in the writing of language should be mentioned, as an example of the inventiveness of individual geniuses and to underscore the importance of writing systems. During the period 1809–1821 a Cherokee Indian named Sequoya became so impressed with the great power and importance of written language as it operated among White people who were steadily forcing his people from their lands and livelihood that he determined to create a system of writing for his people. Sequoya did not simply readjust the English alphabet to the special sounds and requirements of Cherokee, as the Romans had done with the alphabet they got from the Greeks. Instead, he transformed the whole alphabet idea into a SYLLABARY. The system is partly an adaptation from the English alphabet, but a syllabary requires an extensive inventory of symbols in order to manage the rather large number of two-

Adaptation Through Learning and Communication: Homo sapiens sapiens

1. *[Cherokee syllabary]*
2. na s gi ya | na s quo | a ni ya to hi hi | ge tsi lv quo di
3. that | also | deacons | they like them
4. Deacons | likewise | must be | serious,

1. *[Cherokee syllabary]*
2. ge se s di | v tle s di | gu da le nv dv | i ya ni we s gi
3. it is | not to be | different thing | they said it
4. | not double-tongued,

1. *[Cherokee syllabary]*
2. yi ge sc s di | a le | v tle s di | gi ga ge a di ta s di
3. than it is | and | not to be | red blood of drink Lord's Supper
4. | not addicted to much wine,

1. *[Cherokee syllabary]*
2. u ni ga na si s gi | yi gc se s di | tle s di | lc gv wa tsa di
3. no good for you to be liking | they are | not to be | values
4. | not greedy for much

1. *[Cherokee syllabary]*
2. un ri gv si s gi | yi ge se s di
3. presidents | they are not;
4. gain;

9.10 Example of writing using the Cherokee syllabary: 1. Passages from the Bible in Cherokee; 2. Approximate pronunciation of the syllables; 3. Literal translation. (Courtesy of Janet Jordan)

9.11 Mayan hieroglyphics in the Dresden Codex. This writing system has not yet been fully deciphered.

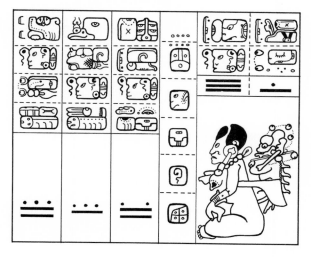

and three-phoneme clusters (syllables) on which a language such as Cherokee is built. Sequoya's Cherokee syllabary is still used today.

Writing in New World Indian Civilizations

Of all the American Indian civilizations the Mayan is perhaps most celebrated for its intellectual-technological developments. In addition to the sculptures, monuments, and other stonework, they developed a complex mathematical system and an intricate calendar for recording cycles of sacred events and secular (especially political) progressions. And they had a system of hieroglyphic writing that

185

Speech, Body Language, and Writing

as yet is only partly translated. It remains an exciting puzzle for those specialists who have devoted their careers to the unraveling of Mayan cultural history. As evidence has accumulated concerning the meaning of the Mayan hieroglyphics, it is becoming more probable that the system is a mixture of phonetic and ideographic elements. There is no alphabet as such nor any other kind of key to translation of the Maya texts, so the intricate mixture must be worked out piece by piece like a jigsaw puzzle. There is a fairly rich body of materials to work with, because the hieroglyphics are found on stone carvings, as well as on screen-folded manuscripts of bark, paper, and cloth. The best specimen of these, the so-called Dresden Codex, is about 20 cm high and stretches out for several meters of text.

The Binary Code: Language of Computers

Alphabetic writing was a remarkable technological achievement. When combined with the printing press, invented some three thousand years later, it made possible a fantastic increase in communication and storage of human knowledge. The results are visible in our massive libraries of printed works. In the last half of the twentieth century a new revolution in information storage and retrieval took place in the form of electronic computers. For the computer to be effective a new language notation system was devised that would permit incredibly rapid processing with minimal error of electronic impulses.

The new "writing system" is built up from the simplest possible units, for it employs only two symbols, zero and one. This BINARY CODE is employed mostly for numerical notation but can, of course, be used for writing in ordinary language, as all of us know who have seen our names, Social Security numbers, and other personal information printed out on paychecks or down at the local bank.

But where did the idea for the binary code come from in the first place? In the fascinating history of modern technology it turns out that the binary code was invented at least four different times by individuals with quite different purposes in mind. The philosopher-scientist-politician Francis Bacon (1561–1626) developed a binary code for conveying secret messages. A Frenchman, Josef Marie Jacquard (1752–1834), invented an ingenious system of binary-coded cards for controlling the warp and weft of mechanical looms. His were the first binary-controlled production machines. An English mathematician, George Boole (1815–1864), developed a new kind of algebra using a binary system. And a French engineer, Emil Baudot (1845–1903), developed a binary code that brought about the major breakthrough in telegraphy.

Because the binary system has only two symbols, they must be combined in complex combinations if a large array of numbers or other ideas must be symbolized. This is how our standard decimal system of numbers looks translated into binary:

Decimal Code	Binary Code
0	0
1	1
2	10
3	11
4	100
5	101
6	110
7	111
8	1000
9	1001

Whereas we can go all the way to 99 in our decimal system using only two symbols, by the time we get to 40 in binary we already have six (101000). What is 99 in binary? (Heath, 1972:76–83)

186

Mayan civilization had fallen into decay centuries before the coming of the Spaniards to the New World. The great religious centers in the jungles of the Yucatán and of Guatemala had been given back to the encroaching jungle, and the thousands of Mayan-speaking peoples of those regions lived in relatively small village clusters without the pomp and circumstance that had once been Mayan civilization. Many of them lived under the partial control of the spreading Aztec empire of central Mexico—a militaristic group recently risen to power. Their writing was a pictographic rendering of military exploits, religious ceremonies (including human sacrifices), and other significant concrete events. Perhaps their writing system was at the point of transition where, had the Spaniards not interfered with the process, they might have soon developed a writing system more flexible for expressing abstract ideas.

Paper and Printing

The major revolutionary implication of alphabetic writing is that information can be stored indefinitely in physical (written) form; the written information can be recovered later, centuries or millennia later, even though everyone who knew the information has long since been reduced to dust.

But the singular advantages of alphabetic writing would be of much less significance if it were not for two other crucial technological developments —paper and printing.

Paper is an invention that helped make modern industrialized society possible. Some kind of cheap, portable, relatively enduring, flat-surfaced form had to be developed if immense quantities of information were to be recorded, manipulated, distributed to great numbers of people, and stored for future use.

The ancient Chinese inscribed their prose on palm leaves and on harder materials like bones. They then began writing on silk, because they had some new and finer hair brushes for stroking the thousands of characters of written Chinese. Then in about 105 A.D. (it is said) paper pressed from shredded rags and nets and bark was invented.

Paper was imported as a luxury novelty toward the West, and the slow pace of diffusion of paper manufacture testifies to how different the world was

some centuries ago. Here is A. L. Kroeber's reconstruction of the spread of this crucial invention:

Dates for paper manufacture: A.D. 105 invented in China. 264 in use in Sinkiang, Chinese Turkestan. 751 Samarkand, Russian (then Arab) Turkestan. 793 Baghdad, Iraq. Ca. 900 Egypt. Ca. 1100 Morocco. Ca. 1150 Mohammedan Spain. 1189 France. 1276 Italy. 1391 Germany, 1494 England (introduced after printing). 1690 Philadelphia. (KROEBER, 1948:491)

It is not surprising that the invention of multiple production of written works also occurred in the Far East. Because they had the paper to do it on, the Chinese found that they could press moist paper against inscribed slabs and then run a pen smoothly over the paper to produce a reversed white-on-black copy of the original inscription. Multiple production in quantity was taken up by eager missionaries bent on spreading their religions. Taoists and Buddhists, competitively missionizing in the period 500–700 A.D., rolled out large numbers of prayers and charms by means of cylindrical seals, usually made of wood. Block prints, rubbings, and other reproduction techniques were also used. By 700–800 block printing, particularly of religious texts, was widespread in China and Japan, and a whole book printed with block prints, the Buddhist *Diamond Scriptures*, dates from 868.

To set up a printing press with movable type is a formidable task, given the Chinese writing system, so it is no wonder that this development did not occur until the eleventh century. The inventor Pi Sheng baked his characters in clay and then set them up on a gum base. Later, metal was used in place of those earlier clay characters. Because it takes several thousand Chinese characters to operate an effective movable-type system, Chinese printing continued to favor whole-page blocks, while printing presses in Europe, when they finally were developed, took the form of movable type since the Western alphabets needed only twenty-six letters and a few additional items. In Europe the earliest block prints date from the early fifteenth century. There is an interesting parallel between East and West in the fact that these European block prints, like their Eastern counterpart, were mainly religious in nature.

There was a growing demand for books in Europe after about 1400, and the block printers did what they could to meet it. The invention of movable

187

type came quickly. In conventional history, Johann Gutenberg "invented" type printing in Mainz in 1450. Probably a number of other printers contributed to the invention, however, and it is very possible that Pi Sheng's invention four hundred years earlier was carried to Europe along with other details of paper and printing for which Western European civilization owes so much to the Chinese.

9.12 The Gutenberg press. (Lessing, Magnum)

Three crucial inventions came together in Western Europe to produce ultimately an immense and far-reaching growth of information storage and distribution. Alphabetic writing, paper, and printing with movable type make up an extremely efficient system for transmitting information and ideas. Recent developments such as photocopying, paperback books, and various new electronic printing equipment are but frosting on the cake, although their considerable influence on information processes keeps us reminded of the importance of information-processing technology as a central feature of modern industrialized society.

Reflections on Speech and Writing

Human societies are held together with language —and other means of communication. The fact that human social systems are often very much larger than those of other animals is based, above all, on our complex systems of communication. In face-to-face interaction it is always possible to express a good deal of subtle difference in social interaction patterns by means of body language—the chimpanzees are probably more effective than humans in this respect. Beyond body language, the human language system, with all its richness, provides a means by which people can convey very elaborated information. Furthermore, subtle language clues can refer to sex, age, marital status, degree of formal acquaintance, and many other features of social situation.

1. If social systems are highly stratified, the differences in social position will be reflected in customary modes of speech.

2. People in higher social categories of socioeconomic privilege will regard their modes of speech as "superior" or "more correct" than those of the people in lower socioeconomic categories. Formal systems of education frequently reflect these attitudes about "correct" speech.

3. People who act in two or more different social systems generally will use different language forms to convey information in the different social contexts.

4. Most people in complex societies are skilled in codeswitching—especially between the more formalized and the relatively informal sectors of their social systems. A prime example of such code switching is that of the college student who uses a particular style of speech in an academic setting and a different grammar, pronunciation, and vocabulary among nonacademic peer groups and among friends back home.

5. The design feature of displacement—the quality of referring to things and events out of sight and out of time—reaches its ultimate expression in writing systems, whereby people can displace their narratives to inform people far from the original point of action, and perhaps even many generations later. "Social tradition" takes on very powerful added meaning when it can all be written down, as in a political constitution or a last will and testament.

6. So powerful is the transmission of information through writing that the Cherokee genius, Sequoya, saw this feature of White people's technology as the key to their power and so decided that his people were helpless unless he created a similar system.

7. Ideas of how to do things, transformed into technical form, are the main stuff of which cultural evolution has been fashioned, and it can well be argued that the idea of effective writing (syllabary, alphabet, or other) still ranks as the technological invention that most transformed human lifeways. But that's not a fact—it's simply a topic for discussion.

Part
Four

The Material
Dimensions
of Adaptation:
Homo faber

From the body of that gemsbok the Bushmen had bailed out several bucketfuls of liquid, enough to supply them for almost a week. They cut the meat into strips which they would dry in the sun and use as they needed them, also enough for a week or perhaps even longer, as there were only a few people and the gemsbok was almost as big as a cow. (THOMAS, 1965:49)

It is the hunting way of life that has really molded man, to the extent of making him a large-brained biped, a tool making cooperative carnivore, and perhaps most important, a linguistic creature. (PILBEAM, 1972:4)

Our ancestors began to hunt animals for food perhaps as early as 3 million years ago. Those ancient hunters, in East Africa and elsewhere, were probably able to kill only young, small animals, in addition to which they may have scavenged some meat from the kills of other animals. Over the millennia human hunting skills and equipment were refined and developed to the point where Ice Age hunters were more than a match for the huge mammoths, mastodons, and other large and fierce game. The hunting-gathering mode of food getting has contributed significantly to shaping fundamental aspects of "human nature," and it is therefore important for us to review the main features of this way of life.

The evidence we have to work with comes from two main sources: (1) the archaeological record of bygone times and (2) data from modern hunting-gathering peoples recorded by nineteenth- and twentieth-century ethnographers. Fortunately, anthropologists have had the opportunity to study a number of such societies in considerable detail. There are, for example, a number of excellent studies of Inuit communities, as well as a great deal of information concerning the !Kung Bushmen of the Kalahari Desert in South Africa. In a recent review John M. Whiting reports finding data on seventy-four societies in which subsistence is or was recently more than 75 percent dependent on hunting, gathering, and fishing. This number is surprising considering that less than .001 percent of the people living today are hunter-gatherers.

Today hunting-gathering peoples are found, for the most part, in very marginal areas in which food production through plant and animal DOMESTICATION is not easily achieved. For example, the desert areas of Australia and the Kalahari have pro-

Survival Without Crops: The Hunting-Gathering Way of Life

10.1 Tasadai girl gathering fruit in the Philippine tropics. At the time of their recent discovery, the Tasadai made their living from food gathering. (John Nance, Magnum)

vided territories not easily reached by plow and not yet overwhelmed by cattle herders and sheepmen. "Arctic deserts" are another type of area that have been beyond the reach of agricultural peoples until quite recently. A third kind of environment is that of the tropical jungles. The Pygmies of the Congo Basin, some marginal groups in the Amazon basin, and people like the Semang of the Malay Peninsula are examples of these jungle dwellers.

We cannot assume that any contemporary groups represent a way of life that is "the same as" that of 20,000 or 200,000 years ago. *All* of the hunting-gathering societies that have persisted into recent times have, to a greater or lesser extent, been influenced by the cultural ways (perhaps especially the predatory ways) of their settled, food-producing neighbors. So our analysis of the characteristics of these latter-day hunting-gathering peoples must accept them for what they are—a number of small populations who have managed to maintain themselves in a foraging way of life. The study of the similarities and variations among these peoples can permit us to make some guarded hypotheses concerning the limits of variation and the range of probabilities of cultural patterning characteristic of our evolutionary past.

10.2 **Australian hunter with spear thrower. (Courtesy of the American Museum of Natural History)**

10.3 **Approximate areas of hunter-gatherer (including fishing) peoples before the spread of European conquest. People living in the unshaded areas had subsistence economies based on various combinations of domestic plants and animals.**

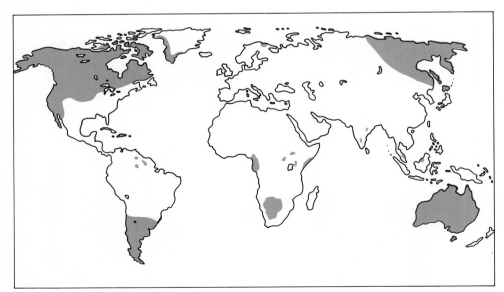

The Material Dimensions of Adaptation: Homo faber

Table 10.1: Population Densities in Some Hunting-Gathering Societies

Society	Density of Population
Australian Aboriginies	
Favorable areas	One person per two sq. miles
Unfavorable areas	One person per 30–40 sq. miles
!Kung Bushmen	One person per 18 sq. miles
Inuit (Eskimo)	One person per 30–35 sq. miles
Shoshone (Great Basin)	One person per 20–30 sq. miles

Small Nomadic Bands

Although there are a few exceptions, hunting-gathering peoples have usually had to move from place to place several times a year in their search for food and water. The movements of nomadic hunters are not, however, random wanderings about the landscape. Usually their movements are quite regular and planned in relation to seasonal changes in the locations of game, vegetable foods, and other supplies. Some special times of the year may have presented enough riches of food so that the nomads could settle down for several weeks, as in the time of pine nut harvesting in the American Southwest and the coming of the spring caribou herds in some parts of the Arctic. Other seasons require more frequent moves, as the available food supplies are sparse and elusive. Related to this adaptation of nomadism is the fact that the primary face-to-face community (the BAND) usually numbers no more than forty to sixty persons. In the seventy-four cases reviewed by Whiting, only 24 percent maintained groups larger than a hundred.

The small nomadic bands of hunter-gatherers tend to be very thinly settled on the land, and population densities are often considerably less than one person per square mile. Table 10.1 shows the estimated population densities for various hunter-gatherer groups. Although these estimates are certainly subject to error, it is important to stress that encounters with other persons—especially strangers—in the course of the day's activity are very much less frequent in a hunting and gathering way of life than in practically all food-producing societies. The contrast with modern, urbanized living is overwhelming.

No Way to Monopolize the Means of Production

The "means of production" among hunter-gatherers consists mainly of human skills (including cooperative skills) in killing animals, catching fish, and finding roots, nuts, and other vegetable foods, and in fashioning tools, weapons, containers, and other items from wood, stone, bone, and assorted locally available materials. A particularly important feature of the hunting-gathering way of life is that most of the food and other scarce resources are thinly spread in unpredictable arrays across the

10.4 **Arunta hunter with boomerang. (Courtesy of the American Museum of Natural History)**

195

landscape and can be exploited only through the skill and perseverance of individuals and small groups. Since the location of game and other food supplies is not easily predictable and, in many cases, water supplies and other scarce resources are also changeable, there is generally no way for individuals or groups of individuals to exercise long-term monopolistic control or ownership over these supplies. In some cases, though, rich vegetable food sources, like groves of nut trees in Bushman territory, are "owned" by bands.)

Julian Steward has provided a most interesting analysis of food resources and human population among the aboriginal Shoshone of the Great Basin (Utah, Nevada, eastern California, and adjacent areas). A main staple food of the Shoshone and their

10.5 A stone axe like this one can be hafted and made ready for use in less than twenty minutes. (John Nance, Magnum)

neighbors was the pine nut crop from the tree *Pinus monophylla.* As many organic food enthusiasts know, pine nuts are rich in protein and other nutrients, and in most years they are found in abundance in the pine groves in the upland areas of the Basin. However, in any given year some groves have pine nuts in abundance; others are barren. The small bands of Shoshone who inhabited these areas could never depend on any of the groves for a guaranteed supply. Rather, each year they scouted anew for these elusive food supplies. Steward reports that rabbits, too, were available in abundance in certain valleys to which groups of Shoshone came for rabbit drives. Since the cooperative rabbit drive was usually a highly successful team effort, the rabbit "crop" was severely decimated after each such drive, so the locations of drives shifted from year to year. Cooperative antelope drives displayed the same pattern.

From Steward's analysis, it appears that any effective localized control or monopoly over these food supplies was impossible. Hence the pattern of organization among the Shoshone was that small groups, varying from single families or pairs of families to larger aggregates that came together in varied combinations for rabbit drives, antelope hunts, and pine nut gathering and dispersed in a constantly varying, kaleidoscopic fashion—in unending adjustment to the environment. (Steward, 1955)

Flexibility: The Primary Design Feature of Hunting Ways of Life

Many popular descriptions of non-Western peoples have given the impression that the technologically simpler peoples of the world have been uniformly docile servants of their cultural traditions, unthinkingly following the wisdom handed down by their grandparents. Such a characterization of so-called primitive peoples is a generally false and insulting one and appears to be especially wide of the mark when applied to hunting and gathering peoples. The facts of life of hunting-gathering appear to require a great amount of self-reliance from every individual. In part it is simply a matter of numbers: the individual hunter, fisherman, or collector cannot expect that there will always be people around to help when he or she runs into problems. Decisions must often be made alone; unforeseen circum-

The Material Dimensions of Adaptation: Homo faber

10.6 This painting in a Spanish cave may be the oldest evidence of use of bows and arrows (probably late Pleistocene). Reprinted from *Prehistoric Europe: The Economic Basis* by J. G. D. Clark with the permission of the publishers, Stanford University Press, and Associated Book Publishers Ltd. Copyright 1952 by J. G. D. Clark.

stances must be resolved with no help from "the gang back home." Nelson has made this point quite clearly with regard to patterns of adaptation among the Inuit:

In situations where needed materials are not at hand, one must attempt to push his imagination beyond its usual limits. Outsiders often do not see an obvious solution as a feasible one, because they simply assume that it is impossible to deviate so far from convention with any hope of success, or they resign themselves that the situation is hopeless. An Eskimo will never do this. A familiar example from the literature is making an emergency sled from pieces of frozen meat. When the cross-hairs of a telescopic sight are broken, they can be replaced on the spot with thin strands of dental floss (which is carried for sewing), or when a hole is torn in the skin cover of a boat, a small board can be quickly nailed over it as an effective repair. Non-essential pieces taken from other equipment are often used for improvisation. An iron rod from the grid of a camp stove can be removed and used to clear the barrel of a jammed rifle, or shaped into a serviceable gaff hook. One who has not grown up to think in this way will not equal the Eskimos, but it is easy

to improve one's own ability markedly by forgetting about conventional solutions and allowing one's inventive imagination greater freedom. (NELSON, 1969:378)

The importance of flexibility in individual behavior, so necessary for successful hunting and foraging activities (as compared with the more routinized work of cultivators, for example), is underscored by the great flexibility of membership, as well as in the size and composition of local groups. Colin Turnbull has described "the importance of *flux*" for the Mbuti Pygmies of the northeastern Congo. He notes that they are

able to maintain a fluid band composition, a loose form of social structure, and to utilize flux as a highly effective social mechanism . . . [with] constant changeover of personnel between local groups and the frequent shifts of campsites through the seasons. This apparent instability is, in fact, the very mechanism that gives . . . [Mbuti society] . . . cohesion. (TURNBULL, 1969:132)

The flexibility of hunting and gathering societies is partially a reflection of the weekly and seasonal changes in availability of food. There are, however, additional factors. One of the main ways of resolving conflict among such groups is avoidance: one or the other party to a dispute leaves the group to join a different band. If entire families are in conflict, the kin groups may split up into separate bands until tensions are forgotten or resolved.

Among the Mbuti:

The focal point of the process is the honey season, during which the net hunters spread out into fragmented sub-bands, sometimes uniting siblings, sometimes dividing them, but always separating antagonistic elements. At the end of the honey season, the band begins to reform, carefully avoiding any lines of fricture that remain unhealed. The net hunters normally form bands larger than those of the archers, for a net hunt demands cooperation between a minimum of six or seven nuclear families, and allows a maximum of thirty. The honey season, they say, is a time of such plenty that the game can easily be caught by hand and there is no need for the large cooperative net-hunt. During the previous ten months, the necessity of constant cooperation, and the proximity and intimacy in which all band members must live with one another, invariably gives rise to numerous latent antagonisms

Survival Without Crops: The Hunting-Gathering Way of Life

10.7 Bushman women filling ostrich eggs for carrying water supplies. Kalahari Desert of South Africa. (Courtesy of the American Museum of Natural History)

and even a few open hostilities. If hostilities were to go unchecked, it would destroy the essential unity of the band and consequently ruin the success of the hunt. Thus, the honey season is an important safety valve, allowing for the radical reconstitution of face-to-face groups. (TURNBULL, 1969:135)

Generally there are no political obstacles of authoritarian headmen, boundary-maintaining policemen, or other "officials" that would screen or interrupt an individual's free movement from one band to another. It is especially striking to note that in many hunting-gathering societies, individuals are not powerfully constrained by kin group membership in their choice of living groups. Contrary to impressions given in many earlier ethnographic descriptions, hunting and gathering peoples are apparently very loosely bound by ties to particular kin. Kin ties are important in establishing one's relationships to a particular local group, but each individual usually has kinsmen on "father's side" and on "mother's side" in a number of different bands. In addition, for a married person the spouse has an additional network of kinsmen to whom a married couple may turn if they decide to shift their residential allegiances.

The flexibility of social organization in many hunting-gathering groups is clearly adaptive in many ways and reflects a close relationship with the physical environment. In the Shoshone example the size of local groups was adjusted quickly and effectively, throughout the seasons, to available food resources and the types of cooperation needed to get those foods. In times when group cooperation could gain a fine harvest (e.g., in the rabbit drive or antelope hunt), then more people got together. At other times, when available foods were best obtained through individual efforts, the people spread out very thinly in small family clusters to maximize the food-getting possibilities. Not all hunting and gathering groups have had such flexibility of social organization. Among the Australian aboriginal peoples, for example, social alignments appear to have been more fixed and responsibilities to particular kinsmen more exacting.

The flexibility of group membership and individual activity has far-reaching consequences for other aspects of the hunting-gathering way of life. The following points may be kept in mind as likely consequences of this flexibility, though their application may vary from one group to another:

1. There can be very little authoritarianism of leadership in a group in which membership is so voluntary and control of productive activity so individualized. In fact, in many groups leaders have

The Material Dimensions of Adaptation: Homo faber

been described as men or women whose behavioral examples were often followed and their advice heeded, in spite of the fact that they possess no authority to "command" another person to act.

2. Although there are no rulers, judges, courts, or policemen, individual antisocial troublemakers become quickly known "through the grapevine" to everyone in the region. There is no place to hide. A wrong doer may find sanctuary in a different band, but if he does not mend his ways he will be considered *persona non grata* among all of his people. If he is considered dangerous, the more influential members of the band may have to take action, and the most effective action is for someone to kill the "criminal." Such a proceeding runs the risk of exciting the anger of kinsmen of the "defendant," so the organization of public opinion in such cases usually requires that some understanding be reached with the culprit's nearest relatives.

3. Where property cannot easily be monopolized, and an individual can shift membership from group to group, inheritance is of little consequence. When a person dies, his worldly possessions may be destroyed so that their "souls" may accompany him to whatever happens in the hereafter; or the person's few possessions may be distributed—often to people who are not even close kin.

4. When we recognize that the exercise of authority by one person over another is extremely rare,

we should not be surprised that such areas of morality as sexual codes would tend to be quite flexible as compared to the more "puritanical" tendencies in complex societies. Premarital sexual freedom is the general practice among hunting and gathering groups, and adultery, easy divorce and separation, and other flexibilities of marriage and sexual relationships are typical.

Although sexual behavior tends toward a good deal of freedom, sexual conflicts are nonetheless among the prominent reasons for fighting and feuding. In many hunting and gathering groups conflict over sexual partners is the main reason for intergroup hostilities, as quarrels over economic assets are usually pointless.

5. Sexual division of labor, plus the more obvious differences of behavior associated with differences in age, make up the only significant specializations among most groups.

This is not to say that the lines of sexual division of labor are always strict. Like everything else in the hunting and gathering way of life, flexibility is the order of the day. There are always occasions when women join in hunting and when men engage in activities usually carried out by women. In reading the ethnographic accounts one gets the impression that with hunting-gathering peoples the mere symbolism of sex-typed roles must often give way to practical, adaptive action.

199

Survival Without Crops: The Hunting-Gathering Way of Life

10.9 Kamloops Indian woman gathering roots with a digging stick. British Columbia. (Courtesy of the American Museum of Natural History)

The phrase "hunting and gathering" is applied here to a wide variety of societies, some of which have been quite specialized toward hunting (e.g., Inuit and the Upper Palaeolithic hunters of Western Europe), whereas others, like the Shoshone, the Paliyan of India, and some California Indian peoples, depended much more on collecting than on hunting. A third variety, of course, is the cultural system oriented mainly toward fishing and hunting sea mammals. The people of the Pacific Northwest Coast are examples of this third type.

Sedentary Hunter-Gatherers

Food resources and other materials are unevenly distributed in the world. The Near East, for example, seems to have been an area with unusual abundance in pre-agricultural times, permitting an almost fully SEDENTARY life in some areas. The Indians of the Northwest coast of North America occupied another such region of plenty, although their maritime food resources were not always consistent and predict-able. Similar areas of abundance, especially in sheltered coastal waters like the islands of Japan and some favorable locations around Denmark and Great Britain in the North Sea region, may have allowed a density of population, with periods of leisure based on stored food supplies, that permitted greater complexity of social organization, experimentation with invidious social inequalities, and that special human luxury, warfare. People who grow no domesticated foods usually cannot spend the whole annual cycle tied down to a single geographic location, but there can be a lot of politics, ceremonialism, and fun during the weeks and months when stored foods are plentiful.

The Kwakiutl of Pacific Northwest Coast: Sedentary Hunters and Gatherers

The habitat of the Kwakiutl in southwest British Columbia is a rugged coastline with many small islands and steep, rugged mountains in the background. The traditional communities of the Kwakiutl were located in narrow inlets, where boats and people were protected from the rougher coastal waters and where the mountains protected the houses from the sharp force of winds, rain, and winter storms. The warming influence of the Japanese Current, flowing up from the South Pacific, makes the climate relatively mild with little seasonal change, but it also brings heavy rainfall throughout much of the year. The average annual rainfall is well over a hundred inches a year. Coastal vegetation is rich with giant fir, cedar, and spruce, beneath which the forest floor is covered with ferns, mosses, and other moisture-loving plants. In some areas this vegetable environment is a kind of northern temperate jungle.

But the land environment was perhaps less important for the Kwakiutl and their neighbors than the coastal waters with their abundance of food resources. Each year millions of salmon appeared in the in-shore waters for their migration to spawning areas. A variety of smaller fish, including candlefish, herring, and smelt, also spawned along these shores. Mussels, clams, sea urchins, crabs, and other forms of shore-dwelling food supplies supplemented the Kwakiutl diet. Out in the deeper waters the hair seals, porpoises, sea otters, and other marine animals contributed to the abundance of the region.

The Material Dimensions of Adaptation: Homo faber

There were also land animals, including deer, elk, and mountain goat. The Indians had direct competition for some of these food supplies, for wolves, black bears, grizzly bears, and other carnivores (including the mountain lion) preyed on these same high-protein foods.

Even today the Pacific Northwest Coast region is not particularly good for crop growing (except in a few especially favorable valleys and pockets of coastal plain), so the well-endowed aboriginal Indian groups would have gained little from adoption of plant and animal domestication.

In response to the abundant food resources of the region, the Kwakiutl and their neighbors developed a complex technology—especially for spearing and trapping the larger sea creatures. They had several types of harpoons, nets, and traps. Fish weirs were constructed in small streams to divert fish into spots where they could be easily harpooned, netted, or trapped. There were dip nets, gill nets, and sometimes long sweep seines. Long, tubular nets were used to capture candlefish, and a somewhat similar device was used for herring.

In the hunt for sea mammals they had a variety of harpoons with attached lines that prevented the quarry from escaping once it was speared. Use of this equipment depended on the large sea-going canoes carved from huge red cedar trees. Their boat makers were equipped with adzes, hammers and nails, drills, chisels, wedges, and a variety of knives.

Their principal wood-carving tool, the adze, was usually of jadeite, shell (of a deep-water clam), or horn, but some iron was available for tools long before the coming of White people to the region.

In addition to the canoes, which were sometimes large enough to carry thirty to fifty seafarers, the elaborate wood-carving technology of the Northwest Coast people was particularly evident in their houses. To protect themselves from storms and frequent rain and to reflect the social prestige of various kin groups, they built large, rectangular plank houses that were sometimes a hundred feet or more in length. The heavy weight of the planks was borne by massive timbers—demonstrating both high technical skill and spare time for complex constructions.

Areas of population concentration among the Nootka, Kwakiutl, and their neighbors may have had at least one person per square mile, perhaps ten to twenty times the population densities of fully nomadic groups. Although the magnificence of their houses gives us the impression that the Northwest Coast Indians were completely sedentary, their villages were generally seasonal headquarters, occupied mainly during the winter ceremonial and social season. During other parts of the year the various kinship groups scattered out to their fishing locations, inland hunting sites, and other food-getting areas. The concentrations of population during the winter season were made possible by the fact that they were able to preserve and *store* (e.g., in wooden

10.10 Northwest Pacific Coast village with totem poles. Queen Charlotte Island, British Columbia. (Courtesy of the American Museum of Natural History)

201

boxes) relatively large quantities of food during the months of abundance.

What is especially significant is that the ecological situation of the Northwest Coast peoples made possible quite clear definition of property in the form of lands, fishing sites, and man-made possessions such as houses and canoes. The lands and goods were owned, however, not by individuals or NUCLEAR FAMILIES, but by the larger extended kin groupings. Membership in these local groups implied participation in a complex display of social management, including warfare, administration of justice, and the colorful round of winter rituals.

Wealth was a very important concern of these people, giving their way of life a tone much different from the general run of relatively propertyless and egalitarian hunter-gatherers. Not only did the Northwest Coast peoples have complex forms of

wealth, but the members of local groups were ranked in terms of their degree of nobility and general social excellence. Each individual was accorded a unique position in the scale from highest to lowest, and no two persons were exactly social equals, except the slaves, who were not considered to be members of the local group.

An individual's social STATUS was determined to a very considerable extent by inheritance, which could be both from one's father and from one's mother. RANK and privileges were also conferred through adoption. From one's father (and sometimes from one's mother) an individual inherited the rights to certain songs, the use of particular ceremonial designs and masks, and socially recognized names, as well as the rights to perform in symbolically important ceremonies. These rights, however, had to be validated and verified through impressive public displays of feasting, conspicuous waste and consumption, and exchanges of property with other persons, all of which made up the system known widely as the POTLATCH.

10.11 Potlatch scene in which the speaker is representing the chief (seated behind the blankets) who is giving away the pile. Fort Rupert, British Columbia. (Courtesy of the American Museum of Natural History)

To put on a successful potlatch feast, an individual had to have support from his kinsmen, and some of this support certainly depended on his record of generosity to kin and other people. Furthermore, astute "wheeling and dealing" in a debt and credit system affected people's abilities to accumulate the food and goods for a significant wealth display. Potlatches were an important social institution among all of the groups from the Tlingit and the Tsimshian in Alaska, down the coast of British Columbia, to the Indians around the coasts of Washington and Oregon. Powerful rival chiefs sometimes destroyed large amounts of property, especially canoes and blankets. The Kwakiutl, the Haida, and other Northwest Coast peoples had ceremonial "coppers," hammered out of the costly metal in a shape something like a combination shield and medallion. The height of reckless potlatch competition was reached when a chief would break or chop up a "copper" or throw it into the sea.

When the potlatching ceremonial was first popularized in ethnographic literature, it was considered an example of "anti-economic" behavior among non-Western peoples. However, further analysis makes it appear that the socioeconomic system of the Northwest Coast peoples made good sense, in an earlier day, in relation to the boom-or-bust economy. Natural fluctuations in plant and animal populations produced a situation of alternating abundance and scarcity. The potlatch, with its feasts and exchange of items, served to redistribute scarce goods among the people—from the "haves" to the "have nots."

Slavery is so uncommon among hunting and gathering peoples that its presence among the Northwest Coast groups deserves a note. Slaves were usually captured in warfare, though in some areas the failure to pay damages for some offense could lead to slavery. Normally an individual captured in warfare could expect to be ransomed by his kin group, unless they were economically destitute. However, long-range raiding sometimes netted captives who were so far from home that their kin groups could make no contact with them. Possession of slaves was socially significant both as evidence of war-making powers and as a mark of wealth. There were not large numbers of slaves in those Northwest Coast groups, and their economic importance was probably not great. They generally carried out housekeeping chores and other work alongside their masters.

The Variable Food Supplies of Hunter-Gatherers

One of the major misconceptions about hunting societies is the idea that their diets consist mainly of meat. It's true that the most highly publicized of all hunter groups, the Inuit, have maintained a food

10.12 Andaman Islander shooting fish. (Courtesy of the American Museum of Natural History)

Survival Without Crops: The Hunting-Gathering Way of Life

system that is undoubtedly the world's champion in high fat-and-cholesterol animal diet. Maritime peoples, like the Kwakiutl and other Northwest Coast Indians, also have generally had a very high proportion of meat and fish in their regular food intake. On the whole, however, the common pattern, especially in warmer regions, is more like that of the Bushmen of South Africa, the Australian Aborigines, and the Hadza of East Africa: 60 to 80 percent of their daily food intake is from roots, berries, nuts, and other vegetable materials, and only perhaps 20 to 40 percent (variable with the seasons) is in the form of meat and other products of the hunt.

The Shoshone and Paiute peoples of the Western Great Basin region had less big game than did most other hunting peoples of either the Old or New Worlds. Their major staple was the pine nut, but they also gathered many roots, seeds, berries, and greens in season. In some areas they got fish from the interior rivers, but the scarcity of game animals (e.g., antelope and deer) led them to utilize many small animals, as well as some insects, for protein foods.

The mixed diet of most hunting-gathering groups has been a major reason for their adaptive success— "success" because, as more than one writer has put it, hunter-gatherers may be considered the original "affluent societies." Contrary to the image of hunters constantly on the go, half-starved, and worried about where the next mouthful is coming from, Richard Lee has demonstrated that modern !Kung Bushmen (men and women), for example, need spend an average of *only about twenty hours per week* in the food quest. The same sort of working schedule applies to the Hadza of East Africa and some recently studied aboriginal groups in Australia. Much of the time people are to be found loafing around the camp. Hadza males spend a great deal of time in a gambling game, only occasionally picking up their bows and arrows for expeditions to look for game. Their hunts, moreover, are usually unsuccessful! Meanwhile the gathering of plant foods is quite productive and predictable, so there is generally no fear of starvation.

The meat from hunting is, of course, a highly important part of the diet even when it constitutes only about one fourth of the average food intake.

This is a major source of protein and other nutrients essential for adequate nutrition. Richard Lee made careful estimates of the dietary intake of the !Kung Bushmen and found that their average daily intake was about 2,140 calories and included 93 grams of protein, which is well above estimated minimum daily requirements. Thus people like the Bushmen not only need work rather short hours per week— they eat quite well indeed. Many peasant peoples would certainly envy them their leisure time!

The affluence of these hunter-gatherers is in leisure time and social freedom rather than in material goods. No social system has successfully promised *both* leisure and material affluence for everyone, at least not for long.

Observations on the Hunter-Gatherer Way of Life: Summary Comments

1. Because hunter-gatherers do not till the soil, build large houses, or make other large-scale modifications of their environment, their ways of life are more directly geared to the physical characteristics of the landscape (water, animals, vegetation, and so on) than is true of more complex societies.

2. Individual Bushmen, Inuit, and other hunter-gatherers must have a very well-developed knowledge of the flora and fauna, physical geography, weather, and other environmental features in order to ensure survival.

3. The fact that they do little to transform their natural environments through permanent settlement means also that they exert less fixed control, including property rights, than do food-producing peoples.

4. The near absence of fixed, monopolizable property results in social organizations that are, on the whole, egalitarian.

5. Individualism and social flexibility have been characteristic of many hunting-gathering societies, mainly because of the need for ready adjustments to the variable demands and resources of their environments.

6. Although some hunter-gatherer groups occasionally face grave problems of food shortage, many of them maintain good diets, with spare time for recreation, storytelling, and other enjoyments of life.

204

The archaeological evidence thus far accumulated indicates that the DOMESTICATION of plants and animals was begun perhaps ten thousand to twelve thousand years ago. This portentous change in human culture was achieved by *Homo sapiens* whose physical and mental equipment were not different from those of modern humans. All the significant features of human biological evolution had occurred many thousands of years before the rise of food production. There are two important points here that must be underlined:

1. The biological evolution of *Homo sapiens* was, for all practical purposes, accomplished while humans were hunter-gatherers. Thus, our "human nature" is basically that of a hunting-gathering animal, living in small, usually nomadic, low-density groups.

2. The immense variety of lifeways developed among humans during the past ten thousand to twelve thousand years appear to be largely cultural developments of people with essentially similar *biological capacities*. All of the differences among recent human societies are the result of differences in cultural histories and developments and are *not* due to genetic, biological differences.

If genetically inherited physical and mental capacities do not account for the differences in behavior and life style of hunter-gatherers, peasant plowmen, and modern suburbanites, then how can these differences be explained? First we should go back to the point made in the preceding chapter—that one of the most important features developed during the hunting-gathering way of life was *adaptive flexibility*. With that behavioral flexibility in mind, we can examine something of the information concerning the first steps toward food domestication and the first drift toward complex, sedentary social systems.

In the period of fifteen thousand to ten thousand years ago, as the last glacial ice disappeared from Europe and North America, large-scale climate changes in these regions brought about greatly altered ecological conditions to which humans had to adapt. In some areas, big-game–hunting techniques were rendered obsolete by the disappearance of the mastodon, the mammoth, the woolly rhinoceros, and other large animals. Either the hunting techniques were so effective that they wiped out the big animals or else the changes in climate went beyond the adaptive range of the great beasts. At the same time, the great herds of wild reindeer retreated

The Domestication of Plants and Animals

11

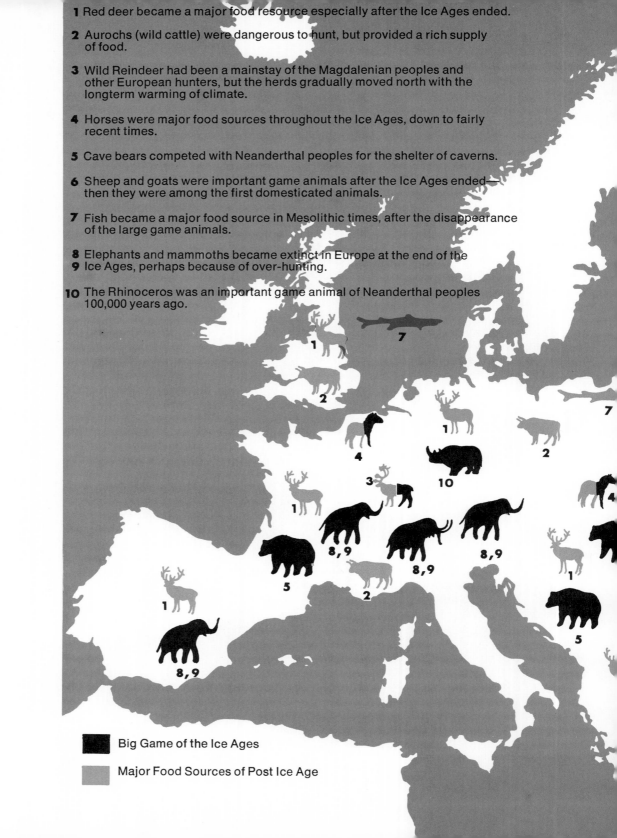

1 Red deer became a major food resource especially after the Ice Ages ended.

2 Aurochs (wild cattle) were dangerous to hunt, but provided a rich supply of food.

3 Wild Reindeer had been a mainstay of the Magdalenian peoples and other European hunters, but the herds gradually moved north with the longterm warming of climate.

4 Horses were major food sources throughout the Ice Ages, down to fairly recent times.

5 Cave bears competed with Neanderthal peoples for the shelter of caverns.

6 Sheep and goats were important game animals after the Ice Ages ended— then they were among the first domesticated animals.

7 Fish became a major food source in Mesolithic times, after the disappearance of the large game animals.

8 Elephants and mammoths became extinct in Europe at the end of the
9 Ice Ages, perhaps because of over-hunting.

10 The Rhinoceros was an important game animal of Neanderthal peoples 100,000 years ago.

Big Game of the Ice Ages

Major Food Sources of Post Ice Age

11.1 Changes in main food animals hunted by peoples of Europe in the later part of the Ice Age and after. Large game animals, like the mammoth and the elephant, became extinct near the end of the Pleistocene, possibly because of overhunting. In the final phase of the Pleistocene, the reindeer was an important game animal, along with the horse. In Mesolithic times fishing became a major food source. Red deer, auroch, and other animals were hunted.

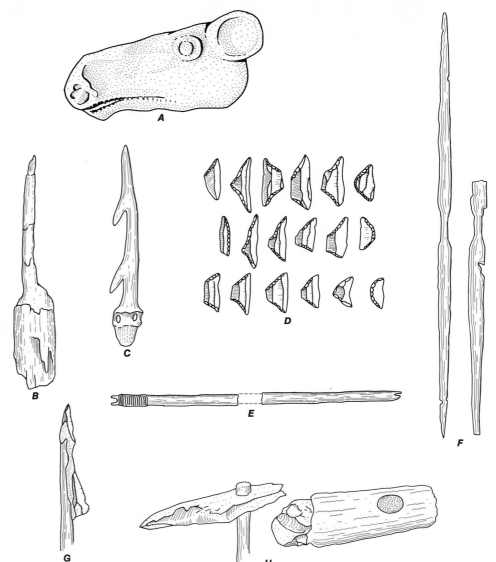

11.2 Some items from the technical inventory of Mesolithic peoples. A. Stone mace head from Finland. B. Wooden paddle found in North Germany is evidence of use of boats. C. Bone harpoon head from Sweden. D. Microliths (small flakes of flint and other stone) were used in a wide variety of projectiles and cutting implements. Note the similarity of the microliths from Star Carr, England (first row), Spain (second row), and Jarmo, Iraq. E. Arrow shaft from Denmark. F. Wooden bows found in Holmegaard, Denmark. G. Arrow tip with microlith from Sweden. H. Elk antler mattock from Star Carr and adze head mounted on elk antler from Denmark.

toward the north, leaving the plains of Europe to game animals with different habits and characteristics.

The period of time after the end of the Pleistocene and before the advent of earliest food production in the Near East saw a variety of different local adaptations of peoples to the changed climate, vegetation, and animal life. In many parts of Northern and Central Europe, hunter-gatherers settled around lakes and rivers, as well as along the ocean shore, where they developed a heavy reliance on fish and other aquatic life. In many places it was possible to make a good living from a combination of hunting (deer, wild pigs, elk, and birds) plus the regular harvests from nets, weirs, and other fishing equipment. The remains of an ancient fish net, estimated to be six thousand to eight thousand years old, have

208

The Material Dimensions of Adaptation: Homo faber

been found in a clay deposit in an area near Lake Ladoga (now in the USSR), and constitute material evidence of this new kind of human adaptation.

The distinctive tool equipment of the postglacial hunter-fisher-gatherers includes many small flakes of stone, often as sharp "teeth" imbedded in the cutting edges of harpoons, knives, arrows, and "sickles." The bow and arrow was invented sometime in this period, and there is also archaeological evidence of boats, complex harpoons, and other refined equipment.

Hunter-gathers throughout Europe undoubtedly used a good deal of wood and bone for their cultural equipment, but usually there are no remains of these materials preserved in archaeological sites. However, under rather unusual circumstances, when wood and bone materials become covered over with clay deposits at lake-shore or sea-shore locations, even wood and bark have occasionally been preserved from human living sites several thousand years old. Starr Carr, near the east coast of England, is one of these remarkable archaeological finds where such materials have been discovered. It was apparently occupied about 7500 B.C. by a small group of coastal hunter-gatherers. There are abundant remains of birch bark, as well as the bones of the fish and animals these people hunted. Red deer were a major food source, and the Starr Carr people apparently practiced a sort of herd conservation, for the kills are mostly males. Starr Carr is also archaeologically important for the oldest Eurasian evidence of a domesticated dog. This, our children's best friend, became domesticated at least ninety-five hundred years ago. (Actually there is even older evidence of domestic dogs in the New World, from a place in Idaho that has been radio-carbon dated to 8400 B.C. [Higgs, 1973:4].)

Settlement, Villages, and Farming

Before continuing with information from the archaeological record about the rise of food-producing societies, we need to dispel some widely held myths about the "origins of civilization."

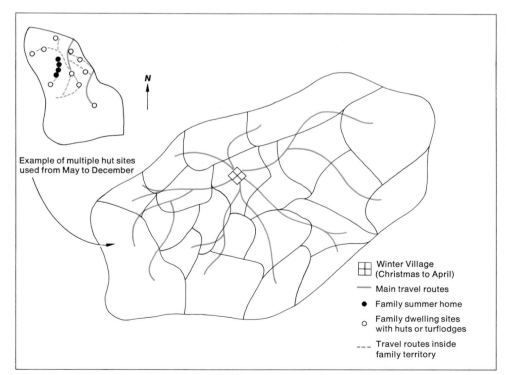

Example of multiple hut sites used from May to December

N

Winter Village (Christmas to April)

— Main travel routes

● Family summer home

○ Family dwelling sites with huts or turflodges

--- Travel routes inside family territory

11.3 Schematic map illustrating arrangement of Skolt Same family territories prior to World War II. Families had cabins or huts at the winter village but spent most of the year (May to December) herding their reindeer and fishing at locations in the individual territories. Each territory had a number of living sites for use in different seasons.

The Domestication of Plants and Animals

1. It is not correct to say that "food production made it possible for people to settle down in villages." In especially favored locations people have maintained settled villages without cultivating crops or keeping domestic animals. The Indian people of the Pacific Northwest, for example, were in such a well-endowed area that their hunting of sea and land mammals, plus extensive fishing, made possible the maintenance of fairly considerable population density, and the people lived in large, well-built houses. (See pp. 200–203.)

2. The presence of clusters of houses, which we call villages, does not mean always that people live in them on a year-round basis. The Skolt people of Finland, for example, maintained a fishing and herding way of life during the nineteenth and early twentieth centuries that required seasonal movement throughout their territory, yet they maintained a winter village with substantial log cabins and outbuildings. The winter village was only occupied from the middle of December to late April, after which the families spread out to their spring calving and fishing locations for the rest of the year (cf. Nickul, 1948; Pelto, 1962). There are many other examples of peoples who *seem* to have sedentary villages but in actuality carry out considerable seasonal nomadism. This pattern must be kept in mind in the interpreting of prehistoric remains.

3. Crop growing does not absolutely require that people settle in villages. Many crop cultivators in Africa, for example, live scattered widely across the landscape in individual family homesteads. The same is true of many farming areas in Europe, and in much of Northern Europe farming spread into the more distant, marginal areas in scattered, one-family migrations, so that cultivated fields were widely spaced throughout the forest.

With these points in mind we can return to the archaeological record as it has thus far been put together in the Near East.

The Fertile Crescent: A Heartland of Food Domestication

Most anthropologists and historians believe that the earliest domestication of food resources, and hence the first steps toward population growth and complex social organization, occurred in the Near East in the region of the Tigris-Euphrates rivers. This area, from Palestine and Jordan to Turkey and Iran was rich in a number of wild grasses (ancestors of wheat and barley) and wild sheep, goats, and other animals. There is much archaeological evidence that the people living in the region some ten thousand to twelve thousand years ago were able to manage a semisedentary way of life, deriving part of their food from harvesting the abundant wild grains.

The plant scientist J. R. Harlan set out one day to test the possibilities of "making a living" from harvesting wild einkorn wheat and found that he could collect a kilogram in an hour. He calculated that a family of four persons would have harvested a metric ton in about three weeks, so that it would have been possible to support a fully sedentary life style based on harvesting wild grains.

The archaeological village sites in Palestine where these ancient harvesters lived have been given the label "Natufian." The remains in these villages, which probably housed twelve to twenty families on the average, include grinding stones, clay-lined storage pits, and flint-bladed sickles and knives with a PATINATION that suggests that they were used to cut grasses, most likely wild grain. The Natufian sites and other preagricultural living places probably began as base camps near areas of good wild stands of grain. From the base settlements hunters went out in pursuit of game, and they maintained seasonal hunting camps, often at considerable distances from the base settlements.

The characteristics of the preagricultural Natufian settlements of the Near East have been analyzed in detail by Kent Flannery in an attempt to develop hypotheses about the kinds of social organization that might have fitted with the hard materials and physical features dug up by the archaeologists. One of the important features of those earliest hamlets is that the dwellings are rather small and have a *circular* design. These semisubterranean huts might well have been intended as the quarters for one or two persons each, Flannery notes, and a cluster of such huts could well have been the home of a POLYGYNOUS EXTENDED FAMILY. Flannery's evidence for these ideas is derived from numerous examples of similar habitation patterns in Africa and elsewhere among peoples whose social organizations and family patterns have been described in ethnographic reports. (Flannery, 1972)

Michael Robbins (1966) has demonstrated statis-

210

tically that, on the whole, circular dewllings are most common among nomadic or *recently* nomadic peoples, whereas practically everywhere long-term sedentary housing tends to develop into larger, more rectangular architecture (at least until geodesic domes came along). This is partly because nomadic peoples are used to building huts or tents of skins, brush, or other impermanent materials, which are structurally most easily organized in a circular or oval pattern. As nomadic people settled down, they often started out by reproducing their circular tents or huts in the small-scale dwellings of wattle and daub, mud bricks, or stone. Many of these early houses were semisubterranean as an added protection against cold.

When people became more fully sedentary, and perhaps had need to develop more substantial houses, they discovered through trial and error that circular architectural design is fairly limiting as to size of dwellings. Larger multiroom, multifamily structures are easier to put up in a rectangular pattern. Figures 11.4 and 11.5 show the floor plans of dwellings in prehistoric villages in the Near East, illustrating the transition from the prefarming hamlet of Eynan to the small farming village of Jarmo.

Throughout much of the Near East, as elsewhere

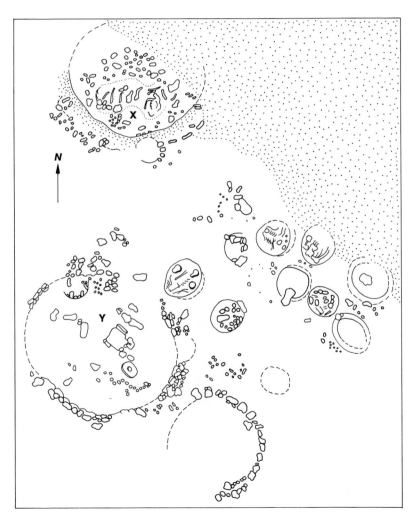

11.4 Diagram of portion of a Natufian (preagricultural) village at Eynan (Israel), with houses, storage pits, the grave of a special person (X), and a hearth (Y). Storage pits were often used for burying the dead. (Simplified from FLANNERY, 1972:34)

211

The Domestication of Plants and Animals

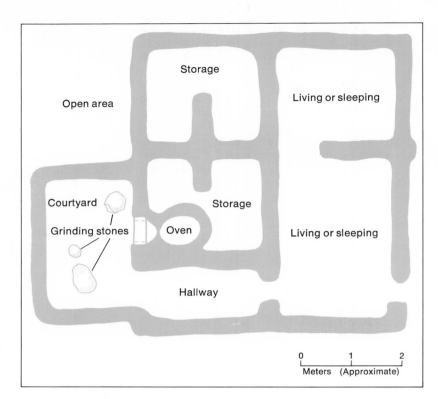

11.5 Diagram of rectangular house at Jarmo (Iraq). Jarmo was evidently quite sedentary, with domesticated plants and animals. The transition to fully sedentary life in many areas was accompanied by a change to larger, rectangular dwellings. (*Source:* FLAN-NERY 1972:42)

in the world, the transition from semisedentary to more fully settled living styles shows up in the archaeological record as a development to larger clusters of more clearly rectangular dwellings. These villages were established, and full-scale crop growing with domesticated varieties of wheat and barley had been developed, at least two thousand years before the beginnings of cities down in the fertile *lowlands* of the Tigris and Euphrates.

In Turkey, at a place called Cayönü Tepesi, the archaeologists Halet Cambel and Robert Braidwood uncovered a village dating from at least 7000 B.C. in which there are remains of stone architecture; signs of a primitive form of wheat; bones of domesticated dogs, sheep, pigs, and probably goats; and, most interesting of all, some objects made of copper that the excavators report as the oldest known examples of metal use (Cambel and Braidwood, 1970).

In the uplands of Iraq, Robert Braidwood and his colleagues excavated a village site called Jarmo

which dates from about 7000–6500 B.C. The village of Jarmo contained about two dozen mud-walled houses, with a total of perhaps 150 people. Domestic CEREALS included two-row barley (a very primitive form) and two different types of domesticated wheat. Goats, dogs, and possibly sheep were domesticated, but wild animals were also hunted, and a variety of nuts, acorns, and other wild foods contributed to the diet.

In both Jarmo and another farming village of the same age, farther to the southeast, there are numbers of small female figurines which the researchers interpret as "fertility goddesses" because the figurines often appear to be pregnant. A large variety of figurines and sculptures, as well as wall paintings, have also been found at other NEOLITHIC sites. They were usually found with the special structures that the excavators have identified as shrines. There are many evidences of a rich symbolic and religious culture in these early Neolithic communities.

212

The Transition from Wild Cereals to Domesticated Crops

The Near East, from the shores of the Mediterranean east to the Caspian Sea, was an especially favored area for the beginnings of cultivation because of the profusion of wild wheat and barley varieties, as well as other edible plants. The transition from gathering these wild grasses to the full-scale planting and cultivating of domestic crops was a gradual process, and data from archaeological excavations cannot pinpoint precisely when and where the change took place. Hans Helbaek (1959) has suggested some of the steps and some of the reasons that might have brought about this revolutionary change in human food-producing capabilities.

In the first place, wild wheat and barley generally drop their seeds quite easily, as the dried grains are loosened by the winds and rains. Some mutant plants, however, develop heads of grain that are resistant to such easy loss. Such genetic mutants were certainly among the harvest gathered by those Natufian foragers. Over time the grain harvesters

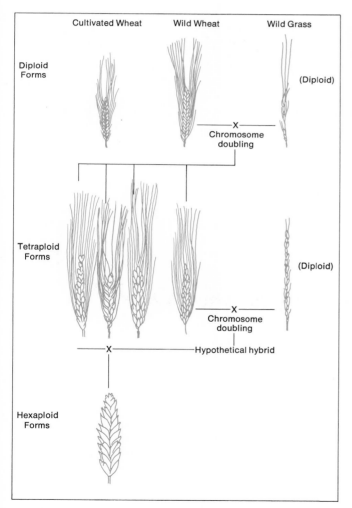

11.6 **Comparisons of cultivated and wild wheats and grasses. Cross breeding of the more primitive forms may have led to the evolution of modern (hexaploid) wheat varieties.**

213

might well have been selecting, accidently, the "hard-headed" seeds;[1] also, over time, quite a few of these seeds got scattered around their dwelling areas. The grain probably grew well in those spots where people left their excrement, garbage, and other waste materials. If, at some time, the harvesters decided to throw out a few extra handfuls of seed grains into the patches of grasses near their homes, Helbaek notes that they would very likely have sown a selection of seeds that included higher than usual proportions of the "hard-headed" varieties.

The early developments in plant domestication in the Near East apparently took place in the uplands and not in the fertile lowlands, which required a much more sophisticated system of agriculture—a later chapter in this story. As Kent Flannery points out, the hamlet-dwelling people, who were able to maintain a near-sedentary way of life from wild grains (plus hunting), had a definite stake in protecting and preserving their production places from intrusion from "foreigners." As their populations increased, so did their dependence on particular locations of abundant wild crops. Unlike the free-roaming game animals, the favorable patches of wheat and barley do not move about from year to year, so it was possible for the people to establish control and "property rights" over them, especially by maintaining their hamlets near the best "fields."

Continued dependence on particular favored locations may have been an important motivation for experimenting with improvements in the wild harvests and then the gradual development of regular reseeding operations to improve on nature's handiwork. From such reseeding, it's but a step further to establishing a full cycle of planting, tending, and reaping of the half-wild, half-domestic varieties of wheat and barley.

Plant Domestication in Other Parts of the Old World

The Near East is almost certainly *not* the only place where domestication of plants was developed,

nor is it without doubt the earliest place. Other areas may yet turn out to be earlier than the Near East as "cradles of food production," although there is much less archaeological data at present to evaluate the question of greater antiquity. From some sites in Thailand there are remains of domesticated peas and beans that have been dated (by radio-carbon technique) to earlier than 8000 B.C. In areas of Ethiopia, north China, and northern India, there are places where the wild cousins of modern domesticated plants grow in great variety, and some botanists and geographers have argued that these will turn out to be the heartlands of early domestication. We will have to wait for more archaeological evidence before these theories can move out of the realm of speculation.

It is evident, however, that some areas of the Old World developed food crops that were different enough from the mainstays of domesticated food production in the Near East, so that they may well have had quite independent origins. Rice, for example, was probably first cultivated in the Indonesian-Malaysian region, and the origin of domesticated root crops (including such foods as yams and taro) was probably somewhere in Southeast Asia (Chard, 1969). There is also evidence of an independent development of some food crops in West Africa.

From the initial centers of experimentation the idea of plant domestication spread in many directions. In the Near East upland cultivators improved their techniques and moved their production down the slopes into areas where the soil was more fertile and they could have better control of water supplies for their crops. It took more organization, more manpower, and a developed technological tool kit to transfer their grain-growing practices to the bottomlands of the Tigris and Euphrates rivers. By 4000 B.C. these valleys were becoming well settled with cultivators, and the first urban centers were coming into being.

By 2000 B.C. an agricultural complex that included wheat, millet, cattle, and sheep was developing in north China. Many prehistorians believe that the beginnings of food domestication in China derived from the spread of cultural ideas from the Near East, but the paths of the spread and conclusive evidence of this CULTURAL DIFFUSION have not been clearly demonstrated. The rise of a separate Chinese civilization more than thirty-five hundred years ago certainly received impetus from Southeast Asian food

---

[1] Wind, rain, and other natural events scatter the "loose-headed" grains, leaving higher proportions of the "hard heads" for the people to harvest.

The Material Dimensions of Adaptation: Homo faber

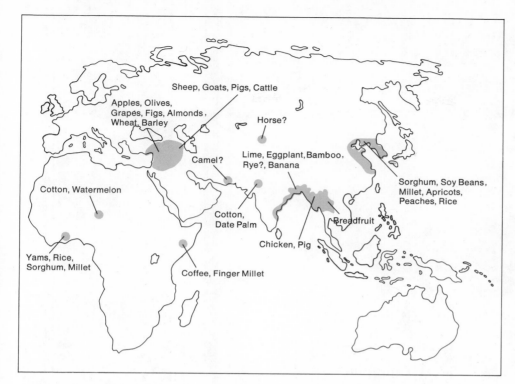

Sheep, Goats, Pigs, Cattle

Apples, Olives,
Grapes, Figs, Almonds,
Wheat, Barley

Horse?

Lime, Eggplant, Bamboo,
Rye?, Banana

Camel?

Cotton, Watermelon

Cotton,
Date Palm

Sorghum, Soy Beans,
Millet, Apricots,
Peaches, Rice

Breadfruit

Chicken, Pig

Yams, Rice,
Sorghum, Millet

Coffee, Finger Millet

11.7 Major early centers of plant and animal domestication (shaded areas). Archaeological and botanical/zoological evidence indicates that several different parts of the Old World may have developed food domestication systems independently. Many of the locations of first domestication of the various plants and animals are somewhat speculative.

technology (e.g., rice, Asian pigs, and chickens), in addition to the items that may have spread from the Tigris-Euphrates region.

The spread of food production northward into Europe required some modifications to fit with the more difficult, or at least different, climatic features of these regions. In much of Europe there is a good deal more rainfall than in the Near East, and Europe was in those days covered with woodlands and undergrowth that left little room for profuse growth of natural grasses and grains. Land had to be cleared and the open areas wrested from woodland environments that were not always amenable to the growing of wheat and barley. Some of the "weeds" turned out to be hardier and more effective than the barley and wheat. Among these weeds were oats and rye. Wheat did not spread into Northern Europe until new varieties were developed; barley was more versatile; but rye and oats became the main cereals in many areas.

By about 4000 B.C. there were food cultivators living close to the North Sea in Northwestern Eu-

rope, and some had even crossed over into England. That was, however, at least three thousand years after plant cultivation was under way in places like the little village of Cayönü Tepesi in Turkey. Farming had reached Denmark by at least 3000 B.C. and, in the more southerly parts, perhaps by 3500 B.C. The spread into the cold north happened later than this, for it was not until about 1500 B.C. that settled or semisedentary farmers established themselves in the more favorable bottomlands of southern Sweden and Finland.

Domesticated animals were actually more important than cereal grains in the northward spread of cultivation. Early European farmers often burned off areas not for field crops but to provide pasturage for their cows, sheep, goats, and pigs. By the time farming was well under way, milking had developed, and it is rather hard to see how the whole farming complex could have penetrated the forests of the cold north if people had not been able to depend on milk products for an essential part of their food supplies (Sauer, 1969:98–99).

215

The Domestication of Plants and Animals

11.8 Rice paddies in Korea, showing intensive, irrigated food production. (René Burri, Magnum)

Domesticated Animals

When people began to improve the grasses and the vegetation around their base settlements, they naturally attracted some of the grass-eating animals. Some writers have argued that the lure of crops was the primary factor bringing sheep, goats, and other domesticable animals into close association with human groups.

Dogs were actually the first animals to be added to people's households, probably during Mesolithic times before any crop cultivation took place. Dogs were, no doubt, interested in all those bones that humans had around their hunting camps, and we can imagine that some people captured the cubs of wild dogs, just as people today sometimes capture and tame the cubs of wolves, lions, and other wild animals.

Evidence of domesticated food animals in the Eastern Mediterranean area presents a somewhat confused picture, since there is some indication that pigs and cattle may have been domesticated in Greece and adjacent areas before they were domesticated in the Near East. On the other hand, sheep and goats may have been domesticated first in the Near East (Iran) about 8000 B.C. The oldest evidence of domesticated cattle appears to be from Argissa-Magula (Greece) with radio-carbon dates of 7000 B.C. (Protsch and Berger, 1973).

Goats may have been among the very first food animals domesticated, for they are extremely versatile in their eating habits and other characteristics. In some areas people with no other domestic animals have kept at least a few goats. Goats have apparently held some sort of fascination for a long

The Material Dimensions of Adaptation: Homo faber

11.9 Pounding kafir corn in South Africa. (Courtesy of the American Museum of Natural History)

The Domestication of Plants and Animals

11.10 Reconstruction of a Neolithic village in Switzerland. (Courtesy of the American Museum of Natural History)

time—the god Pan is goatlike, the ritual fool or ritual loser as "the goat" is a very old idea in cultural history, and in Mediterranean cultures the use of goat symbolism for a husband victimized by adultery also has a considerable antiquity. The idea of a "scapegoat" is found, for example, in the Old Testament (Leviticus).

The ass was apparently first domesticated in Africa (in Nubia) and served as a beast of burden for people long before the horse and the camel came into the domestic scene. As Carl Sauer (1969:93) notes, "it is the original pack animal of the old civilizations and probably the earliest riding animal." Horses may have been domesticated first by noncultivator peoples of Central Asia or perhaps by farming people in the south Russian Caucasus. Domesticated horses had come to play a role in the early civilizations of Mesopotamia by the third millennium B.C. and also show up in the Harappan civilization in north India of about the same time. This is of great importance, for the horse, until very recent times, has been a major technological factor in warfare, first as the musclepower for war chariots and then as the mount for swift-moving cavalry. Horses have been a major food source among people of Central Asia, and throughout Eurasia horsemeat

was an important food item until Christians banned the eating of horseflesh as "pagan."

Camels were domesticated even later than horses. The points of origin are thought to be somewhere

11.11 War chariots were among the early uses of the domesticated horse. (Erich Lessing, Magnum)

The Material Dimensions of Adaptation: Homo faber

in Arabia for the one-humped variety and farther east in Asia Minor for the two-humped (Bactrian) camel. The use of camels in extensive western Saharan trade seems to have developed around the first century A.D. and made possible a significant expansion and intensification of commerce, because camel caravans are much more effective means of transport in arid regions than are humans, horses, and asses. In the Bible Abraham is supposed to have owned a few camels in addition to his sheep, goats, and other animals, but for the most part the "ship of the desert" was the special concern and possession of the more nomadic Bedouin peoples of Arabia throughout biblical times.

In the New World, the llamas, alpacas, and vicuñas domesticated by the Andean peoples of South America are relatives of camels but are not large enough to serve really effectively as draft animals.

The origins and antiquity of reindeer domestication have been a matter of great dispute among anthropologists, particularly because there are few archaeological remains to testify unambiguously about early reindeer husbandry. The hunting of wild reindeer was of great importance in the late- and post-Pleistocene period in Europe, and since wild reindeer were common throughout parts of Northern Europe and much of Siberia until the nineteenth century, it is likely that reindeer herding, as opposed to hunting, arose only in recent centuries. This development may have occurred independently in two different areas—in Lapland (northern Finland and Scandinavia) and in northern Siberia. The practice of reindeer herding is generally thought to be a "copying" of the cattle-keeping practices of more southerly populations.

East of the core areas of domestication, some very interesting domesticated animals such as the yak of high-altitude Tibet and the water buffalo of India and Southeast Asia have also long been food sources (both are milked) and beasts of burden. We know rather little of when the yak, for example, was domesticated. Zebu cattle in India are another prime source of power for threshing, turning water wheels, plowing, pulling carts, and other hard work.

Chickens and other fowl seem to be Asiatic in origin, possibly coming first from Southeast Asia. The geographer Carl Sauer cites fairly strong evidence for a native South American variety of chickens, for while on a field trip in Chile he reports,

11.12 The "ship of the desert" made possible large-scale changes in desert travel and commerce. (Elliot Erwitt, Magnum)

"We were served boiled blue and olive green eggs at an inn. I was surprised at seeing them . . . and learned that the Indians . . . Araucanians . . . raise a breed of chickens that lays such eggs" (Sauer, 1969:58–59). From that clue Sauer went on to find that Magellan's round-the-world expedition party secured supplies of chickens on the south coast of Brazil in 1519, before any Europeans had set foot in that region. Henry Cabot's men in 1526 also got hundreds of fowls from the natives along the coast of southern Brazil.

The Domestication of Plants and Animals

11.13 **Among the reindeer herds, Finland.**
(Werner Bischof, Magnum)

Food Domestication in the Americas

While there may still be some doubt about the independent origins of plant and animal domestication in areas such as Southeast Asia and West Africa, there is no doubt about the separate invention of food domestication in the New World. The Indian peoples in Mesoamerica (Mexico and Central America) and in the Peruvian area of South America developed high-level food production systems based on a series of food plants native to the Americas and largely unknown in the Old World. In the Mexican area the principal crops were maize, beans, squash, and chili peppers, with a variety of secondary foods. The South American agricultural system, on the other hand, was based heavily on potatoes, sweet potatoes, quinoa, manioc, peanuts, and a number of other distinctively South American foods. In addition, they had nearly the entire Mesoamerican list of crops, which underwent a separate line of development in the South American habitat.

The hunter-gatherer peoples who came over from Siberia to North America at least twenty thousand

The Material Dimensions of Adaptation: Homo faber

years ago (perhaps earlier) had spread throughout all the Americas by at least fourteen thousand years ago. Archaeological sites at the tip of South America, at Fell's Cave, and Palli Aike, have materials dating from over ten thousand years ago. Throughout most of the millennia since those hunters first set foot in the New World the basic way of making a living was through hunting and gathering.

By 7000 B.C. the large game animals—mammoths, horses, and camels—had become extinct and, to the extent that they had been a focus of hunter-gatherer adaptations, the people probably had to turn toward a variety of more modest sources of plant and animal foods. (So far there is no clear evidence that American hunters were ever as specialized in big game hunting as were, for example, some of the European hunters of the Upper Pleistocene.)

The first signs of food cultivation appear to be in the central Mexican area, where food gatherers in the Tehuacan Valley area apparently cultivated squash and avocados at least eight thousand years ago, nearly as early as the first food cultivators of the Near East (MacNeish, 1964:266). By about 3000 B.C., and perhaps even earlier, the Tehuacan Valley

people were cultivating a wide variety of foods, including squash, chili peppers, avocados, maguey, amaranth, gourds, beans, zapotes, maize, and cotton. They also still depended on hunting wild animals (mostly deer) and the population was rather sparse, with groups numbering perhaps five to ten families in small hamlets. Clearly the total amount of food available in the central Mexican highland area, even with cultivation, did not nearly measure up to the abundance of the Mesopotamian areas.

In the Old World, in Mesopotamia, the productivity of the land meant that villages could grow relatively rapidly once farming techniques were well in hand, for the number of calories produced per unit of land was greater than that available to hunter-gatherers or even foragers of wild grain. Between 8000 B.C. and 5000 B.C. villages housing between one-hundred to three-hundred persons developed all about the region, and during the millennium 4000–3000 B.C. there was rapid growth of towns and cities. In Mesoamerica, however, it took very much longer from the first domestication of plants to the development of large settlements.

The Tehuacan Valley area was perhaps not the

Turkey, Maize, Beans, Squash, Avocado

Lima Beans, Tomatoes, Potatoes, Cotton, Llama, Guinea Pig

11.14 **Major centers of plant and animal domestication in the Americas. These New World centers developed independently of Old World systems of food production.**

The Domestication of Plants and Animals

first heavily agricultural region in Mesoamerica, but there is very little sign of well-developed villages in the entire region until about 1400 B.C. Flannery has excavated a substantial village site, near Oaxaca City in Southern Mexico, named San José Mogote. He reports that "At 1300 B.C. it was a village of at least fifteen to thirty households covering 1–2 hectares. In the central part . . . was an area of 200–300 m² of lime-plastered 'public buildings' of undetermined function. . . . by 900 B.C., San José Mogote covered 20 hectares and must have had in the order of 240–320 households" (Flannery, 1972:44).

The slow development of settlement complexity in Mesoamerica would appear to be a direct reflection of food production limitations, at least in the early phases. There are several reasons for the limited productivity, as compared with that of the Near East.

In the New World the archaeological data indicate that the cultivators continued to rely, to a considerable extent, on the hunting of wild animals (especially deer) for several millennia after they had learned how to grow crops. One of the main reasons for the continued dependence on hunting for sources of animal protein is that the New World lacked domesticable animals. There were no wild sheep, goats, or cattle that could be gradually converted to domestic use. With the exception of some fowl and dogs all of the familiar barnyard animals in the Americas were brought over to the New World by European colonists. Aboriginal domesticated animals in the New World were limited to guinea pigs, bees, the long-haired creatures of the high Andes (llamas, alpacas, vicuñas, and guanacos), as well as chickens, turkeys, and dogs (cf. LANNING, 1967:14–18). None of the animals gave people a comfortable feeling of a rich and reliable food supply, and they were not strong enough to serve as draft animals.

Another important factor is that maize, the mainstay of most American food systems, did not at first have high productivity comparable to that of wheat and barley. Maize is genetically much more difficult to develop than are the "noble cereals" of the Old World, and apparently it took thousands of years for maize to develop the large ears that we now take for granted. Wild varieties of corn, from which the ancient Indian peoples developed the first domesticated varieties, have ears "no bigger than the filter tip of a cigarette," to quote Richard MacNeish, one of the leading archaeologists working on the evidence of early plant domestication in Mesoamerica.

The first domestication of maize, at least in the Tehuacan area, was probably about 5000 B.C. The

11.15 Major food domesticates of the New World.

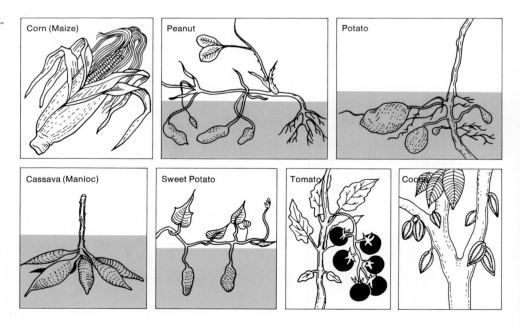

The Material Dimensions of Adaptation: Homo faber

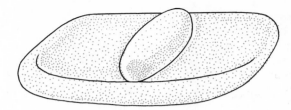

11.16 Grain-grinding equipment of Central American peoples includes the *mano* and the *metate* (grinding platform or basin), forms of which are common in archaeological sites, especially in Mayan areas.

tool kits of the Tehuacan peoples in the time period from about 5000 B.C. to 3400 B.C. contain grain-grinding equipment, including *manos* and *metates* not so different from the types one sees today in the marketplaces of Mexican towns.

Some of the earliest evidence of plant domestication in Peru is from a rather small and insignificant location along the central coast. It is called Pampas and dates from about 4000–3500 B.C. The people who lived there got most of their sustenance from the sea—fish, sea lions, clams, mussels, and birds. But they also grew a lot of squash, in addition

to gathering wild crops. As the centuries wore on, they seem to have given up all or most of their squash cultivation and specialized more fully in gathering the rich marine harvest.

Another site along the coast, dated from around 3600–3200 B.C., also shows a strong orientation toward marine foods, but the people there also grew gourds, guavas, and chili peppers for foods, in addition to which they cultivated cotton to use for making textiles and fishnets.

From 2500 to 1800 B.C. the coastal areas of Peru developed rapidly into farming communities and fairly large permanent settlements grew up. Temples, pyramids, and altars were among the more notable public works that marked this increased density of settlement. The entire area appears to have become a series of settled villages and towns in the space of about five-hundred years. Food crops had become much more varied, now including squash, lima beans, chili peppers, avocados, guavas, and maize. Much of the food supply came from fishing and other coastal marine life, however. The population of several of the coastal Peruvian settlements was probably between five-hundred and a thousand people (Lanning, 1972:64).

In the highlands of Peru the development of agriculture ran a rather different course from that along

11.17 These terraced agricultural lands were part of the Inca food production system before the Spaniards came. (Magnum)

223

the coastal regions. Evidence of domestication shows up at about 1500–1000 B.C. at the village of Chiripa, in which llama bones were found, and it is presumed that potatoes were a staple, though no direct evidence of potatoes was found in the site itself.

Summary

By the time Columbus was fitting out his ships for the long voyage west, domesticated food production had spread to every continent except Australia and Greenland. Actually some foolhardy Viking voyagers had even established food cultivation on the coast of Greenland before 1000 A.D., but their settlement was gradually eliminated, perhaps by a worsening climate.

The maize-squash-beans complex from Mesoamerica had spread widely throughout North and South America, reaching up to the Iroquois and Huron in northeastern North America, and large-scale social systems had developed in what is now the southeastern United States, based on intensive agricultural techniques. Indian groups in the Northern Plains cultivated maize and other foods in the fertile river valleys.

In large regions of North America there were still hunter-gatherers. These included the Inuit far in the arctic north, many Athapaskan and other Indian groups in the subarctic forests, and stretching south to along the West Coast and all the way into California. Practically all the Indian peoples in California lived by hunting and gathering, except for a very small corner in the southeast, adjacent to the maize growers, where the Pueblo peoples lived. The Great Basin area around Nevada, Utah, and adjacent regions was also an area with no crop growing or domesticated food animals.

In South America most peoples had taken up food cultivation long before the coming of Europeans, though a few small groups in the Amazon jungles, and the Ona and Yahgan peoples at the southern tip of the continent, were hunter-gatherers.

The food-growing complexes of the Old World had eliminated hunting-gathering economies practically everywhere that crops could effectively be grown. In Africa the cultivators of warm-climate foods—mainly root crops plus millets and sorghums—had pushed the hunter-gatherer Pygmies into a dependent, marginal position in the Congo forests; and the Bushmen and Hottentot hunter-gatherers of southern Africa had been displaced in most areas where crops and cattle could be maintained, leaving them with the arid semidesert regions of the Kalahari Desert. A few other remnant peoples still lived a hunter-gather way of life in East Africa, in the areas too inhospitable for herders and cultivators. East African subsistence economies are particularly interesting because of the large numbers of people who had adopted nomadic or seminomadic pastoralism with their herds of cattle. Many of these people, like the Masai, the Turkana, and others, have stoutly resisted pressures to settle down to crop growing, even though national governments are pressuring them to give up their nomadic ways.

In Oceania the planting of yams, taro, sweet potatoes, breadfruit, manioc, and other food crops had spread widely among the islands of Polynesia and Micronesia and all the way to Hawaii and Easter Island, carried by Malayo-Polynesian–speaking sailors. In the New Guinea area and adjacent larger islands of Melanesia, food production probably came in even earlier, with various root crops plus the highly important domestic pig. Australia and Tasmania were practically unique in the region in their absence of food production systems before the arrival of the Europeans. The only domesticated product of the Australian aboriginal peoples was the dog.

The spread of food production technologies around the world has produced a great variety of subsistence systems. Differing culture histories, variations in rainfall and seasons, and many other factors have combined to create many unique contexts for making a living from combinations of food gathering and production. In the next chapter we will review some of the principal types of basic food production economies.

The Material Dimensions of Adaptation: Homo faber

The development of plant and animal domestication has often been called the NEOLITHIC REVOLUTION. This is certainly somewhat misleading when we consider that the "revolution" took thousands of years to come to fruition in many areas and was especially slow, for example, in the Americas. On the other hand, once set in motion, the changes arising from food production so altered human social life that all manner of new developments came into being. Many more people established sedentary village ways of life, followed by population growth, the beginnings of real social inequalities, and increasingly complex forms of social organization.

As the various food production systems arose in different parts of the world and spread into new regions, they were transformed in myriad ways by local environmental conditions. Through the centuries several main types of societies developed as *relatively* stable adaptations based on complex interactions of food technology and environmental possibilities. None of these social and cultural systems was fixed and unchanging, of course, but there are enough similarities among variant forms so that some common features can be described—not forgetting the many exceptions to our generalizations. In the following discussion of "types of societies" based on food-getting styles, we will leave out the hunter-gatherers because we have described that basic foundation "type" earlier. We are concerned here with the various kinds of cultural and social systems that developed as a result of food production.[1]

Part-time Cultivators

In the long, drawn-out cultural transformation after the first domestication of foods, there must have been many small groups who made their living by hunting and gathering supplemented by cultivated crops. The earliest *protoagriculturalist* peoples of the Near East probably expended only small amounts of energy in preparing garden plots and planting them with seeds, after which they moved on to a round of hunting-gathering activities that

[1]In discussing features of the social systems there will be introduced a number of terms about social organization, such as *clan, nuclear family,* and so on. These are defined in the glossary, but they will be more fully described in a later section on the social dimension of human adaptation.

Food Production Systems: Foundations of Cultural Complexity

12

12.1 Slash-and-burn cultivation is a productive way to grow crops in areas of dense vegetation. Family clearing a field for planting in Mexico. (Arthur Trees, Magnum)

kept them occupied and nourished until they returned many weeks later to check their harvests, if any. If their harvests were poor, they continued the whole year as hunter-gatherers; in years of abundance, they did not have to spend much time in the chase.

Some of the people in Africa and South America whom we customarily label hunter-gatherers plant a few crops, and in former times may have been even more dependent on agriculture than they are now. For example, the Sirionó of the northeastern Bolivian tropical forests have been primarily hunter-gatherers in recent times, but they depend to a minor extent on harvests of maize, sweet manioc, camotes, and papaya. (In addition they grow some cotton and tobacco.) (Holmberg, 1960). They also plant calabash and uruku trees, both of which appear to have been introduced very recently. Usually it is a man-and-wife team that works to clear and burn off the small jungle plots (usually no more than fifty feet square) using the simplest possible technology—a digging stick and (more recently) iron machetes. Since seasonal change is of little significance in this tropical region, the Sirionó can plant their little gardens almost any time, though it is usually done at the beginning of the rainy season. After the crops are planted, they spend very little time on their gardens until harvest time.

Allan Holmberg, who lived with the Sirionó in 1940–1941, noted that some of the harvested maize was occasionally stored at the garden site in baskets and was available as food the next time hunting brought the family to the same area (Holmberg, 1960:29). The storage of food, however, was relatively minor because the people often preferred to stay at their garden site until they had consumed what they had grown. Storage of larger amounts of food at the garden site was more than a little risky, and carrying a heavy harvest any great distance was obviously out of the question.

The Sirionó hunted and fished mainly with bows and arrows, and they killed a wide variety of game—several species of monkeys, peccaries, tapirs, alligators, anteaters, armadillos, and a variety of other small game. They gathered a variety of wild plants, especially fruits and nuts from several kinds of palms, and also dug up edible roots. Honey from wild bees was their only sweet and was especially important for making mead, their only alcoholic drink. Thus the Sirionó had a rather simple array of technology for food getting and food storage. Their scheduling and adaptive strategy were for the most part geared to hunting and gathering; the marginal agricultural activity was a distinctly secondary occupation.

The Sirionó, during the time of Holmberg's observations, lived in a small number of bands of kin-related people. One band had ninety-four persons, including twenty-five adult males, thirty adult females, eighteen preadult males, and twenty-one preadult females. Another group contained fifty-eight persons. The larger of the two bands consisted of seventeen nuclear families, grouped into five EX-TENDED families. Individual families or even groups of families sometimes changed band membership, especially when there were disputes. The composition of Sirionó bands was relatively flexible, much like other hunting and gathering groups. Their population density was also quite low—Holmberg estimated that it was about one person per twenty square miles.

Among the relatively simple societies that pursue a mix of foraging and cultivation there is a range of variation from groups like the Sirionó, whose adaptation is geared mainly to hunting and collecting, to the other extreme in which crop cultivation sets the schedule and tone of daily work, although hunting-gathering activities are essential to the maintenance of the society. Some of the Semai groups of Malaya appear to be adapted to their tropical environment in this second style. Their cultivation of gardens in the tropical forest strongly affects the shape of social groupings and movements. As small clusters of semisedentary peoples, their emphasis is somewhat more on village life than is true of the Sirionó. On the other hand, their population density is about the same. (Dentan, 1969).

In seeking to understand the transition from hunting and gathering to sedentary agriculture, we should keep in mind that crop cultivation requires important shifts of behavior patterns and poses new adaptive risks that hunter-gatherer peoples may feel are not worth it. The balance sheet of costs and gains in some tropical areas does not seem to offer enough rewards from cultivation to induce hunters to settle down near their fields. Among the Semai and others like them, the balance of risks and opportunities may be more nearly 50–50, and the people cannot afford to give up the shifting cultivation or the considerable dependence on hunting. In other

12.2 Cultivating a field, Mexico. (Arthur Trees, Magnum)

adequate crops for a few years through techniques known as SLASH-AND-BURN (or SWIDDEN) agriculture.

The term *slash-and-burn* refers to two important aspects of land preparation. First, trees and undergrowth are "slashed" or cut and allowed to dry; then this material is burned off, leaving a residue of ash that helps to fertilize the crops. After periods of use, varying from one to several years depending on local ecological conditions, the soil is exhausted and new fields must be slashed and burned. This method of crop growing, with its many variants, was widespread throughout pre-Columbian America, Africa south of the Sahara, and in the Southeast Asian islands; it was also used by earlier peoples throughout Europe and continued in some northern areas until very recent times.

Slash-and-burn agricultural techniques require a fair amount of unused land that can be utilized in turn as the productivity of current fields is exhausted. In the tropics and subtropics, horticultural peoples must move their villages every few years as the lands near their home bases become progressively depleted. Some of the highland New Guinea peoples typify the characteristics of this kind of food-getting system. The Kapauku in the Kamu Valley region of western New Guinea will serve as an example.

The environment has high mountains, deep valleys, relatively heavy rainfall, and mild climate. There is plenty of vegetation but not much in the way of game animals. The Kapauku grow crops, both on the valley floors and on the mountain slopes, which they farm by the extensive slash-and-burn method. Pospisil has described their cultivation methods in detail:

The man, with the help of his wife, first clears the underbrush from a selected site. He then cuts down the forest with a stone axe and machete, trims off the branches, and processes the wood so that it can be used to build a fence. When this work is finished, the uprooted underbrush and the branches form a continuous layer of dry debris that covers the garden area. In order to protect the crops from destruction by marauding wild boars and domesticated pigs the Kapauku farmer must build a sturdy fence around his property. . . . After this fence is completed and the plot safely enclosed the native farmer, often aided by his wife, removes the dry debris from the vicinity of the fence and sets the whole garden area on fire. Since

areas of the world, the people have found that the gains from cultivation were sufficient to enable them to reduce their nomadic hunting and gathering activities. Naturally the possibilities of food storage also strongly affect people's adaptive strategies in these small-scale societies.

Horticultural Societies

In many parts of the world different peoples developed food-getting systems that involved relatively little capital investment in irrigation work, draft animals, or implements of cultivation and harvesting. These cultivation complexes, which we frequently label HORTICULTURAL SOCIETIES, are well adapted to the somewhat poorer soils found in heavy tropical and subtropical rain forests. The soils do not support continuous intensive agricultural activities, but they can be made to produce quite

227

Food Production Systems: Foundations of Cultural Complexity

12.3 A Hopi village, situated for effective defense against raiders, Arizona. (Courtesy of the American Museum of Natural History)

the surrounding jungle is always damp from the frequent tropical rains, there is no danger that the fire will spread into it. With the firing process the man's work is completed, and the female takes over the care of the newly created garden. On the next day she appears with bundles of shoots of sweet potato vines, which she plants in shallow holes by means of a dibble stick (digging stick). The abundant moisture and sometimes daily tropical rains cause the shoots to root and grow fast. . . . It is the woman's task also to keep the gardens clean and to weed them at least three times during their growing period. Only such care assures an adequate harvest. Most of the harvesting

is again accomplished by the woman who digs out the ripe tubers with a short pointed digging stick. The harvest of sweet potatoes is a protracted affair. . . . Consequently, sweet potatoes are dug from the same garden for a prolonged period of time. Usually the whole area is gone over three times before all of the tubers are extracted and the plot is abandoned as fallow land to the pigs and the jungle. (POSPISIL, 1963:6–7)

The mountain slopes must be left to nature for eight to twelve years before they can be used again. The Kapauku also use slash-and-burn techniques to clear the valley flatlands for garden plots. Because the soil is richer, a variety of crops, including sugar cane, taro, bananas, several types of greens, cucumbers, gourds, and native beans can be planted on these valley lands. It takes a great deal of heavy work to maintain drainage ditches and to put up fences to keep out the pigs. This greater investment of labor is rewarded by a richer variety of crops, and through crop rotation it is possible to use the same lands several times before they must revert to fallow.

The Kapauku practice a third type of cultivation, which must be characterized as intensive, complex cultivation. It involves the use of green fertilizer (grasses, reeds, and leaves) in relatively small beds surrounded by drainage ditches. Fire is not used for clearing these grounds since the fertility of the soil is maintained by green manuring.

The Kapauku, like many other New Guinea peoples, cultivate a large variety of garden crops, but nine tenths of their cultivation efforts go into sweet potatoes. The sweet potatoes are not only used for human food, they are also the mainstay of the pigs—the prime focus of Kapauku economic activity. Pigs are not simply a source of protein; they are significant economic and social investments. The attention to pigs as a major social-economic-ceremonial concern is widespread in the Melanesian area. Individual wealth is generally measured in number of pigs; the magnificence of ceremonial events can be read in the number of pigs brought to slaughter; and a major motive for a man to seek more wives is their importance as caretakers of pigs. Among the Kapauku "breeding and trading pigs is an activity which, properly executed, may bring a Kapauku esteem from his neighbors, wealth, and the highest status in his society, namely that of *tonowi*, a rich man and a political leader" (Pospisil, 1963:11).

The Material Dimensions of Adaptation: Homo faber

The Kapauku number some forty-five thousand individuals with a population density about ten per square mile. Thus their food production system can support at least ten times as many people in a given area as does the hunting-gathering subsistence style. The area is dotted with small villages, each with a population of fifty to a hundred people, and generally each village is the home of a single, extended kinship group. Very likely the Kapauku must work harder than hunter-gatherers to extract sufficient food from their environment, but their methods are very effective even though their cultivation equipment is simple. All of their complex crop growing is carried out with digging sticks, stone axes, machetes, and a few other miscellaneous tools. The system is one of backbreaking toil, especially for the women, but the rewards are large and dependable supplies of food. If there were no pigs, the Kapauku would perhaps have some preservation problems with their sweet potatoes and other crops, but pigs on the hoof are an excellent means of storage.

Dry Land Cultivators: Pueblo Peoples of the Southwest

The many Pueblo Indian groups of Arizona and New Mexico are generally divided into the western and the eastern (Rio Grande) Pueblos. We will focus here on the Hopi and Zuñi, the best-described communities of the western Pueblos. The earliest census figures, from about 1630, list ninety villages of Pueblos, with perhaps sixty thousand inhabitants (Dozier, 1970:125). As of 1968, the Hopi population, with a number of separate villages, numbered some five thousand peoples, and the Zuñi Pueblo group numbered approximately the same. In contrast to the wet land cultivation of the Kapauku and most peoples of the South Pacific, Southeast Asia, and central Africa, the Pueblo peoples plant their crops under semidesert conditions, in which the principal concern is getting water. Although some eastern Pueblo peoples have complex irrigation works, the western Pueblo peoples have not, and rely on flood-water irrigation from the uncertain rains of the Arizona–New Mexico area.

In pre-Columbian times to till the soil they used simple digging sticks, wooden shovels, stone axes, and other simple implements comparable to the technological inventory of the Kapauku. Their inventory of food crops was very different, however.

The Pueblos depended mainly on maize, beans, gourds, squash, and a few other New World plants that had spread to their region from the centers of civilization in Mexico. Their domestic animal was the turkey, used both for food and for feathers. Compared to New Guineans, the Pueblos had relatively little in the way of a domesticated meat supply. On the other hand, their chances of getting meat from hunting were undoubtedly greater. There were rabbits, deer, and antelope in the nearby hills, and some Pueblo groups made periodic trips into buffalo-hunting areas as well.

There is another feature of Pueblo life, past and present, that contrasts sharply with the life of the Kapauku. The Hopi and Zuñi villages are comparatively permanent, complex adobe and stone structures, often with multistoried apartments. Population sizes are much greater than in the hamlets of the Kapauku. The typical Hopi village, for example, contains at least several hundred persons. The Zuñi peoples are now clustered into a single town numbering at least twenty-five hundred persons. The surrounding dry lands around the villages, on the other hand, are relatively empty and inhospitable to settlement.

Social Organization of Horticultural Peoples

Whereas the New Guinea horticulturalists have a social organization based firmly on small, village-based kin groups, the Hopi and Zuñi peoples have, to a considerable extent, subordinated their kinship groups to the solidarity of village integration. The complex religious ceremonials of these peoples reflect as much their striving for intravillage cooperation and harmony as they do the needs for supernatural help with the crops.

Compared to the New Guinea peoples, Pueblo communities are highly "communalistic" and solidary, with great emphasis on conformity and adherence to group-oriented goals. It has frequently been said that even today it is very difficult to get Pueblo individuals to compete against one another—for example, in foot races—given their noncompetitive training. The open and individualistic struggle for political power and prestige, as well as for wealth in pigs, in the Melanesian area would be quite foreign to the lifeways of the Hopi and the Zuñi.

229

These two contrasting examples of horticultural societies are far from exhausting the range of variation in this broad and amorphous level of food-getting technology. Many horticultural peoples (especially in some of the tropical forest regions of the world) have extensive lands in which to exploit their shifting methods of cultivation. Population densities vary a good deal, but tropical forest regions usually do not carry more than twenty-five to thirty persons per square mile. On the other hand, horticultural peoples on the small islands and atolls of the South Pacific (Micronesia, Polynesia, Melanesia) have established sedentary villages on tight little islands, sometimes with very little elbow room. For example, Romonum in the Trukese Archipelago has less than a square mile of land space, on which there dwells a population of two hundred persons. This is high population density and, of course, would be impossible without the resources in the sea around them. Many of the Oceanian horticultural societies are compact and highly structured societies that resemble, in social cohesion, the Pueblo peoples more than they do the Kapauku and their neighbors.

In some areas of Africa horticultural food-getting methods in fertile regions can maintain fairly dense populations, many of them organized into complex multivillage political systems. In East Africa, before European intervention, there were a number of kingdoms, such as the Bunyoro, the Ganda, the Acholi, and others. The Bunyoro, in what is present-day Uganda, now number about 110,000 people, with a population density of 25 per square mile. Instead of clustering in villages—like the Pueblos, the Kapauku, and many other horticulturalists—the Bunyoro and their neighbors live scattered out in homesteads, which typically consist of one or two mud-and-wattle houses around a central courtyard. Nyoro farmers cultivate millet, sweet potatoes, casava, and varieties of peas and beans, and bananas, used primarily for beer. They have goats, chickens, and sheep. In areas that are free from the tsetse fly, some farmers have great herds of cattle. In recent decades the people have begun to grow cotton and tobacco as cash crops in their increasingly modernizing economy.

Very large numbers of African peoples, therefore, make their living with food-getting methods that are not much more complex than those of the Pueblos and the Kapauku. However, their past histories and the broader environmental situations have led to complex political structures—kingdoms with bureaucracies, armies, royal capitals, and other features that underscore the great range of variation possible in social systems based on horticulture. Similarly, the Mayan peoples in Mesoamerica apparently built a complex, stratified civilization on a comparatively simple base of swidden horticulture.

Similarities Among Horticultural Societies

The sometimes bewildering variations in the adaptive systems of horticultural peoples should not prevent us from seeing essential similarities. In the first place, horticultural societies around the world are basically nonindustrialized, and for the most part their modes of food getting require that the great majority of people be employed in food-getting tasks. However, there are usually a few important specialists. The various craftsmen can spend their time in metalwork, wood carving, and other pursuits because their families take care of the crops and produce the household food supplies. Specialists in trade and marketing may spend much of their time "on the road" or in the marketplace, yet they too rely on their families for their food needs, rather than on their commercial transactions. The vast amount of craft and other products of specialists in horticultural societies is, in part, made possible by their relatively sedentary life in permanent villages. There is, thus, a dual reason for the large material inventory of horticultural people: they can afford to feed non-food-producing specialists, and they don't have to worry about transporting their worldly goods as do hunters and nomadic pastoralists.

Another feature that appears to be widespread among horticulturalists is the elaboration of kinship organization as a major social structural feature, accompanied by a corresponding elaboration in the complexity of religious structures, which on the one hand are a reflection of social organizational complexity, and on the other hand seem to be a reflection of the search for adequate "crop insurance." In drier areas there are continuing negotiations with the gods to obtain water for the crops; in other places where water is not such a problem there are various other chance factors over which people try to get supernatural control.

The Material Dimensions of Adaptation: Homo faber

Other similarities among horticulturalist groups include the following:

1. They have a relatively high concern for ritual and other dealings with the supernatural compared with hunter-gatherers and pastoralists. They also frequently display greater fears of witchcraft and sorcery, perhaps because their compact villages and sedentary lives give people fewer chances to move away from each other to avoid disputes.
2. Headmen in horticulturalist groups often have considerable authority, for there are more legal disputes to settle, more decisions to make on behalf of the entire community, and perhaps more enemies "out there" to deal with.
3. The villages and fields of sedentary cultivators provide targets that attract the attention of people of other regions, hence chances of serious warfare are greater than is the case among hunter-gatherers.

Horticultural peoples in warm climates often can depend upon multiple crops per year. In temperate areas, on the other hand, the growing season starts sometime in the spring and terminates with an autumn harvest festival. Even in multicrop areas there is need for storage of food supplies. The wattle-and-mud granaries in many African groups are a major feature of the landscape; many societies have underground storage pits. The storability of different crops varies widely. The hard-kernel maize that was the mainstay among American horticultural Indians is particularly easily stored, along with its coequal in nutrition, beans. One other note should be added about food and storage among horticultural peoples: compared to hunters and gatherers their diet tends to move away from high protein content, and protein foods may be in especially short supply in famine times. Horticultural peoples run double risks when their food supplies are threatened: they are likely to be short of calories in general, but the slim meals they eke out may be nutritionally inferior compared to the daily fare of hunters and gatherers.

Nomadic Pastoralists: Protein on the Hoof

In the historical progression from simple to more complex food-getting systems, pastoralist, animal-keeping societies appear, in general, to have developed their specialized food-getting systems as a symbiotic reaction to the growth of efficient sedentary agricultural systems. Those societies, past and present, that have specialized in making their living from nomadic animal husbandry have had to locate in land areas with sufficient space to meet the food needs of their herds. They often make use of areas with insufficient rainfall for crops. Animal-keeping peoples often have been partially dependent on the plant foods grown by their more sedentary neighbors. In addition, some pastoralist peoples grow plant foods of their own, although they generally subordinate cultivation activities to the work and mobility demands of their animals. The Barabaig cattle herders of East Africa are a good example of this type of society.

The Barabaig pastoralists number some twenty thousand persons in a semiarid area of perhaps sixteen hundred square miles in Tanzania. Their population density may be perhaps ten to fifteen persons per square mile, certainly less than the population concentrations among the more sedentary cultivators in East Africa. The mainstay of their economy, and their principal ritual and emotional focus, is their zebu-type cattle—those colorful animals with large fleshy humps over their shoulders, and sporting a fold of loose skin under the neck (dewlap). They also keep sheep, goats, and donkeys, of which the goats are perhaps the most important because they supply both milk and meat (Klima, 1970:10–15). Compared to the diet of most sedentary peoples, the Barabaig diet is rich in dairy products—milk, curdled milk, and butter—as well as a mixture of milk and blood. Blood is extracted from the jugular vein of live animals, usually bulls, by means of a specially designed arrow. Meat from the cattle is used only when an older animal dies or when cattle are sacrificed for ritual purposes.

The high-protein diet of the Barabaig does include some plant foods, especially maize, which has increased in importance as a food supply in recent times. Hunting and gathering activities also provide some additional food, and the Barabaig gather wild honey, principally for beer making.

The entire East African cattle area from prehistoric times to the present has been a scene of continuing conflict among competing pastoralists and the sedentary cultivators of the region. For the Barabaig, the Masai warriors have been special threats over the years, as the competition for grazing lands

is a constant source of conflict between the two peoples. Some of the social organization of these peoples, therefore, represents a response to the general warlike conditions under which they have maintained themselves and their herds. Thus both the physical environment (especially for their animals) and the social environment (of neighboring warlike groups) pose special problems for these kinds of societies.

The Barabaig cattle herders are organized into a number of kinship groups that make up the main structure of their society. The members of each CLAN claim to be descended from a common ancestor, and the cattle are considered to be legal property of the clan. Five of the Barabaig clans are composed of ritual specialists who offer their services to promote human and cattle fertility as well as giving other ritual help. The other fifty-five clans are the "laity" served by the ritual specialists.

The society also includes two castelike groups that are socially distinct from the Barabaig clans. These are a group of arrow-poison specialists (they also perform circumcision) and a blacksmith CASTE that make spear blades, arrow points, branding irons, women's iron bracelets, and other metal products. Both these groups of craft specialists are looked down upon as social inferiors by the Barabaig populace.

12.4 Skolt Same woman fishing with gill nets under the lake ice. (P. J. Pelto)

12.5 Among some East African cattle people the animals are a main focus of ritual, social relations, and economic wealth. (Marc Riboud, Magnum)

Contrasting Case: Tibetan Nomads

A few comments about the high-mountain nomadic peoples of Tibet will serve to emphasize a main point about pastoralist peoples—namely that the interrelations between animals and terrain have powerful effects on the life styles of these peoples. Nomadic pastoralism in Tibet has been markedly different from cattle keeping in East Africa, mainly because of the extremes of topography and of temperature at the "roof of the world." The Tibetan pastoralists are highly specialized in making their living at the extremes—at the twelve-thousand-foot to seventeen-thousand-foot level, beyond the reach of agriculture. There the nomadic tribesmen herd their yak, sheep, cattle, and horses. Of these, the yak are the most important and are the best adapted to the extremes of altitude and cold. They are the animals that give the special flavor to Tibetan nomadism.

Yak are large, heavily built "country cousins" of

cattle, and hybrid yak-cattle are especially powerful and valuable. Both the yak and the hybrids have furry coats and great lung capacity as well as remarkable agility for maneuvering in the mountains. Nomads sometimes open up snow-blocked mountain passes by driving their herds of yak back and forth to trample down the deep snows (Ekvall, 1968:11–15).

In contrast to the mud-thatched homesteads of the East African cattle people, Tibetans live the year round in heavy felt or cloth tents, that facilitate frequent movement in search of new pasturage for the animals. Seasonal changes require moving the animals up and down the high slopes. Winter is endured in the lower valleys at locations where hay has been stored for feeding the animals when pastures are depleted. This pattern of seasonal movement in connection with animal husbandry is often referred to as TRANSHUMANCE.

The Tibetans plant no crops, but they purchase barley, dried fruit, and tea from more settled peoples. Hunting is an important secondary source of food in some areas, especially those in which wild yak are still found. The diet is high in protein from milk, meat, and blood; yak milk and milk from cattle are processed into butter, cheese, and yogurt. Barley is the chief cereal, and special ceremonial meals include some rice and white-flour noodles.

The social organization of Tibetan nomads is rather loose and flexible compared to the clan-and-LINEAGE structuring of pastoralists in East Africa and Central Asia. A basic unit of the society is the tent household, often a nuclear or POLYGAMOUS family (see Chapter 14). The tent households are usually grouped into encampments numbering from five or six to as many as eighty households. The size, composition, and location of these groups change with the season, though some of them are sufficiently permanent to have headmen who represent the groups to outsiders.

The home areas of the Tibetan nomads have in the past been sufficiently remote so that warfare from the outside was not a constant threat. Enemy armies have, on occasion, penetrated the areas, but the more immediate problems of self-defense have been from the night raids and other yak-rustling activities of their fellow pastoralists from "the other side of the mountain." In some areas "range wars" have been endemic; in others, predation is limited to the rustling of a few stray animals.

Comments on Pastoralists

Pastoralist societies are of some importance for highlighting a number of ideas about human adaptation. In the first place, they provide us with clear illustrations of how physical environments affect the course of human adaptations. Many pastoralist groups must move from place to place in response to their animals' needs, and they develop great sensitivity to these needs. For example, Same reindeer herders used to move with their animals from spring calving grounds, to open-air uplands in summer

12.6 Horse race among Mongolian pastoralists. In earlier centuries the ancestors of these people conquered vast areas from China to Europe with their superb cavalry. (Henri Cartier-Bresson, Magnum)

where insects are not as numerous, then on to other locations for the fall rutting season and winter pasturage. Some ink has been spent in argument over whether the Same peoples' reindeer herds decided on these courses of migration or whether it was the human societies that shaped the semidomesticated reindeer to these patterns. The answer appears to be that animals and people worked out the migration patterns together, with compromises on both sides, in response to the ecological pressures of the environments.

In some areas more favorable to agriculture, animal-keeping peoples (such as the Barabaig) have enough of a stake in cultivated crops so that they do not move around very much. Actually many different strategies have been adopted by herdsmen. Some are highly dependent on their animals. Others have various combinations of animals, crops, hunting, fishing, and other pursuits; each combination results in different patterns of movement, social organization, and other aspects of life style.

There are many other areas of contrast among pastoralist groups. Kazak and Kirghiz horsemen of the central Asian steppes not only have kept animals for food, clothing, and shelter but have maintained mounts for warlike pursuits. Many pastoralist peoples are thought of as warlike, and possession of horses for rapid transportation certainly enhances war-making capabilities. East African cattle peoples usually did not have mounts, although they frequently engaged in warfare anyway. At the other extreme are people like the Same of the European Arctic, who have seldom engaged in group fighting and usually have retreated into more distant backlands in response to the pressures of their more warlike European neighbors. Many of the cultural and even psychological differences among pastoralists are direct or indirect reflections of the habits and requirements of the different kinds of animals.

Pastoralists often have well-earned reputations for fierce independence and disregard for land boundaries. As world populations have increased sharply in recent centuries, claiming more lands for food cultivation, the world of pastoralist nomads has shrunk and in many areas pastoralists have entirely disappeared. Policies of almost all modern governments from West Africa to the Soviet Union (and elsewhere) are to settle these independent people and fence in their unruly herds so they don't interfere with more sedentary peoples' activities. The law is usually on the side of the settlers and their fields, and pastoralists must shift their activities to more and more inhospitable areas. Pastoralists still have some independence in parts of North and East Africa, in the more rugged desert areas of the Near East, and in the mountains of Iran, Afghanistan, and some neighboring areas.

Complex Agriculture, Peasants, and Cities

The development of crop growing in fertile areas such as the Near East, the heartlands of Central Mexico, and the west coast of South America, as well as in many parts of India, Southeast Asia, and China, opened up a process of social change involving population growth, technological developments, and new forms of economic and political systems. Even with relatively simple agricultural techniques, as in parts of Africa south of the Sahara, especially favored regions could support stable and dense populations characterized by kingships, bureaucracies, and other features of nationhood. The social evolution that accompanies the development of really complex and intensive agricultural techniques is especially visible in the rise of towns and cities.

All human societies known to us (except possibly a few extremely isolated, unusual cases of Inuit hunting communities in the nineteenth century) have been and are dependent on other societies—their neighbors and their enemies—in exchanges of goods, spouses, social visits, and aggressive actions. Nonetheless, the types of societies we have been reviewing thus far have usually had the luxury of being *relatively* self-supporting and autonomous in governing their own affairs. Hunting and gathering bands, horticultural societies, and other intermediate or mixed "types" of small-scale societies have generally produced most of their own food supplies and, for the most part, have organized their social interactions and behavior patterns through *local* social control and localized ENCULTURATION to conform to the group's own particular lifeways. With the coming of more complex STATES and centralized political controls, this autonomy was no longer granted to local food-producing communities; rather they were required to produce surpluses to pay the price of the specialization inherent in growing URBANIZATION. Ironically, the PEASANT peoples,

12.7 **The versatile camel is used by Arab peasants for many tasks, including plowing. (Erich Hartmann, Magnum)**

garded as superior in many ways to the life style of the rural food-producers. Peasants, though often highly ambivalent about city ways, have sought to acquire some of the culture of the cities, and at the same time they have more and more acquired the language of the dominant political state. Many peasants first learned their national language through conscription into military forces.

According to many anthropologists, peasant villagers around the world are often considered "part-societies with part-cultures" (Kroeber, 1948:284). However closed the internal workings of community life in peasant villages, many features of their lives are powerfully influenced from the outside. At the same time, those things of the outside world, including the national language and the national religion, are given special and unique stylizing in the local scene. For example, some forms of Catholicism practiced in peasant villages often differ from those same forms as practiced in the cities. Local village dialects of national languages are sometimes so different from those of their urban counterparts that city and country folk can hardly speak to one another without interpreters.

In most parts of the world today, former horticulturalist peoples have become peasants; in some areas though, they have been peasants for millennia. Because peasant forms of social organization are so widespread and are the conditions of life for a large segment of the world's population, they have been extensively studied by social scientists, and especially by anthropologists.

Tepoztlán: A Peasant Community in Mexico

The community of Tepoztlán is perhaps the most famous peasant community in all ethnographic literature. It was first described by Robert Redfield, who did fieldwork there in the 1920s, and it was later restudied (in the 1940s and again in the 1950s) by Oscar Lewis. These studies have traced the progression of changes in a peasant community adapting to a nation undergoing rapid modernization. These modernizing influences actually get to Tepoztlán rather quickly, for it is located only about sixty miles from the cosmopolitan bright lights of Mexico City.

Like a great many peasant villages, Tepoztlán was a community of food producers long before a com-

the food producers, who have had to suffer the ever-increasing burdens of providing more and more surplus commodities for their urbanizing rulers, have at the same time become greatly inclined to look to the cities for both cultural ideas and new kinds of material possessions. As the nations of the world, with their various capital cities and other urban clusters, have grown in power over the centuries, the life of city peoples has come to be re-

235

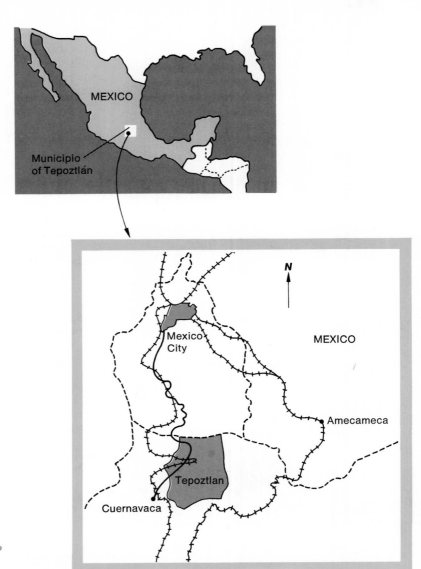

12.8 **Central Mexico, with the** *municipio* **of Tepoztlán just to the south of the capital city area.**

plex political system and economic network drew the people into peasant bondage. The ancestors of these peasant people were probably once autonomous horticulturalists with their own localized culture and concerns. As a progression of larger and ever more powerful empires (long before the Spaniards) succeeded one another in the Central Mexican region, Tepoztlán became a dependent food-producing unit within a larger structure. The burdens of tribute, taxes, and forced labor that the Tepoztecans had to pay to their Spanish conquerors were not so different from the burdens they had endured earlier under the mighty sovereigns of Tenochtitlán and perhaps the Toltecs of Tula. In a still earlier time, nearly two thousand years ago, influence from the coastal lowlands of what is now Vera Cruz had reached inland as far as Tepoztlán—possibly those ancient Olmec political influences

The Material Dimensions of Adaptation: Homo faber

had reduced Tepoztecan autonomy centuries before empires developed in Central Mexico.

In 1944 the village of Tepoztlán had a population of some thirty-five hundred people. The "aboriginal" Nahuatl Indian language was still in frequent use in the 1920s, when Robert Redfield studied the community, but by 1944 only about half of the villagers spoke some Nahuatl, and Spanish was predominant among the villagers (Lewis, 1960:6). The gradual deterioration of the local native language in favor of the national language is a nearly ubiquitous feature of peasant communities. Another quite typical feature of peasant communities was evident in the fact that the younger people in Tepoztlán were quite ashamed of speaking their Indian language in the presence of outsiders.

Food production in Tepoztlán and surrounding communities was (and is) carried out in both the ancient slash-and-burn horticultural style and with the more complex plow cultivation introduced by the Spaniards. The simpler food production style was essentially geared to the subsistence needs of the people, whereas plow cultivation was directed toward production of surpluses for the wider market. In the 1940s both wooden and steel plows were used by the Tepoztecans, and the power for pulling these implements was usually provided by oxen. Fifty-seven percent of the landowners had oxen in 1944. There, as elsewhere in Mexico, tractors have come into fairly common use in more recent times, though most peasant farmers cannot afford to buy the machines.

As in most of the rest of Mexico, the chief crops of Tepoztlán are the time-honored maize, beans, and squash, as well as chilis and a variety of other vegetables. Maize is the mainstay. Because Tepoztlán is located at the junction of hot land and high-altitude temperate cultivation, the people can grow a wide variety of fruits and vegetables, including bananas, oranges, lemons, limes, grapefruit, mangoes, avocados, squash, tomatoes, and sugar cane. Protein foods from animals are relatively less abundant in the Tepoztlán subsistence, for in recent times they have had relatively little livestock.

In the matter of diet, only a few of the Tepoztecan families could afford to eat much meat or other high-protein animal products, and the very poorest families had to subsist on maize tortillas, beans, chilis, and a few other vegetable products. While the food systems of simpler societies have tended on the whole to maintain egalitarian food intake (partly through extensive food sharing and redistribution), peasant societies like Tepoztlán often have very marked inequalities in food use, with near starvation for the poorer families, unrelieved by any compulsory generosity on the part of the rest of the community. There are some exceptions to this pattern, but it is interesting to note that the sharp

12.9 Street scene in Tepoztlán. (P. J. Pelto)

237

inequalities between city and rural village imposed by the growth of political systems are often reflected in a similar trend to inequality *within* the local communities themselves. In many parts of the world the rich and mighty landowners in peasant villages are actually agents of the central governments that are in charge of local governmental policies. This was already true in Tepoztlán in earlier times, when the local ruling elite was a representation from the Spanish colonial system.

12.10 **The sap of the *maguey* plant is collected in a large gourd and then placed in vats to ferment into *pulque*, a drink that was celebrated by a whole pantheon of gods in pre-conquest Mexico. (J. Anthony Paredes)**

Compared to the types of societies discussed earlier in this chapter, peasant societies are especially distinctive with respect to the central importance of land and landownership. The fact that Tepoztlán has been an inhabited village continuously for perhaps two thousand years should make clear their attachment to a particular portion of the earth's surface for food production. Their slash-and-burn cultivation techniques, of course, depend upon extensive exploitation of the local hinterlands. On the other hand, plow cultivation involves more intensive and continual use of productive bottomlands. Historically, landownership, then, has been one of the main features separating the rich and the poor in Tepoztlán, and significant historical events, like the Mexican Revolution, begun in 1910, were particularly focused on the existing inequalities of land control in Tepoztlán as elsewhere in Mexico.

The Spanish who had come into the area and conquered the Indian peoples had grabbed up the lands for themselves in large and powerful hacienda estates, forcing the peasants into situations of ever-deepening servitude in PEONAGE, while communities, whether of Indian- or Spanish-speaking peasants, were left with only very marginal agricultural lands for their own subsistence cultivation. Even though the Revolution in Mexico was fought for redistribution of land, Tepoztlán, like most peasant villages in Mexico, is still faced with serious overall inequalities in the ownership of agricultural lands.

Among the Tepoztecans, "an individual's primary loyalties are to his nuclear family" rather than to some broader kin grouping (Lewis, 1951:41). Outside the nuclear families, individuals owe some secondary loyalties to kinsmen on both maternal and paternal sides, and there are feelings of loyalty or "in-groupness" with regard to neighborhoods, or BARRIOS, within the town. Tepoztlán is divided into seven such *barrios*, each with its own patron saint, internal organization, and ceremonial features. Kinship and marriage ties tend to be strongest within the *barrio* structure, and people with houses in a particular *barrio* must show their loyalty to the neighborhood through contributions to the neighborhood chapel. The elaborate and colorful fiestas that mark the saint's day celebrations of many communities in Mexico are ceremonial features that underline the importance of allegiance to particular local groups, and in Tepoztlán this means especially the *barrio*.

In Tepoztlán, as in most peasant villages around the world, there were by 1943 a large number of outside social institutions reflecting the policies and problems of the wider society. There were the schools to which children went to learn the culture, language, and lore of the wider nation; police with the uniforms of national authority who enforced both local and national laws; tax collectors and their accessories; and, to increasing degrees, storekeepers selling the modern goods from the city and foreign places. Those commercial transactions required money, which meant that there were people in the village who acted as bankers and moneylenders.

The Material Dimensions of Adaptation: Homo faber

Peasants generally operate within a cash economy, even though much of their food getting is outside the monetary system. There are many other needs for cash besides that of buying food, and in Tepoztlán:

There are a few money lenders . . . who make loans at an interest rate of 10 and 12 percent a month. The money lenders are extremely cautious about making loans and are careful about choosing a good risk. . . . A practice of pawning property as security for a loan is common. Usually land, oxen or . . . trees are pawned, but smaller items such as an iron, or even a woman's *rebozo,* may be pawned for small loans from neighbors. (LEWIS, 1951:172)

Peasant Communities and the National State

Because peasant communities are by definition under the powerful influence of their national governments, it makes a good deal of difference what kinds of policies those national governments operate under. Many of the nations in Latin America continue to have military dictatorships in which privileged landholding aristocrats dominate over the masses of relatively landless and oppressed peasantry. On the other hand, in newly communist nations such as Cuba and China, policies of the national government are much different, and there are attempts toward rapid development of education, medical services, and other benefits, accompanied by agents of ideological enculturation. Among communist nations peasant life can be much varied, as Soviet collectivizing is a quite different patterning of influence from the social influences of Maoist policies in China. For obvious reasons, American and European anthropologists have had few opportunities to study in detail the living patterns and life styles of peasants in these communist nations.

When anthropologists from Europe and the Americas have opportunities for thorough study of rural agricultural (peasant) communities in mainland China, the data should be especially fascinating, for some excellent studies of prerevolutionary rural Chinese communities (e.g., Yang, 1937) provide a baseline for comparison from which the revolutionary changes can be measured. In Yang's prerevolutionary village, many of the prime features of

12.11 Peasants at work in the fields of Yunnan, China. (Marc Riboud, Magnum)

239

the peasant life style were clearly evident: the central importance of landownership as the measure of wealth and prestige was clearly expressed; the landholding by kin groups, with very strong focus on males and male succession to landownership, was clear; at the same time, the powerful influences of the outer world as they impinged on local politics and economic transactions gave the village of Taitou a character that would have seemed familiar to a peasant visitor from India, Mexico, or nineteenth-century Europe. This is not to say that all peasant communities have the "same culture," for there are a great many differences in language, food styles, religious institutions, and many other things in different regions of the world.

Most peasants in the twentieth century have lived and are living in nation-states of great historic depth and social complexity. Peasant communities in China, India, Latin America, and other parts of the world are participants in extremely complex, large-scale social systems that have generally not been the focus of interest or specialization of anthropologists. No particular type of social scientist can claim to have sufficient skills to study the "full social system" of these large nation-states. Thus, for the most part, as social systems have advanced to great complexity, beyond the level of the nonindustrialized, pastoralist, and cultivating societies, anthropologists and other researchers have had to concentrate on selected features of these societies rather than trying to study them as sociocultural wholes. Some anthropologists have, however, attempted the monumental task of describing the social systems of, for example, African kingdoms and other complex societies. These studies give us some of the flavor of complex states with heterogeneous, multitribal populations.

Bornu: A West African State

The arid and semiarid regions of North Africa, from Ethiopia and Egypt on the east to Morocco, Algeria and Nigeria on the west, have for a thousand years and more been the scene of a conglomeration of kingdoms, emirates, and multitribe empires whose boundaries shifted frequently and sharply throughout the centuries of Moslem conquest and other political turmoil. Powerful states such as Ghana, Mali, Songhai, and others rose to power and then disappeared—some of them have been resurrected, at least nominally, in the form of newly independent modern nation-states. Some of these complex societies were practically unknown to Europeans until the period of colonization in the nineteenth century; yet their capital cities and military histories extend far back in time. Bornu is one of these states. It is located in the northeastern corner of Nigeria, and it has maintained its sovereignty for a thousand years or more and continues to exist as a semiautonomous province.

The people who call themselves Kanuri—"the people of Bornu"—number about 900,000 to 1 million in population. At least one quarter of them live in cities with populations of at least 10,000 inhabitants. Their capital city is Maiduguri, with a population (1960s) of about 80,000 people. Bornu consists of about twenty-four thousand square miles, and in addition to the Kanuri, there are perhaps 200,000 Fulani and Shuwa, who are seminomadic cattle herders. Another 200,000 to 300,000 people belong to various small "pagan" groups in the south, and there are perhaps 5,000 real "foreigners" from Europe and North America. Thus Bornu, like most states large and small, includes a diverse population, with a number of different languages and cultural groups.

The overall population densities of Bornu range from perhaps forty to sixty persons per square mile. Thus, it is interesting to note that Bornu is not as densely populated as are many areas with much simpler social systems in East and Southeast Africa, for example. Sheer density of population is not, therefore, the "cause" of Bornu social complexity.

The land that the Kanuri inhabit is for the most part open savanna, and there are few barriers to the rapid movements of both horsemen and destructive windstorms. Rainfall ranges from about twenty-two to twenty-seven inches per year, but most of it falls in the summer months, leaving the rest of the year a time of drought, heat, and windstorms.

The more rural Kanuri produce subsistence crops of millet (the major staple), guinea corn, ground nuts (major cash crop), and a number of other vegetables and gourds. Cattle, sheep, chickens, ducks, and goats are kept in considerable numbers, and in recent times a number of deep wells have been sunk in some areas, providing possibilities for a greatly expanded cattle industry. Compared to technologically and politically simpler societies such as horticulturalists and pastoralists, the Kanuri have a great many people engaged in crafts, including metalwork,

The Material Dimensions of Adaptation: Homo faber

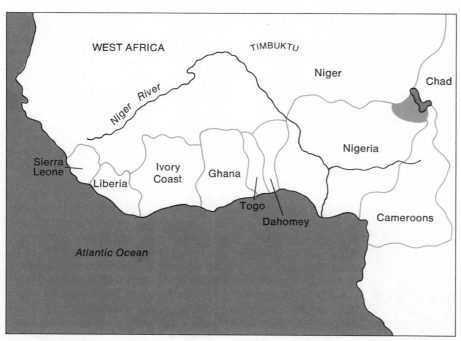

12.12 A Greek peasant woman irrigates her small garden plot. (Constantine Manos, Magnum)

12.13 Location of Bornu in northeastern Nigeria.

Food Production Systems: Foundations of Cultural Complexity

leather craft, tailoring, hat making, carpentry, dyeing, and so on. Other occupational categories that may be either full or part time include a variety of merchants and traders, various categories of civil servants, and the higher-level politicians of the bureaucracy.

As among peasant peoples everywhere, rural Kanuri households rely on their own cultivation for a considerable part of their food supplies but supplement their farming with produce purchased in the market. In addition they must have cash for purchasing other necessities in the complex economic system. Households, therefore, have quite diversified economies, and maintenance of the system depends upon large amounts of materials imported from outside Bornu territory.

The Kanuri household reflects the economic complexity of a society in which agricultural activities must be supplemented with craft specialization, trading, and political activities. Many households are POLYGYNOUS, for the multiple economic pursuits of a family put a premium on the household labor force, and additional woman power is a distinct asset. The economic and political power of individual households is frequently linked into systems of three, four, or more kin-related households, especially if there is a senior man with leadership abilities to manage the multihousehold association.

Above the household and multihousehold kinship level, however, political and economic structures in Bornu take on more and more nonkin trappings. Neighborhoods of villages are headed by *bulamas* (headmen). These local headmen with their local political responsibilities are subordinate to village headmen (*lawan*), who are local tax collectors and maintainers of law and order. Each such village headman has a retinue of followers who serve as administrative staff.

The village or local headman in Bornu may *seem* to be no different from his counterpart in a horticultural or pastoralist society. There is, however, a big difference. In a state-organized system such as Bornu, local headmen are the appointees and repre-

12.14 In the Sudan of West Africa there is extensive trading of goods between different ecological zones. (George Rodger, Magnum)

sentatives of the *central government*, and their tax collecting and adjudication of disputes, as well as punishment of crimes, carry the full weight of institutionalized law maintained by the organized and specialized police and legal system. They are the local embodiment of the national political bureaucracy, rather than simply lineage or clan elders whose chief responsibilities are to their local network of kinsmen.

Above the local level the bureaucratic organization of Bornu has a series of districts, each with a principal village or capital in which one finds the district courthouse and other governmental installations. At the head of the Bornu government is the *Shehu*. His palace is in the royal plaza in Maiduguri, and beside the palace stands a mosque symbolizing the official state religion of Islam. The court is a place of pomp and circumstance: "The people, including the nobles, go down on their knees to the monarch, stand when he stands, remove their shoes in his presence, and speak to him only indirectly, using terms of reverence and respect" (Cohen, 1967:106).

In actual day-to-day political affairs the *Shehu* shares power with the Native Authority Council under the direction of a chief minister. Governmental affairs are handled by a number of departments with a growing mass of salaried bureaucrats, most of whom have some education in European schools. As in much of the rest of the world, young men with political and economic ambitions must get some education if they are to further their careers. Education, however, is not enough—political influence is often the essential lever for getting a position in government.

The turbulent history of Nigeria, with its internal warfare and rapid growth of modern political parties and governmental structure, naturally has an influence on Bornu politics. In fact, the politicians of Bornu are part of the Northern Peoples Congress Party, which has been a dominant element in the federal government in Nigeria. Thus the *Shehu* and his people in Bornu can play a considerable role in the Nigerian national political system, even though maintaining their semiautonomous rule in the northeastern corner of the nation.

The complexities of the Bornu sociopolitical system must, of course, depend upon a food production system that feeds a great number of nonfood-producing specialists. The food production system is really not all that complicated. In fact, it is quite comparable to the crop-growing and animal husbandry systems of many relatively simpler societies in Africa and elsewhere. The complexities of Bornu society appear to have arisen in part from Bornu's strategic position with regard to trade routes across the Sahara Desert as well as from the waves of conquest and other military action that have crisscrossed North Africa. The political control by the rulers of Bornu apparently developed to meet the requirements of military defense and offense in complex international struggles.

Complex States and Industrialization

The Bornu state, with its semifeudal political machinery, is a relatively simple social system compared to the wide-flung Roman Empire, the massively stable and enduring Chinese civilization, and the dozens of other large political and economic dynasties that make up the history of civilization. On the other hand, the nations large and small that came and went up to the eighteenth and nineteenth centuries were generally made up of two essential social components: the city communities with their political machinery, commercial establishments, military garrisons, and complex religious organization; and the food producers of the countryside, with small-scale, face-to-face life styles usually far removed from the increasingly impersonal and highly stratified culture of the urban sectors. Communications and transportation systems were slow; products and people moved across the land with animal and human muscle power. On water, travel depended on the energies of the winds and the currents.

In the nineteenth century the distances between peoples—and the separation between urban and backland populations—began to close up, as the invention of steam-powered and internal-combustion machines radically changed transportation systems. At the same time, growth of factories producing all kinds of commercial goods brought about increasingly rapid growth of cities as manufacturing centers, offering employment to the sons and daughters of the rural folk. The INDUSTRIAL REVOLUTION produced a variety of new types of social systems, all of them interconnected by elaborate communi-

Food Production Systems: Foundations of Cultural Complexity

cation and transportation systems. In later chapters we will examine some of the significant effects of industrialized societies as they reach out and engulf the smaller low-energy societies.

Summary and Conclusions

Our focus in this chapter has been on the various ways in which human societies since the Neolithic revolution have made their living. The foundations of "making a living" are in food getting—the technical activity in which *Homo sapiens*, like most animals, has had to spend most of his time. It is only in recent centuries that large numbers of people have been freed from the food-getting tasks to spend their time on other pursuits. But the fact that many people do something else besides producing food does not change our basic point: that the technology and social organization of food getting have powerful effects on practically all aspects of cultural and social systems. So it is useful to categorize the various human societies around the world in terms of their subsistence systems—as long as we keep in mind that these are only broadly useful guidelines.

We have looked at the types of subsistence systems approximately in their order of appearance in human cultural evolution. Hunting and gathering was first. The subsistence systems based on cultivation of crops and the keeping of animals are quite recent developments in human history, but their appearance has brought profound changes in human lifeways. Certainly since the Neolithic revolution the varieties of human social systems have been greatly increased, and the potentialities for our present sociocultural complexities depend on those massive changes in food-getting systems. At this time, all of these different types of subsistence systems are still to be found somewhere on earth. The hunting and gathering societies are doomed to disappear soon. This process is already evident in some hunt-ing and gathering groups that are being decimated by interference from the complex nation-state systems into which the world is now divided. Pastoralist societies too are rapidly being brought under control and "settled down," as their independent ways interfere with the affairs of nations.

As long as we focus our attention on *subsistence technology*, we can use descriptive labels such as "simple societies" and "more complex systems." However, these terms should not be applied loosely and automatically to refer to all features of societies. Although the material inventories of hunting and gathering peoples and many other small-scale societies may be relatively uncluttered compared to the masses of material goods produced in agricultural states and industrial nations, their systems of kinship and marriage may be extremely complex (as among many Australian groups); the religious ideas and practices can also be quite varied; and it is clear that the modes of thinking and rational problem-solving are complex in all societies, regardless of the extent of their tool kits and armory of weapons.

Also, we make no value judgments when we refer to technological systems (or anything else) as "simple" or "more complex." There is nothing inherently inferior about simplicity; complexity is neither better nor worse in any absolute sense; in moral or judgmental terms they are all equally human, and for people who use them, they are all equally adaptive in that generations of men and women have lived their lives based on those subsistence techniques. There are nonetheless differences in the qualities of living characteristic of the different subsistence technologies. And there are absolute limits in the shapes that social behavior can take in the different forms of food getting. Hunting economies cannot maintain urban-settled populations, nor can systems of shifting slash-and-burn cultivation. These things make a difference, and many of the features of cultural and social systems we will examine in later chapters are based on these differences.

The Material Dimensions of Adaptation: Homo faber

Some philosophers and optimists are fond of referring to *Homo sapiens* as "the philosophical animal," or perhaps *Homo idealisticus*. It is certainly true that humans are the only animals who philosophize, compose symphonies, and write poetry. It is equally true, however, that humans are the only animals who accumulate great masses of things that they carry around with them, lay claim to ownership of, and frequently fight over. So without denying the idealistic side of *Homo sapiens*, which we will discuss in later chapters, this chapter will be devoted to some of the important aspects of human materialism, especially the matter of socially defined ownership and distribution of material things.

It appears to be a nearly universal principle in preindustrial societies that individuals have special rights and privileges with respect to the things they create or produce by their own labors. Such rights and privileges are never absolute, for there are many rules and expectations concerning sharing, loaning, and reciprocity that affect individuals' "property rights."

The Sirionó (discussed in Chapter 12) are much like other small nomadic groups in the way they view the ownership of things:

Since the material apparatus is sparse, holdings and moveable property are few. As regards all of these possessions, however, individual rights of ownership are recognized and respected. Thus a man is owner of his bows and arrows, the animals which he kills, the maize or manioc which he raises; a woman is the owner of her pots, calabashes, baskets, necklaces, feather ornaments—in fact, all of the things which she herself makes and collects. (HOLMBERG, 1960:21)

Inheritance of personal private property among nomadic groups is naturally a rather simple matter. With the Sirionó:

When a person dies most of the things with which he has had intimate contact are placed with the body or thrown away. Thus, one's pots, calabashes, pipes, and feather ornaments are left at the site where the body is abandoned. Exceptions include hammocks, necklaces, cotton strings, and sometimes a man's arrows, particularly if he has been a good hunter. These may pass to his son or to his brother, while the few possessions of a woman usually pass to her sister or a co-wife, although they may also be inherited by a daughter. (HOLMBERG, 1960:21)

Homo sapiens: The Great Materialist

13

The Sharing of Food

Most nomadic hunters and gatherers, as well as the simpler cultivating peoples, cannot rely to any extent on the preservation of food. Though drying and smoking and other means of preservation can be fairly important under some circumstances, the proceeds of the hunt are much more easily disposed of as fresh food. If fresh-killed meat is to be eaten right away, the food is usually widely shared, often by everyone in camp. Here is an example from the Semai, as described by Dentan:

After several days of fruitless hunting, an East Semai man kills a large pig. He lugs it back through the moist heat to a settlement. Everyone gathers around. Two other men meticulously divide the pig into portions sufficient to feed two adults each. (Children are not supposed to eat pork.) As nearly as possible, each portion contains exactly the same amount of meat, fat, liver, and innards as every other portion. It takes a couple of hours to cut the pig up into portions that are exactly equal. The adult men of the house groups take the leaf-wrapped portions home to redistribute them among the members of the house group. . . . The question that immediately occurs to people brought up in a commercial society is, "What does the hunter get out of it?" The answer is that he and his wife get a portion exactly the same size as anyone else gets. No one even says Thanks. In fact . . . saying thanks would be very rude. (DENTAN, 1968:48–49)

Among the Semai, as in a great many other groups, one is supposed to share whatever food he can afford to give up. If a hunter brings home a relatively small animal, he might share it only with his nuclear family; but if he makes a larger kill he shares it with a larger group of people, and if possible with the entire settlement. Whenever someone is cooking or eating and another person stops in, the guest should be fed if there is enough to spare. Again, as in all societies, "There are . . . 'stingy' and 'selfish' people who do not share what they can afford . . . on the other hand, although 'generosity' is the mark of a 'good heart,' sharing more than one can afford is plain 'dumb.' " (Dentan, 1968:49)

The pig that was so carefully distributed in the Semai example would, no doubt, have spoiled if the hunter had kept it for his immediate nuclear family and tried to make it last several days. If there is some assurance that others will reciprocate it is much more economical and adaptive for the entire group to share fresh meat so it can be eaten before it spoils. The hunter who has invested in future reciprocities from his fellow food getters does not have to be concerned about a return of generosity from any *one* other individual. He is only concerned that *somebody* with food to spare will share with him when he has been unsuccessful in the hunt and does not have food for his family.

In this system, which we can call GENERALIZED RECIPROCITY, the members of the community can feel secure that they will receive food if there is any to be had. They do not necessarily all come out "even" in these exchanges, however. There are always some hunters who are more capable (and lucky) than others, and some cultivators and vegetable food gatherers may occasionally be more productive than their neighbors. Such individuals may gain a special measure of prestige from contributing more than their share of food supplies.

The excellent hunter could, of course, gorge himself frequently and be better fed than others, but there are limits to how much that display of greed would do for a person, whereas the prestige of being able to do more than one's share in providing food is an important and scarce commodity among hunting and gathering peoples. Frequently the most prestigious individual is the one who is the best hunter.

Ownership of Scarce Production Resources

When we view the uses and the social distribution of wealth in more complex societies, we are struck by the fact that differences in wealth are often due to peoples' different (unequal) relationships to natural resources of land, water rights, mineral deposits, and other natural features. The foundations, then, of wealth production in human society are in the relationships to the *essential means of production.* Many who have written about territorial behavior in hunting and gathering peoples have suggested that individual small bands of hunter-gatherers "own" their production territories and protect their territories against invasion or trespass by other groups. If this were true, we could say that each hunting and gathering band owns and controls its own production area. However, a number of recent studies suggests that such a picture is misleading.

In our discussion about the Shoshone (pp. 196,

246

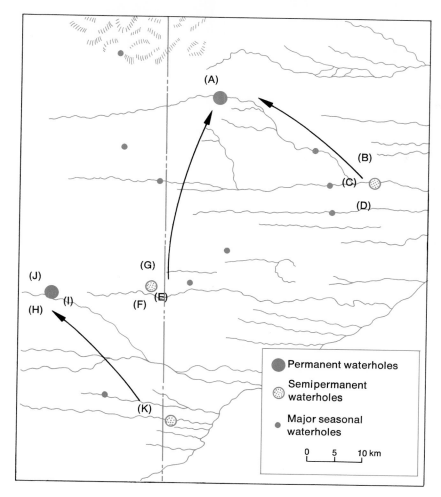

13.1 **Movements of Bushmen bands in times of drought. The bands (A)–(K) each have their traditional water holes, but (as shown in the figure) they may regroup in different patterns when some waterholes become dry. (Adapted from LEE, 1972:141)**

198) we noted that the locations of bountiful pine nut harvests shifted markedly from year to year and that locations of other food supplies of their region were similarly unpredictable. Therefore it would have been foolish for families, or small bands of families, to lay claim to a particular territory. In response to the shifting and relative unpredictability of food sources, Shoshone bands had to be extremely flexible in membership and unconcerned about exclusive rights to particular resources. When two different groups of Shoshone approached the same pine nut areas and some friction developed, there could occasionally be brief disputes over USE RIGHTS, but these were generally brief and unimportant (Steward 1955:105–108).

An extreme in nonexclusiveness of resources is probably that of the Inuit, among whom the idea of exclusive control over particular territories was almost completely absent. Among the Mbuti Pygmies of the Congo, the !Kung Bushmen, and other African hunting and gathering groups, small bands maintain use rights within particular territories, but they do not hold a monopoly over their resources. Woodburn, in his discussion about the Hadza in East Africa, reports that they:

Assert no rights over land and its ungarnered resources. Any individual may live wherever he likes and may hunt animals, collect roots, berries, and honey and draw water anywhere in Hadza country without any sort of restrictions. Not only do the Hadza not parcel

247

out their land as resources among themselves, they do not even seek to restrict the use of the land they occupy to members of their own tribe. (WOODBURN, 1968:50)

Among some hunting and gathering groups there can be individual claims to ownership of particular trees or groves of nuts, and some local groups may lay claim to certain water holes. However, these "privately owned" resources are usually available to other persons simply for the asking. For example, visitors in the territory of a particular Bushman band can ask for the right to use the water from the water holes "owned" by the local band, and the request will not be refused.

Property Among Nomadic Herdsmen

Domestication of animals brings about a measure of potentially monopolistic control of food resources. Herdsmen *own* animals, which they control and maintain for food supplies and other needs. We are all familiar with the fact that American Western ranchers use brands to identify their animals. Similarly many herders in other parts of the world use ownership brands. Among East African cattle peoples, for example, brands identify not individual ownership but also clan or lineage membership.

13.2 **Branding cattle in the American Southwest. (Erich Hartmann, Magnum)**

13.3 **A Skolt Same marks the ears of a reindeer calf with his personal property identification.** (P. J. Pelto)

Klima reports the following identification markings among the Barabaig:

Another way in which easy identification of livestock is achieved is through the culturally standarized use of cattle brands. Every bovine animal (that is, cow or bull) carries a set of three distinctive brands on some part of its body. Wealthy cattle owners sometimes apply a fourth brand which identifies the livestock as belonging to a particular family. Otherwise, no family name brands are used. While all cattle are owned and controlled by individual families, the cattle are ultimately the property of a larger social grouping, such as a clan and lineage. Each clan has its own distinctive cattle brand which is burned into the flesh of all cattle born into a family herd. A specific area on the animal's body is reserved for a particular clan. One clan's brand will always be placed on the left side of an animal's neck while another clan will customarily burn its brand into the right rear flank. Cattle brands, therefore, serve to prevent cattle theft and aid in identifying the animals on occasions when they are used in various stock transactions which occur during the lifetime of their owners. (KLIMA, 1970:27)

The control of food on the hoof necessitates some kind of control over grazing lands and water holes. Nomadic pastoralists therefore need to assert greater control over particular territories than do hunting and gathering peoples. At the same time, the quality of grasslands and other kinds of grazing areas

Among the Same of Northern Europe, where reindeer have been a mainstay of the economy, the animals have usually been owned by individuals and families rather than by larger groups. In order to identify the ownership of particular animals, the Same developed, over the centuries, a system of earmarks much like the marks on sheep and other domesticated animals elsewhere in Europe. Figure 13.4 illustrates some of the marks used to identify individual ownership. Nowadays the various different ownership marks among the Same and their neighbors must be registered with the reindeer associations. The number of earmarks has greatly increased, partly because of increases in the population and partly because it has become customary to register separate ownership marks for children. Consequently, there are hundreds of different earmarks in use in every reindeer district in northern Finland and Scandinavia, and the reindeer men must be able to remember many dozens of these ownership marks in their daily herding activities. No herdsman, of course, can remember every one of the hundreds of earmarks that are used in his own district, but some exceptionally capable herders can identify as many as two hundred to three hundred earmarks without the need to consult the little black registry books that these men often carry with them.

changes from time to time and season to season, so pastoralists must be able to shift their locations to meet the food needs of their animals. In their concern for adequate grazing, they may come into conflict with neighboring groups, and in recent times they have increasingly encountered problems with the rules, regulations, and police forces of more sedentary populations.

The fact that the ecological adaptation of pastoral nomadism is strongly oriented to ownership of animals and control over access to grazing areas and water rights means that there can be a great deal more inequality of wealth among pastoralists than is found among hunting and gathering peoples and simple cultivators. Part of this unequal distribution arises because wealth in the form of animals can be stored indefinitely, unlike bountiful harvests of yams and other perishable foods. It is also important to note that herds of animals are easily divisible into identifiable "ownable" units, thus encouraging interest in property and inheritance.

The nature of pastoral nomadism is such that changes in the size of herds of different families, lineages, and communities can be rather rapid. Droughts, warfare, theft, and disease, as well as other misfortunes, can bring about rapid decimation of herds so that a wealthy herdsman can be impoverished practically overnight. On the other hand, maintenance of herd sizes depends a good deal on the labor resources within the families, so that a

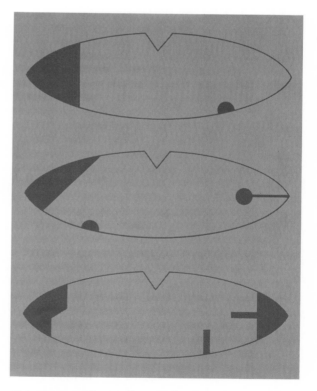

13.4 Ownership marks cut in the ears of reindeer. Different shapes and sizes of notches make up a series of codes that permit thousands of different unique combinations.

Homo sapiens: The Great Materialist

household with several able-bodied males and females can build up herds fairly rapidly, particularly if animals can be acquired by purchase and other transactions. Of course, one person's loss is another person's gain in rustling and other theft, so that some wealthy families have been known to build up wealth quickly through illegal means.

The fluid nature of ownership among pastoral nomads has another important aspect. In general, the control of grazing and water resources is such that no individuals are deprived of access to them. Any newcomer to a region, if accepted socially within the local group, can have access to grazing and water if he accumulates a herd. Similarly, the sons of impoverished families can gain access to grazing and water resources if they are able to accumulate animals. Access to the scarcest essential means of production is not, therefore, generally monopolized and tightly restricted among pastoral nomads, even though wealth differentials may be substantial.

Among the Barabaig, poverty in cattle is looked upon as unfortunate, and "a man who has lost his herd through improvidence and irresponsibility will not be helped by kinsmen and will become an object of ridicule and derision" (KLIMA, 1970:32). A man who is rich in animals, on the other hand, will be envied and may become the object of theft and other social controls unless he is also generous. To be wealthy and to use the wealth in socially acceptable ways, especially through generosity in sharing food and drink, is the main road to prestige and social acclaim in a great many herding societies. It is obvious that attitudes of reciprocity and food sharing among herdsmen are different from those among hunting and gathering and cultivating peoples. It would not be possible to build up large individual herds if an ethic of complete sharing within the local community were upheld. Pastoralists permit themselves a certain amount of "stinginess" and indifference to the food needs of their neighbors, or else they would never accumulate large herds. On the other hand, the wealthy herd owner can generally be approached for gifts to the more unfortunate members of the community. Needy persons in the pastoral community can usually rely on *some* generosity from rich herd owners, but it is generally expected that those herd owners will not deplete their herds significantly for the sake of other people. Furthermore, the wealthy cattleman or reindeer herder will not extend his generosity equally to every member of the community but will generally reserve it for particular kinsmen and in-laws on a selective basis.

It is important to note that differences in attitudes toward property and degrees of sharing and generosity among peoples are not abstract qualities that develop through some ethereal religious beliefs or psychological sets. Rather, these differences in attitudes toward ownership are reflections of ecological situations—of the potentially monopolistic control of resources and the adaptive strategies available in human groups for maintenance of stable economies, given their techniques and the nature of the local natural resources.

Wealth and Property Among Cultivators

We have noted that land as a fixed and exclusively controlled property and source of wealth is almost absent from hunting and gathering peoples, and is generally not a source of much social differentiation among pastoralists. Among many simpler cultivating societies, too, land by itself is not worth monopolizing. Under conditions of shifting cultivation (see pp. 227–231) ownership of particular parcels of land may not be nearly as important as control over the labor to clear, burn off, and cultivate new plots. In many cultivating societies individuals and families have only use rights (sometimes called USUFRUCT) to the particular plots of land that they have currently under cultivation, and their ownership over such lands lapses when they give up crop growing in that particular place. The use rights to various portions of community lands may be controlled by kinship groups, which allocate these resources to their members. Since every kinship group within the local community has access somewhere to lands, no individuals are deprived of access to places where they can grow crops. Among the Semai of Malaya, Dentan reports that:

There is no permanent ownership of fields among the Semai. A nuclear family "owns" land which they have cleared and from which they are still getting crops. The fields are usually marked off into nuclear family plots by fallen logs or lines-of-sight between two landmarks. If for some reason a man is unable to clear a

The Material Dimensions of Adaptation: Homo faber

plot, he asks for part of the field of a kinsman or housemate. . . . To refuse such a request would be . . . an extremely serious breach of proper behavior. If someone outside the nuclear family helps clear the family plot, the head of the family supplies him with tobacco and feeds him a meal when the work is finished or gives him some rice and tobacco to take home. . . . Before a settlement moves, people clear fields near the site of the settlement, which may be a couple of miles from the old one. (DENTAN, 1968:43)

Although some forms of individual landownership and other "private property" occur among cultivating peoples, CORPORATE kinship control of production property is probably more common. Such corporate ownership of resources is particularly significant in societies with limited land, as in the islands of Oceania. Many of the island communities of Micronesia, for example, consist of small coral atolls, often with only a few square miles of total land surface, only part of which can be cultivated. The atoll of Ulithi, for example, consists of a series of small islands around a central lagoon with a total surface of perhaps 5 square miles. The largest island has 1.8 square miles of land surface. Here crop lands are owned by the lineages, although use rights are allocated to individuals. Since the Ulithians are dependent on fishing for a significant part of their protein intake, canoes are another important production resource. These, too, are owned by corporate kin groups rather than by individuals.

The island of Moala in Fiji provides another interesting instance of the relationship of landownership to environmental conditions. Moala is of volcanic origin, some twenty-four square miles in area. The island is rather hilly and has a population of about twelve hundred people, settled in eight coastal villages. The people grow root crops such as taro, yams, sweet potatoes, and sweet manioc using slash-and-burn cultivation techniques. Land on Moala is claimed by the different villages, and village lands are "owned" by individuals who have use rights over the plots they cultivate. Although individuals are said to own their crops and their own labor resources, many of the Moalans live in extended families in which all resources are pooled. The extended family is "usually composed of a man, his wife, his unmarried daughters and sons, and married sons with their wives and children." (Sahlins, 1957:450)

In Moala:

The traditional extended family pools its property resources as well as its labor resources. Each mature man has a yam garden, taro patches, and plots of other plants which he calls his own, but the products are not his to dispose of. All gardens of family members are subject to the control (lewa) of the family head. He determines where and (formerly) when gardens are to be planted, when they are to be weeded, and when crops are to be harvested. Since the food produced is for a common hearth, and since control of the plots is centralized, the various gardens are in effect joint property. As one informant puts it, "We are planting for one pot. The gardens are separate, but they are as one garden. Any one of us can and does take without permission from any of these gardens." (SAHLINS, 1957:454)

It is interesting to note that in the villages on Moala that do not need to cultivate distant lands there has been a tendency for the extended families to fragment into separate nuclear households. Thus it seems that ownership and organization of production in the extended family form (with several adult males and females in residence) are adapted to situations in which productive properties are scattered about in a variety of places; if production lands become consolidated close to home, nuclear families (only one married couple plus offspring) can manage them quite effectively.

Landownership and Complex Agriculture

As agricultural techniques have become more refined over the centuries, cultivators have developed irrigation systems, methods of fertilizing the soil, and other means whereby productivity per acre is increased and the same fields are used over and over, year after year, instead of being left to revert to forest land. Permanent, intensive agricultural land use naturally results in heightened value of land as property, and possession of cultivation lands often becomes the main mark of social wealth. As intensive cultivation practices spread in ever-widening circles from the origins in the Near East, Southeast Asia, and the nuclear agricultural areas of the New World, control of land as property became a central feature of complex social systems. We are all familiar with the histories of the European nations, in which conflicts over rich agricultural lands often motivated

251

wars among dukedoms, kingdoms, and other governments, and in which there grew up a complex FEUDAL social system based on landownership. Gradually an aristocracy of landowners developed, with systems of reciprocal relationships between them and the people who tilled the soil.

Landed Aristocrats, Peasants, and Serfdom

Ownership of large tracts of rich agricultural land is meaningless unless the owners can find people to work to convert its potential productivity into negotiable wealth. Landlords can always offer the land to peasant cultivators in return for rent, but throughout history the owners of agricultural lands have found it useful to develop means to insure that their agricultural workers stayed at home and in the fields, rather than wandering on to greener pastures. The development of the Russian system of SERFDOM is an interesting example of this tendency. Until about the sixteenth century agricultural workers using the lands of the privileged aristocracy were not bound by any permanent ties to their landlords. However, with increased population and increased competition among the aristocratic landlords for profits, the institution of debt bondage began to develop. Lands were loaned out to peasants, along with money and seed, to be paid back with crops, money, and obligatory labor for the landlord. As long as there was open frontier in Russia—through the sixteenth century—peasants could move out from under these debts to find new areas of cultivation, and landlords had to compete with one another for their services. However, by the middle of the seventeenth century the government had passed laws restricting the peasants' rights of movement. Peasants were legally tied to the lands on which they worked, and running away was severely punished. By the middle of the eighteenth century, over half of the rural population of Russia were serfs, legally bound to the land they cultivated.

Thus, in Russia as elsewhere in developing agricultural states, ownership of large landholdings generally meant control not only of the cultivable lands but also of the labor force for exploiting these properties:

Throughout the nineteenth century, there was a tendency to raise the amount of peasant labor on squire land from three days a week to four, five, or even six days. In addition, peasants had to work on construction projects and in brick making, while women produced linen and woolens. Peasants also had to supply carts and manpower to carry the squire's produce to market, an obligation which consumed 30% of their working time in winter, 8% in the summer months. On some farms, the squires were even successful in converting labor dues into outright wage labor, in which the worker did not have access to land, but received payment in food and clothing for work on the lord's domain. (WOLF, 1969:54)

The Material Dimensions of Adaptation: Homo faber

13.5 Terraced fields represent countless hours of labor for both construction and maintenance. Yunnan, China. (René Burri, Magnum)

No wonder, then, that throughout the centuries of Russian history peasant populations rose up again and again in an attempt to throw off the oppression of the landlords and the system of bondage that tied them to the landed estates. For example, between 1826 and 1861 (when the first major reforms in the system were attempted) there was an amazing total of 1,186 different peasant uprisings—with a steady increase over time (Lyashchenko, 1949:370).

Prior to the Mexican revolution of 1910, a very small aristocracy controlled most of the arable land in Mexico, and millions of peasants were tied in debt peonage to the haciendas. It has been estimated that at the end of the dictatorship of Porfirio Díaz, just before the revolution, there were 8,245 haciendas in Mexico, of which 300 contained at least 10,000 HECTARES, 51 had approximately 30,000 hectares each, and 11 contained no fewer than 100,000 hectares. One man, Luis Terrazas,

archetype of the Porfirian hacienda owner, had fifteen holdings, comprising close to 2 million hectares. People

253

Homo sapiens: The Great Materialist

joked that Chihuahua [state in northwestern Mexico] had less claim to him—as its native son—than he had claim to Chihuahua. He owned about 500,000 head of cattle and 250,000 sheep, exporting between 40,000 and 65,000 head of cattle annually to the United States. . . . The average hacienda was probably close to 3,000 hectares. (WOLF, 1969:16–17)

These illustrations from feudal landownership systems of past centuries illustrate an important aspect of landownership: where land is the scarcest essential production resource, it is extremely subject to monopoly by a few privileged landowner-aristo-crats. Unlike herds of cattle or other domesticated food resources, agricultural lands do not move about; it is possible to build fences around fields, to build fortifications to defend them against ene-mies, and to develop complex systems of ownership and inheritance. Land does not diminish in size and

13.6 Harvesting in west Finland. Until this century many Finnish peasants cultivated lands owned by well-to-do landowners. (P. J. Pelto)

13.7 Plow agriculture in Chile. (Sergio Larrain, Magnum)

its productivity can be expanded by improved food-producing techniques, so fixed amounts of land tend to increase in value, constantly inviting greater monopolistic control. The absolute ownership of land in complex agricultural states thus takes on significant dimensions entirely unlike the looser forms of landownership found in simple cultivating communities.

The distinctive feature of property ownership in complex society is that large segments of the population are deprived of direct access to production resources and must pay "rent" for the use of the resources or are forced to work as laborers for those who own lands and other properties. A further change from the economic organization of simpler societies is that individuals no longer own the products they themselves produce. Thus there is a profound change in individuals' relationships to the means of their own subsistence.

Money: "The Filthy Lucre"

Wherever extensive exchange of goods takes place among peoples, there is a need to establish customary rates of exchange for different goods. Rates of exchange are often managed more easily if there is some basic standard of value—some kind of scarce good in terms of which the "prices" of various commodities can be set. Although there are exceptions to this, the valuable things that become the standards of exchange are generally portable and relatively permanent. (It would not seem practical to have tomatoes or fresh fish as standards of exchange, for example.) Accordingly, valuable metals have often been used as standards of value and exchange. In Africa south of the Sahara, for example, brass rods have been widely used as money, as have various iron objects, such as hoe blades and spear points. In many parts of the world various kinds of shells—especially cowrie shells, dentalia, and occasionally even clam shells—have served as money. All these items are durable and easy to carry around and can be hoarded for long periods of time without deterioration.

The idea of money as objects that could be used in exchange and could be hoarded as wealth was a major cultural focus among some of the Indians of Northern California, especially the Yurok. Their dentalium shells were grouped into five different

grades and generally kept on strings. The longer the dentalium shell, the higher its value. These shells were widely traded all the way to the Missouri River and north to Alaska in aboriginal times. There was a correspondingly wide range of use in the eastern half of the United States of WAMPUM made of marine shells found off the coast of New England and the Middle Atlantic states. In the early periods of trade between the Iroquois Indians and the White settlers, wampum became widely accepted as a standard of value by Whites and Indians alike. However, the White peoples' metal tools made the manufacturing of wampum so simple that a rapid

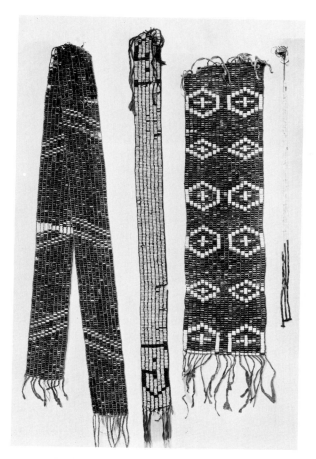

13.8 Belts of wampum, money among Northeastern Indians. (Courtesy of the American Museum of Natural History)

255

Homo sapiens: The Great Materialist

13.9 Dogs' teeth and shell money exchange hands in this Manus ceremony, Admiralty Islands. (Courtesy of the American Museum of Natural History)

inflation took place, and wampum gradually became completely worthless.

In Central America the chocolate bean (cacao) was widely used as a medium of exchange, especially as a handy means of giving "change" when articles of unequal value were traded. The beans, like many other items of food that have been used as money, have the advantage of being edible if the wealthy person is hungry.

Among animal-keeping peoples, live herds often serve as "money on the hoof." Many transactions—from bride payments to payments for injuries—are regularly paid off in animals, and when one herdsman works for another, he often prefers to accept payment in animals. The usefulness of animals as money depends, of course, on the size and value of the animals. Bullocks, camels, and even elephants, can serve as wealth, but they are not particularly handy for day-to-day transactions in the marketplace because each individual animal is so valuable. Among many herding peoples a variety of animals are kept. Cattle serve for larger transactions,

and smaller exchanges may be in terms of goats or chickens. Among Same reindeer herders, payments for services, as well as gifts at weddings and other occasions, have usually been in the form of reindeer calves, since the value of a calf is small enough to be useful for a variety of different transactions. Animal hides are also fairly handy as a type of stored wealth and medium of exchange. The use of beaver pelts as a quasi money was widespread during the heyday of fur trapping in North America, and squirrel skins served as "money" in Northern Europe and Siberia.

Special-Purpose and All-Purpose Money

Nowadays we are used to the idea that money is a fully generalized medium of exchange, good for anything that "money can buy." In many nonindustrialized societies objects that serve as money have had quite restricted uses. Cattle and other large

256

animals are awkward as a medium of exchange because they are not easily transported, and it's hard to "make change." The famous ceremonial coppers used in the Northwest Coast potlatches were mainly ceremonial and could not serve for ordinary economic transactions.

Recently Stuart Berde has described the complexities of a ceremonial "monetary" system on Rossel Island in Melanesia. The coins, made from spondylus shells, are called *ndap* and make up a series of ranks or values from 1 to 22. Although the lowest pieces in the series are used for small-scale economic transactions (e.g., purchases of baskets and tobacco), most of the *ndap* currency is used only for ceremonial exchanges, especially in connection with obtaining brides. Furthermore, the lower orders of *ndap* are not exchangeable for the more valuable pieces in a strict fashion, like our "small change." Actually the Rossel Island *ndap* currency system is a set of symbols concerning social support, social relations, and social obligations. As Berde expresses it, the "value" that is symbolized in the Rossel Island ceremonial money "is the *number of occasions* that one can involve oneself in economic transactions" (Berde, 1974:27).

There are many other exchange systems in the world that involve some sort of special-purpose money. One could argue that our economic system has several different types of special-purpose money, whose utility is sharply restricted by circumstances. The various kinds of green stamps, red stamps, and other trade stamps are examples, and of course our personal checks and credit cards also represent money in special ways.

Trade and Circulation of Goods

In most societies, even those with very simple technologies, barter and trading take place both within and among communities. Even though meat and most other foods may be shared in systems of generalized reciprocity of the sort described above (p. 246), there are usually some kinds of goods (both

---

Real Money in a Stone Age Society

The Kapauku of New Guinea are an excellent example of a non-Western, nonindustrial people with a fully developed use of money. It appears that Kapauku transactions in pigs, land ownership, and other things are sufficiently complex so that there is good reason for them to have developed a common medium of exchange that simultaneously serves as the measure of value for things. Cowrie shells and two types of necklaces are used by the Kapauku for food transactions, the sale of animals, and as the measure of value of crops, lands, and artifacts. They also can be used for payment for work in the gardens, magical curing, and other services. Damages and fines are also calculated in terms of cowrie shell standards.

The cowrie shells come in several denominations. The largest denomination is the *bomoje*, an angular cowrie with a lot of bumps and depressions. There are two types: a yellowish-white *bomoje* and a dark-bluish one of slightly higher value. The more valuable *bomoje* has a value of approximately twenty *kawane*, which is the Kapauku small change. The slightly "cheaper" *bomoje* is worth about fifteen *kawane*.

The Kapauku use several other kinds of shells in their monetary system, giving them greater flexibility than if they were simply using the two main types of shells. All of these shell valuables are imported into Kapauku territory from coastal regions, so the amount of money in circulation is limited. When Leopold Pospisil carried out his research among the Kapauku he found that they readily gave customary prices for various resources. For example, the price of a nine-hundred-square-meter plot of land was quoted as five *bomoje*, while lease of the same land for a crop would cost one *bomoje*: "A piece of pork of about 2 kilograms should sell for 1 *bomoje*, an introduced steel ax costs 5 *bomoje* and a steel machete 3 *bomoje*. A male pig of approximately 90 kilograms weight which is destined for slaughter sells for 20 *bomoje* . . . and the customary price for 30 rats is 1 *bomoje* . . ." (POSPISIL, 1963:19).

257

Homo sapiens: The Great Materialist

raw materials and finished products) that change hands through regular trading relationships. For example, special high-grade stone for making hand axes, missile points, and other tools and weapons is often found only in certain locations, and the people living near those locations have often taken advantage of these natural resources to trade with more distant communities, sometimes with coastal peoples for fresh fish; with people in tropical areas for bird feathers or other exotic products of the forest; or for the furs of animals more plentiful in one region than in another.

In the Pacific Northwest, in what is now southern Alaska, the Chilkat people were widely known for their excellent blankets made from the hair of mountain sheep and mountain goats, mixed with the inner bark of cedar. Chilkat blankets were widely traded among different tribes of the Pacific Northwest. Many other kinds of goods were involved in these trading activities.

Long before the coming of White people to North America, Indians had discovered large deposits of

13.10 Valuable Chilkat blankets were important in the economic transactions of Pacific Northwest Coast peoples. (Courtesy of the American Museum of Natural History)

13.11 Trading expedition in the Solomon Islands. (Elliot Erwitt, Magnum)

The Material Dimensions of Adaptation: Homo faber

13.12 Sailing canoes from Paneati Island, eastern New Guinea, on a trading expedition. (Stuart Berde)

copper near the south shores of Lake Superior. Both the raw metal and objects shaped from it were traded for hundreds of miles in all directions from the mine locations. There were several other copper centers—one in the Appalachian Mountains, one in southeast Alaska, and another among the Inuit on the Copper Mine River, which flows into the Arctic Ocean.

In the southeastern part of the United States salt was produced by evaporation in special pottery pans, an activity of part-time specialists. The salt was widely traded among different groups, for, like metal objects, it is easily portable and relatively high in value per unit of weight. Various wild plants, both food plants and especially herbs and other medicinal roots, seeds, and other items, were frequently traded among North American Indians and widely in other parts of the world as well.

Trading Areas in Melanesia

New Guinea and the nearby islands making up the Melanesian CULTURAL AREA have particularly intensive and complex trading networks. Thomas Harding has studied a trading system that links several hundred communities on both sides of the Vitiaz Straits, a rough and difficult stretch of water,

thirty or forty miles wide, between the Bismarck Archipelago and mainland New Guinea. Traders, operating with large two-masted canoes, move back and forth across the rugged strait, as well as along the coasts, linking their trading activities with inland exchange systems. Harding estimates that about 150,000 people live within the area of this trade system, most of them horticulturalists who produce not only extra food but also pots, bows and arrows, drums, various wooden items, and other trade goods.

Many of the communities in the Vitiaz Straits region specialize in one or two trade commodities. For example, the people of Bilibili Island are principally specialized in earthenware pots, whereas the Tami islanders trade carved hardwood bowls, as well as pots they pick up from the Huon Gulf people.

Trading activities depend on the excellence of seagoing canoes, some of which are up to sixty feet long with a depth of four to five feet, and one-half foot of hull. The island people from Bilibili, Tami, and Siassi supply themselves with trading canoes, but other people in the network who do not have suitable timber for canoes must rely on trade relationships to get canoes and canoe-building materials. The larger canoes are capable of carrying as many as twenty persons along with a goodly cargo—a cou-

259

ple of tons of taro, or two hundred to three hundred clay pots. The canoes are traded over a wide area, often in return for substantial numbers of pigs.

Pigs are a major object of wealth in the area and are obtained from the mainland interior. Not surprisingly, young pigs under a year in age are the most frequently traded animals, as they are easier to manage on long trips. Nowadays, the prices of pigs are quoted in modern Australian monetary values: "the more or less standard equivalents are five pounds [Australian] for a one-year-old, 10 pounds for a two-year-old, and fifteen pounds for a three-year-old. [In 1963–1964, the Australian pound was valued at U.S. $2.24.]" (Harding, 1967:35).

The market networks of the Vitiaz Straits area involve, then, a good deal of production specialization. For example, people of Umboi Island say of the Siassi islanders that "We are their parents, we give them food." The people of Siassi say, "They originate from us." What they mean by this is that the Siassis are the sources of the wooden bowls and clay pots that are the principal wealth objects involved in the marriage relationships of the Umboi people. These wealth objects legitimate marriages and thus the offspring of the Umboi people. On the other side of these transactions, the food that comes to Siassi from Umboi (and other places) is not just for calories. The shiploads of taro are combined with cocoanuts in ceremonially significant "puddings" that assume a central place in the rounds of politically significant Siassi feasts (Harding, 1967:154–159).

Traders must voyage widely and actively to keep up their place in the trading networks. The profits from their commercial expeditions are brought home, where they can be expended in feasting and other celebrations—which win prestige and power on the local scene. The profits from trading are not directly reinvested in expanded commercial enterprise but are consumed in conspicuous wealth displays that have political meaning within the local community. Individual big traders—who are at the same time the big men in local politics—must continually return to trading expeditions in order to maintain wealth and power.

While the basic structure of these trading patterns involves competition for political power among the traders, their connections are established primarily by means of kinship relationships. Each trader has "trade friends" at various points throughout the network, some of whom he inherited from his father or uncles or other patrilineal kinsmen, some of whom may be his mother's kin, and others established through marriage ties. Not all of the trade friends need be kinsmen—some are contacts that have been developed through other means.

The Growth of Trading Cities: Timbuktu

As trading activities developed in intensity because of improved transportation systems and new kinds of trade goods, some locations became especially favored as transshipping points, central nodes in complex multidirectional trade networks. In the case of the Siassi, as well as the ancient Phoenicians, the home bases of the most active merchants have often been small islands or other constricted locations situated at convenient points of articulation between different ecological zones. In Northwest Africa, the ancient city of Timbuktu developed as a commercial center at the point where the tropical environment of West Africa met the broad expanses of the Sahara Desert. The Niger River provides a convenient highway for goods and people, and camel caravans bringing goods across the hot desert from points in North Africa could trade for goods from the tropical areas on the shore of the river—at a point that was once simply a seasonal camp of the nomadic pastoralist Tuareg. There is an old Arabic manuscript that says, "In the beginning it was there that travelers arriving by land and water met. They made it a depot for their utensils and their grain. Soon this place became a crossroads of travelers who passed back and forth through it. They entrusted their property to a slave called Timbuctoo" (quoted in Miner, 1965:1–2).

Because Timbuktu borders on two different ecological zones, it is not surprising that it also has been the meeting ground of several different cultural groups. To the north, on the desert side of the triangle, are the Tuareg pastoralists. The first traders to settle in Timbuktu are supposed to have been from the west, from among the Bambara peoples, one of the numerous Mandingo tribes of the western Sudan. The Mandingo empire grew rapidly in the early part of the thirteenth century as they pushed eastward to establish political control over a domain geographically similar to the present newly created state of Mali in West Africa. Influences from the east reached Timbuktu from the ancient Songhoi capital of Gao, two hundred miles beyond Timbuktu.

The commercial activities of modern Timbuktu are probably a pale reflection of the bustling trade of bygone centuries, but some of the goods and activities of the marketplace still reflect the centuries-old interactions among diverse ecological zones. Along the river and in other regions favored with sufficient rainfall, the people grow millet, guinea corn, rice, peanuts, melons, and other crops. From the desert oases of the north come dates, and the caravans from farther north bring tobacco, European trade goods, and various other trade commodities. From the desert side of the landscape, the Tuareg herds and flocks are a major source of hides, wool, meat, and milk. Raw cotton is imported from locations to the west, and many other goods flow into the city from various areas.

From the earliest days of Timbuktu, a major commodity in the city's commerce was rock salt, which was mined in the central Sahara and brought by camel caravan to the city. The salt mines, especially those of Taodeni in the central Sahara, are of such importance that major military activities have been undertaken in struggles for control of these resources. Modern Timbuktu is still highly dependent on salt trade, and at the time when Horace Miner carried out his original anthropological research in the region (1940), the salt mines of Taodeni were still worked largely by Black slaves.

We are all aware of the fact that commercial transactions offer quick roads to the amassing of personal fortunes. Wealth accumulated through commerce, as practiced in Timbuktu, requires no land base, and the sharp commercial operator sometimes need make no great effort of labor in order to turn a profit. The scarce essential resources from which profit and wealth are derived in a place like Timbuktu consist of *social* connections with sources of supply and markets for delivery of goods (whether individual trade friends who seek particular goods or general public markets with consumption needs) plus some kind of liquid capital with which to buy access to the market transactions.

In spite of the risks and uncertainties in commercial ventures, it has always been apparent to youths seeking their fortunes that successful trading activities are a much quicker and grander (and perhaps less energy-consuming) way of getting wealth than is the slow process of accumulation through crop growing and rent collecting on one's hereditary farm land. Many a younger son of aristocratic background has found it more attractive and exciting to go into commercial activity than it is to stay down on the farm with the older generation. This is part of the original motive force for the rapid spread of European adventurers around the world as they found that the New World of the Americas and the hitherto unknown regions of South Africa and Oceania were full of a great variety of goods that would turn a handsome profit in the cities of Western Europe, if only one survived the long sea voyages to get them there.

While individuals spread out around the world in search of the profits of commerce, nations, especially of Western Europe, sent forth their armies and navies to protect their native-son entrepreneurs. Such protection of commercial activity usually necessitated laying claim to those "foreign lands" and subjugating their peoples to the flag and rule of their commercial masters, the Europeans. Great trading companies were organized to finance the ships and buy the supplies and men (and arms) for consolidating overseas commercial activities in India, West Africa, and other parts of the globe. Many great and envied fortunes were built by the more fortunate British, French, German, and other entrepreneurs, and, at the other end of the commercial network, more and more of the world's populations were drawn into the orbit of organized, "westernized" commerce.

The Public Marketplace

Until the urbanization and heightened commercial complexity of recent centuries, a large part of the exchange of goods in the world probably occurred in the context of open-air markets—established locations in town centers, village greens, and special areas where vendors and buyers meet to haggle, bargain, and deal over their goods. Such marketplaces are widespread today in Mexico and other parts of Latin America, usually convening once a week in each particular location. Each town or other market location has a market day. Neighboring towns usually hold markets on different days

261

13.13 **Market scene in Bali, Indonesia. (Magnum)**

13.14 **Fish seller in a Mexican market. (G. H. Pelto)**

so that vendors and buyers can travel from one location to the next, making the market circuit on a weekly basis.

In Timbuktu, as elsewhere, the marketplace is the retail center of trading. Most people in Timbuktu are engaged in commerce of one kind or another; but males are the main protagonists in the large-scale wholesale and export-import trading, whereas the smaller-scale transactions that are the life of the marketplace are defined for the most part as "women's work." This sexual division of labor in African markets is quite variable, however. For example, in a series of markets in the Rhodesian copper belt, more than half of the sellers were males (Miracle, 1965:304).

One of the chief features of open markets in most parts of the world is that it costs very little to become a vendor. Often the vendor must pay a fee for entry into the market, but the fee is usually nominal and is paid for that particular market day only. This is a market tax, collected by the local officials who regulate the market days and who are in charge of law and order in the area. Many of the sellers bring to the market goods they have produced themselves on their own garden plots or by their own handicraft activities. Thus they need not have invested much cash in entering the marketplace. Also, only the somewhat more affluent vendors expend much money for construction of selling booths. The poorest vendors in the marketplace simply spread their goods out on the ground, perhaps protected by a cloth. In addition to the fact that different types of goods occupy different areas of the marketplace, in many cases the poorer vendors tend to be segregated to some extent from the sellers with larger stocks of merchandise.

As European and North American communities have become more thoroughly commercialized and "modernized," open marketplaces have given way to established business enterprises, which are heavily regulated by governmental rules and taxation and which require very much larger investments before one can begin to engage in commercial activities. In this situation the entire society tends to be separated into "the business world" and the "consuming public." The economically less privileged part of the population has nothing to sell and could not enter the commercial arena even if it did have something to sell. The older system of open markets is, in that respect, much more democratic, for nearly

13.15 Indian woman vendor in a Mexican marketplace. (P. J. Pelto)

anyone can enter the market scene as a seller. In fact, there are individuals who come to the marketplace to buy sufficient quantities of merchandise (or even take them on loan from a larger vendor) simply to turn around and try their hand at selling. Small-scale, "semiprofessional" vending in the marketplace can be a crucial source of additional income that helps peasant populations and other economically marginal peoples to fill part of the economic gap between subsistence needs and meager incomes.

Silent Barter

The Carthaginians also relate the following:—There is a country in Libya, and a nation, beyond the pillars of Hercules, which they are wont to visit, where they no sooner arrive but forthwith they unlade their wares, and having disposed them after an orderly fashion upon the beach, leave them, and returning aboard their ships, raise a great smoke. The natives, when they see the smoke, come down to the shore, and, laying out to view so much gold as they think the worth of the wares, withdraw to a distance. The Carthaginians upon this come ashore and look. If they think the gold enough, they take it and go their way; but if it does not seem to them sufficient, they go aboard ship once more, and wait patiently. Then the others approach and add to their gold, until the Carthaginians are content. Neither party deals unfairly by the other; for they themselves never touch the gold till it comes up to the worth of their goods, nor do the natives ever carry off the goods til the gold is taken away. (HERODOTUS, trans. by RAWLINSON, 1945:363)

SILENT BARTER of the sort described by Herodotus occurs widely in the world, particularly in locations where the partners to the exchange are markedly different in culture and in the goods they have for exchange and where at least one partner to the exchange takes a relatively noncommercial view of the whole business. For another example, the Pygmies of the Congo forest often "silently" exchange meat and other animal products of the hunt for agricultural products, factory-produced goods, and other items from their more sedentary Bantu neighbors.

263

Homo sapiens: The Great Materialist

The Evolution of Trade and Commerce

In the general sharing of food and other resources characteristic of social systems like those of the Semai, the Bushmen, and the Inuit, the accumulation of wealth is not practical. Hunter-gatherers and other small-scale communities "enforce" this ecological factor by directing public opinion against the individuals who are stingy hoarders. Accusations of witchcraft and sorcery can help to pry loose the extra food or other goods that some individuals may accumulate from time to time.

More sedentary peoples, with greater resources and wider social contacts, can frequently afford some accumulation of goods; but the publically approved way of managing wealth often takes the form of "conspicuous distribution," in return for which individuals and kinship groups gain prestige and social influence. The "big men" in the Vitiaz Straits trading communities do not generally seek to accumulate goods in order to hoard property. Ceremonial sharing, with lavish distribution of food, converts wealth into the valuable coin of social honor and recognition, plus leadership in political decision-making.

Ceremonial distribution and exchange of goods have often been described by ethnographers in ways that attempt to demonstrate that the economic systems of nonindustrialized peoples are qualitatively different from "modern" distribution systems. The differences, however, are matters of degree. In the first place, the ceremonial circulation of goods in the form of reciprocal exchanges is a prominent feature of our own sociocultural system, especially around Christmas time. Like most "nonmodern" exchange systems, our Yuletide circulation of goods operates in a basically kinship-oriented fashion, and the intended effects of the giving and receiving are nonmaterial social relationships. Many other aspects of our contemporary arrangement of commerce have "noneconomic" elements—including special trading with kinfolk (even in major corporations) and the conversion of economic wealth into political and social power.

On the other hand, some of the most distinctly "nonmodern" systems of distribution appear to reflect the law of supply and demand and show individuals calculating gains and losses in ways like those of old Scrooge, Shylock, or J. P. Morgan. Among the Kapauku of New Guinea, for instance, Leopold Pospisil found that customary prices of pigs, land, and other goods fluctuated in response to available supplies, and individual entrepreneurs appeared to act as "rational economic operators" in planning their investments and transactions.

There are, nonetheless, some major changes in distribution systems that have come about through centuries of sociocultural evolution:

In the simplest, face-to-face social systems, like those of hunting-gathering bands, generalized reciprocity is a common feature of the distribution system. In somewhat more complex societies, economic goods are distributed through systems of greater formality, often through redistribution of food and other things at elaborate feasts and other ceremonial occasions. The potlatch system of the Pacific Northwest Coast, for example, (pp. 202–203) served to redistribute goods in ways that tended to balance out the effects of occasional large surpluses and occasional food shortages in individual communities within the larger regional system.

The development of large-scale societies based on complex agricultural systems has necessitated the growth of market exchange systems, which gradually developed more and more impersonalized features, including the use of versatile, all-purpose money. Whereas the accumulation of wealth in horticultural societies, like those of Melanesia and most of aboriginal North America, was of little consequence except as it could be converted into *social* prestige (through redistribution and conspicuous giving), the complex economic systems in agricultural and industrial societies make hoarding and control of wealth to some extent an end in itself. The rise of complex market systems of exchange does not, however, eliminate the operation of ceremonialized redistribution and reciprocity in some social contexts.

Growth of economic complexity has also been accompanied, as we noted, by increased possibilities for monopolizing scarce production resources. Such control of vital resources, in turn, provides direct and indirect control over *people*, so that ownership of capital goods can bring political and social power, even without any conspicuous comsumption or other ceremonial redistribution.

264

The Rise of Industrialization: New Kinds of Wealth and Resources

The Industrial Revolution of the past two centuries has brought with it a rapid increase in new kinds of production resources and new ways of accumulating wealth. The whole fabric of the Industrial Revolution is so complex and interrelated with other aspects of social relations and culture that we cannot go into any full-scale analysis of these processes here. But it is interesting to look at some instances of embryonic industrialization in order to identify certain common threads that might apply widely around the world.

In many parts of the world industrialization—the production of goods for commercial sale through the harnessing of new energy sources—has developed out of specialized handicraft activities. Features that appear to be essential in the beginnings of industrialization include:

1. Some kind of concentrated, harnessable energy source—wind to power windmills, water to turn waterwheels and later for generating electricity, fuel to power steam engines and internal combustion engines, and others.
2. Craftsmen with skills for producing products.
3. Sufficiently high agricultural productivity, freeing many people from the necessity of food production.
4. Raw materials for producing goods.
5. Potential buyers for the goods and ways of transporting the goods or bringing the buyers to the goods.
6. A medium of exchange—money or its equivalent—to facilitate the exchange of the goods for other wealth or goods or services.

The Development of Small-Scale Manufacturing in a West Finnish Parish

Until the late nineteenth century the inland parishes (counties) of West Finland were nonindustrial agricultural communities. As was typical of nineteenth-century Europe, a small number of families owned the major agricultural lands, part of which they rented out to crofters under long-term tenancy contracts. Kurikka was one such typical agricultural parish. Until the 1880s, and even later, the population of Kurikka could be divided into the following social categories:

1. A few professional and "aristocratic" families, including the parish priest.
2. The wealthy landowners and their families.
3. Tenant crofters who owed taxes in both cash and work days to the landowners.
4. Craftsmen—tailors, smiths, barrel makers, carpenters, and others—who lived partly from their own small gardens and partly from their regular production of goods and services for the rest of the population.
5. Poor "shack dwellers" and other landless peasants, who made their living through working for the wealthier part of the populace, plus begging and miscellaneous other activities.
6. Beggars, indigents, and other poor, supported partly by the church and partly by donations from the more fortunate families of the county.

Within this rural community we note first that there was a population of craftsmen who could make things for other people. The smiths, for example, made sleds for winter travel and horse-drawn buggies and wagons for summer travel and transportation. A large part of the clothing worn by the people of Kurikka in the nineteenth century was homemade, and some of it was made by the shoemaker, the tailors, and other craft specialists. Another interesting feature of the social system of Kurikka was that there were periods of enforced idleness throughout the long winter because no work could be done in the fields. During this period craftsmen could spend almost full time making things.

During the 1870s, one of the smiths living in the village of "Smithville" made a rather fancy horse-drawn carriage with a new type of spring system, which he hoped would produce a more comfortable ride on the bumpy back roads of rural Finland. He painted this buggy and took it to the Midsummer's market days in Vaasa—the largest annual market event in west Finland. He quickly found a buyer for his buggy. He also got the impression that others

265

13.16 Paneati Island people preparing their pigs for an important exchange ceremony. (Stuart Berde)

13.17 The New York Stock Exchange after hours. (Charles Harbutt, Magnum)

The Material Dimensions of Adaptation: Homo faber

would be interested in buying his product if he could produce more. The following autumn, when the crops had all been gathered and field work had ended for the year, Harjan Jaakko went back to work in his smithy, this time bringing in additional help from kinsmen and neighbors.

That winter Jaakko and his helpers made several carriages of the same model as the first one, painted them, and again headed for the Midsummer's Eve market days in Vaasa. The fashionable city dwellers of Vaasa quickly bought up the few available buggies, and there were orders for more. The new fashion was spreading, and the Kurikka buggy was gaining a reputation as a desirable luxury item. They came to be known as *Kurikkalaiset*, after the community in which they were built, and the reputation of the manufacturers spread through west Finland. Most of the smiths in Kurikka busied themselves making carriages throughout the winter, hiring their friends, neighbors, and kinsmen to help out in the process. In the ensuing years, these peasant manufacturers did not rely solely on the Midsummer market days for sale of their product. The smiths, as well as some of their relatives, traveled widely throughout western and southern Finland, and during the best days of summer they drove far to the north, selling their vehicles wherever they encountered people at market days and county fairs.

In time, styles changed and, shortly after World War I, gasoline-driven, horseless carriages began to appear. The market for the *Kurikkalaiset* waned. The smiths of Smithville evidently did not have the financial resources, the knowledge of gasoline engines, and other essentials for transforming their carriage manufacturing into an automobile industry.

All through the parishes of west Finland a similar process of embryonic industrialization took place during the nineteenth and early twentieth centuries. Craftsmen of various kinds began producing both luxury and utilitarian goods for an ever-larger market. After World War I, especially, many of these cottage industries developed into small factories, some of which have gradually grown into nationally known industrial enterprises. There are still some families in these west Finnish parishes whose wealth is in the form of agricultural lands, but landed wealth is now relatively insignificant, except in those cases where landholdings have been combined with ownership and control of factories or other industrial facilities.

Summary and Conclusions: The Transformations of Human Materialism

We are all of us concerned with our own survival. In that sense every human being is selfish at heart, although individual self-interest seems frequently to dictate impressive acts of altruism toward other persons, especially loved ones. People in cultures technologically less complicated than our own are not exceptions—they, too, look out for their own-self-interest. The generosity of food sharing among people like the Bushmen and the Semai is based on an ecologically enlightened self-interest. Giving food to

13.18 Private property becomes more and more economically significant as production systems become more complex. (Erich Hartmann, Magnum)

PRIVATE DO NOT ENTER

other members of the local band without any immediate return is part of longer-term personal insurance. Selfish hoarding is both technically and socially unfeasible. This type of general reciprocity is usually confined to small-scale communities, where practically everyone can claim kinship links to others within the group. Of course some small-scale societies display a certain amount of low-level greediness and antisocial hoarding (e.g., as among the Sirionó, who will sometimes eat their fill out in the bush rather than share with hungry relatives in camp). Hunter-gatherers are not, by any means, all alike in economic behavior.

In theorizing about the differences between modern and nonmodern life styles, some people seem to place major weight on attitudes, beliefs, and personalities in explaining different styles of ownership and exchange. But where do these differences in mental states come from? They surely do not "just happen." Careful analysis of different socioeconomic systems has accumulated evidence to support

13.19, 13.20 The many faces of poverty. The faces have more scars in inner-city scenes. (Magnum)

The Material Dimensions of Adaptation: Homo faber

the general idea that people act differently because their relationships to physical, biological, and social environments are different.

Relationships to the physical and social environment are mediated by technical culture, especially the means of food getting and the manufacturing of equipment and supplies. Throughout human history, storage and transportation have been especially influential in affecting the possibilities for inter-community exchanges of goods. Some easily portable and durable items have been trade items for thousands of years—the best examples are amber, seashells, and high-grade stone, such as obsidian, flint, and slate.

The other major dimension of the evolution of human materialistic activities is that complex matter of ownership and control of scarce economic resources. The growth of large, sedentary populations has generally been accompanied by increased possibilities for economic control by the few, the "owners" of production resources. Whenever the accumulation of wealth in individual hands is technically possible, people will apparently react (at least some of them) by becoming greedy for extra material possessions and power at the expense of fellow citizens, even relatives. Some hunter-gatherers have turned to wealth hoarding in unusual situations, but in cases in which the hoardable wealth is mainly food, there is little point in any individual's hoarding beyond his powers of consumption. Far better to convert that extra food into social capital through ceremonial and ostentatious distribution to other people, even one's enemies. The widely celebrated potlatch of the Northwest Coast peoples is an example of a situation in which temporary food surpluses were converted into social and political power through ceremonial redistribution.

In our complex, industrialized economy we have such a highly developed sense of "property" that we tend to think of everything as owned by someone, at least everything that is at all scarce. The widespread pattern of treating land as non-property—among hunting-gathering groups, pastoralists, and simpler cultivators—has often mystified Europeans, especially those who are the descendants of land-hungry peasants. The lack of clear property attitudes among people like the Inuit and the Hadza (and many others) is not a sign of simplemindedness or "poverty of culture." Rather, the ecological adaptations of nomadic and seminomadic peoples, as well as shifting swidden-cultivators, make human labor and skills the scarce means of production—so scarce, in fact, that land is left a free good. The intruding Europeans, on the other hand, with a technology for intensive cultivation tied to a more complex social and economic system, focused their attention on the best agricultural lands (e.g., in North America) and thereby converted real estate into a scarce and monopolizable resource, to be "purchased" or stolen outright from the Indians.

Concepts of property and rules of commerce are the distillates of social and ecological relationships. Property and wealth are always relative to the social and cultural context. In small-scale social systems individual property is involved with kinship obligations; in larger systems with centralized political administration property is under the control and taxation of the government and subject to many kinds of restrictions, from zoning to pollution control, in the "public interest."

The development of potentials for the unlimited accumulation of material property has had profound effects on human lifeways. The fundamental egalitarianism of social relationships in small-scale societies has given way to the elaboration of social inequalities and socioeconomic stratification in every sector of social life. No other aspect of human activity so clearly illustrates the significance of socio-cultural evolution in changing human behavior. Security for the hunter-gatherer, in the long run, depends on social credit, for each individual knows that sooner or later there will be times when it will be impossible to feed one's family by one's own production efforts. When that happens, one can count on help from others, based on the credit one has accumulated in the general system of reciprocity. When, in more complex sociocultural systems, it is possible to accumulate wealth in the form of both natural resources and money, it is possible for people to take the more "modern" attitude expressed (for other purposes) by Omar Khayyam: "Take the cash and let the credit go."

Homo sapiens: The Great Materialist

Part
Five

Perspectives on Social Organization

From Egg to Chicken: Organizing to Perpetuate the Species

Human Organization: Marriage and Family Life

14

One measure of adaptation, which is the most important measure from a biological perspective, is successful reproduction. As part of the study of human adaptation we need to examine the organization of reproduction from both biological and social points of view. We should be concerned not only with birth (and the physical processes of reproduction) but also with social patterns of mating, as well as with the care and upbringing of new members of the species—with bringing the infant to adult reproductive capacity.

In the evolution of ever more complex life forms, changes in reproductive processes have played a critical role. With increasing complexity the "value" of each individual life form increases. For millions of years the only medium for the growth of the embryonic forms was water, just as it was the only medium for animal life. Eggs with soft, vulnerable outer shells, had to be produced in huge quantities in order for a sufficient number to survive to guarantee a future generation. With the evolution of a hard protective shell some 300 million years ago, the depositing of eggs on land (where they were safe from water-living predators) increased the probability that the fertilized eggs would survive. The impact of this evolutionary advance is clearly evident in the contrast between the number of eggs laid by water-dwelling fish (carp lay half a million, sturgeon over 3 million) and the number of hard-shelled eggs deposited by animals such as the turtle (up to one hundred).

The mammalian pattern of reproduction, in which the fetus is nourished within the mother's body, changes very drastically the life chances of any one offspring. Instead of producing hundreds of babies, as does the turtle, mammals produce offspring in numbers ranging from one to fifteen or twenty per birth. In adaptational terms, the differences in number of offspring of different species represent differences in the probability of survival of individual offspring. The higher the probability that any given infant will survive the rigors of gestation and birth, the fewer the number required in each reproductive episode.

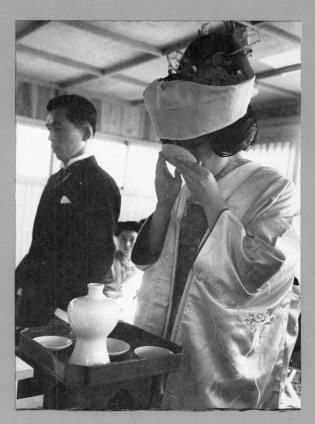

14.1 The Japanese wedding ceremony includes many symbols of social obligations to a network beyond the nuptial couple. (Werner Bischof, Magnum)

The larger issue, of course, is bringing the new generation from birth to reproductive capability. The chances of surviving to adulthood are as critical as surviving birth, and the number of total offspring per adult female also reflects variations in life chances among different species. Many factors influence survival. Among the more important are the abundance and reliability of the food supply and the potential for harm from negative environmental features, especially predators. In the complex equations of survival yet another variable is the extent to which the newborn can take care of itself and the degree of continuing protection it requires.

In many egg-laying species, including fishes such as the salmon, the parent provides no protection at all for its offspring; once the eggs have been deposited, parental responsibility ends. We may note, however, that countless years of natural selection have affected egg-laying behavior to increase the environmental protection greatly; the instinct-guided journey of the salmon to the upriver spawning grounds is itself a kind of act of parental responsibility. In a scale of protectiveness, the next step is represented by creatures like the catfish (which gives birth to live babies); the mother provides some protection for the newborn, remaining near her offspring and attacking threatening predators.

In the evolution of greater complexity, the next stage is the large number of species that not only protect their infants but also feed them. The significance of parental action for the survival of offspring is most marked in those species in which parents not only protect and feed but also teach their children survival skills. While learned behavior is clearly paramount for survival in humans, there are numbers of other species in which learning (and therefore parental "teaching") plays a significant role in survival.

The care and protection of offspring are at the heart of human social organization, but many other biological factors enter the picture. In any case, we will begin our examination of social organization from this fundamental biological perspective. The social relations that are essential to our primate survival include the following functions:

1. Sexual mating between male and female in order to start the reproductive process.
2. Nurturing the newborn infant through several years of dependency.

3. Protecting dependent infants and, at least to some extent, their mothers from predators and other external dangers.
4. Care and feeding of individuals who are temporarily incapacitated.
5. Cooperation (including some division of labor) in food getting and obtaining other necessities such as water and shelter.
6. Training the young to carry out their roles in biosocial activities successfully.

There are many other "motives" for social organization, but these six items seem especially important for understanding the kinds of social groupings of primate, and particularly human societies. Various monkey, ape, and human societies put different emphases on these essential functions, in part because their environments have different challenges and resources. For example, baboon social organization in East Africa is strongly affected by the presence of dangerous predators, whereas chimpanzees and gorillas have few external threats. In Chapter 3 we discussed some of the important adaptive features of nonhuman primate social organization. Here we turn our attention to mating, marriage, and family life among humans.

Getting Together for Reproduction: Marriage

Mating to produce offspring often seems a pretty casual affair among many of the primates, especially the chimpanzees. Among most human groups, also, mating frequently takes place on a fairly temporary basis; "premarital" and "extramarital" intercourse are not particularly "against the rules" in a great many populations. Nonetheless, in almost every human society there are special customs for regularizing and socially validating those relatively long-term, legitimate sexual relations between males and females that we call marriage. We have to say "almost every human society" because there are some groups that are so casual about "marriage" that it is hard to identify a clear ritual recognition of the marital state. Robert Dentan says of the eastern groups of Semai people (Malay Peninsula) that they "have no wedding ceremonies. As a result, it is sometimes hard to tell whether a couple are 'married' or just having an affair. Temporary separations are equally hard to differentiate from divorce. . . . Sometimes

the Semai themselves seem unsure about whether a certain person is married or not" (Dentan, 1968:73).

People who have very elaborate ideas about marriage are usually found in situations in which property is very important, kinship relations are complex, and social inequalities affect the definition of "good" and "not-so-good" marriage arrangements. In trying to understand why some people have elaborate wedding rituals the first question to ask is: "What difference does marriage make in this particular society?" (Sometimes the question has to be looked at in historical terms—referring back to the significance of marriages in earlier times.) The great pomp and circumstance of a royal wedding in England, viewed all over the world on television in 1973, was not because that marriage changed the course of English history—but it did reflect the fact that many earlier weddings among the royalty of England and Europe had profound political consequences.

Among many landowning, sedentary agricultural peoples—especially those with social differentiation between higher and lower strata of the population—weddings are carefully planned, selection of appropriate mates for young men and women is worked out by the family elders, and the rules of married life are strict, especially for females. Among the Rajput caste in a North Indian village, as described by Leigh Minturn and John Hitchcock:

275

Human Organization: Marriage and Family Life

When a girl is old enough to be married, her family must begin the search for a suitable groom. Marriage negotiations are sometimes conducted by the girl's father. . . . But it is more usual for the father to obtain the help of elderly relatives . . . the selection of a suitable groom requires a delicate balancing of many factors. The reputation of the groom, his age, health, looks [and]. . . . the relative social and economic standing of the two families must be weighed. (MINTURN and HITCHCOCK, 1966:57)

In a caste-organized social system such as India's marriage is allowable only between members of the same caste, and when things are that complicated it is no wonder that the choice of marriage partners is completely in the hands of the elders, the young newlyweds-to-be having little say in the negotiations.

In many societies weddings are the main festive celebrations. Like other human activities, the ritual enactment of marriage can serve other purposes besides getting two people wedded. The entertainment value of weddings is generally so high that many people have mock weddings for recreational and dramatic purposes. Some of us who were in grade school in the 1930s remember such rituals, especially the emotional shock of seeing one's secret sweetheart (age nine) "married off" in full ceremony to that snot-nosed kid on the next block.

No matter how elaborate the religious rites and other pageantry, people do not lose sight of the fact that the central object of the wedding celebration has to do with sex and procreation. The main preoccupations of the celebrants often focus on the question of the bride's virginity (totally unimportant in many societies) and the virility of the groom. Both these problems can be tension-filled, especially among those many people who have strong male-female antagonisms.

Among the Gusii people of East Africa, for example, the bride is expected to resist the sexual advances of the groom as long as possible. The Gusii bridegroom can generally expect help from his male friends and kin in getting the bride undressed and forced into the bed. If need be, the young men also hold her forcibly in position so the groom can make the first penetration. "Once penetration has been achieved, the young men sing in jubilation and retire from the house to allow the groom to complete the nuptial sexual relations" (LeVine and LeVine, 1966:48).

At first glance this example of male-female antag-

onism on the wedding night might seem just a "quaint custom" in a little-known social group, but it is mentioned here to point out that complex ritual celebrations generally tell a good deal about all kinds of social relationships. The kin affiliations of the wedding guests, the social identities of major actors in the drama (including who pays what parts of the wedding costs), and the types of extra ritual situations (e.g., bridal showers and bachelor parties) mirror special aspects of social structure and style.

Selection of Marriage Partners and Who Pays What

In most human societies there are some expectations about appropriate marriage partners, even in those many cases in which the young people themselves make the choice of mates. Among the Ojibwa peoples of the Upper Great Lakes region, for example, the ideal mate for a young man was either his mother's brother's daughter or else the daughter of his father's sister. Both of these preferred marriage partners are CROSS COUSINS (see Figure 14.4). The idea that the preferred mate for a male should be a cousin, often specifically a cross-cousin on the "mother's side," is fairly widespread in human groups. Sally Moore (1963) has listed a total of forty-three such groups, in addition to which there are a few, but only a few, societies in which the father's sister's daughter is the preferred or prescribed marriage partner. A great amount of anthropological quibbling has been spent in theoretical argument over the presumed causes of such a preferred marriage pattern. For some people the answer lies in a supposed knitting together of kinship groupings through marriage, while another suggestion is that a young man has a special emotional relationship to his mother's kinfolk, so they are the approachable ones when it comes to finding a wife. Of course it also depends on who is making the decisions, the parents or the young people who are getting married. A further element in the matter can be the kinds of economic assets—for example, land—controlled by particular kin groups.

Preferred marriage to a PARALLEL COUSIN is not so widely practiced, though it is well known in the Bible and is a significant cultural idea among some Moslem peoples. In the Bible, Isaac, son of Abraham, married his father's brother's son's daughter Rebekah; Isaac's son Jacob, in his turn, married his parallel

Perspectives on Social Organization

cousins Leah and Rachel. Some anthropologists have suggested that parallel-cousin marriage is a way of solidifying the social bonds in small-scale male-centered kin groups in situations where there is conflict with nearby competitors for grazing lands or other scarce resources. Many of the people who have preferred this type of marriage alliance, from the time of Abraham to the present day, have been pastoralist keepers of animals with plenty of jostling over scarce real estate.

Wait a moment, the careful reader says—if Isaac's son Jacob *continued* a pattern of PATRILATERAL parallel cousin marriage, then he was also marrying his mother's brother's daughter! In fact, that's just what Isaac told Jacob to do, according to the Bible: "Take thee a wife of the daughters of Laban thy mother's brother" (Gen. 28:2). Figure 14.5 shows these interesting complexities of marriage and kinship.

In many European folk legends a man doesn't win the hand of a desirable damsel until he has shown his courage and prowess in some exciting feats of strength, like killing the dragon or crossing the flaming river. The point is that it is generally the people with the daughters that have the upper hand in the bargaining and exact some sort of demonstration of excellence or payment for the hand of their fair daughter. Among the cattle people of East Africa a man is unlikely to get himself a good-looking bride unless he and/or his family pay a number of cattle in BRIDE PRICE. In 1956–1957 the young men among

the Gusii were likely to pay something like ten or twelve cattle for a bride, even though the national law allowed only a payment of eight cows.

In some areas the effect of modernization and commercial expansion has been to drive up the price of brides; witness this 1970 UPI bulletin from Port Moresby, New Guinea:

The price for a bride reached a new record Tuesday in New Guinea—$6,900. The bride's father, Toua Kapena, said he had accepted the offer in cash and goods for his teen-aged daughter, Dia Toua, from the family of Gave Ovia, 18.

Kapena is a member of the New Guinea legislature and the Port Moresby City Council and, ironically, has been a leader in a campaign to lower and stabilize the increasing cost of purchasing brides in this South Pacific island. He said he had been forced by the tribal custom of bidding for brides to accept the highest price offered for his daughter. . . .

In his successful bid, Ovia made a down payment of the equivalent of $3,700 in cash plus $960 worth of goods.

The interpretation of the exchange of valuables in connection with marriage has been a point of debate in anthropological theory, for many anthropologists have apparently found it necessary to develop some idealistic explanation for the apparent crass materialism of selling young girls off as brides. The most usual explanation is that bride price is paid over to the bride's parents in return for the warranty that she will produce children for the family and kin group that receives and supports her. The payment is also viewed, then, as a symbolic demonstration that the children born to her "belong" to the husband's kin group. The payment of a bride price is seen as cementing a social contract between the kin groups of bride and groom.

14.4 **Cross cousins and parallel cousins from the point of view of a female "ego."** (Note that cross cousins and parallel cousins are not necessarily of the same generation as "Ego." Thus, X and Y are also patrilateral parallel cousins of Ego.)

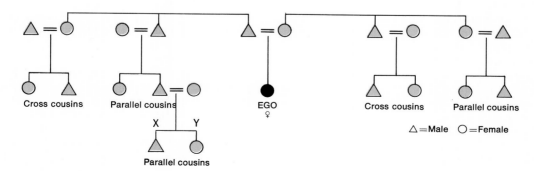

Cross cousins   Parallel cousins   EGO ♀   Cross cousins   Parallel cousins

X   Y   △=Male ○=Female

Parallel cousins

Human Organization: Marriage and Family Life

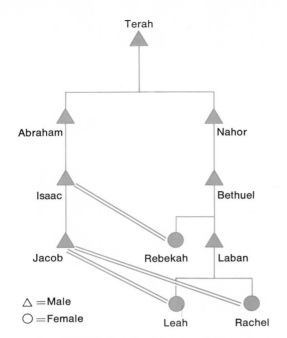

Terah

Abraham   Nahor

Isaac   Bethuel

Jacob   Rebekah   Laban

△ =Male
○ =Female

Leah   Rachel

14.5 **"And Isaac called Jacob, and blessed him, and charged him, and said unto him ... 'Arise, go to ... the house of Bethuel thy mother's father; and take thee a wife ... of the daughters of Laban, thy mother's brother.'" (Gen. 28:1-2).** (From *Anthropology: The Study of Man* by Edward A. Hoebel. Used with permission of McGraw-Hill Book Company.)

If a woman does not produce children she may be returned to her people and the bride price returned. That much is clear. But the claim that the bride price is "not really" buying a bride seems a bit stretched. Anthropologists appear to have been unwilling to admit the extent to which males have dominated over females in social affairs and, when expedient, used their daughters as pawns in economic and political manipulation.

Since the custom of bride price payments in connection with marriage is widespread, it is interesting to look at variations on the theme. Among many hunting and gathering groups the groom and his people have not had to pay bride price, but the groom himself has gone to his bride's people to serve them for a period of time. Among some Bushmen, Lorna Marshall notes, "!Kung society rigorously, and without exception, requires that all men, in first and subsequent marriages, go to live with the par-

ents of their brides, and give them bride service. The service is essentially hunting. 'Our daughter's husband must give us meat.' 'We shall soon be old; we need a young man to hunt for us'" (Marshall, 1965:261). The opposite side of the coin, the situation in which the bride's family offers some material rewards to the bridegroom, is also found in a number of societies, and it is particularly widespread in the stronghold of male dominance in the Mediterranean region. Accumulation of DOWRY for sisters is one of the major themes in accounts of Greek and south Italian migration to the "promised land" of North America. And we recall that New England farmer of colonial days who offered his somewhat homely and overweight daughter in marriage with a promised dowry of her weight in pine tree shillings.

In a cross-cultural survey of the distribution of bride wealth and dowry, the anthropologist Jack Goody found that the latter practice is limited to Europe and Asia. He suggests that the dowry, which can be thought of as a kind of premortem inheritance, occurs in stratified societies and creates special kinds of tight bonds between the married pair, particularly related to property distribution. Goody concludes, "If one wanted a facile distinction between bridewealth and dowry, one might say that in one case [bride wealth] the woman was paid for and in the other paid off" (Goody, 1973:46).

Exogamy and Endogamy

Although many peoples have expressed preferences for certain special types of cousin marriage, there are also many societies in which marriage with a first cousin, or even a second cousin, is forbidden. Many people have cultural rules forbidding marriage between persons who are thought to be related in any manner through kinship.

In those societies with well-organized kin groups it is quite usual that individuals must find marriage partners from *outside* their own kin group. Such marriage regulations are usually referred to as lineage or clan EXOGAMY. Also, some peoples have cultural rules, or at least strong preferences for, VILLAGE EXOGAMY, in which marriage partners must be from separate communities. In many Chinese communities surname exogamy is observed—bride and groom should not have the same last name. Euro-American cultural rules are similar to those of many other

Perspectives on Social Organization

peoples, frowning on marriage with close kin (e.g., first cousins).

ENDOGAMY refers to the rules prohibiting marriage outside one's social group. Among many agricultural villages of Mexico, there are strong tendencies to marriage within the local community. In the community of Tepoztlán, described by Oscar Lewis, 90 percent of marriages were village endogamous. Village endogamy is often simply a strong preference instead of a hard-and-fast rule. Many states within the United States have had until recent times laws forbidding marriage between Whites and Blacks. Such laws are expressions of racial endogamy.

Preference for endogamy or in-group marriage was very strong among the Hebrews, as described in the Bible. Esau, son of Isaac, took to wife two Hittite girls, "and they were a bitterness of spirit unto Isaac and to Rebekah" (Gen. 26:34–35). Seeing that his parents were so upset, Esau married a third wife, the daughter of Ishmael, Isaac's brother (Gen. 28:8–9). Preferences for in-group marriage are usually strongest among people who have some vested economic interests or elaborate religious rituals and beliefs. Jewish and Catholic peoples have usually had strong objections to interfaith marriage, whereas groups with less elaborated and exclusive religions have been somewhat less worried about "marrying foreigners."

Forbidden Fruit: The Incest Taboo

The tragedy of Oedipus Rex was that he unknowingly had sexual relations with his own mother. Such an act of INCEST aroused revulsion and fear among the Greeks, as it does among most peoples. All human societies forbid sexual relations between mothers and sons, fathers and daughters, and brothers and sisters (there have been exceptions in the latter case under very unusual conditions[1]). Various

[1] The universality of incest taboos prohibiting the mating and marriage of brother and sister can be questioned, for it has occurred as the special and honored prerogative of royalty. The heads of the Inca empire were so far removed from ordinary mortals that the only "fit" marriage was between brothers and sisters. The same pattern occurred among the deified pharaohs of Egypt—Cleopatra was the descendant of a long line of brother-sister mating. Native Hawaiian royalty also permitted brother-sister marriage. These cases seem to represent the power of high and godlike royalty to go against the "laws" that bind ordinary mortals.

other combinations of kin can also be included in incest prohibitions, but these are quite varied from one society to another. In most groups incest is thought to lead to dire consequences for those who engage in it and more especially for the offspring of incestuous unions. Among the Ulithi Islanders of the South Pacific, "the physical results of incest are illness in either the offenders or their close relatives . . . and takes the form of headaches, boils or yaws. It is said that the child of an incestuous marriage will be mentally deficient, its toes webbed together, its fingers twisted and bent, and its buttocks shriveled" (Lessa, 1966:90).

Explaining the universality of incest taboos is another popular topic that has resulted in an outpouring of anthropological theory over the years. In most societies the "folk theory" agrees with the Ulithians—that children from incestuous unions are likely to show mental deficiencies and other genetic defects usually seen as the direct work of the gods. Anthropologists, on the other hand, have tended to disagree with the folk theories, claiming that close inbreeding will not usually result in *noticeable* genetic problems.

Some theorists have argued that people have a "natural aversion" to sexual relations with persons of their own household. Others point to the advantages of intergroup marriage for political and peace-keeping purposes. And still others, with a psychological bent, argue that sexual relations among sisters and brothers and between parents and children would be disruptive of family harmony and cooperation because of role conflicts and sexual jealousies. Although the "natural aversion" idea seems fallacious (given the evidence that quite a few people are regularly tempted into incestuous relations despite the taboos), the other social and psychological arguments all appear to make some sense, though there is no way to "prove" any of them.

But what about the folk wisdom concerning the genetic dangers? In recent times geneticists have come to the conclusion that each of us carries many more potentially harmful recessive genes than previously thought. As we noted in Chapter 5, the rate of new genetic mutations in human populations has been estimated to be rather high; perhaps at least one out of five of us is a carrier of harmful recessive genetic material. Some evidence concerning the genetic dangers of inbreeding has been uncovered by pediatricians, who made a detailed examination of

279

eighteen children born of incestuous mating in Michigan. Six of these were from father-daughter unions, and twelve had resulted from brother-sister intercourse: "Seven of the children were normal. One child had a severe bilateral cleft lip; one had a unilateral congenital hip dislocation . . . two died neonatally; one of these . . . showed respiratory distress syndrome. . . . Two of the children were severely mentally retarded . . . four others had IQs of under 70" (Adams and Neil, 1967:265). They compared this incest-born group of children with a group of illegitimate children of mothers matched in socioeconomic background, age, height, ethnic origin, and IQ. In the control group there were no deaths, and all the children had IQs over 80. Overall there were, even in this small sample, rather striking numbers of genetic defects associated with the incestuous (inbreeding) unions.

Very likely the worldwide popularity of incest taboos arises from a combination of biological and sociocultural effects. One of the small communities in which we have personally carried out ethnographic fieldwork includes two persons who are known to be the offspring of brother-sister incest. One of these is a completely normal, functioning member of the community; the other is a severely retarded person who is unable to do any but the simplest activities, though he can feed and clothe himself. The evidence concerning possible biological consequences of incest would not have to be very widespread to become widely noticed by the "folk theorists" in every society.

Fathering and Mothering

Students of sociolinguistics are fond of reminding us of that intriguing fact about human life, that language reflects social structure and ideas. In this regard a bit of semantic exploration of the meaning of two verbs, to father and to mother, provides an interesting commentary on the English (and European) view of parental role differentiation. In popular usage, to father someone (or something) is essentially a procreative act; to say of a man that he "fathered a child" is to suggest that he was the biological father. Such a statement implies virtually nothing about his social role with respect to that child. On the other hand, when we mean that a man provided nurturance or protection or displayed

other social behavior, we are much more likely to turn to a nominal or adjectival use of father, such as "he was a good father," "he acted in a fatherly way toward the boy," and so on.

Although it is technically quite correct to use the verb mother to refer to a female's role in procreation, in popular usage we usually refer to the nonbiological side of mothering. When it stands alone, we will most likely take the expression "she mothered the child" to mean that she provided warm, loving, nurturant support rather than that she was the biological PROGENITOR. The difference in the common usage of these two terms clearly reflects differences in our concepts of parental roles. It is the mother who has the primary responsibility for nurturant care. In the cultural systems in which these usages developed fathers have tended not to participate actively in the hour-by-hour care and protection of their children. Typically, mothers stay home and take care of the kids, while fathers go off to "earn a living" and to protect the family from its enemies.

14.6 Pigmy marmoset fathers carry their young around much of the time, only giving them over to the mother at feeding time. (San Diego Zoo)

280

In cultural systems such as our own this sharp division of labor between fathering and mothering is often seen as the "natural way"; whether one appeals to divine law or natural law, the fact that women have primary responsibility for child rearing is usually viewed as the consequence of biological differences that are true not only for human beings but for most other animal species as well. We are, if anything, prone to believe that nurturant behavior on the part of human fathers represents something of a departure from the more common animal state, in which males are presumed to be more or less totally indifferent to their offspring. Certainly this assumption is justified with regard to many animal species. However, it is instructive to remember that in the evolution of some species of animals, natural selection has favored male "mothering." In still other species cooperative sharing of child-rearing responsibilities has evolved. The ethological literature is full of fascinating examples of these unusual adaptations:

The royal albatross of New Zealand pairs monogamously for life. Once every two years the pair returns to the nesting area where, after the female lays the egg, the two take turns sitting on the nest for eleven weeks (one of the longest incubation periods for any birds). Once the chick has hatched both parents share the task of taking care of the baby. When the little one is old enough to take care of itself, but long before it can fly, the parents leave the infant and fly off to sea. (DURRELL, 1966:56)

Among the emu of Australia the males have practically full responsibility:

The marital life of an emu is one that would delight the most militant of suffragettes: having enjoyed all the pleasures of the nuptial couch (as it were) the female then lays her eggs and forgets about the whole sordid business. It is the male who constructs the nest (if it can be dignified with that term), collects the eggs, sits on them devotedly—without food—until they hatch out, and then takes charge of the youngsters and looks after them until they are old enough to fend for themselves. (DURRELL, 1966:157)

Among the Hamadryas baboons males often take an active interest in infants. It is quite common to see them carrying infants in their manes when the group is traveling from one feeding area to another.

14.7 Father and daughter, U.S.A. (Leonard Freed, Magnum)

14.8 Father and son, Northern Territory, Australia. (Courtesy of the American Museum of Natural History)

Human Organization: Marriage and Family Life

Some males are particularly receptive to infants and the youngsters seek them out. An interesting feature of Hamadryas social organization is that a motherless infant is usually adopted by a young male; he carries the infant around, makes sure that it doesn't move too far away from him, and in other ways offers "motherly" protection (Kummer, 1971).

Regardless of how much nurturance is provided by fathers, aunts, uncles, grandparents, and others, the major social tie that is prominent in all human groups (as in most other species) is the mother-child bond. That special relationship, which is essential for the health and well-being of newborn infants, is another dimension in which we find many parallels among other animals, yet the mother-child bond is much more long-lasting in human groups than among other animals. This is because of the long period of dependency of our young ones. *Homo sapiens* children are physiologically, emotionally, and sexually immature until well past the age of ten. As society has grown more complicated, so has the period of social dependency of the young, so that we now generally consider children to be legally dependent until age eighteen. Actual dependency may last much longer.

The point is that human social organization is based on long-term relationships among biologically related people, and the most important of these is the mother-child bond. The bond between "man and wife" or the sexual bond that leads to pregnancy and childbirth is also frequently of long duration in human societies; but in some communities relationships between males and females are relatively short-term and flexible, much less essential than the mother-child bond.

The Nayar people of Southwest India are a famous example of an extreme case that demonstrates how human families can have clear and long-term structure without making much of the husband-wife bond. As Kathleen Gough has described them, the Nayar caste in former times lived in extended family units based on a strong matrilineal set of kinship ties. The basic property-owning kinship group traced descent and group membership through female lines (see pp. 301–302). The girls in these households were married to ceremonial "bridegrooms" but they did not settle down to connubial bliss with these husbands. It was simply a ceremonial rite of passage essential for the social position of the girls:

14.9 Mother and child, the fundamental social unit in human and other primate societies. (Deana H. Hoffman)

At a convenient time every few years, a lineage held a grand ceremony in which all girls who had not attained puberty, aged about seven to twelve, were on one day ritually married by men drawn from their linked lineages. The ritual bridegrooms were selected in advance on the advice of the village astrologer at a meeting of the neighborhood assembly . . . the ritual husbands left the house after the four days of ceremonies and had no further obligations to their brides. A bride in turn had only one further obligation to her ritual husband: at his death, she and all her children, by whatever biological father, must observe death-pollution for him. (GOUGH, 1971:367–368)

The Nayar girls were seven to twelve years of age at the time of this ceremony, and after that they were socially ready for sexual and reproductive functions. It was a kind of coming of age for the girls. They continued to live at home, and, of course, the younger ones did not enter immediately into sexual relationships with males. They were, however, free to receive male visitors, with whom they might establish fairly enduring sexual ties. A woman had as many as a dozen lovers, although Gough reports that three or four regular "husbands" might have been most typical. These "husbands" of the Nayar women did not assume any significant economic obligations for children born of the unions, nor did they support their "wives":

Perspectives on Social Organization

A husband visited his wife after supper at night and left before breakfast next morning. He placed his weapons at the door of his wife's room and if others came later they were free to sleep on the veranda of the woman's house. Either party to a union might terminate it at any time without formality. . . . At the start of a union it was common although not essential for [the husband] to present the woman with a cloth of the kind worn as a skirt. Later he was expected to make small personal gifts to her at the three main festivals of the year. . . . Most important, however, when a woman became pregnant it was essential for one or more men of appropriate sub-caste to acknowledge probable paternity. This they did by providing a fee of a cloth and some vegetables to the low-caste midwife who attended the woman in childbirth. (GOUGH, 1959:369)

That acknowledgement of paternity by some socially appropriate "husband" was very important, for if no man stepped forward to claim responsibility, it was assumed that the woman had had sexual relations with some low-caste person, for which she would be expelled from her kin group and perhaps killed by matrilineal kinsmen.

In modern times these family patterns of the Nayar have been changed a good deal, especially because of pressures from moralistic British colonial administrators. In spite of the fact that the special structure of the Nayar family no longer exists, it is an important example of how, in some societies, the sexual relationships between husband and wife may be considered insignificant as compared with the kinship relationships between mothers and their children, as well as with the wider networks of relationship in lineages, clans, and other types of kin groups.

In a number of modern societies, particularly among some poverty-stricken groups in the Caribbean and in Central America, a fairly high proportion of households are headed by women who have relatively temporary relationships with the men who are the biological fathers of children born into these households. Very often it is the economic marginality of these households that forces the males into migratory labor, frequent changes of residence, and a pattern in which the "fathers" are of little economic significance to the maintenance of the children. Such women-headed families in the Caribbean area and among some Central American Indians and other groups illustrate the fact that economic conditions may sometimes make permanent sexual ties between males and females economically disadvantageous. This is the case among some of the most economically deprived segments of North American society as well. Usually these so-called MATRIFOCAL families are a minority within a larger social system in which nuclear families predominate. The existence of matrifocal families demonstrates that the family structure we take for granted—married pair plus children—is not necessarily always feasible or "natural" at all times and places.

The Nuclear Family

In spite of the exceptions we have just noted—and there are others of equal importance—in a great many human societies of various levels of complexity, a family group made up of both the mother-child bond and the male-female sexual bond is a primary social unit. Such a married-pair-plus-unmarried-children family is referred to as a NUCLEAR FAMILY and is the most usual and typical family in North America, most of Europe, and nowadays in many other parts of the world as well. It is the most usual social unit among hunting and gathering peoples. In fact, the structural importance of the nuclear family as a basic unit is one of the curious ways in which our modern society resembles that of the simplest hunting-gathering people.

In societies with predominantly nuclear family

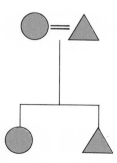

14.10 **The nuclear family: usually defined as a married pair and their unmarried offspring.**

Human Organization: Marriage and Family Life

organization, each individual lives out his or her formative years as a dependent in one's "family of orientation," and then leaves this family to establish a "family of procreation." In other societies, with larger and more and more complex family structures, some individuals remain in their natal families even after they marry and have children.

Extended Families

In many preindustrial societies, households consist of several married couples, generally linked together through ties of kinship. The most common arrangement is that a household contains an older married couple plus married sons with their wives and children. This type of unit is referred to as a PATRILOCAL EXTENDED FAMILY.

14.13 Patrilocal extended family in Delhi, India. (Marilyn Silverstone, Magnum)

14.11 North American nuclear family—suburbia. (Rosen, Magnum)

14.12 North American nuclear family—inner city. (Charles Gatewood, Magnum)

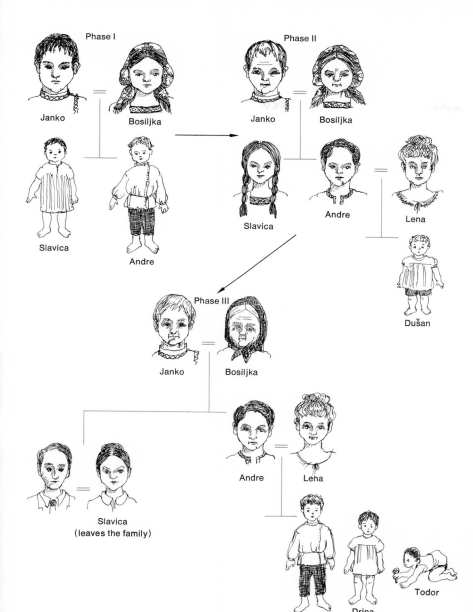

Phase I

Janko = Bosiljka

Slavica

Andre

Phase II

Janko = Bosiljka

Slavica

Andre = Lena

Dušan

Phase III

Janko = Bosiljka

Slavica
(leaves the family)

Andre = Lena

Dušan   Drina   Todor

14.14 Phases in the life cycle of an extended (patrilocal) family. In Serbian peasant villages, as in many other communities, the extended family can sometimes be very large, with many daughters-in-law and hence several component nuclear families.

If the daughters, rather than the sons, stay home after marriage, and the sons-in-law come to live in their wives' parents' house, we call it a MATRILOCAL EXTENDED FAMILY.

Joining a family is, of course, a matter of degree. Among the patrilineal Mayan-speaking Indians of Zinacantan married sons live with their parents' household but not necessarily in the same building. Sons often build houses in close proximity to their parents' house and maintain separate cooking areas and other domestic features.

There are many other ways in which households

285

Human Organization: Marriage and Family Life

and family groupings may be formed to include more than one married couple and related children and other kin. Among the very flexible Semai the people living together in a long house may be two or three brothers and their families, but inclusion of a brother-in-law is not unlikely, and additional people may also be included through a variety of other kinship ties.

The *zadruga* of some Serbian peoples is a particularly interesting example of a patrilineally extended family:

In some houses there are four or five married men, and one-family households are rare. There are as many vajats [sleeping quarters used by married couples] as there are married men, and the house itself is only for communal eating and the place where the old women and old men sleep; all others sleep each with his own wife and children in his own vajat, without fire in both summer and winter. Around some prosperous houses are groups of vajats and other outbuildings (for example, corn cribs, grain storage sheds, and houses with porches) like a small settlement. . . . Each household has a staresina [headman] who governs and guides the household and all its property; he directs the adults and young men . . . [and] he deals with the Turks and attends village and district meetings and conducts business. . . . In zadruga households each woman spins, weaves, and prepares clothing for herself and her husband and children; as for food preparation, each in turn does the job a week at a time . . . usually the wife of the staresina is a woman who all summer supervises the preparation of food for the winter. (HALPERN and HALPERN, 1972:16–17)

Polygyny and Polyandry: Families with Multiple Spouses

Contrary to the attitudes of most Americans and Europeans, humans do not overwhelmingly consider monogamy the most preferable form of married life. Among most human groups multiple spouses are permitted if one can afford them. For example, with many hunting and gathering peoples only the very best hunters can effectively maintain more than one wife. Among the Shoshone and Paiute peoples of the Great Basin area, there were occasionally males who had more than one wife; usually the two wives were sisters. Also, a woman occasionally had more than one husband, usually a pair of brothers or other closely related individuals. These instances of PO-

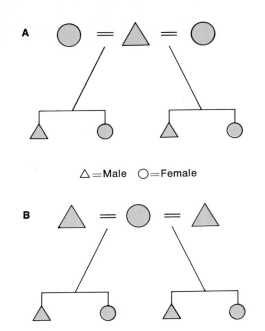

△=Male ○=Female

14.15 Among most human groups multiple spouses are permitted if one can afford them. Polygynous family organization (A) is much more common than is polyandry (B), in which a woman has more than one husband.

LYGYNY (multiple wives) and POLYANDRY (multiple husbands) fitted well with the general flexibility of marital and sexual arrangements among these hunting and gathering peoples.

Often the situation of multiple spouses among egalitarian peoples came about because of the expectation that when a man died his closest kin, usually his brother, had the responsibility of looking after his widow. Assuming that responsibility over a brother's widow generally took the form of marriage. This cultural practice is called the LEVIRATE and is well known in the Bible.

In societies where women's labor assumes great importance for the maintenance of crops and animals, the pattern of multiple wives takes on competitive significance as each additional wife gives a man more direct control of production for wealth. As noted earlier, the Kapauku of New Guinea seek wealth and prestige through pig raising, and a young man can hardly get into the business of adult life unless he has a wife to care for his pigs. As Pospisil

Perspectives on Social Organization

notes concerning the principal male socioeconomic activity:

Since all this is woman's work [caring for the pigs] the obvious course is for the young man to buy himself a wife. In this way the basic economic cycle of an increase in Kapauku production is completed. Ideally, it may be repeated as long as one has women to marry and luck with pig breeding: the more crops one grows, the more pigs can be produced, through whose sale one acquires money for the purchase of additional wives. Practically, however, this economic cycle cannot be continued indefinitely. Since a Kapauku wife is not a chattel, but a human being with a high degree of personal freedom and independence, she makes certain social demands on her husband. . . . Consequently there is a limit to the number of wives he can take. An extreme in this respect was achieved by Awiitigaaj, a rich head man of the village of Botukebo, who married ten native women and in 1959 contemplated marrying the eleventh. (POSPISIL, 1963:11–12)

Polyandry—the marital arrangement in which a woman has more than one husband at a time—is much rarer in the world than is polygyny. Polyandry has occurred among some hunting-gathering groups such as the Shoshone, but more frequent occurrence of multiple husbands is found in South Asia, among some nomadic people in Tibet, the Todas of South India, and some of the Paharis of North India.

The most frequent form of polyandry is fraternal. That is, the multiple husbands are all brothers married to the same woman. Often the oldest brother is the "number one" husband, and his younger brothers have a somewhat lesser status, although each of the brothers has sexual access to the wife and they all have some responsibility for the economic and social welfare of the children. Generally the cohusbands do not know for sure who the biological father of any particular child is, and in some cases all of the children are said to be the children of the oldest brother, the "chief husband."

The many different forms of marital and family arrangements in human groups are generally supported to some degree by emotion-tinged cultural norms and explanations. But in most instances we can discern significant practical, economic reasons for extended families in some societies, nuclear families in most industrialized urban contexts, and polygynous families in yet other ecological settings. In a worldwide sample of 854 societies, the frequencies of the different types of marriage are as follows:

Types of Marriage	No.	%
Monogamy	137	16
Monogamy with polygyny	333	39
Polygyny	376	44
Polyandry	8	1

Source: From BOURGUIGNON and GREENBAUM, 1968:48.

Divorce, Separation, and Other Hi-jinks

Most branches of the Christian religion have had a very strong antagonism toward divorce. Permitting legal termination of marriages has come only in very recent times in some Catholic countries, and some of them permit only annulments. Among different human societies powerful taboos on divorce are relatively unusual. Most people look upon divorce as acceptable and necessary, however unfortunate it may be for some of the participants.

For the biblical Hebrews, with their male-dominated institutions, divorce was legally the prerogative of the husband but not the wife. A man

14.16 **Woman with her two husbands, a polyandrous family among the Toda of south India.** (Arthur Trees, Magnum)

could divorce his wife by giving her a written "bill of divorcement" as in Deuteronomy (24:1–4):

When a man taketh a wife, and marrieth her, then it cometh to pass, if she find no favour in his eyes, because he hath found some unseemly thing in her, that he writeth her a bill of divorcement and giveth it in her hand, and sendeth her out of his house.

Although the law in biblical times completely favored the husband, other passages in the Bible demonstrate that a woman's father, or other kin, could interfere to some extent on her behalf. Only the womin without close kin was entirely at the mercy of her husband.

Practically all industrializing nations have sharply rising divorce rates, and the rates are especially high in the United States; so it is commonly assumed that nonindustrial peoples have much lower rates. The actual *rates* of divorce in different societies are not generally available, but from ethnographers' descriptions we can surmise that in at least some societies the rates are much higher than those on our North American cultural scene. Ronald Cohen reports that the Kanuri people of northeastern Nigeria have exceptionally easy and frequent termination of marriage, so that:

About eighty to ninety percent of all marriages end in divorce, probably because it is such a simple affair.

The husband in most cases simply tells his wife to go, saying "I divorce you". . . . About one-third of all divorce pronouncements end in reconciliation . . . on the other hand. . . . Only rare Kanuri have not been divorced once or twice during their lifetimes, and . . . eight or nine divorces is not uncommon. When explaining divorces, husbands complain about their wives cooking badly . . . they also complain of visits to relatives and friends . . . of their wives being dirty, or of adultery. . . . Wives . . . complain of their husbands' intolerance, of their activities outside the household, their stinginess, or their lack of sexual attention or skill . . . extra-marital affairs . . . co-wives . . . or . . . lack of appreciation . . . especially of their cooking. (COHEN, 1967:44–45)

The almost total casualness of marriage that Robert Dentan reports for the eastern Semai in the Malay Peninsula would lead one to expect that divorce is fairly frequent: "Consequently, there are few east Semai adults who do not report that they have been 'married' and 'divorced' more than once, occasionally as many as eight or nine times." (Dentan, 1968:74)

Among those societies in which kinship relations are reckoned through female kin (see p. 300), we would expect that women would have more rights (including divorce rights). Also, it has often been suggested that men in such societies have conflicts of interest, with obligations and rights in both their

"Family" and "Household"

The examples we have been examining of *family structure* in different societies all illustrate the core definition of FAMILY that we are using here. *Family* in the usual anthropological usage means a group of people related through kinship, marriage, or fictional kinship (adoption, godparenthood, and so on.) *who live together as a social and economic unit.* Like all definitions, this one has to be stretched a bit from time to time, but the main idea is that *family* does *not* refer to those of our relatives who are scattered out all over the continent, coast to coast. There is a clear distinction between those very visible, relatively permanent coresidence groups based on kinship and the nonlocalized networks of kin.

In European and North American social systems, *family* and HOUSEHOLD mean almost the same thing. The difference between the two is especially clear around college campuses, however. *Household* refers to any collection of people who live together, eat together, and share at least some economic tasks and resources. If three or four people get together to rent an apartment and share their food, they immediately become a household—no matter how temporary the arrangement might be. Sometimes people who start out as a *household* (just living together) begin talking of permanent relationships and marriage, so the household may become a *family* in terms of our definition here.

288

own kin groups and those of their wives. In many such groups—e.g., the Hopi of Arizona, the Trukese people of the South Pacific, and others—divorce is quite frequent and can easily be initiated by either husband or wife. Among the Hopi and other Pueblo peoples a man might come home from the fields to find his little bundle of possessions sitting outside the door, and he gets the point—go home and don't come back! The same situation was true among the Iroquois Indians of upstate New York, in which group women had quite a lot of power in all aspects of life.

Marriage and Family in Experimental Communities

In nearly all communities where people have attempted to experiment with new forms of social organization, the reorganization of the family has been a major focus of attention. In the following section we will describe some of the alternative family forms that have been the result of conscious, direct attempts to set up new arrangements of the primary social bonds.

"Complex Marriage" at Oneida

One of the most unusual experiments in family organization was carried out in the Perfectionist colony at Oneida, New York. The commune was founded by John Humphrey Noyes in 1848, based on principles that were derived from his unusual theology. Among other things Noyes believed that monogamy and romantic love were manifestations of selfishness and possessiveness; ideally all men should love all women and vice versa. Consequently, monogamous marriage was not allowed in his community and romantic attachments were sharply discouraged. In place of monogamous marriage, the practice that was instituted was group marriage or, as Noyes called it, "complex marriage."

All of the members of the community lived together in one very large house. Each adult, male and female, had a room of his or her own. In theory, sexual contact was encouraged and possible between any two members of the opposite sex. Contact was usually initiated by the man. If a man wanted to have sexual intercourse with a particular woman, he went to the central committee of the commune to present his request. The committee would then approach the woman to ask for her consent. If she agreed, the man would then go to her room, later returning to his own to sleep. The committee system acted as a kind of protective device, enabling a woman to turn down a man with whom she did not want to have intercourse. The extent to which the committee was used to arrange meetings between couples who had already had contact is not known, but presumably more informal, direct contact also occurred. However, any sign of the development of strong emotional attachments was quickly discouraged, and if criticism was not enough to stop the budding romance one of the two offending people was sent to live at the colony's "outpost" in Wallingford, Connecticut.

A clear distinction was drawn between sexual intercourse, which was viewed as an expressive extension of the love that all members of the community were supposed to feel toward each other, and reproduction. Noyes had read Charles Darwin and Francis Galton and felt that reproduction should be approached scientifically. He developed a program of eugenics, called *Stirpiculture*, in which fifty-three women and thirty-eight men were chosen to be the parents of the next generation. The program was instituted some twenty years after the founding of the colony. For the first two decades members were prohibited from having children on the grounds that the colony was not yet economically in a position to support young additions. Once the program was put into practice fifty-eight children were born to the community in the decade before they disbanded. During all of its existence the method of birth control practiced by the colony members was coitus reservatus, a method that was apparently viewed "not only as an effective method of birth control but as a means of *emotionally elevating* sexual pleasure" (Kephart, 1972:71).

Infants were cared for by their mothers for the first fifteen months of life, after which they went to live in the children's section of the large mansion that housed the colony. Although all ties between children and parents were not cut off, the community made an effort to develop bonds among all adults and all children, and the children were thought of as belonging to the community. Recalling early experiences, one "child of the community" interviewed by William Kephart said, "Everybody was good to us. You knew you were loved because

289

it was like a big family. Also, there were so many activities for the youngsters, so many things to do, well—believe me—we were happy children. Everybody around here will give you the same answer on that!" (Kephart, 1972:72).

The "Family" in Shaker Society

In the late eighteenth century the United Society of Believers in Christ's Second Appearance—better known as the Shakers—established communities in the United States in which celibacy and communal ownership were key elements of social organization. The Shakers believed themselves to be above the "rudimental state of men," and, because they regarded marriage as a convenient screen for "brutish lusts," they prohibited it in their communes. Unlike the Catholic church, in which celibacy is facilitated by institutional separation in convents and monasteries, the Shakers placed men and women together in very close proximity. The communities were organized in terms of "families," the name given to the social unit of men and women who lived together in the same house. The families varied in size from just a few individuals to groups as large as eighty or more people. Within the house strict segregation was maintained; men and women were not allowed to visit with each other alone, to shake hands, or even to pass on the stairs: "The two sexes ate, worked, worshipped, and walked apart, and in all things maintained distance and reserve towards each other, in spite of the fact that, in their quarters, they were separated only by corridors and the common consent of both parties" (Holloway, 1966:67).

In each family the women were collectively responsible for the preparation of food, the maintenance of order and cleanliness in the house, the laundry, sewing, ironing, and other routine household tasks, and the men had charge of all agricultural and manufacturing activities. Each woman, or "sister," was assigned to a particular "brother," for whom she had certain responsibilities, principally taking care of his clothing and making sure that he was neat and orderly.

Since the Shaker communes were not self-perpetuating in the usual manner of human societies, they had the problem of recruiting new members to their ranks. Sometimes converts were made from married couples who joined the community, bringing their children with them. Children were also apprenticed to the community by non-Shaker families. In later years many communities changed their policy with regard to accepting apprenticed children, for they found that these children tended to become discontented and leave the society when they grew up. According to one Shaker elder, "When men or women come to us at the age of twenty-one or twenty-two, then they make the best Shakers" (Nordhoff, 1966:158). There were always some children in the communes, and schools were maintained for their education (boys went to school in winter, girls in summer). However, it is probably fair to say that child rearing played only a minor role in the life of Shaker families. Among other things, the Shaker communities can be thought of as an experiment in a nonconjugal, nonsexual, nonconsanguineous organization of family life. It is significant to note that the "experiment" lasted for 150 years, the last families surviving into the 1940s.

Marriage and Family in the Kibbutz

In analyses of fundamental principles and ideas of communal movements there is frequently some comment about the incompatibility of nuclear family structure and kinship relationships and the needs of the collective. The opposition or tension is seen as basically a structural problem: family ties are particularistic while the collective demands loyalty to the whole group; families interpose themselves between the individual and the group and thus weaken the group's ability to command and hold the individual's loyalty.

With the establishment of the collective agricultural villages, the kibbutzim, in Israel, a number of factors combined to produce a strong antifamilistic bias. The founders of these settlements were mainly young people who immigrated to the Middle East from Europe and North America, motivated by their desire to build new communities based on equality and communal brotherhood. In addition to their belief that there was a fundamental conflict between the interests of the collectivity and nuclear family loyalties, another ideological aspect of their antifamilism was the belief that the nuclear family structure was largely responsible for the subjugation of women and the perpetuation of bourgeois philosophy. In their new communities women were to be relieved of the responsibility for raising their own children; child rearing was to be a collective responsibility. Furthermore, children were to be reared collectively so that group loyalty and communal spirit, rather than selfish individualism, would be reinforced.

In their early pioneering years most kibbutzim were characterized by extreme liberalism with regard to sexual relationships. Bourgeois sexual restrictiveness was to be eliminated and love and/or erotic gratification, not formal marriage contracts, were viewed as the legitimizing basis of sexual activity. Premarital sex was not censured and free love was an explicit doctrine. At the same time there were other factors at work that some observers of the kibbutz scene feel acted as a kind of counterbalance to permissive sexuality. First of all, most of the members came from traditional Jewish backgrounds that tended toward extreme modesty and reserved sexuality. Second, the socialist philosophy to which they subscribed emphasized ascetic dedication and self-denial. Also, some kibbutz practices, such as identical work clothes for men and women, absence of cosmetics and jewelry, and shared bathrooms and living quarters, have been interpreted as having a "deeroticizing" effect. Couples avoided any public show of affection and actually attempted to keep their relationships secret, even though they would have been socially approved. There were, then, emphasis on free love and elements of constraint operating at the same time.

Nowadays when a young couple in a kibbutz decide that they want to make their relationship more permanent and to have children, they apply to the kibbutz for a room of their own. Residence in a common bedroom is a kind of public announcement of marriage. When a child is born, it does not live with its parents. On returning from the hospital the child is placed in the infants' room of the children's section of the kibbutz. A young baby is not taken from the nursery until the age of six months, so the mothers go to the nursery to feed their babies. While they have a child they are nursing, women are excused from several hours of labor in their regular jobs. Weaning is begun early, at about the age of three months, and is usually completed by the time the child is nine months old, at which time the mother returns to a regular work schedule.

Although the biological mother has an important responsibility toward her infant, especially in terms of feeding it, throughout the child's life the major responsibility for its care and upbringing belongs to the kibbutz rather than to the biological parents. The children eat, sleep, and spend many hours of their day in special children's houses, where they are tended by nurses, nursery school teachers, and teachers. The children do not live in one large school but rather are segregated into small groups by age. Each age group occupies a separate cottage and enjoys a high degree of autonomy. The entire educational system of the kibbutzim, which includes child care as well as more formal educational activities, is known by the term *chinuch meshatuf,*

14.17 Army women at kibbutz Ein Gedi return from work in the fields. (Leonard Freed, Magnum)

or "collective education." Just as the form of marriage and the sexual norms reflect the ideological principles of the pioneering founders of the kibbutzim, so too, the child-rearing–educational system in operation in the kibbutzim reflects ideas about the ideal way to raise children who will be responsible to the collective.

Many observers of kibbutz life have noted that the collective education system has strengthened parental ties rather than weakened them. Freed from the pressures of full responsibility for a child, parents in the kibbutz have been able to enjoy warm, loving, and extremely egalitarian relationships with their children. Although children eat, sleep, and spend many hours a day in their own cottages, they also spend quite a bit of time with their parents. When the adults return from work in the late afternoon, the "children's hour" begins. For the next two hours the parents can devote their attention exclusively to their children. When it is time for the children to go to bed, the parents accompany them back to their cottages, and young children are frequently put to bed by their own father and mother. Parents and children are also together on Saturdays and holidays. Children refer to their parents by the terms for father (*abba*) and mother (*imma*) and are in turn referred to by their parents as son (*ben*) and daughter (*bat*). Furthermore, the nuclear family group is referred to by a special term, *mishpacha*, so that it is recognized as a distinct unit within the larger kibbutz structure.

In many kibbutzim there has been a trend toward greater autonomy of the nuclear family. In others, however, including some of those in which the shift to prominence of the nuclear family (e.g., in meals, child care, and so on.) had become quite pronounced, there has been a countermove back toward a more communal emphasis. It is to be expected that flexibility and shifting patterns will continue to be true of the kibbutzim for some time to come as they attempt to work out the problems of the role of the nuclear family in a communal society.

Family in the Soviet Union

The socialist theories that played an important role in the organization of family-in-relation-to-society for the kibbutzim were also very significant influences in the Soviet Union. Following the Russian Revolution, laws were passed to grant women equal status in economic terms; marriage and divorce were to be easily arranged; abortions were freely available; and there were communal facilities for the care, feeding, and training of preschool children.

The disruptions and civil strife following World War I and the economic hardships of the 1920s and 1930s led to large-scale social disorganization in the Soviet Union, and in the 1930s the party leaders instituted changes that appeared to reestablish some of the foundations of the nuclear family that previously had been downgraded. The emphasis was shifted to reproduction, the centrality of the nuclear family for the socialization of children, and other policies that seemed not very different from "family policy" in noncommunist nations.

The Soviet Union has now passed through the turmoil of World War II and its aftermath and has continued to experiment with policies affecting family organization. By 1964 women in the Soviet Union constituted about 48 percent of the labor force, urban inhabitants had grown to 51 percent of the total population, and large numbers of preschool children were being cared for in day nurseries, boarding schools, and other public facilities. These community child-care facilities, like those in the kibbutzim and other collective societies, are supposed to train the young to be good citizens. At the same time they make it possible for Soviet mothers and fathers to work in factories or at other jobs and ease tight household budgets.

Meanwhile, many Soviet writers and citizens have complained that there should be more contact between parents and children, and official Soviet policy appears to favor some sort of combination of parental, nuclear family influence and the training at day-care schools, boarding schools, and other institutions.

The desirable combination from the Soviet point of view might be the ideal described by a woman correspondent for *Pravda*, who wrote:

And you know what I'm dreaming about? . . . A house. . . . In the house families are living. Next door not far away there is a building in which a boarding school complex is situated. Children from nursery to senior high age spend their entire day there, but in the evening, when their parents come home from work, they meet with their children. On those evenings when the parents are busy with civic obligations or go to the theater, the children remain in their

14.18 Wedding, Soviet Russian style. This is an entirely civil ceremony. (Constantine Manos, Magnum)

boarding school. They stay there too when Mother goes to a hospital or travels somewhere in connection with her job. . . . I know that this is the dream of many and many a mother. (Quoted in BRONFENBRENNER, 1970:90)

Contemporary Communes and Group Marriages

North America, like much of the rest of the industrialized world, is full of small-scale social experiments in communal living. Many of these new communes are found in the vicinity of college campuses; others are back-to-the-land organic farms in New York, Vermont, California, and elsewhere; and not a few of them have experimented seriously with the prospects and problems of group marriage. Some of them were directly influenced by the fictional writing of Robert Rimmer in *The Harrad Experiment*. Others got into group marriages through general share-and-share-alike philosophies.

The large numbers of group marriage experiments, along with the widely practiced "swinging," depart from the earlier North American family and sex practices in their openness and their philosophical searching. Robert Houriet, in his book *Getting Back Together*, described the relationships among the six

"multilaterally married" people in an experimental family in California. One obvious problem in group marriage was solved in a rather straightforward and simple manner: "'In the beginning we tried to do without a chart, but we found that we spent the whole day mousing around, trying to figure out who was going to sleep with whom that night. It's just easier this way. And it's fair; no one is *supposed* to get jealous . . . the sleeping chart puts a lot of people off. . . . But there's really no other way to do it'" (Houriet, 1971:260).

It is, of course, very difficult to get any really reliable information on the numbers of such group marriage experiments, but so far it appears that most of them don't last very long. Houriet reported one small study of sixteen group marriages of which only half made it through their first year. It is interesting to note that many of these multimarriage groups are *not* "hippie" groups but rather nonhip, middle-class sorts of people. One of the most interesting comments from the data reported by Houriet was the impression that the most durable multimarriage arrangements seemed to be triads consisting of a man with two women (Houriet, 1971:248–249).

The apparent fact that most group marriage attempts do not last very long underscores two impor-

293

Human Organization: Marriage and Family Life

tant problems: long-standing emotional training concerning sexual behavior is not easily erased in even the most "liberated" minds, and isolated social experiments that arouse anxieties among the more orthodox neighbors often have extra disadvantages in the form of adverse social pressures from the outside.

Summary

The examples of family organization in communal societies and special cases such as the Nayar illustrate the great flexibility of primary human social groups. In some of these examples the nuclear family has been eliminated as a basic unit of economic organization and child socialization. Many writers have commented that the nuclear family is

14.19 A North American family. (Leonard Freed, Magnum)

14.20 The successful maintenance of a nuclear family's economic adaptation requires close coordination. This young Mexican wife has taken time off from her household duties to bring food to her husband at his lunch break. (Deana H. Hoffman)

Perspectives on Social Organization

under pressure in both socialist and capitalist nations; some people argue that it is obsolete under modern living conditions. Social reform movements in North America, Europe, and the Far East are experimenting with various modifications of domestic structures, and the dream of the Soviet woman does not seem far removed from the ideas of many North Americans on possible family organization. Although the primacy of the mother-child bond can hardly be dispensed with, it appears likely that as industrialized, urbanized living conditions continue to change, further modifications in family and kinship organization will develop, possibly along some new and different lines.

15

Kinship Beyond the Family: Kindreds, Lineages, and Clans

Among practically all human groups there are significant kinship ties that unite people of many different households or families. This is true even in societies with large extended families, like the Serbian *zadruga*, for each *zadruga* generally has important ties with other related *zadruga*, often living in close geographical proximity. Ties to kinfolk have two different modes: in many societies there are links or alliances between *groups* of related kin; in others, the significant social relationships, are links between *individuals*. The particular shapes and sizes of kinship groups have, to a considerable extent, developed in response to the adaptive challenges of different social and physical environments. People who make their living from hunting and gathering usually have kinship systems that are quite different from those of sedentary cultivators. In this chapter we will examine some of the ways in which kinship relationships are structured in various kinds of societies and the ways in which these patterns relate to other aspects of social and ecological conditions.

Bilateral Kin Relations

Most of us have relatives on both "mother's side" and "father's side." In our usual Euro-American kinship system, both sides of an individual's kinship network tend to be of equal importance, even though there are times when some individuals lose contact with one side or the other. Our common-sense definition of "our relatives" evokes a picture of a somewhat vague network of kin, stretching out in all directions from a single individual as point of reference and with very hazy boundaries. Some of you reading this book will be able to name forty, fifty, or more relatives in your network; others see kinship in a much more restricted way and include only a small collection of first cousins, aunts and uncles, nephews and nieces, and grandparents.

The type of kinship network of most Euro-Americans corresponds roughly to what anthropologists refer to as the KINDRED. Figure 15.1 shows the general idea of kindred, with the following features:

1. A kindred is always based on an *individual* as point of reference. That is, the kindred exists only in the sense of the network linked together through relationship to a given person (EGO).[1]

[1] Anthropologists use the term "ego" for the individual who is the point of reference in charting a system of kinship relationships, kinship terminology, or individuals' social networks.

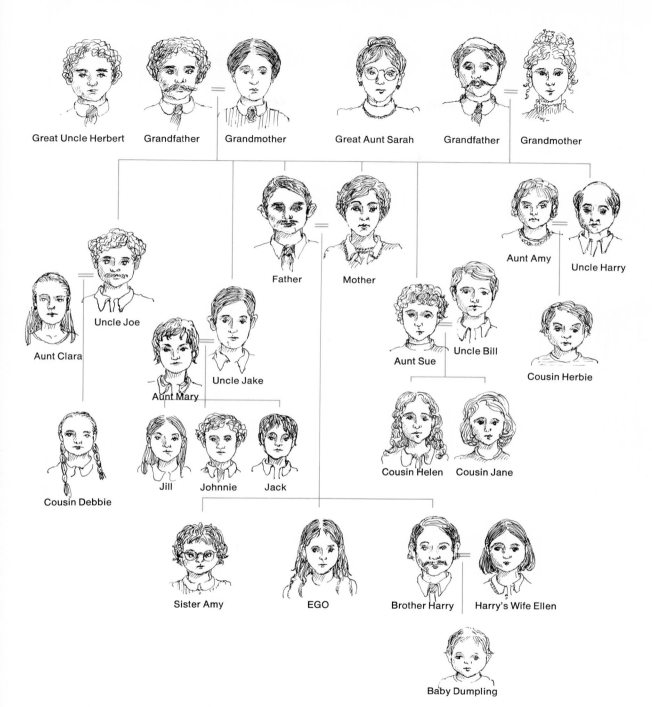

15.1 The kindred: an individual's bilaterally extended network of kin.

297

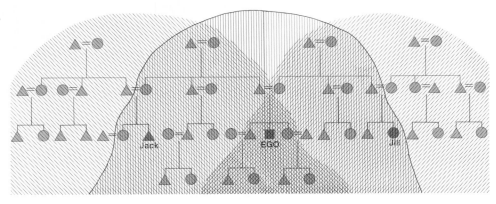

15.2 Everybody has a different kindred. In this diagram ego has several cousins, including Jack and Jill—they are members of ego's own kindred (outlined in black). We see in this diagram that Jack has a different kindred network from that of ego, because he has a whole set of kin on his father's side who are not ego's kind. Similarly Jill has a unique cluster, or network, of kin.

2. The kindred is BILATERAL. Relationships are traced equally through male and female links and thus equally through the mother's side and the father's side.

3. Usually the term *kindred* is applied only to persons who are consanguineously related, that is, related through *biological* ties. However, North Americans, for example, make no sharp distinction between CONSANGUINEOUS aunts and uncles and those "aunts" and "uncles" related to us by marriage.

4. Because each kindred is defined in relation to a *particular individual* (ego), only SIBLINGS have the same kindreds, and even brothers' and sisters' kindreds are different after they have children and grandchildren.

5. Since each individual's kindred is different from everybody else's, kindreds cannot usually be effective social groups with important economic and political functions.

6. The significant functions of an individual's kindred come into play at important crisis points or rituals of great significance to the individual. We expect, for example, that a considerable part of the kindred of each of us will surface and be visible at our wedding and sometimes at very important birthdays. For young Jewish boys, the kindred is often of significance in the celebration of their Bar Mitzvah. For Catholics and other Christians, quite a few members of the kindred may show up for one's confirmation. The final roll call of the active mem-

15.3 Schematic diagram of the Semai *jeg* (ego-centered kin network defined as all the descendants of ego's great-grandparents). Among the Semai, "the trustworthy people, kinfolks are referred to as one's *jeg*. . . ."

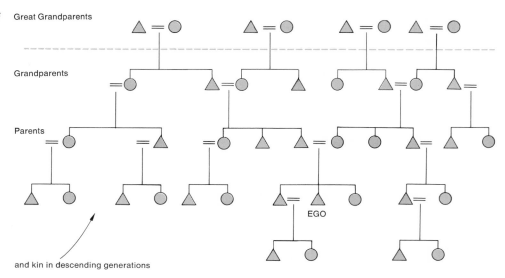

Perspectives on Social Organization

bers of our personal kindred is likely to be at our funeral.

Most, if not all, human groups have some concept of the kindred, even if it is blurred by other, much more significant, rules and ideas of kin relationships. Among the Semai of Malaya, for example, individuals speak of *mai*—those people who are strangers or in no way one's consanguineous kin. If two people meet, they will try to trace out their relationships to see if they can establish a biological link. If they do find such a kinship tie, "however tenuous the relationship, people will cling to it because it transforms the visitor from a potentially dangerous *mai* person to a more trustworthy kinsman" (Dentan, 1968:72). These trustworthy people, one's kin, are referred to as one's *jeg*. The *jeg* includes "the set of all the descendants of one's greatgrandparents, not including the greatgrandparents themselves." (Dentan, 1968:72). Figure 15.3 shows schematically the types of people who would be included in a Semai's *jeg*. You will note that this restricted network of kin includes second cousins (in our own terminology) but not third cousins. The Semai, then, recognize a more restricted kindred than do many Euro-Americans.

Bilaterally (or Multilaterally) Organized Kin Groups

From our description of the bilateral kindred, it should be clear that a community or social system cannot be neatly divided into discrete, separate kindreds. They are endlessly overlapping, since each

individual belongs to as many *different* kindreds as he has relatives. In some societies, however, bilateral organizations are maintained as distinct groups, but they are *not* ego-centered networks.

Among some Malayo-Polynesian peoples there are kin groups defined as "all those persons, both male and female, who are descended from a common ancestor." Such a kin group principle is found, for example, among the Gilbert Island people, the Ifuga-ons (Philippines), and other South Sea island communities. Among Gilbert Island people all the descendants of a particular common ancestor belong to the same *Oo*, which we can label an "unrestricted descent group." Like the ego-centered kindred, these groups are endlessly overlapping in membership, for each person belongs to several different descent groups through lines of ancestors.

The *Oo* descent groups among the Gilbertese are very important in land ownership. Each individual *potentially* has rights in land in several different *Oo*, but in practice, he or she inherits land from some *Oo* and not from others. If the controllers of particular *Oo* lands die out, the others who claim descent in the *Oo* can activate their rights to the land (Goodenough, 1955).

The reindeer-herding Swedish Same, like many other nomadic or seminomadic peoples, have very flexible ideas about residence practices. A newly married couple may join the wife's family (if they have extra pasturage and need of herdsmen), or they may choose to join with the husband's father or brothers. Any particular herding band, therefore, has a mixture of people from several different family

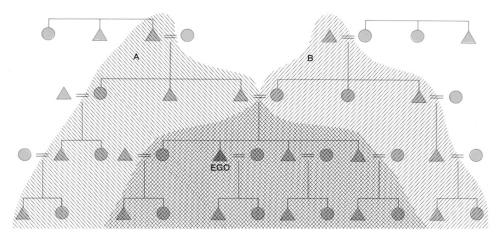

15.4 In the Gilbert Islands all the descendants of a particular ancestor belong to the same *Oo*, which we can label an unrestricted descent group. Each person belongs to several different descent groups. In the illustration ego belongs to the descent group of both *A* and *B* (and he also belongs to many other such unrestricted descent groups).

299

Kinship Beyond the Family: Kindreds, Lineages, and Clans

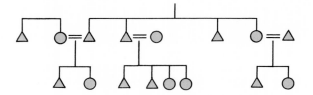

15.5 Structure of a Same reindeer herding group. The core of such a group is often a set of brothers and sisters, with in-marrying spouses.

lines. Thus the bilateral social structure of the Same herding band might look like Figure 15.5.

Robert Pehrson has studied the Swedish Same herders and found that they generally conceive of the core group in a particular herding band as a cluster of siblings, with perhaps a few attached in-laws. The fact that the membership of the group can be expanded by the addition of brothers-in-law gives the bilateral band much greater flexibility than would be the case if they had strict rules of patri-local residence (Pehrson, 1954).

The Idea of Unilineal Descent and Lineages

Kindreds, as we noted, are really not groups at all; they are quasi groups because each person belongs to as many different kindreds as he has relatives, and each of those kindreds is a different list of persons. The way to divide an entire community or larger society into clearly definable, exclusive (non-overlapping) groups is to adopt the rule that each individual inherits membership into *only one specific group*. Furthermore, lines of individual group membership are clearest if a uniform rule is used that one acquires group membership *only* through males or *only* through females.

By far the most common rule of UNILINEAL descent is based on male lines and we refer to it as PATRILINEAL descent. In this type of system all children (male and female) born to a couple are considered members of their *father's* kinship group. Thus the woman, as wife and mother, "contributes" offspring for the continuance of *her husband's* social group rather than to her own kin unit. Brothers, but not sisters, add their progeny to the family line. When social membership is assigned through male lines only, the kin groups are called PATRILINEAGES. The opposite system—in which kin group membership is traced through females only—results in MATRILINEAGES.

In societies in which the patrilineal principle is strong, there is often an equally strong tendency for males related through common patrilineage membership to live in geographic proximity, so that the division of the society into kin groups corresponds, to a relatively high degree, with the actual geographical division of humans on the landscape. The maintenance of clear patrilineal boundaries is generally accomplished through a rule of patrilocal mar-

15.6 The principle of unilateral descent unites individual kin who are linked by descent *through one sex only*. When social membership is assigned through male lines only, the kin group is called a *patrilineage*. The opposite system, in which kin group membership is traced through females only, results in a *matrilineage*.

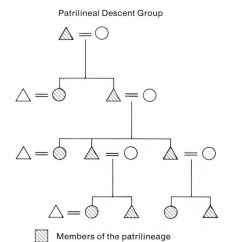

Patrilineal Descent Group

Members of the patrilineage

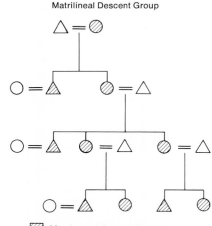

Matrilineal Descent Group

Members of the matrilineage

300

Perspectives on Social Organization

riage, in which each newly married couple takes up residence with or near the husband's family. Not all patrilineally organized societies have strict rules of patrilocal marriage, and in cases in which they do not, both males and females of the patrilineage tend to be geographically scattered so that the lineages themselves are likely to be less important as economic and social units. (Membership in a lineage is generally a lifetime assignment, and it applies equally to males and females. Thus the women who marry into other patrilineages and take up residence with their husbands' people do not thereby drop their membership in the lineage to which they were born.)

The Kapauku are an example of patrilineal organization of the entire social system. As already noted (pp. 227–229), the Kapauku live in small villages, usually about fifteen houses, numbering perhaps 100 to 130 persons in all. In most cases the Kapauku residential group is a single lineage or perhaps a branch of a lineage. Groups of villages jointly occupy lands identified as lineage territories. The Kapaukus' patrilineally organized villages and groups of villages act together in warfare and other dealings with other patrilineages belonging to adjacent villages and territories. Often several patrilineages may band together in a confederacy, especially for defense and offense against more distant villages. Figure 15.7 illustrates the relationship of lineages to territories in societies such as that of the Kapauku.

The Matrilineal Principle

The Greek historian-anthropologist Herodotus was perhaps the first researcher to describe the workings of a matrilineal society. The Greeks, like most other Mediterranean peoples, tended toward patrilineal principles of social organization, so the opposite—a society organized through female descent lines—must have seemed strange indeed:

They have, however, one singular custom in which they differ from every other nation in the world. They take the mother's and not the father's name. Ask a Lycian who he is, and he answers by giving his own name, that of his mother, and so on in the female line. Moreover, if a free woman marry a man who is a slave, their children are full citizens; but if a free man marry a foreign woman, or live with a concubine, even though he be the first person in the state, the children forfeit all rights of citizenship. (HERODOTUS, Book I:89)

Herodotus was wrong when he said the Lycians were unique in the world in their matrilineal descent, for there were (and are) matrilineal societies in many parts of the world, although they are far fewer than patrilineal societies. The matrilineal principle is quite common among American Indian peoples, including the Crow, Iroquois, Creek, Cherokee, and several of the Pueblo peoples in the Southwest, notably the Hopi and the Zuñi, as well as people in parts of Africa and Oceania.

Although we might think of a matrilineal system as being simply the mirror image of a patrilineal society, there is one very important difference that possibly accounts for the relative scarcity of matrilineal societies. Even in matrilineal societies political and economic decision-making tends to be in the hands of men. The leaders are often the "elder brothers" or "uncles," the senior male members of

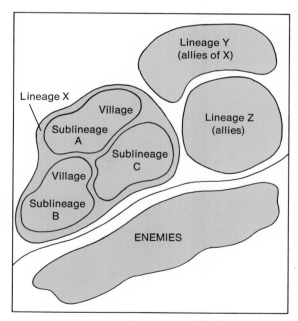

15.7 Among the Kapauku each sublineage has its own territory, a segment of the area occupied by the whole patrilineage. The geography of settlement patterns reflects the social geography.

301

Responsibilities   EGO   Responsibilities

Ego's natal kin group   Wife's kin group

15.8 "The matrilineal, matrilocal dilemma." In societies with matrilocal residence patterns, married men have many social and economic obligations to *both* their own matrilineage and to the wife's kin group.

the matrilineages. The significant difference between the two types of unilineal systems should be evident: in the patrilineal societies the lines of descent and the lines of political and economic authority are in the same hands—the males', whereas in a matrilineal system the lines of descent (and hence group memberships) follow female lines, *but authority remains generally male.* This means that, for example, the headship of a patrilineal group can be inherited directly from father to son, but in a matrilineal group the headship, as well as significant property control, is inherited from a man by his *sister's son,* since a man's own son is not a member of his matrilineage by definition.

Matrilineal societies frequently have matrilocal rules of marital residence. Males of a lineage continue to play an important role in their own kin groups, so it follows that a man who goes to live with his wife's people and works for them must also maintain active participation in his own matrilineage. This poses the matrilineal dilemma. Whereas in a patrilineal society a man generally has undivided loyalty and responsibility within his patrilineage, the male in a matrilineal society goes through life balancing his responsibilities and activities between two groups: his own matrilineage and

his wife's matrilineage, in which he lives and works. The solution to the matrilineal dilemma requires that the separate matrilineages not be geographically far apart, so that a man can maintain both sets of responsibilities without too much strain. Matrilineal societies are often fairly compact village groups, such as those of the Hopi in Arizona.

There are a few societies in the world that employ both matrilineal and patrilineal principles in social organization. Such societies may be referred to as duolineal or as having DOUBLE DESCENT. Among the Yakö peoples of eastern Nigeria, for example, there are patrilineal groups that are the basic political and landholding units. At the same time, each individual is born into a matrilineal group, which regulates the inheritance of movable property and also maintains the shrines to founding ancestresses. Thus the duolineal system is based on a kind of "division of labor" between the two opposite principles of kinship.

Corporate Kin Groups

The groups that are created through patrilineal or matrilineal descent do not depend for their existence or definition on any one individual, so they can be perpetuated through the generations as long as new members are born into them. Because the rules of membership are clear-cut and the group has a perpetuation beyond the lives of individual members, it is an ideal social unit for landownership, religious ceremonials, political organization, and many other activities. In many small-scale horticultural societies, it is the lineages that, at least in theory, own the cultivated lands. Among the Micronesian island people of Ulithi the matrilineages control garden plots, sailing canoes, and other production property. Furthermore, important political and ceremonial activities, as well as the settlement of disputes, are organized by heads of matrilineages. Whenever kin groups have significant property and prerogatives of this sort, we speak of them as being CORPORATE kin groups. They are, in a sense, supra-individual corporations, around which social and cultural behavior is played out. In contrast, the bilateral kindreds discussed above are not corporate groups, for two reasons: (1) they are not perpetuated through the generations, and (2) they do not generally own property or other significant cultural materials.

Most societies in which one finds unilineal descent groups, either patrilineal or matrilineal, consist of several levels of such groupings—sublineages, lineages, maximal lineages, clans, and so on. Because a lineage is defined as "all of those people who trace their descent back to a known, common ancestor," the size and "depth" of a particular lineage depend partially on how far back people decide to trace their ancestry. Among people with written records, like the Chinese, the tracing of descent can go back many generations, so that large groups of people may all see themselves as belonging to the same kin group. Their common kinship, however, rests on their relationship to a founding ancestor in the distant past, so that the relationships among more recent ancestors can be of considerable social importance in day-to-day affairs, including factions and cleavages within the larger group. In southeast China, for example, some branches within a larger kin grouping may become wealthy and powerful and decide to establish their own religious and political separateness. Their separateness is generally defined as "common descent" from a *particular* ancestor— perhaps one of the sons or grandsons of the original founder. As significant linking older relatives die off

generation after generation, the groups may split into more fragments or segments, although still recognizing that they are all ultimately descended from that original founding figure.

Some societies are so neatly organized in terms of several levels of lineage membership that they may consider their entire society to be descended from a single founding ancestor. This is the case, for example, among the Tiv people of Nigeria. All the people consider themselves to be descended from the original ancestor, Tiv. Naturally a population of several hundred thousand persons must have gone through a number of generations to reach its present size. Nonetheless, the Tiv theory of social organization is based on the assumption that the currently existing lineages can be arranged in different levels of segmentation stretching back to that original ancestor, seventeen generations ago. Figure 15.9 illustrates the point in shortened form; the schematic system of "nested," or segmented, lineages corresponds generally to the subgroups, groups, and larger units of Tiv making up the traditional territory. Two small sublineages adjacent to one another (a and b in our diagram) are likely to be so closely related that they can quite accurately demonstrate their descent from a common ancestor, perhaps only three or four generations ago. Being close neighbors, a and b may have some land disputes with one another, but if they have political or economic difficulties with people from c or d, they (a and b) are likely to unite in opposition to those more distant relatives. Such a dispute would then involve conflict between the two larger lineages, 1 and 2. By the same logic, those larger lineages would unite along kinship lines for mutual defense if they got into a dispute with people from lineages 3 and 4. And so on up the line.

The SEGMENTARY lineage structure of societies such as the Tiv and other African peoples is an extremely effective device for mobilizing people at various levels of conflict. Whole armies organized in terms of their kin relations can take to the field in an organized manner in territorial disputes with other tribal groups. In fact, the superior military forces of the Central Asian steppe peoples who have, from time to time, waged highly successful warfare against European populations, as well as against the Chinese, appear to have been organized into fighting units in terms of patrilineal kinship lines. The segmentary kinship lines fit well, then, with segmented

303

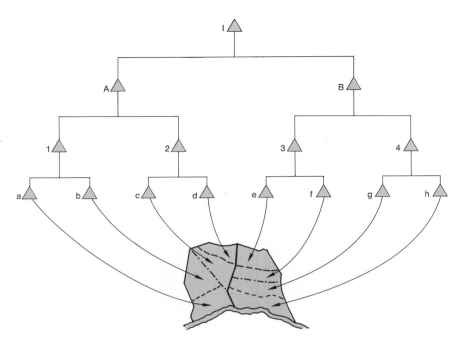

15.9 In a segmentary lineage system the schematic system of "nested" or segmented lineages corresponds generally to the subgroups, groups, and larger units that make up the entire population. In this illustration the minimal lineages *a* and *b* occupy adjacent lands, and are likely to unite in conflicts against people in neighboring groups (e.g., *c* and *d*). However, if there are conflicts with more distant kin (e.g., in lineage *B*), all the minimal lineages, *a*, *b*, *c*, *d*, are likely to band together in opposition to their opposite numbers, *e*, *f*, *g*, and *h*. Against more distant groups the large lineages, *A* and *B*, are likely to unite for common defense or offense, because they are all descendants of *I*. (*Source:* Adapted from Bohannan, 1965:532)

military organization in which one has various levels from platoons and companies up to divisions and armies.

Clans and Phratries

In many societies with unilineal descent groups as major social building blocks, groups of lineages that are *not* territorially adjacent may be affiliated through myths of descent from some supernatural ancestor or ceremonial figure. Often the mythical ancestor is an animal, a plant, the wind, or some other natural feature. These larger groups that are linked through descent from a mythical ancestor are often referred to as CLANS.[2] Among the Hopi peoples of Arizona, for example, there are a Bear clan, a Snake clan, a Sun clan, and others. The same principle is found among the Kapauku in New Guinea—localized lineages have lineages of kin in other areas with whom they are linked through diffuse clan membership. In some cases it would appear that

clans are the descendants of what once was a large lineage of which the human ancestral origins have long been forgotten. On the other hand, it is perfectly possible that, in some cases, separate lineages may become affiliated in warfare or other social action and then later create a fiction of descent from some supernatural source to account for their social ties.

Sometimes the clans or other large kinship bodies in societies are grouped in loose ways into confederations or coalitions called PHRATRIES. These affiliations, like those of clanship, may be based on some special social unity that arose from previous geographical proximity, cooperation in warfare, or some other social situation. In some cases these large, geographically dispersed subdivisions of a society may take the form of two halves referred to as MOIETIES (named from the French word for "half"). Among some of the Pacific Northwest Coast Indian groups, for example, the entire social system was divided into the Wolves and the Ravens. MacKenzie Inuit society had Ravens and Cranes. Many of the California Indian groups had moieties, which were most visible in athletic games and in certain types of ceremonial occasions. In fact, the association of the moiety idea with athletics is so widely found

[2]Some anthropologists use the term SIB in place of *clan* and refer to patrisibs and matrisibs, depending on which unilineal principle of descent is involved.

Perspectives on Social Organization

in the world that one can consider moieties to be somewhat analogous to the National League versus the American League in professional baseball. Another usual social task of moieties has been to bury one another's dead; moieties as complementary "burial societies" were important in earlier times among the Chickasaws and the Choctaws in the southeastern United States.

Labeling Kin: The Tangle of Kinship Terminology

One of the most persistently fascinating areas of research for anthropologists is describing and analyzing the great varieties of ways in which different groups categorize their kin. The importance of kin-naming systems was recognized by Jesuit priests in the eighteenth century when they found that North America Indians had ways of classifying kinsmen that were very different from the customary terminology of European systems. One of the "founding fathers" of anthropology, Lewis Henry Morgan, car-

ried out a study of different kinship terminology systems around the world, trying to classify them into major types. He became interested in the fact that people like the Iroquois referred to their "fathers" and a number of other senior male relatives by the same term. Morgan thought this curious system of kinship labels was a "survival" from an earlier time of group marriage, when all of the males of the kin group supposedly shared in mating with their women—hence distinct paternity was not known.

In more recent times, anthropologists have found that the logic of lumping people whom we would refer to as "father" and "uncle" under a single kin label makes sense in relation to the special social importance of corporate, unilineal kin groups. The social and economic relationships that one has with the senior, male members of one's patrilineage, for example, are of great significance whenever the most important forms of property ownership and social control are in the domain of the lineages. It has been demonstrated that societies like the Iroquois and many others who classify parents together with

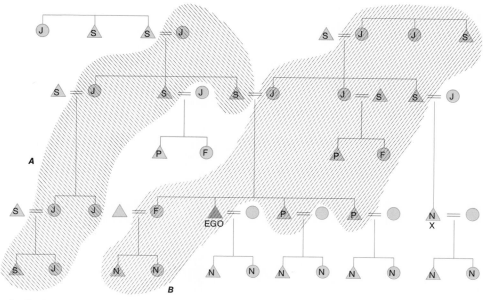

15.10 **Schematic diagram of Truk kinship terminology. (Consanguineal kin terms in the diagram: J = jinej; S = semej; P = pwiij; F = feefinej; N = neji.) Members of ego's** *father's* **matrilineage (A) are** *all* **honorifically considered to be in a generation senior to ego. Kin in shaded area** *B* **are all members of ego's** *own* **matrilineage. Note that ego's mother's brother's son X is called** *neji* **("child") by ego, mirroring the fact that X refers to ego as** *semej* **("father").**

J = Jinej
S = Semej
P = Pwiij
N = Neji

305

other categories of kin are usually those in which lineage and clan organization is a major feature of social organization.

Figure 15.10, which shows the kin labels that are used by the Trukese People of Micronesia, is an example of kinship terminology in a society with corporate matrilineages. We note that a number of people are lumped under the same terms as those used for one's biological "father" and "mother," so that in kin terminology one's nuclear family is merged with other types of people. There is another interesting feature of this system. Among the Trukese, the labels that are applied to "father" and "mother" are applied to a number of persons in the diagram who are of the same generation as ego, or even of a younger generation. This interesting deviation from Euro-American systems puzzled earlier travelers and anthropologists in their encounters with some North American Indian groups. Why should someone use a term that means "father" to refer to a little child? The logic is that the little tad, much younger than the speaker, is referred to as a "father" because he is a member of the *speaker's father's matrilineage*—a group of people that are of great social importance to the individual, even though he is not himself a member of that matrilineage. *All* members of the speaker's father's matrilineage are classified as "father" and "mother," symbolizing the social respect and importance that the speaker recognizes in his or her father's lineage. The kinship system of the Trukese is referred to as a Crow-type kinship classification because it was first identified among the Crow peoples of North America.

In the English-speaking system of kin labeling we always distinguish our own biological parents from our parents' brothers and sisters, but note that we do *not* distinguish between father's siblings (brothers and sisters) and mother's siblings. Instead we lump them all under two labels: "aunt" for females and "uncle" for males. There is an easygoing and clear-cut bilaterality to the way in which those labels apply equally well to father's side and to mother's side.

There are many kinship systems in Europe, on the other hand, that distinguish between mother's brother and father's brother terminologically. For example, in the Finnish language, the father's brother is *setä*, whereas the mother's brother is *eno*. These are two distinct types of people in the Finnish terminology, corresponding to something that was of great social importance in the bygone generations of Finnish cultural history. In the past Finnish families often included more than one generation, usually based on patrilocal rules of marital residence. For a child growing up in the extended family there were several adult males in addition to the father who might discipline him or her. If one's father's brothers tended to be immediately present disciplinarians, then one's mother's brothers were quite different kinds of people, for they were in other households, perhaps in other villages, and one knew them only from social visiting and pleasant, nonworking activities. In fact, one's mother's brother in many patrilocal societies tends to be a friend and confidant—a special source of help, advice, and even financial support. One can run away from home and go to his mother's brother's house. In some African

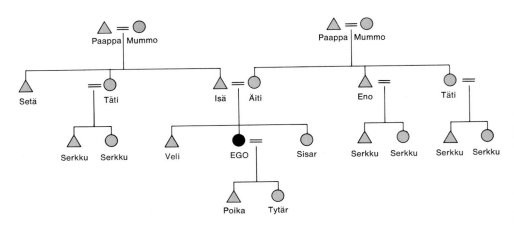

15.11 Finnish kinship terminology (major consanguineal terms). Note the differentiation of father's brother and mother's brother.

306

Perspectives on Social Organization

societies one can even steal his mother's brother's cattle, and mother's brother isn't supposed to care, but laugh at the joke. The Finnish terminology is not based on any deep-lying patrilineal system, as in many African societies, but reflects a past history of patrilocally oriented household structure.

Many other examples could be given of the ways in which kinship terminology gives us clues about important lines of social organization and family structure. Terminology changes slowly so that kin labels persist for generations after the social conditions that gave rise to them have disappeared. That is one of the reasons why the study of kinship terminology has claimed so much anthropological attention; it provides important yet subtle clues about social structure, both past and present.

Fictional Kinship: Blood Brothers and Godparents

The idea of kinship is so powerful in human groups that a great many peoples have invented ways to extend kinship relations to other people through special ceremonies and ritual contracts. The idea of "quasi kinship" will be familiar to college students who belong to fraternities (composed of "brothers") or sororities ("sisters"). There are also "house mothers," and "house fathers." In many ways we extend family relationships, or a part of them, symbolically to other persons with whom we have close emotional interactions. Of course, the institution of adoption, found throughout the world, is a clear example of *socially* constructed kinship.

Among the Vikings of Northern Europe, men sailing out to distant shores and dangerous battle often sought close associates with whom they made binding ritual vows of mutual defense by means of BLOOD BROTHERHOOD. Blood brothers swore to fight to the death to defend each other, to share misfortunes, and to maintain powerful support for one another because they had, in solemn ritual, mingled their flowing blood.

The swearing of ritual or "blood" brotherhood is an idea found widely in the world, including in such groups as the Kpelle in Liberia, the Kamba in East Africa, and the Serbians of Southeastern Europe. Among Serbians, *pobratimstvo* was particularly invoked if a person fell seriously ill and needed supernatural help. The sick person asked a friend to go to the graveyard with him to swear an oath in a setting where the family ancestors could spiritually witness the act. After such a ceremony the blood brothers were supposed to have a close relationship for life, and their children were not supposed to marry each other as they were considered to be very close kin.

Another form of ritual kinship, "godparenthood," is also very widespread in the world, although we often think of it as associated with Christian church beliefs and practices. The theological interpretation of godparenthood, in Christian thought, has to do with ritual and social protection of the godchild, but in many Latin American societies the most important social tie is between the godparents and the parents of the godchild. This is the relationship of COMPADRAZGO, or ritual "coparenthood." *Compadres* ("coparents"), once established, have a lifetime special relationship that is not dissolved even if the godchild dies or moves away. This special social relationship is often established by people to develop economic relationships, close political alliances, and other significant secular ties. George Foster has commented on the use of *compadrazgo* among the people of the town of Tzintzuntzan in western Mexico:

In former years muleteers carried pottery on journeys that sometimes lasted up to a month, passing through distant towns in the *tierra caliente.* They tried to establish compadrazgo relationships in each town where they stayed so as to have a place to pass the night and a support in case of trouble with local authorites. Long distance muleteering is a thing of the past, but a related pattern persists, in that a number of potters have established compadrazgo relationships with pottery merchants in Patzcuaro, to whom they deliver most of their wares. Moreover, within the village pottery merchants who have highway stands or who carry goods to Mexico City buy much of their merchandise from compadres. There is a strong feeling that a satisfactory commercial relationship is bolstered by a baptism or a confirmation. (FOSTER, 1967:81–82)

It should be pointed out that, particularly in Catholic Latin American families, children can be very real social and economic assets for the establishing of *compadrazgo* relationships. The childless family, or a family with only one or two children, is not only poor in terms of its household work force, but even more important, it has few opportunities to cement ties of ritual kinship.

While the institution of *compadrazgo* in Latin America generally involves the flexible manipulation of individual DYADIC ties between sets of nuclear families and individuals, in Serbian Yugoslavia ritual godparenthood is closely linked to patrilineal kinship, so that the honored position of godparenthood, *kumstvo*, is inherited in the male line. Being a *kum* ("godfather") is an honorific and prestigeous position and is "owned" in families, so that if the family head cannot attend a baptism or marriage another male from that same family can enact the ceremonial role just as well.

In earlier times Serbia, as well as neighboring areas, was a feud-ridden region, as patrilineal family groupings (and larger social units) frequently engaged in armed conflict over women, land, and other valuables. As in other parts of the world, feuding between families could sometimes be terminated through exchange of women in marriage. (This solution should have occurred to the heads of the Montague and Capulet families in the case of Romeo and Juliet.) Among the Serbians the offer of *kumstvo* could also be a way of ending blood feuding. Eugene Hammel quotes the following story of some Serbian peace negotiations:

"The Kovacevici, who owed the blood, came with a baby in a cradle. When they were 300 meters from the house of the Vukovici they got down on their knees and pushed the cradle ahead of them, crying, 'In the name of God and Saint John, accept kumstvo!' Then they baptized the baby. The widow of Milos saw the boy of the Kovacevici and said, 'So this is the smrkavac [literally, "snot-nosed brat"] who killed my fine Milos!' And she wept. And then many people wept. Then the priest cried out again that the blood had been pacified and called down curses on those who would break the peace—bad luck would come to them, their children would die. And the people cried, 'Amen.' And the priest spoke some more, and the people cried 'Amen.' This is the way the Vukovici came to be the kumovi of the Kovacevici." (HAMMEL, 1968:84)

Ritual kinship is certainly not restricted to peoples with Christian theologies. In many societies around the world, individuals and/or families ask for ritual sponsors on important ceremonial occasions. Ritual kinship is a way to expand and modify the ties among social groups and between individuals. It builds on basic ideas of "real" kinship but is more flexible because one can *choose* ritual kin, whereas biological kin are an inflexible set of persons, unmodifiable except through the slow processes of birth and death.

The Evolution of Kinship and Family Organization

In industrialized societies it often seems as though the organization of social action in terms of kinship ties has been displaced or even rendered obsolete by the increasingly depersonalized modes of social relations characteristic of modern lifeways. In less complex social systems the tasks of socialization of the young and of social control were important functions of extended kinship units and households. Now many of these functions have been taken over by school systems, police and court systems, and other bureaucratic devices. Where in earlier times the family was the basic economic unit on the farm or in family-owned businesses, such activities are now largely dominated by corporate organizations, even displacing one-family farms in most areas. It is sometimes difficult for industrialized, urbanized people to understand the social behavior of people whose lives and behavior are orchestrated in networks of kinship. Yet, paradoxically, few human societies place more emphasis on the primacy (and even "sacredness") of the nuclear, monogamous family than do the industrialized peoples of Europe and North America. In recent times, too, studies have shown that kin relationships are much more important in structuring the lives of metropolitan people than had previously been realized.

Kinship in Hunting and Gathering Societies

It has long been taken as axiomatic that nonindustrialized people structure their economic activities and other social behavior in terms of kinship relationships. This idea has led to the assumption that there is a great fixity and pattern to life in nonindustrialized communities, which is part of the general stereotype of uninventive, custombound, routinized tribal life. It may be, however, that the social behavior and organization of economic activity of hunting and gathering peoples have frequently

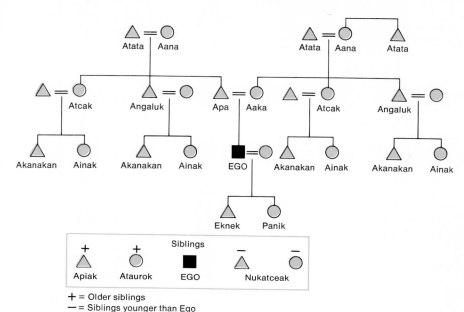

Siblings

+ Apiak   + Ataurok   EGO   Nukatceak

+ = Older siblings
− = Siblings younger than Ego

15.12 Nunamiut (Inuit) kinship terminology. Like the system of English-speaking Euro-Americans, the Inuit system is bilaterally symmetrical, and close lineal kin (father, mother, siblings, and so on) are distinct from more distant kin, such as cousins, aunts, and uncles.

been as flexible and individualistic as our own are touted to be. Hunting and gathering peoples interact frequently with kinsmen and cooperate with them in hunting and other activities because in very small societies nearly everybody is related to everybody else. The very pervasiveness of kinship ties may account for the fact that the composition of local groups and cooperating work units has frequently been extremely flexible and bilateral in organization.

The language of kinship designations is instructive in this matter. The Inuit, who represent an extreme case of adaptation to a hunting way of life, use a system of kinship terminology that is much like that of Euro-Americans. Their labels for various kinds of relatives vary somewhat in different regions of the Arctic, but in general they display a bilateralism of kin relations and emphasize the unity of the nuclear family in contrast to all those other kinsmen—a characteristic in keeping with the flexibility of membership in local groups.

Table 15.1 shows the distribution of different types of kinship organization among hunting and gathering systems that anthropologists have studied. Compared to the worldwide distribution of kinship systems, past and present, the hunters seem to be unusual in the prevalence of bilateral structure as compared with patrilineal and/or matrilineal modes of social organization. This bilaterality fits in with the flexibility requirements described earlier.

Sedentary hunting and gathering peoples can usually maintain more complex kinship organization than people who must move far and wide in search of food. The Kwakiutl and their sedentary neighbors on the affluent coastlines of the north Pacific had kinship structures that contrast markedly with those of most hunting-gathering peoples. Many of these sedentary, maritime hunters were basically matrilineal in social organization. The Kwakiutl them-

Table 15.1: Types of Kinship Organization of Hunting-Gathering-Fishing Peoples

Type of Descent System	Number of Societies
Patrilineal	19
Matrilineal	13
Bilateral	61
Duolineal (Double descent)	8
Total	101

Source: Adapted from ABERLE, 1973:677.

309

Kinship Beyond the Family: Kindreds, Lineages, and Clans

selves show some tendencies to patrilineal organization, though it appears that they were not particularly fussy about maintaining a strict unilineal principle of recruitment to kinship groups. Various theories have been advanced to account for the matrilineal tendencies of the Haida, the Tlingit, and other Northwest Pacific Coast peoples, but the point that concerns us here is that their relative affluence made possible a structured organization that encouraged the development of strong corporate kinship groups.

Kinship Among Cultivators

With the invention of plant and animal domestication, the greater population mass and fixed settlement produced conditions that affected kinship organization in several ways. One effect is the greatly increased probability of warfare among horticultural people. Both the tendency toward warfare and the labor organization needed in gardening, as well as the fixity of settlement patterns, tend to place considerable emphasis on stability and "mobilizability" among cultivators. Horticulturalists *need* fixed social groups much more than do the hunters and gatherers. As already suggested, one of the easiest ways to gather groups of people for either work or combat is through kin relations.

Table 15.2 shows the kinship types found among horticultural peoples of the world. Most of the matrilineal societies in the world are horticulturalists. Although it *cannot* be said that most horticulturalists are matrilineal and matrilocal, in those cases in which matrilineal principles of descent are principal organizing features, the subsistence technology is very often horticulture rather than either hunting-and-gathering or intensive food growing.

The tendency toward a positive association between simple cultivation technology and matrilineal organization suggests a causal relationship between kinship organization and division of labor. The work of horticultural food production is very often female-dominated. Men may have the work of clearing the fields and burning off the vegetation, but the arduous, day-by-day tasks of hoeing, tending, and then harvesting are often assigned to women. In addition, especially in those tropical areas where the preparation of the food from the gardens involves a great amount of further processing—grating, chopping, and other tedium (e.g., with manioc and taro)—a premium is placed on the contributions of women (and the working relationships among females) as major elements in the structure of work.

The need to keep effective work groups of females may lead to the desire to have one's daughters stay at home, working with their mother and aunts even after they get married. If one's married daughters stay home, a residential situation of *matrilocality* has been established. If such a system is established

Table 15.2: Types of Kinship Organization Among Horticultural Peoples

Type of Descent System	Number of Societies
Patrilineal	109
Matrilineal	57
Bilateral	86
Duolineal (Double descent)	15
Total	267

Source: Adapted from ABERLE, 1973:677.

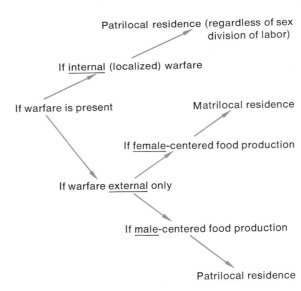

15.13 **Warfare and residence patterns.** Matrilocal residence patterns are most likely to be found in societies with female-centered food production *and* external warfare. (*Source:* Adapted from Ember and Ember, 1971:584)

Perspectives on Social Organization

Table 15.3: The Statistical Relationship Between Warfare (External and Internal) and Residence Rules

	Societies with Matrilocal Residence	Societies with Patrilocal Residence
Purely External Warfare	5	3
Warfare with localized conflict	1	24

$\phi = .65$
$p < .01$

Total cases: 33

Source: Adapted from EMBER and EMBER, 1971:585.

and institutionalized for an entire community, the "custom" of matrilocal residence comes into being. In time this can lead to a reckoning of descent matrilineally to coincide with the clustering of females as the core kinship groups.

If the division of labor between the sexes were the only factor affecting the organization of households and kin groups, we would expect that wherever women are dominant in food production activities, the kinship system would be matrilocal and matrilineal. However, most peoples of the world who maintain a principle of unilineal descent are patrilocal and patrilineal, even in situations in which the women are the major workers in food production. Clearly there is some other major causal variable working, and it appears to have a good deal to do with warfare. Through analysis of a large sample of the world's societies, Melvin and Carol Ember have demonstrated that wherever there is *local* warfare or conflict people are likely to maintain solidary kin groups of males through patrilocal residence and patrilineal descent. (See Table 15.3) It's not warfare, as such, but *local* conflict that puts such a premium on patricentered organization.

When we recall where a man's kinsmen are located in a matrilocal society, we are struck with the possibility that in localized feuding among neighboring villages a man could easily find himself fighting *against* his brother or cousin living in one of those other communities. Under the rule of patrilocal residence, on the other hand, male kinsmen are geographically together.

From their cross-cultural statistical analysis Ember and Ember (1971) derived the diagram in Figure 15.13 to illustrate their theory.

The sexual division of labor in food production is a significant factor affecting tendencies toward matrilocal versus patrilocal residence, but the Embers' work demonstrates that the matter of external versus internal warfare must also be taken into consideration. The prevalence of patrilineal kinship organization in much of New Guinea and in Africa south of the Sahara appears to reflect the prevalence of local warfare in those areas, as well as other social and cultural factors.

Kin Groups in Pastoralist Societies

People who make their living from keeping large herd animals are distinctive for the decided degree to which they are patrilineal. It is possible that among the pastoralists the factors of division of labor and of warfare operate in the same direction, instead of being at odds with one another as in horticultural societies. That is, the division of labor in primary food production is often male-dominated among pastoralists (in some groups it is taboo for women to have anything to do with the herds), so that food-getting activities may be more efficiently maintained through groups of solidary, related males, as in strong patrilineal systems.

Herding societies are often societies in which there is a fair amount of warfare. One of the reasons for this tendency toward warfare is the ease with which military expeditions can have positive economic consequences for the victors through the capture of herd animals. Also, herders have frequent cause to dispute with their neighbors concerning

311

control of grazing areas. For a number of reasons, then, herdsmen are often somewhat militaristic and, as already noted, militarism tends to foster patrilineal organization. In general, the greater the reliance on large animals as a food source, the greater the tendency to patrilineality in human societies.

Kinship in Intensive Agricultural Societies

By this time the discerning reader would be ready to make the prediction that plow agriculturalists and other intensive cultivators, who produce high population densities and complex social organizations, are likely to have patrilineal tendencies in their orga-

15.14 **Modern family scene, Egypt.** (George Rodger, Magnum)

nization of social groups, at least in their preindustrial stages of growth. Like their animal-keeping counterparts, the agriculturalists with systems of intensive food production have historically been relatively warlike (including localized fighting), and these militaristic tendencies must certainly have been conducive to patrilineal organization. The work of food producing in plow agricultural societies is often male-dominated activity, especially when the care of large animals as beasts of burden and pullers of plows is part of the picture, for usually that is men's work and women have a much smaller role in the food-growing activities than is the case among hoe cultivators.

There is another reason for intensive agriculturalists to have kinship organizations different from those of horticulturalists. With complex agriculture, including irrigation systems, crop rotation, and other new technological measures, the value of land rises steeply, and the ownership and control of land by kin groups becomes a crucial element. As a general proposition, it can be suggested that extended kin groupings based on principles of patrilineal descent (in order to make individual memberships clear and the boundaries of kin groupings unambiguous) are particularly well suited to the land-intensive systems of agricultural states. Most of the peasants of the world (e.g., in China, Japan, India, and large parts of the Moslem world) have continued to be patrilineal in their basic kin groupings.

Kinship in Industrialized Societies

The growth of industrialization and city life has tended to cause a decline in the importance of extended families and wider networks of corporate kinship. This process is not inevitable or uniform throughout the world, but in a great many instances, in both East and West, the new production systems built around high-energy manufacturing and large-scale commerce give adaptive advantages to smaller, more mobile family groups. Sons who have chafed under the control of their parents can take their wives to the city and find factory employment. The decline in importance of agricultural landholdings leaves the heads of kinship groups with less economic power over younger members since the focus is no longer on "who will inherit the land" or "who will control the family herds."

Getting jobs in factories and finding the right political connections in the city often depend initially on kinship ties; but later on factors such as education, contacts with nonkin employers, and activity in nonkin organizations like unions, political parties, and mutual benefit associations play

Perspectives on Social Organization

increasingly significant roles. Beyond a certain level of complexity there are forces that work against the maintenance of strong kinship organization of the types that have been so well adapted to preindustrial food-producing societies.

Some exceptions to the trend away from larger kin groups have appeared in places like Sumatra (Bruner, 1973) and Japan. In these instances of East Asian and Southeast Asian modernization it appears that new kinds of solidarity of extended kin groupings are developed in response to industrialization and modernization, and these ramified kin relations have been successful in helping people adapt to conditions in the cities. There is always the possibility that the continuance of extended kinship organization in these cases is a temporary phenomenon. However, we should note that complex kinship organization among the Chinese in modernizing urban conditions, including the Chinatowns in San Francisco and New York, also seems to be a well-adapted mode of behavior and has been maintained for a long time.

People who move into industrialized, urban surroundings do not cut off *all* of their kinship ties. In fact, kin relationships may be important at every stage of the modernization process—as people rely on some of their kinsmen for support and for information about jobs in the city, the locations of housing, and other important items.

One of the main ways in which kinship organization takes on a different structuring in urban conditions is that corporate groups of kinsmen tend to be replaced by flexible *networks* of kin organized and interacting in terms of the needs and ambitions of particular individuals rather than, as traditionally, in terms of long-enduring families. Thus kin relations in "modernizing" societies tend to become more ego-centered or nuclear-family–centered, in place of the group-centered systems that were the mainstays of both peasants and urban elites in agricultural states. Rapid communication, by telephone, automobile, and other means, has increased the possibilites of contacts in our own kin networks.

Industrialization and Matrilateral Kinship Ties

A number of researchers have found that kinship ties in modern urban settings tend to be slightly tipped in favor of relatives on the mother's side. This is not matrilineal kinship, because it does not refer to kin groups but to the ties that each individual or nuclear family has with other kinfolk. When systematic surveys of North American families are made, we find that on the average there is more contact (social visiting) with the mother's kin than with the father's side of the family. This MATRILATERAL ASYMMETRY appears to be related to another tendency: the tasks of communicating with kinfolk (through telephone calls, letters, and Christmas cards) are most frequently female activities (Poggie and Pelto, 1969).

Various explanations for this "female bias" in kinship contacts have been offered, but the question is open to more research. Some researchers have suggested that keeping up ties to kinfolk beyond the nuclear family is an "expressive" rather than a practical or "instrumental" task and that females are generally allocated the more "expressive" roles in our social system. On the other hand, it can be argued that women are more dependent on the long-term maintenance of ties to their own kin because the high frequency of divorce and separation, together with economic discrimination against women, makes them potentially vulnerable to economic and social isolation. The divorced or widowed woman, especially with children, may have to depend on at least partial economic support from her relatives if she does not have an occupation or a personal income.

Summary: Nuclear Families Versus Corporate Kin Groups

Families are always parts of larger social groups in all human societies. Like the one-male groups of Hamadryas baboons, the small family unit is not strong enough and flexible enough to insure adequate food supplies and protection from enemies. Among hunting-gathering peoples the nuclear family groups, based on the husband-wife relationship, are generally dependent on the flexible, reciprocal sharing of food (and protection) in small local bands. The nuclear families are not subservient to the local band or encampment, however. Families or parts of families can shift membership from one local band to another to adjust to the availability of food supplies or to avoid interpersonal conflict.

313

15.15 The modern Chinese family often includes several adult members and is not just a married couple with their children. (René Burri, Magnum)

The relative freedom of choice and movement of nuclear families is considerably lessened in more sedentary, cultivating societies, in which larger kin groups are often the primary units and control lands and other resources. Larger kin groups enhance continuity of land control, as well as succession in leadership. There tends to be an inverse relationship between the importance of the nuclear, husband-wife unit and the importance of extended families and lineages. Furthermore, there are often conflicts between nuclear family and extended family loyalties. Martin C. Yang has described the tensions between the demands of the extended family and the husband-wife relationship in a pre–World War II Chinese peasant village:

It is true that when parents find a wife for their son they hope that the couple will be compatible and are pleased on the wedding day to receive such congrat-

ulations as "Harmony in one hundred years." . . . However, the parents are displeased when the young couple are too devoted to each other, for this menaces the relationship between parents and son, especially that between mother and son. . . . We . . . pointed out how a father's instruction may be neglected, rejected, or misinterpreted if his son listens too attentively to his wife's words. (YANG, 1945:67)

Powerful corporate kin group organization seems to have been especially suited to stable, sedentary agricultural societies in which land ownership was a basic production resource. Tending herds or flocks, with frequent raiding among neighboring groups, also favors the maintenance of strong corporate kin organization. The spread of industrialization and related "modernization" has tended to undermine the larger kin groups because they are often not flexible enough to adjust to rapid socioeconomic changes.

The nearly worldwide decline in the importance of extended kin organization has been accompanied by the increased autonomy and significance of the nuclear family unit as the fundamental economic "corporation" within which resources of food, shel-

Perspectives on Social Organization

15.16 Ceremonial dinners are occasions that bring scattered family members together. (Roger Malloch, Magnum)

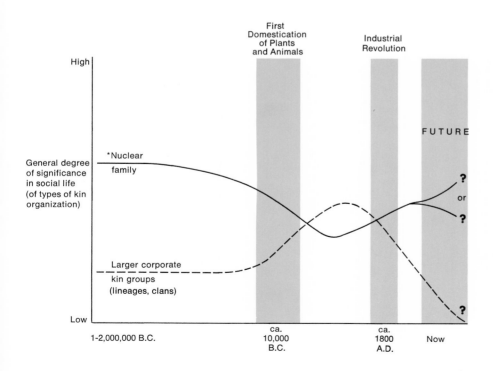

15.17 Evolution of kinship and family structure. The importance of the nuclear family appears to vary inversely with the rise and decline of larger kin organizations.

315

ter, and luxuries are shared. Decisions concerning the socialization and training of children are still made to a considerable extent within the circle of the small family, and, most important, the husband-wife bond is the nexus of emotional and social support. Beyond the nuclear family there are loose social ties to other kin, but major features of economic and political organization have passed over to totally nonkin systems. In some respects the shift toward nuclear family autonomy represents a return to the family organization of the hunter-gatherers, but in a vastly changed context.

Perspectives on Social Organization

Men and Women in Groups: Beyond Kinship

16

As we all know from our own experience, the organization of social relations along kinship lines is inherently restricted and inflexible. Although the organization of social life in terms of kinship appears to be highly adaptive under many circumstances, in many non-Western societies some organizational arrangements have developed that cut across kin groups to form other types of ASSOCIATIONS for specialized purposes. For example, there are many African and North American Indian societies in which the principle of age became institutionalized as a primary marker for grouping people. Another primary principle along which groups have been formed is sex: men's and women's organizations have important duties and activities in some societies.

The idea of organization based on a single principle such as age or sex was certainly available to human groups thousands of years ago. In more recent times, as the division of labor in human societies has grown in complexity, potentialities for developing voluntary societies or specialized groups on the basis of other criteria of selection have greatly increased. In modern societies we take for granted that special-interest groups will be formed in terms of hobbies (ski clubs, stamp clubs, debating societies, gourmet cooking circles, and so on), special occupational groups (plumbers, sociologists, truck drivers, and so on), and political action organizations (Democrats, SDS, Constitutionalists, and so on). These are of increasing importance in our pluralistic social systems. Groups with special interests have grown up in some non-Western societies as well, although they have not been major organizational features until fairly recently in human history. In this chapter, we will review some of the important aspects of these different kinds of "voluntary associations," noting their general importance in human biocultural evolution and the ways in which their structures and activities have become more and more prominent as social systems have become urbanized and industrialized.

Age Sets and Age Grades

Among nonhuman primates groups are often formed on the basis of age and sex. Juvenile age groups are common among many monkeys, and single-sex (temporary) bands are frequent among

16.1 The solidarity of the men in an East African community is symbolized in the ceremonial leopard skins. (George Rodger, Magnum)

chimpanzees, for example. Probably all humans have some feeling of social solidarity or at least some vague special interest in members of their society who are the same age as themselves. "The class of '66" from many high schools in North America probably decided to hold ten-year reunions for 1976. Such AGE SET reunions are perhaps slightly trivial but are nonetheless real expressions of the tendency for people of approximately the same stage of development to identify with one another and later to reminisce together over their common experiences. This tendency for people in a similar stage of the life cycle to feel social bonds of solidarity has been institutionalized in a great many societies in such a manner that cohorts of a particular age (often

all the youths in a society, who were all initiated at the same time) are grouped together in named and organized age sets; and the entire society, or more likely the *males* of the entire society, is grouped in terms of the succession of age sets that spans the living generations of the society.

We can take an example from the system of the Samburu, a patrilineally organized society of cattle pastoralists in East Africa. Male initiation rites are very important for the Samburu, and all of the men initiated in a certain period (a span of about twelve to fourteen years) comprise an age set—a group of males who have feelings of solidarity with one another *across* kin groupings and communities and who advance together through AGE GRADES, the recognized stages of the life cycle.

When Paul Spencer was living among the Samburu from the late 1950s through 1960, all of the male Samburu could be grouped into six age sets, as shown in Table 16.1.

318

Perspectives on Social Organization

Ordinarily there are six age sets at any given point in time. However, because a major initiation of boys in the Samburu communities took place in 1960, there were temporarily seven instead of six age sets in existence as a few old men of the Marikon age set had not yet died. Even though the members of an individual age set differ from one another in their actual age, all of the Kimaniki, for example, are socially equivalent and are expected to act together and support one another on many occasions. The immediately senior age set must receive respect from all the members of a junior age set (for example, the Kishili must show respect to the Kimaniki members). In addition, there are special relationships between *alternate* age sets. Thus the Mekuri age set was the *ritual sponsor* of the new group, Kishili, and because of its ceremonial relationship to the junior group, Mekuri are morally and spiritually responsible for the conduct and maturation of the Kishili. To exert moral authority over the younger age set, the senior sponsoring age set members have the power to lay potent curses on the juniors as punishment for misconduct.

We note from Table 16.1 that in 1960 there were two age sets, Kimaniki and Kishili, in the life-cycle stage of *moran*, or young, unmarried men. Actually, by 1960 a few of the Kimaniki were already getting married and becoming elders. The *moran* age mates within particular kin groups act together in raiding for cattle and herding cattle, and in times gone by they were the warriors in battle. Within each patrilineal clan of the Samburu the *moran* of an age set can be regarded as an organized club, and the unmarried girls of the clan are associated with the club

16.2 Boy Scouts and Girl Scouts, voluntary associations based on age and sex. (Wayne Miller, Magnum)

Table 16.1: Male Age Sets of the Samburu: 1960

Stage of Life Cycle	Name of Age Set	Date of Initiation
Elders	Marikon	ca. 1880
	Terito	ca. 1893
	Merisho	ca. 1912
	Kiliako	ca. 1921
	Mekuri	1936
Moran (young men/warriors)	Kimaniki	1948
	Kishili	1960

Source: From SPENCER, 1965:81.

and are the mistresses of the *moran* members. Because these clan-based *moran* clubs are extremely possessive of their mistresses—and also aggressive and predatory toward the girls of other clubs—a good deal of fighting and other interclub mischief occupy the attentions of the *moran*. The *moran* clubs of individual clans also hold frequent dances, which involve songs of rivalry between the sexes. Samburu clans are generally dispersed over a number of communities in a region, so the *moran* clubs are correspondingly dispersed geographically. Dances and other get-togethers sometimes involve gatherings of several different clubs, especially on the occasions of a girl's circumcision and marriage.

Whenever a society such as the Samburu has organized groups based on age, there will nearly always be some kind of hierarchical series of these organizations with ceremonial relationships among the several "levels." The usual situation is that the age group of "active young men" (the *moran* of the Samburu, for example) has relatively little political importance. Graduation from this stage of nonpolitical involvement comes when a new group can be initiated into the "young man" category. The organization of societies in terms of age sets is a device that has been particularly associated with peoples who do a lot of fighting. In fact, among the Zulu, the Swazi, and other Bantu peoples of Southeast Africa, age sets were the backbone of very effective military organizations as each new set of initiated youths formed regiments of the royal armies. Special ceremonial activities of groups such as the Samburu *moran* enhance their willingness to fight together in dangerous military expeditions; and ceremonial rivalry between the males and the females, as in the *moran* clubs, adds further motivation and emotional fervor to the young men's fighting and cattle raiding.

Men and Women in Groups: Organizations Based on Sex

In most societies there is a considerable division of labor and other activities separating the sexes. In some, differences are further emphasized through ritual rivalry and antagonism. In many societies the differences and the hostilities between the sexes are further enhanced through ceremonial organizations that, in effect, create clubs or associations of males and, sometimes, of females.

Often people with exclusive men's organizations and esoteric initiation rites have separate "men's houses," where the males congregate to lounge around, transact political business, and carry out ritual activities. The men's houses are often sleeping dormitories as well, married men visiting their wives at mealtimes and at night for sexual intercourse. In societies such as the Mundurucú of the Brazilian Amazon, women are forbidden to enter the men's house on threat of death or at least the pain of mass rape.

Where men are organized into exclusive activities separated from women and children, women often develop social clubs or associations, sometimes based on ritual or work activities. Among some tribes of Plains Indians, for example, there were women's craft guilds that maintained control over specialized economic information relating to the preparation of buffalo and deer hides. Cheyenne women and women of the Oglala Dakota had a variety of craft organizations that were concerned with the skills of quill embroidery, moccasin work, and tipi making, and a woman could gain entrance to a particular craft guild only through large financial payment.

Among the Mandan Indians of the upper Missouri River region, there were in the prereservation period a number of women's societies of great ritual importance. The Goose Society danced and performed other ceremonies in order to enhance the success

16.3 Men's house on Selio Island, New Guinea. Symbol of sex-role solidarity. (Courtesy of the American Museum of Natural History)

of the corn crops, and the White Buffalo Cow women were especially important in luring the buffalo to the hunters. These Mandan women's societies were in certain respects parallel to the series of male organizations whose ceremonials were primarily concerned with hunting and warfare.

Throughout Africa there was, before the coming of White domination, a very great variety of ritual associations and clubs of all types. The majority of these showed the exclusive-male features that are often described in connection with male circumcision and other initiation rites (see pp. 409–411). In a number of cases, though, parallel women's associations—some of them powerful secret societies—have also been common. Among the Mende peoples in Sierra Leone there is a powerful and feared secret men's society called the Poro. This is balanced off by a ritually powerful women's group called the Bundu:

No man would under any consideration venture to approach the closed "bundu bush," for the mystic workings of the "bundu medicine" upon any delinquent are firmly believed to be exceedingly severe; and this belief is so firmly rooted in the minds of all men that Bundu girls when under the protection of the bundu medicine can walk about unattended within bounds, knowing that they are perfectly secure from the smallest molestation. (LOWIE, 1961:309–310)

In some areas of West Africa males who accidently penetrated the secrets of women's societies ran the risk of being put to death, just as women had reason to fear for their lives if they intruded on men's secret meetings.

One of the most unusual women's organizations is that of the *Tirgwaged Gademg* ("council of women") of the East African Barabaig cattle herders. The Barabaig council of women reflects and enhances the generally high status of women in the society, for they act as a court to regulate the behavior of men toward women. The council hears cases brought to it by women complaining against their husbands or wrongdoing by other males. The power of the women is well illustrated in a case that happened in 1955 in which a man refused to pay fines assessed by the women's council. His refusal brought on a stiffer fine and a ritual curse of lethal power. But the women didn't rely simply on supernatural sanctions. They tore up his homestead and sent his

16.4 The carvings and other paraphernalia within the men's house are strictly forbidden to the sight of women. (Michael Rockefeller, Magnum)

wives back to their families. The male offender's wives stayed away for a whole year and could not be returned to him until the death curse was lifted and new fines were paid. He finally agreed to the stiff demands of the women's court and normal social relations were at last restored. The anthropologist George Klima, who lived among the Barabaig during 1955–1956 and again in 1958–1959, suggests that the power of the women's council among these people may be unique in Africa (Klima, 1970).

Men in Groups: Instinctive Male Solidarity?

Although there are many examples of women's organizations, it appears that among non-Westernized peoples male associations have been much more common than female societies. Some theorists,

321

Men and Women in Groups: Beyond Kinship

16.5 Nandi spearmen—males organized for war. (Courtesy of the American Museum of Natural History)

16.6 Sisterhood is powerful. African women on their way to market. (Magnum)

including the German Heinrich Schurtz at the turn of the century and, more recently, the anthropologist Lionel Tiger, argue that this disparity—the preponderance of male groups—reflects basic differences in the psychology of males and females. Tiger bases his argument on the idea of "male bonding," which he says has arisen from the ecological-economic patterns in the long, long period of hominid hunting and gathering:

Males dominate females in occupational and political spheres. This is a species-specific pattern and is associated with my other proposition: that males bond in the variety of situations involving power, force, crucial or dangerous work, and relations with their gods. They consciously and emotionally *exclude* females from these bonds. The significant notion here is that these broad patterns are biologically based, and that those various different expressions of male dominance and male bonding in different communities are what one would expect from a species highly adaptable to its physical and social environments, and where learning is a crucial adaptive process. To use Court's term, male dominance and bonding are features of the human "biogram." (TIGER, 1970:143–144)

Tiger feels that his biological, economic-ecological explanation of male dominance and male "groupiness" is stronger than psychological explanations based on unconscious personality themes or other purely mental mechanisms.

Some of the key ideas in Tiger's argument deserve careful attention. His language includes the ideas of "genetic programming" and "species-specific behavior." Thus Lionel Tiger's "men in groups" must in some sense be considered as representing instinctual "imperatives" something like Robert Ardrey's "territorial imperatives" and Konrad Lorenz's "aggression instincts." We have the same objections, then, to Tiger's theories as we do to those of Lorenz and Ardrey. Although we need to emphasize the importance of the human biological past in shaping our genetic programming, we feel that the claims for the genetic programming of male bonding ignore the wide range of variation and adaptive flexibility that seem pervasive in all human behavior, as well as in the behavior of other higher primates. As we noted in an earlier discussion, our nearest primate relatives, the chimpanzees, have very flexible social adjustments—some temporary clusters of chimps consist of mothers with children, others are all male, and still others are mixed male-female groups.

The impression of a species-specific pattern of male bonding can be given if one selects only cases of male solidarity and exclusively male organizations found in many parts of the world. But cataloguing all of the examples of such behavior is very misleading if other types of societies—those with strong female organizations or with *neither* male nor female associations—are ignored. In fact, most hunting and gathering groups for which we have good ethnographic data demonstrate relatively little in the way of *exclusive* male groupings, and the ties between particular males in the form of "male bonding" are surprisingly loose. If we were to accept the biological theories of Tiger, we would have to assume that the women's councils of the Barabaig are in some way "unnatural" since the "genetic programming" of males and females is sup-

posed to prevent any such aberrations from the male way of doing things.

What about these "exceptions"? The rigidly programmed instinctivist must always invent special mechanisms or less-than-natural processes to account for the things that don't "fit" with the theory. For example, Tiger has to resort to some curious reasoning: "Where females have some success in politics, this appears to result from a self-conscious process of planned change rather than 'organic' development" (Tiger, 1970:141).

Tiger goes on to give the example of a campaign in Norway that is aimed at drawing more women into local and national politics through a process of discriminating against male politicians. According to his theory, it is apparently a "natural process" for the males in many societies to exclude women forcibly from all political participation, whereas it is "not natural" for a society to attempt to change sexual imbalances in politics through active discrimination against males!

The most distinctive feature of the human "biogram" is changeability—the production of new social and cultural forms in response to new situations and contingencies. We must keep in mind that those societies with strong women's organizations or mixed and egalitarian male-female associations are just as natural as the much more numerous societies used as examples of male bonding. They are the result of the same processes of human adaptibility in response to varying social and physical environmental conditions.

Societies of Military Glory Among Plains Indian Groups

When anthropologists first delved deeply into the study of the Plains Indians of North America, the Cheyenne, Sioux, Arapaho, Blackfoot, and other buffalo-hunting tribes had recently been put on reservations by the conquering White peoples' armies. The older men of these tribes reminisced freely about the grand old days of buffalo hunting and intertribal raiding that had lasted up until the 1850s, and even as late as the 1870s and 1880s in some areas. Some of them also proudly recalled that brief moment of glory when they defeated Custer's armies on the Little Big Horn River.

The young anthropologist Robert Lowie had finished his Ph.D. in 1908 and was beginning his long-

Men and Women in Groups: Beyond Kinship

time association with the Crow Indians, whose language he learned to speak. He was especially impressed with the humor and the bravery of the Crow peoples as celebrated in tales of the activities of the military "clubs" or societies. He found that most of the Plains Indians still had these military associations as part of their reservation social organization, even though their raiding activities were now sharply curtailed by the reservation situation. Some groups, like the Mandan, Hidatsa, and Blackfoot, had military clubs that were age graded, something like the age sets of the East African Samburu. Each organization had a name: there were the "Little Dogs," "LumpWoods," "Half-Shaved Heads," "Black Mouths," "Bulls," "Ravens," and so on.

In other Plains Indian groups, such as the Crow and the Cheyenne, the military associations were not age graded, and the societies were competing clubs that rivaled one another in military exploits and took turns in carrying out policing actions within their tribes. The clubs were not military units like the Zulu and Swazi age regiments of southeast Africa. Warfare among the Plains Indians was generally a much looser and more individualistic activity, and war parties were generally formed from spur-of-the-moment groups that volunteered to follow some individual warrior on a raid. War parties were generally made up of members from a number of different clubs. They competed against one another in demonstrating their bravery and recklessness in battle—through such exploits as touching a live enemy, cutting loose the enemy's horses, and taking vows of "no retreat," which sometimes amounted to a kind of honorific military suicide. The warriors back at camp lounged around in their tipi club houses, talking about their military exploits, generally having a good time, and occasionally slipping out to try to seduce one of the women of a rival club. Especially among the Crow peoples sexual rivalries were as exciting and important as the military campaigns, while the neighboring Cheyenne were much more prudish in their ideas concerning the proper behavior of girls and married women, and seduction was a serious offense.

The Foxes, the LumpWoods, the Little Dogs, and other clubs each had its special insignias, clothing, and songs to celebrate military honors. In a way, these groups could be compared to the VFW and the American Legion because their main activities were to celebrate and talk about military exploits in order to maintain the fighting "honor and prestige" of the tribe.

On certain occasions, such as a collective buffalo hunt, a march to new territories, or the putting on of a large celebration, the Foxes, the LumpWoods, and other organizations had special public duties. Among the Crow peoples the chiefs each spring designated one or another of the military societies to act as the police force throughout the summer season. In the collective hunt their task was to keep reckless individual young men from going out prematurely and frightening away the buffalo herds. On one occasion, related to Lowie, some young "juvenile delinquents" chased a small group of buffalo through camp, tearing up some tipis and frightening the women and children. The "police" fined the youths and banished them from camp for a month or more. This would have been fairly serious punishment if their girl friends hadn't collaborated in smuggling food out to the young criminals. Police duties ended in the fall when the large tribal groups broke up into much smaller bands for the winter season. During the winter there was much less time for play and the glories of warfare, as the quest for food required the full attention of the hunters.

16.7 Boy Scout troop in an Indian community, Southwestern U.S.A. (Dennis Stock, Magnum)

Voluntary associations are all those different kinds of social groupings whose memberships are not automatically recruited at birth through kinship ties and relationships. Membership in such organizations is defined as an *achieved* status in contrast to a status automatically *ascribed* because of one's sex, color, kin group membership, or place of birth. By this definition there are types of associations that are really intermediate—for example, the male solidarity "clubs" in many societies, which include for practical purposes every male of the community beyond a certain age. Thus the term *voluntary* is not completely appropriate for those societies, although a male is not automatically a member until he has "achieved" the initiation rites. Similarly, in age-set societies, every male becomes a member of a particular age set and passes through a series of fixed statuses through his life cycle. There again the transition process is not absolutely automatic but must be achieved through initiation ceremonies and other ritual.

Most voluntary associations are identifiable because they have names (such as the Foxes, Alpha Kappa Lambda, the Soyal Society (Hopi), the American Legion, the Democrats, and so on). They also often have special emblems, perhaps items of clothing, badges, and other ritual identification markings. They often further identify themselves with songs, secret languages and slogans, special rules and procedures, and other unique activities. Especially in contemporary contexts, voluntary associations usually have officers, selected by the membership, and they have treasuries, dues, and other financial arrangements.

The military clubs of the Plains Indians are of special interest as a type of social organization because they illustrate the ways in which *non*kinship groupings can be developed in fluid, changing societies to accomplish special purposes in a manner quite different from kinship groups like clans and lineages. The Foxes, the LumpWoods, and other groups among the Crow and their neighbors recruited their memberships from many different kin groups, competing with one another to initiate the bravest and flashiest of the young men. In some groups entry to the clubs required heavy outlays of wealth as initiation fees. Once the clubs had become well organized and numerous, they were quite flexible and adaptable for new tasks and activities, including police work and other organizational needs among the tribes. The fact that these military clubs had memberships that cut across the kin groups made them ideally suited for the organization of social control. Robert Lowie and other anthropologists have argued that organizations like the Plains Indian military societies represent some of the alternative political-social structures that later developed into complex, bureaucratic state organizations. In any case, these nonkinship voluntary organizations are one mode of transition away from kin-and-clan–dominated social systems.

Street Gangs: Adaptations to Internecine Warfare?

In most larger North American cities there are large numbers of voluntary associations that police and some other people refer to as street gangs or fighting gangs which other people refer to as boys' clubs or social clubs. These groups have become prominent in the newspapers in recent times, mainly because of intergroup warfare, including bloody fighting with occasional killings. In some instances they have also captured attention because the gangs that were formerly concerned primarily with recreation and defensive and offensive fighting have taken an interest in the politics of social change and have become political action groups on behalf of the marginal and economically deprived populations from which they arise. The well-known Blackstone Rangers of Chicago have received grants of money and other support for community development in the city of Chicago and have carried out boycotts and picketing on behalf of increasing labor opportunities for Black people in their city.

The street gangs of New York, Chicago, and other cities have colorful and sometimes frightening names, such as the Egyptian Cobras, Satan's Disciples, the Latin Counts, the Vice Lords, and so on. Often the

325

Men and Women in Groups: Beyond Kinship

16.8 Signatures of Chicago street gang members, with the formidable Blackstone Rangers' presence prominently displayed. (P. J. Pelto)

16.9 The territory of the Vice Lords in West Chicago, showing the separate "branches" and their locations. (From *The Vice Lords: Warriors of the Streets* by R. Lincoln Keiser. Copyright © 1969 by Holt, Rinehart and Winston, Inc. Reprinted by permission of Holt, Rinehart and Winston, Inc.)

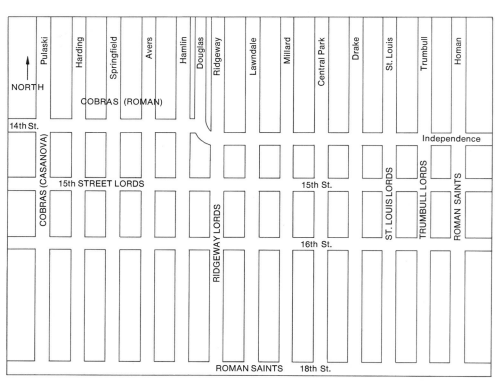

gangs are identified with particular ethnic groups and maintain a belligerent possessiveness over their "territory," or "turf," usually an ethnic neighborhood in the inner city. This ethnic territorialism is, in fact, one of the most interesting features in the behavior of the street gangs, although their territorial behavior varies somewhat in different environments.

The territoriality of street gangs has been mapped out in detail by Gerald Suttles in his study of *The Social Order of the Slum* (1968), which deals with West Side Chicago. He studied in detail the territorial demarcations among the various gangs, focusing on an Italian area, surrounded by a variety of other gangs of diverse ethnicity. He noted that in public places such as the city parks, where the gangs tended to congregate, various sectors of the park "belonged to" particular groups and that trespass in these "miniterritories" by adjacent gangs was often the signal for trouble.

The Conservative Vice Lords of West Side Chicago have been studied in detail by Lincoln Keiser (1969). His description of the origins and growth of the Vice Lords is especially interesting because it shows how city gangs form in response to conflict-ridden interaction with gangs from other neighborhoods. In part, groups like the Vice Lords provide a self-defense adaptation for the boys of a particular neighborhood. Self-defense often converts to offense, however, as a group grows and prospers. The most successful gangs, like the Vice Lords, invade adjacent neighborhoods, often through conquest and annexation. At the time Keiser studied the group the Vice Lords had several branches—the Monroe Street Lords, the Lake Street Lords, the Madison Lords, and so on. The core of this gang empire was Vice Lord City, located at Sixteenth and Lawndale Streets.

Street gangs very frequently develop age-set organization. Each age set is actually an independent organization but is affiliated in name and spirit with the related age sets. Graduation from one age set to another is not automatic, but it does occur. In the hard life of the streets, girls are not exempt from the need to organize or participate in the fighting gangs as auxiliaries. Most of the gangs have their "ladies' auxiliaries," with names such as the Latinettes and the Vice Ladies.

Gangs like the Vice Lords and scores of others representing different neighborhoods and ethnic groups are nothing new in North American cities. In 1927 the sociologist F. M. Thrasher carried out an extensive study of the gangs of Chicago. As he pointed out, gangs generally develop as an adaptation to the complexities and dangers of the inner city, where crime, drugs, and other social problems are the order of the day. As new migrants come into the city, their young people find themselves objects of scorn and occasionally physical abuse from already-established youth groups. Whether or not they are attacked by organized gangs, the newcomers on the scene find that for their own protection they are well advised to organize in mutual self-defense. Thus each new ethnic group in turn develops its own internal groups, whose recreational activities may be seen by local police as a dangerous threat to law and order.

Not all boys' gangs are street fighters, however, and not all the activities of even the supposedly most aggressive groups are lawless and dishonorable. For example, in the late 1960s, after community development funding had become widely available in inner-city areas, the Vice Lords entered into cooperative arrangements with one of their traditional enemies, the Egyptian Cobras, as well as with the West Side Organization and several other West Side Chicago groups. This consortium of Black organizations became known as the West Side Development Corporation, which established a number of commercial enterprises in the Near West Side Chicago Black area.

Social Change and Voluntary Societies

The military societies of the Plains Indians and the age-graded organizations of East African peoples appear to have arisen in contexts of rapid social change. On the Plains, the growth of these groups was associated with the adoption of horses and a shift from an agricultural way of life to an economy based on buffalo hunting. In East Africa, before the coming of Whites, there was a period of rapid expansion of cattle-keeping peoples toward the southeastern portions of the continent, along with a growth of warfare and raiding related to the slave trade.

In both cases, then, there was reason to "experiment" with new social forms, and the new social

327

organizations were related to military activities. There are, in fact, some remarkable parallels in the types of organizations that were developed in the two regions (e.g., the age-set military societies). There were, of course, great differences as well, for the East African peoples with their kingly bureaucracies had much larger and more complex societies than those of the Plains Indians.

Whereas relatively stable, cultivator societies might adapt to change through long-term adjustments of their kin organization, the more rapid and sweeping transformations that were going on in Africa and on the High Plains of North America favored the more flexible, nonkin types of organization. We should note, however, that some sedentary cultivators have developed complex associations—notably, the Pueblo Indian communities. Currently, with the fantastic acceleration of social change now going on throughout the world, the social adaptations of many peoples are most visible in the growth of voluntary societies, clubs, unions, guilds, mutual benefit associations, and other quite flexible organizations. Clubs and societies can raise their membership from zero to thousands in a few weeks or months. It is not just a matter of numbers, however. Voluntary organizations can recruit new members from like-minded individuals in order to promote ideological solidarity, and they can recruit people with special skills for particular tasks. There are other advantages that voluntary associations have as compared with kinship organizations, not the least of which is the fact that a special-purpose club can get people together for some short-term, highly specific goal, ignoring all other aspects of life style and social commitment.

Ethnic Associations

For many North Americans, some of the most familiar examples of the growth of social clubs and societies in times of cultural change are the ethnic and minority organizations that have sprung up in our cities as immigrants from foreign lands or from rural backlands have searched for ways of adapting to the complexities of modern city life. The examples are numerous: in areas where Northern Europeans migrated to North American cities, there are the Sons of Norway, the Finnish Kaleva Brothers and Sisters, and a great number of Swedish, German, Danish,

Polish, and other social clubs. Many of these European-American social organizations arose as forms of social insurance for people who had left the kin groups and village solidarities of "the old country" and found that as individuals they had insufficient means to cope with the problems of the New World. Sickness, disease, and death were among the problems that required group cooperation; it came as a great shock to learn that the sorrows of death were compounded by the high cost of dying in an industrialized society. One of the first aims of many ethnic societies in North America was to use the money collected from individual dues as a fund for payment of funeral expenses of the membership. Health insurance was an equally important concern, and many of these organizations have pioneered in the provision of financial support for people who suddenly encounter large doctor bills and hospital expenses. Other types of social insurance have also been characteristic of North American ethnic associations.

Summary and Conclusions: Voluntary Associations and Cultural Evolution

In commenting on the social organization of non-human primates, we noted that the primate *biogram* (general pattern of adaptive behavior) is based on a great amount of social learning and social interaction in groups. Most primates, including humans, are intensely social animals. The basic social groups of the primates appear to be the more-or-less territorial geographic groups, like baboon groups and hunting and gathering bands, as well as the smaller clusters of various types of family groups, as among some chimps. While bonds of biological relationship, especially mother-child ties and mate pairing, tend to be the primary linkages among individuals in the simplest primate organizations, some other kinds of associations, often of a temporary nature, must have been important adaptive mechanisms for early humans, as well as for our ape relatives millions of years ago. Some people have argued that the cooperating hunting group of males is the prototype for the varieties of fraternities, societies, clubs, and other associations of more recent times. However, the demands for flexibility and mobility in hunting and gathering groups suggest that pre-Neolithic men and

16.10 Motorcycle groups are examples of new modes of social organization in industrialized urban settings. (Magnum)

women had relatively little need to form special-interest associations except among perhaps the most affluent hunting groups, such as the well-to-do Northwest Coast peoples and the buffalo hunters, the prereservation Plains Indians.

Voluntary associations are not usually of much importance in most simpler cultivator societies, for the intricacies of politics and economic organization are generally well handled by kin groups. There are a lot of interesting exceptions, of course, and the Pueblo cultivators of Arizona and New Mexico are an example of a group of societies in which religious fraternities and sororities developed, along with kinship groupings, especially to manage Pueblo ceremonial and religious life. Pastoral herdsmen, too, tend to be dominated by kin groups rather than associations, although the East African cattle-herding peo-

ples are notable for their age-set organizations, which have been of great importance in warfare and cattle management. One special feature of those age-set organizations, however, is that they are not truly voluntary: every individual male must in his turn be initiated into his particular age set and passes automatically through the recognized age grades whether he likes it or not. Incidentally, in age-set societies advancement to the role of "retired elder" often operates automatically, something like forced retirement at age sixty-five. There are studies that indicate that such forced retirement can be as anxiety-provoking and unwanted in those African societies as it is for many North Americans.

Voluntary associations of the type so familiar to us in industrialized societies have, for the most part, come into their own after cityward and intercontinental migration on a massive scale have produced dramatic changes in human lifeways. These associations do not take over all aspects of social life for city folk, and the ties of kinship, especially in the nuclear family, remain part of the social network of nearly everybody. The additional complexities that arise in urban and especially in industrializing surroundings, along with the reduced contacts with kin and clan caused by migration, require additional forms of organization, and for many people the clubs and mutual-help associations meet their needs. For some people, the core of such voluntary associations is built around religious worship; others are drawn to labor unions and occupational groups; and to an increasing degree political groups and movements are the major organizers of peoples. In contemporary urbanized and industrial society, it is the unusual person who does not belong at least nominally to a voluntary association. Many people, especially at the "middle-class" level of society, belong to dozens of such groups.

In summarizing the materials in this chapter, we see the following as general points:

1. From the evidence we have from past history, and from the different societies around the world today, it seems clear that the role of voluntary associations in human social organization increases greatly with social complexity, especially in connection with urban migration and the development of industrialization and complex nations.

2. Since membership in voluntary associations is recruited through interest and participation rather than by birth, these organizations can be much more

Men and Women in Groups: Beyond Kinship

flexible than kin groups in expanding or contracting or changing while adapting to social processes and conditions.

3. Voluntary associations generally take over many of the functions or activities handled in traditional societies by kin groupings, but they do not totally replace kinship organization.

4. Although historically there seem to have been more male clubs and other organizations than either mixed or female associations, it does not seem necessary to postulate any genetically determined programming such as "male bonding" or other special biological characteristics to explain these male-female differences.

Perspectives on Social Organization

Many Europeans and North Americans experience such consistent patterns of male and female behavior that they get a strong impression that these differences in psychology and temperament are biological, inborn characteristics of our species. On the other hand, anyone who is familiar with some of the ethnographic literature from other parts of the world is aware that the patterning of female versus male activities can vary a good deal from one society to another, depending on the situations and demands of their environments.

Margaret Mead was the first anthropologist to focus on the extremes to which different societies are able to bend the definitions of appropriate male and female character. In New Guinea she found three societies that were quite strikingly different from one another in sex roles. The mountain Arapesh appeared to favor a gentle, cooperative style of behavior in both males and females. There was not much contrast between the sexes in either activities or personalities, for Mead found them both showing a "mild and loving attitude," "little sense of struggle in the world," and an "easygoing acceptance of the individual's own wishes" (Mead, 1935:100–105).

The Mundugumor, a warlike and cannibalistic tribe on the Sepik River, contrasted sharply with the Arapesh in their definitions of male and female roles, for among these people, *both* males and females were "expected to be violent, competitive, aggressively sexual, jealous, and ready to see and avenge insult, delighting in display, in action, in fighting" (Mead 1935:158). As a characterization of New Guinea males, this description is perhaps not all that surprising, for there certainly is a great deal of competitiveness, warfare, and overt sexuality in the lifeways of many New Guinea peoples. The more interesting thing, though, is that the Mundugumor women were expected to be as aggressive as the men.

Just a little way up the river from the fierce Mundugumor was a group called the Tchambuli, who provided yet a different style in sex roles and temperament. These were a patrilineal people, so we might expect that the emphasis on male ancestors, the men's club house, and other man-centered features would be accompanied by an aggressive style of male behavior. On the contrary, Mead found that it was the Tchambuli women who were the dominant, entrepreneurial managers of the economy and household affairs: "The women's attitude toward the men is one of kindly tolerance and appreciation" (Mead, 1935:176). The women showed a sort of surface deference to the males, but they apparently felt some amusement at the Tchambuli men's preoccupations with art and ceremonial. Every man was supposed to be an artist and to excel in everything from painting to carving to dancing. They were vain and self-decorating in all kinds of ways, hence expressing personality features that some people derogatorily assign to modern North American women.

Since Margaret Mead first published these observations in her book *Sex and Temperament* (1935), there has been a great deal of argument and disagreement concerning both her data and her interpretations of them. Mead has said that this was her most misunderstood book. Many people interpreted these three strikingly different cases as proof that there are *no* biologically derived differences in temperament between males and females. But that, said Mead, was not the conclusion she herself intended; all she was pointing out was the great degree to which human groups, with their distinctive cultures, can "push around" the raw biological materials of male and female temperament. Her emphasis was on the cultural-social malleability of human males and females.

Regardless of the criticisms that might be made of Mead's pioneering work, and even if the descriptions of these three peoples are somewhat exaggerated for the sake of emphasis, the Arapesh, Mundugumor, and Tchambuli must serve as a very powerful warning for us as we try to sort out "basic, sex-determined" behavioral features. If in those non-Westernized societies such great differences in life styles of males and females can be fostered by the social system, then it may be extremely difficult for anyone to disentangle the genetically programmed biological sex differences from the complex of social and cultural forces.

Chromosomes and Hormones

The difference between male and female *Homo sapiens* begins with the genetic coding carried in the sex-determining chromosomes. The two types of chromosomes are conventionally labeled X and Y—an individual who receives an X chromosome from each parent becomes a female (XX), whereas maleness is determined by the XY combination. As only males have both X and Y chromosomes, the determination of sex depends on which type of sperm, an X or a Y, fertilizes the ovum in the female reproductive system. The X and Y chromosomes are very different from one another. The Y chromosome is very small and carries very little genetic information other than sex determination. The X chromosome, on the other hand, is very large and has a number of genes affecting other kinds of biological functioning besides sex. This difference between X and Y chromosomes has a number of side effects, including, apparently, the greater susceptibility to disease and death in males. Any genetic flaw carried on the X chromosome is potentially dangerous for males. The reason is that many of these genetic flaws are recessive in nature (see p. 102), so their presence is masked by the *other* X chromosome in females. Males do not have a "shielding" second X chromosome, so the recessive, harmful genetic materials in an X chromosome can show their true nature. Thus there are those diseases, including hemophilia, that appear only in males.

Primates and Sexual Dimorphism

The size differences between the sexes in *Homo sapiens* are not as pronounced as in many of the other primates. Among baboons and gorillas, for example, males are generally twice as big as the females. Here again the chimpanzees are closer to us humans.

		Average Adult Weight			
Sex	Humans	Chimpanzees	Gorillas	Orangs	Baboons
Male	65 kg	45 kg	175 kg	75 kg	35 kg
Female	58 kg	40 kg	85 kg	37 kg	14 kg

Perspectives on Social Organization

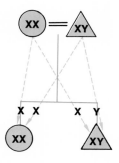

17.1 Sex determination: the combination of X and Y chromosomes.

The greater vulnerability of males to disease and death affects all ages and is balanced off by the fact that more males than females tend to be conceived, by an estimated ratio of approximately 120 to 100. Since more males die even prenatally, the ratio in newborns is about 106 to 100. Throughout life, males in all societies tend to be more vulnerable than females to a variety of diseases and problems ranging from heart attacks and ulcers to various viral infections and cerebral palsy (Hutt, 1972:23–24).

The physiological differences between males and females brought about by the sex-determining chromosomes are in the chemical messengers called hormones. Male hormones are called ANDROGENS, of which the most important is testosterone. These chemical substances produced in the interstitial cells of the male gonads (testicles) are already present in the unborn male child.

The female gonads (ovaries) produce two types of hormones: PROGESTERONE and the ESTROGENS. The estrogens are important for the development of the reproductive tract of uterus, vagina, and oviducts. Progesterone is more directly concerned with pregnancy. The sex hormones, like a number of other hormonal secretions in the human body, are under the control of secretions from the pituitary glands, located at the base of the brain.

Some people have argued that these genetic differences, especially differences in hormones, are responsible for supposed differences between male and female in temperament, interests, and skills. Others have suggested that men and women are not really different in biological personality and behavior and that social conditioning, laced with male dominance, causes most of the apparent differences. Considering the importance of the sex hormones in affecting the physiology of males and females, and considering the relationships of hormones to behavior (e.g., adrenal secretion and arousal to fight and flight), it would be very surprising if there were *no* behavioral differences between males and females. On the other hand, a great many differences or variations among individuals are socially trivial, even though they may be quite noticeable. It is much like the problem of racial characteristics: skin color and hair texture are probably relatively unimportant biologically, yet social importance is attached to them in most societies. Let us look at the two views of male-female differences.

The Argument for Biopsychological Differences

Corinne Hutt, a psychologist and ethologist at Oxford University in England, has discussed some of the principal evidence on the side of physiologically determined male-female differences. She refers to a considerable body of psychological research, her own as well as that of others, that shows a great difference between males and females, not only in British and North American populations but in non-Western societies as well. Some of these studies have shown that practically from birth on females tend to be more sensitive to sound than are males, whereas males are apparently more attuned to visual stimuli. According to various kinds of tests, females, on the average, do better than males in verbal skills. On the other hand, males tend to perform better than females in tests concerning spatial relationships and arithmetic. (This would suggest the possibility that females *might* be more "left-hemisphere dominant" in brain functioning—see pp. 146–147.) There is even experimental evidence that these male-female differences are found in chimpanzees and other animals.

One of the spatial relations tests in which males tend to do better than females is the Embedded-Figure Task. Figure 17.2 illustrates an embedded figure in which the problem is to find a specific design that is disguised within the larger framework. Ability to see the design within the larger figure is referred to as *field independence* and is related to one's capabilities of maintaining spatial orientations

Female and Male: Vive la Différence?

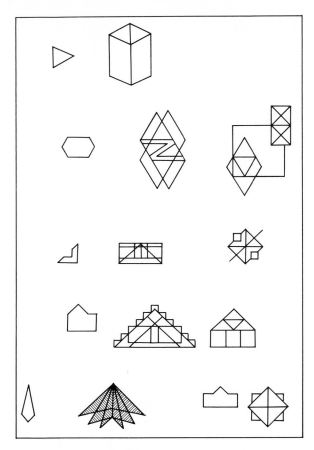

17.2 **Examples of embedded figures.**

and recognizing relationships in spite of distortions and distracting background.

Another major difference between males and females that has been found repeatedly in human populations, as among other animals, is in aggressiveness. Many experiments and physiological tests have shown relationships between level of aggression and level of male hormones. For example, female monkeys injected prenatally with androgens fight more and play more roughly than do females not injected with male hormones. Conversely, males deprived of androgens at a critical period (e.g., through castration) tend on the average to show lower levels of aggression than do their normal age mates. While many of these male-female differences in aggression have been isolated in monkeys and

other animals, the experimental evidence from human subjects also supports these generalizations about sex differences in aggression, as well as the influence of male hormones on aggression levels.

For those researchers who emphasize the behavior *differences* between males and females, the explanation is based on the role of hormones in affecting all parts of the body. Professor Hutt cites evidence that structures in the brain of males are different from those of females because of the effects of sex hormones during the critical earliest months of development. The importance of the sex hormones in connection with sensory performance has been noted in much folklore—for example, in the widely current notion that pregnant women are often extremely sensitive to smells that they tolerate nicely when they are not pregnant. It has been experimentally demonstrated that sense of smell is related to the presence of estrogen (females have a sharper sense of smell than do males generally). Because estrogen level is heightened during pregnancy, this would account for the special sensitivity of women at that time.

Social psychologists have turned up fascinating differences between males and females in response to experimental crowding. J. Freedman and his associates set up experimental groups, some of which engaged in competitive activity, whereas the other groups played cooperative games. The experimenters also put some of the groups into large rooms and other groups into relatively crowded conditions. They found that males were more competitive in the smaller room, whereas females tended to show more competition under *less crowded conditions.* Several other related studies have repeated the same results—crowded conditions tend to bring out aggression and antagonism in males, whereas females expressed more positive emotions toward others under the same crowded conditions (see, e.g., Freedman, 1972).

Generalizing from a number of these studies, some social psychologists have suggested that, in general, females are more used to body contact and closer interactions with persons, whereas males tend to be more defensive about their "personal space" and feel uncomfortable (and possibly hostile) when they are crowded into small spaces. This last example, we should note, seems especially related to the *social learning* of appropriate behavior, and the results might be quite different in other societies, especially in non-Westernized groups. Very little cross-cultural research of this sort has been carried out, however.

The Other Side: Basic Psychosocial Similarity

Many anthropologists, psychologists, psychiatrists, and others have argued that males and females are basically similar in their psychological, behavioral qualities at birth but that the heavy hand of social learning and cultural expectations *trains* the sexes differently, so that pervasive differences are present by the time adulthood is reached. J. Money and A. A. Earhart (psychiatrists) have argued that males and females may have some biological differences in behavioral tendencies at birth, but the major differences arise from social learning. They refer to cases of female hermaphrodites, genetic (XX) females in which secondary masculine characteristics were developed because of androgen hormone influence. In some cases, the individuals showing both female and male characteristics were raised as females; in other cases they were defined socially as males, although their genetic-hormonal conditions were approximately the same. Professor Money and his colleagues found that both the social male and the social female careers of these hermaphrodites were fairly successful and well adjusted (Money and Earhart, 1972).

If these "intermediate" male-female individuals can become *either* socially female or socially male, depending on the roles assigned to them by their parents and other people, then the power of environmental, nonbiological forces must be very great indeed!

Anthropologists in their ethnographic work around the world have found that in most societies males dominate over females in the most important political decision-making, fighting and defense, and other power-oriented activities. Because females are, *on the average*, smaller and physically weaker than males and have lesser tendencies to aggressive behavior, it is not surprising that males have nearly always maintained the upper hand and exploited females at least to some degree. The female child-bearing and child-care activities have also added to their vulnerability to restrictions imposed on them by males.

The tendency for males to dominate over females and to define female activities and products as socially inferior, would naturally be expected to have powerful effects on the personalities and behavior of women of all ages. By this argument, then, many of the divergences between male and female performances on tests and in other situations can be seen as the results of social learning that begins in

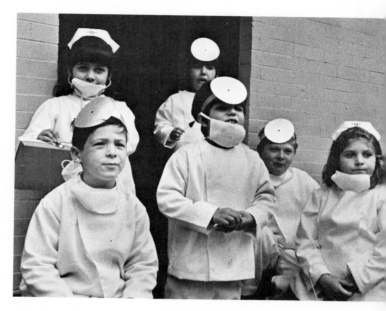

17.3 Sex stereotyping occurs frequently in schools and play groups. Here these children express the common North American idea that boys aspire to be doctors, girls to be nurses. (Magnum)

the cradle and follows women throughout their lives. Because of the social organization imposed on them by dominant males (and the generations of females who have been trained to accept the status quo), the social-role training of girls is nearly always bent toward submissiveness, lesser creativity, and interest in socially defined "female" activities such as cooking, child care, nurse and caretaker activities, and general homemaking. These forces of social training are so powerful that they can affect physiological processes. Therefore, it is argued, what appear to be genetically programmed differences be-

335

Female and Male: Vive la Différence?

The Sexual Equality Amendment

tween males and females are really deep-lying, socially trained role behaviors.

At this point we reach something of an impasse. Many scientists have demonstrated behavioral differences between males and females that "hold good," on the average. Further, some of these behaviors, such as aggressiveness, have been experimentally linked to hormonal activity. On the other hand, there is a great deal of convincing evidence to show that these same behaviors are *very heavily* influenced by learning and social experience. Therefore, we really cannot know the extent to which biology versus learning has produced the patterns of differences we can observe. Probably we will not have even tentative answers to these difficult questions until significant social experiments have truly altered our social environments to achieve greater sex equality of opportunities for learning and development. For reasons that we will see in the following sections, there are very few societies in the world that are so egalitarian and nondifferentiated in male and female roles that we can test the two sides of the argument.

"Matriarchal" and Matrilineal Societies

From time to time some writers and social philosophers have referred to supposed matriarchal societies of bygone times. These social myths refer back to "Amazons" or other societies of women who were dominant over males, who removed their right breasts in order to improve their archery style, and who were fierce warriors and hunters. In some of these mythical communities males were crippled at birth so they would remain docile servants for the women. A variety of other fanciful stories have cir-

culated from time to time concerning female-dominated societies.

To the best of our ethnographic knowledge, there never have been any such matriarchal societies. What has perhaps led to some confusion, especially in older times, is that there are numbers of societies around the world in which kinship relations are reckoned through lines of female descent and in which property and some other prerogatives are said to be "owned" by females (see pp. 300–302).

The question arises: Who has the authority and what kinds of prerogatives do women have in matrilineal societies? As has already been suggested, in many matrilineal groups political and social authority appear to be exercised mainly by the *male* members of the matrilineages; that is, by the uncles (mothers' brothers) and the brothers of the matrilineally related women. When it comes to the matter of a woman's rights in marriage and family affairs, the matrilineal society offers two alternatives: she may be under the "legal" authority of her brothers and other kinsmen throughout her life, or she may on marriage come under the authority of her husband. Professor Alice Schlegel has recently completed a study of matrilineal societies in which she finds that matrilineal household and marital organization varies from "husband-dominated" to "brother-dominated" but that there are some intermediate societies in which there is a "compromise" of authority between husbands and brothers. It is in these *intermediate* matrilineal societies that women tend to have the most freedom and social rights. The Hopi Indians of Arizona are a good example of one of these "women's rights" societies. Although there is no doubt about male domination of the political structure and major religious organizations, Hopi women have a good deal of freedom in many aspects of life. They can divorce their hus-

336

bands quite easily; much of the important property in land and houses is conceptualized as "owned by females"; and, as Schlegel notes, the Hopi women generally "rule the roost" in their households.

Of her sample of sixty-six matrilineal societies from all parts of the world, Schlegel found that in thirty of them women had substantial control of property rights, although in only six of these cases (including the Hopi) was female control of property not shared with the husband or brother (Schlegel, 1972).

Although matrilineal kinship, especially under conditions of matrilocal residence, tends on the whole to present the potential, at least, for a "better deal" for women, it is infrequent that the powers and privileges of women in the household are extended into the broader political sphere.

The prereservation political organization of the Iroquois Indians of Upstate New York was one of those relatively rare cases in which women exercised a great deal of direct political influence. Like the Hopi, the Iroquois were matrilineal in kinship organization, but their granting of prerogatives to females went further than among the Hopi. In addition to owning land and houses, Iroquois women appear also to have exercised control over the arrangement of marriages. Some of the important ceremonial organizations were managed by the women, and incumbents from these women's organizations were also important in the decision-making structures of the matrilineal kin groups. In the general politics of the tribe, women nominated candidates for vacancies in the council of chiefs, and they apparently could impeach chiefs who failed to live up to the standards of office. Thus the Iroquois women exerted a very large political influence behind the scenes, even though they did not themselves directly sit in chiefly councils.

Among the many kingdoms and other complex societies of Africa, social systems from household to head of state have generally been male-dominated, but there are some interesting exceptions. In a number of kingdoms of the nineteenth century and later, women exerted important political power. Among the Swazi of southeast Africa, the king shared his authority with his mother, who had the title of Indlvukati. The Indlvukati had a separate village of residence from that of the king, her own court, and her own following of officials. It appears that in some ways the political powers of the Indl-vukati were balanced with, or complementary to, the sphere of influence of her son, the king. An example of this balance of power is that "the king controls the entire army, but the commander-in-chief resides with his own regiments in the capital of the queen-mother, while she has regiments under the leadership of princes at the capital of the king" (Lebeuf, 1971: 99–100).

The joint sharing of power between king and queen-mother has also been noted in other African kingdoms. At least in former times the Ruanda had this kind of monarchy. Among the Bamileke in Central Africa, the mother of the sovereign has a separate residence, as among the Swazi, and "She directs all feminine activities, thereby controlling the agricultural work of the whole country" (Lebeuf, 1971:100). She also participates in political councils and has direction of the women's secret societies.

Perhaps the most striking example of a woman head of state in recent African politics is that of the Lovedu people in the northeastern Transvaal. During the past century, a succession of three women have ruled the Lovedu kingdom of about forty thousand inhabitants. This female rule is particularly interesting because the people are patrilineal with patrilocal residence; yet the status of women in general is quite high. According to Dr. Lebeuf, "The prestige of the queen rests primarily on the supernatural power with which she is invested" (Lebeuf, 1971:98).

In bygone times the Lovedu were ruled by kings, and important men of the districts sent women to the capital as tribute to the king to become his wives. This system of female tribute to the sovereign continues, and the women sent to the capital are conceptualized as "wives" of the queen. She not only claims kinship links to her important subjects through her "wives," but she can also marry off some of these "wives" to important men, thus establishing further important social ties. The Lovedu queens are so well known in the southeast African area that a number of other groups have emulated their example.

In some of these cases of high-ranking female political figures, the family and other levels of social organization are male-dominated. This curious paradox has also occurred among European nations. Catherine the Great of Russia and Elizabeth of England are only two of the more famous women rulers in European history, and the social systems they

337

ruled over were largely male-dominated in terms of property rights, occupations, and social privileges. Indira Ghandi, as head of state in India, and Golda Meir of Israel are two contemporary examples of this pattern.

These examples are sufficient to point out that there is a considerable difference between the general level of women's rights and social roles in a society and the occasional appearance of women as heads of state. Those occasional queen-mothers, queens, and empresses have usually been defined as "completely different" from the rest of the people of the nation. They have been treated as divine or are thought of in some other way as outside the usual rules of social interaction. It would not be expected, therefore, that such female sovereigns would exert great effort toward the liberation of their sisters. For the most part, their roles as divine rulers have been endorsed by traditions, which also endorsed the maintenance of male-centered patterns in other aspects of daily life.

Cultural Evolution and the Status of Women

Basic subsistence and economic systems have a powerful influence on the degree to which male dominance and exploitation of women is characteristic of particular societies. The egalitarianism in property and social relations in most hunting and gathering groups is often extended to relations between the sexes. At least males have not generally placed great restrictions on the freedom of movement and social interaction of women. In matters of extramarital sex, for example, hunting–gathering groups have tended to be quite relaxed, and sexual freedom has applied equally to females and males. Also, the few important specialized roles, such as the shaman curer, have been open to females, and women often have been important and prestigious practioners. Of course these societies are quite varied, and some are more egalitarian than others concerning the status of women.

The Ituri Pygmies as described by Colin Turnbull seem to exemplify the egalitarian end of the human continuum in matters of sexual roles:

The woman is not discriminated against in Bambuti society as she is in some African societies. She has a full and important role to play. There is relatively little specialization according to sex. Even the hunt is a joint effort. A man is not ashamed to pick mushrooms and nuts if he finds them, or to wash and clean a baby. A woman is free to take part in the discussions of men. (TURNBULL, 1962:156)

The Paliyan peoples of South India exemplify near-complete sex egalitarianism. According to Peter Gardner (1966) there is rather little hunting to be done in the Paliyan environment, so they are much more gatherers than hunters. Their individualism of social action is so complete that there is little food sharing. Women, thus, gather their own food supplies, with little dependence on the men. Marriage relations are fairly flexible, so a woman who feels she is being mistreated can easily leave her husband and take up relations with someone else. (The same, of course, applies to the men.) Thus there are practically no mechanisms whereby men can dominate women politically or economically.

In some other hunting-gathering groups there is a much clearer division of labor, hunting activities being largely male activities, whereas women do much of the gathering of vegetable foods. That is the pattern of work, for example, among the Bushmen. Vegetable foods make up about three fourths of their diet, so the economic productivity of women is correspondingly important, and the patterns of daily life are relatively egalitarian. Women do, on occasion, participate in some hunting activities in most such societies, but much less than the men.

Still other hunting-gathering groups show more male dominance. The Australian aboriginal groups are perhaps the extreme case, in which the authority of the old men is very important. They dominate over both the younger males and the woman. Elaborated ritual activities, especially surrounding the male initiation ceremonies, express the strong segregation of male and female worlds, and the dominant political theme is GERONTOCRACY (rule by the old men).

With the evolution of food production systems, some of the social innovations that arose included the invention by males of new ways for exploiting females. Some of these activities—for example, the development of male solidarity groups—appear to have arisen, at least in part, because of the increased importance of military activities. Military exploits, in their turn, have tended to produce an exaggeration of aggressive, supermasculine behavior patterns that are often accompanied by predatory and demeaning attitudes toward the supposed "weaker sex." Thus some of the most militaristic societies have tended to be the most male chauvinistic ones.

This hypothesis requires some qualifications, however. The effects of military activity on social organization depend a good deal on what kind of warfare people are engaged in (as demonstrated on pp. 310–311). The Gusii people of Kenya are a type of patrilineal society with a long history of warfare that seems to be associated with sexual antagonism and relative male dominance over females.

Among the patrilocal Gusii, a young woman's disadvantages relate to the fact that very often her marriage is arranged without her consent, for her

17.4 In some Middle Eastern societies the laws and customs still favor strong male dominance, and these two wives are maintained under strict seclusion by their husband. (Bruno Barbey, Magnum)

brothers and father are most eager to marry her off to someone who will pay a satisfactory amount of bride price in the form of cattle. Women occasionally elope in order to avoid unwanted marriages, but antagonistic relationships between the sexes mean that girls usually do not have many chances to find attractive elopement partners. The cattle that are paid over to a woman's family in the marriage contract give the husband legal custody of all children born to her, as well as exclusive sexual rights over her. As is typical in a great many societies around the world, males may engage in extramarital affairs, but natural and supernatural punishment will fall on the woman if she engages in adulterous relationships.

As women bear children and become older and more established members of their husbands' households, they are accorded more prestige and develop their own informal means of exerting social influence. Nonetheless, the dependent status of a woman is legally evident in the case of her husband's death, for she is not free to remarry but remains a ward of his kin group.

There are some changes in Gusii lifeways in recent times that suggest some slow steps toward greater recognition of women and their social status. In the past females were generally excluded from beer-drinking groups, which are among the main recreational activities of the males. In more recent times, women have been permitted some marginal part in drinking sessions, but the following comments show that women's liberation hasn't necessarily progressed very far yet:

A woman enters the room, stands by a man whom she knows well, takes his [drinking] tube when he is resting between drafts, and drinks some of the beer. She does not sit down, and she usually leaves in a few minutes to rejoin the women in the other room of the house, where they are boiling water and preparing food. If the liquid in the beer pot runs down, the men may shout at the women to bring more hot water. Occasionally an intoxicated man barks abusively at the women and tries to chase them out of the room. (LeVine and LeVine, 1966:61)

There are a number of ceremonial occasions when women are allowed to act out their antagonisms toward males and to make obscene remarks and gestures. Such rowdy behavior by the women is especially evident on the occasion of girls' initiation

339

rites (the ceremony consists of the clitoridectomy genital operation); the women sing lewd songs, dance around feigning intercourse with one another, and insult or embarrass passing males. In day-to-day life such open mention of sexuality, along with immodest body exposure and other behavior, would be considered extremely shocking.

The example of the Gusii is instructive because it would appear that neither the patrilineal-patrilocal kinship system nor prevalence of raiding and warfare, by themselves, necessarily brings about strong male dominance. The two factors *together*, however, make strong male dominance more likely.

The rather extreme social stratification characteristic of preindustrial agricultural societies has often been accompanied by marked discrimination against women. The elites in high-productivity agricultural societies have had the spare time and the opportunity to restrict their females to subordinate, servile positions—expressed in such extreme devices as the practice of binding girls' feet in China (supposedly to make them more attractive; at the same time practically crippling them). Until the nineteenth century, Hindu women in caste-structured India were supposed to cremate themselves on their husbands' funeral pyres to continue their devotion and loyalty into the next life. Forbidding the remarriage of widows has been common in many male-dominated societies. The seclusion of women behind veils and behind closed doors in the inner rooms of their homes—the custom known as *purdah* in India and in much of the Islamic world—is another expression of the same orientation. Patrilocal residence practices naturally add their weight to the subordination of women, for, wherever the newly married female must leave her home and kin group to join her husband's household, she is effectively without social support and must submit to the discipline of her husband's people. In patrilocal extended families such as those in peasant India and China (and many other societies) older women past childbearing age finally are relieved of some of the features of servitude when they get a daughter-in-law to dominate; but the structure of inheritance, politics, religion, and nearly everything else favors the prerogatives of males.

Powerful male dominance in highly stratified societies, including preindustrial Europe, has usually been most pronounced in the upper classes and castes, for they could afford to keep their women economically unproductive and sheltered. The customs of *purdah*, for example, are not so strictly observed in the lower castes in India or among the lower social strata in Moslem societies, for their women must go out of the house to work, to go to the market, and to carry water, firewood, and other goods. Poor people cannot always afford the luxuries of male dominance.

In postrevolutionary China the binding of girls' feet is no longer practiced. Widows in India no longer cremate themselves on their husbands' pyres. Among Europeans laws have gradually changed over the past two hundred years, giving women citizenship and rights of control over some of their economic property, and other steps toward equality have been taken. Modernization and industrialization do not, however, automatically bring sexual equality. In matters of occupations, behavioral styles, political participation, and other things the relations between the sexes have taken different shapes in response to economic, cultural, and political variations in complex societies.

The Status of Women in the Kibbutz

From its inception the kibbutz movement has involved a movement for women's liberation, for the founders of the kibbutzim intended that women, as well as men, should benefit from the egalitarian principles they sought to put into operation. The system of child care and education, as well as the development of communal dining and clothing facilities, was designed in part to facilitate the entrance of women into full-scale participation in all aspects of kibbutz economy. In the earlier years of the kibbutz movement women were particularly adamant in asserting their equality in all things, and they took part in all aspects of work, including building construction and road making. We should note that Israeli women's attitudes concerning their equal responsibilities, in addition to their equal rights, were not limited to the women of the kibbutz. To this day army service is mandatory for both sexes, and women continue to play a role in the defense of the nation.

In spite of the liberalized intentions and the dedication of the early kibbutz women, the position of women in the kibbutzim today presents some serious problems. The situation at Kiryat Yedidim is

340

17.5 Same woman at reindeer roundup. In a relatively egalitarian society, women can participate in activities that are predominantly male-oriented. (P. J. Pelto)

17.6 Chinese women building a factory in Layang. Sex-role stereotyping of occupations is under attack in China. (Marc Riboud, Magnum)

illustrative. The American anthropologist Melford Spiro found, for example, that of 113 physically able women only 12 percent worked permanently in agricultural production and that the vast majority of women worked in service branches, such as child care, laundry, and cooking. Since the service jobs are often more routinized and more boring as well as lower in prestige, the women feel that they are not getting equal treatment in the economic sphere. Furthermore, about 40 percent of the women in Kiryat Yedidim have no steady work assignments. They are assigned to one job and then another and moved around as the work chairmen see a need; so they do not have the satisfaction of seeing a job completed and developed. In part as a result of their work roles, women are seriously underrepresented in executive and administrative posts. In short, women in the kibbutz are mainly involved in traditional women's roles in spite of the explicit emancipatory philosophy.

How did the present, unsatisfactory situation develop? Spiro suggests that the answer is quite simple and straightforward:

For obvious biological reasons, women could not undertake many of the physical tasks of which the men were capable; tractor driving, harvesting, and other heavy labor proved too difficult for them. Moreover, women were compelled at times to take temporary leave from that physical labor of which they were capable. A pregnant woman, for example, could not work too long, even in the vegetable garden, and a nursing mother had to work near the infants' house in order to be able to feed her child. Hence, as the kibbutz grew older and the birth rate increased, more and more women were forced to leave the productive branches of the economy and enter its service branches. But as they left the productive branches, it was necessary that their places be filled and they were filled by men. The result was that the women found themselves on the same jobs from which they were supposed to have been emancipated. (SPIRO, 1956:225)

An Israeli scholar, Yonina Talmon, takes a similar position. She suggests that "Sex differentiation in the occupational spheres was kept at a minimum as long as the women were young and had few children, and as long as all efforts were concentrated on pro-

341

Female and Male: Vive la Différence?

17.7 Hasidic Jews in Jerusalem maintain strict segregation of the sexes. (Leonard Freed, Magnum)

duction and the standard of living was kept very low" (Talmon, 1965:273). In more recent years, the birth rate in the kibbutzim has increased, and the process described by Spiro has escalated correspondingly. (Of course many people would dispute Spiro's basic assumptions about "biological reasons" in the statement above.)

The Israeli sociologist M. Rosner and his associates interviewed several hundred male and female kibbutz members concerning their attitudes about the status of women. In general he found that both men and women tended to respond in terms of an ideal of egalitarianism (e.g., men and women are seen as equal in intelligence, administrative capability, and most personality traits). However, he also found, as have other researchers, that the present-day situation does not conform to the ideal, and he has expressed concern that the present process of role differentiation may finally lead to the development of nonegalitarian ideas. The more women are left out, the more incipient stereotypes (for which he also found evidence) are reinforced so that "the differentiation itself leads to the development of inequality as regards experience and spheres of interest" (Rosner, 1967:63). Here, then, we see the

beginnings of reestablishment of the classic problem of the excluded group: they are perceived as inferior in some particular set of characteristics, and because they are excluded from participation in particular spheres, they fail to gain the experience of the skills by which they can demonstrate that they are, in fact, equal.

The implication of the Spiro and Talmon analyses is that role differentiation and the consequences of this differentiation are somehow the result of a "natural" process. They are seen to arise from the needs of the group as a whole. As Talmon suggests, "When practical considerations of utility take precedence, considerable sex differentiation in job allocation comes to be regarded as inevitable" (Talmon, 1965:273). However, we should also recall that the Judaic tradition in which the older generation of kibbutz members was raised is strongly patriarchal, and the Mediterranean and Middle East are among the most thoroughly male-oriented areas of the world. We would suggest, then, that "practical necessity" interacts with ideas of long standing to produce the present situation. Rosner notes with concern that in some kibbutzim up to 30 percent of the women feel discriminated against, a percentage that

342

is high for an "egalitarian" society. To us the message seems clear: it takes more than ordinary measures to establish new social relationships. In the case of the agricultural kibbutzim the core of the problem concerns work in the field. Granting that there are physical differences between men and women that affect their capabilities in agricultural work, there is considerable evidence from other areas of the world to counter Spiro's claim that "tractor driving, harvesting, and other heavy labor proved too difficult for them [women]." If work in the so-called productive branches is not only more prestigious but also essential for the acquisition of leadership positions, and if pregnancy and lactation are seen as the major deterrents to work in the productive branches, then a clearly established policy of pregnancy leaves with return to field labor jobs would help toward establishing an egalitarian social structure that parallels the egalitarian ideals.

The Women's Liberation Movement

In the play *Lysistrata*, written by the Greek writer Aristophanes (411 B.C.), Athenian women united to deny their husbands sexual satisfaction until the men granted the women's request to stop the war in which they were engaged. Very likely this was not the first instance of a women's movement aimed at forcing some changes in a male-dominated world. Moreover, in classical Greek times male philosophers sometimes wrote in favor of equal rights for women as we see in the following conversation between Socrates and Glaucon (from Plato, *The Republic*):

S. To conclude, then, there is no occupation concerned with the management of social affairs which belongs either to woman or to man, as such. Natural gifts are to be found here and there in both creatures alike; and every occupation is open to both, so far as their natures are concerned, though woman is for all purposes the weaker.
G. Certainly.
S. Is that a reason for making over all occupations to men only?
G. Of course not.
S. No, because one woman may have a natural gift for medicine or for music, another may not.
G. Surely.

S. Is it not also true that a woman may, or may not, be warlike or athletic?
G. I think so.
S. And again, one may love knowledge, another hate it; one may be high-spirited, another spiritless?
G. True again.
S. It follows that one woman will be fitted by nature to be a Guardian, another will not; because these were the qualities for which we selected our men Guardians. So for the purpose of keeping watch over the commonwealth, woman has the same nature as man, save in so far as she is weaker.
G. So it appears.

The male-oriented Greek society of Plato's time must surely have been shocked by such near-egalitarian ideas about women. Since Plato's day other

17.8 Parental influence is a strong element in teaching sex roles. (Abigail Heyman, Magnum)

343

Female and Male: Vive la Différence?

writers and other social movements have occasionally contributed a nudge here and there toward greater rights for women. The French Revolution brought about important advances in women's rights, until Napoleon reversed much of this trend.

Various socialist reformers of the early nineteenth century advocated women's rights, and many North American communal societies, such as the Oneida people, attempted to create social systems in which women had substantially the same rights and duties as men. The French socialists François Fourier and Claude Henri de Rouvroy Saint-Simon advocated complete sexual freedom, an end to marriage and family, and other sweeping changes that horrified the staid bourgeois citizens of Europe. However, another well-known radical socialist, Karl Marx, was not a particularly strong advocate of women's rights. His views of the sexes are perhaps made most clear in a letter he wrote to Friedrich Engels in 1851: "My wife has been delivered, unfortunately of a girl and not a boy."

In 1840 antislavery reformers in England organized a worldwide Anti-Slavery Convention, to which several North American groups sent women delegates. Despite their avowed reformist and democratic ideals, the English convention organizers denied credentials to the women and made them sit in the visitor's gallery! Evidently North American liberals were more liberal than their English counterparts. Meanwhile, the legal and economic status of women in "the land of the free" was far from free, for "in the eyes of the law, all (white) men were entitled to equal justice, but women, slaves, Indians, children, and idiots did not stand on the same level with them" (Paulson, 1973:11).

After the democratic reforms of the American and French revolutions had come and gone, the next phase of "radical agitation" to include a women's rights movement developed in connection with the abolitionist movement of the 1830s and 1840s. In England John Stuart Mill and Harriet Taylor (later his wife) wrote essays favoring equality of the sexes during the 1830s, although they didn't publish them until later. Mill, like many other women's advocates of the mid-nineteenth-century, put most of his faith in "education for women"—he didn't particularly go along with Harriet's views that women should enter the world of economic productivity and contribute to the family income. Mill's position was typical of Enlightenment thought—that reason is the basis for equality and justice, hence a main step toward equality of the sexes required equal opportunity for education and knowledge. One of the very earliest woman writers on behalf of equality, Mary Wollstonecraft, wrote *A Vindication of the Rights of Woman* in 1792, arguing for the education of women, saying "consequently the perfection of our nature and capability of happiness, must be estimated by the degree of reason, virtue, and knowledge." It is therefore not surprising that one effect of the embryonic campaign for women's rights in the early nineteenth century was the establishment of a number of women's colleges in England and North America.

The first women's rights convention in North America was held in 1848, in Seneca Falls, New York. The organizers were Lucretia Mott and Elizabeth Cady Stanton. Of the two leaders, Stanton took the more radical position and pressed for a resolution in favor of women's right to vote:

With the support of Frederick Douglass, the black abolitionist, she secured endorsement of the resolution by a narrow margin. A hundred brave souls (sixty-eight women and thirty-two men), about a third of those present, signed the declaration, and the convention ended . . . the declaration and reports of the meeting unleashed an avalanche of criticism, fun-poking, and ill-humored editorials in the press. Some of the signers withdrew their endorsement. (PAULSON, 1973:32)

The United States Congress was finally pressured to adopt the Women's Suffrage Amendment in a special session held in May 1919. In Europe most nations had granted women this fundamental right by 1930, but in a few places this aspect of the battle for women's equality was won much earlier. In New Zealand women were granted the right to vote in 1893—not, however, because of a strong women's movement but because of a struggle between political parties concerning the legal control of alcohol. In Finland legislation permitting women to vote was passed in 1906 in connection with a political battle with czarist Russia.

Campaigns for women's rights have developed effective strength mainly in connection with larger social turmoil—world wars, the abolitionist movement, and various internal political upheavals. And it was in connection with the internal struggle and political confusion of the late 1960s and early 1970s

344

that the women's movement again fired up large numbers of people in North America. By 1974 there were large memberships in women's organizations, a mass media magazine, *Ms.*, and women's studies programs had been inaugurated in a number of universities. A new women's rights amendment had been passed by Congress, and the events of the 1970s will test the strength of the women's movement in getting the enactment ratified by a sufficient number of states.

The effect of the women's movement on anthropology itself is likely to be far-reaching. Of the behavioral sciences, anthropology has been the most committed to a global, cross-cultural view of "human nature." Also, anthropology has been the most persistent of the sciences in seeking to combine the biological side of humanity with sociocultural data in a general theory of behavior. Reexamination of cross-cultural data on male and female roles, now ongoing, will result in significant changes in our perspectives concerning the range of variation in women's activities in different societies and the ways in which biological factors and sociocultural learning interrelate in different environmental settings.

Unfortunately it must be admitted that much of earlier anthropological research (with notable exceptions such as Margaret Mead's important work) has been male-oriented. Many ethnographic descriptions contain surprisingly little about women's

17.9 In a strong social movement, opposition often serves to strengthen the resolve of members. (Leonard Freed, Magnum)

17.10 In many societies women work at heavy physical labor, as in this housing construction project in Ghana. (Marc Riboud, Magnum)

345

activities, and often the data are presented as seen from a male viewpoint. This has come about because most anthropologists are males, and the male world is often more accessible to ethnographic study by outsiders. There are, therefore, some distressing misconceptions and stereotypes current in our ethnographic literature, which will have to be modified in the light of new research. Such studies give us little inkling of the many ways in which women's activities are of great importance, often in rather subtle ways, in affecting the style and shape of cultural behavior. Much of anthropological theory will have a different look in the late 1970s and 1980s, reflecting the inclusion of new data about the female experience in different cultural scenes.

Summary

From the cross-cultural data we have reviewed in this chapter some tentative generalizations seem appropriate:

1. As in all other aspects of human adaptation, flexibility is a principal feature of sex role patterning. Margaret Mead's examples from the Tchambuli, Arapesh, and Mundugumor peoples are only a small sampling of the evidence concerning the very wide diversity in peoples' definitions of "proper" male and female conduct and character.

2. The ways that people make their living, and the special characteristics of particular environments, are powerful factors influencing the cultural shaping of sex roles, as we note from the differences in, for example, degree of male dominance under various kinds of subsistence systems.

3. It appears that growth in societal and technological complexity, from small-scale hunting-gathering bands to large agricultural societies, generally has led to greater male dominance and restrictions on women's social prerogatives, particularly because of the effects of endemic warfare, heightened concern about control of property, and increased social and economic inequalities.

4. Although there has probably never been a true "matriarchy" (woman-controlled social system), among human societies past and present there are examples of groups in which women have held substantial political power, social prestige, and economic prerogatives. The Iroquois peoples appear to be an outstanding example of such a system.

Although our first anthropological task is to find out what *has been possible* in different human groups, in matters of sex roles as in other behavior, the cross-cultural data also aid our understanding about what *can be possible* in human social systems of the future. In evolutionary perspective, the structuring of male and female roles appears to be one aspect of behavior in which there is cause for optimism about social experiments that are as yet untried.

Perspectives on Social Organization

Social Inequalities

18

Among the most pervasive features of complex socio-cultural systems are the discrepancies between rich and poor—the often gross inequalities in economic and social position in most present-day societies. An important clue to understanding this aspect of social systems is the fact that institutionalized social and economic inequalities are relatively rare in nomadic hunting-gathering populations.

If the people who practice little or no agriculture or animal keeping have been generally egalitarian in nature, what about the rest of the nonindustrial peoples of the world? Many of the cultivator societies of the South Seas, South America, and parts of North America have exhibited tendencies toward social differentiation without clearly developed social classes. In some groups in Micronesia, for example, certain lineages, clans, or other kin groups are considered more "noble" than others, and there are chiefs, subchiefs, and other honorary titles that express inequalities of prestige. On the other hand, the differences in prestige are often more ceremonial than economic. There are (or were) no deprived or economically depressed categories of people. Anthropologist Morton Fried has referred to these kinds of communities as RANK SOCIETIES, in which *some* exclusiveness of prestige positions is found without any monopolizing of the means and products of production. Rank societies are a step in the direction of significant social inequality. However, since people in such societies have more or less equal access to production resources, there is no development of serious, life-limiting economic deprivation (Fried, 1967).

The Causes of Social Inequalities

Many scholars in the social sciences have devoted whole careers to the study of social stratification—its causes, dynamics, and consequences. There are many different theories about this important problem, of which the best known and perhaps most widely accepted (counting all parts of the world) stems from the work of Karl Marx. Following Marx's pioneering work in the nineteenth century, there has been a great deal of modification, reinterpretation, and extension of DIALECTICAL MATERIALIST THEORY. There is now a wealth of information about non-Western, nonliterate social systems that was not available to Marx and other nineteenth-century theorists, so a number of political and economic anthropologists have been especially concerned with analyzing and modifying Marxist ideas in the light of this data. Regardless of the extent of agreement or disagreement with his theories, Marx has had a powerful effect on the development of an evolutionary, ecological perspective in anthropology.

One of the most thoughtful and carefully prepared theoretical essays on the rise of social inequality from an anthropological perspective is Morton Fried's book *The Evolution of Political Society* (1967). The argument is based on an evolutionist point of view. It begins with the premise that serious inequalities do not develop from some accidental racism or ideology of superiority, nor from abstract religious ideas. Rather, stratification arises from ecological relationships in which important resources are scarce and monopolizable and where there are so many people dependent on one another that they cannot simply break into small foraging groups.

Looked at in this way social stratification is probably a rather late-blooming characteristic of human societies. Until domesticated plants and animals made possible the heavy concentrations of population and the beginnings of urbanization, pervasive social inequalities among people were rare in human societies. Marshall Sahlins (1958) has demonstrated the relationship of economic productivity to degree of stratification in a careful comparative study of fourteen Polynesian societies.

Before continuing we should make clear that we do not deny that there are individual differences of prestige and "dominance" in all human groups, as well as in other primate groups. There are always some individuals who are more successful than others and who dominate in various economic, political, and psychological ways. What we are dealing with in this section are those social inequalities that go beyond simple dominance and prestige differences, to cause significant differences in the foods people eat, the adequacy of their clothing and shelter, and their opportunities to make a living.

Fried's basic theory holds that population pressure is a chief force that brings about stratification. The forces of population pressure operate in many ways, not the least of which is through the significance of land tenure. It is when food production systems become sophisticated, and population can be increased in more favored agricultural areas, that scarcity of prime lands leads to more and more complex landownership systems and usually to inequalities between the landed and the landless. Fried quotes from a pioneering study by C. K. Meek in British Colonial Africa:

If land is plentiful, population sparse, and the people are still content with a subsistence economy, then it is possible to practise a system of shifting cultivation without the necessity of imposing rigid rules of tenure. But when the population becomes denser, or for some reason there is a marked increase in the area of cultivated land, it may become necessary to devise more settled systems of holding land. (MEEK 1946:1–2; cited in FRIED 1967:201)

In our earlier discussions of subsistence systems (Chapter 12) and property (Chapter 13) we noted the ways in which landownership becomes more fixed with increased population. It is not only land by itself that may be at the core of social stratification. In some cases, especially in most fertile areas of the early civilizations, intensive agriculture came to be dependent on irrigation projects, which required a good deal of organization, construction

Social Stratification

We define SOCIAL STRATIFICATION as existing when some category or segment of a society holds direct control over at least a portion of the means of production, while other people in the social system are barred from direct access to those resources. In many preindustrial societies the important means of production is land for cultivation and pasturage. Whenever there is clear-cut individual and family ownership of land, there is usually some category of people who are landless. Other important, scarce means of production may include water (especially for irrigation), fishing locations, hunting territory, special equipment, and special knowledge and techniques. Social stratification is almost always accompanied by differences in economic power, social prerogatives, prestige, and other benefits.

348

18.1 Pre-Hispanic site of Machu Picchu was apparently an Inca colonial administrative center. (Cornell Capa, Magnum)

expertise, and long-term governmental control. Anthropologist Karl Wittfogel has studied these irrigation societies in some detail (he calls them "hydraulic societies") and has suggested that:

the raw materials for making the hydraulic installations (earth, stone, and perhaps timber) either are communal property—that is, owned by nobody or everybody—or if they are found on land held by a particular individual, family, or clan, are taken over by the community. And the end products of the community's coordinated effort, the ditches or canals, do not become the property of the individual farmers or farming families that participated in the work, but . . . they are controlled ("owned") by the community's governing agency. (WITTFOGEL, 1958:234).

Thus the secondary features that are required in intensive food production, such as the irrigation and water control systems, may require a degree of coor-

dinated, managerial, and political work that brings into power some particular group of "specialists" or "politicians" who have social power over the ordinary farmers, who must rely on the irrigation system and the "government" in order to water their individual crop holdings. There are, of course, other kinds of managerial tasks that may have similar effects in connection with intensive agriculture.

Warfare and Stratification

Many recent writers have pointed out that complex societies tend to have bloodier and more economically significant warfare than do simpler societies and that social stratification is, in some ways, related to this trend toward military activity. The history of the early civilizations of Mesopotamia and

349

Social Inequalities

Egypt, as well as those of the New World—especially around the Valley of Mexico—illustrates the ways in which intensive agriculture makes some lands and locations so valuable that people will go to war to try to win these from one another. In the very earliest history of Uruk, Sumer and other ancient cities along the Tigris and Euphrates rivers it appears that with the growth of irrigation works, the beginnings of urban life, and the opening of trade routes linking the growing population centers, there was a steady growth in military defenses around the city-states. This was accompanied by increased influence of the warriors—who became more and more socially dominant as the defenders of local populations.

The histories of conquest and bloody warfare in both the Middle East and pre-Hispanic Mexico give evidence that the growth of concentrated and urbanizing wealth at places like Teotihuacán, Uruk, Babylon, and Montezuma's capital of Tenochtitlán generated pressures for conflict both within the centers themselves and in the hinterlands. In the first place, the rulers of the new cities often found that the growth of wealth and fame through internal development was a much slower process than was the conquest or pillage of weaker neighbors. Urban centers, moreover, require ever-growing lists of raw materials, including precious metals, construction materials, and other supplies. In some cases the easiest way to get those supplies was to take them away from those other people "out there," beyond the rim of the growing city-state. Also, the increasing food needs of the city folk "required" collecting tribute from unwilling farmers of the outlands. There are always ambitious younger princes, nobles, and other impatient would-be autocrats who are ready to push for military expeditions to supply the food and wealth to maintain the growing population, and enhance their own prestige at the same time. When these expeditions are successful, the results are the further subjugation of rural populations (including a further erosion of the peasants' rights to the fruits of their labor) and increased wealth for the urban dwellers, especially for the leaders of the military units and their sponsors in the aristocracy.

Concomitant with these *internal* tendencies toward social stratification and military adventure in

Social Inequalities in Prehistoric America: Etowah

The Etowah site in northwest Georgia is one of the more famous and imposing evidences of cultural complexity in North America before the coming of White people. Overlooking the Etowah River the ancient inhabitants had built a large plaza and beside it an impressive ceremonial "pyramid," flanked by smaller temple mounds approximately 150 feet square at the base. Archaeologist Lewis Larson, Jr., found that the smaller temple mound was some kind of ceremonial burial ground, containing more than 350 individual graves. These burials were significantly different in style from contemporaneous burials in other parts of this prehistoric complex. Evidently the people buried in this mound were somehow special. Many of them had copper and stone axes that appear to be more ceremonial than functional. There were also some pottery vessels, shell bowls, and in some cases stone paint palettes. The people who were given special burials in this mound seemed, according to Larson, to represent a special group that:

had exclusive access to a range of exotic goods that were employed both to legitimatize and emphasize their position in the society. The marine shells, sharks teeth, sea turtle shell, and minerals, as well as the other materials listed above, are all largely exotic . . . [and] the burials in the final mantle are tentatively interpreted as the remains of a descent group that occupied a superordinate position in the total society. The occupants of the burial pits in the village area were, following this interpretation, a subordinate group. . . . Therefore, within the total society there existed stratification, and within the descent group there was internal ranking. (LARSON, 1973:280–282)

350

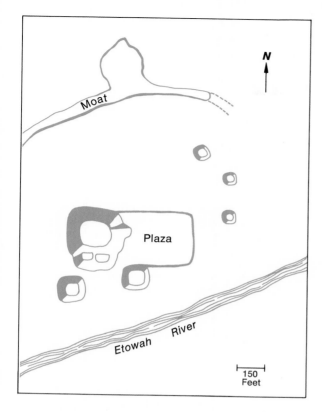

systems. One of the results of military conquest has always been the tendency for conquered peoples to be relegated to low social positions in increasingly unequal economic and political systems. Slaves were often taken from conquered peoples, and the rapid increases in manpower needs that came with social complexity meant that slaves were put to hard work.

18.2 Schematic plan of the mounds and related features at the famed Etowah archaeological site in Bartow County, Georgia, U.S.A. (*Source:* LARSON, 1973:270)

18.3 Diagram of Mound C at Etowah. A and B are burials in which the elaboration of the grave and grave goods suggests that they were for especially high-status persons, compared to the other burials around the edges of the site. (*Source:* Adapted from LARSON, 1973:272)

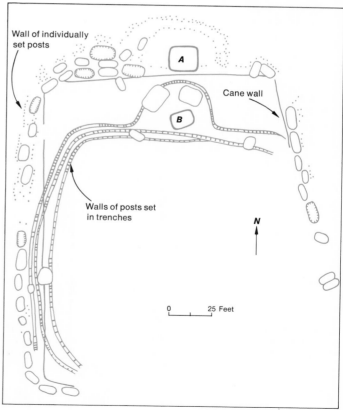

city-states, there seems to have been a counterforce in the backlands, from all the people who resented and despised the city and the centers of power. Throughout history the capitals of the world have been fair game for the attacks of roaming backlanders, whether they were Tartar hordes from the Central Asian steppes, Arab tribesmen from the interior of North Africa attacking North African cities, Germanic tribes battering at the degenerate capitals of the Roman Empire, or the Chichimec and other tribesmen descending on the Valley of Mexico. It is not hard to imagine the motivations of those people in their military expeditions against the "centers of culture."

From the evidence of archaeology and historical analysis of the growth of city-states in the Near East and in the Valley of Mexico, it appears that military conquest added to the tendencies toward social inequality that grew along with the advancing technologies of food production and the rise of city social

Social Stratification in Burundi

In a number of areas in Africa social systems developed that featured a sharp social stratification based on the dominance of cattle-keeping people over the physically smaller peasant agriculturalists, with a lowest stratum of craftsmen and semioutcasts. This pattern of social stratification is especially notable among the Rundi and Rwanda kingdoms of East Central Africa. Their marked social stratification appears to have developed, at least in part, from the military expansion of the pastoralists, the Tutsi, whose oral traditions tell of their emigration from areas farther to the north, somewhere around the Nile Valley. It is worth noting that the population density of the Rwanda and Rundi peoples is quite high—at least 220 persons per square mile, ranging up to 450 per square mile in some of the best lands. The people are scattered across the land in small homesteads and until very recent times did not develop highly concentrated urban centers.

As is typical in highly stratified societies, the Tutsi pastoralist-warriors were a minority, comprising perhaps 16 percent of the total population. The agriculturalist Hutu people comprised over 80 percent of the population, and the outcast, bottom-of-the-ladder Twa people, who were mainly hunter-gatherers, made up apparently less than 1 percent of the population. The backbone of the Rwanda and the Rundi social systems has always been the agriculturalists, who grow beans, peas, pumpkins, millet, and many other crops. Animal protein (especially milk) has been available mainly to the Tutsi pastoralists.

The political dominance of the Tutsi leaders had strong economic implications, for economic surpluses from the peasants were paid over to the military-administrative leaders. A complex of rituals and administrative functions in the king's court naturally required a lot of economic exploitation of the agriculturalists. The king of the Rwanda peoples, like many other rulers, was considered to be a divine being with theoretically absolute power over his subjects. The divine king shared his royal prerogatives with a queen-mother, who was either the king's own mother or a woman specially chosen (D'HERTEFELT, 1965:422).

In theory all land and cattle were owned by the king, so he could transfer these economic resources from one household to another to manipulate his political followers. In turn, his political followers in higher administrative and military offices passed on royal lands and cattle to their own followers, thus maintaining control over their subject peoples and forcing them to perform services whenever the officials needed them. Followers used their lands and cattle to produce crops and milk products for their own purposes, but rebellious followers always ran the risk of having their cattle and lands taken away from them.

The Hutu and lower Tutsi followers supposedly received the benefits of protection by their powerful lords, as well as access to significant economic resources, as long as they behaved themselves and worked hard for their masters. Some of this service to the lord included carrying him on a litter wherever he traveled, for the ruling people naturally had to give the appearance of regal style in their visits to court as well as among their subjects.

The caste stratification of the Rwanda and Rundi operated within the context of a patrilineal descent system. Thus each Tutsi official of any significance was the head of his own patrilineal kin group. There were about a dozen Tutsi lineages of high aristocratic importance and political power deriving from their significant ritual connections with the divine kingship at court. The system of patrilineal inherit-

18.4 High chief in Dahomey with entourage, music, and other signs of high status. Bronze casting, West Africa. (Courtesy of the American Museum of Natural History)

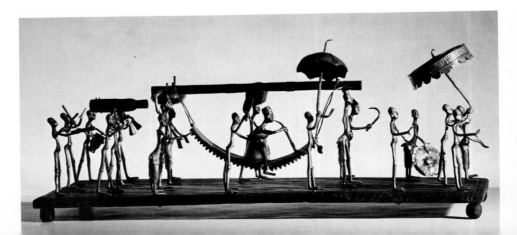

ance meant that relationships of CLIENTSHIP, or chief-follower linkages, were inherited from father to son.

The apparently docile subservience of the Hutu and the Twa to their Tutsi lords and masters was not destined to go on for all time, however. New political developments and independence for African peoples resulted in social movements designed to throw off *both* the power of European colonists *and* the minority oppression of overlords such as the Tutsi. In Rwanda a Hutu rebellion was started in 1959, followed by elections in 1960 in which the Hutu won clear political majorities. The Tutsi royalty, followed by quite a number of Tutsi officials, fled into exile. In some areas large numbers of Tutsi have been killed or driven away and their cattle confiscated by the openly rebellious Hutu peasants. In the past, the Hutu had been unable to unify because they were divided among so many different districts, but now the social divisions of the Hutu are breaking down in the face of nationwide political movements. It appears, then, that the Hutu of Rwanda have fairly successfully ended their subservient caste status.

The rigid and pervasive system of social inequalities that grew up among the Rwanda and the Rundi peoples was not associated with irrigation systems or other large-scale "managerial" construction enterprises. In fact, this social system was not even associated with urbanization, though population density was clearly a factor. It is probable that the social stratification systems that developed in East Africa involved two major features: (1) the high population density and productivity of food growing and (2) the military conquest and warlike tendencies brought into the area by the Tutsi pastoralists.

Trade and Social Inequality

In western Africa, around the ancient city of Timbuktu and in the old Bornu kingdom of northeastern Nigeria, systems of social stratification grew up in a somewhat different pattern. Contrasted with the East African scene, the "westerners" developed cities, particularly as fortified bastions dominating trade routes. Widespread trade in all kinds of goods linked Central Africa to the West African cities, which in turn were the anchor points of caravan routes that reached to the Mediterranean shores and ultimately linked up with European consumers. Those caravan routes, of course, required military protection, as did the market centers and warehouses in cities like Timbuktu and Birni Ngazargamo, the capitol of fifteenth-century Bornu (Cohen, 1967). Ronald Cohen, who has studied the history of the Bornu peoples, found evidence of the growth of central organization as loose federations of kin groups banded together to defend themselves and to carry on trade relations. Leading lineages in the federations grew to be the royal heads of state.

It is interesting to note that these West African stratified societies grew up in situations that apparently did not have heavy population pressure as a factor. The population density of Bornu today is only some twenty-five to forty persons per square mile. Of course, population density is a relative matter, depending on the fertility of cultivatable lands. But it does appear as though people like the Kanuri of Bornu have not been pressured by population densities nearly so much as they have been subject to the hazards of economic conflict over trade routes and advantageous military locations.

Caste Stratification: Fossilized Differentiation

A central feature in many instances of CASTE-structured societies is the domination of the subordinate castes by some ruling group who came from somewhere else as conquerors and whose members often have a physical appearance that is notably different from the people over whom they dominate. In East Africa it is the taller, slimmer, cattle-keeping military conquerors who have imposed caste stratification on the shorter Bantu peoples. In India, a significant part of caste structure appears to derive from conquest by lighter-skinned Indo-European warrior groups who imposed their political power and cultural ideas on a shorter, darker-skinned population, at least parts of which were non-Indo-European in origin. The most widespread caste structuring in the world today is based on the White/non-White distinction that arose as European colonists and conquerors spread their domination to the rest of the world.

The essential features of *caste structure* as we are using the term here include the following:

353

1. Two or more strata (in socioeconomic and prestige terms) are present in a society, with very limited mobility between strata.
2. Assignment to a particular stratum or caste is hereditary and fixed for life.
3. The separate castes or strata are in principle endogamous—that is, one is expected to marry within one's own caste.
4. Social contacts between castes are restricted by means of rules such as separation of castes in public places, avoidance of foods touched by other castes, and general avoidance of social contact.
5. Each caste generally has a name and a separate social identity. Frequently they have internal organization (but not always) and marks of caste status that identify individuals to their own caste and to outsiders.
6. The castes are generally identified with particular socioeconomic positions, sometimes with hereditary occupations.
7. In many areas the entire caste structure is supported by complex religious and philosophical ideas.

By this definition of caste, the social boundaries that separate Blacks, Whites, Indians, and, to some extent, "Orientals" in North American society are caste lines. Marriage across these so-called racial lines is unusual and frowned upon. The much-awarded movie *Guess Who's Coming to Dinner* was an artistic portrayal of the tendencies toward endogamous marriage maintained even by supposed "liberal" White and Black families.

In the North American instance, the division between Black and White castes is more easily maintained because of the culturally defined physical differences that distinguish the two groups, but our definition of caste does not depend on physiological distinction. Perhaps the most striking example of caste structure *without* clear physiological markers is that of the outcast Eta people of Japan, who are indistinguishable from the ordinary Japanese on the street. In that case, the maintenance of endogamous marriage rules concerning the castes depends on careful genealogical work by the marriage arrangers and the parents of the prospective bride and groom. The anthropologist-psychologist research team of George DeVos (University of California) and Hiroshi Wagatsuma (University of Hawaii) have described this unusual situation of caste stratification in their book *Japan's Invisible Race* (DeVos and Wagatsuma, 1966).

Caste in India: The Textbook Example

Although there are caste-structured societies in many parts of the world, the most famous and most thoroughgoing system of caste stratification is that of India. In embarking on a description of caste in India some writers start by recounting the religious beliefs in terms of which people are divided into the five caste categories: Brahmans (priests), Kshatriya (warrior-rulers), Vaisya (merchants), Sudra (artisans, servants, and laborers), and the Untouchables (the lowest—people regarded as being outside the whole system of caste stratification). For some this division into social categories is seen as arising from religious beliefs, and therefore understanding the system requires an understanding of Hindu religious philosophies. But to focus on the religious beliefs associated with caste stratification in Hindu India is, it seems to us, to put the cart before the horse. The religious beliefs certainly rationalize the existence of differential social, economic, and sacred position, but the origins and social meaning of this stratification derive from much more mundane facts of life.

The Rājpūts of Khalapur, India (Minturn and Hitchcock, 1966) provide an example of some of the possible historical background to Indian caste stratification. Khalapur, in North India, is an area that was in the path of numerous military campaigns throughout the centuries. Sometime, perhaps four hundred years ago, the ancestors of the people who now call themselves Khalapur Rājpūts conquered and took over the lands of the present community, having successfully defied the power of the Muslim rulers who had reigned over much of northern India. The warrior-conquerors claimed the status of high-born caste ranking and established the genealogical documentation to support their social claims. In the struggles for social status that go on in caste-ridden societies almost everything depends on the demonstration of the right ancestry, but the "right ancestry" is somewhat easier to lay claim to if one's group is already in a position of social and economic power. The records can always be altered to fit the social facts.

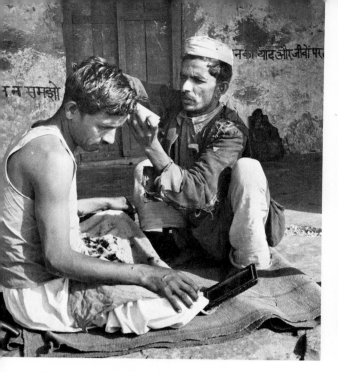

18.5 Caste stratification in India includes a system of hereditary occupations. Here a member of the barber caste cuts the hair of a higher-caste individual. The basket maker is a member of the Bajgi ("drummer") untouchable caste. The Rājpūt man and woman are relatively high caste, though not as ritually pure as the Brahmans. (Gerald Berreman)

The invasion and successful takeover of Khalapur, which is simply one of hundreds of thousands of small Indian villages, was a fairly recent episode in the long line of military conquests and reconquests in the Indian subcontinent. Sometimes the invading victors were of the same physical appearance and language as the people they came to dominate; in other cases the physical and cultural differences were sharp. Over time this process resulted in a series of social categories, ranging from the elites to the exploited lowest status groups. It included intermediate social categories, privileged to serve the elite and partake of their relatively high status if their services were of sufficient importance and tendered with appropriate loyalty to the ruling groups.

Hindu villages of India are composed of more

than just the five basic categories outlined in Hindu sacred scriptures. In any particular village the segments of castes are interconnected through economic ties based on hereditary occupations. Leigh Minturn and John T. Hitchcock described the Khalapur web of social interdependence as follows:

Each Rājpūt family is dependent for services on families belonging to nine other caste groups, and these families in turn are dependent on the Rājpūt families they serve for most of their food. Water carriers and sweepers come to a Rājpūt house every day, the former to bring the daily water supply—a task of special importance, for wives cannot leave the courtyard—and the latter to clean the latrines or carry off refuse, a job which only an Untouchable can do. Every family, in addition, is served by a carpenter, blacksmith, barber, potter, washerman and leatherworker. Carpenters and blacksmiths make and repair agricultural implements; barbers shave, cut hair and fingernails, and play a key role on ceremonial occasions; potters make a large variety of clay pots and other utensils, including the jugs in which water is carried and stored; the washerman washes clothing and bedding; sweepers make cow dung cakes and carry away refuse, and the women also act as midwives. The leatherworker removes dead cattle and supplies his clientele with a few simple leather articles, such as a whiplash and parts of the bullocks' harnesses. . . .
Each family also has a Brahman priest who assists on ceremonial occasions. (MINTURN and HITCHCOCK, 1966:17)

Khalapur, like other typical Indian communities, is composed of a set of subcastes, each of which has a well-known and long-standing position within the hierarchy of social excellence. Many anthropological studies of Indian villages have examined the question of social consensus concerning subcaste rankings. Usually the villagers are clear about the relative positions of almost everybody, but there are often one or two subcastes whose positions are in some doubt—sometimes because the group itself has organized a concerted drive to upgrade their status by some new claims concerning their ancestors and their religious purity. The higher the subcaste, the greater their concern about "polluting" contacts with lower subcastes. (see Table 18.1).
The importance of the caste hierarchy system in Indian villages is particularly evident when we note that, for example, in Khalapur the dominant Rājpūts owned over 90 percent of the cultivatable land at the time that Minturn and Hitchcock made their study of that community. In general, the sacred and ideological rank orders of prestige of castes in Indian communities follow along the lines of economic power and political influence.

As a general point, we suggest the possibility that in India as elsewhere conquests of some peoples by others have ultimately resulted in a very unequal division of economic resources. Among those who are relatively deprived of economic resources there are always some who have found intermediate niches or social stations, especially the artisans and the craftsmen, whose services can be of great value to dominant military elites. When these differences in social position become strongly fixed in social custom, they have often been explained by the religious leaders (who generally shape their sacred ideologies on behalf of the wealthy) as divinely ordained relationships among peoples—the will of the gods. Regardless of the vicissitudes of various conquering political forces, if an economic structure based on intensive agriculture remains relatively unchanged over the centuries, there is always the possibility that the eternal verities of the occupations will become enshrined as religious principles by the people who hold the political power, as in India.

There have been writers, including some anthropologists, who have described the interdependencies among the different caste groupings of Indian villages as a relatively benign or even democratic division of labor. The more subservient castes, such as the potters and the barbers, for example, have a clear and secure place in the traditional life of their communities, and they are assured that the landowners and higher-caste folk will provide them with grain and some other economic returns for their services. It is argued that the system seems to operate well and that the high-born castes are generally not simply sitting in idleness while the lower castes do all the work. In fact, in Khalapur, as elsewhere in Indian villages, the wealthy, landowning Rājpūts work hard, though they are somewhat ambivalent about the status of agricultural work as compared to the former glories of warfare and conquest.

Any romanticized description of the security and harmony of caste-stratified Indian villages should not be allowed to obscure some essential facts about this stratification: that a particular stratum of the society owns and controls most of the basic produc-

356

tive resources and that the people at the bottom of the stratification ladder suffer from many social deprivations and insults in addition to fairly regular hunger and even starvation.

In recent decades the Indian government has en-acted legislation in an attempt to abolish the worst inequities of caste stratification, especially to promote a measure of social and economic justice for the Untouchables at the bottom of the ranked system. Increased industrialization and urbanization in

Table 18.1: Scale Picture of Responses Indicating Ritual Distance[a]

Item Castes	13	10	1	2	7	11	4	8	6	9	12	3	5	Score
Rājpūt	X	X	X	X	X	X	X	X	X	X				10
Merchants	X	X	X	X	X	X	X	X	X	X				10
Water carriers	X	X	X	X	X	X	X	X	X	0	X			10–11
Goldsmiths	X	X	X	X	X	X	X	X	X					9
Genealogists	X	X	X	X	X	X	X	X	X					9
Barbers	X	X	X	X	X	X	X	X						8
Goosaaii	X	X	X	X	X	X								6
Shepherds	X	X	X	X	X	X								6
Carpenters	X	X	X	X	X	X								6
Potters	X	X	X	X	0	X								5–6
Washermen	X	X	X	X	X									5
Grainparchers	X	X	X	X	X									5
K.B. weavers	X	0	X	X										3–4
Joogiis	X	0	X	X										3–4
Mus. Rājpūts	X	X	X											3
Oilpressers	X	X												2
Miraassiis	X	0	X											1–2–3
Ch. weavers														0
Shoemakers														0
Ag. laborers														0
Sweepers														0

Identification of above items:
13 Can touch our children.
10 Can accept dry, uncooked food.
1 Can touch me.
2 Can sit on our cot.
7 Can smoke bowl of pipe.
11 Can take water from his hand.
4 Can touch our brass vessels.
8 Can accept fried food from him.
6 Can smoke our pipe.
9 Can accept boiled food from his hand.
12 Can touch our water vessel.
3 Can come on our cooking area.
5 Can touch our earthenware vessels.

[a]The caste of the informant, a Brahman female, is omitted from this analysis. It is the highest caste.
X = yes   0 = no
Source: Pauline Mahar, ''A Ritual Pollution Scale for Ranking Hindu Castes,'' *Sociometry,* Vol. 23, 1960, p. 303. Reprinted by permission of the American Sociological Association.

India have contributed some changes toward greater social mobility, but the movement toward reform is a painfully slow process.

Caste and Class: North American Social Inequalities

Under conditions of industrialization and urbanization, economic and social differentiation has become so complex that it is quite difficult to sort out clear "social classes" corresponding to the sharp differences between the aristocrats, the commoners, and the other categories in many nonindustrialized societies. Relationships to the sources of wealth, to political power, and to general social prestige are so many-stranded that we find an unbroken continuum of socioeconomic status from the top "power elite" to the bottom levels of the unemployed poor. The picture is further complicated by the way in which the White/non-White caste division cuts across the social stratification.

Despite the gradation of socioeconomic position that characterizes our modern industrialized social systems, there are categories of people who share some similarities of life styles and economic prospects—for example, factory workers, small-scale storekeepers, "white-collar" office employees, and "the power elite" of managers, bankers, and millionaires. In the most general terms, these categories refer to differences in access to economic resources. Anthropologist W. L. Warner, in his book *Social Class in America*, described communities in which he felt it useful to divide up the population into six classes—upper upper, lower upper, upper middle, lower middle, upper lower, and lower lower. Such distinctions, or "class" categories, made by social scientists and others are usually based on criteria of education, occupation, income, and neighborhood of residence.

The basic social class division identified by Karl Marx and Friedrich Engels is frequently cited, though many people have pointed out that Marx himself was somewhat vague and inconsistent in his definition of social class. In the *Communist Manifesto* Marx identified five social classes in Western Europe: (1) the (noble) aristocracy, (2) the bourgeoisie, (3) the petty bourgeoisie, (4) the proletariat, and (5) the ragged proletariate. The most important

18.6 Residential locations are often prime markers of socioeconomic status. (Arthur Tress, Magnum)

division in Marxist theory is between the capitalists (who own the productive resources) and the proletariat. However, in discussing particular societies then existing in Western Europe, Marx noted that these categories do not completely correspond to all the various types of people in the socioeconomic system.

The confusion about "how many social classes there are" in different industrial urbanized societies arises because different criteria can be used to identify and describe social differences in our populations. People of high occupational prestige are not necessarily always those with the most money, for example. Since social differentiation based on occupation, education, income, and other usual criteria forms an unbroken continuum or gradation from the very poorest people up to the very wealthiest in North American society, it follows that concepts such as "middle class" or "working class" or other subdivisions of our society are theoretical abstractions constructed of arbitrary criteria and arbitrary divisions. In older times, on the other hand, the difference between the nobles (generally landowners) and the peasants was for the most part quite clear, and social mobility upward into the noble

Perspectives on Social Organization

ranks was relatively infrequent. In many parts of old European society a third category of persons—the urban merchants—grew up over time and contributed to the gradual blurring of the distinctions between the elite and the common people.

Life Style, "Social Class" and Stratification in North America

Even though social stratification in North America and other industrialized societies shows no sharp break between one social stratum and another, there are "typical life styles" that tend to identify some of the major "check points" in the social differentiation. For example, in most towns and cities there are certain residential areas that are the special domains of the elite. North Americans are especially notable for the amount of wealth spent in private homes for the maintenance of an "appropriate" standard of living. Often the elite families of our towns and cities have their homes placed at some distance from the noise and air pollution of downtown.

Zoning ordinances in elite suburban residential areas are often quite strict, so that each home must occupy at least two or three acres (only the very wealthy can afford to pay for that much space), and in various other ways the exclusiveness of residential areas is maintained.

At the other end of the scale of housing and residences is the core of the inner city, with varying degrees of deterioration. In general the amount of floor space per person is a great deal less, and play and recreational areas outside may often be nearly nonexistent except for sidewalks and streets. In every way the residential scene for the lowest socioeconomic levels is a more crowded place than are the home sites of the wealthy.

Differences in the healthfulness of living conditions, in food intake, and in access to medical facilities have important effects on the healthiness of different social strata. In the United States, the differences in health between Black and White populations are quite striking, reflecting the overall lower socioeconomic status and unhealthy living conditions suffered by the majority of the Black population. Lower-status Blacks still show a considerable incidence of tuberculosis, for example, which has been brought under control for North American, nonpoor, White populations: "At the turn of this century, the average nonwhite American at birth had a life expectancy between 32 and 35 years, 16 years less than that of the average white American. By 1960, this life expectancy had risen to from 61 to 66 years . . . [But] there is still a discrepancy of six to eight years" (Pettigrew, 1964:99).

Studies of differences in infant mortality rates, tuberculosis incidence, and other disease rates comparing Black and White populations in North America have demonstrated that, except for a few hereditary diseases such as sickle-cell anemia (predominantly in Black populations) and phenylketonuria (predominantly in Caucasoid populations), most differences in health between Black and White populations reflect inequalities in socioeconomic status.

18.7 Poverty is different today because the world of affluence is constantly available as a reminder—through television. (Constantine Marcos, Magnum)

359

The Culture of Poverty: A Mistaken Idea

During the 1960s anthropologist Oscar Lewis introduced the idea of "the culture of poverty" in an effort to explain and describe behavior characteristics of certain types of economically deprived peoples. He felt that:

the culture of poverty is both an adaptation and a reaction of the poor to their marginal position in a class-stratified, highly individuated, capitalistic society. It represents an effort to cope with feelings of hopelessness and despair which develop from the realization of the improbability of achieving success in terms of the values and goals of the larger society. Indeed, many of the traits of the culture of poverty can be viewed as attempts at local solutions for problems not met by existing institutions and agencies . . . for example, unable to obtain credit from banks, they are thrown upon their own resources and organize informal credit devices without interest. (LEWIS, 1970:69)

Although Lewis intended to show the *positive* side of poor people's ways of doing things, his writing on the subject had some unfortunate connotations. What came to be a chief focus of attention was his discussion of poor people's cultural behavior as a "subculture" that:

once it comes into existence . . . tends to perpetuate itself from generation to generation because of its effect on the children. By the time slum children are six or seven years old, they usually have absorbed the basic values and attitudes of their subculture and are not psychologically geared to taking full advantage of changing conditions or increased opportunities (LEWIS, 1970:69)

This idea, in turn, was interpreted as Lewis's belief that poor people maintain a poverty syndrome or way of life by *training and socialization* of the young, so that the idea was easily converted into a claim that the poor people are that way *because of their own conscious culture patterns* rather than because of the effects of the socioeconomic system that offers them few chances of economic advancement.

In a book-length critique of the "culture of poverty" concept, Eleanor Leacock has said:

The fact is that, through the "culture of poverty" and similar notions, the nineteenth century argument that the poor are poor through their own lack of ability and initiative, has reentered the scene in a new form, well decked out with scientific jargon. . . . The major assumption made by many "culture of poverty" theorists is that a virtually autonomous subculture exists among the poor, one which is self-perpetuating and self-defeating. (LEACOCK, 1971:10–11)

A major flaw in the idea of the "culture of poverty" is the unchanging homogeneity of behavior and thought that it implies. Furthermore, this theoretical idea is often used in a manner that assumes that people act the way they do because of ideas, opinions, and "personality traits" in their heads, relatively independent of the complex network of environmental forces that impinge upon them. That is, the idea of a culture of poverty is actually a nonecological theoretical model since it sharply underestimates the importance of social and physical environments in shaping people's ongoing behavior.

Even in Oscar Lewis's own research in urban families there was a great amount of heterogeneity of behavior. If we look carefully at studies of urban poor people, we might easily derive the hypothesis that there is greater behavioral variation among the poor than in suburban middle-class populations. Part of that heterogeneity derives from the strong effects of ethnic diversity in inner-city populations. In many areas there are first-generation Greeks, Italians, Puerto Ricans, Mexicans, and Black families recently immigrated from the rural south, and diverse other ethnic groups, making for real richness of ethnic mixture. The cultural differences between first- and second-generation ethnic peoples add to this diversity.

Cultural descriptions of ethnic groups and other cultural enclaves, especially those embedded in the social complexity of modern, industrialized social systems, have practically all been deceptively oversimplified and stereotyped. Cultural stereotypes of "Black people," of "Jewish culture," of "Swedish-Americans," and of Indian groups on reservations have frequently erred on the side of oversimplifications that lead to a misunderstanding of behavioral complexities. For example, in a small community of Chippewa Indians in the northern Minnesota town of James Lake, we found that despite what, at the first hasty glance, appeared to be uniform poverty and social marginality, the Indian families had in-

360

18.8 Low-income people in some areas maintain extended families as an adaptation to economic necessities. (Arthur Tress, Magnum)

comes ranging from something over $6,000 per year to a truly poverty-stricken low of $700 (in 1965). Some of the Indian people were Episcopalian, others were Catholic, several had recently joined the Mormon church, and other religious denominations were represented. Some families reported frequent and pervasive unemployment, others had experienced much less unemployment.

One of the highly significant seasonal occupations of Chippewa Indians in northern Minnesota is the late summer harvesting of wild rice. "Ricing" is one of the major focal points of Indian identification in the changing socioeconomic scene of the northern Midwest. Not surprisingly, we found that some individuals and families had intense involvement in the rice harvest, whereas others participated minimally or not at all.

As we see it, the idea of the culture of poverty, suggested by Oscar Lewis and taken up by many other social scientists, is simply one example of an unfortunate stereotyping to which anthropologists have contributed because the general idea of "culture" has been used to convey the mistaken impression that people with a particular ethnic or cultural label all think and behave alike.

A more reasonable view, insofar as people in poverty-stricken communities are concerned, is that within even the most homogeneous-appearing small populations there are very great differences in the *ways* that the overall social and economic system— the surrounding social environment—affects individuals. All of these kinds of differences are *intra*-cultural variations, and focusing on these intracommunity variations and their patterning helps to make sense of how people manage to cope with economic marginality in a highly stratified and unequal social system. That is why, we feel, the idea of the culture of poverty went so far astray and

361

Social Inequalities

became such a negative influence in social thinking, even though Oscar Lewis had originally intended the idea as a weapon to be used on behalf of people living in poverty.

18.9   Chippewa Indians collecting wild rice in northern Minnesota. (G. H. Pelto)

18.10   The Andean hacienda, or plantation, like this one at Huapra, Ancash, Peru, features the traditional manor house located in the bottom lands with the Indian huts on the hillsides near the land utilized by the serfs for their own subsistence. This hacienda was the site of a peasant uprising in 1960, when three were killed and five wounded by police. (Paul Doughty)

Summary and Conclusions

Unraveling the various factors leading toward social inequalities in different societies will require a great deal of more specialized research than has been done thus far. In fact, until recently anthropologists have tended to underplay the importance of stratification and systems of oppression. The examples we have looked at here are but a small sample of the many different contexts and patterns of social stratification in Africa, Asia, and elsewhere. In general, it is beyond dispute that the development of clear-cut social inequalities has come about only in those societies with a sufficient population mass and productive capacity so that there are plenty of material goods to be unequally distributed. In the absence of material goods social stratification is practically meaningless.

Although incipient tendencies toward inequalities were evident in especially favored hunting-gathering peoples, such as in the groups of the Northwest Pacific Coast and in a few horticultural societies, the first social systems to develop thoroughgoing, deep-lying social inequalities were the large-scale plow agriculturalist city-states of Mesopotamia and Egypt and, somewhat later, the social systems in India, China, and the Americas. In these societies the control over permanently cultivatable lands, especially irrigated lands, was at the foundation of highly stratified social orders.

As long as land remained the main productive resource, stratification tended to become more and more fixed until, in many instances, membership in social strata became largely hereditary, thus becoming a caste system of stratification.

A high point of social stratification was reached in those systems in which people were assigned to a particular social stratum from birth to death and in which people in the lowest castes were legally bound to serve and obey their masters. Thus legally maintained serfdom and other forms of servility represent something like the epitome of social differentiation.

In recent decades there have been some important

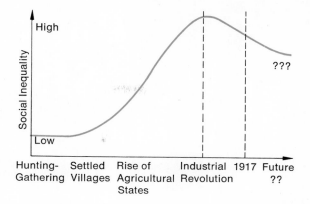

18.11 The evolution of social inequality. Note: The degree of social rigidity in this diagram is defined in terms of the degree of rigidity, individual immobility, and servility built into a social system.

changes in the shape of social stratification as the world has become more industrialized. Among the large populations of Russia and China the worst features of social stratification were removed through social revolutions, and revolutions have diminished stratification, to some degree, in many other countries as well. Even in nations that have not experienced violent revolutions, there has been some progress in eliminating the legal basis for slavery and serfdom. Figure 18.11 illustrates the general point about the sharp rise and then some tapering off of *rigid* social stratification.

We do not deny that very serious and pervasive social stratification still exists in most of the world's societies. Even with massive efforts at societal reorganization it has been extremely difficult to eliminate large social inequalities wherever large populations, urbanization, and extensive division of labor are found. In a later chapter we will return to this problem of social stratification and examine some of the social movements that have arisen as people in various parts of the world have attempted to bring about changes in the structure of their societies.

363

Part
Six

Perhaps the most complex part of human behavior and belief is that which we label MAGIC and RELIGION. Often we contrast these two with the idea of "science," and many people assume that the center of gravity of human knowledge and thinking shows a gradual shift toward more and more science and less and less belief in supernatural forces. (The evidence is ambiguous, however.)

Religion is a complex topic because the effects of religious beliefs penetrate into many other aspects of cultural and social life. Art and literature have been shaped by religious beliefs to a large extent; much of the monumental architecture of the world was religiously inspired; and many of the most persistent political and international conflicts have had (and continue to have) religious features.

Religion and magic are also difficult to deal with because they mean different things to different people: some think of religion mainly in terms of ritual enactments; to others it is all a matter of belief—of explanations of life after death, the meaning of existence, and other philosophical problems; still others equate religion and morality, seeing religious beliefs as the essential cement of morally correct behavior.

Religion has all these different aspects and more. In some societies religion is healing of sickness; in militaristic societies religion has been the source of inspiration before battle, courage on the battlefield, and the medium for triumphant congratulations or comforting solace afterwards—whichever was in order.

Some social philosophers have looked upon religion as communal and group-oriented in its essence and as the expression of social solidarity. Thus the French anthropologist Émile Durkheim wrote, concerning the religious organization of Australian aboriginal peoples:

"[The totem] . . . is the outward and visible form of what we have called the totemic principle or god. But it is also the symbol of the determined society called the clan. It is its flag; it is the sign by which each clan distinguishes itself from the others, the visible mark of its personality, a mark borne by everything which is a part of the clan under any title whatsoever, men, beasts, or things. So if it is at once the symbol of the god and of the society, is that not because the god and the society are only one? . . . it is unquestionable that a society has all that is necessary to arouse the sensation of the divine in minds, merely by the

19.1 In ecclesiastical religious systems priests minister to individuals, as well as performing public ceremonials for their congregations. (Burt Glinn, Magnum)

power that it has over them; for to its members it is what a god is to his worshipers. . . . Since religious force is nothing other than the collective and anonymous force of the clan, and since this can be represented in the mind only in the form of the totem, the totemic emblem is like the visible body of the god." (DURKHEIM, 1915; quoted in LESSA and VOGT, 1958:74–75)

On the other hand, there are anthropologists, philosophers, and theologians, especially in modern times, for whom religion is an intensely personal and individualized phenomenon concerned with relationships between individuals, their personal philosophies, and their unique existential destinies.

Some Definitions

Perhaps the best course in defining religion is to offer several different ones from which the reader can take his pick. One definition, set forth by a leading figure in nineteenth-century anthropological work, E. B. Tylor, suggests the minimal definition of religion as "belief in spiritual beings." The definition does not say *whose* beliefs in spiritual beings are referred to—an individual's private beliefs, the ideas of a particular small community, or the special dogmas of a worldwide ecclesiastical system. Some people would argue that this minimal definition

must be stretched to include not just beings but essences or forces, for there are people who see themselves as imbued with religious faith not in "beings" but in some kind of supernatural processes or powers that permeate the universe.

Durkheim's definition of religion, focusing on social groups and their solidarities, takes the following form: "A religion is a unified system of beliefs and practices relative to sacred things, that is to say, things set apart and forbidden—beliefs and practices which unite into one single moral community called a church, all those who adhere to them" (quoted in Lessa and Vogt, 1958:69). Durkheim pointed out that the second part of his definition "is no less essential than the first; for by showing that the idea of religion is inseparable from that of the Church, it makes it clear that religion should be an eminently collective thing" (Lessa and Vogt, 1958:69).

Another useful definition is that given by Marvin Harris: "To the extent that beliefs lack a basis in the systematic, controlled methodology characteristic of modern science, they may be regarded as constituting a broad realm of religious phenomena. A religious belief, in other words, is any culturally patterned belief about man, culture, or nature that is not a product of scientific research" (Harris, 1971:536). To this Harris adds that "Religious and scientific beliefs may be distinguished in this sweeping fashion only if it is emphasized that neither science nor religion enjoys a monopoly on truth.

19.2 Modern "Jesus freaks" in Redondo Beach, California. (Hiroji Kubota, Magnum)

Both science and religion may consist of false as well as true beliefs. The difference between them is the method underlying the establishment of any particular belief, be it true or false" (Harris, 1971:537). In general, the nature of science includes refined ways of empirically testing and revising our knowledge, whereas religious systems are much less subject to systematic revision.

Magic Versus Religion

Many anthropologists of earlier times, notably Sir James Frazer and Bronislaw Malinowski, made a rather sharp distinction between the idea of magic and that of religion. For Malinowski:

Magic changes its forms; it shifts its ground; but it exists everywhere. In modern societies magic is associated with the third cigarette lit by the same match, with spilled salt and the need of throwing it over the left shoulder, with broken mirrors, with passing under a ladder, with the new moon seen through glass or on the left hand, with the number thirteen or with Friday. . . . Black magic is practised in the slums of London by the classical method of destroying the picture of the enemy. At marriage ceremonies good luck for the married couple is obtained by the strictest observance of several magical methods such as the throwing of the slipper and the spilling of rice. . . . The saints of the Roman Catholic Church become in popular practise passive accomplices of magic. They are beaten, cajoled, and carried about. They can give rain by being placed in the fields, stop flows of lava by confronting them and stop the progress of a disease, of a blight or of a plague of insects . . . the gambler at Monte Carlo, on the turf, or in the continental state lottery develops systems. Motoring and modern sailing demand mascots and develop superstitions. Around every sensational sea tragedy there has formed a myth showing some mysterious magical indications or giving magical reasons for the catastrophe. Aviation is developing its superstitions and magic. Many pilots refuse to take up a passenger who is wearing anything green, to start a journey on a Friday. (MALINOWSKI, 1931:635–636)

Malinowski suggested that magic consists of the superstitious acts and beliefs through which individuals try to control nature when their technology and rational techniques are insufficient. He found that in the Trobriand Islands people did not use any magical safeguards to aid their fishing within the sheltered lagoons. However, when they went out

Relationships with the Supernatural

onto the high seas, where even their considerable navigation abilities could not protect them from the dangers of unexpected winds or other problems, fishing expeditions were accompanied by magical acts. Malinowski theorized that the function of these acts was to alleviate anxiety in the face of uncertainty.

19.4 **Modern shamanistic supply house, Nigeria.** (Marc Riboud, Magnum)

In contrast to his view of magic, Malinowski saw religion as: "intrinsically . . . connected with man's fundamental, that is, biological needs. . . . Religion is not born out of speculation or reflection, still less out of illusion or misapprehension, but rather out of the real tragedies of human life, out of the conflict between human plans and realities" (Malinowski, 1931:641). Thus religion is largely concerned with the making sacred of the crises of human life: "Conception, birth, puberty, marriage, as well as the supreme crisis death, all give rise to sacramental acts" (Malinowski, 1931:641).

In the views expressed by Malinowski and others magical acts involve a manipulative attitude that is thought to be very different and to arise from different psychological and social origins than the more prayerful, humble, and reverent attitude in religious worship. Perhaps in modern Euro-American culture

these differences are fairly clear, at least some of the time. People who engage in small magical acts and superstitions do not ordinarily consider them to be in the same realm as their reverent religious observances. Nonetheless, in many social systems the contrast between magic and religion often fades away, although any ritual event with a large number of participants is generally regarded as "religion," whereas the beliefs and practices that are specially individual and private may more often be derogatorily labeled as "magic" or "superstition."

Witchcraft and Sorcery

Humans everywhere fear the spirits and the gods for the harm they can cause. Also, in nearly every society there are some concerns about the nonnatural ways in which some of our fellow mortals can inflict harm, and in many cultural groups illness and misfortune are thought to be caused by the supernatural malevolence of people, not the gods or the spirits. Some of those people who cause misfortune and illness may do so because they have mystical psychic powers over which they may have little control. Carriers of psychic evil are usually referred to technically as WITCHES. In many societies witches can cause illness by looking at a person, for they have an "evil eye."

In a remarkably large number of societies witches are said to change themselves into animals (e.g., werewolves) during their evil activities. Among the Lugbara people of East Africa, witches "walk at night, often in the guise of a rat or other night animal, or as a moving light; others walk about and defecate blood on their victim's compound. In the morning the victim wakes up aching and sick, and may die unless the witch removes his witchcraft" (Middleton, 1965:81).

SORCERERS are individuals who practice evil magic and countermagic using material objects. Whereas no one knows for sure who the witches "really" are, sorcery is more detectable. Continuing with the Lugbara example, the sorcerers prepare harmful materials "from snakes and other evil creatures, which they sprinkle in their victims' food or drop in their compounds or fields. . . . Women sorcerers are co-wives who are jealous of each other." Other sorcerers are young men "who are thought to buy poisons from the Congo and south-

370

Sacred and Secular Realms of Adaptation

ern Uganda" (Middleton, 1965:83). Their targets are often senior people of the patrilineages who do not give them respect, even though the young men have gained wealth through migrant labor.

Witchcraft and sorcery are difficult to detect, so the accusations of these activities are likely to be leveled at persons who "act different" or who are known to be envious or malicious. If we reflect on this for a moment, we can see that the *accusations* of witchcraft or sorcery can themselves be an extremely effective form of malicious harassment. Accusations of witchcraft are often directed toward people who have "gotten ahead" or who are thought to have excessive wealth. The patterning of witchcraft accusations is likely, therefore, to highlight points of social tension and unexpressed hostilities.

S. F. Nadel has compared witchcraft accusations in four African societies, with interesting results. Among two neighboring peoples in the Sudan he found that in one, the Korongo, there were practically no witchcraft fears or beliefs; among the Mesakin, their neighbors, witchcraft was rampant—especially as practiced by older males against their sisters' sons. In this matrilineal society young men inherit cattle from their mothers' brothers, and the uncles are supposed to acknowledge this fact with gifts of cattle. But cattle gifts are, at the same time, a signal of old age and "retirement," which the elders resist as long as they can. There is considerable tension between the generations for that reason, and if a young man falls ill or suffers misfortune, his mother's brother is very likely to be accused of supernatural foul play (Nadel, 1952).

Equally interesting is Nadel's comparison between

Witchcraft and Hallucinogenic Drugs

Witchcraft, in most cases, exists only in the imaginations of the accusers. Yet there is much evidence that *some* of the people who were accused of witchcraft during the Middle Ages and after were "up to something" and thought themselves to be witches. In connection with these self-identified warlocks and witches there are some fascinating themes of behavior that deserve further exploration. What about those broomsticks they rode on, the near-universal stories of magical flight, copulation with the devil, and other bizarre episodes? How could individuals believe those things happened to themselves?

Michael Harner has suggested that many of the fantastic experiences of witches are suspiciously similar to the well-known effects of powerful hallucinogenic drugs. Moreover, the literature about witches includes mention of such hallucinogens, especially *Datura*, henbane, and deadly nightshade. Harner quotes a report from the physician of Pope Julius III, who was in Lorraine in 1548 when an old couple were seized as witches and accused of burning grain, killing livestock, and sucking the blood of children. They confessed. The physician reported that a jar of greenish ointment was found:

whose odor was so heavy and offensive that it showed that it was composed of herbs . . . soporiferous in the ultimate degree, which are hemlock, nightshade, henbane and mandrake. . . . From all this we can conjecture that all that which the wretched witches do is phantasm caused by very cold potions and unguents: which are of such a nature as to corrupt the memory and the imagination, that the wretched ones imagine, and even very firmly believe, that they have done in a waking state all that of which they dreamt while sleeping. (Quoted in HARNER, 1973:135–137)

According to Harner:

The European witches rubbed their bodies with a hallucinogenic ointment containing such plants as *Atropa belladonna, Mandragora,* and henbane, whose content of atropine was absorbable through the skin. The witch then indeed took a "trip"; the witch on the broomstick is a representation of that imagined aerial journey to a rendezvous with spirits or demons, which was called a Sabbat (HARNER, 1973:129)

371

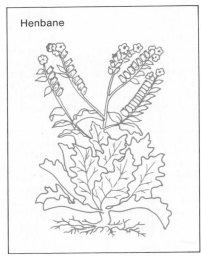

19.5 Some powerful hallucinogenic drugs used by shamans and other curers, as well as by "witches" of the Middle Ages in Europe.

the Nupe and Gwari people of Nigeria. Among the Nupe, the women have a good deal of economic power, for many of them are itinerant traders in the marketplaces. They also have a great deal of freedom of movement. Here witchcraft accusations are leveled at the women, according to Nadel, and these witches are said to have an organization, much like the women's trading association. To counter the dangers of female witchcraft Nupe men have a secret organization that threatens individual women and goes about the business of periodically "cleansing" the community.

Among the nearby Gwari, on the other hand, women do not engage in trading activities away from home. Here witchcraft is a milder problem, with little evidence of sexual antagonism. Both men and women are equally likely to be accused, and the men do not have an exclusive witch-hunting license.

These cases illustrate an important social control feature of witchcraft beliefs. Accusations of witchcraft can be leveled at anybody, but they are most likely to be directed at people who deviate too much from the wishes and expectations of others in the

372

Sacred and Secular Realms of Adaptation

community. Because witches can be legitimately punished or executed, it behooves a Nupe woman or a Mesakin mother's brother to take care that public opinion does not begin to go against her or him.

Not surprisingly, a high rate of witchcraft accusations is very common in societies in which there is no superordinate, centralized political authority with police powers. To some extent the constant possibility of being accused of witchcraft or sorcery can keep individuals from treading on too many toes or from being too different.

Witchcraft in the recent history of Europe and North America fits the same pattern to a considerable degree. Joan of Arc dared to be different and to challenge some male prerogatives, so she was burned as a witch. The great numbers of other people, both males and females, who were burned or drowned or tortured to death by our Christian fathers for alleged witchcraft were often individuals who challenged "the establishment" or the accepted social practices.

It is interesting that the term *witch hunt* has played such a large role in recent North American politics. People appear to recognize that the hunt for Communists in our social system is frequently a social control device whereby people with deviant political and social attitudes can be harassed or even jailed as "dangerous to the community." Sometimes these modern victims of witchcraft accusations are persons who "go too far" in campaigning for various humanitarian causes. Thus moderate or liberal anti-racism in political speeches or writing is perfectly respectable, but going out and actively working for elimination of discriminatory economic and political situations can lead to accusations of "radicalism" or "Communism," the twentieth-century equivalents of witchcraft.

Individualistic Religion

In all societies there are religious forms that refer directly to the well-being of individuals. It is not enough to celebrate communal relationships with the supernaturals; the maintenance of ritual relationships between groups and their deities does not satisfy all of the religious needs of individuals. In many hunting-gathering groups among which there are no corporate kin groups that maintain common

religious perspectives or observe rites for a founding ancestor, religious observances are largely directed to individual life crises or to the problems of small family groups. The nature of religious ideas and systems in such societies is quite different from the religious institutions that Euro-Americans are most familiar with.

Guardian Spirits Among North American Indians

The individualism of many Northern American Indian groups of the Great Plains and the North was exemplified by a system of religious beliefs in which visions were sought in order to achieve a "contract" between the individual and a supernatural guardian. From childhood, boys were trained for the time when they would go out on a "vision quest." Normal practice among societies like the Crow was for a young man to go into seclusion at some lonely spot where he fasted and prayed to the spirits. Sometimes self-mutilation (such as cutting off a finger joint) was used to get the spirits to take pity on the supplicant.

The vision usually appeared on the fourth day—often in the shape of an animal who announced himself as a guardian spirit. The spirit taught the young man a sacred song, instructed him in how he must dress in battle, and imposed taboos concerning food and other behavior. There was a great variety of spirits—buffalo, elk, bears, eagles, hawks, dogs, rabbits, and so on. Among the Cree there is a story about a mosquito that was a spirit helper of a chief, and Crow stories of the vision quest include one about a rabbit that was being pursued by a hawk, stopping long enough to tell the young vision seeker that he would give supernatural power to him if the youth shielded him from the bird of prey (Lowie, 1954:157–161).

In some cases abstract concepts became embodied as spirits, as in the case of an Ojibwa spirit named Miserable Poverty:

a young man rejected a marriage offer made by a girl's midé-shaman father. As the man had passed summer nights with the girl, to everybody's knowledge, the father became furious. So during the winter he magically caused game and fur to avoid the young hunter. After twenty days of winter starvation and semi-illness, the persecuted hunter came upon a mournful, skeletal

373

19.6 An 1892 photograph of the Blackfoot Sun
Dance. The self-torture was enacted to gain
closer rapport with the supernatural world.
(Courtesy of the American Museum of Natural
History)

figure with vast, empty eye sockets, and asked, "Who
are you?"

"I am Poverty, miserable Poverty. . . . I am the failure of hunters. Some old woman (mother of the rejected girl) told me to follow you for a month. So if
you hold out ten days more, then do as I say, I'll be
able to help you."

The hunter doubted his endurance and begged Poverty to quit now. But the terms were fixed. At month's
end, the hunter still lived, again met Poverty, and
agreed to his conditions.

"I am not really a *manito*," said the figure, "but I
help Indians who remember me (with offerings). I
mourn because they pass by me. I stretch out my hand
for tobacco but always find it empty. So I fell away
to a skeleton and I shrink into corners. Now it will
be different. . . . Offer me tobacco when you start out

hunting. When you are successful, leave me some
grease. That is all I ask. Tell others to do the same
and they will find luck. And I will give you this
(hunting) medicine."

So the hunter grew renowned despite the shaman.
(LANDES, 1968:23)

The highly individualistic religious practices of
the Indians of the Great Plains were not by themselves sufficient to manage all aspects of adaptation
to the natural and supernatural environment. Curing serious illness required the services of a
SHAMAN, and occasionally one's guardian spirit was
not powerful enough to defend one against the evil
of a medicine man; in this case a rival medicine
man had to be hired for protection. Also, among
some groups there were important communal rites
for which incipient priesthoods were developing.
The Cheyenne were notable for their important
Arrow Renewal Ceremonies, celebrating the unity
of the Cheyenne people. These ceremonies were part

374

Sacred and Secular Realms of Adaptation

of an impressive round of ceremonials that emphasized communal rather than individual concerns and well-being.

Shamans and Shamanism: The Universal Religion

At the level of "practical religion," certain patterns have been so widespread as to be near-universal in human culture. Shamanism, usually devoted particularly to the curing of illness, is one such near-universal feature. A shaman is an individual who claims the power to cure and affect other aspects of life because of powers gained through *direct* contact with the supernaturals. Across societies of the world there are many variations in the amount of training a shaman is thought to need, the level of his prestige within the group, the prerequisites for "office," and other features, but in all societies it is the shaman's capacity to communicate

19.7 A Siberian shaman with his drum. (Courtesy of the American Museum of Natural History)

with the supernatural that forms the core of belief and practice.

The !Kung Bushmen of the Kalahari Desert believe that there are two gods somewhere up in the sky, the great god in the eastern sky and a lesser one in the west. The great god is the creator of all things, including himself. The Bushmen pray to these gods, asking for help in important matters including food getting, sickness, and death. In the sphere of health maintenance the Bushmen gods have given special powers to the people, that they might maintain the physical and mental capabilities needed to sustain their lifeways. The powers given by the gods come to people during singing and often manifest themselves in the form of a trance. The trances come to the men who are the shamans—and they include most of the men in the society. Unlike shamans in many societies, the !Kung medicine men generally practice no evil magic and they receive no payments or special privileges.

Two or three times a month the people gather to dance. There are always several shamans performing in the dance, and they progress to deeper trance states as the night wears on. The medicine man places his hands on his patient, flutters his fingers, and thus:

draws the sickness, real or potential, out of the person through his own arms into himself. To demonstrate that this is in fact going on and is hard to do, he grunts with shuddering grunts that intensify in tempo and pitch into shrieks and reach a high piercing, quavering yell. Finally the medicine man throws up his arms to cast the sickness out, hurling it into the darkness back to [the spirits] who are there beyond the firelight. . . . In the course of a dance, these medicine men approach everyone present, even the infants, thus cleansing the people of potential sickness. (MARSHALL, 1965:271–272)

The word *shaman* is a Tungusic word from Siberia and was adopted into anthropological usage from descriptions of elaborate shamanism among the Tungus and other groups of Siberian peoples. Siberian shamans were skillful performers who demonstrated superb verbal and manual skills—ventriloquism, sleight-of-hand—and a sense of drama that made their performances high entertainment as well as a convincing demonstration of their curative powers.

In Siberia, as in many other parts of the world,

375

a shaman is "called" through dreams or visions, often experienced during illness. He (or she) is considered to be psychologically strange by the local people. He may be moody, careless of his life, or highly introverted. Among the Chukchee the shaman was often a homosexual. Although the shaman is often considered psychiatrically abnormal by his neighbors, it is also true that the skills of the shaman can be taught and are sometimes transferred by sale or inheritance from one person to another. Among the Siberians the shaman often chose one of his sons to carry on his traditional role. In many societies the shamans are mainly male, although in some groups female shamans have achieved renown. Shamans are thought to differ greatly in their powers, and only a few achieve widespread reputations for supernatural greatness and curative powers.

In a great many different cultures the shaman must travel to the realm of the supernaturals in order to accomplish his mission of curing. Often the shaman's "trip" is helped along with narcotics or other special materials. Siberian shamans used tobacco and a dangerously poisonous mushroom, fly agaric. (*Amanita muscaria*). Shamans in many parts of Mexico and the Southwest use peyote, various mushrooms, and other botanical aids. The powerful shamans of the Jivaro of the Ecuadorian Amazon drink preparations of a powerful hallucinogen that has effects similar to LSD.

During fieldwork in the upper Amazon basin Michael Harner had occasion to drink the hallucinogen and:

for several hours after drinking the brew, I found myself, although awake, in a world literally beyond my wildest dreams. I met bird-headed people, as well as dragon-like creatures who explained that they were the true gods of this world. I enlisted the services of other spirit helpers in attempting to fly through the far reaches of the Galaxy. Transported into a trance where the supernatural seemed natural, I realized that anthropologists, including myself, had profoundly underestimated the importance of the drug in affecting native ideology. (HARNER, 1968:60–61)

The writings of Carlos Casteneda in the *Teaching of Don Juan* and other books gives support to this same view.

When we come to "modern" societies, as among the urbanized and industrialized people of North America, shamanism does not disappear but most of these practices go "underground." Most North Americans belong to regularly constituted religious denominations in which priests and ministers without supernatural powers officiate in the regularized religious services; for the curing of illness they rely on medical professionals who claim to accomplish their healing arts without direct divine intervention. But belief in direct contact with the supernaturals is quite common, and many people patronize "spirit mediums," "spiritualists," and other latter-day shamans for purposes of health maintenance, for securing supernatural intervention in family quarrels, or perhaps simply for seeking messages from the recent dead. Faith healers abound, some of whom closely approximate the old-time shamans in their behavior, beliefs, and curing methods. The "laying on of hands" is practiced by modern Christian faith healers in a manner that reminds us immediately of those benevolent shamans of the Bushmen in South Africa.

Religion in the Family Circle

Worship of supernaturals built around the co-dwelling family or other localized kinship group is one of the most widespread religious forms. In many patrilineal and matrilineal societies the focus of religious observance is on the lineage ancestral shrine.

The British social anthropologist Meyer Fortes has described the religious institutions of the Tallensi of Nigeria, an excellent example of lineage-based religious structure.

He notes that a typical patrilineal joint family is generally a branch of a more extensive patrilineage, which may be able to trace its ancestry back ten or twelve generations. Lineages tend to be geographically localized, but:

its essential focus of unity and identity is the cult of the lineage ancestors. Just as there is a hierarchy of lineage segments of greater and greater inclusiveness, until finally the entire lineage is included, so there is a hierarchy of ancestors and ancestor shrines. Members of the smallest segment worship the founding ancestors of their segment, join with the members of the next more inclusive segment to worship their common founding ancestors, and so on till the most inclusive unit, the maximal lineage as a whole, is reached. The lineage ancestor cult is by definition a

Sacred and Secular Realms of Adaptation

cult of the patrilineal male ancestors. But the ancestress of a lineage or segment is almost as important as the founding ancestor, and the spirits of maternal ancestors and ancestresses play as large a part in a person's life as his paternal ancestor spirits. (FORTES, 1960:17)

The religious system of the Tallensi fits neatly with their social structure. Their homesteads have many shrines, constructed of dried mud and adorned with a variety of relics—each symbolizing a particular ancestor spirit. They contact their ancestors with prayers, offerings, and other means, but contact with the supernatural generally requires consultation with a religious diviner first. The diviner's intervention is necessary in order to determine which ancestors are involved in a given situation and what they want. In the case of childbirth, sickness, or death; in public crises such as drought or the seasonal events of sowing and harvesting; and before hazardous undertakings of hunting or other activities, diviners are consulted on behalf of individuals or kinship groups.

The Tallensi, like most of their neighbors in West Africa, have some beliefs concerning witchcraft and a variety of ideas about various dangerous qualities of trees, animals, and other natural phenomena. However, their cosmology is overwhelmingly dominated by beliefs and practices related to ancestors. Thus peoples' fates among the Tallensi are caused and affected not by strangers from other groups, or the witchcraft activities of dangerous persons, but by the social relationships of their highly structured patrilineal system. In their social life as in their religious beliefs individuals must accept responsibility for their own actions and their own failures. But the structuring of their religious beliefs provides a way to face the trials and tribulations that most individuals must endure.

And the irritations and complaints of the ancestors at various points in an individual's life reflect the lines of patrilineal (and occasionally matrilineal) kinship on which practically all activities are structured: "Submission to his ancestors is symbolic of his encapsulation in a social order which permits of no voluntary alteration of his status and social capacities" (Fortes, 1960:40).

Traditional Chinese society is another example of a religious system in which ancestor worship plays a central role. Religious devotion to the ancestors

19.8 Toda priest in front of the sacred dairy— scene of milk and cattle rituals. South India. (Arthur Tress, Magnum)

has taken a variety of forms at different periods in China's complex history, and it appears that in earlier times attention was devoted particularly to the venerable ancestors of the large patrilineal kin groups. In his time Confucius inculcated the worship of ancestors as an act of filial piety, as a continuation of the respect and devotion that a good son owed to his parents during their lives. Ancestors of the kin groups were worshiped at shrines and temples, and images were erected in their memory and honored with regular sacrifices to obtain their blessings. In later times inscribed wooden tablets generally replaced the earlier ancestral images. Throughout the centuries Chinese religious practices have greatly increased in complexity with the advent of Buddhism and Taoism and other religious move-

377

ments, but the veneration of the ancestors continued into recent times.

In the Manus society of the South Pacific the sacred ancestor worshiped by an individual or a family was made concretely manifest by placing the skull of that person in a wooden bowl within the house. This spirit protector, referred to as "Sir Ghost," was expected to prevent accidents, bring wealth, and prolong life.

As is the case with most ancestors, Sir Ghost was concerned about the moral behavior of his wards and punished their misdemeanors. When Sir Ghost failed to protect individuals, as he often did, he was berated for his carelessness, and the death of an individual was the final proof of Sir Ghost's failure to protect. This usually resulted in the skull's being removed and perhaps thrown into the sea. The moral laxities that Sir Ghost was particularly concerned with were in the realms of loose sexual conduct and economic irresponsibility. These concerns, as those among the Tallensi, usually came to light if someone suffered misfortune in the form of illness, poor fishing, or other difficulties. In these cases diviners (men) or mediums (women) would be called in to find out what Sir Ghost was complaining about. The earthly intermediaries then informed individuals of the sexual trangressions or economic derelictions that had aroused the anger of the ghost. Few secrets could be kept in this relatively close-packed community, so the diviners always had something to go on as they interrogated Sir Ghost about the causes of illness or misfortune. Persons guilty of sexual or other sins had to confess; otherwise the sick person might die. Those who failed to confess were open to the charge that they had caused the death of the person who lay ill.

When we consider these forms of family-structured worship and veneration of ancestors, we are struck with the extent to which such a system must be conservative in its nature. Fortes's analysis of the Tallensi system emphasizes the dependence and subjugation of the individual in a tight-knit kinship system. The Manus ancestor worship was perhaps more flexible, reflecting the greater individualism of their social system. Nonetheless, the transgressions of social behavior that the ghosts supposedly punished were interpreted by diviners and mediums who, as older members of the community, had the greatest stake in a conservative interpretation and maintenance of the status quo. The conservativism

of these systems of ancestor veneration is aimed primarily at the maintenance of established kinship and family relationships rather than the general solidarity of the wider social system. In fact, ancestor-oriented religious practices can sometimes be inimical to the interests of wider community unity because there is always the possibility that a particular group of ancestors will invoke their supernatural powers on behalf of a factional, intracommunity split. Nasty feuds can result from such narrow-minded attitudes of the ancestral spirits or ghosts.

Ancestor cults and family worship are often only parts of a larger, more comprehensive religious system. For example, when the far-flung Inca empire was beginning to rise in the fifteenth century, the emperor Pachakuti'inka Yupanki (1438–1471) reorganized the entire religious system of this pluralistic empire by imposing a new priesthood and theology on the existing localized religious practices of the many peoples the Incas had conquered. Shrines of only local importance were maintained, as always, by kin groups, and these local shrines were attended by low-level priests who interpreted oracles, heard confessions, and made sacrifices and offered up prayers on behalf of the individuals who paid for these services.

The official Inca religion required elaborate temples, a complex, hierarchically organized priesthood, and frequent ceremonial observances, but the imperial religion did not eliminate kin-oriented, localized religious observances.

Priests in Service to the Community: The Hopi Way of Religion

In some nonstratified societies we find communities that are tightly structured and "theocratic" in the sense that religion and ritual are central elements of their lifeways. In such religiously oriented societies there is need for a well-organized and dedicated priesthood, but the priests must be drawn from the populace, and socioeconomic differentiation and stratification are usually discouraged or prevented altogether. The Pueblo Indian communities of the Southwest are examples of such "egalitarian theoracies."

Throughout the Hopi ceremonial cycle, for example, a number of religious leaders take their turns in being responsible for relationships to the supernaturals. These "priests" are not regarded as sanctified or holy, and they do not wear distinctive dress except on ceremonial occasions. Ritual responsibilities throughout the year rotate among different religious societies, and each of these organizations with its associated ceremonial rites belongs to a particular clan.

The organizations that have charge of the different ceremonial events are nominally voluntary secret societies, to which individuals can seek admission by asking members in good standing to sponsor them as ceremonial "fathers." At the age of six or eight, children are initiated into the Katchina society, after which girls can be initiated into one or more of the three women's secret societies. Boys generally join one of the two Flute societies and then either the Snake or the Antelope group. As they progress through adult life, Hopi males who seek prestige and social approval join other religious fraternities and serve in them as ritual functionaries.

Among the very large number of ritual enactments that still take place in the Hopi villages, the best known to outsiders is perhaps the snake dance. Before the ceremony takes place, members of the Snake society go out to gather all the reptiles they can find and bring them to their *kiva* (underground ceremonial center) for "baptism" and for the public performance on the ninth day of their ceremonials in mid-August:

There is some preliminary singing by both groups, following which the Snake line breaks into pairs, with each couple dancing in a circuit about the plaza. When a pair reaches the bower, the front man kneels, receives a live snake, puts it between his lips, and goes on with his dance. This continues until all of the captured snakes have been danced with, whereupon four runners hurry to release the reptiles at designated shrines, with prayers for rain, crops, and good health." (TITIEV, 1958:537)

The snake dance, like the many other Hopi rituals, emphasizes the Hopis' close dependence on nature and their links with the world of the supernatural; as long as the Hopis perform these rituals in good order, the gods are thought to be quite benevolent toward their earthly wards.

Cargo Systems: Voluntary Religious Service in Mexican Villages

The CARGO SYSTEM, or civil-religious hierarchy, found in most Indian communities of Middle America is an interesting example of the maintenance of complex religious rituals with a system of volunteers. It also represents a thoroughgoing mixture of Christian and non-European religious elements.

The *cargo* system, as it is practiced in the community of Zinacantan in southern Mexico, has been described by a Harvard University anthropological team led by Evon Vogt. The people are Mayan-speaking Indians, and their religious system reflects some features that were developed during the height of the Mayan civilization over a thousand years ago.

The Zinacanteco people conceive of themselves as living at "the navel" of the universe, and a small shrine at their ceremonial center receives the offerings of candles, *copal* incense, and prayers directed to this navel of the world. Their cubical world is thought to be carried on the shoulders of the Four-Corner Gods, and other important deities are the "father-sun" and "our holy mother," the moon. The Catholic influence has supposedly shifted the identities of these deities somewhat, for the sun now supposedly represents God and the moon is associated with the Virgin Mary. There are many other lesser gods in the Zinacanteco pantheon.

It is noteworthy that, like the ancestors of the Manus, the Chinese, the Tallensi, and others, the ancestral gods of the Zinacantecos become angry at antisocial or "anti-Zinacaneco" behavior and punish transgressors with illness and misfortune. The ancestor spirits meet and deliberate about their living descendants at a large number of shrines throughout the area marked by Christian-like crosses. Much like the kin-group–defined shrines of the Tallensi, the various shrines of the Zinacantecos are the special concerns of various patrilineal kin groups.

Whereas the animal guardian spirits and ancestral gods reflect kin groups, water hole groups, and individual persons, the unity of the entire community of scattered hamlets is ritualized in the *cargos*, or religious offices, that Zinacanteco men assume. Each *cargo* requires a full year of service, and there

379

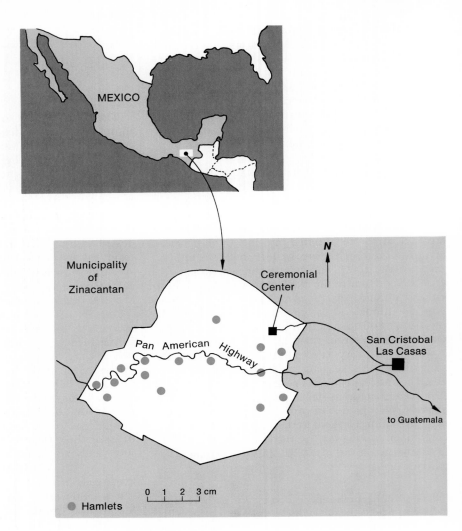

19.9 Location of Zinacantan in southern Mexico (from Vogt, 1970).

MEXICO

Municipality of Zinacantan

Ceremonial Center

N

San Cristobal Las Casas

Pan American Highway

to Guatemala

0 1 2 3 cm

● Hamlets

are sixty-one of these positions, making up four levels in a ceremonial ladder (see diagram). The main road to prestige and social approval (as well as to maintaining good relationships with the supernaturals) is for a man to work his way up this ceremonial ladder with the aim of one day serving as an *Alcalde Viejo* at the top of the hierarchy. But these religious services are extremely expensive. The *cargo* holders must spend large amounts of money for food, liquor, ritual paraphernalia (e.g., candles and incense), and fireworks. Some *cargos* cost a person as much as 14,000 pesos (over $1,000 U.S.).

When a man feels he can accumulate the money necessary to serve a *cargo*, he asks to be put on the waiting list. Finally, when his time arrives, the new *cargo* holder and his wife move to the ceremonial center and live there throughout the year of service. The *cargo* holder wears special costumes and enjoys special prestige. If he is one of the twelve *Mayores*, he serves as a policeman and errand boy for the civil officials of the town and performs some ceremonial duties. If he starts as a *Mayordomo*, he will care for one of the saints in the church in all the major ceremonies. In older times service in the religious hierarchy alternated with service in the civil government of the town. Thus only those who had given

Sacred and Secular Realms of Adaptation

religious service were eligible for positions as secular officials.

There are not enough *cargos* for all the adult males of Zinacantan to participate fully. Only a small number of persons make it to the top and serve their year as *Alcaldes Viejos*. They are the most honored and prestigious of the older men, and they have much influence in the social and political life in the community. This achievement of religious service costs so much in economic terms that it cannot be done without intensive economic cooperation with a wide-ranging kin and nonkin network. In any case, service in a *cargo* puts a man in debt for many years.

Because of these economic costs, it was formerly argued that this religious system represented an effective "leveling mechanism" that prevented social stratification within the community. It is true that without the *cargo* system some individuals might become economically wealthy without much redistribution of wealth to the rest of the community. This system apparently does result in some sharing of the wealth, but it has also been demonstrated that there is a socioeconomically successful stratum in Zinacantan that is able to assume the burdens of the higher *cargos* and still maintain their economic position and to offer a fair chance that their sons as well will assume *cargos* when their time comes. There are differences of wealth among the Zinacantecos, although the religious system is still an organization of voluntary service. (Cancian, 1965)

19.10 Procession of Zinacanteco *cargo* celebrants performing their voluntary service in the religious system. (Frank Cancian)

Table 19.1: The Religious *Cargo* System of Zinacantan.

	2 *Alcaldes Viejos*	(1 *Alcalde Shuve*—terminal *cargo*)
	4 *Regidores*	
2 *Escribanos*		
2 Musicians	14 *Alféreces*	
4 *Sacristanes*	28 *Mayordomos* and 12 *Mayores*	

Source: Adapted from VOGT, 1970.

Relationships with the Supernatural

The Rise of Ecclesiastical Religions

ECCLESIASTICAL RELIGIONS are those with a full-time, or nearly full-time, priesthood composed of persons who are responsible for managing religious ceremonials and other aspects of relationships to the supernatural world on behalf of an entire society or subunit within a society. From the archaeological evidence it may well be that priesthood (instead of prostitution) is the oldest profession. Certainly the earliest evidences of complex architecture and new social organization at the predawn of civilization in the Near East, as elsewhere, took the form of increasingly elaborate temples and other religious works; and the earliest written records, both in the Near East and in the civilizations of the New World, reflected powerful priesthoods at the center of the growth of cultural complexity. It was to the temples that the peasants brought their grain and paid their taxes; and in mundane secular activities the people around the temples developed systems of mathematical notation and writing for the maintenance of the temple records.

V. Gordon Childe has described the archaeological evidence of growing theocracy at Erech in Mesopotamia as follows:

the ruins of successive settlements had already formed a tell some sixty feet high. At the top, one is no longer standing in a village green but in the square of a cathedral city. In the foreground lie the ruins of a gigantic temple measuring over all 245 feet by 100 feet . . . later dedicated to the goddess Inanna. Behind, attached to the temple of Anu, rises an artificial mountain or *ziggurat*, thirty-five feet high. It is built of mud and sun-dried bricks, but its steeply sloping walls have been consolidated by hammering into the brickwork while still wet thousands of pottery goblets. A flight of steps leads up to the summit—a platform covered with asphalt. On it stands a miniature temple. . . . The walls, of whitewashed brick and imported timbers, were embellished with niches and buttresses and pierced with clerestory windows; the doors were framed with imported pinewood and closed with mats.

The erection of these monumental temples and artificial mountains, the manufacture of the bricks and pottery goblets, the importation of pine wood (from Syria or the Iranian mountains), and of lapis lazuli, silver, lead and copper to adorn the shrines presuppose a substantial labor force—a large population. In point of view of size the community has expanded from a village to a city. It has grown rich too.

The artisans, laborers, and transport workers may have been "volunteers" inspired by religious enthusiasm. But if they were not paid for their labor, they must at least have been nourished while at work. . . . The fertility of the soil that enabled the farmer to produce far more than he could consume supplied this. But its expenditure on temples suggests what later records confirm, that "gods" concentrated it and made it available for distribution among their working servants. Perhaps these gods were projections of ancestral society and were regarded as the creators, and therefore the eminent owners, of the soil that society itself had reclaimed from desert and marsh. . . .

But the gods, being fictions, must have had real representatives, normally their specialized servants, who must have done much to give concrete form to the imaginary beings, and by interpreting must have invented their desires. Temples presuppose priesthoods. . . . By the beginning of historical records the Sumerian priests formed corporations as eternal as the gods they served and maintained; individual priests might die, but the vacant seats would find new occupants. (CHILDE, 1946:84–85)

There were several interrelated reasons for the growth of religious power in the early civilizations. By developing fixed settlements with relatively large population concentrations, people were much more dependent on their annual crops than their nomadic ancestors had been. They were therefore much more vulnerable to droughts, famines, floods, and other disasters. Furthermore, the increased interdependence of people required some kind of common understanding about collective vulnerability and collective interests, which could be expressed in a supernaturally prescribed ideology. The people served the gods, and those gods, in turn, protected them from disasters. The names of the gods point to their close relationships to the regulation of natural events: the name of the goddess Inanna may be derived from reference to the ripening of dates; Dumuzi is "he who quickens the young ones;" Enki was the god of the sweet waters (at Eridu, the earliest city in the Sumerian creation epic); the name of the god Ashman is the word for grain; Lahar stands for sheep; and Sumugan refers to wild asses and gazelles. In Central Mexico the first great New World city, Teotihuacán (100 B.C.–750 A.D.), was apparently ruled over by a pantheon of whom the *rain* god (later Tlaloc) was the most important.

In the Near East, Middle America, India, and the Far East, gods of war and conquest made their appearance as expansionism and lethal rivalries got out of hand among the competing centers of socioeconomic power. In Central Mexico there was little evidence of military activity and warrior gods at Teotihuacán; but later, at Tula, the Toltec empire appears to have developed increased separation of sacred from secular powers and a corresponding increase in the gods of war. The growth of empire in Central Mexico, culminating in the magnificence of the Aztec civilization, was accompanied by a rather steady growth in the military aggressiveness of the gods, including their increased demands for human sacrifices.

The development of complex food-producing societies, accompanied by sharp increases in socioeconomic stratification, made life increasingly hard for the people in the lowest socioeconomic strata of society. The peasants and other toilers harbored considerable resentment against those people who controlled the wealth and the "good life" in their midst; but some of the discontent of the lower classes could be diverted in other directions if the priests could offer consolations in the form of splendid ceremonial displays as well as promises of a better life in the hereafter. How else can we understand the sacrifices of the lower classes of the Aztec empire, for example? And how else can we understand the willingness to believe that the world would come to an end unless large numbers of human sacrifices were offered to the gods? In part the power of the Aztec leadership and the Aztec religious belief system must have depended on the awful emotional power of those huge religious observances in which so many human lives were sacrificed in a gory offering to the supernaturals.

Almost all complex agricultural state societies,

19.11 In complex societies full-time priesthoods are usually part of the elite social structure. An ordination ceremony in Bombay. (Marilyn Silverstone, Magnum)

Relationships with the Supernatural

19.12 **Modern druids at Stonehenge. (George
Rodger, Magnum)**

then, have been theocracies—political systems in
which secular control and religious organization
were fused into a single authoritarian bureaucracy.
At least that is the picture one gets from archaeological and ethnographic evidence of the earliest
civilizations.

Religion Versus Practicality in Nonindustrialized Societies

Non-Western peoples have often been portrayed
by Europeans, even by anthropologists, as steeped in
religious and supernatural beliefs, employing supernatural means for adaptive problems that we "moderns" regard as amenable to scientific control. Many
of our social philosophers have theorized that progress and modernization have been constant ad-

vances away from some sort of dark age of superstition toward greater empiricism and science. For
example, Auguste Comte, the founder of modern
sociology, suggested that the evolution of human
intellectual styles and concerns can be described in
three stages—magic, religion, science.

Although it is true that there are many societies
that have been dominated in their organization and
day-to-day preoccupations by religious concerns, we
must regard with caution the descriptions of the
"spirit-ridden" life of non-European peoples, for
many reports have come to us from missionaries
and administrators who felt that their own religious
beliefs and magical practices were the only true
ones.

The technologically simplest societies in the
world—those that might be regarded as most at the
mercy of the environment—often appear to have a
rather pragmatic mode of adapting to their environments, with a willingness to adopt new technologies
and new belief systems as circumstances arise. It is

Sacred and Secular Realms of Adaptation

possible that on the whole, hunting-gathering peoples have not been particularly concerned with religious matters and that much of the elaborate religious beliefs, superstitions, and other supernatural concerns developed among settled peoples, especially in relation to increased population density and sociocultural complexity.

With regard to the supposed pervasiveness of religion and magic among simpler societies, the Sirionó of eastern Bolivia are an instructive case, for their beliefs and practices concerning the supernatural appear to have markedly little elaboration. Allan Holmberg suggested that the little magic that the Sirionó practice is concerned almost exclusively with success in hunting; and the attitudes of the Sirionó must give pause to those people who argue that the source of religious belief is in concerns about death:

Upon inquiring of informants as to the fate of their souls after death, I was almost always given the answer that they did not know. There seemed, however, to

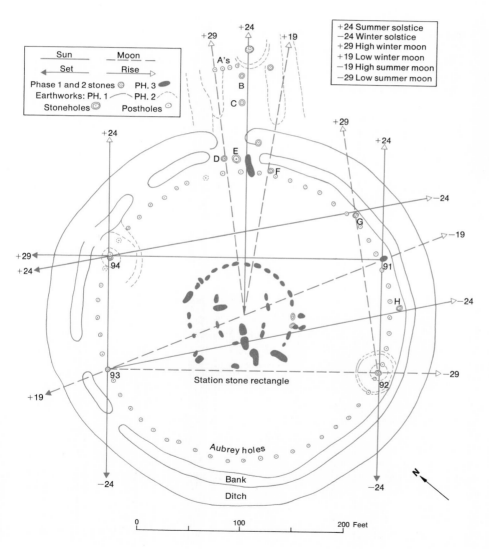

19.13 Diagram of main features of stones and earthworks at Stonehenge. The alignments of the stones suggest that the entire site may have been built in such a manner that prehistoric priests could organize ritual (and perhaps secular) activities in accord with the yearly cycles of summer and winter solstice, as well as the phases of the moon. (*Source:* Baity, 1973:392)

+24 Summer solstice
−24 Winter solstice
+29 High winter moon
+19 Low winter moon
−19 High summer moon
−29 Low summer moon

Relationships with the Supernatural

be general agreement that the soul of the deceased may become an abačikwaia (evil spirit) or a kurúkwa (monster), but this form of survival informants were reluctant to contemplate for their own souls . . . it vaguely appears that the soul of a "good" man, i.e., one who has abided by tribal custom and has the respect of his countrymen, does not return in the form of an evil spirit or monster to harass his surviving relatives. . . . Informants . . . were never able to supply me with any clean-cut ideas as to what happens to the soul of a "good" person after death. One thing seems clear as regards eschatological belief: there is no afterworld to which the soul departs. (HOLMBERG, 1960:92)

The Kapauku of New Guinea are basically pragmatic in their religious views. According to L. Pospisil the Kapauku believe that the world and all existence was created by Ugatame, their principal god, who is manifested as the sun and the moon. They believe that both "evil" and "good" were created by Ugatame. Logically, then, Ugatame is neither good nor evil, and "good" and "evil" are themselves relative terms. From his many months of fieldwork among the Kapauku, Pospisil argues that "in other words in his religious philosophizing, a Kapauku is basically logical; he refuses to accept dogmas that either oppose clear empirical evidence or that contradict his common sense and logic" (Pospisil, 1963:85).

There is a powerful contrast between the pragmatic religious individualism of many small-scale societies and the theocratic societies that developed where food production techniques permitted the rise of states and empires. In the preceding section we discussed a number of factors that probably contributed to the rise of ecclesiastical religion in the developing states. It is interesting to note that the past four hundred to five hundred years of Euro-American life has been a time of the growth of technological industrialization and rational science *and*, at the same time, a history of unparalleled growth of religious complexity, magical beliefs, and other evidences of tremendous concern with the supernatural world. There were witch hunts all over Europe and the bizarre outbreaks in Salem, Massachusetts, as well as religious persecutions such as the Spanish Inquisition.

Spirit possession, "possession by the devil," and a great many other kinds of supernatural visitations are still common in Europe and North America (and note the great impact of the movie *The Exorcist*). Trancelike states of possession, speaking in tongues (glossolalia), and related manifestations of "possession" are common, even on the increase, among a number of religious movements. Many observers have noted a considerable increase in interest in astrology, spirit mediums, and Ouija boards, not to mention the widespread adoption of

19.14 The Pyramid of the Sun at Teotihuacán is 210 feet high and 689 feet along the side, and is estimated to have required the labor of ten thousand workers for twenty years. (Erich Hartmann, Magnum)

19.15 The colossal statues on top of a ceremonial structure at Tula, Mexico represent warriors with spear throwers. (P. J. Pelto)

19.16 Reconstruction of the Great Temple of Tenochtitlán from descriptions of Spanish conquistadores and Aztec accounts. Reconstruction by Ignacio Marquina. (Courtesy of the American Museum of Natural History)

Relationships with the Supernatural

19.17 Oral Roberts, charismatic religious leader. (Eve Arnold, Magnum)

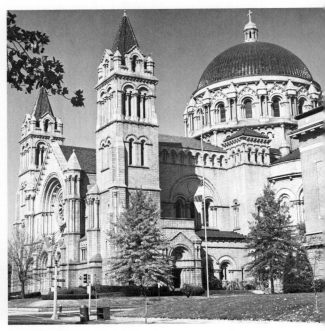

19.18 Established religion, Saint Louis. (American Airlines)

the "new mysticism" of Zen Buddhism and other Eastern faiths among segments of our North American and European populations.

Perhaps the dominance of religious and magical ideas and practices has waned a bit in the lives of Europeans and North Americans since those hag-ridden earlier centuries, but it is premature to claim that an "age of science" has replaced religion and magic in the modern industrialized societies of Europe and North America.

Summary and Conclusions

Some generalizations about religious systems can be offered, although the subject is so wide-ranging that every general proposition must be regarded with caution:

1. Religious beliefs and practices arise from the practical adaptations of people to their environments. The Hopi direct most of their religious concern to matters of rains and crops; fishing people seek supernatural aid in getting the fish; and people about to go to war seek the aid of war gods.

2. Among some people relations with the deities involve prayerful submission; other peoples see their supernatural world as much less authoritarian, hence more subject to human control and manipulation.

3. Important aspects of social organization are mirrored in religion. For example, when extended kin groups are major elements of a society, religious observances will reflect their importance.

4. For many social systems, religion is a form of "cultural cement," as, for example, in the thousands of small Jewish communities scattered around the world. On the other hand, there are also many societies in which there is no overarching set of religious practices but rather the expression of religious practices on the level of individuals, families, and other subgroups.

5. There are no societies without religious systems, although some modern societies seem to be able to replace sacred ideologies with secular beliefs.

388

Sacred and Secular Realms of Adaptation

19.19 The inner cities of North America have hundreds of store-front and apartment churches. (A. Devaney, Inc.)

6. The religious systems of most peoples appear to be quite open to additions of new practices and ideas. For example, many peoples of the world have accepted new elements from Christianity without giving up their non-Christian ideologies.

7. Religious systems among many peoples are eclectic mixtures of ideas about supernaturals, concepts of taboos and other practices expected to please the gods and spirits, and a variety of cere-monies and other behaviors. They are seldom fully worked-out "systems" of philosophy and world order. Also, they are not clearly separate from the ordinary, practical knowledge of the world. "Science" and "religion" are not clearly separate, even in complex modern theologies.

8. Among nonmodern peoples there is considerable individual variation in religiosity and degree of interest in religious ideas. In his book *Primitive Man as a Philosopher* Paul Radin observes that people who speculate about the unknown, about the gods, and about the hereafter are generally a small minority of persons in any society. There are also variations in degrees of belief. Among the Gururumba peoples of New Guinea there is a belief in "lightning balls" that result when lightning strikes a tree. People patiently dig a lot of holes looking for these prized objects. One day when a group of Gururumba were busy digging, "a man named DaBore came along and sat down beside me. He asked the men in the hole what they were doing, and after they explained, he turned to me and said: 'There are no lightning balls.' He then got up and walked away" (Newman, 1965:104).

9. Religious practitioners, too, are extremely varied in their social roles. Shamans are thought of as individualistic and personalized in their ministry, but some also act as priests in performing rituals for larger congregations. There are also diviners, soothsayers, *gurus*, sorcerers, and a great variety of other magic-religious performers.

In this chapter our focus of attention has been on the relatively stable aspects of religion and on religious systems as stabilizing, conservative forces in sociocultural systems. In a later chapter (Chapter 27) we will turn to the radical and revolutionary aspects of peoples' relationships to supernaturals.

Relationships with the Supernatural

20

Subjective Culture: The Expressive Side of Life

A major aspect of human lifeways is the EXPRESSIVE CULTURE, which includes oral and written literature, dramatic performances, music, games, visual arts, and other symbolic productions. Anthropologists have approached the study of expressive culture from a number of theoretical perspectives, but for several decades psychoanalytic theory dominated the interpretation of the arts. There was a time in the history of Freudian thought when not just the artwork and the mythology of human groups but almost everything in their cultural symbol systems was interpreted as an expression of psychodynamic problems. In this vein the psychoanalyst-anthropologist Geza Roheim developed the theory that plow agriculture arose as a psychic sublimation of forbidden sexual wishes and that plowing "mother earth" is symbolically analogous to sexual activity with a mother figure.

The Concept of Projection

Very few theorists other than psychoanalysts have been so bold as to derive all of human cultural activity from psychic foundations. On the other hand, many activities are tinged with ritual, ceremonialism, and other features that reflect the subjective experiences of people. Our subjective thoughts and psychological predispositions are always present to some degree, coloring our perceptions and shaping the style and patterning of even our most routine activities. The general idea is that people PROJECT their own psychological characteristics and expectations into their cultural activities. Also, people select activities and produce works of art that "fit with" their own personalities. Here are some simple examples:

1. Persons who are rather introverted may tend to enjoy solitary activities such as reading and bird watching.
2. Children who are fascinated by automobiles may tend to draw pictures of cars when their teachers say, "Now children draw a picture of anything you'd like to draw."
3. People who admire extreme order and neatness are likely to get aesthetic pleasure from Japanese gardens.
4. Mathematicians tend to prefer abstract, complex musical compositions such as chamber music.

5. In writing plays and novels, people who are fascinated by interpersonal antagonisms may tend to stress this as a prominent theme in their writing.

Although some of these examples are perhaps debatable, they illustrate processes of projection. In each case, something about the individual is projected outward, either affecting the individual's preferences and choices or appearing in a transformed way in the individual's creative endeavors. Just as individual activity and productivity can reflect psychological predispositions, the concept of projection has been employed in research on societies with some very interesting results.

The Personalities of the Gods

Based on the concept of projection, we could hypothesize that the supernatural creatures that humans invent to explain the nature of life must be, in some respects, like the people themselves, perhaps incorporating some of the forbidden and not-so-forbidden wishes of the soul derived from life experiences. This idea might be expressed in the paraphrase: "People create their gods after their own images." Of course in some cases the gods and their emotional and expressive qualities are so much in the service of a particular class or privileged group within a society that they look more like impression management than innocent projection. "The gods demand that we go to war against the Assyrians" smacks more of press conference manipulation than a sincere projection of human attributes onto the supernaturals.

Several cross-cultural studies have produced evidence that supports the idea that people's views of the gods have a relationship to childhood experiences with parents. Like most hypotheses about human psychic universals, this one is very difficult to substantiate with hard evidence. Nevertheless, it is interesting that researchers such as M. Spiro and R. D'Andrade (1958) found that in societies in which children are warmly indulged in their early years, people tend to have beliefs that their gods will be friendly to humans, provided one performs the right rituals. In a similar vein, another study shows

20.1 Volleyball game in the park. (Elliot Erwitt, Magnum)

391

that societies in which infants are harshly and painfully treated tend to have supernaturals that are considered aggressive rather than benevolent toward human beings (Lambert, Triandis, and Wolf, 1959).

The gods of the Pueblos of the Southwest are an example of religious supernaturals who demand a great deal of attention—prayer, ceremonial observances, and other ritual—but who, on the whole, are relatively benevolent if they are treated right. In keeping with the findings of these cross-cultural studies, ethnographic reports of the Zuñis' child-rearing practices say that they grant infants and small children considerable freedom and license and that they feed them well if they possibly can. These are features of child rearing that reflect general indulgence and warmth toward children.

We would not argue that people have created their religious systems as a direct reflection of childhood impressions of parents. Many other factors play a part in affecting the nature of religious beliefs. However, we do suggest that *some* of the features of religions may be a reflection of the shared life experiences of individuals.

Games People Play

Games and other recreational activities provide another area that can reflect psychological predispositions. For example, it is likely that people who love to watch boxing and wrestling may have greater tendencies toward interpersonal hostilities than do persons who prefer sports like long-distance running and tennis. And surely there are interesting psychological processes at work in the current great interest in American football.

John M. Roberts has devoted more research and theoretical effort to the study of expressive culture than has perhaps any other contemporary anthropologist. A key concept in his theory is "conflict enculturation," and he begins with the observation that most people experience conflict situations in their childhood that they seek to resolve through a variety of means. Conflict-producing situations from childhood experiences set the themes that affect individual expressive preferences, according to Roberts. We seek out games and other recreational events that provide relatively nonthreatening reenactments and "practice" sessions with the same

20.2 Games of strategy, like chess, have apparently been popular favorites mainly in more complex societies, especially those with social stratification. (P. J. Pelto)

20.3 Card playing is an important expressive pastime among the Skolt Same. (P. J. Pelto)

characteristics as our individual psychosocial conflicts.

Games and other recreational activities are thus MODELS of real-life dramas. Chess is a model of strategic warfare; boxing is a model of lethal hand-to-hand combat; and bingo is a model of life in which the whims of chance control outcomes much more than our personal capabilities and skills do. It is interesting that the Crow Indians called stick ball "the little brother of war."

John Roberts's models are, in a sense, projections.

Sacred and Secular Realms of Adaptation

Table 20.1: Social Complexity and Games of Strategy in Societies Around the World

	Games of Strategy Present	Games of Strategy Absent
Societies with low social complexity	5	18
Societies with complex social organization	14	6

Source: Adapted from Roberts et. al., 1956:600.

But they are projections with a purpose. The models are situations in which we can rehearse our skills (and our anxieties) for the main arenas of practical action. In this view games really become very important experiences and not just frivolous pastimes.

If games are models for behavior, we would expect that they must be different in hunting-gathering societies, as contrasted with industrial societies, because the hangups and conflicts are different. Roberts and his research collaborators suggest that games of strategy:

which are models of social interaction should be related to the complexity of the social systems; games of chance which are models of interaction with the supernatural should be linked with other expressive views of the supernatural; and there's a possibility that games of physical skill may be related to aspects of the natural environment. (Roberts, Arth, and Bush, 1959:599–600)

Table 20.1 presents cross-cultural data that show that as a general proposition the *more complex societies tend to have games of strategy* (like chess, checkers, backgammon, and so on), whereas in societies with a low degree of political integration and with no clear stratification there tend to be no games of strategy. In egalitarian societies games tend to concentrate on physical skills, such as competitive shooting, races, and wrestling.

In other research Roberts and his associates found that in societies that stress *obedience training* for children there are many games of strategy, whereas societies that train their children for *independence* tend to have games of physical skill. Because a number of studies have shown that boys and girls in our

Table 20.2: Number of Games Differentiating Between the Sexes at $p < .05$ or better

Game Classes	No Differences	Girls Prefer	Boys Prefer
Strategy	Beasts, birds, fish; dominoes; chess; Parcheesi; Scrabble; tic-tac-toe; Clue; Monopoly	I've Got a Secret; Name that Tune; checkers; twenty questions; I spy	0
Chance	Coin matching; forfeit; cards; 7-up	Bingo; spin the bottle; post office; musical chairs; letters; colors; initials	dice
Pure physical skill	Quoits	Hop scotch; jump rope; jacks; tiddlywinks	bowling; horseshoes; racing; tug-of-war; darts; shuffleboard; bows and arrows; throwing snowballs; shooting
Physical skill and strategy	handball; tennis; volleyball; prisoner's base; fox and hounds; ping-pong	pickup sticks	marbles; wrestling; boxing; basketball; football; capture the flag; punt back; pool; billiards; baseball; soccer

Source: Adapted from Roberts and Sutton-Smith, 1962:177.

393

Subjective Culture: The Expressive Side of Life

own society tend to experience differences in socialization (with girls being rewarded for obedient behavior and boys for independence), Roberts argued that American girls should show a greater preference for games of strategy and chance and boys should prefer games of physical skill. Such preferences, if they occur, could be due, then, to differences in subjective experiences of socialization rather than simply differences in physical strength. Table 20.2 shows the game preferences that Roberts and Sutton-Smith collected from 1,900 schoolchildren.

Naturally many other factors besides psychological interests in strategy, chance, or physical skill affect people's game playing. However, people who are interested in redefining sex roles in modern society would do well to look at features of children's and adults' games, as these are important socialization models affecting role behavior. In recent times there have been heated arguments—even court cases—concerning the right of girls to participate in Little League baseball and football, for example. From the point of view of John Roberts's theory of games these are not trifling questions about "mere entertainment" but are part of the socialization situations that help shape adult personality and behavior.

Songs People Sing

Song styles, both words and music, are sensitive indicators of people's moods, aspirations, and dreams. We are so accustomed to associating music with particular expressive scenes that we often have the feeling that the language of music is indeed pure "human nature." Thus martial music is loud, brassy, and relatively simple. Funeral music is slow, "minor key," and somewhat muted. Love and romance are themes that would seem to require fairly softspoken, lilting, melodic lines without much heavy drumming or other percussion—or so we thought until the advent of rock 'n' roll.

Perhaps the large-scale shifts in musical styles during the past fifteen years are enough evidence for us to become cautious indeed with regard to generalizing about "panhuman musical expression." Styles and fashions change a good deal in music, and what sounded so naturally romantic to people in the roaring twenties had no "sex appeal" to the moderns of the 1940s and 1950s. Some people have pointed

to the differences in musical preferences as one of the more obvious evidences of the generation gap. The electrically amplified joys of the present generation are frequently perceived by the tribal elders as simply a lot of noise and confusion.

All of us have had enough experience with music to know that tastes and preferences are extremely sensitive to sociocultural learning and habituation. At an early age we learn to identify the types of music that are fashionable within our own social traditions. As old songs go out of style and new ones take their place, most persons adjust their cultural tastes accordingly, although there are always some unusual individuals who don't go along with "the crowd" and maintain their own individual musical preferences.

All too little research has been done examining music as an expression of personal identification, but the fit between the cultural in-group and their music preference is often very evident. The spread of Euro-American "modernization" throughout the world is evident to the alert-eared traveler in the widespread prevalence of music from the Beatles, the Rolling Stones, and other "superstars" in distant corners of the globe. We have watched young reindeer herders dancing to this new "music of the world" on a chilly arctic night while northern lights flickered across the skies. We found that one of the juke box favorites in a rural Mexican village during the summer of 1970 was "Let It Be," side by side with some traditional and modern Mexican music. In many parts of Europe the new international musical preferences have all but eliminated localized folk musical forms, so that one must go to special tourist places if one is to listen to the old-time Swiss yodelers, German polka bands, or Norwegian fishermen's songs. As the new mass-media dance music replaces old forms, traditional music is preserved and elaborated by those people who seek out symbols expressive of special ethnic and cultural identifications.

Even the most serious and pragmatic social movements develop identifying symbolism through special music. The "Internationale" of the Communist movement is sung in many different languages around the world as an expression of the general idea "workers of the world unite;" and revolutionaries and ex-revolutionaries still express the pathos of the Spanish Civil War by singing (in many different languages) songs like "Viva la Quince Bri-

Sacred and Secular Realms of Adaptation

gada'' and ''Los quatro Generales.'' Not only German peasants but many other kinds of people have raised their morale and hurled their defiance with the stirring words of ''Die Gedanken Sind Frei'' (Thoughts Are Free). The song is over five hundred years old and appears to derive from the days of the peasant wars. It was used by a German poet Schiller in one of his plays, and university students in many lands have sung it as they wave their beer mugs in innumerable toasts to free expression of ideas. Quite predictably, Adolf Hitler banned this song:

Die gedanken sind frei,
My thoughts freely flower,
Die gedanken sind frei,
My thoughts give me power,
No scholar can map them,
No hunter can trap them
No man can deny,
Die gedanken sind frei.

I think as I please,
And this gives me pleasure,
My conscience decrees,
This right I must treasure;
My thoughts will not cater
To duke or dictator
No man can deny—
Die gedanken sind frei!

From Blues to Soul Music: Music of Black Political Expression

Many writers have commented on the importance of music in connection with a rise of political consciousness referred to as the Black Power movement. Michael Haralambos examined some of the differences between the soul music of the 1960s and the earlier blues styles that he feels were characteristic of the cultural expressions among Black people in an earlier time. He suggests that:

Blues relates to a time of hardship and sadness which many don't particularly want to be reminded of. It is a musical form that starkly relates experiences and feelings without generally offering any hope of future improvement. As such, blues is a recognition and acceptance of the situation. The heritage of blues and its present-day expression is neither in tune with the material conditions of many in the northern ghettos, nor in harmony with their aspirations, expectations and general mood. (HARALAMBOS, 1970:372)

20.4 **The pipe or flute is one of the most ancient musical instruments. Above, Indian flute player, Southwestern U.S.A. (American Museum of Natural History) Below, Sherpa herder in Nepal. (Arthur Tress, Magnum)**

395

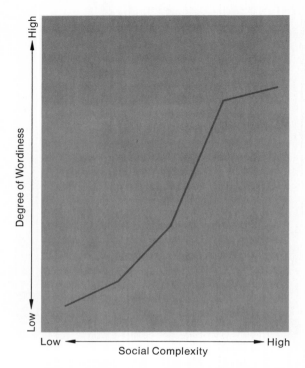

20.5 **The wordiness of songs as related to the economic system. High-production systems (plow and irrigation agriculture) have greater wordiness than do societies with less complex economies. (Based on Lomax, 1968)**

Haralambos surveyed the music on Black radio stations in a number of northern cities and found that soul music was increasing in popularity at the expense of the blues. A Detroit disk jockey explained the reasons:

"You try to push it [blues] out of your life. . . . In the old days they were really in a blues bag. The man was treatin' him so bad that he had to sing the blues, but it's not like that anymore so they don't have a leg to stand on." (HARALAMBOS, 1970:371)

The new mood—a revolutionary change in the expressive culture of Black people—expresses many themes of new self-confidence. Among Indian peoples, too, the music and dance forms of the modern powwow celebrations express a growing Pan-Indian network of contacts and identification. The basic

dance steps and musical style were earlier identified only with some Plains Indian groups.

In examining various aspects of human sociocultural systems (such as kinship organization, religious organization, and social stratification) we have seen the ways in which these are patterned in social evolutionary terms. We would expect, therefore, that expressive culture is also patterned in different ways in, for example, hunting and gathering as compared with agricultural societies.

Alan Lomax and his associates have studied the singing and the instrumental music of a great many societies in order to look for generalizations about relationships of social facts to musical styles. With a method they call cantometrics, they have examined ethnographic data in terms of "complexity of

20.6 **The language of the dance, India. (M. Silverstone, Magnum)**

20.7 Trance dance in Bali, Indonesia. (Cartier-Bresson, Magnum)

songs," "degree of embellishment," "repetitiousness of songs," "varying uses of melodic intervals," "unison singing," "unison orchestral rhythm," "counterpoint," and a great variety of other musical characteristics.

They find that complex societies on the whole have much wordier songs than the simplest societies and that the "precision of enunciation" tends to increase from simple to complex societies (Lomax et al., 1968:131). Although people with complex social systems tend to be more precise in their pro-

nunciation, the highest levels of precision singing are not found among Europeans, according to Lomax. The social significance of precision singing is evident in the following:

The ethnographic distribution of precise singing offers support to the notion that this trait reflects the communication demands of societies with complex orderings. Of all style regions, Oceania scores highest for precision. . . . Ethnologists . . . have remarked that Polynesians attach great value to early mastery and

Did Humans Sing Before They Learned To Speak?

Singing is different from ordinary human speech in several ways. Much of it is quite simple in vocal character, and it is often repetitive and ritualized. At the same time, song is not so very different from some of the calls of nonhuman primates. Further, many creatures, especially birds, sing even though they seem not to "converse" very much. The communication capabilities of yodeling, hog calling, and other song forms are obvious; and we should also keep in mind that the early protohumans, like *Australopithecus*, probably ranged rather widely in their daily food quest, especially as they developed greater inclinations toward hunting game. Frank Livingstone (1973) has suggested that human communications systems evolved from primate calls to song calls before the development of full speech capabilities. Is it possible that a step toward opening up the prehuman communication system was a song-yodel calling the scattered members to dinner?

397

Subjective Culture: The Expressive Side of Life

felicitous use of language. The Maori, for example, send their children to school to learn genealogical chants from an adept, whose duty is to teach them to pronounce the traditional poems with such exactness and clarity that they acquire a magical power. . . . Around the world, however, heavy loading of exactly articulated bits of information in a song style indicates a high level of productive complexity. (LOMAX et al., 1968:131)

Lomax and his associates have also analyzed a considerable body of information about dance styles around the world. In general they feel that greater societal complexity gives rise to greater complexity of movements in the dance. For example, they suggest that "looped movements" are absent among simple cultivators but are a prominent feature of Oriental dance.

Oral Literature: Myths, Tales, and Other Lore

The telling of myths and tales is an expressive pastime in all human societies. Often the stories hark back to the supernatural and account for why things are the way they are:

There was once a time when there were but two persons in the world, Old Man and Old Woman. One time, when they were travelling about, Old Man met Old Woman, who said, "Now, let us come to an agreement of some kind; let us decide how the people shall live." "Well," said Old Man, "I am to have the first say in everything." To this Old Woman agreed, provided she had the second say.

Then Old Man began. "The women are to tan the hides. When they do this, they are to rub brains on them to make them soft; they are to scrape them well with scraping-tools, etc. But all this they are to do very quickly, for it will not be very hard work."

"No; I will not agree to this," said Old Woman. "They must tan the hide in the way you say; but it must be made very hard work, and take a long time, so that the good workers may be found out."

"Well," said Old Man, "Let the people have eyes and mouths in their faces; but they shall be straight up and down."

"No," said Old Woman. "We will not have them that way. We will have the eyes and mouth in the faces, as you say; but they shall all be set crosswise."

"Well," said Old Man, "the people shall have ten fingers on each hand." "Oh, no!" said Old Woman.

"That will be too many. They will be in the way. There shall be four fingers and one thumb on each hand."

"Well," said Old Man, "we shall beget children. The genitals shall be at our navels." "No, said Old Woman, "that will make child-bearing too easy; the people will not care for their children. The genitals shall be at the pubes." (Blackfoot Indian myth, Radin, 1956:127)

In this myth we have some clues to male-female relationships as well as some ideas about Blackfoot attitudes toward supernatural creation.

Legends and tales, whatever else their purpose, must be entertaining for the listeners—they often have heroes and beautiful women, great deeds and dreadful dangers, and all the other stuff of drama. And it's hard to put together a legend or a tale of any length that doesn't have some extensive travel in it. Some of the most elaborated sagas in traditional cultures have been preserved by people who had some chances to specialize in storytelling and who must have had audiences who cared about the heroism and grace elaborated in these tales. A number of very long Nordic sagas are widely known; the British are justly proud of *Beowulf*; and the *Iliad* and the *Odyssey* were repeated from generation to generation for centuries before writing things down became a regular habit in the Mediterranean.

Among the Finns of northern Europe a long and beautiful legend of heroes and heroines was handed down through the generations, chanted and sung by old gray-beard tellers. Probably no one of these Finnish singers ever knew all—the full fifty cantos—of the *Kalevala: Land of Heroes*. In 1835 a Finnish country doctor, Elias Lönnrot, began to collect these oral presentations during his medical rounds in the eastern Finnish backlands. By 1849 he had accumulated the 22,795 lines of epic poetry that make up the present written version of the *Kalevala*. (Longfellow copied the style and cadence of the *Kalevala* in his famous *Hiawatha*.)

In the *Kalevala* there are great shamanistic performances, the wooing of beautiful northern women, the brewing of excellent mead, steambaths (saunas), the magical mill that turns the sea to salt, and hundreds of other fantastic adventures. Unlike the heroes of the Mediterranean region, the *Kalevala*'s heroes did not have great ships or magnificent palaces, nor did they muster large armies, though

398

they engaged in plenty of fighting. One of the *Kalevala*'s heroes, Lemminkainen (about whom the composer Sibelius composed his tone poem "Lemminkainen's Homeward Journey"), lived a year on an island full of women, whose menfolk had gone off to war. The hero slept with each of them (except one) during three marvelous summers until the men returned. Although the women pleaded for him to stay, the lively Lemminkainen pushed off with his magic boat back to his homestead, with its wild strawberries and yard full of cackling chickens.

Among the great cultural achievements of the *Kalevala* people, none had more significance for the future than the invention of beer (mead) by the woman Osmotar:

. . . And the beer at length fermented,
And the fresh drink now foamed upward,
From within the new-made barrels,
From within the tubs of birchwood,
Foaming upward to the handles,
Rushing over all the edges;
To the ground it wished to trickle,
And upon the floor ran downward.

But a little time passed over, . . .
When the heroes flocked to drink it,
Chief among them Lemminkainen,
Drunk was Ahti, drunk was Kauko,
Drunken was the ruddy rascal,
With the ale of Osmo's daughter,
And the beer of Kalevatar.

Osmotar, the ale-preparer,
She, the maid who beer concocted,
Uttered then the words which follow:
"Woe is me, my day is wretched,
For I brewed the ale so badly,
And the beer so ill concocted,
That from out the tubs 'tis flowing,
And upon the floor is gushing."
From a tree there sang a bullfinch,
From the roof-tree sang a throstle,
"No, the ale is not so worthless;
'Tis the best of ale for drinking;
If into the casks you pour it,
And should store it in the cellar,
Store it in the casks of oakwood,
And within the hoops of copper,"

Thus was ale at first created,
Beer of Kaleva concocted,
Therefore is it praised so highly,

Therefore held in greatest honour,
For the ale is of the finest,
Best of drinks for prudent people;
Women soon it brings to laughter,
Men it warms into good humour,
And it makes the prudent merry,
But it brings the fools to raving.
(*Kalevala; Land of Heroes*, Runo XX: lines 382–424)

Many peoples of the world regard the supposed creators of their world with awe and reverence, trembling before the altars of their gods like Dorothy's little troupe before the Wizard of Oz. But many North American Indian people took fairly lighthearted attitudes toward some of their supernaturals, especially toward that scatalogical trickster god. The idea of the Trickster is practically universal among North American Indian groups. On the Northwest Coast the Trickster was Raven, in other areas it was Coyote; others had Trickster gods not clearly identified with a particular animal. Winnebago Trickster stories are a particularly rich illustration of the mixture of god-creator-fool-clown typical of many Indian groups. The Trickster in stories collected by Paul Radin had a very, very long penis, which he often carried around in a box. Unfortunately, one day he stuck it into a hollow tree to scare out a chipmunk.

Then he kicked the log to pieces. There he found the chipmunk and flattened him out, and there, too, to his horror he discovered his penis all gnawed up. "Oh, my, of what a wonderful organ he has deprived me! But why do I speak thus? I will make objects out of the pieces for human beings to use." Then he took the end of his penis, the part that has no foreskin, and declared, "This is what human beings will call the lily-of-the-lake." This he threw in a lake near by. Then he took the other pieces declaring in turn: "This the people will call potatoes; this the people will call turnips; this the people will call artichokes; this the people will call ground-beans; this the people will call dog-teeth; . . . this the people will call rice." . . .

What was left of his penis was not very long. When, at last, he started off again, he left behind him the box in which he had until then kept his penis coiled up.

And this is the reason our penis has its present shape. It is because of these happenings that the penis is short. Had the chipmunk not gnawed off Trickster's penis our penis would have the appearance that Trickster's first had . . . it would not have been good had

399

our penis remained like that and the chipmunk was created for the precise purpose of performing this particular act. (RADIN, 1956:39–40)

MYTHS are stories about the past that are intended to justify some feature of the present life of people. Thus as long as North Americans kept Black people as slaves, they supported this inhuman practice with stories and tales about the alleged lowly origins and mental capacities of their subordinate population. The caste-stratified inequalities of India are supported by religious myths that impress on the people the idea that everyone's station in life is ordained by the gods. In North America the dominance of the Whites over the Indians is often supported by mythological versions of Indian-White encounters in pioneer days.

The study of myths has provided rich entertainment for generations of psychologists, philologists, litterateurs, and anthropologists. The psychologist Carl Jung searched mythologies for the "archtypal" mental characteristics of people, Freudians examined myths as a key to universal psychodynamics, and in recent times the French anthropologist Claude Lévi-Straus has become widely known for his structural analyses devoted to the exploration of psychic universals and the basic (mental) structures of humans.

People create myths to explain themselves and to absolve themselves of the contradictions between their ideals and realities. Myths also give people courage in the face of hardship, as in the case of the Jews, who through many centuries of life in hostile surroundings clung to their myth of the Jewish people as the chosen people in order to ease the pain of persecution.

We should remind ourselves that the definition of myth does not state that myths are untrue. Some myths are manifestly factual, including some of the myths of suffering and struggle that have kindled the spiritual fires of protest in the Black Power movement, the Chicano "La Raza" organizing, and the great labor struggles of earlier decades.

The truth or falsehood of myths is not the main issue; the more important questions are: How do the myths become established as widely accepted explanations, and what are the powerful qualities of myths that provide some sort of psychic energy for the people who believe in them? Here the word-of-mouth narratives of ancient peoples joins hands with the press agent's efforts of today's ephemeral celebrities—each in their own way creating something of the psychic atmosphere infecting the practical courses of human action.

Clowning and Ritual Humor

Clowning around probably occurs in all human communities, and very often buffoonery has an important place in peoples' public ceremonies. Clowning is often designed to arouse ridicule and scorn, as the words and actions of the clowns lampoon significant aspects of the local scene.

In Zinacantan (Mexico) the celebration of the Christmas season includes a series of humorous episodes involving masqueraders who play the bull (*torito*) and its owners, the Grandfathers and the Grandmothers. All the players are males (*cargo* holders as outlined on pp. 379–381), so the really high humor involves the behavior of the Grandmothers. They clumsily demonstrate spinning and weaving, bragging about their skills (very inappropriate conduct for Zinacanteco girls and women), and then insist on riding the "horses" that the Grandfathers have purchased. Naturally they fall off the horses; their skirts fly up, uncovering their buttocks (demonstrating that women should keep in their proper place and not try to assume male roles). The Grandfathers also fall off their horses and must be "cured." They have to get their "bones" put back in place. The curer's recitation of the therapeutic formula is actually a clever double entendre, referring to sexual intercourse:

Find your place, bones!
Find your place, muscles!
Don't leave your hole, muscle!
Don't leave your hole, bone!
(Etc. in the same vein . . .)
Don't go to another hole, muscle!
Don't leave your hole empty, bone!
(BRICKER, 1973:23)

Victoria Bricker, who has made an extensive study of humor among the Mayan communities of Chiapas in southern Mexico, notes that the dramatic portrayals of the Grandmothers are not intended to make fun of women—but they remind women, in a variety of ways, that they should not act in an "unfeminine" manner.

400

Sacred and Secular Realms of Adaptation

20.8 Ritual clowns (including the grandmother) in Zinacantan ceremonial scene. (Frank Cancian)

20.9 Ngatatjara artist with rock painting. Warburton Ranges, Australia. (Courtesy of the American Museum of Natural History)

Graphic Arts: The Wide-Canvas Medium

The word *art* often is used to mean paintings, sculptures, and other visual creations. Yet in Indo-European languages *art* refers to a great many other areas of expressive culture, from drama to politics. The portrayal of "pictures" in stone sculptures, paintings, and carving on bone, antler, wood, and other materials—as well as the decoration of implements with lines, diamonds, and other nonfunctional decor—is very old in human culture. We have discussed earlier the cave paintings of the late Ice Ages. Even before that period of great artistic expression there were certainly many signs of human tendencies to decorate their material surroundings.

Some graphic art is meant for practical purposes. As already described, cave art was very likely intended for hunting magic—at least it was *not* for home decoration since the caves and their brilliant art were far underground. Similarly, decorations on harpoons and other implements were very possibly meant for magical purposes.

Subjective Culture: The Expressive Side of Life

20.10 Modern sculpture, Finland. (P. J. Pelto)

20.11 Polynesian tattooing. (Courtesy of the American Museum of Natural History)

On the other hand, decorations can also be used to mark ownership or identify kin groups, as with the crests and totem pole carvings of the Indians of the Northwest Pacific Coast. Also, pictures are sometimes created for entertainment or for prestige enhancement through telling about historical events of courage and heroism.

In the Mortlock Islands of the South Pacific people carved elaborate scenes on pieces of wood to illustrate stories of the past. The painting of stories on Plains Indian tipis (see p. 182) allowed individuals the opportunity to tell about their prestigious exploits in a manner that brought admiration from other members of the group.

The painting of the body to attract admiration and attention has been an extremely widespread practice among all kinds of people. Tattooing was developed to a fine art by the Japanese and other peoples, even though it has the obvious drawback that the pictures (or inscriptions) are distressingly permanent. Our North American folklore is full of sailors and other heroes who got "Lola" or "Betty" or "Mary" tattooed onto exposed skin surfaces, only to find themselves with a desperate need to erase it so they could write in "Suzie," "Jane," or "Anne."

South American peoples have been particularly elaborate in their body art, often painting large parts of the near-nude anatomy with attractive designs. Many peoples in Africa and other parts of the world also have been notable for their self-decoration through body painting. The modern use of lipstick and eyeshade is but a pale reflection of the widespread human tendency to seek improvements of natural beauty through cosmetic means. It's hard to decide whether humans have spent more artistic energy in honor of the gods or in honor of self—possibly it comes out about even in the full range of human societies.

Midway between self-adornment and art for the gods is the widespread use of masks for the imper-

402

Sacred and Secular Realms of Adaptation

20.12 Masks of the Kwakiutl, British Columbia. (Courtesy of the American Museum of Natural History)

20.13 Mud face masks in New Guinea. (Burt Glinn, Magnum)

sonation and portrayal of the supernaturals in dramatic action. Mask art has reached great heights in many parts of the world, most notably in Melanesia and parts of West Africa and North America. Among the Kwakiutl, masked dancers portrayed supernatural deities in the winter ceremonies; Hopi and Zuñi dancers put on Katchina masks and headdresses to bring deities into direct participation in village life; and among the Iroquois the False Face society put on dramatic shows that were intended as illness-curing ceremonies.

Charles Valentine, describing the masked performers of the Lakalai people of New Britain, was moved to write that:

masks have a special appeal which is difficult to describe. The feeling is often expressed that these objects are endowed with a singular preternatural quality. The beholder of the mask is moved to attribute a life of its own to the object. The feeling arises that a masked performer has somehow undergone a metamorphosis and assumed in living form the qualities of his disguise. The watching audience, knowing that what it sees is a person wearing something which he can again take off, nevertheless is captured by the illusion that the mask somehow belongs to the figure and expresses its nature. Wearers of masks, on the other hand, often report that they feel more or less transformed by the image they are wearing, so that they are moved to act according to the characteristics which are associated with it. (VALENTINE, 1961:2–3)

No wonder our small children sometimes react with horror and fear to masks and cannot be comforted even when it is demonstrated repeatedly to them that the masked figure is really just big brother. Perhaps our little ones "know" in some way that big brother really *does* turn into a monster when he puts on the false face!

Subjective Culture: The Expressive Side of Life

Are There Universal Standards of Aesthetic Appreciation?

Artists do not intend that everything they create should be "beautiful." Nonetheless, the appreciation of excellence—manifest in emotional reactions of pleasure and excitement—is an extremely widespread reaction among sensitive people, even though individuals and groups differ widely in their definitions of aesthetic beauty. Much anthropological ink has gone into discussions of "cultural relativity," in terms of which there cannot be any such thing as universal standards of art because different people have different ideas about the good, the true, and the beautiful. Radical cultural relativism has, however, received some serious setbacks. In the first place, the art and music of the East have become greatly appreciated in the West, and, conversely, non-Western peoples have accepted art forms of Euro-American origin. In the amazingly rapid "delocalization" of artistic expression, perhaps the symbol of our era is the "jam session" played by Ravi Shankar on the sitar and Yehudi Menuhin on the violin.

Some researchers have found significant evidence of cross-culturally similar standards of aesthetic judgment. In one study judgments of the aesthetic qualities of a group of Bakwele masks (Africa) were collected from sixteen Bakwele elders and from a panel of art experts in New Haven. It was found that "the consensus of the sixteen Bakwele . . . showed significant agreement with the consensus of the New Haven experts" concerning which of these finely carved masks were regarded as artistically superior (Child and Siroto, 1965). In a similar study six Fijian expert carvers were asked to make judgments about a series of abstract paintings presented as postcard-sized pictures. They also were asked to make aesthetic judgments of a series of Bambara antelope headpieces (Africa). As in the Bakwele study, the Fijian art experts' judgments were quite similar to the critical opinions of that panel of New Haven art experts. The same results were found in the judgments of a group of potters from a relatively remote island in Japan. (New Haven "art experts" crop up in all of these comparisons simply because Irvin Child and his colleagues are located at Yale University.) Child and his fellow researchers pointed out that these cross-cultural similarities in aesthetic judgments were found among *experts;* the opinions of "nonexpert" high school students showed a much lower degree of agreement with either the art critics or their fellow critics from Japan. These studies of cross-cultural similarities in art appreciation do not prove that people everywhere are "the same" in their viewing of works of art. The studies do, however, suggest that there may be a much greater than expected agreement among various peoples of the world with regard to what is or is not beautiful.

Summary and Conclusions: Perspectives on Expressive Culture

Humans and many other animals expend a great deal of time in expressive activities that are not immediately "practical" acts of food getting, providing shelter, or satisfying other obvious physical needs. Kittens, dolphins, baboons, and humans spend great amounts of time in "play" activities, ranging from play fights to sliding, jumping, racing, mimicking, and sometimes just clowning around. In addition to play and amusement human groups create special "things" in the form of pictures, songs, tales, drama, and other productions we loosely lump together as "art." Other animals do not seem to go in for very much artistic production, though chimpanzees paint pictures if one hands them paint and brush, and they seem to consider their works of art to be "meaningful" representations.

In recent years there has been some significant progress in careful empirical study of various forms of artistic expression, but the scientific study of emotive culture is still in its infancy. The following generalizations are made mainly to point out some possible directions for anthropological research:

1. Games, artistic works, and other aspects of expressive culture appear to fulfill some very significant emotional-cognitive needs of individuals. At least it is significant that all human societies have games and art.

2. All of these aspects of expressive culture take a great variety of forms, and their varieties tend to have predictable patterns. Particularly, the progression from simpler to more complex societies tends to predict significant trends in games, music, and other expressive forms.

20.14 Japanese ceremonial theater. (Erich Hartmann, Magnum)

20.15 Monkey dance in Bali. (George Rodger, Magnum)

3. The forms of games and artistic works in particular societies appear to have some relationship to the psychological dispositions of people, so that some aspects of art and games provide clues to people's basic motives or important psychic conflicts—people project important psychic content into their art and games.

4. According to at least one body of important research (including that of Roberts and his associates), many forms of expressive culture provide "models" or "surrogates" for real-life experiences and allow people to practice or rehearse these experiences.

5. The forms of games and artistic works also reflect significant social relationships within the society. Myths and folklore project images of sex roles, relationships among subordinates and superordinates, and other social features; graphic arts tell about the attributes of the gods as well as of the priests; and songs can express everything from despair and depression to buoyant hope and braggadocio, depending on the inclinations of the singers.

6. In almost all societies the forms of artistic expression tell something about the people's views of the supernatural world. Magic and religion inspire much of the world's artistic effort, but secular art, too, is found in all societies, the simpler and the more complex.

7. Art is often used to express political ideas, as, for example, in the works of Diego Rivera and in the many examples of colorful political messages painted on the walls of buildings in the city by Chicanos, Blacks, and other minority groups.

8. The favored forms of art in different societies depend, of course, on the available materials. Scattered nomadic bands of hunters do not put on Wagnerian operas—they lack the personnel and the equipment. The much-appreciated wood-carving art of the Northwest Pacific Coast Indians was possible because of very rich supplies of suitable wood, tools for carving, and an at least periodic abundance of food supplies.

9. The artists in any society tend to be a minority of special producers who, for whatever reason, find it interesting and profitable to develop the extra skills and proficiencies (and special knowledge) requisite to artistic production. In societies with very complex art there are very special, highly trained performers. On the other hand, practically all individuals produce *some* artistic works—at least putting a special bit of effort into self-adornment from time to time.

10. Judgments about artistic goals differ widely from one cultural milieu to another, and each major area of the world has developed creative traditions refined through centuries of cultural evolution. Nonetheless, it is quite possible that there are universal forms in expressive culture—reflecting universals in human social life, panhuman cognitive features, or other aspects of our biopsychic unity.

406

Sacred and Secular Realms of Adaptation

In his book *Civilization and Its Discontents* Sigmund Freud made much of the fact that "culture," embodied in the relationships among people in a social system, imposes tensions on individuals and that social norms, practices, and expectations are a major source of psychological stress. Freud was not alone in his concern, and many philosophers from ancient times to the present have theorized about the tensions and contradictions between the needs of the individual and the demands of society.

Cultural norms, patterns, and expectations take different forms in different societies, so individual responses—in psychological characteristics as well as in "typical" stresses and coping responses—also can be quite varied. Some social systems are quite individualistic, allowing people a good deal of latitude in choosing their own behavior patterns within the opportunities available in the environment. Other societies are much stricter and insist on firm disciplining and control to make each individual fit into the goals and tasks of the system.

The Skolt Same of northeastern Finland are an example of a rather individualistic society, for their modes of adapting to the environment permit each person—even small children—much flexibility and independent decision making. Very few productive tasks require intensive cooperation, and the ownership of resources (reindeer and fishing gear and other equipment) is individualized. The emphasis on self-reliance and individual decision making is reflected in the laissez-faire attitudes toward child training.

On the other hand, social systems such as those of the Pueblo Indian communities of Arizona and New Mexico, the island communities of Micronesia (e.g., Truk, Ulithi, and other tiny atolls), and many of the more densely populated peasant communities, exhibit strong demands for a "conformity orientation" that would seem like unpleasant regimentation to a reindeer-herding Same and to many hunting-gathering peoples, like the Bushmen, the Hadza, and the Paliyan people of South India.

Child Training and Group Adaptations

The degree of social pressure on individuals is often most clearly visible in childtraining practices, for parents and other adults usually impose on their

21.1 Skolt Same children are given their own reindeer at an early age. (P. J. Pelto)

children a pattern of social learning that will gradually transform the unpredictable and undisciplined little ones into responsible, productive members of the adult world. The discipline may be most noticeable in chores, baby tending, and other work, but the training is also often reflected in parents' permissiveness or strictness in feeding, toilet training, management of interpersonal aggression, and other behavior.

Often the impact of the parental generation on the socialization of their children has ramifications that are quite different from the conscious intentions of the mothers and fathers. The size of households, the demands of agricultural work, the physical dangers of the environment, and many other ecological features all help shape the "training program" that eventually leads to particular behavorial styles and expectations in each new generation. For example, Cora DuBois pointed out that the demands for women's labor in food cultivation among the Alorese of eastern Indonesia severely limit the amount of attention that mothers can give their infants. The Alorese people do not really intend that children should *learn* anxiety and distress about food and other needs—but that's the message they get as a result of the food production system that requires so much work from the women.

Differences in environmental conditions, economic systems, and many other features have resulted in a wide range of differences among societies in child training. In some societies children are breast fed until the age of three or four years, whereas others are less indulgent. Like many other aspects of socialization, toilet training varies from the lenient style characteristic of the Sirionó ("An infant receives no punishment if he urinates or defecates on his parents" [Holmberg, 1960:75]) to the "uptight" attitudes reflected among the Tanala of Madagascar, among whom "anal training is begun at the age of two or three months, and the child is expected to be continent at the age of six months. If after this time the child soils its mother, it is severely punished" (Whiting and Child, 1953:74).

When a number of aspects of child rearing are considered together it appears that, in general, hunting-gathering peoples place more emphasis on independence and self-reliance than do people who cultivate crops. People with complex food systems and large population masses have several converging motives for emphasizing obedience training. For one

thing, they do not want their children in trouble with nearby neighbors.

Cross-Cultural Studies of Child Training

Cross-cultural studies of psychological characteristics are based on the assumption that, if there are basic psychic unities among humans, they cannot be in particular personality traits but must lie in the basic processes by which personality constellations are formed. In the early 1950s a team of researchers, led by anthropologist John M. Whiting and psychologist Irvin L. Child, analyzed a sample of seventy-nine societies from around the world,

Sacred and Secular Realms of Adaptation

focusing on relationships between child training and adult personality as expressed in particular cultural patterns. They reasoned that childhood experiences would be reflected in adult life and adult cultural forms. For example, they hypothesized that high oral gratification would be expressed in expectations of oral gratification in adult cultural systems. To test this hypothesis they suggested that people who have learned to expect oral gratification will use oral means for bringing relief from the anxiety-producing situation of illness. In examining the data from seventy-nine societies they found that there was indeed a tendency for societies that they rated high on oral gratification to have expectations of effective curing by oral means.

Whiting and Child tested a number of similar hypotheses and found further confirmation of their ideas, although some of their hunches did not pan out. Many other studies similar in design to the Whiting and Child study have contributed to the evidence about cross-cultural, and perhaps pan-human, similarities in personality development and psychological functioning. In most cases the theoretical ideas that have been tested cross-culturally in this manner are derived from ideas that first received considerable support in psychological studies within our own society. An example of this kind of psychocultural research is that of Ronald P. Rohner at the University of Connecticut. Rohner wanted to test the idea that rejecting, hostile, or indifferent behavior of parents toward their children will tend to produce a series of personality characteristics including dependency, hostility, lack of initiative, and so on. He found that in societies in which parents tend to act in a rejecting manner toward their children, adults (who were presumably also subjected to the cultural pattern of rejection as children) tend to show the psychological characteristics predicted by his theory. (ROHNER, 1970)

Initiation Ceremonies: Introduction to Adult Life

There are wide differences in the extent to which males participate in the early training of their children, but among many peoples the first years of a child's life are mainly involved in the women's world. Little children cannot follow their fathers in distant hunting activity, nor are they permitted to go out to battlegrounds or on cattle raids. In many societies, then, especially those with sharp sex-role distinctions, there comes a time when young boys are symbolically (and sometimes physically) separated from the women's circle in which they spent their early years. Male initiation ceremonies are one means of accomplishing a rapid role switch.

Initiation rites, which often include circumcision or other painful hazing, are widespread in Africa, in Oceania, and among some Indian peoples of

21.2 (Opposite) In North American society many parents put pressure on their children to conform to "proper eating" behavior beginning at an early age. (Charles Harbutt, Magnum)

21.3 Learning "appropriate" sex-role behavior in a middle-class North American family. (Leonard Freed, Magnum)

21.4 Male initiation ceremony among the Fulani of Nigeria. (Marilyn Silverstone, Magnum)

North and South America. In a cross-cultural study Frank Young points out that male initiation ceremonies are often found among societies in which there are strong male clubs or organizations. Writing about initiation among the Kurnai people of Australia, A. Van Gennep suggested:

The intention of all that is done at this ceremony is to make a momentous change in the boy's life; the past is to be cut off from him by a gulf which he can never re-pass. His connection with his mother as her child is broken off, and he becomes henceforth attached to the men. All the sports and games of his boyhood are to be abandoned with the severance of the old domestic ties between himself and his mother and sisters. He is now to be a man, instructed in and sensible of the duties which devolve upon him as a member of the Murring community. (VAN GENNEP, 1960:75)

A number of common features are found in male initiation practices in many parts of the world. These are as follows:

1. The ceremony includes some physical marking, such as circumcision, SCARIFICATION, filing the front teeth, or cutting hair. Additional markers, such as changes in dress style, may be used to identify the initiated.

2. Initiation does not necessarily correspond with physiological puberty; in many societies a group of boys ranging in age from eight or nine to their early teens will be initiated at the same time.

3. Especially in African societies, boys who go through the ceremony together form an "age set" that remains a cohesive group throughout their lives (Cf. the Samburu, pp. 318–320).

4. If the initiates are in their teens, the ritual transition generally makes them eligible for participation in adult sexual activity.

5. The ceremony is often associated with schooling in both practical and ritual activities. In many societies in which secret, sacred information is controlled by males, boys are introduced to that knowledge during the initiation period.

6. In many societies there is more than one level of initiation, and several transition points may be

410

21.5 A Bar Mitzvah in Israel. (Ian Berry, Magnum)

21.6 Women's initiation dance in Australia. (Courtesy of the American Museum of Natural History)

celebrated. Religious practices of Christians and Jews constitute such a sequence; for Jews circumcision, eight days after birth, is the first initiation rite, followed thirteen years later by the Bar Mitzvah, which marks the major transition to manhood.

7. After the ritual status change, the initiates are often expected to take at least some part in food production activities.

Female Initiation Rites

Female initiation ceremonies, with many of the same characteristics as male rites, occur in many parts of the world. However, following the logic of male initiation, we would expect fewer societies to have ceremonies for girls. Since girls grow up surrounded by female role models, they do not require the same kind of dramatic announcement of adult sex-role status, and in statistical terms there are fewer societies that celebrate the initiation of girls as compared to boys.

For females the role change is from "girl" to "potential married woman," and the beginning of menstruation is often used as the marker of status change. Among many North American Indian groups the onset of menses signaled a time for special ritual observances to protect the girl and all the people around her from the spiritual dangers attributed to menstruation. The Apache people of the Southwest have had elaborate puberty celebrations for their girls, which brought people together from miles around for dancing and celebrating in honor of a girl's first menstruation. In recent times the ritual has become more group-oriented, for they now celebrate the girls' puberty rites in groups on July 5 as part of the Fourth of July celebration. Often there is a rodeo, with men competing in steer roping, bull dogging, and other sports—all to celebrate the young women's coming of age.

The Stresses of Life: Adulthood

Whatever the actions of people in training their children and initiating their youth into full participation in the adult world, there are often all kinds of escapes in play, leisure, and adult protection—until full adult status is achieved. With adult-

411

21.7 **The beginning of a fight? (Bill Stanton, Magnum)**

hood, the kinds of stresses that individuals experience, as well as their sources of reward and satisfaction, vary a good deal from one social system to another. Nonetheless, there are certain kinds of conditions that are likely to induce stress in individuals everywhere.

1. Servitude and other severe inequalities. One of the most stress-inducing situations is that of being dominated by another person or group, particularly if the dominance-subordination relationship is of long-standing duration. Such stress-producing systems are very widespread in human societies, as we have noted elsewhere, for they include practically all systems of serfdom, slavery, and caste and class stratification, as well as male dominance over females and various other authoritarian relationships.

2. Warfare and other intergroup conflict. In warfare and in other large-scale conflict individuals are often placed under severe strain because of the danger of physical harm and loss of loved ones; stress manifests itself in such phenomena as "shell shock," "combat fatigue," "war neurosis," and other psychological problems.

3. Competition for scarce resources (intragroup conflict). It can be argued that all individuals seek to maximize rewards (food, sex, and so on) and to minimize the discomfort (stress) of hunger, cold, wounds, illness, and the other punishments of mind and body. (In many instances, however, the seeking of higher goals will induce individuals to withstand severe pain.) Within any society there exist scarcities of means and enjoyments, and people compete for these. Some people fight; some groups go to court; others simply quarrel a lot. Although a certain amount of such in-group competition is undoubtedly beneficial for the human organism and is in any case unavoidable, in-group competition can be psychologically painful for most individuals.

4. Restraints on sexual drives and other impulses. This is the stress of civilization that Freud especially singled out as significant in complex societies. Anthropologists have been quick to note, however, that restraints on sexual impulses are severe in a variety of societies, from simple to complex.

21.8 **Playing cards provides a means of human contact at Attica prison in New York State. (Cornell Capa, Magnum)**

5. *General pressures to conform.* The case of sexual restrictions is only one of a much larger class of restraints, prohibitions, or taboos imposed on individuals to varying degrees in all societies. For example, there may be fasting regulations or restrictions on the type of clothing worn, and in some societies (e.g., Java) one must exercise extreme care in the use of language. Social systems vary widely in the extent to which conformity is demanded of individuals.

6. *Expectations of performance.* The opposite of cultural restraints is the long list of expectations of performance of particular acts for other individuals and "for the public good." The society, in the form of the individuals within it, may expect a person to work when he is tired, to give up some of his possessions for feasts and celebrations (as in Zinacantan), to perform rituals when he is not inclined to participate, and to carry out many other activities that he may not desire to do.

7. *Violations of privacy.* Human groups differ widely in the importance placed on privacy, but in many societies interactional phenomena (such as intruding, keeping a person waiting, and interrupting activity) can produce stress upon the personal "life space" of individuals.

8. *Monotonous routine.* It is often noted that humans, like other animals, seek change, novelty, and new stimuli. In many societies individuals are exposed to a good deal of monotony, especially of work routines, which can become highly stressful.

9. *Conflicting expectations.* Societies undoubtedly vary considerably in the degree to which individuals encounter conflicts or irreconcilable discrepancies in role expectations (as in the "matrilineal dilemma," p. 302). In most societies individuals are likely to experience conflicting expectations—for example, between one's immediate family and spouse versus other kinsmen or between one's brothers and sisters and other age mates and the senior generation. Anthropologists have studied a number of situations in which conflicting expectations arise because of rapid culture change. For example, social conformities derived from traditional religious beliefs may be incongruent with the prescriptions of newly introduced norms, or cash-and-carry market economies may be in conflict with traditional ceremonial exchanges.

10. *Deprivation of social interaction.* Research on sensory deprivation shows that when individuals are deprived of stimulation from their environments there can be marked strains, to the point of serious mental breakdown.

The extreme of social isolation may be that experienced by persons who are exposed to "voodoo death," during which the "bewitched" individual's friends and relatives withdraw support from him and prepare for his funeral, believing that his death is imminent. Painful social isolation may be one of the most frequent stresses experienced by people in our complex North American scene.

11. *Stress of social interaction.* Most of the items listed involve types of social interactions that are stressful, at least in some circumstances. Along with these we must keep in mind the possible stresses of crowding. High levels of social interaction may be experienced as stressful by people even when the specific nature of the interaction includes nothing that is seen as negative.

On the other hand, in complex urbanized societies the stress of social interaction that we experience most is the high frequency of encounters with strangers, with whom we must transact business and successfully communicate without prior preparation.

All human activities, of course, involve people in stresses of various kinds. At the same time, humans, like other animals, are goal-oriented and tend to select means of attaining their goals in a manner that gives optimal "benefit" in the balance of gratifications over the physical and psychological costs. Humans do not, therefore, seek to *eliminate* stresses, but must try to *schedule* the psychological and physical demands on their systems to avoid chances of breakdown through wear and tear. However, human groups have also developed a wide variety of countermeasures against the stresses of life.

Cultural Mechanisms for Adapting to Stress

There are many "built-in" mechanisms that societies have developed to alleviate socially induced stress. In many mammalian groups, *territoriality* is a stress-reducing mechanism, for systems of spacing provide the means for avoiding, or bringing an end to, hostile interactions. *Patterns of dominance* also have stress-reducing aspects, and patterns of *defer-*

413

21.9 The grape harvest festival in Russia. (Inge Morath, Magnum)

21.10 For many North Americans the five o'clock cocktail hour is the major cure for the day's tensions. (Leonard Freed, Magnum)

ence and politeness serve to reduce the friction of social encounters.

Rituals of social solidarity reduce tension through reaffirming relationships among groups; and *vacations and holidays* offer relief from usual work routines. *Joking, playing, and laughter* are used in many kinds of situations as tension-reducing devices. Many writers have pointed out the importance of *magicoreligious beliefs and practices* for reducing the stresses of life, and *alcohol and narcotics* are widely used chemical modifiers of human behavior.

Unusual psychological states (including mental disorders) are among the most commonly cited indicators of individual psychic stress. At the same time, many psychologists and anthropologists have noted that these same phenomena can be mechanisms of escape from intolerable stress. The case of "wild man" behavior among the Gururumba of New Guinea is one example of the possible tension-reducing functions of special psychic states:

One day, in the late afternoon, I was sitting in the front door of our house talking to a group of children when Gambiri approached carrying a small bowl in one hand. When he stopped to listen, one of the children began asking him for food. Gambiri indicated he did not have any food, but as usual the child did not accept this first denial and snatched the bowl away to examine it for himself. There were further demands and further denials. Tempers rose and the child finally ran off with Gambiri's bowl with Gambiri chasing him.

A few minutes later Gambiri again appeared at the door. He was carrying a bow and a sheaf of arrows in one hand and a long-knife in the other . . . when he began rummaging about in our personal belongings . . . I asked what he was doing. He replied by demanding in a loud voice that I give back the bowl I had stolen from him. . . . Then he saw a plastic pot used as a toilet for one of our children and said in Neo-Melanesian, "There's my bowl. I can take it and throw it away in the forest. It is not heavy." By this time it was becoming clear that something was radically wrong. This was apparent from his aggressive behavior and from the agitated character of his actions. Someone said, "Gambiri ahaDe idizi Be" and someone else referred to him as "longlong," Neo-Melanesian for "crazy" or "insane." . . . In a short period of time (about an hour) his actions became known to a wide audience. It was not more than ten minutes after Gambiri was recognized as "longlong" that men who happened to be on the scene began calling out to other villages informing them of what was happening. . . .

During [the next phase] Gambiri acted out the pattern throughout the territory. . . . He moved hurriedly from place to place, ending up wherever his attacks led him. Once in a place, he would force his way into a house, demand some small item as his, stuff it into the stolen net bag, and engage in aggressive verbalizations or actions until diverted. He frequently made quick, assertive moves as if to attack other persons, and although most of these forays were not consummated with blows, he did occasionally strike someone. . . .

On the evening of this [third] day he ran into the forest and was not seen again until the next morning when he walked past the outer fringe of the village, without his net bag, and called to the men's house that he was going to a place on the other side of the Bismark Mountains near Bundi, a journey of at least two days, to collect pandanus nuts. . . .

Gambiri was not seen again for thirteen days. (NEWMAN, 1964:2–5)

Why did Gambiri go "longlong" and what happened to him? Philip Newman, the anthropologist who observed this instance of "nervous breakdown," pointed out that Gambiri, a married man in his mid-thirties with one small child and another on the way, was experiencing serious social and cultural pressure. Young men among the Gururumba incur heavy financial debts and social obligations in order to get married. To pay these off they must work hard and be successful in their economic activities, otherwise they will fall more deeply into debt and become economically dependent on other, more successful men.

As a result of the "temporary insanity" displayed by Gambiri he was able to redefine his social position and obligations within his social network. Because he had been "longlong" the people to whom he owed obligations no longer pressed for payment, and he no longer was required to meet the expectations demanded of ordinary persons in the community. He still contributed to village and kin group activities, but people did not pressure him to contribute beyond his meager means.

The case of Gambiri sounds familiar, for in some ways it resembles the syndrome of "nervous breakdown" found among some busy executives, overtaxed housewives, harassed students, and other people who find themselves under too much pressure and desperately seek relief from overwhelming burdens. A case that has remarkable similarities to that of Gambiri is that of a young social science professor

415

21.11 Shooting up with drugs is one of the more extreme reactions to the stresses and pressures of modern life. (Ian Berry, Magnum)

at a large university who fell further and further behind in his writing and research while he struggled to improve his teaching. He was also under pressure to carry out administrative duties in his department, and his family was putting pressure on him to "spend more time with the kids." As these accumulating pressures and expectations became too much for him, he became quite suddenly hyperactive and aggressive toward his family and some other persons, somewhat as Gambiri did.

Instead of being allowed to run off into the forest, however, this case of "wild man behavior" resulted in his being placed in a psychiatric hospital for a period of some weeks. He rapidly recovered and returned to his position at the university, where people ceased to put pressures on him and allowed him to find a new adaptation at lower levels of performance, at least for the time being.

If signs of psychological distress reflect the degrees of social and cultural pressures put on individuals, then we should expect that different types of sociocultural systems would be likely to have different patterns of mental illness and different parts of their populations "at risk." In some societies it may be the eldest sons who are especially under pressure; in our own society some segments of the older end

of the population appear to be experiencing significantly heightened levels of sociocultural stress. We must also keep in mind that individuals differ a great deal in their degrees of "inner strength," some of which may reflect biologically inherited, genetic foundations. The relationships, therefore, between mental illness and social and cultural systems and other factors are very complex.

Social Inequality and Mental Illness

We have already noted that servitude and severe inequalities are important sources of socially induced stress. In Gambiri's case his failure to meet his economic obligations and continuing subordinate status appear to be the precipitating causes of his temporary mental illness. In highly stratified societies we might expect to find the stresses of exploitation reflected in higher rates of mental illness among the exploited classes.

A. B. Hollingshead (sociologist) and F. C. Redlich (psychiatrist) carried out a large-scale study of psychiatric cases *in treatment* in the New Haven area of Connecticut in order to examine the relationship

Sacred and Secular Realms of Adaptation

of mental illness to social inequality. (Hollingshead and Redlich, 1958) They searched for all the psychiatric cases they could find in mental hospitals, in private physicians' care, and in other institutions. They divided up the total community into five socioeconomic or "social class" categories and found that there were significant differences among these socioeconomic classes in their rates of *treated* mental disorders: "For example, class I (the highest class) contains 3.1% of the community's population but only 1.1% of the pyschiatric cases. Class IV on the other hand includes 17.8% of the community's population, but contributed 36.8% of the psychiatric patients." (Hollingshead and Redlich, 1953:167) Table 21.1 shows the relationships of the psychiatric percentages to the population percentages in this study.

The Hollingshead and Redlich study is interesting because it not only demonstrates the differences in percentages of people in psychiatric care from different segments of the population, but it also shows that there are significant differences in the *types* of treatment. Treatment by psychotherapy (requiring intensive contact with psychiatrists and other specialists) was used in over 75 percent of the cases in the two highest social classes but diminished sharply in the lower classes and was found in only 16 percent of the cases in class V. More striking is the finding that more than 50 percent of the people in category V were receiving *no treatment whatsoever* in a community with well-developed, modern medical facilities.

Rural Marginality and Psychological Stress

It is frequently assumed that life in the rural areas of North America is more satisfying, more peaceful, and less stressful simply because it is far from the "rat race," the air pollution, and the other hazards of city life. On the other hand, many rural areas face severe economic problems coupled with high rates of migration out, especially of the young and able-bodied. Increasingly, the rural regions of the United States, especially those lacking in valuable resources, are reduced to economic and social marginality.

During the mid-1960s a group of anthropologists and psychologists from the University of Minnesota, including the authors, joined with the staff of a mental health clinic in northern Minnesota to study the psychological impact of economic marginality.

North Central Minnesota first experienced extensive White settlement and economic development around the turn of the century with the expansion of large-scale lumbering. Following the decline of the lumbering industry, many people turned to small-

Table 21.1: Socioeconomic Status and Psychiatric Patients in the New Haven Metropolitan Area

SOCIAL CLASS	NORMAL POPULATION[a]		PSYCHIATRIC POPULATION	
	No. of Cases	%	*No. of Cases*	%
I	358	3.1	19	1.0
II	926	8.1	131	6.7
III	2,500	22.0	260	13.2
IV	5,200	46.0	758	38.6
V	2,037	17.8	723	36.8
Unknown	345	3.0	72	3.7
TOTALS	11,422	100.0	1,936	100.0

[a]The "normal population" in this study was a 5 percent random sample of households in the community from the 1951 New Haven City directory. This random sample of the New Haven population was drawn in order to establish the percentages of persons assignable to the different social class categories. Socioeconomic class was established by means of an index based on occupational status, education, and neighborhood of residence.
Source: HOLLINGSHEAD and REDLICH, 1953:167.

Society and the Individual: Stresses and Responses

scale farming. However, the soil was poor and the growing season short. Frosts in late August sometimes decimated the crops, and the long, hard winters made animal husbandry a tedious occupation. The area has experienced a steadily worsening economic situation for several decades. Some small-scale lumbering continues, but the harvesting of second-growth pole timber is just as economically marginal as the farming activities.

21.12 Dilapidated housing is one aspect of poverty in a marginal rural area of Minnesota. (G. H. Pelto)

The northern Minnesota area can be labeled a "twilight zone of poverty." Although the median income of this population in the mid-1960s was only slightly over $3,000 per year, most families owned their own homes and had plenty of food. Many people grew at least a part of their own food supplies, and they got meat and fish from the forest and streams and lakes of the region. They did not spend as much for services as people in the cities, for they repaired and maintained their houses and much of their equipment themselves. Thus their $3,000–$4,000 per year went further than comparable city incomes. Nonetheless, people generally lacked many of the conveniences and luxuries associated with the American "mainstream" life style.

We selected a series of households in several different communities in order to get in-depth data about their social, cultural, and economic situations, as well as an assessment of their "psychological well-being." For the psychological data we used the Minnesota Multiphasic Personality Inventory (MMPI), partly because its usefulness as a "psychiatric inventory" was based on a complex standardizing procedure that was carried out in the state of Minnesota.

Psychiatrists in the mental health clinic had a strong impression that many of the people of the area showed signs of depression. That is, people who came for psychiatric help to the clinic often complained of lack of energy, feelings of pessimism, hopelessness, poor self-esteem, and other symptoms of depressive tendencies. Our "personality inventory" survey in the nonclinic populations bore out the mental health staff's observations. The people in general showed a noticeably higher tendency to give depressive responses on the MMPI questionnaire than the average Minnesota population.

Besides the general tendencies toward depressive reactions in this marginal population, we found that the *people who were the poorest in income and material goods showed greater tendencies toward depressive symptoms* than the people who were relatively more affluent. The second cluster of factors that appeared to be significantly related to depressive tendencies was "social marginality." We found that people with small families and with few relatives left in the area were more likely to show signs of psychological stress than those who had more kinsmen and friends about them.

One of the most important results was that people who reported considerable religious participation tended to be less depressed, with fewer psychiatric symptoms. "Religious participation" was not associated with any particular religious denomination but was found equally among Catholics, Lutherans, and the other Protestant denominations. Our measure of "religious involvement" included frequency of church attendance, statements about the importance of religion in their lives, membership in church organizations, and habits of daily prayer, grace at meals, and other items. We do not know exactly

Sacred and Secular Realms of Adaptation

which of the many facets of religious participation might be more important in buffering these people against psychological depression. It may be that their faith in a supreme being who will protect the individual against disaster in his present life, or bring a better life after death is the most important. Or it may be that the people are gaining social support from the congregation, the minister, and other personal involvements in their church. Or perhaps their resistance to depression comes from a philosophy that places less stress on material success and more on "living the good life." More likely, a combination of these different aspects of religious participation is the explanation for these results. In any case, it is clear that religiosity is an important element in the maintenance of psychological well-being in north central Minnesota.

In sorting out these several different factors affecting psychological well-being among the marginal people of northern Minnesota, we were struck with the importance of considering the entire *system* of contributing causes. No one of these factors by itself tells us very much about which people are likely to show psychiatric symptoms in the population. Only when we consider the economic factors, the social marginality, and the religious and other features in an interrelated system do we begin to approach an understanding of factors for and against psychological well-being in this kind of environment.

Male Chauvinism, Female Status, and Mental Illness

In keeping with the idea that a position of subservience or socioeconomic inferiority is likely to be psychologically stressful, we would expect special psychiatric problems among females in societies in which the subservience of women is strongly maintained.

The Zulu of southeast Africa appear to be an example of a strongly male-dominated society. As J. B. Loudon (1959) and others have described their daily life in the past and down to recent times, Zulu women have experienced very powerful social and cultural pressures:

Women are thus excluded altogether from any dealings with the preeminent economic and ritual activities—whether their own kin group or that of her husband.

On the other hand they are expected to carry out all the other economic activities of the household that have no ritual significance.

The daily life of the Zulu woman is thus most arduous, and her activities are little diminished even by pregnancy or the need to care for young children. In either case she merely has an added weight to carry with her on her household and agricultural tasks and expeditions. (LOUDON, 1959:355–356)

In spite of the strong male dominance, one of the most important ritual events, until about fifty years ago, was the Nomkubulwana ceremony, performed completely by women. This ritual was performed at the time of new crops to ensure fertility. It is interesting, then, that the ritual was a striking instance of "role reversal" in which women assumed some of the important features of male behavior and of male clothing. Their usually modest deportment was cast aside, and in the ritual the women acted out flagrantly obscene movements laced with profanity.

In the Zulu Nomkubulwana ritual, as in some other "rituals of rebellion," the participation of the women in behavior sharply different from that usually expected of them may act as a psychological catharsis. Now that this ceremony has not been performed much for several decades, what effects, if any, can be discerned among the Zulu women?

In recent times there has been a sharp increase, Loudon claims, in a specific form of psychogenic disorder that is much more common among women than among men. This disorder includes severe anxiety and other characteristics that European psychiatrists label "conversion hysteria." Loudon suggests that the problems exhibited by the Zulu psychiatric patients (including their dreams) suggest that the *ufufunyana* syndrome is at least in part produced by the pressures experienced by the females in their markedly deprived social status and that the increase in the incidence of this psychiatric syndrome is related to the fact that the cathartic ritual rebellion ceremony is no longer performed.

Identification, Social Mobility, and Psychological Stress

There is increasing evidence from a number of different kinds of research that a major type of psychological stress born of sociocultural processes

419

(naturally enough) comes from the thwarting of legitimate aspirations. Of course everyone's goals and aspirations are thwarted to some degree. Very, very few of us become millionaires, movie stars, presidents, or nationally known heroes. Expectations and aspirations are geared, however, to some kind of "fit" with the situations and perceptions of people's "reference groups." If everyone else in an individual's social network is satisfactorily employed at an income of $10,000 a year, then relatively unsatisfactory employment at $8,000 a year is frustrating because of obvious comparisons within one's peer group. The anthropologist-sociologist research team of S. Parker and R. Kleiner gathered data from a large sample of Black people in Philadelphia, with a total of over 1,000 mentally ill respondents and a comparable sample (1,489) drawn from the at-large Black community. The mentally ill sample was drawn from persons in treatment at both public and private psychiatric facilities during the period March 1, 1960, to May 15, 1961. The researchers examined a number of hypotheses concerning factors in mental disorder and found support for the general proposition that persons who are socially mobile (both upward and downward) tend toward higher rates of mental disorder than persons of stable social status. Parker and Kleiner noted that such social mobility tends to be associated with the loosening of ties to individual social networks and reference groups. They also found strong support for their hypothesis that mental illness is related to "goal-striving stress" as well as to more generalized "reference group discrepancy" (Parker and Kleiner, 1966).

The contribution of frustrated expectations to psychological problems is evident in the adjustment of Navajo Indian migrants to the city, according to research by Theodore Graves and his associates (1970). These researchers were particularly interested in examining *intra*group differences in drunkenness and drinking-related arrests, a serious problem for migrants.

The researchers note that the

> role of economic marginality in the migrants' adjustment problems is fundamental. . . . Repeatedly factors such as marriage, peer pressures, and a variety of personality variables make their primary contribution to the migrant's drinking problems, whether this contribution be positive or negative, when the migrant has a *poor and unstable income.* (Italics added, GRAVES, 1970:52)

Part of the team's conclusions include the key idea that:

> when goals are strongly held for which society provides inadequate means of attainment . . . the resulting means-goals disjunction produces pressures for engaging in alternative, often nonapproved adaptations, of which excessive drinking is one common form. . . . This means . . . that the anticipated rewards (goals) for engaging in socially approved behavior (means) are relatively low. The resulting disappointment and frustration leads to the selection of *other* courses of action (such as drunkenness) that may not be so highly approved but provide substitute rewards. (GRAVES, 1970:42–43)

Some of the indicators of "relative deprivation" that Graves and his associates found to be significant included relatively higher education (high school education); a low-paying job in the city after a higher-paying job on the reservation; a low-paying job compared to the father's higher-paying job; and other such discrepancies.

Does Rapid Social Change Equal Psychological Disturbance?

Many writers have suggested that sociocultural changes that result in a disintegration of the previous economic and cultural system lead to great increases in sociocultural and psychological stresses. The case of Indian communities within the United States is particularly clear, in terms of their increasing rates of suicide as well as other signs of psychocultural stresses. In the cases of some Indian communities most of the viable and interesting socioeconomic roles of the past are no longer relevant, and access to new "modern" and economic activities and social roles is extremely difficult. But is *all* sociocultural change and modernization psychologically disturbing and stressful, leading to increased rates of mental illness and other symptoms?

Answers to this question are difficult because a number of studies in different kinds of social contexts suggest that many different dimensions are involved in the psychiatric effects of social change. Most of the cases of sociocultural change and "modernization" that have been studied in terms of psychological impact have involved, at least to some

Sacred and Secular Realms of Adaptation

degree, dominant-subordinate socioeconomic relationships among ethnic and racial groups. In the case of sociocultural change among North American Indian populations, in most instances "modernization" includes the tightening of the net of dependency and economic marginality over the previously autonomous social and cultural system of the Indians.

In an attempt to sort out the effect of rapid social change, per se from the additional elements of marginalization, the case of the Manus in the Admiralty Islands is very instructive.

In 1953 Margaret Mead returned to the Manus peoples of the Admiralty Islands in the South Pacific, twenty-five years after her first fieldwork. The events of World War II had extensively disrupted and transformed the situation of the Manus Islanders. Their previously autonomous and relatively peaceful life was suddenly altered by the invasion of Japanese, Australian, and United States troops with their fantastic inventories of material equipment. The peoples of Oceania have experienced mind-boggling social change in connection with the war and events since then.

Although there are no "before and after" psychological data, Mead suggested that the people of Manus were adapting quite successfully to the rapid metamorphosis of their social system. They had in one fateful moment of cultural decision decided to cast the material paraphernalia of their religious system into the sea in favor of new religious practices (Christian), and they had, at the same time, decided to build their houses on dry land and abandon the pile villages jutting out into the bay. If sociocultural changes, as such, are psychologically disruptive to human beings, then surely the Manus peoples should all have been candidates for mental institutions. Margaret Mead found, however, that they were adjusting well and that perhaps the very precipitancy of the changes—the sort of total commitment to a new life style—enhanced the possibilities of psychological adjustment to the new social situation.

Mental Illness Among the Hutterites: Does the Communal Way of Life Prevent Psychiatric Disorder?

The Hutterite groups of the western United States and Canada have a religious communal system of living that provides each individual with adequate food, shelter, and other necessities, as well as the security of firm membership in a tight-knit social group. Some visitors to these colonies on the northern plains have said that the Hutterites have practically no mental illness. On the other hand, the self-denial and discipline necessary for maintenance of the Hutterite religious tenets are experienced as a psychic strain by at least some members of the colonies. Even the strict forbidding of aggressive tendencies might for some people be highly frustrating.

Control of impulses rather than expression is the rule. Enjoyment of food, drink, music, and sex are rather frowned upon, and are not spoken of publically. No

21.13 Cooperative work in a Hutterite kitchen. (John Williams, Magnum)

421

Table 21.2: Types of Psychiatric Cases in Selected Societies

Community or Region Studied	Total No. of Diagnosed Cases	Percent Schizophrenia	Percent Manic-Depressive	Percent "Other Disorders"
Hutterites	53	17	74	9
Formosa Chinese	76	57	17	26
Area in northern Sweden	107	87	2	11
Williamson County, Tennessee	156	27	26	47
Baltimore	367	43	11	46
Thuringia (Germany)	200	37	10	53

Source: Adapted from EATON and WEIL, 1955.

fighting or verbal abuse is permitted. A spirit of compromise, of giving in to one's opponent, is the accepted guide for interpersonal disagreements and frictions. It is expected that a Hutterite man will not get angry, swear, or lose his temper. (KAPLAN and PLAUT, 1956: 19–20)

Hutterites themselves recognize that mental illness does occur among their members. They consider such disorders to be trials of faith imposed by God (similar to the tests of faith experienced by Job in the Bible).

The sociologist-psychiatrist team of Joseph Eaton and Robert Weil carried out an extensive "casefinding" survey among the Hutterites during the early 1950s and found that there were, indeed, mentally ill among these people but that psychiatric symptoms were on the whole less extreme than those of the mentally ill in other populations. The preferred treatment was to keep them in their social group and maintain strong emotional support, with religious counseling and confession of sins, and to encourage them to work if they felt so inclined.

The researchers also found that the most "typical" or statistically usual mental breakdown among the Hutterites was quite different from the usual pattern in other European and North American communities. In most sectors of our Euro-American social system the most frequent type of serious mental breakdown is some form of schizophrenia, involving confusion of thought processes and emotions, violent outbreaks, and various other behavioral disturbances. Eaton and Weil found that the Hutterite

pattern of mental illness showed a much greater tendency toward "depressive" psychoses than is common in other populations.

When individual Hutterites experience serious psychocultural stress, their most frequent reaction is to feel guilty and depressed. The feeling of serious guilt and sinfulness is well recognized by the Hutterites, and they label it *anfechtung*, or "temptation by the Devil." Much of Hutterite psychotherapy is adjusted to the cleansing of guilt and sin, helping people to get rid of the "Devil's temptations." Their treatment of the mentally ill is apparently very successful, for despite the tendencies toward feelings of guilt and depression among Hutterites, suicide, the most extreme manifestation of aggression turned inward, is almost unknown.

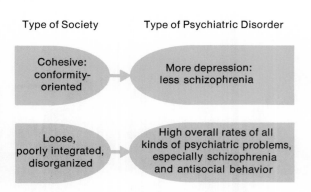

Type of Society	Type of Psychiatric Disorder
Cohesive: conformity-oriented	More depression: less schizophrenia
Loose, poorly integrated, disorganized	High overall rates of all kinds of psychiatric problems, especially schizophrenia and antisocial behavior

21.14 **Suggested relationship between type of social system and forms of mental illness.**

Sacred and Secular Realms of Adaptation

As can be seen from Table 21.2, the Hutterite pattern of mental illness contrasts sharply with that of both the modern urban scene (e.g., Baltimore) and the rural farm people in "typical" European and North American hinterlands. Many people in our rural regions live on isolated farmsteads and are not part of a cohesive social system. The impact of social isolation is evident in the high rate of schizophrenia compared to depressive psychoses in the north Swedish region. Figure 21.14 illustrates the general theory concerning types of psychosis suggested by Eaton and Weil in their conclusions about the Hutterites.

Cultural Patterning of Mental Illness: The Case of Windigo

Although there are many cross-cultural consistencies in the ways people adjust to or fail to adjust to social stresses, there are significant differences as well. In some societies people have developed fairly specialized ideas of psychiatric symptoms and there are quite clear ideas about "how to behave if one becomes mentally ill." The WINDIGO, or *wiitiko*, psychosis found among Chippewa, Cree, and other Indians in the subarctic areas of Central Canada is one example of a culturally patterned obsession. Windigo psychosis is characterized by cannibalistic impulses and delusions. Of the seventy-odd cases collected by Morton Teicher from travelers' accounts, missionaries' diaries, and other sources, forty-four actually involved some form of cannibalistic act. In the others the obsessed person either recovered or was killed, as in the following case reported by the explorer David Townsend in the late eighteenth century:

One morning a young man of about twenty years of age on getting up said he felt a strong inclination to eat his sister; as he was a steady young man, and a promising hunter, no notice was taken of this expression; . . . he said the same several times a day for a few days. His parents attempted to reason him out of this horrid inclination; he was silent and gave them no answer; his sister and her husband became alarmed, left the place and went to another camp. . . . His father and relations were much grieved; argument had no effect on him, and he made them no answer to their questions. The camp became alarmed, for it was doubtful who would be his victim. His father called

the men to a council, where the state of the young man was discussed, and their decision was, that an evil spirit had entered into him, and was in full possession of him to make him become a Maneater (a wiitiko). The father was found fault with for not having called to his assistance a Medicine Man, who by sweating and his songs to the Tambour and rattle might have driven away the evil spirit before it was too late. Sentence of death was passed on him, which was to be done by his father. The young man was called . . . [and] . . . informed of the resolution taken, to which he said, "I am willing to die"; the unhappy father arose and placing a cord about his neck strangled him, to which he was quite passive; after about two hours, the body was carried to a large fire, and burned to ashes . . . this was carefully done to prevent his soul and evil spirit which possessed him from returning to this world. (From DAVID TOWNSEND'S narrative, quoted in HALLOWELL, 1936: 1308–1309)

Several anthropologists and psychiatrists who have sought explanations for Windigo have pointed out that these northern Indian groups frequently experience serious food shortages and must cope with the ever-present threat of starving to death. This would appear to be a reasonable explanation except that Inuit also frequently face prospects of starvation, and they do not have cannibalistic compulsions, although they do have psychotic breakdowns. There is no way to reconstruct the origins of this psychological syndrome, but once the idea took hold the fact that starvation is a realistic fear among these people gave the obsession a realism that caught on and spread widely.

Nutritional Deprivation as a Source of Stress

The role of food in mental disturbances in extreme environments may go beyond psychological stress. The medical profession has recently become more interested in the possibility that various kinds of malnutrition and shortage of important vitamins may be implicated in mental disorder. Megavitamin therapy for treatment of mental illness is a subject of much debate, and it is possible that some nutritional factors play a role in psychiatric symptomology. The likelihood of malnutrition in subarctic and arctic conditions is very high, especially in the winter and early spring.

423

It is interesting that the "cure" for the Windigo psychosis was frequently dietary. Several reports on the Cree mention that the ingestion of melted bear grease brought about recovery from incipient Windigo possession. Vivian Rohrl (1970:97–101) has pointed out that high fat intake is particularly essential for effective adaptation to cold areas and that fat usually contains some crucial vitamins in addition to its significance as caloric intake. As Rohrl notes, "Most psychiatric diseases are remarkably influenced by the diet. As a general rule, diets high in protein and fat must also be better with respect to vitamins and other nutrients. These diets allow the natural recovery rate to emerge" (Rohrl, 1970:100, quoting A. Hoffer).

A nutritional factor has also been suggested in another unusual culturally patterned mental breakdown—the *pibloqtoq* disorder among the Inuit. This syndrome, for example among the polar Innit, shows itself in irritability and withdrawal from social interaction, followed by violent shouting, the tearing off of one's clothes, and running about, after which the subject may have convulsive seizures and then fall asleep.

Anthony F. C. Wallace (1961) has suggested that some of the features of *pibloqtoq*, especially the occurrence of muscular spasms and convulsive seizures, result from temporary calcium deficiency. Of course periods of malnutrition might well involve deficiencies in many other essential vitamins and minerals besides calcium. The focus on calcium deficiency is particularly indicated because the body needs vitamin D in order to utilize calcium, and that vitamin is very likely to be lacking in wintertime.

Recently Edward Foulks made an intensive medical and psychiatric study of ten Alaskans who had experienced *pibloqtoq* episodes. He found little support for the specific hypothesis of calcium deficiency. However, he did find abnormal *electroencephalograms* in three of the cases, as well as other signs of organic contributors. Most interestingly, *all ten* victims had experienced serious inner ear infections (*otitis media*), with some loss of hearing as well as other side effects. On the social and psychological side he found that all ten individuals had some serious social problems, for "All of these individuals at some point experienced the anxiety of being inadequate and helpless in maintaining a way of life that others in their village would find acceptable and admirable. They were insecure as to their identity" (Foulks, 1972:108). The *pibloqtoq* attacks seemed to reflect complex interactions of physiological factors (including possible dietary deficiencies) with especially negative or traumatic social histories.

Stresses and Responses: A Summary

The occasional stories of "wolf children," "gazelle boys," and other wild creatures raised outside human contact serve to remind us that the special features of our human way of life require a certain minimum network of interacting people as the life support system of each individual. A large part of the beautiful narratives people have created—both oral and written—have their meanings in the painful dilemmas that confront us all: we need each other, yet the demands of the social system with all its complex cultural norms and expectations put great strains on individuals.

The pressures of social interdependency weigh unevenly, for some societies demand levels of conformity and obedience that would drive other, more independent, peoples up the nearest wall. Training for these different situations begins in earliest childhood, and new demands and expectations dog our steps until the final hour. The first requirement of human coping is adaptation to the immediate social surroundings, and the network of cultural expectations gradually expands as the individual grows to adulthood. The bittersweet reciprocity between individual and society, between each self and all the others, has many outcomes, but these adaptations are never wholly without struggle. In all societies there are casualties.

In this chapter we have looked mainly at the psychic casualties, noting that some social contexts and environments take a heavier toll than others. All this is complicated by cultural differences in the definitions and treatment of the casualties. Here are some things to think about:

1. Some sociocultural environments are very stressful for individuals, whereas others are by comparison quite "benign."

2. Regardless of how secure and comfortable the

424

lives of some people might seem, all human societies produce some casualties in the form of people with identifiable mental illnesses.

3. Biological inheritance and other constitutional factors (including nutrition) may play a considerable part in some mental illness, but interpersonal stresses seem pervasive as contributing factors.

4. In most societies there are categories of persons who experience seemingly more stress and may be more "at risk" of mental impairment than others. But outcomes of the stresses vary, depending on the cultural defense mechanisms available.

5. The more exploited portions of complex populations often run greater risks of psychic problems: in male-dominated societies it may be the females; in highly stratified societies it may be the bottom rungs of socioeconomic status; in societies that emphasize personal social mobility it may be the people with thwarted expectations.

6. Socioeconomic success and high prestige do not purchase freedom from the stresses of society, though the nature of the demands on individuals of high status may take a different shape, and the treatment of casualities may be markedly different from the therapies practiced among the poor.

7. In societies very different from our own it may be extremely difficult for "Western-trained" observ-

ers to identify the actual stress points, symptoms, and sufferers of cultural pressures. In any case, very little in the way of reliable, quantified cross-cultural research on mental illness has been produced, though descriptions of individual "cases" are available from a wide variety of different kinds of populations.

8. In many societies mental illness is not considered a separate category of sickness because most diseases and ailments exhibit both mental and physical components.

9. The experiences of childhood have long-lasting effects on individual personalities, and in different social and physical environments the forms of psychic conflicts can vary as a reflection of those early patterns of rewards and punishments.

10. Whether or not mental problems are recognized as a separate category of experience, all societies have healers whose therapeutic practices appear to have effects on the mental well-being of their patients. The "nonmodern" strategy that treats nearly all illness as essentially psychobiological appears to have been fairly adaptive for many peoples, and there is no doubt that various peoples' treatment of illnesses have been successful in improving the "peace of mind" and adaptive resolve of their clients.

425

Society and the Individual: Stresses and Responses

22

The Maintenance of Health: Disease, Diet, and Medical Practice

Other than the quest for food, the struggle for maintenance of a sound body and mind has perhaps been the major adaptive concern of humans from earliest times. The importance of good health is evident in the fact that a very large part of religious activity is concerned with the maintenance of health—hence, the term *medicine man* is a rather apt label for designating the major religious-magical practitioners in many societies. In many societies religious ceremonials are to a great extent devoted to protection from illness, and a common reason for seeking the services of a shaman is to offset the mysterious and unpredictable effects of sickness and accident.

Until recent times, diseases and injuries brought death at an early age. In addition to high rates of infant mortality in most preindustrial populations, the average life span was much shorter than today. The age at which an individual died can usually be determined to within a few years by examination of the teeth, the sutures in the skull, and other features of the skeleton. Table 22.1 gives some of the evidence concerning the short life spans of some earlier populations.

It is interesting to note that among most premodern populations the life expectancies for males were somewhat greater than those for females, quite the opposite of the situation in modern populations. The difference is probably explained by the considerable risks that females encounter in childbirth. Table 22.2 shows the mean age of death for adults in some selected populations that illustrate this point.

Health and Illness Among Hunter-Gatherers

The life expectancies shown in the tables are certainly short by modern standards, but we should point out that the life expectancies of hunting and gathering peoples have not been much different from those of food producers until *very recent* times. The chances of a newborn's living to "a ripe old age" were very slim indeed until the nineteenth century. If we judge from their respective longevities, hunting and gathering peoples probably enjoyed at least as much bodily health as food producers in most premodern societies. In some respects their chances of good health may have been better than those of many food-producing peoples. Among the

22.1 Drainage ditches were one of the many public health features developed by the Inca empire, although open water such as this can also be a source of infectious disease. (Sergio Larrain, Magnum)

Table 22.1: Life Spans of Early Populations

	PERCENTAGE OF PERSONS DEAD BY THE AGE OF		
Group	30	40	50
Neanderthals	80	95	100
Cro-Magnon	61.7	88.2	90
Mesolithic	86.3	95.5	97
Tepe Hissar	48.3	78.9	99.3
Anglo-Saxons (Caister)	57.4	81.8	97.5

Source: WELLS, 1964:177.

present-day Kalahari Bushmen (1963–1965), for example, in a group numbering 466 persons there were 46 individuals who were over sixty years old. Thus at least some hunting and gathering populations in favorable environments may have maintained a level of health that permitted a life span longer than that of most cultivators. The people of the Aleutian Islands are another interesting example of longevity, for records in the early nineteenth century showed that a considerable proportion of the Aleuts were at least fifty years of age at the time of death, and there were a number of individuals who lived to be nearly a hundred years old! (Laughlin, 1968:242).

Nomadic hunting peoples have often maintained more balanced diets than have sedentary people. They usually get enough meat to have a high-protein diet much of the time, and the meat protein is usually supplemented by such high-protein sources as nuts, seeds, and fish. In the warmer parts of the world, starvation is a rare occurrence. Among the

Table 22.2: Mean Age at Death of All Adults Who Attained at Least the Age of 18 Years

Group	Male	Female
Chalcolithic Anatolians	35.8	27.9
Anglo-Saxons (Norfolk)	38.1	30.4
Early Texas Indians	41	33.9
Ancient Romans	33.4	28.6
Modern British	70.3	75.6

Source: WELLS, 1964:179.

arctic peoples, such as the Inuit, on the other hand, starvation has been quite frequent—sometimes whole populations have starved to death when the weather was extreme and no hunting could be done.

Accidents of drowning, falls, exposure to extremes of cold and heat, and attack by animals are serious threats to health in some hunting and gathering populations. Snake bites as a cause of death have been frequent among Australian Aborigines. Attacks by other kinds of animals are apparently rare in almost all parts of the world. To the urbanized European the jungles of Africa's Congo seem full of dangers, but Colin Turnbull has commented on the relatively low incidence of accidents among the Pygmies. He does report occasional falls from trees, attacks by animals, falling on a spear, bee stings, and snake bites as health hazards (Turnbull, 1965).

The low population densities and open-air living of hunting-gathering groups tend on the whole to reduce the possibility of virulent epidemics and plagues such as have swept through settled Eurasian populations time and again through the centuries. Food gatherers do not remain in one place long enough to accumulate infestations of rats, mice, lice, and other disease carriers. Their food and water supplies are generally less contaminated by human habitation than is true in most settled populations. Of course the kinds of infections and diseases found among peoples in the tropics are much different from those of temperate and arctic regions. People of desert environments are threatened by fewer infectious diseases and parasites than are people living in wetter areas.

Diseases of Settled Life

Sedentary life in the villages of cultivating peoples increases the dangers of disease in several important ways:

1. Almost all domesticated animals can act as hosts for bacterial parasites, as well as for lice, fleas, and other parasites that are themselves the carriers of serious illness. The scourge of typhus fever, for example, is caused by a tiny bacillus called *Rickettsia*, which spends a good deal of its lifetime in the bodies of lice, fleas, and rats. The *Rickettsia* is carried from place to place by rats and is transmitted from one rat to another by fleas. But the rat fleas can transmit typhus to humans, and then the typhus

427

is spread from person to person by human lice. (When we consider the great human achievements of animal domestication we usually think of all those wonderful food animals and beasts of burden, momentarily forgetting that our sedentary food producing civilization has also resulted in the "domestication" of immense numbers of rats, mice, and other creatures of dubious value—living in our houses and barns and other buildings, eating our food, and from time to time biting our children.)

2. Accumulated human wastes and garbage are loaded with many disease-producing agents, from which flies and other insects can carry their dangers directly back to humans—for example, by contaminating food supplies. Of course water supplies are even more quickly and thoroughly contaminated by the waste products of sedentary humans.

3. The clearing of lands for cultivation, including the cutting down of the forests, and the use of irrigation systems greatly increased the numbers of mosquito- and fly-borne infections such as malaria, relapsing fever, and sleeping sickness. Schistosomiasis, a disease carried by snails infected with schistosomes (blood flukes), is an endemic problem in many African irrigation areas. The schistosome-bearing snails like the quiet, slow, warm waters of the secondary and tertiary canals and ditches in irrigation areas. Thus some of our environmental modifications related to agriculture have produced just the sort of environmental conditions favoring infectious disease as well.

4. Large human settlements produce disease reservoirs large enough to maintain some infectious diseases such as typhoid fever, measles, and smallpox. These diseases ordinarily do not maintain themselves for long periods of time in other animals and require a certain minimum population density to perpetuate themselves.

5. Sedentary peoples accumulate extra clothing, various possessions, and permanent reusable bedding, all of which provide a happy environment for infestations of worms, body parasites, and a variety of bacteria as well. The habit of wearing a lot of clothing further contributes to the germ-carrying capacity in our settled life styles.

6. In many sedentary communities water becomes such a precious· and scarce resource that bathing becomes practically obsolete and antisocial. These effects became most notable with the rise of European cities and the squalor of medieval living conditions.

Many human diseases leave no trace in skeletal materials, so that we have no idea what their history might have been in those populations of the past that lack written records. The ravages of infectious diseases appear early in written histories, however, so we may surmise that a variety of bacterial and viral infections had been around on the face of the earth for a long time before anyone got the opportunity to write about their fearful destructiveness.

For those diseases that leave their marks in human bones, on the other hand, there are some interesting historical trends. It is noteworthy that some of the most striking deficiency diseases that have afflicted recent groups are extremely rare in the skeletal records. For example, rickets was scarce until city life, especially the crowded and sunless urban life of European peoples, brought about conditions conducive to a severe vitamin D deficiency. Professor Calvin Wells, M.D. and anthropologist, says of the history of rickets that:

It is preeminently a disease of the twilight, the perpetual twilight of dark tenements and city slums. As long as human beings huddle in ill-ventilated basements where rag-hung, grime-crusted windows keep out whatever light drifts through the smoke-laden murk of factory chimneys far above them, there, inevitably, rickets will be found. It is a disease of infants and children, and its cauldron is the teeming soot-choked city of the Industrial Revolution. Only in the last two generations have changing social customs and the advance of medical science slaked its onslaught from the high peak of the nineteenth century until it is now on the way to join such other dead diseases as the green sickness (chlorosis), the dancing mania (tarantism), and "the vapours." . . .

. . . constant sunshine in the Nile Valley combined with the dietary habits of the people was powerfully prophylactic and throughout the long corridor of Egyptian history human cases were extremely rare. Under the somber skies of higher latitudes, where a swaddle of clothing muffled out the light, we should expect it to be more lavish. It [rickets] was scarce at first but from the Neolithic period onwards a trickle of cases seeps out of Norway, Sweden, and Denmark until with the late Middle Ages the disease becomes plentiful, at least in cities, across all northern and central Europe. (WELLS, 1964:116–117)

428

Tuberculosis is another disease that leaves its traces in the bones, and it has been identified in various long-dead populations. Some medical authorities believe that tuberculosis is the oldest of the specific infections that can be diagnosed and identified in written and unwritten materials. It was described by the Greek physician Hippocrates and is identifiable from bones of at least Neolithic age. Although tuberculosis was among the diseases that spread widely and quickly in New World populations after White contact, some skeletons that were laid in the ground long before Columbus discovered America show signs of this disease. Like many other diseases, it was probably endemic in many populations in both the Old and New Worlds. But new and more virulent forms were introduced by White people to the Indians and the Inuit as part of a veritable plague of new diseases that rapidly killed off a large portion of the American Indian population in the first two centuries after Columbus's voyages.

The total population of the New World before the coming of White people has been estimated from 8 or 9 million up to (probably much exaggerated) 90–110 million. Most of the population was concentrated in the two areas of greatest cultural development—the Mesoamerican area (mainly Mexico and Guatemala), with perhaps 12 to 15 million persons, and the Inca Empire region of Andean South America, with about 6 million people (Sanders and Price, 1968:74–97). These areas of dense population were the ones that the Spanish took over quickly and in which the newly introduced European diseases (measles, influenzas of several types, smallpox, new types of tuberculosis, typhoid fever, and many others) quickly became virulent epidemics. Long before these epidemics had run their full course, the population of Mesoamerica had been reduced to an estimated 3.5 million persons—more than two thirds of the population had been wiped out in the first 150 years of colonial rule (population figures from Moreno, 1965:263).

As a general rule, the older the disease in a human

1520   **First smallpox epidemic brought by a sailor on Cortez's ship (Cortez landed at Vera Cruz, March 1519). Some estimates say that 50 percent of the population of New Spain died of this "great leprosy."**

1531   **"Tepitonzahuapl"—"the small leprosy," probably measles.**

1545   **According to the friar Geronimo de Mendieta, 150,000 died in Tlaxcala, 100,000 in Cholula, and similar proportions in other provinces. Symptoms: congestion, fever, bloody stools, blood from the nostrils. Zinsser believes this was typhus.**

1564   **Another decimating epidemic of undeterminable nature.**

1576   **Another epidemic like the 1545 disease.**

1588   **Typhus, especially in the valley of Toluca.**

1595   **Measles, mumps, and (typhus?).**

The Marqués de Varinas, who wrote a description (in 1685) of the effects of the 1630–1633 epidemic, estimated that only 20,000 Indians remained of over 2 million who had inhabited a region of Mesoamerica. This estimate suggests a depopulation ratio of 100 to 1.

From 1870 to 1950 the Ona of Tierra del Fuego suffered a depopulation of about 50 to 1 over the eighty-year period. Their population has been estimated to have been as high as seven thousand to nine thousand in 1871.

The European invaders knew that they had significant advantages in "germ warfare," for as the biologist René Dubos has noted:

The Europeans soon became aware of the fact that smallpox was one of their most effective weapons against the Indians and they did not hesitate to spread the infection intentionally by means of contaminated blankets, always on the pretext that it helped to destroy the enemies of the faith. God is always on the side of the strong battalions, even when they are made up of microbes. (DUBOS, 1959:229)

429

The Maintenance of Health: Disease, Diet, and Medical Practice

population, the milder its form. That is, death-dealing pestilences and plagues kill off large parts of the population only when they are relatively new and the receiving population has had little chance to develop immunities. In time people develop at least partial immunities to diseases that have been present a long time, and there is evidence that the diseases themselves become transformed. A microorganism that kills all its hosts will die itself, so the most "successful" bacteria, viruses, and other parasites are those that permit their hosts to live on to another day. By this logic, the microorganism that causes the common cold must be the most successful of all disease entities. Diseases such as measles, influenza, and scarlet fever were once death-dealing and much-feared sicknesses, but over the centuries their potency has diminished.

On the other hand, some diseases occasionally develop new and startling destructive powers even after they have been present for a considerable time. Some medical theorists believe that syphilis had been endemic in both Old World and New World populations for a long time before it developed a new and frightening destructive power early in the sixteenth century. As this "rejuvenated" disease swept through populations in Europe, it *seemed* like a totally new disease. A number of populations, however, have been found to have endemic forms of syphilis with little external sign of illness. Some Guatemalan Indian people, for example, show a relatively high percentage of positive presence of syphilis spirochetes but little reaction to the microorganisms.

Still other diseases have caused high mortalities and then apparently disappeared. Between 1485 and 1551 there were several epidemics of the dreaded "sweating sickness" in England and nearby areas of Europe. Many people died and the disease was feared as much as the smallpox and the plague. But it disappeared completely in less than a hundred years and has apparently never recurred. Very possibly the microorganisms of "sweating sickness" live on in some milder form in present-day populations.

22.2 Dental arch and skull of "Rhodesian Man," showing the severity of his dental problem. (Courtesy of the American Museum of Natural History)

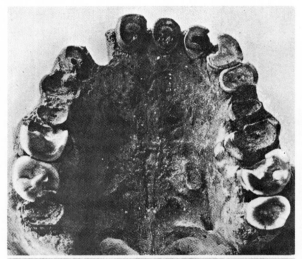

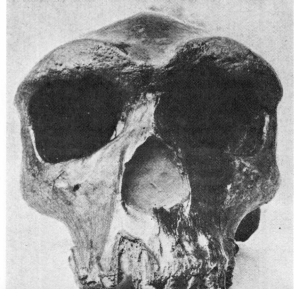

The Perennial Toothache

For there was never yet philosopher that could endure the toothache patiently. (SHAKESPEARE)

One of the more famous toothaches in prehistory is that of Rhodesian man, a Neanderthal-like fossil. This poor fellow must have lived out his last days in an agony of toothache and mastoid infection. He was not, however, the first human to suffer from serious tooth decay, for dental cavities have been found in the teeth of South African *Australopithecus* fossils perhaps a million years old. However, *rates* of tooth decay among earlier peoples appear to have been markedly lower than those of recent

430

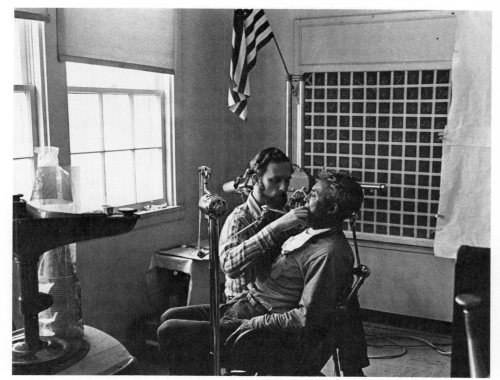

populations. There is, of course, considerable variation. For example, Indians in prehistoric California appear to have had rather high rates of tooth decay (about 25 percent of the skeletons have some tooth cavities), which sharply contrast with extremely low rates of tooth decay among the buffalo hunters of the Plains such as the Sioux. Some populations of maize growers in the New Mexico area show evidence of tooth decay in 75 percent of the prehistoric population. In general, flesh eaters appear to have had fewer tooth problems than people who eat lots of carbohydrates. Other cultural factors also have significant effects on dental health. People such as the Inuit used their teeth a great deal for all kinds of work with leather, bone, and other materials. This kind of activity has beneficial effects on the teeth and gums, up to a point, but heavy pressure on the teeth can cause cracks and other damage leading to increased danger of abscesses.

In contemporary populations the effects of modernization are sometimes strikingly evident in the rapid deterioration of teeth as people develop a taste for candy and other sugar-loaded foods. A survey of 422 Guatemalan schoolchildren aged four to six showed an average of 2.4 cavities per child, whereas their older brothers and sisters aged thirteen had an average of about 1.5 cavities per child. These rates were considered exceptionally low in the light of the serious malnutrition in many Guatemalan Indian communities. The unexpectedly low rate of cavities appears to be best explained by the fact that these children had had very little contact with refined carbohydrates (Scrimshaw and Tejada, 1970: 203–225).

The Same of Northern Europe have in earlier times been famed for their healthy teeth. Studies of Same skeletal materials from the eighteenth century showed a rate of cavities as low as 1.5 percent of the total number of teeth. This compares with Danish teeth from the Middle Ages with about 6 percent cavities and other populations of Northern Europe of that period who approached 10 percent cavities.

431

The Maintenance of Health: Disease, Diet, and Medical Practice

The diet of Same in former times was very heavily based on meat and fish with extremely low proportions of carbohydrates, whereas now they have adopted much greater use of refined carbohydrates in their cooking, along with candy, soda pop, and other sugar-flavored pleasures. The results are striking. Recent studies of Same in some areas show such high rates of tooth decay that the investigator described it as a "dental catastrophy." In some boarding schools children between the ages of seven and sixteen have averages of as high as 85 percent of all teeth with cavities. In the exceedingly short period of time of one or two generations, the diet of the Same has changed drastically, and so has the number of toothaches.

Food, Nutrition, and Health

From the data we have reviewed thus far, it seems likely that greater dependence on cereal grain crops and other high carbohydrate foods has undermined the health adaptations of food-producing populations, unless they are able to maintain a balance between meat animals and their relatively low-protein crops. The production of wheat, barley, potatoes, and other vegetables and cereals yields many more "calories per acre" than does the keeping of livestock, so that only societies with *relatively* low population densities can afford to eat a good deal of meat. Of course, wealthy communities can trade for meat supplies or other food supplies from other areas. Modern American middle-class populations in urban areas eat plenty of meat imported from the wide-open spaces of the underpopulated Midwest and western regions of North America.

For millions of people in India, Southeast Asia, China, and much of Latin America, meat protein is too expensive to play much part in the daily diet. In some areas fish provide a more than adequate source of protein, especially among coastal and island peoples. In still other areas various nuts and seeds provide good sources of protein.

22.4 **Fishing adds an important protein supplement to the diet of many agricultural peoples. In Mexico (P. J. Pelto), in Egypt (Elliot Erwin, Magnum), and in East Africa (Bruno Barbey, Magnum).**

Sacred and Secular Realms of Adaptation

Some societies with relatively meager sources of animal foods can get adequate protein nutrition from special combinations of protein-containing vegetable foods. This is especially true among Middle American populations where the combination of maize and beans, both of which contain incomplete proteins, taken together results in fully adequate protein intake because the maize and the beans complement each other in their protein composition. Many anthropologists and historians have argued that the Aztec, Maya, and Inca civilizations of the Americas could not have been developed if these people had not had unusually good sources of vegetable proteins.

Some peoples of the world maintain high-protein diets through the intake of dairy products—milk, cheese, yogurt, butter, and eggs. High dependence on dairy (and the associated poultry) products is especially characteristic of some regions in Northern Europe. Although people like the Danes, the Swiss, and some of the cattle-keeping peoples of East Africa may keep their livestock alive and draw off the proteins in milk products, the maintenance of the animals still requires relatively large acreage. In "calories per acre" dairy products cost more than cereal grains and other vegetable foods.

Social Stratification and Nutrition

In addition to changes in the types of foods available, the Neolithic revolution and its aftermath, as we have noted, brought about increasing social inequalities for larger and larger numbers of humankind. Food sharing has been so pervasive in most simpler societies that for the most part everybody had approximately the same diet. Even in societies with incipient stratification, such as is widespread in the islands of the South Seas and New Guinea, differences of social status between "big men" or chiefs and the ordinary population have not usually been accompanied by marked differences in access to food.

The changes of dietary habits that came about in connection with the growth of stratified societies were themselves very complex, but a major fact of life of these social systems was the gradual development of political means by which the more privileged classes were able to extract taxes, tribute, and

rents from the working and peasant populations, gradually undermining both the diet and the general health of the commoners. Deterioration of diet and health standards in agricultural societies is a result not simply of greater population densities but of serious imbalances in access to the available foods and other resources. William Haviland has argued that such a process played a part in the decline and fall of the Mayan civilization.

In the Early Classic period (about 250–550 A.D.) the average Mayan male in the large community of Tikal was about 165 centimeters in stature. Then in Late Classic times, Haviland finds, there was a marked reduction in stature to an average of about 157 centimeters, which is not much bigger than some groups of Pygmies in Africa. He argues that this reduction in stature was due to an increasingly poor diet, brought about by the greater population densities plus the growth of a complex, stratified social system. While the *average* stature of the population was declining, the ruling class people *gained* in physical height, averaging about 170 centimeters. Haviland suggests that the average life span of the privileged people compared to that of the commoners showed some similar differences, reflecting the privileged population's greater access to food and health resources. (Haviland, 1967:316–325).

Nutrition and Health in Modern Times

In connection with the Same example above, we noted that one of the more predictable and consistent effects of "modernization" in previously non-industrialized societies is the great increase in tooth decay caused by dietary changes. In some cases dietary changes are not totally detrimental to all aspects of health, especially in situations in which modernization has brought general *diversity* of food resources because of the importation of "foreign" products, supplementing traditional local foods. Throughout much of Northern Europe, for example, a large number of new vegetable crops have been introduced in recent centuries, probably improving the overall diet of many peoples—even while great increases in sugar usage have had obvious deleterious effects on the teeth.

Recent research in northeast Brazil illustrates how

433

22.5 Modern drive-ins have significant effects on North American diets. (Bruce Davidson, Magnum)

technological "modernization" can have serious detrimental effects on a population. Because of the dryness of the climate much of the region had been devoted to ranching and to small-scale farming until changes in the world market for heavy twine made from the sisal plant brought a rapid spread in the cultivation of this cash crop during the 1950s. It is a hardy crop and requires little tending, but the

22.6 New religious movements in North America are in the forefront of change in dietary habits, especially in the spread of vegetarian and health food ideas. (Dennis Stock, Magnum)

stripping away of the outer part of the sisal to get at the commercially valuable fibers is a hard job even though it is done with a diesel-driven leaf-stripping machine. During the 1950s and 1960s a large number of these decorticating machines were introduced into Baía, the major state of northeastern Brazil. Daniel Gross (1970) studied the impact of this new technology and new economic activity in northeastern Brazil. He found that the conversion of small-scale household economies to dependence on sisal production results in a very high demand for nutrition intake for the male worker (he needs about five thousand calories a day), and the marginal receipts from the sisal sales do not permit sufficient high-nutrient food for the worker unless there are cutbacks in the caloric intakes of the women and the children. Height and weight studies among the children of the subsistence farmers show that the recent years of economic and technological development have been paid for in part through decreases in the nutrition and health status of a significant part of the population (Gross and Underwood, 1971; Gross, 1970).

The advent of cash cropping in many parts of the world is likely to lead, at least temporarily, to serious nutrition and health problems. The cash crops frequently require massive diversion of energy from growing subsistence foods to the time-consuming cultivation of plants for cash.

The pattern goes something like this:

1. Before the coming of the "new economy" the local population's main concentration of effort (and land) is on growing food for domestic purposes.
2. The introduction of a cash crop is attractive first to those few wealthier families who have land to spare—they make some extra money.
3. Other people follow suit, sometimes with the help of government loans or other inducements, and plant part of their slim acreage in the cash crop, hoping that they will manage to get enough to eat from the rest of their traditional planting.
4. The needs for cash increase, in part because of food shortages and the necessity to *purchase* additional food, so *more* of the precious land is planted in the cash crop in order to pay the bills.
5. Often the cycle results in the abandonment of subsistence farming in favor of purchasing food from the stores.

22.7 **Skull from Peru showing trephination.** (Courtesy of the American Museum of Natural History)

The new dependence on purchased food supplies in exchange for the cash from commercial agriculture works well as long as the world market prices for the product (e.g., sisal, sugar from cane, cotton, and coffee) remain high. But the instabilities of world market prices for these products sooner or later put the marginal farmers into deep trouble. As the world market prices dip lower, they find they cannot pay their loans, and inevitably there is a cutback on the purchases of food at the stores. Frequently, as in the Brazilian example, the women and the children suffer most from this loss of nutritional independence.

The Search for Health

Just as some evidence about bygone diseases and other threats to health can be found in the skeletal remains and other traces left by the ancients, there are also clues that give us a glimpse into ancient medical practices. For example, dental work, including some fairly fancy gold bridges, have been found among the Etruscans. One of the most dramatic and well-documented ancient medical practices is that of TREPHINATION, which consists of cutting one or more holes in the skull as a treatment for head injuries. Precise directions for this major operation were given by Hippocrates and later added to by medical men such as Celsus (about 42 B.C.–37 A.D.) and Galen (130–201 A.D.). (Galen claimed that the special trephination instrument he had developed was so safe that no damage would result "even if the surgeon is half asleep" [Wells, 1964:142].) Some of the best-known examples of clearly successful trephination of human skulls come from ancient Peruvian skeletons. The surgery was often performed on heads broken by slingshots and the notorious star-headed maces that the Inca peoples and their predecessors used so effectively.

Evidence of the success of a trephining operation is generally quite unequivocal. If the patient lives, the edges of the bone begin to knit back over the hole. If the patient does not recover, the hole resulting from trephination remains sharp and unhealed, just as the ancient surgeon's knife left it. Perhaps the most successful trepanners were the ancient Peruvians, who may have had a recovery rate of 75 percent in their operations. Some of those skulls have been found with several holes representing operations at different times.

Successful trephination of human skulls appears to date from at least early Neolithic times. It is curious that people in ancient times developed this particular surgical skill, whereas the rest of their surgical and medical knowledge remained rudimentary. The amputation of fingers and occasionally of larger sections of limbs is testified to by Stone Age materials, but other evidence of any high art of surgery in ancient times is lacking.

The ancient Egyptians are supposed to have had medical practitioners of great fame, as commented on by such well-known roving reporters as Homer (about 1000 B.C.) and Herodotus some five hundred years later, both of whom spoke of Egyptian physicians as among the best in the world and of the population of Egypt as being particularly healthy. Inscriptions dating back to nearly 3000 B.C. mention physicians and dentists, including such exotic ones as "shepherd of the anus."

After the ancient Egyptians, the Greeks assumed prominence in medical matters, particularly through the work of Hippocrates (although there were a number of other famous Greek physicians). The medical knowledge and sophistication of the Greeks was remarkable and probably unsurpassed by more recent medical people until the Renaissance. Al-

435

22.8 Blood-sucking leeches were used to cure illness in ancient Egypt. (Elliot Erwitt, Magnum)

though the Greeks had some interest in gods and other supernatural influences on health and illness, the medicine of Hippocrates and the other Greek physicians was to a considerable degree based on a rational, naturalistic approach. Apollo had been regarded as the god of disease and healing in earlier times, but in the fifth century B.C. he was replaced by Asclepius and that famous medical symbol—the staff and holy snake. Numerous healing temples were built in honor of Asclepius, where patients were treated in part through supernatural intervention. Parallel to this religion-based medicine was the naturalistic observation of different diseases and discourses and experiments with various treatments. At least three different "schools" were well known in Greek medicine, and the Hippocratic school was the most important of these. Some fifty to seventy books that are attributed to Hippocrates were proba-

bly the collected works of a number of different men who aligned themselves for the most part with a Hippocratic orientation, although the writings also show influences from the other schools of medicine.

The basic philosophy of the Hippocratic physicians of ancient Greece emphasized treatment of the "whole individual" rather than focusing on some special part of the body. Disease was considered to be caused by disharmony among the "humors" in the body, and health was to be restored through the reestablishment of bodily balances—especially through manipulation of the diet.

After Hippocrates and a line of other well-known physicians, the different schools of Greek medicine were brought together in a unified synthesis by Galen of Pergamum (130–201 A.D.). He had studied medicine at Smyrna and Alexandria and returned to his home town to become a physician to gladiators. Later he gained fame as a physician and lecturer in Rome and became the physician of the emperor-philosopher Marcus Aurelius.

The medical contributions from Roman times

Sacred and Secular Realms of Adaptation

include some very important public health measures, including the magnificent aqueducts, sewage systems, and bathing places. Some of the Roman architects accepted the hypothesis that malarial fever was produced by small creatures that came up out of the swamps. They therefore planned some of their building programs to prevent malarial invasions.

The health practices and medical knowledge of the Greeks and the Romans were in many ways superior to the health adaptations of medieval Europe. Gradually, medical practice and study fell into the hands of the priests, and health maintenance and concepts of illness came again to be riddled with magical and religious practices. With some exceptions the early Christian priests were much more concerned with matters of the soul than they were with bodily ills. Disease came to be seen as punishment for sins, possession by the devil, or the result of witchcraft. Therapeutic methods for curing then naturally called for penitence and prayers to saints for intercession. Curing illness in this system of medicine was more the miraculous work of the deities than the operation of natural processes.

Every society has developed its own theory of illness and system of curing. Many local traditions have been strongly influenced by the medical systems of the great centers—in Greece, China, India, and the Middle East—as cultural beliefs and practices spread widely with invading armies, traders, visiting scholars, and other agents of contact. On the other hand, there are many societies that developed and maintained their own systems relatively intact until recent centuries.

In a great many societies around the world—

22.9 The oldest medical amphitheater in existence. Padua, Italy. (Lessing, Magnum)

among them the Chukchee, Inuit, Tungus, and other Siberian and North American groups—it was believed that illness is caused by evil spirits, the magical intrusion of evil substances by "black magic," or through "soul loss," in which the spirit of a sick individual leaves the body, wanders away, and gets lost, causing the person to fall ill. When a person became ill, he consulted a shaman for help. The shaman entered a trance (often induced by drugs) and embarked on a dangerous journey, most often in quest of information about the wandering spirit of his ailing patient. Sometimes the object of the journey was simply to locate the "lost soul," but more often effective therapy required propitiating

The Invention of the Water Closet

That classic triumph of modern plumbing—the water closet—was apparently invented by a poet, Sir John Harrington, who included it in an appendix to his *Metamorphosis of Ajax* under his butler's name. Henry Sigerist reports that Queen Elizabeth "was impressed by the new invention and had it installed in Richmond Palace, 'with a copy of the *Ajax* hanging from the wall'" (SIGERIST, 1943:37). The water closet was a great advance over earlier plumbing arrangements but could not be applied on a large scale until the water systems and sewer complexes were developed in the nineteenth century. Actually, sewage disposal systems including "inside" toilet facilities appear to have been developed in ancient Egypt and in the early civilizations of the Indus River, but these sanitation arrangements had no influence on European practices.

437

22.10 Kwakiutl shamans. (Courtesy of the American Museum of Natural History)

Ojibwa of Canada and the Great Lakes states had a curing society called the Midewiwin. Ruth Landes, in her study of *Ojibwa Religion and the Midewiwin* (1968), reported that individuals seeking relief from illness or misfortune always went to a shaman first. If the shaman was unable to cure the patient, he might be referred to the Midewiwin society. The society included a number of shamans of different grades of power. Very few medicine men cared to achieve the top (seventh and eighth) levels of the Midewiwin, for that involved deep immersion in sorcery and other dangers.

A Midewiwin curing generally lasted seven or eight days. The supernatural spirits had to be invoked again and again. The doctors recited portions of the origin myths of the society. Then on the third day a sweat lodge was built and complex ceremonials were carried out in the lodge by the Midewiwin medicine men. This was to increase their powers and to purify them. The patient did not participate in the sweat lodge ceremonials. Dancing and singing were a prominent part of the Midewiwin ceremonies, and one entire session was devoted to

some offended and offending spirits who were responsible for causing the person's soul to wander.

Among the Inuit, especially those of central Canada, sickness was usually thought to be caused by evil spirits who had been angered at the breach of certain taboos. Part of the shaman's medical performance included killing as many of the evil spirits as possible after he had enticed them into the igloo. Often, though, a main feature of shamanistic curing included searching out the taboo violations or other problems (including interpersonal tensions) that had angered the spirits. Confession of taboo violations was therapeutically important.

Possession by spirits (or ghosts) is another of the most common and widespread theories of disease among both modern and nonmodern peoples. Actually, the idea of possession possibly reached its peak in the thought of Europeans during the late Middle Ages. Certainly, possession by the Devil was the usual explanation for a variety of mental ailments, hence our familiar expression "he acted as if possessed."

Among many groups with well-developed shamanistic curing methods, there were occasions on which medicine men referred patients to one another, and occasionally they got together on particularly difficult cases and split the fees afterward. The

22.11 The False Face Society of the Iroquois performed rituals that provided cathartic psychotherapy for their people. (Courtesy of the American Museum of Natural History)

438

Sacred and Secular Realms of Adaptation

The idea of health adaptation as a problem of equilibrium between "hot" and "cold" forces was part of ancient Greek medical theory. The idea was considerably elaborated in ancient times, and was later transmitted by the Arabs to Western Europe, where the hot-cold theory was part of prevailing medical belief among people who embarked on the conquest of the New World. Thus the ancient Greek view of things came to be widely accepted among the peasants and the Indians of Latin America under Spanish influence, and these ideas persist to the present day in many areas. All over Latin America, especially in rural areas, most foods, beverages, herbs, and medicines are classified as either "hot" or "cold." The designations do not refer to any particular observable characteristics of form or actual physical temperature. Rather, the designation, for example, of peanuts, pork, coffee, most chilis, and beans as "hot" and of eggs, rice, potatoes, pork lard, beer, and tomatoes as "cold" by people in the community of Tzintzuntzan is based on the role of these foods in the maintenance of the balance of nature (FOSTER, 1967:185).

A variety of diseases are thought to be caused by imbalances of hot and cold in the body, and certain diseases are considered to be by their very nature "hot" diseases, whereas others are considered to be "cold." Various aches and pains, earaches, chest cramps, and rheumatism are all brought about by cold's entering the body. Tuberculosis is also a cold-caused ailment. On the other hand, dysentery is a hot disease often caused by eating too much "hot" food. Any pain in the kidneys is a "hot" pain, and warts and rashes are usually "hot." It is notable that the lists of hot and cold foods vary somewhat from community to community, and there may be fairly sharp differences of opinion even *within* individual communities, although everyone agrees in general on the idea of hot-cold distinctions.

For many Latin Americans health adaptations involve the precarious equilibrium of hot and cold things, and the ministrations of the *curandero* often consist in dietary recommendations and acts designed to restore the overall body harmony that the Greeks wrote about more than two thousand years ago. Ideas of hot and cold in relation to disease and health are important in Chinese medicine and in parts of the complex health ideas of India as well. The hot-cold theory of illness is also found in the Philippines, perhaps brought there by the Spanish explorers.

the complex ritual distribution of fees, which were often quite high. Landes reported on fees during the hard times of the 1930s that included distribution of goods to the amount of about $50, and on another occasion:

five yards of print and a lot of store rice, two new quilts, five or six pieces of quilting, a pair of flannelette blankets costing two and a quarter dollars, a man's new shirt, a common tin pail, tobacco . . . in great quantities . . . , brown sugar, and raisins, besides huge amounts of cooked and canned foods for days and nights of ritual feasting. People had to ask even remote kinsmen for aid . . . and they asked unrelated people also. (LANDES, 1968:57)

The Ojibwa theory of curing was fairly complex. The object of many of their procedures was to se-cure the assistance of well-meaning spirits (especially individual guardian spirits) and to baffle or avoid the evil ones. Various songs and dances were endowed with magical powers, and an individual who had paid for a cure acquired rights to use the songs on later occasions. In general, the Midewiwin rituals were directed more toward general health and well-being than toward cures for specific illnesses. The attitude toward the potentially helpful spirits (*manitos*) was one of humility and supplication, so that a patient seeking to be cured called out: "O, midé manitos! We beg life of you!" (Landes, 1968:56).

Among the Lugbara of East Africa there appear to be at least three major different causes of illnesses, and correspondingly at least three different kinds of approaches to curing. A number of diseases and

439

other problems result because individuals have offended the ancestors and ghosts:

A man aches and grows thin and so knows that the ghosts have sent sickness to him; he aches in his stomach or his bones in the early morning and knows that a witch or sorcerer has affected him; he aches in his head and knows a kinsman has cursed him; his wife does not conceive and he knows a grandmother has cursed him; and so on. He may then consult the oracles to discover two things: the identity of the agent and the remedy. (MIDDLETON, 1960:79)

On the other hand, for diseases that are recognized as being of recent (European) origin, the patient seeks the aid of Western medicine, and for traditional illness that is not handled by the oracles, one goes to a diviner.

Among the Lugbara, as among most peoples, the oracles and the diviners have a fine knowledge of

22.12 The ancient humoral theory of disease was based on the four body substances—phlegm, blood, yellow bile, and black bile. Imbalances of these substances were thought to cause illness. It was also an explanation for different personalities, as in this illustration. The "hot-cold theory" of illness, widespread in many Latin American communities, is derived from humoral theory.

The phlegmatic

The sanguine

The choleric

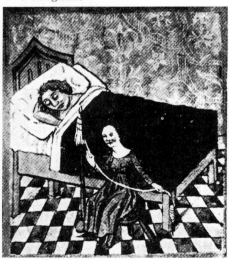

The melancholic

social relationships and of points of tension in the society that may be implicated in visitations of sickness. Once the oracle or diviner has identified the cause of a person's illness, major sacrificial and purification rituals must be enacted in order to make things right with the ancestral spirits. The very great concern of the Lugbara, then, is to maintain a state of ritual purity in the eyes of the supernaturals.

In contemporary peasant societies, medical services and practices nearly always involve a mixture of both "traditional," folk medical healing and the new pharmaceuticals, inoculations, and practitioners of modern medicine. In most cases it appears that peasant peoples make use of both the traditional and the modern health services to varying degrees, depending on types of illnesses and relative costs of treatment.

Although modernization is bringing about an increase in beliefs about naturalistic causes of illnesses and the means to cure them, belief in witchcraft and sorcery and other supernatural illnesses is still common throughout Mexico, as it is in Latin America and widely throughout the rest of the world. Supernatural ailments caused by the evil acts of others cannot usually be cured by modern medicine and must be combated by the traditional means best known to the CURANDEROS and other folk healers.

Some of the illnesses that Mexican rural people regard as curable by *curanderos* rather than medical doctors are thought of as naturalistic ailments that modern doctors "do not understand." These include *susto* (or *espanto*), which is a generalized illness that may include listlessness, lack of appetite, and other symptoms caused by some experience of a frightening nature. It can also be caused by the accumulated frustrations of one's day-to-day-coping. Frequently the explanation given by Mexican people—both in Mexican rural areas and in the United States—is that the *susto* condition is caused by one's soul's leaving the body.

Attitudes concerning "traditional illnesses" and modern medicine are well illustrated in an incident that took place in a rural community near Mexico City during the summer of 1972. The young son of an anthropological fieldworker was bitten by a dog. The local people were in full agreement with the boy's mother that he should be taken to the doctor for immediate treatment, but on his return from the doctor's office it was insisted that the dog-bite victim should then be taken to a *curandero* for treatment

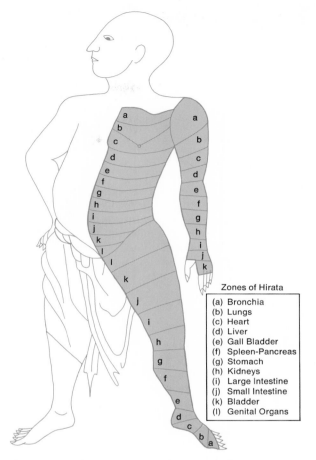

Zones of Hirata

(a) Bronchia
(b) Lungs
(c) Heart
(d) Liver
(e) Gall Bladder
(f) Spleen-Pancreas
(g) Stomach
(h) Kidneys
(i) Large Intestine
(j) Small Intestine
(k) Bladder
(l) Genital Organs

22.13 Acupuncture—a central feature of traditional Chinese medicine—is in some respects similar to humoral theory. The illustration shows the main acupuncture lines used in anesthesia and curing.

of *espanto* because of the fright he must have experienced in being bitten. Another of the same anthropologist's children was treated for *espanto* after falling down and striking her head sharply on a rock. The little girl was not physically injured, but it was felt that the shock from the fall might have caused fright.

The health problems for which the aid of a *curandero* is sought are nearly always those involving a considerable mixture of physical and psychological etiology (causes). Hence the *curandero* is also concerned with people's social interactional styles, even

441

The idea of tiny "animals" as causes of illnesses may have been suggested by individuals in earlier centuries, but a consistent theory of contagion and germs was first set forth by the Italian Girolamo Fracastoro (1484–1553), physician, astronomer, and poet. He concluded that epidemic diseases were caused by small germs that multiplied in the human body. These germs, he argued, were specific to particular illnesses and were spread by contact. Incidentally, the name for one of the important diseases he studied— syphilis—comes from one of his poems. Earlier it had generally been called the "French disease," "Neapolitan disease," or "big pox"—depending on an individual's nationality and point of view.

though focusing on the treatment of specific ailments. Moreover, the course of treatment is likely to include prayer and supplications, as well as herbal remedies and social manipulation. For many Mexican people, Indian and mestizo, religious participation and offering candles in the church are an intrinsic part of their total health adaptation systems.

Major Breakthroughs in Modern Medicine

With the beginnings of the Industrial Revolution the increasingly crowded cities and the increasingly brutalized conditions of work in factories were bringing about a crisis in health for growing numbers of people in Western Europe. At the same time, a number of breakthroughs in medical science began to pave the way toward improved standards of health and curing of disease. Some of the most significant scientific discoveries affecting our health adaptations have included:

1. The establishment of the fact of the circulation of blood by the Englishman William Harvey (1628).

2. The discovery of the microscope and the first description of bacteria by the Dutchman Anton van Leeuwenhoek (1632–1723).

3. The development of inoculation and vaccination, beginning perhaps with Edward Jenner's use of cowpox for protection against smallpox (1798).

4. The development and refinement of the germ theory of disease and pasteurization and other means of control of microorganisms by Louis Pasteur and others, beginning in 1850.

5. The development of asepsis (sterilization of surgical instruments and other equipment in operating rooms and hospitals) by Ignaz Philipp Semmelweis in 1847.

6. The use of ether, chloroform, and other anes-

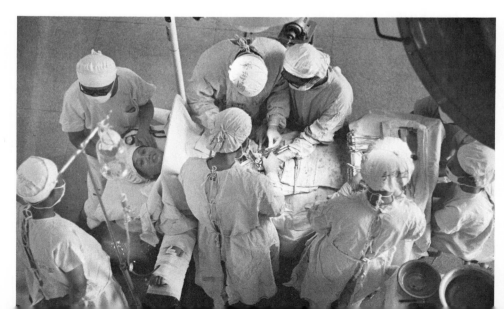

22.14 Scene in a Chinese hospital. Acupuncture is used as the anesthesia for surgery on a woman with a cyst. (Marc Riboud, Magnum)

thesic agents. Apparently the first use of ether for anesthesia was in 1842 by Crawford W. Long in Georgia. However, the beginnings of anesthesic practices are often dated to a famous trial operation that took place in Massachusetts General Hospital in Boston in 1846. The operation was carried out by the famous Boston surgeon John C. Warren.

7. The development of penicillin and other antibiotic drugs, especially penicillin by Alexander Fleming (1928).

This is, or course, a very incomplete list of the breakthroughs that have led to modern medical science and the "great leap forward" in life expectancies of modern Europeans and North Americans. The fascinating point is that the "germ theory" of disease that most people now take for granted has been developed only during the past hundred years. Even after the great medical discoveries of Pasteur and other bacteriologists many of the leaders of the medical profession remained skeptical about the role of bacteria for many years. In retrospect it is incredible that Ignaz Semmelweis was *dismissed from his position* in Vienna as a reward for his demonstration that many of the deaths from puerperal fever in the obstetric clinic were caused by the fact that doctors and medical students *did not wash their hands after coming from the autopsy room.* Evidently for the medical profession as for much of the rest of European culture, cleanliness and sanitation were regarded with suspicion until very recent times.

Health Adaptations in Modern North American Communities

Most North Americans are now so accustomed to nearly complete reliance on licensed practitioners of medicine and dentistry that they fail to realize the extent to which the monopoly of medical practice by M.D.s is a very recent phenomenon—and "we moderns" are often oblivious to the significance of other kinds of "paramedical" practitioners in our health system.

When the first colonists came to North America they were drawn mostly from the economically and socially marginal segments of English and northwestern European populations. Very few trained "doctors" were in those first groups of migrants. Furthermore we must keep in mind that the medical

science of the sixteenth and seventeenth centuries as practiced in Europe was very far from the medical science of today. The practice of medicine in early North American communities was mainly in the hands of individuals who were self-trained in the use of various herbs, practical remedies, superstitions, and the other paraphernalia of folk curing. Some feeble attempts at licensing and regulating medical practice were attempted in the colonies, but the rules were impossible to enforce because so few individuals had any medical training whatsoever. The New York historian William Smith wrote in 1757: "'Few Physicians amongst us are eminent for their skill. Quacks abound like locusts in *Egypt*. . . . This is less to be wondered at as the profession is under no kind of Regulation. Any man at his pleasure sets up for Physician, Apothecary, and Chirurgen [surgeon]'" (Shryock, 1960:12).

Despite the shortage of persons who had any training in medicine, there were many individuals who set themselves up as "doctors." A ratio in 1775 was estimated at about one doctor per six hundred persons, which is exceptionally high by modern standards. The doctors didn't charge high fees for visits, and they made their money mainly from the charges for the drugs they sold. In those days doctors were general practitioners, surgeons, and pharmacists rolled into one. Often the ministers of the gospel practiced some medicine as part of their general services to their congregations. They were often as well trained as most of the other "doctors," although one wonders about this situation when we read that "the favorite remedies of the Reverend Mr. Bulkeley were acquired by him from a Hartford blacksmith!" (Shryock, 1960:16). One critic of American medical practice in 1753 wrote: "'Frequently there is *more Danger* from the Physician, than from the Distemper . . . sometimes notwithstanding the Male *Practice*, Nature gets the better of the Doctor, and the Patient recovers'" (Shryock, 1960:17).

Some medical schools had been established at Philadelphia, Harvard, and elsewhere in the end of the eighteenth and early nineteenth centuries, but with the rapid growth of the new nation standards of training deteriorated. Schools sprang up everywhere, and medical men came to be trained not by apprenticeship but by quickie courses in fly-by-night, commercially motivated "schools." The situation did not improve much until the period immediately following World War I. New regulations on medical schools and the licensing of practitioners were introduced after the famous Flexner Report of 1911; and the quality of training increased rapidly in the 1920s and the 1930s at the same time that a number of the medical "breakthroughs" mentioned above gave well-trained physicians a real edge in curing over the folk practitioners. Until the end of the nineteenth century, on the other hand, the differences between the trained and the untrained, the licensed and the unlicensed, may not have been all that impressive in terms of curative powers.

In spite of the high levels of training, the great advances in surgery, the discovery of antibiotics and other medicines, and many other aspects of medicine, North American populations continue to place reliance on a wide variety of other curers besides the licensed M.D.s. On the side of mental health, for example, many people feel a need to put their faith in religious practices, because the matter of sin and general relationships with spiritual forces is thought to play such a wide role in mental health and often physical well-being as well.

Chiropractors, spiritualists, religious faith healers, and a variety of folk medical practitioners within different ethnic groups in North America make up a very large body of "paramedical" healers whose activities are outside the regular medical professional structure. Many people, of course, cannot afford the high costs of regularly constituted medical care. In fact the present crisis in the American health-care system has, to a great extent, been caused by high medical costs that are an inevitable result of the great increases in technological complexity and professional specialization that characterize modern medicine. Many people turn to other means of health maintenance, including the enormous interest in all kinds of new pills, powders, and other nonprescription products now widely advertised by way of television and other mass media.

Concluding Remarks

Modern medical science is characterized to a very high degree by professional specialization and increased use of a complex technological system, all of which costs money. Also, it involves the development of a category of persons—physicians—with very special training, knowledge, and prerogatives

22.15 The typical North American middle-class medicine cabinet is full of over-the-counter remedies and prescription drugs. (Sepp Seitz, Magnum)

and the possibilities for socioeconomic status far above the majority of the population. The disparity between the social position of the modern medical doctor and the poor segments of our populations is especially marked and poses serious problems to the communication system that is essential for adequate health care. Very often the practitioners of modern medicine have experienced considerable difficulty in bringing about changes of health behavior even when the costs of their medical services were borne by outside agencies instead of the local populations. In part this difficulty is due to serious communication failures because of the large gap between the style of behavior and thought of the outside medical personnel and of the general populace.

In most health adaptation systems religious beliefs, social relationships, psychological factors, and the physical aspects of illness are completely inter-

444

Sacred and Secular Realms of Adaptation

twined. Thus it was natural for the first medical practitioners among the American colonists to be (very frequently) clergymen who ministered to people's spiritual needs at the same time as they attended to physical aches and pains. The fact that modern medical practice sharply separates the physical ailments from the complex network of social and spiritual forces is perhaps one of the reasons why most people in the world still appear to prefer a mixture of the modern and the traditional—if they can afford the high cost of the modern side of this combination.

445

Part
Seven

Homo modernicus: Dimensions of the Contemporary Scene

Aggression, Suicide, and War: Our Most Dangerous Achievements

23

Most mammals defend territories, or at least their young ones, from encroachment by other members of the same species. The establishment of some sort of territorial "proprietorship" (by fighting or threat of fighting) is very often a prelude to mate selection, so the male winners in aggressive encounters are the individuals most likely to mate with the females to produce offspring. Thus, as ethologists have often pointed out, aggressive behavior among animals serves a number of interrelated functions, including spacing individuals and families in relation to the available food sources, selection of the supposedly fittest males for propagating the next generation, and "training" and developing the fighting capabilities of the males for defense against predators. The example of intraspecific aggressiveness among baboons is often given as an example of a selection system that, over time, has produced males with excellent chances of success in facing the dangerous carnivores of East Africa.

Aggressiveness, especially in males, is a common characteristic in primates, as in other animals, so there has been a good deal of theorizing about the supposedly instinctual basis of aggression in humans—as a carry-over from our less humanlike past. Konrad Lorenz, for example, has popularized the view that aggression in humans is an instinctive "drive" or "urge" that serves the same biological functions as in the other animals. This would suggest that warfare and other acts of fighting, brutality, and meanness are expressions of biological forces raging in us all.

The instinct theory has been expressed by Lorenz in this way:

Like the triumph ceremony of the greylag goose, militant enthusiasm in man is a true autonomous instinct: it has its own appetitive behavior, its own releasing mechanisms, and, like the sexual urge or any other strong instinct, it engenders a specific feeling of intense satisfaction. The strength of its seductive lure explains why intelligent men may behave as irrationally and immorally in their political as in their sexual lives. (LORENZ, 1963:271)

On the other side of the theoretical fence many writers have suggested that human expressions of aggression—in killing and maiming with weapons, in destruction of property, in deliberate neglect of people in need of help—are socially learned pat-

23.1 These two gorillas were only playing but the game is getting rough. (Ron Garrison, San Diego Zoo photo)

449

terns. This view has been forcefully expressed by anthropologist Marvin Harris:

There is no greater distortion of the truth about human nature than to blame mankind's record on intraspecific murder and war on an alleged "instinctual" aggressiveness. . . . Man is dangerous to himself because of the loss of genetic control over aggression, the separation of the act of killing from fear and rage, and the substitution of artificial weapons for natural ones. . . . Man's capacity to kill cannot be controlled by "instincts"; it can only be controlled by culture. (HARRIS, 1971:63)

In this chapter we will examine various aspects of human aggressiveness in order to learn more about its scope and patterning.

Variations on the Aggression Theme

In trying to understand human aggression we can start with some peoples among whom aggressiveness is rare, for there are, in fact, many societies in which fighting of any kind is strongly discouraged.

The Russian Ivan Veniaminov learned of no cases of homicide among the Aleutian peoples during his more than twenty years of residence among them in the early nineteenth century. Similarly, Ralph Linton's informants among the Tanala people of Madagascar, a population of about 200,000 people, could report no recent cases of killing. Robert Dentan has described the Semai people of the Malay Peninsula as a "nonviolent people," noting a number of cultural practices and beliefs that serve to cut down the likelihood of in-group hostility. Their strategy for dealing with potentially hostile outsiders in this difficult environment has often been to retreat farther into the more inaccessible parts of the jungle. "In brief, little violence occurs within Semai society. Violence, in fact, seems to terrify the Semai. A Semai does not meet force with force, but with passivity or flight" (Dentan, 1968:59).

The case of the Sirionó is interesting because it involves a group of people apparently living under very marginal economic circumstances with frequent hunger and anxiety about food. Quarreling, principally with regard to food and sex, is frequent, but they seldom resort to dangerous fighting or killing.

One cannot remain long with the Sirionó without noting that quarreling and wrangling are ubiquitous. Hardly a day passes among them when a dispute of some kind does not break out. . . .
Except at drinking feasts antagonisms seldom lead to violence, and even at these the participants are usually so drunk that they are unable to harm one another. On other occasions strong words are used between disputants, but fighting with weapons and clubs is rare. This is especially true of the men, who

23.2 The fighting of these bulls probably has a considerable amount of instinctive patterning. (Marc Riboud, Magnum)

seldom express direct aggression against each other, although among women quarrels frequently culminate in battles with digging sticks.

Men often dissipate their anger toward other men by hunting. One day Eantándu was angry with Mbíku who had hunted coati and given him none. Flushed with anger, Eantándu picked up his bow and arrows and departed for the hunt. When he returned about 5 hours later with a couple of small monkeys, his wrath had subsided considerably. He told me that when men are angry they go hunting. If they shoot any game their anger disappears; even if they do not kill anything, they return home too tired to be angry. (HOLMBERG, 1960:61–62)

Some of the most nonviolent people in the world are to be found among the highly religious, communalistic agrarian societies such as the Hutterites of America's northern plains. Because of the high degree of cooperation required by their social system, open hostility is very much feared in such communities and strong measures are taken to eliminate it. John Bennett, in his descriptions of the *Hutterian Brethren* (1967), notes that the communalistic interdependence of the Hutterite way of life involves great self-sacrifice and self-discipline and therefore creates considerable tensions and stresses among these people.

While the Brethren are thoroughly trained to feel and practice brotherly love, the vicissitudes of daily living and the conduct of a large enterprise inevitably generate tensions and difficulties. The techniques of avoidance serve to prevent these tensions from becoming open, public disputes; but at the same time, such techniques can promote an atmosphere of festering hostility. This is especially true of colonies whose leaders are inept at handling the tensions between families and individuals and internal disagreements over policy. (BENNETT, 1967:138)

Whatever tensions and aggressive emotions the Hutterites feel, they do not often erupt into open violence, and the killing of one Hutterite by another is rare indeed. The religious teaching, coupled with the social mechanisms of dispute settlement and personal avoidance tactics, appears to be quite successful in maintaining a general harmony within each Hutterite colony. The strong social support provided by their way of life is also a positive inducement for maintaining amicable in-group relationships.

Aggression in City and Country

All kinds of aggressive acts—homicide, assault, rape, robbery, and so on—tend to be more frequent in city populations than in rural areas. In the high-density areas of large North American cities, violence has become institutionalized among youths in the form of street gangs mentioned earlier. The heavy involvement in street warfare is reflected in the following reminiscences of a Vice Lord gang member:

"What happened, this guy was coming from school and he was shot and killed. It was in a gray hood [White neighborhood]. There was mostly Polish living over there. I guess they killed him cause he was a Negro. He wasn't doin nothing, just walking down the street coming from school . . . with two other studs. And the Man [the police] didn't know who did it. Anyway, he say he didn't. I guess it could have been anybody in the hood.

"And when this happened . . . well, I don't know just exactly how it was, but everybody just thought the same way. The Lords decided to go on over there, and some kind of way we ended up with the Cobras, too. It was just that everybody was out there, all the groups on the West Side. And we went through the high school over there and the neighborhood every day and every night after that! And we dusted everybody we saw, Jack—tearing up property—we turned over cars—we did everything!

You know, before that, any time we went over there—in South Lawndale—we almost always would get dusted, or maybe even killed. But now they think twice." (KEISER, 1969:7–8)

Institutionalized aggression among rival gangs is not restricted to city life, however. In many rural areas of Europe, for example, intervillage fights were a common feature in earlier times. The development and intensification of village fighting was particularly notable in rural Finland. The Finnish social scientist Eliina Haavio-Mannila (1958) made a survey of intervillage gang fights, intercommune fights, and Finnish-Swedish ethnic gang fights. Fighting was especially frequent in west Finland, an area of population concentration. Brawling frequently took place at weddings and at village centers and crossroads. The participants were mainly young unmarried men, though married men often joined in. Sometimes the fight was prearranged, with appropriate

451

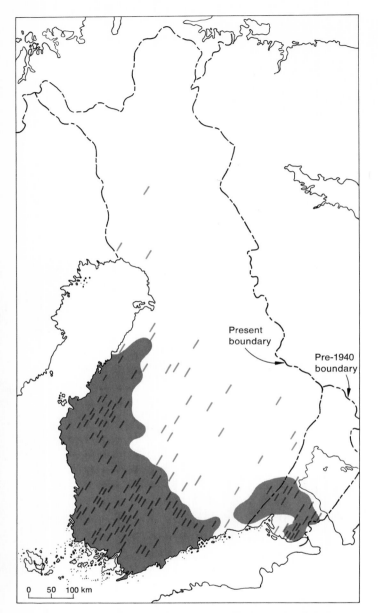

23.3 Village fights as a "cultural norm" in Finland during the nineteenth century. The shaded areas of concentrated agricultural settlement had the heaviest incidence of institutionalized village fighting. (Each colored slash marks a parish in which fighting was prevalent.)

challenges issued. The ostensible reason for the fights generally involved "village honor," and a particularly frequent theme was keeping the boys from neighboring villages away from "our girls." The heroes of these fights were generally much admired by the local populace, just as football heroes are in North American communities.

That the village conflicts had strong sexual overtones is seen in the fact that weddings were the favorite scene of these fights, and the bridegroom was often the intended target. The spirit of the occasion is enshrined in a Finnish folk saying, "It was a crummy wedding; the bridegroom lived."

From Haavio-Mannila's extensive survey, it is possible to match the information about institutionalized fighting with data about population densities in different parts of Finland. It appears that the highest incidence of village fighting in rural Finland developed in the areas of greatest population density, particularly in the west and the south, which comprise the most fertile agricultural areas (Pelto and MacGregor, n.d.).

Aggression in the Long, Hot Summer

Smouldering hate, resentment, frustration, poverty, hopelessness—and a week of oppressive heat and humidity are the complex tangle of motives behind the devastating Los Angeles riots, a social worker and five psychiatrists said Sunday. . . . The weather helped to bring the seething emotions to a boil. "The advent of the heat wave undoubtedly served to fray the nerves of the already angry and frustrated Negro community even more," said Mrs. Esther Fine, social worker and wife of Brentwood psychoanalyst Sidney Fine. Another assistant professor of clinical psychiatry at the University of Southern California, Bernice Innes, was reported to have said, "Climatic factors are important in human behavior. The excessive heat does act as a stimulant and stress on already quite strained individuals. (St. Paul Pioneer Press, August 16, 1965, in news item entitled "Heat Explodes Hate")

The idea of the "long, hot summer" as a factor in inner-city violence has often been put forward in the popular press and is accepted by many people as a contributing factor, though certainly not the

Homo modernicus: Dimensions of the Contemporary Scene

There is a favorite Finnish folk song that recounts a wedding fight:

Härmän Häät

In Härmä the wedding was terrible,
They drank and they fought;
From the parlor to the front steps
They carried out the bodies.

prime cause of the urban riots of the 1960s. There is some evidence that climate and weather do affect people's personalities, including the arousal of aggressive tendencies. The psychologist W. Griffitt and his associates (1969) performed laboratory experiments on human behavior under conditions of heat and crowding. Griffitt asked people to rate other persons in terms of how much they liked them while the subjects were experiencing heat stress. The heat stress situation tended to increase negative evaluations of other persons, and Griffitt concluded that "it seems clear, then, that the individual who feels hot, fatigued, uncomfortable, bad, lacking in vigor, and so forth, may be expected to respond to other individuals less positively than one who feels cool, comfortable, and generally pleasant" (Griffits, 1969:244).

The ecologist F. Sargent surveyed a large body of data and concluded that "hot atmospheres produce real and significant changes in physical and mental performance, behavior, and emotional equilibrium. These alterations accrue from an effect of heat on the nervous system. Circulatory disturbances and salt deficiency may be contributory, especially when the physical conditions are severe or exposure prolonged" (Sargent, 1963:304).

Taking a cue from popular opinion and psychological research, M. Robbins, P. Pelto, and B. DeWalt (1972) examined data about aggression in a sample of societies around the world to see if there is any relationship between hot climate and attitudes toward aggression. It is hard to get direct and comparable information on amounts of aggression in different societies; however, they did find some interesting indications. Since Whiting and Child (see pp. 408–409) had rated their sample of societies in terms of "indulgence of aggression," Robbins and his coresearchers tested the hypothesis that people

in hot climates have more tendencies toward aggression and hence greater general tolerance of aggression than people in colder climates. They found that there was a strong tendency for peoples living in the warmer climates of the world to show greater indulgence of aggression in training their children. They also found a very interesting relationship between climate and human aggression in myths, for people in warmer climates tended to have more myths with human agents of aggression, whereas people of colder climates tended to have aggressive acts carried out by *nonhuman* agents (animals, spirits, ghosts, and so on).

They then turned to information about rates of homicide in different nations as reported in the *Demographic Yearbook* published by the United Nations. Homicide data were available for 1950 and 1965 for thirty-four nations of the world. It turns out that there is a .50 correlation between homicide rate and climate. That is, the nations in hotter parts of the world tend on the whole to have higher rates of homicide than those of nations in colder climates (Robbins, Pelto, and DeWalt, 1972). It is interesting to note that similar results have been obtained in the comparison of homicide rates in different parts of the United States ranging from hot to relatively cold areas. Also, statistical data show some tendencies for homicide rates to change in response to the different seasons of the year and different weather conditions.

We hasten to point out that these effects of climate on human aggression do not mean that climate is a *main cause* of human aggressiveness. As noted in the newspaper article concerning the riots in Los Angeles, heat is best regarded as simply one additional factor that may in some cases be the one that helps trigger human aggressive tendencies built up by many other frustrations.

453

Physiological Mechanisms and Nutrition

In a study in the High Andes (more than twelve-thousand feet above sea level) Ralph Bolton (1972) examined *intra*group variations in aggressiveness among the Qolla people near Lake Titicaca. There is a very high rate of homicide in this area compared to that in other populations, but there are, of course, large intragroup variations in aggressive behavior. Because of the peoples' poor diet, Bolton suspected that hypoglycemia (low blood sugar levels) may be implicated in the triggering of aggressive responses. After obtaining ratings of the males in the village of Incawatana with regard to their degree of aggressiveness in fighting, court battles, and other hostility, Bolton collected blood samples from fifty-four males and tested them for blood sugar levels. He found that the individuals who were relatively higher in aggressiveness in Incawatana tended to be individuals with *moderate* hypoglycemia as compared to fellow villagers. This fit with Bolton's hypothesis that lowered blood sugar levels, up to a point, tend to promote aggressiveness—beyond these moderate levels, low blood sugar is more likely to cause lassitude, depression, and inactivity. (See Figure 23.4.)

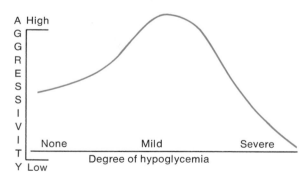

23.4 Hypothesized relationship between aggressivity and hypoglycemia. (Adapted from Ralph Bolton, p. 243.)

But why do some people in Incawatana have lower blood sugar levels than others? A most important factor affecting blood sugar levels is diet. The people of Incawatana, like most of their neighbors, live in marginal areas in which getting food from the soil is a difficult and uncertain task. The farmers have relatively small and inadequate plots of land, and there are few ways to earn supplementary incomes through other labor. The people are very poor, and many of them may be constantly bordering on malnutrition. Although this study suggests hypoglycemia as a *linking* mechanism possibly accounting for some of the variation in aggressive tendencies, this physiological link is activated by differences in food intake (and other factors as well) so that these links must be traced back to social and economic conditions.

Bolton suggests that another factor in the relatively high level of aggressiveness among the Qolla people is the high altitude. Many researchers have noted that lack of oxygen at high altitudes is a stressful condition affecting the body system. Living under these stressful conditions may make the Qolla people and other high Andean peoples especially susceptible to the aggression-provoking effects of other physiological variables, as well as to cultural and social factors in their environment.

The involvement of hypoglycemia as a possible cause of aggressiveness in humans is clearly a biological factor in human behavior, yet it is much different from the "aggressive instincts" biological argument of Lorenz and others. The aggressive instincts theory suggests a constant stream of aggressive tendencies in every human, which may be deflected or influenced by outside factors. On the other hand, the biological factors that Bolton investigated among the Qolla people are *not* given at birth but are the results of individual life experiences. The fact that individuals differ to a very considerable extent in their degrees of and tendencies toward hostility makes this kind of human variability theory much more plausible and useful than the "constant instincts" view of the human condition.

Crowding and Aggression

Psychologists and other social scientists frequently point to the aggression-producing possibilities inherent in our crowded way of life. Well-known experiments with crowding in other animals have demonstrated the possibility that there may be far-reaching and destructive effects if too many individuals are in a confined space. For example, when a group of rats were confined to overcrowded cages, some of

454

23.5 Human aggression is often carried out for instrumental purposes, such as acquisition of property, though many acts of violence seem to arise from emotional outbursts. (Charles Gatewood, Magnum)

groups men respond negatively to crowded conditions; they become suspicious and combative, almost as if they were engaged in the territoriality described in animals. Women respond positively, becoming friendly and more intimate in high density situations. When men and women are mixed there are no effects of density" (Freedman, 1971:86).

In ongoing living situations, however, there does seem to be reason to believe that high population density raises the aggression potential of humans, especially when they are *competing for scarce resources*. Among the Qolla in Incawatana, for example, a major reason for intragroup hostility is that there is very little land and some people have more than others. It is also interesting to note that in recent decades the institutionalized village fights in west Finland have died out, and although population levels have not decreased, many alternative ways of making a living have developed. As wage labor opportunities have increased for rural Finns, competition for scarce resources has no longer been confined to the narrow limits of local agricultural lands. It is also significant that the rigid social hierarchy of landed versus landless peasants broke down rather quickly under the impact of social and economic modernization. Perhaps in many situations human crowding does not matter so much if individuals do not *feel* crowded out of local adaptive opportunities.

Aggression and Ecological Systems

Many people have noted that some kinds of occupational activities seem to be associated with higher levels of aggressiveness than are other kinds. Anthropologists have studied the differences in aggressive tendencies among, for example, farmers versus herdsmen. In 1961–1962 an interdisciplinary team of researchers compared pastoralists and farmers in four groups in East Africa. By comparing farmers and pastoralists who spoke the same language and shared many cultural features, they were controlling for cultural differences in order to examine the effects of differences in subsistence patterns. They found:

The farmers employ indirect action, featuring secrecy and caution; their emotions are constrained and they live with great anxiety. They not only show disrespect for authority, but the prevailing affect between people

the males became uncontrollably aggressive and others became pathologically dependent and passive. The females in these overcrowded conditions became incompetent as mothers, failing to build adequate nests for their young. The "neurotic" males often attacked the females and killed or maimed the children. In other words, the crowded rats exhibited greatly increased rates of rape, homicide, child abuse, and other pathologies (Calhoun, 1962; Hall, 1966).

A number of studies have demonstrated similar tendencies among monkeys and apes. Although it is very difficult to conduct realistic controlled experiments on crowding with humans, there is some research to show that the effects can be quite varied. As we noted earlier (pp. 333–334), Freedman, who argues that crowding is not particularly pathological for humans, reports research in which "in one-sex

Aggression, Suicide, and War: Our Most Dangerous Achievements

is hostility or hatred. They avoid conflict, engaging instead in litigation and witchcraft. Yet, their hostility, anxiety, and sensitivity to insult sometimes produce impulsive physical attack when open aggression does occur. . . . Where the farmers are constrained in their emotions and indirect in their actions, the pastoralists freely express emotions, both positive emotions such as affection, sexuality or bravery, and dysphoric emotions such as guilt, depression, brutality, and fear of death. Where the farmers are indirect in their actions, especially in their actions relating to conflict, the pastoralists act independently and aggress openly. (EDGERTON, 1971:274–276)

Aggression and Socialization

A large body of literature is concerned with the relationship between parental treatment and children's tendencies to covert or overt aggressiveness.

In the study mentioned earlier concerning parental rejection (pp. 408–409) Ronald Rohner placed these psychological results in a cross-cultural perspective. He found that consistent rejection of children by their parents tends on the whole to develop personality features of aggression and hostility in children, and these personality characteristics are carried forward into adult behavior patterns.

Nonviolent peoples, such as the Hutterites and Semai, usually put heavy emphasis on overt training for conflict avoidance. Religious and philosophical principles are brought into play, along with direct punishment for fighting and other conflict behavior. On the other hand, people who place high positive value on aggressiveness and fighting ability usually make these attitudes known to children very early, and practice for adult military action can become a major feature of children's games and pastimes. The film *Dead Birds* (see pp. 461–462) includes a dramatic spear fight among the little New Guinea children, practicing the adult skills called into action in warfare, around which theme the film was produced.

Aggression: The Result of Many Factors

The forms of human aggression are so various and complicated that a variety of causes and forces must be involved. In line with the multicausal approach to other questions taken in this book, let us review some of the different kinds of factors that may be involved in aggression. Incorporating some of the theoretical ideas that have been produced by psychologists, sociologists, and cultural anthropologists, this multifactor view includes the following points:

1. Aggression as an emotional response experienced by human individuals has a biochemical basis and tends to occur as a response to experiences of pain, frustration, and other unpleasant circumstances. In our view, it is not useful to imagine every individual as having a constant amount of aggressive urges.

23.6 Social psychologists have demonstrated that children's aggression is increased by the presence of aggression cues, including guns. (Wayne Miller, Magnum)

456

2. Every individual experiences the emotional state of "aggressiveness" to some degree or other, depending on his or her circumstances. The kinds of circumstances that are *perceived* as frustrating and unpleasant are themselves quite varied, so that different individuals may experience different degrees of emotional aggression in response to the same stimulus situation.

3. In addition to experience-derived differences in the degree of emotionally aggressive response, individuals differ considerably in the degree to which they translate these feelings into concrete action. Some individuals "walk around with a chip on their shoulder," whereas others show extreme patience in the face of all kinds of provocation. Some aspects of early socialization seem to be involved in these personality differences.

4. Beliefs and values—for example, ideologies of nonviolence—can have marked effects on people's tendencies toward violence. These ideological commitments to violence or nonviolence appear to be much affected by degrees of social support and social provocation.

5. Many eternal factors—including environmental features; individual physical states in terms of health, nutrition, and so on; effects of drugs; and all kinds of social and cultural factors—appear to have a part in triggering or suppressing violence among humans.

6. All the cultural, psychological, and biological factors mentioned here (and probably a number of others as well) make up a complex *system* of interacting factors that, together, produce the tremendous variations in manifest aggressive behavior in individuals and among different groups.

Suicide: Aggression Turned Inward

Many social scientists regard suicide as aggression turned against the self. Thus, as a response to sociocultural and psychological stresses, aggression against others and suicide may be looked upon as two alternative "solutions" or responses to serious pressures. Aggression outward (e.g., homicide) tends to vary inversely with suicide. In the "high suicide" nations such as Denmark and Sweden, for example, we find relatively low rates of murder. In North American populations there seem to be higher rates of suicide among White populations than among Blacks; the homicide rates are reversed for these two populations. In those societies in which *both* homicide and suicide rates are high it seems likely that the psychological and cultural pressures on people are especially severe, with correspondingly high levels of all kinds of tendencies toward aggression, both inwardly and outwardly directed. There are also societies, such as that of the Hutterites, in which there are strong prohibitions of both externally directed aggression and suicide.

Among non-Westernized peoples under fairly stable cultural conditions, variation seems to be very great. Among the Tanala people of Madagascar and the Azande people in Africa, ethnographers and officials report suicide rates that were probably less than 1 per 100,000 persons. In Tierra del Fuego: "'That suicide was ever committed in Tierra del Fuego is hardly probable. . . . My informants knew nothing about suicide and my questions confused them so strange a concept did it seem to them'" (Gusinde, 1931:481, 1119; cited by Naroll, 1962:145).

Although many North American Indian groups, such as the Yuma, the Mohave, and the Zuñi, were reported to have very few suicides in the past, some groups on the Great Plains, such as the Cheyenne, the Blackfoot, the Comanche, and the Sioux, approved of suicide as a fitting end for a brave warrior—he could take a vow to die in battle:

One story which is well remembered about two suicide warriors took place before 1851. These two young men, Stands on the Hill and Left Hand, had vowed to be killed in the next battle with other Indians or with the whites. They did not want to be killed right away, but to touch the enemy first with a spear or with their hand. That would bring them the highest honor. And like any warriors, they preferred fighting with other Indians to fighting with white men. . . . Other tribes had this suicide custom too, but the Cheyennes were one of the first. The Sioux learned it from them. It was just one way of showing bravery; there were other ways of doing it. (STANDS-IN-TIMBER, 1967:61–63)

Probably one of the last instances of warrior suicide occurred in the battle against General Custer at Little Big Horn on June 25, 1876. John Stands-in-Timber reminisced about the things the older Cheyenne had told him in his youth about that moment of Indian glory:

Some of the Sioux boys had just announced that they were taking the suicide vow, and others were putting on a dance for them at that end of the camp. This meant they were throwing their lives away—they would fight till they were killed in the next battle. . . .

The next morning the Indians held a parade for the boys who had been in the suicide dance the night before. . . . They paraded down through the Cheyenne camp on the inside and back on the outside, and then returned to their own village. . . . [In the battle the next day] . . . the suicide boys were the last Indians to enter the fight. . . . The suicide boys started the hand-to-hand fighting, and all of them were killed or mortally wounded. . . . At the end it was quite a mess. . . . After the suicide boys came in it didn't take long—half an hour perhaps. Many have agreed with what Wolf Tooth said: that if it had not been for the suicide boys it might have ended the way it did at the Reno fight. There the Indians all stayed back and fought. No suicide boys jumped in to begin the hand-to-hand fight. The Custer fight was different because those boys went in that way, and it was their rule to be killed. (STANDS-IN-TIMBER, 1967:194–202)

The United States Army was quick to take revenge for the humiliation of the Custer massacre. Within a few years the Cheyenne like the rest of their neighbors of the Northern Plains were put on reservations, and their economic life was destroyed.

In prereservation times other kinds of suicide were also found among the Cheyenne; loss of close kinsmen, close friends, or lovers were precipitating causes of these other suicides. Male suicides usually involved the loss of a brother or a close friend, whereas female suicides (mostly by hanging) apparently resulted mainly because of the loss of a husband or a lover.

During the late 1960s the rates of suicides among young Cheyenne men reached such proportions that an emergency appeal was made by health authorities for help from psychiatric and anthropological consultants. The general hopelessness of the socio-economic situation among reservation Indians seems clearly to be at the root of these escalating tendencies toward self-destruction. That suicide among Cheyenne young men is even more frequent than in many other Indian reservation communities may be a reflection of the fact that suicide had been relatively frequent and had been considered honorable in the traditional Cheyenne way of life.

Suicide in Modern Nations

When we turn our attention to modern nation-states, we find again a good deal of variation from one country to another. The Scandinavian countries generally have high rates of suicide compared to other nations. This is especially true in Denmark and Sweden, where suicides have averaged nearly 20 per 100,000 population. The rates of suicide in Japan, Switzerland, Germany, and Austria are nearly as high as those in Sweden and Denmark. Curiously, in Norway, which is culturally closely related to Denmark, suicide rates are currently only about 7.5 per 100,000 population. Nations with quite low suicide rates (under 5 per 100,000 population) include Barbados, Canal Zone, Taiwan, Gibraltar, and Ireland. It is interesting to note that the highest rate of suicide in Europe appears to be in West Berlin, with more than 30 suicides per 100,000 population.

Suicide and Culture Patterns

The work of the French sociologist Émile Durkheim is the most widely known investigation of suicide. From his examination of ethnographic ma-

Climate and Suicide

In the more northern portions of the world many people dread the coming of winter with its frequent gray skies, cold, and long hours of darkness. From Émile Durkheim's time to the present, researchers have occasionally noted the effects of climate and weather in relation to suicide and have suggested that there are higher rates of suicide in colder areas. In a cross-national study of suicide rates and climate Robbins and associates (1972) found that the correlation was .58, so that people in colder climates do, indeed, appear to have higher suicide rates than those in the sunny south! (It should be kept in mind, however, that national suicide data are likely to be somewhat inaccurate, partly because of the stigma that many peoples attach to taking one's own life.)

Homo modernicus: Dimensions of the Contemporary Scene

terials and European suicide statistics (which showed different rates for rural and urban areas, for married versus single people, for Protestants versus Catholics, and so on), he suggested that suicide can be divided into three different types: "egoistic," "altruistic," and "anomic." Altruistic suicide, Durkheim suggested, occurs in cultural groups and social contexts in which individuals are expected to commit suicide for the benefit of the group. The usual illustration of altruistic suicide is the ritual of committing *hara-kiri* among certain classes in Japanese society, as well as going to one's death voluntarily among many military groups. The suicides of aged Inuit for the benefit of their families also fit this category. In general, altruistic suicides supposedly reflect strong integration of individuals in their societies.

Egoistic and anomic suicides, on the other hand, were viewed by Durkheim as the products of *lack* of integration of individuals into their society, or of the disintegration and disorganization of social systems. Durkheim, and other researchers following his lead, have argued that Catholic communities are more organized and integrated than Protestant communities, hence their lower suicide rates. Similarly, in rural communities there is greater social "solidarity" and greater orderliness and predictability of relationships of individuals to their families, neighborhoods, and other parts of the social system, as compared with life in the cities.

Since Durkheim carried out his classic research, many other people have worked on the problem, and many of Durkheim's ideas continue to be generally supported. But there are still many unanswered questions and some suicide patterns that do not fit his theories.

Warfare: Our Most Destructive Activity

Although intragroup aggression and suicide are problems that have excited a considerable amount of attention and controversy, many people regard intersocietal war as the most serious manifestation of human aggressive behavior. There is a thread of continuity that runs from individual aggressiveness to organized warfare. However, when it comes to the more highly developed modern forms of military action, the link between individual biocultural responses and the plans and strategies of warleaders and diplomats is rather indirect, so we cannot regard war as simply individual aggressiveness projected onto a larger screen.

Many social philosophers start with the assumption that all human groups engage in warfare; therefore, *Homo sapiens* is a warlike animal. That idea is a gross distortion of human behavior. There are many human groups, past and present, whose behavioral patterns have been to a great extent peaceful, even when attacked by outsiders.

On the other hand, there have been some groups in the world who are widely known for their warlike behavior and in which a desired goal of men is to be heroic on the warpath and to die in battle. In other societies heroism has been esteemed, yet warfare itself has come to be looked on as a disturbing burden on the people. Here are some examples from the ethnographic literature:

[Among the Crow] War was not the concern of a class nor even of the male sex, but of the whole population, from cradle to grave. Girls as well as boys derived their names from a famous man's exploit. Women danced wearing scalps, derived honor from their husband's deeds, publically exhibited the men's shields or weapons; and a women's lamentations over a slain son were the most effective goad to a punitive expedition. There are memories of a woman who went to war; indeed, Muskrat, one of my women informants claimed to have struck a coup and scalped a Piegan, thus earning songs of praise.... Training for war began in childhood.... On the subject of warfare the older generation, otherwise little inclined to interfere with youth, turned didactic. "Old age is a thing of evil, it is well for a young man to die in battle." (LOWIE, 1935:215–229)

[For a contrasting case] The best evidence we have for the relatively unwarlike character of the Sirionó comes from the culture itself. Here are not found the organization, the numbers, or the weapons with which to wage war, aggressive or defensive. Moreover, war does not seem to be glorified in any way by the culture. A child is not educated in the art of war, nor is there a warrior class among the adults. Furthermore the care with which the Sirionó avoid contact, with other peoples and the fear with which they regard their more warlike neighbors bear witness to the punishment they have suffered as a group in the past (HOLMBERG, 1960:63)

[In the African Sudan] The Dinka allege in their songs that they are never the aggressors but defenders of

459

23.7 These Australian warriors have removed the points from their spears in order to enact a ritual of peacemaking. (Courtesy of the American Museum of Natural History)

honor and resisters of aggression, although in most cases what they consider aggression is emotive and readily conceived:

A man threatened me at the borders,
I thought we were at peace.
Do not provoke me, I am bad.
If I should make it bitter one day,
I will be bad
And I will not be passed by.
All people will avoid me in respect . . .

. . . In the battlefield the opposing groups, standing within throwing distance, dart at each other with their slim medium-length spears and forked clubs. The art of throwing and dodging spears is one a Dinka learns from an early age. In war the value of early training is brought to the test. A few cowards may retire never to recover from the loss of face. Renowned warriors become frenzied with valor. They are usually the ones who kill and remain unharmed. Some individuals become excessively brave—almost suicidal. The particularly brave and dangerous are among the most aimed at by the enemy, but they are also the most covered by their men. (DENG, 1972:76–77)

The frequency of warfare varies greatly among different kinds of nonindustrialized societies, as it does among modern nations. We must examine carefully the evidence from around the world to see if some generalizations are possible about the warlike tendencies of people.

Warfare Among Hunter-Gatherers

Really serious warlike activity has not been a dominant feature of hunting-gathering societies except in unusual cases. There are good, sound ecological and adaptive reasons for this. Looking back at the description of the hunting-gathering way of life, we are reminded that such peoples do not control very much economic property and they often have rather little interest in specific territorial control. Although they inhabit an area they are intimately familiar with, they frequently do not defend such territories against outside encroachment.

There are some other practical matters to consider. Most hunting-gathering groups are so thinly spread across the land that the marshaling of a war party of more than a dozen or so able-bodied males would be a major achievement. Moreover, if a sufficient war party is assembled, the location of the "the enemy" is likely to be some distance away. In this instance a military expedition would require stored food supplies that are often beyond the means of such groups. Finally, hunting-gathering groups frequently have very little in the way of authoritarian leadership, so that persuading men to embark jointly on some military venture is a relatively unusual occurrence. As Julian Steward has noted:

Homo modernicus: Dimensions of the Contemporary Scene

Most so-called "warfare" among such societies is no more than revenge for alleged witchcraft or continued interfamily feuds. . . . Collecting is the main resource in most areas, but I know of no reported defense of seed areas. Primary bands did not fight one another, and it is difficult to see how a maximum band could assemble its manpower to defend its territory against another band or why it should do so. (STEWARD, 1968:334)

Although warfare is not a prominent feature in most hunting-gathering societies, there have been some groups with hunting-gathering subsistence systems who did engage in a great deal of warfare. A number of Plains Indian groups—the Crow, Cheyenne, Blackfoot, Sioux, and others—are well known for their capabilities as warriors and their interest in warfare activities.

In trying to understand Plains Indian warfare as it developed during the eighteenth and nineteenth centuries, a number of anthropologists have pointed to a combination of social and environmental features of that period. In the first place, huge herds of buffalo (they numbered perhaps 10 million head at their maximum) provided an abundance of food resources. This resource, however, was not easily exploited without the horse, so that buffalo did not become the major subsistence item of most groups until Plains Indians acquired horses from the Whites. Furthermore, the buffalo drives required a great deal of personnel so that a buffalo hunt was a time when large numbers of people came together. The combination of large encampments and an abundant food supply provided the conditions that facilitated warfare, while the need for horses, the pressures of White encroachment, and other factors provided the motivations for fighting and raiding.

Although the various hunting-gathering groups of central Australia did not have the abundance of food sources and "monopolizable resources" available to the people of the Plains and the Pacific Northwest Coast, they did have relative stability of food supplies and occasional abundance, permitting temporary gatherings of relatively large numbers of people. Warfare among the Australian peoples did not involve large-scale killing or taking over economic resources or territory. Often their armed combat took the form of ritualized spear throwing and other controlled aggressiveness. But certainly there were deaths from warfare, and raiding was fairly common among some groups.

Warfare Among Horticulturalists

In contrast to hunting-gathering peoples, the ethnographies of cultivation peoples seem warfare-ridden. The cultivators of New Guinea, of the Amazon basin in South America, and of various locations in tropical Africa all seem to have in common a tendency toward internecine raiding and warfare. Napoleon Chagnon's characterization of the Yanomamö as "the fierce people" describes a way of life in which fighting and other aggressive acts dominate. For example, a typical ceremonial exchange between allied villages is intended as a ritual of solidarity; nonetheless, "any Yanomamö feast can potentially end in violence because of the nature of the attitudes the participants hold regarding canons of behavior and obligations to display ferocity" (Chagnon, 1968:117).

The Dani people of highland New Guinea are rapidly becoming the most famous primitive warriors in ethnographic history, on the strength of the documentary film *Dead Birds*. The film depicts two opposed groups of Dani peoples locked in an unending reciprocal raiding based on the belief that their supernatural spirit protectors expect the deaths of enemies in return for their continued supernatural support. If either (human) group falls behind in the killing, they are in danger of losing their spiritual life-force. This ritualistic aspect of Dani warfare suggests that these groups are locked in mortal conflict for motives quite alien to Westerners.

A search for meaning and pattern in human warfare is easily led astray by cases like the Dani as portrayed in this valuable ethnographic film. Like many ethnographic accounts, the film takes up one aspect, a more esoteric one, leaving us uninformed about possible economic and political aspects of this warfare pattern. In an ethnographic description of these same Dani peoples, Karl Heider has described the nonritual side of their conflicts. It turns out that while

the ritual phase of war seems more like a medieval tourney than like what we usually mean by war . . . the nonritual phase of war is just the opposite: short, treacherous, bloody, and with major economic effect.

In 1966 the Dugum Dani were involved in a nonritual war episode, which I learned about in 1968 from the Dani participants and missionary observers. The

461

events of June 4, 1966 could only be called a massacre. At dawn that day warriors from the northern part of the Gutelu Alliance crept through the ground fog to launch a well-planned attack on the compounds to the south of the Elogeta River. The attack lasted only an hour or so, but nearly 125 men, women, and children were left dead or dying, and dozens of compounds were in flames. Other alliances had been informed of the attack and joined in, not so much to kill and burn as to plunder pigs. . . .

The immediate effect of the attack was a major population shift. Most of the survivors left their burned-out compounds on the southern banks of the Elogeta River and moved into the Dugum Neighborhood, or beyond to occupy the old no-man's-land (HEIDER, 1970:118–121)

The population density in the valley where the Dani live is nearly eighty persons per square mile. This is a density *eight hundred times* greater than that of the Bushmen in their most luxuriant areas. This factor of population density must be constantly kept in mind as we try to make sense of this uniquely human activity, warfare.

Compared to hunting and gathering peoples, the unwearying fighters of the Dugum Dani have all the major ingredients that we have suggested as contributing to the probabilities of warfare. They have monopolizable resources in the form of gardening lands as well as pigs. They have the population density from which the personnel for war can be easily conscripted. The work of gardening takes time, but there are plenty of hours and days left over for warfare, especially if it takes but a few minutes to get to the battlegrounds and the enemy appears always willing to meet one halfway. Only during predawn surprise attacks does one have to walk the extra hundreds of yards to reach the enemy's village. Transportation of food and other supplies is not a problem—warriors generally return to their home villages in the evening.

Warfare in Complex Societies

One of the reasons for what appears to be an unceasing persistence of warfare among horticultural New Guinea peoples is that the combatants form rather small alliances of a few villages living quite close to one another. The alliances shift from time to time, and the people are in frequent interaction with one another, so that there are always quarrels, always new disputes arising—always the possibilities for renewed hostilities. Mobilization takes little effort, leadership is flexible, and the processes of peace maintainance are uncertain. It takes a certain amount of centralization of authority, with rulers and established lines of command, before warfare gets very complicated.

In many African states before the coming of the Whites, warfare was no longer a matter of a few dozens or a few hundreds of fighters but of thousands. Such organized combat required the organization of subunits within the military forces, with lines of command, and some attention to problems of supply, scouting, and other elements of sophisticated warfare. In societies such as the Zulu, the Ganda, and others, warfare was clearly for acquisition of territory and economic gain.

Among the people of East Africa, Ganda warfare with neighboring states was organized by the king in consultation with his advisers, some of whom relied on supernatural advice from the deities. A general was appointed, and war drums summoned the peasants to their chiefs, who in turn acted under the command of the centralized authority. The warriors lived off the land as they moved toward battle positions, so large detachments could be a severe economic drain on the food producers. Spoils of successful campaigns were brought back to the capital and distributed among the king and his ministers, as well as to warriors who had distinguished themselves in battle.

Among the most successful of the African war-making groups, the Zulu had regiments that were directly under the king's control and lived in barracks close to the capital. Thus the Zulu had a specialized army *in addition* to the war-making groups in rural regions. Maintenance of permanent regiments required, of course, that the Zulu subsistence system produce sufficient cattle and grain to feed the standing army.

At the time the Europeans spread into sub-Saharan Africa and wrested political control from the local peoples, large-scale population shifts and changes were in process, reflected partly in the extensive military campaigns by some groups and the general expansion of cattle-keeping peoples farther and farther into the south. Some areas undoubtedly suffered overgrazing and population pressures; and

Homo modernicus: Dimensions of the Contemporary Scene

the spread of slaving expeditions by the Arabs and the Europeans had generated unsettled conditions. Increasingly complex military organization was one of the results of these pressures.

The Evolution of Warfare

Several anthropologists have carried out cross-cultural studies of warfare, attempting to generalize from large numbers of ethnographic cases. Keith Otterbein (1970) has tested a number of generalizations concerning the development of warfare and demonstrates the not-unexpected finding that more complex, centralized political communities have more complex organization for warfare. Thus as populations have increased in density as well as food-producing techniques, centralization of authority has arisen as an almost necessary consequence. And no matter how fortunately situated these centralized political systems have been, somehow their long-term adaptations have nearly always led to increased military sophistication, often with increasingly relentless expansionist tendencies.

Most discussions of warfare have noted that hunting-gathering peoples are not nearly as involved in warfare as are many food-producing populations. The causes of warfare, then, are *not* to be found in the habits and social practices developed during the millions of years in which humans hunted for their subsistence in relatively small groups. But as soon as human groups have had possibilities for more settled residential patterns and greater control over localized and exploitable resources, they have become subject to pressures to expand their living space, at the same time experiencing pressures from their neighbors. In areas where very little in the way of centralized authority was to be found, warfare often took the form of continual small-scale raiding back and forth (as in the New Guinea highlands) with occasional larger expeditions leading to real massacres and large-scale political and economic shifts of power.

Escalation of warfare to more serious dimensions depends on the development of more sophisticated war-making powers, in terms of both personnel and material equipment. Societies that have reached that state of technological complexity have almost always come to the conclusion that the gods who protected them approved strongly of heroic military action or perhaps even demanded military conquest and the killing of enemies as a price for continued supernatural support. In any case, practically all troops that have ever marched have done so with complete conviction that their gods were on their side. In some cases, then, military actions have been launched for supposedly religious and ritual motives. But the people who were the victors did not hesitate to reap the economic and political rewards that came with their sacred successes.

Warfare and Individual Aggression

As warfare developed beyond the point of simple individual retaliations among small groups, the business of making war came to be based more and more on the calculated planning of political chiefs and rulers. In most human warfare, then, the *men who make the decisions to go to war generally haven't gotten much into the thick of the fighting themselves;* whereas the ones who face the dangers of combat often have had no part in the decisions. This separation between the aggressive acts and the adaptive decisions of political leaders should be enough to make it clear that warfare cannot be treated simply as an extension of some kind of "aggressive instinct." The men who find themselves in the front lines must rouse themselves to aggressive action when the time comes, and perhaps "aggressive tendencies" are quite useful then, but that is often long after the original war-making decisions have been made, by others.

Summary: A Perspective on Human Aggression

Human aggressiveness, in all its forms, arouses more tension, political controversy, and philosophical debate than any other behavioral category. Probably there is no other aspect of human activity that so thoroughly illustrates the systematic interrelations of physiological mechanisms, cultural expectations and ideals, economic conditions, technological equipment, and environmental features in a single dynamic system. To ignore the biological side, including possible genetic predispositions and

463

differences in arousal levels, is to run the risk of continued misunderstanding and confusion. This applies most especially to the study of the aggressive acts of individuals.

Stresses and frustrations, from economic deprivation to unrequited love (and myriad other culturally defined disappointments), are undoubtedly major factors in building up individuals' angers and predispositions to aggressive action. Deprived of expected satisfactions, some individuals lash out at the people who seem to stand directly between them and their goals; others turn to vent their hostilities on bystanders or other persons who are innocent victims of forces beyond their control. Many battered children in North American homes are victims of such displaced aggression. Aggressive tendencies can be displaced even further, to pets and inanimate objects (like the kicking of a chair) or into fantasy worlds.

Another reaction to overwhelming problems and frustrations is to turn aggressive feelings inward—to blame oneself and perhaps to end the psychological stresses through self-destruction. Suicide is overwhelmingly disapproved of among Euro-American peoples; but in many cultural groups taking one's life has been accorded honored status as a "solution," and the weight of public opinion could help individuals to undertake such a drastic step. The special case of "warrior suicide" was probably the example with the largest amount of social reward and prestige for seeking self-destruction. Maybe some people would argue that it wasn't really "suicide"—it was simply reckless military glory-seeking.

The work of Durkheim, the evidence from many modern Indian groups, as well as other recent work with suicidal people, illustrate the point that our modern society has many sectors in which social control integration and support are lacking, and individuals who find themselves driven to despair by circumstances are not much deterred by the distant and nearly meaningless "prohibition" against suicide. "Anomic suicide" seems to be increasingly common in industrial, urbanized societies.

The close links between life's frustrations and solutions like aggression or suicide must be understood first of all as the adaptive systems of flesh-and-blood individuals, each with a unique concatenation of social situations and cultural-psychological stresses.

The harnessing of peoples' willingness (of varying

23.8 **Watching aggressive encounters in animals and men is a favorite pastime in many human groups. A group in Thailand watches a cockfight. (René Burri, Magnum)**

23.9 **The evolution of destructive warfare in human societies.**

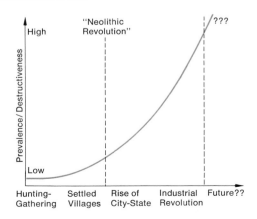

464

degrees) to fight and kill—in the form of organized warfare—takes us into a realm of social action in which military compaigns usually have their origins and outcomes in the combined decision making and strategic modes of many people. Sometimes individual war leaders play a large role in initiating a war. But even the wars of Alexander, Caesar, Napoleon, and Hitler involved the plans and efforts of many other leaders, to say nothing of the different kinds of motivations and attitudes of the followers.

In all except the very simplest instances of warfare the practical economic gains of conquest have played a significant part, and the development of political centralization, hand in hand with social stratification, has also been a significant background feature affecting the likelihood of war. Beyond a certain level of military sophistication, leaders of political states have probably made most of their decisions for war in an atmosphere of calm, practical reflection about military strategies, while the effectiveness of their troops depended much more on the discipline, equipment, and supply lines than on their levels of "aggressiveness." Somehow, though, the emotional moods of hatred and antagonism are brought into the picture in modern warfare, and able politicians play on individual aggressive tendencies when they want to arouse their people to support warlike activities. Once the soldiers are out there fighting, the "primitive" emotional responses of aggression might even be detrimental to effective action—at least for those people who manipulate complex electronic machinery of killing.

Aggression, Suicide, and War: Our Most Dangerous Achievements

24

City and Country: Pathways to Modernization

When the first urban centers developed in the Near East, over five thousand or more years ago, a new dimension in human social relations came into existence. Cities are, generally, densely settled communities in which a large proportion of the people do not grow their own food but depend on imports of grain, meat, and other foodstuffs from rural food-producing areas. The maintenance of non-food-producing communities requires some means of political and economic control that reaches out to the rural villages—cajoling, bribing, taxing, or otherwise convincing the peasants to produce extra foodstuffs so that the city folk can maintain their living. The beginnings of city life thus correspond quite closely to developments in multicommunity political organization as well as to heightened social stratification, with the creation of an elite social category freed completely from the supposed drudgeries of farming.

The identification of "the first city" is a matter of definition. How many houses, how many people, what special structural features are necessary to fulfill the idea of *city?* The archaeologist James Mellaart has described the rich archaeological site of Çatal Hüyük on the Anatolian plateau as a city because of its evidence of "extensive economic development, specialized crafts, a rich religious life, a surprising attainment in art and an impressive social organization" (Mellaart, 1964:120). Çatal Hüyük comprised at least two hundred living quarters covering more than thirty acres. The site also contains over forty shrines (areas with statuettes, figurines, wall paintings, and other artifacts suggesting religious motifs). Çatal Hüyük flourished for at least a thousand years, from nearly 7000 B.C. until some time after 6000 B.C. Mellaart believes that trade in valued objects, especially obsidian, accounted for the growth and wealth of Çatal Hüyük. However, whatever their economic base and social system, the impressive Neolithic communities in Anatolia did not develop into larger and larger city-states, and they did not develop techniques of writing to pass on to later generations the shape of the social and moral world they had created.

So far as we know, Mesopotamia was the first area to develop long-lasting cities, with large aggregates of people and the political-economic clout to go out and conquer neighboring populations. In the region of the Tigris and Euphrates rivers, the growth of those first large settlements around 4000 B.C. led to

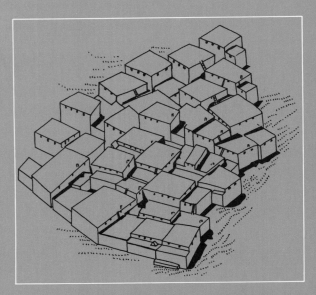

24.1 An artist's conception of Çatal Hüyük, one of the first "proto-cities" of the Near East.

466

ever more impressive urban centers, until, at the dawn of written historical records, a whole new city way of life had been created.

Early dynastic Uruk covered more than a thousand acres and had perhaps fifty thousand inhabitants (Adams, 1960:143). As was probably the case in many early cities, most of the inhabitants were still cultivators of the soil. But there were many nonagricultural specialists around: "One temple archive, for example, records that 90 herdsmen, 80 soldier-laborers, 100 fishermen, 125 sailors, pilots and oarsmen, 25 scribes, 20 or 25 craftsmen (carpenters, smiths, potters, leather-workers, stonecutters and mat- or basket-weavers) and probably 250 to 300 slaves were numbered among its parish of around 1200 persons" (Adams, 1960:143).

From those ancient days human life styles took on a duality that remains deeply significant to this day: the bipolarity of urban versus rural. Even the earliest writing reflects some of that dichotomy, and the suspicions of peoples always cut both ways: the rural peasants distrust the sophisticated urbanities, and the city people have anxieties about unknown hordes somewhere "out there" who might one day swarm in and ransack the city. Time and again the cities were, in fact, assaulted and pillaged by noncity folk, such as, for example, some of the Semitic nomads from the Arabian desert referred to as the Amorites in the Bible.

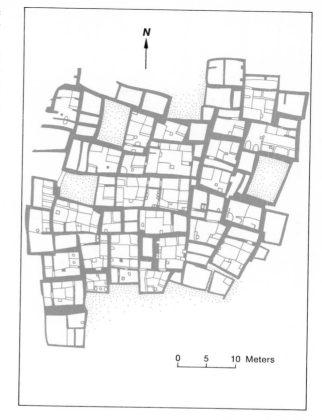

24.2 The "city plan" of Çatal Hüyük in about 6000 B.C., with apartments and shrines. (*Source:* Adapted from Mellaart, 1965:92)

24.3 Some wooden vessels from Çatal Hüyük.

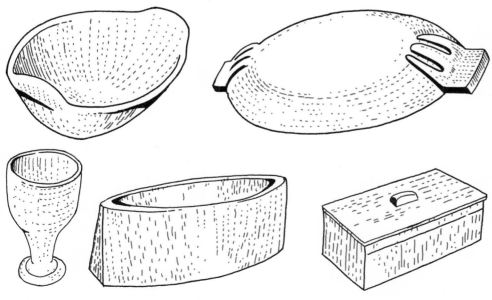

467

City and Country: Pathways to Modernization

On the other hand, the cities have always exerted a powerful attractive force—especially for the young and adventurous. But until the Industrial Revolution the growth of cities was a slow process. As the Industrial Revolution gained momentum the picture changed, as there were increasing numbers of jobs available in urban factories, and peasants were drawn to the new possibilities of city life. At the same time, they experienced a push from behind because of growing population pressures. Also, many systems of rural servitude were loosened by the revolutions of the nineteenth and twentieth centuries, so that both political and economic factors helped to break the peasants' ties to their home villages, adding to the sharply increased flow of populations to the cities.

There are a great many ways in which cities as social-cultural systems are different from the small-scale communities of the rural countryside. Our focus here will be on some of those features that anthropologists have been most interested in, which are often quite different from the interests of sociologists, economists, and other social scientists.

For one thing, anthropologists have often arrived on the urban scene (in their research) by following the migration pathways of rural populations. Many of the recent important studies of African urbanization, for example, have been carried out by people who first got into research in nonurban communities. It is natural, then, that their studies are concerned with the processes of adaptation of the immigrants—people from rural areas.

24.4 Ellis Island arrival of the *S. S. Prince Frederick Wilhelm* (1915). Migration of peoples is age-old, but the scope and extensiveness of migration in the twentieth century is an unprecedented index of modernization. (UPI Photo)

24.5 People migrate to the city in search of better jobs and higher wages, but their dreams are not always fulfilled. Rio de Janeiro. (René Burri, Magnum)

Squatter Settlements

In areas of the world where resources have not been plentiful and where the massive migrations from the countryside to the city have occurred quite recently, the development of housing has not kept pace with the flood of cityward migration. The result, in many areas, has been a development of so-called SQUATTER SETTLEMENTS around the peripheries of the cities, often developing into aggregates of hundreds of thousands of people. These squatter settlements are identified by many different labels in different parts of the world: in Brazil they are referred to as *favelas*, in Peru as *barriadas*, and in parts of North Africa as *bidonelles*.

The squatter settlements on the outskirts of

most of the major cities of Latin America, Africa, and Asia, as well as the Near East, are generally built up of homes put together from various kinds of scrap, ranging from cardboard cartons and sheet iron to sturdier materials such as stone and mortar. Sometimes these settlements are constructed in a single day or two, as groups of people go out en masse to a preselected building site—usually on some kind of governmental or public lands. Since squatter settlements involve living conditions that are thought to be far inferior to the usual pattern of city-dwelling comfort, these "suburbias" are often seen as wretched slums, supposedly full of crime, prostitution, and related social disorganization. Recent anthropological research has demonstrated, however, that the situation is often quite different from what has been expected.

William Mangin and Paul Doughty, in their research in the *barriadas* of Peru, found that there is often a considerable social organization and amount of planning in the building up of squatter settlements and that the squatters are frequently employed and upwardly mobile citizens of their urban communities.

Mangin has described the case history of Carmen and Blas, a young couple who, born of highland Quechua Indian parents, settled down in Lima to hard work and saving until they could make the big move, out to a new *barriada*. Their life in the inner

city was unsatisfactory due to the stresses of crowded conditions:

There was no place for the children to play and the petty bickering over jurisdiction of the small sidewalk was a constant irritant. (MANGIN, 1973:50)

A colleague of Blas's in the restaurant had spoken to him about a group to which he belonged. The members were organizing an invasion of state land to build houses and they wanted fifty families. The group had been meeting irregularly for about a year and when Blas was invited they had forty of the fifty they sought . . . their spokesman and leader was a bank employee who was also a functionary of the bank employees' union. (MANGIN, 1973:50)

Each family bought its own straw mats and poles for a house, and small groups made arrangements for trucks and taxis. Each household was asked to get a Peruvian flag or make one of paper. . . . A newspaper photographer was notified by the invaders and he arrived about the time the houses were being finished. . . . By early morning when the police arrived there were at least thirty one-room straw houses flying Peruvian flags and the principal streets were outlined with stones. (MANGIN, 1973:51)

Some houses were built during one night and the number built increased quickly in the ensuing weeks. The new suburbanities, proud of their little neighborhood, worked during evenings and Sundays

469

City and Country: Pathways to Modernization

to put up brick walls and other more permanent structures. Two years later Carmen and Blas were able to afford a concrete roof. At the time of Mangin's fieldwork, Carmen and the children operated a small shop in the home while Blas continued with his job as waiter in the city.

Not all *barriadas* in Peru have been established in the orderly, planned fashion illustrated in this brief vignette. But the importance of the squatter settlement process is underscored by the fact that slightly over 400,000 of Lima's 2.5 million inhabitants live in the *barriadas* ringing the city.

24.7 A barriada ("squatter settlement") at the outskirts of Lima, Peru. Built of bamboo matting in a matter of days, the houses are inhabited by migrants to the city seeking to establish themselves on public, unused lands. (Paul Doughty)

Kinship and Ethnicity in the City

Cityward migrants do not usually cut their ties to kinsmen and neighbors when they leave home. The kinship ties and bonds of friendship of migrants extend in both directions: back to the home regions and into networks of association in the new and unfamiliar environment of the city. Frequently, kin groups and village or regional or tribal groups organize mutual benefit associations seeking to improve their adaptations to city life. This is not a new, twentieth-century idea, of course. The many ethnic associations formed by European migrants to North America in the eighteenth and nineteenth centuries are illustrations of this same phenomenon. The parallels between the Polish, Greek, Italian, German,

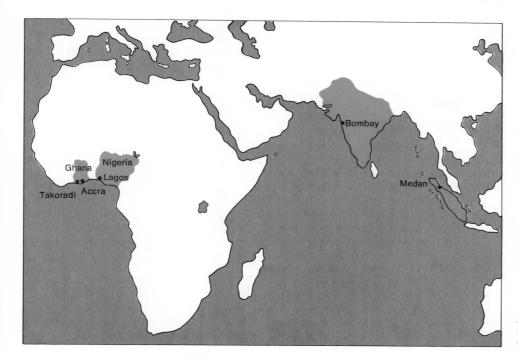

24.8 Location of some rapidly growing urban places discussed in this section.

Scandinavian, and other ethnic associations of North American cities and the new tribal and kinship and regional associations in West African cities are striking. Some of the new organizations growing up in West African cities are particularly interesting and have been intensively studied by the British social anthropologist Kenneth Little (1965).

The men and women who migrate from their traditional native areas to the cities come in search of money-earning opportunities, and they quickly encounter the difficulties of adapting to ethnic diversity and bureaucratic complexity. In most cases, however, individuals who move to the cities do so in contact with relatives and friends from their home village or at least from their native tribal region. These contacts are maintained, and as the urban population of a particular kin group or tribal-linguistic grouping increases, people develop more formalized societies and clubs to help one another in protecting themselves against the difficult aspects of metropolitan life. For example, Ibo peoples moving into Nigerian cities in the past thirty years have tended to form associations of Ibo "to protect themselves from the hostile way in which they were received by the local inhabitants when they took jobs as clerks, policemen, traders, and labourers" (Little, 1965:26). In the late 1950s there were nearly a hundred different tribal associations in the city of Accra (Ghana) alone.

In the city of Takoradi on the Ghana coast there

Urbanization

In about 1900 Great Britain became the first nation in the world to have over half its population living in cities—hence it became the first "urbanized nation" in the world. Since that time most European nations, and quite a few in Latin America, have become urbanized in that sense. By 1960 one third of the entire world population was living in cities. This rapid urbanization is largely the result of migration rather than of differences in birth rates.

471

City and Country: Pathways to Modernization

is a Fanti Union to which all people from the Cape coast are eligible for membership. Professor Little reports that at the time of his study there were about three hundred members in the Fanti Union. Every other week the union holds a general meeting, opened with a hymn and prayer, in which business is transacted in the Fanti language. Strikingly parallel to the ethnic associations of the Italians, Norwegians, Germans, and other migrants to North America, the benefits of membership in the Fanti Union include funeral benefits in the case of death of a member. (Little reports the funeral benefit of a member as 7 pounds, 4 shillings; and a lesser amount of 2 pounds, 2 shillings if a member's wife, husband, father, or mother dies). If a member of the union falls ill, he receives a sick benefit. Recognizing the importance of education in getting better jobs in the city, the union has planned to raise funds for scholarships.

Many of these new societies among West African urbanizing peoples are relatively egalitarian with regard to the sexes, and membership tends to be based on families. Other organizations, however, are more specifically women's groups, such as the Ewe Women's Association, the Family Welfare Society (operated by Akwamu women), and an association of Kru women. Kru women have developed their organization in part as a response to the fact that their menfolk are sailors who are absent from home for long periods. As in many of the other associations, funeral benefits are a significant aspect of their functioning (Little, 1965:30–31).

When rural people move to the cities their ideas about forming clubs and mutual aid societies or other adaptive organizations can come from many sources. The types of kinship organization and other social relationships in the home areas certainly affect the patterning of urban adaptation. The examples the newcomers encounter in the cities among other ethnic and minority groups also provide models to emulate. Often people who have been organized in corporate kin groupings tend to perpetuate these kinship organizations in modified form in the cities. In Indonesia, for example, the Batak peoples are organized in strong patrilineal lineages and clans in their traditional agricultural villages. When Batak men and women migrate to the rapidly growing cities they join social organizations already established by their kin groups. The lineages maintain mutual aid and employment

services for their memberships, and often the first wage job of an urban newcomer is working for a wealthy and well-established fellow kinsman whose commercial or manufacturing operations depend on the inexpensive and loyal labor force of migrating relatives.

Medan, Indonesia, is perhaps unusual in the degree to which social relationships are influenced by ethnicity. The Toba Batak and other Batak subgroups are the largest single ethnic category in this city of over 500,000 inhabitants. There are also indigenous Malays, Minangkabau, and Atjehnese from Sumatra; Javanese; and some Chinese and Indians. Since the Batak are Christians, religious themes underlie some of the conflicts with the other ethnic groups (most of whom are Muslims). Because so much of the quality of social interaction follows kinship and ethnic lines, "Positive ethnic identification is not just a matter of convenience or politeness in Medan but is rather an economic and political necessity" (Bruner, 1973:388). Thus, as reported by Edward Bruner, the entire fabric of life in Medan is composed of the interweaving of kinship and ethnic relations.

City and Caste in India

Something of the rapidity of worldwide urbanization is evident in the history of Bombay, India. In the late seventeenth century it was a "heterogeneous, dangerous, and lively town of 10,000 population, settled somewhat precariously on seven distinct islands" (Rowe, 1973:216). In the mid-nineteenth-century it was a major cotton mill town with a population already over 800,000 in 1864, and by 1961 there were well over 4 million people in the city, reflecting its importance as a port city and an industrial center.

As the neighborhoods of Bombay grew, they developed into political wards that approximated the caste composition of the city. (This is quite different, for example, from Medan, where the ethnic groups do not generally form distinct neighborhoods.) As William Rowe notes, "In discussing caste associations it is difficult to avoid mentioning political activity of a formal sort, for the two are closely intertwined" (Rowe, 1973:234). Each political subdivision of the city tends to be dominated by one or two caste groups, so there is heavy in-

472

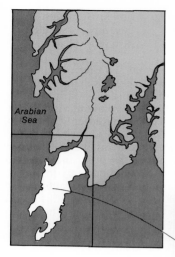

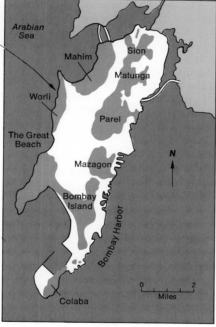

24.9 Bombay was originally settled on a series of islands in the Arabian Sea, off the west coast of India. The harbor was ideal for commerce. Gradually the flats between the islands were filled in to provide more space as the population continued to increase. The original islands are no longer identifiable, but their names are preserved as the names of neighborhoods in Bombay. (*Source:* Adapted from Rowe, 1973:217)

volvement in political affairs, and voting often follows caste lines.

Rural peasants migrating into Bombay seldom do so alone. Generally groups of people arrive together, and "Each residential migrant group has a leader who acts as a source of authority for the group and represents it in dealings with outsiders (landlords, police, merchants, employers) in much the same way the head of a family or the headman of a caste might function in the rural setting" (Rowe, 1973:231). In addition to the organization of migrants in terms of caste and kinship, there is a

sense of "brotherhood" among people from the same rural village that cuts across caste lines.

The caste associations have grown up in urban Bombay as major adaptive structures affecting the lives of individual migrants. The associations are often employment agencies for newcomers; they have cooperative housing; and the larger and wealthier associations operate educational facilities, scholarship funds, and other resources for "getting ahead" in the city.

Because the various caste associations tend to be the "employment agencies," there is a strong corre-

473

Table 24.1: Relation Between Caste and Occupation Among Migrants from One Indian Village

Caste/Village Occupation	Bombay Occupation
Warrior/landlord	Tram conductors
Cowherders/farmers	Dairy workers
Grain parchers	Grain shopkeepers, parched-grain hawkers
Barbers	Barbers
Farmers/earthworkers	Parched-grain hawkers, dairy workers
Washermen	Washermen
Weavers	Millworkers

Source: Adapted from ROWE, 1973:230–231.

lation between caste identity and occupational placement. The list in Table 24.1 shows the occupations of a number of migrants from one North Indian village.

Peasant Urbanites in Yugoslavia

Anthropologists Eugene Hammel, Andre Simič, and others have studied the processes of urbanization in modern Yugoslavia, noting that kinship ties play a large role in adaptations within the city, perhaps more than in many other parts of Europe. As we noted earlier, Serbians (and other Yugoslav peoples) have maintained strong patrilineal kinship groups in rural areas. The economic and ceremonial significance of these kin relationships continues in the urbanward migration of the younger generation.

24.10 Old and new in Belgrade, Yugoslavia. (Andre Simič)

In addition to the activation of kinship ties on arrival to the metropolis, for example in Belgrade, close ties are maintained with home villages:

Visiting patterns between rural and urban kin may be quite intense, with almost weekly exchanges, or may be limited to a trip home during the yearly summer vacation. . . . Perhaps the most common visiting pattern consists of the exchange of children. Urban parents send their sons and daughters to spend the summer with village grandparents or other kin. Children on a "vacation" in the village are fully incorporated into peasant life, and are expected not only to participate in agricultural labor but also to conform to village norms. Teenagers who dance to "beat" music and contemporary rhythms in Belgrade join in the village line dances (*kola*) with equal enthusiasm. Thus, a law student may pasture stock and work in the harvest. (SIMIČ, 1973:114)

Urbanization of North American Indians

Beginning in the 1950s and 1960s Indian peoples in North America have been migrating to the cities in greatly increased numbers. These newest candidates for urban assimilation have often found adaptation to city life somewhat unrewarding. Unemployment rates have been high, and in many aspects of life the migrants see themselves shut out from social and economic opportunities that seem to be open to other kinds of people. There seem to be many reasons for the difficulties the Indians encounter in their adaptation to the city, not the least of which is that they have been arriving in the cities at a time when opportunities and employment possibilities are shrinking for all groups.

Not all Indian people find the move to urban life so negative, however. The Mohawk people in New York, for example, have for a long time been famed as a high-steel workers and have carved out a special economic niche and a special life style in New York City, with fairly secure jobs and a maintenance of Indian ethnic identity (Freilich, 1970). Some Kiowa people, similarly, have found urban life in the San Francisco Bay area somewhat to their liking, "With an average family income of $7,600 many of the Kiowa own their own homes, dress well and participate in many Indian events" (Krutz, 1973:135). To some extent the San Francisco area appears to have less employment discrimination against Indian people than is found in the rural areas from which they migrated.

The rapid growth of urban Indian populations, together with the growth of pan-Indian political and social consciousness, has led, at least in some cases, to a resurgence of interest in traditional culture. Krutz reports of the Kiowa that:

At first they avoid the pow wows. . . . However, through the persuasion of Indian church friends, they begin to attend pow wows in the city. It is during this experience that they learn that they know very little about traditional Kiowa activities. The Kiowa group studies literature and consults with elders on how to represent the Kiowa at Indian events. . . . Old photographs are carefully studied in the construction of dance costumes, and visiting elders teach the words of the traditional songs . . . the migrants demonstrate Kiowa patterns of generosity at give away dances and within the mutual aid system of the kinship network. (KRUTZ, 1973:136–37)

Transition from Ethnicity to Social Class

A great many migrants to the urban scene are relatively poor and enter the metropolitan social system somewhere near the bottom layer of social stratification. Even when rural people have some economic means they are often considered "lower class" in terms of their dress, manners, and language. Although the examples from Medan and Bombay illustrate ways in which the difficulty of entrance into city life may be cushioned by strong ethnic and caste associations, from a longer-term perspective social class alignments and differences play an increasingly important role in affecting relationships among city dwellers.

In the small Ugandan city of Mbale, David Jacobson found that the types of kinship relations and support systems among urban dwellers were quite different depending on which social stratum—elite or working class—they were part of. Jacobson's informants expressed the view that "There are classes in Mbale, but they don't mix. The lower-class man moves with his own people, his fellow tribesmen, and he fights with others. Upper-class men, the educated people, speak English, so they can get together, regardless of their tribes" (Jacobson, 1973:39).

Independence for Uganda (in 1962) produced a rapid growth of governmental agencies and offices, which provide the economic basis for a substantial African government-employed elite in urban centers like Mbale. In contrast with the nonelite people, the bureaucratic corps in Mbale see themselves as a category of sophisticated persons with a command of English, book learning, and knowledge of the wider world.

Civil servants in Uganda are frequently transferred from place to place, so Jacobson found that 73 percent of the elite Africans in Mbale "had worked and lived in the town for less than three years" (Jacobson, 1973:35). Furthermore, "within the six-month period of field work, almost 40 percent of the senior civil servants have been transferred from Mbale" (Jacobson, 1973:35). As a consequence of their rapid geographical mobility, which led Jacobson to use the title *Itinerant Townsmen*, the elite Africans in Mbale are highly attuned to cultivating friendships among nonkin *within* their social stratum. It is this group that provides the supporting network of social contacts within their mobile ranks. Often men who knew each other in the past will meet again in some new post or use their former contacts to make new friends.

We note in this Ugandan example that under some conditions ethnicity is played down for certain segments of the new urban population, whereas it remains strong for the working-class people.

From City to Country: Modernization in Rural Areas

Comparisons of urban adaptations in Indonesia, India, Latin America, and North America suggest that the processes and forms of people's coping with the metropolis can be quite different, depending on the forms of social organization they carry with them from their home villages and towns into the heart of the city. Almost always the requirements of city environments have powerful effects on social forms developed in rural regions, but they do not, as we have noted, result in a single, uniform worldwide style of urban life.

While the pull of the city lights has strong effects on previously nonindustrialized populations, the rapid MODERNIZATION of the world is having pro-

475

found effects in the rural environments also. In addition to the roads cut through tropical jungles, arctic backlands, and other areas previously inaccessible by vehicle, many regions are now actively and heavily exploited for raw materials—the furs of exotic animals, lumber from previously untouched forests, and minerals from under the soil. Melanesian Bougainville—the home of peoples with a simple horticultural way of life well into the twentieth century—is rapidly becoming a wage-labor center of bauxite mining. Other areas are being dramatically changed by large-scale hydroelectric dams and new tourist resort facilities, not to mention the superdestructive effects of high-explosive warfare.

The term *modernization* is often used by economists, developers, politicians, and others to refer to changes that are supposedly progressive "improvements" in people's life styles. In these formulations the wearing of Western-style clothing, the adoption of monogamy, the conversion to Christianity, and other features of Western cultural behavior are also regarded as evidence of "modernization." In our use of the term, we don't attach any value judgments to these processes of change, for in many cases it is not clear that people are better off or worse off under the "modern" conditions. Also, we don't emphasize "Westernization," for some of the new kinds of things going on in many parts of the world include the adoption of cultural items from *other*, non-European sources. For example, modernization in some parts of East Africa includes the adoption of Congolese or "southern" music and other cultural items. In China and India modernization includes a *reaffirmation* of some rather ancient medical practices; acupuncture in China and Ayurvedic medicine in India are part of the wave of modern life. Modernization among North American Indians includes the pan-Indian powwow network.

A great many different, interrelated concepts have been used by social scientists to describe some central features of modernization, including "loss of autonomy," "integration into national systems," "development of cash economies," "growth of political dependence or interdependence," "articulation to the macrocosm," and so on. These and many other similar ideas can be lumped together under the label DELOCALIZATION. Here are some other items illustrating the scope of delocalization:

1. Inuit people in treatment for tuberculosis (and other ailments) in Oregon, California, and other urban hospitals.
2. Oceanian peoples on their islands waiting for shipments of "welfare food."
3. Beatles music and rock records on juke boxes in small Mexican towns.
4. Peasants far in the backlands listening to agricultural prices on their transistor radios.
5. Thousands of Samoans adjusting to a new way of life in San Francisco and other California cities.
6. CIA and other "foreign agents" dropping in on various rural areas and playing various parts in political movements in which the writings of Marx, Lincoln, Mao, Freire, and Fanon are argued over.
7. Small Indian villages in Mexico making fancy pottery for regular export to fancy stores in Mexico City and the United States.
8. Women in a small rural town in Mexico using microscopes to assemble delicate core units for a New Jersey computer firm.

Tappers and Trappers: Effects of Delocalization

As the forces of modern commercialization and other activities reach out to the hinterlands, there are certain general, predictable consequences for previously autonomous or semiautonomous peoples. Robert Murphy and Julian Steward noticed that there were similarities in the changes that were brought about by the effects of delocalization on both the Northeastern Algonkian (Montaignais) peoples (with whom Steward was familiar) and the Amazon Basin Mundurucú with whom Murphy had

24.11 Television has come to Kuwait and to practically every other corner of the world. (Bruno Barbey, Magnum)

476

done fieldwork. Both groups had local raw products of interest to the wider world—furs among the Algonkians, rubber trees in the Mundurucú area.

Murphy and Steward (1956) made a formal comparison of the two cases of modernization and found the following parallels:

1. "the displacement of aboriginal crafts by commercial goods better suited to meet local needs, both old and new, inexorably led to increased dependency" on the outside world.
2. "increased dependence on trader."
3. "after the breakdown of extended kinship bonds in both groups, individuals traded completely on their own."
4. The fully developed situation of delocalization found local chiefs of both the Montaignais and the Mundurucú acting as intermediaries with the Euro-American outsiders (government agents, missionaries, and so on). (Murphy and Steward, 1956:345–349)

The effects of outside influences on the social and cultural systems of the Montaignais and the Mundurucú were profound, for the new age of reliance on traders and other outside agents changed family organization, the political system, and practically everything else. To a large extent, Murphy and Steward argued, the changes followed directly from the *economic* influences introduced by Euro-American traders seeking local raw materials for marketing. A key feature in both situations, reflecting the new cash economy, was that "both became involved in a mercantile, barter economy in which the collector of wild products was tied by bonds of debt and credit to particular merchants" (Murphy

24.12 Modern road-building equipment makes possible the penetration of tropical rain forests and other geographical barriers. (René Burri, Magnum)

24.13 Modern powwow dancing at the Rosebud Sioux Reservation. Similar scenes are found in many different Indian groups across the country from Rhode Island to San Diego. (Gary Renaud, Magnum)

24.14 Transistor radios have greatly increased the spread of news and other communications into remote areas. (Leonard Freed, Magnum)

24.15 Delocalization: peasant women in a rural Mexican village assemble complex computer core units for an electronics firm in New Jersey. (P. J. Pelto)

and Steward, 1956:347). This credit dependency on outsiders is a widespread phenomenon in many parts of the world and reflects how local peoples stop producing their own essentials of production, sacrificing their previous energy-independence in favor of the apparent efficiencies of factory-produced goods. Generally the short-term efficiencies of the factory-produced goods (guns, traps, clothes, snowmobiles) are quickly apparent, whereas the hidden costs of dependency on the traders are not evident until later.

Reindeer Herders and Snowmobiles: Energy Delocalization

The Same reindeer herders of northeastern Finland are an example of what happens when a new item of technology is adopted into a socioeconomic system that was previously based mainly on local energy sources. Until 1960 the major energy source on which the Same of northeastern Finland depended in their daily travel in reindeer herding,

24.17 Skolt Same herdsmen on skis. (P. J. Pelto)

24.16 The use of skis for arctic travel dates back at least two or three thousand years, yet they remained a mainstay for hunters and others until the 1960s. This rock carving from Karelia (USSR) probably dates from at least two thousand years ago.

478

24.18 Same herdsman with his draft reindeer. (P. J. Pelto)

families in the Sevettijoivi area, and every one of them had some reindeer, though four or five families (especially those of widows without able-bodied sons) could be regarded as relatively "poor" because their herds were so small. These households, like all of the others, had ready access to the fish in the local lakes, wood from the forests, and other natural resources, which provided most of their subsistence needs. Some of the people did go out to work for wages, especially in the summertime, to supplement their reindeer and fishing economies.

Many changes were in the wind for the European Arctic, but none was as potentially far-reaching as the new technological "breakthrough" shaping up in a small town in Quebec. A French Canadian, Armand Bombardier, had been working for years in trying to develop a versatile and economical snow vehicle so that people in the snow and ice of the northlands might have a speedy means of transportation that even the "common man" could afford. Bombardier's first successful one-man snowmobile—now widely known around the world as the "Ski-Doo"—became marketable at the beginning of the 1960s and very soon was available throughout the Arctic (Pelto, 1973).

The Same and their neighbors in northeastern

hauling wood and supplies, and just visiting around from place to place was provided by draft reindeer. By 1960 there were government snow vehicles and occasional automobiles, trucks, and light aircraft hauling goods and passengers in the region, but each household's daily affairs depended upon the energy output of at least two or three—and sometimes up to fifteen or twenty—domesticated reindeer.

In 1960 there were approximately fifty Skolt Same

24.19 Herding reindeer with snowmobile. (J. Trobitzsch)

479

City and Country: Pathways to Modernization

24.20 **The mechanized Same herding economy is now dependent on outside energy resources.** (Ludger Müller-Wille)

Finland quickly adopted snowmobiles—so quickly, in fact, that by 1967, when we briefly visited the area to find out what had happened, anyone still driving around with reindeer sleds in the old, slow, reliable way was considered to be curiously archaic. Not everybody was able to afford the $1,000–$1,400 for a snowmobile, however. In fact, among the Skolt Same about half of the households had machines in 1967, whereas the others frequently hired the services of their neighbors (sometimes their kin) for hauling supplies from the store, for quick transportation to reindeer roundups, and other uses. The poorer families—those without snowmobiles—were in effect helping to subsidize the machines for the others.

In 1971, when we visited Lapland again to find out more about the "snowmobile revolution," we found that all except about a dozen families had machines and that there were already over a dozen two-snowmobile families. Reindeer herding was completely transformed after about 1965 or 1966—for the delicate balance of relationships between herders, animals, and their physical environment was upset by the change from silent, slow-moving reindeer sleds to noisy, swift-moving "Ski-Doos."

Instead of close interaction between humans and animals, with long-term winter herding and "home care" of herds, the whole system changed to a "quick roundup" and "turn 'em loose again" mode of reindeer economy. As far as northeastern Finnish Lapland is concerned, by 1971 there was almost no such thing as "domesticated" reindeer—only small herds of wild and unapproachable creatures that had to be driven by force and fear to the roundup corrals for slaughter.

The biggest change was that more than two thirds of the Skolt Same households had been forced completely out of reindeer herding. The high cost of snowmobile ownership and maintenance for reindeer herding was simply not economically feasible for most families. They were better off seeking work for wages or getting on the unemployment rolls of the Finnish government. Only a small number of the more affluent families could maintain themselves in the reindeer economy, and even they had to struggle to make it pay. There were other factors that brought about a need for cash in the local Skolt Same way of life, but the snowmobile was by far the most important single factor.

The effect of the snowmobile—one single techno-

480

Homo modernicus: Dimensions of the Contemporary Scene

logical item that cost plenty and depended on *out-side* fuel sources—was enough to transform the Skolt Same society from a relatively nonstratified, part-cash, part-subsistence system to a community with increasing economic inequalities, great dependence on money for food and almost all other necessities, and rapidly growing dissatisfaction with what "modernization" had brought about.

This case is important not only because of the striking effects of a single technological device but also because it illustrates so clearly the unforseen effects of delocalization—a loss of local semiautonomy, especially as it applies to sources of energy. Until the advent of the snowmobile the Same in northeastern Finland, as well as in many other parts of the European Arctic, relied mainly on their own energy resources to maintain the economic and social system. They did rely on some food imports, but most of their transportation, heating of houses, cooking, and other subsistence activities operated with local energy resources, mainly "reindeer power." The opportunity to purchase snowmobiles for more rapid transportation seemed to the Same, and to everybody else, to offer only convenience and economic advantages. They had no way of forseeing the extensive social and economic changes that *had* to result from this modification of the ecological system.

Modernization Comes to the Miskito Indians of Eastern Nicaragua

The Miskito Indians number some thirty-five thousand people along four hundred miles of the Caribbean coastline. Their abundant subsistence economy was based in former times on hunting and fishing as well as the slash-and-burn cultivation of manioc, bananas, and other crops. Bernard Nietschmann, a geographer from the University of Michigan, recently studied the impact of modernization on the Miskito peoples and found that population growth and the commercialization of hunting and fishing have combined to bring about rapid changes in the interactions between the people and their natural environment. In recent times the Miskito have found ready markets for green turtles, hawksbill turtles, coconuts, and jaguar and ocelot skins, as well as some of their crops.

In 1969 and 1970 two turtle meat companies (both foreign-owned) began operations in the Miskito area, buying turtles from the Miskito hunters. Turtle hunting more than doubled in the first six months of 1971, and "market sales outside of the village have increased 1500% while consumption of turtles in the village declined by 14% . . . the Tasbapauni Miskito are catching and selling more green turtles but eating less" (Nietschmann, 1972:62). As the Miskito hunting and fishing efforts have become commercialized, "populations of hawksbill turtles, crocodiles, caimans, fresh-water otters, jaguars, ocelots, margays, and lobster are all severely depleted or almost exterminated over much of eastern Nicaragua" (Nietschmann, 1972:63). The green turtle is now an endangered species.

It's only a matter of time before the high-protein diet of the Miskito is but a fond memory of days

24.21 **Miskito hunters are rapidly depleting the green turtle populations because of the commercial demand for their shells. (Bernard Nietschmann)**

gone by. In the past most members of the Miskito Indian population were linked through kinship obligations to the immediate sources of meat from the forests and from the sea. Now, however, those kinship obligations are not holding up, as hunters sell more and more of their products directly to outsiders. Families cut off from meat supplies are forced to go down to the store to buy food, much of it, of course, heavy in carbohydrates and low in protein—and all of it expensive. Meanwhile the population is rapidly increasing. Of course the poorer families can turn more and more to their subsistence crops, but the products of their slash-and-burn agriculture are poor in protein and other nutrients compared to the meat supplies they formerly depended upon. Professor Nietschmann sums up the general situation as follows:

> In general, the maladaptive trends presently evident in Tasbapauni and for all Miskito populations are as follows: 1.) Increasing simplification of the variety of subsistence; 2.) the transition of a stable subsistence economy into an unstable cash economy based on local subsistence resources, with potentially adverse nutritional consequences; 3.) loss of local autonomy . . . ; 4.) a trend toward hypercoherence . . . which makes the local system too vulnerable to extraneous fluctuations in outside systems . . . ; 5.) and the overall tendency toward reducing the Miskito's general purpose system organized around subsistence . . . to a specific purpose system oriented toward differentiated access [the beginnings of social stratification]. (NIETSCHMANN, 1973:243)

Not all of the Miskito want to go along with the trend toward commercialization. One older man said:

> "In the beginning there was no selling business here. When it came, the Indians grumbled. They said it was spoiling the place. Now that they're playing with the scale, everyone is selling. The Indian doesn't like that. I'm not going to give them meat; let them cook the money." (NIETSCHMANN, 1972:66)

24.22 One of the first shops in Saint Pascal before the industrialization of the 1960s. (Gerald Gold)

24.23 Modern shop in Saint Pascal, Quebec. An expansion from a small family shop of earlier decades. (Gerald Gold)

Saint Pascal: Rural Industrialization in French Canada

The rural communities of French Canada have, at least until recently, lived somewhat apart from the rapid industrialization in much of North America. A number of writers claimed that the cultural patterns among the French Canadians denigrated commercial enterprise, bestowing prestige

mainly on the traditional roles—priests and doctors, as well as "aristocratic" landholders. But French Canadians are not all alike, and in any case things are changing in French Canada as elsewhere.

The town of Saint Pascal, studied by Gerald Gold in the late 1960s, is perhaps not completely typical of French Canadian towns, but it is extremely interesting in its high degree of small-scale industrial and commercial activities. Out of the traditional agriculture-based society a small group of entrepreneurs began, in the 1950s, to develop small-scale manufacturing enterprises. These included a furniture shop, a candy factory, a tannery for leather goods, and a small tire-recapping factory. By 1969 the labor force in the factories and shops of Saint Pascal had grown from *five* men to a total of over four hundred employees in seventeen enterprises with products valued at over $7 million.

The larger industrial enterprises in Saint Pascal (the town had a population of 3,486 in 1966) are relatively modern enterprises, linked to national and international financial dealing. Most of the Saint Pascal businessmen make business trips to Quebec City at least once a month, and twelve of them use sales catalogs in promoting their wares. It is interesting, however, that only 20 percent of these French Canadian entrepreneurs use English in their daily business transactions. They are still very much French Canadian in their cultural orientation. Language does not, however, pose any real problem for their commercial enterprises, given the fact that the next step up in merchandising from Quebec City is in the heavily French-speaking Montreal.

The effects of the growing industrialization of Saint Pascal, along with related trends of modernization, have brought about the creation of a new and more flexible social system within the community. Industrialists and other commercial operators are the core of the new modern elite of the town, and a substantial middle class has grown up composed of teachers, white-collar workers, and other employees. The factory workers, with their relatively steady but by no means affluent incomes, make up the lower end of the middle range of social stratification, while day laborers and farmers are an economically depressed lower stratum that is on the losing end of the scale of prestige these days. Formerly, farming was the backbone of the area and an honored and basic family-oriented enterprise; but those days are gone.

Delocalization and Inequality

Everywhere the advance of technological change and other aspects of "modernization" bring about changes in life styles as well as significant shifts in social relationships. Among the Inuit in northern Canada, for example, the spread of technology and commerce has brought wage labor opportunities for some people, causing a sharp differentiation between "employed Inuit" and hunter-trappers. In many instances it's the wage earners who can afford to buy snowmobiles and other new technology, furthering the socioeconomic differential between them and their "nonmodernized" kinsmen. In some areas, too, government housing projects have been introduced, especially in the new arctic towns, but not all Inuit families can afford the new housing: "Probably the commonest way in which a native family acquires a dwelling in town is by accepting employment with the federal or territorial government, thereby becoming eligible to rent a government-owned home" (Honigmann, 1972:235). As John Honigmann has noted in his studies of Inuit in Inuvik, "Housing, with it's attendant rules or priorities, has brought out stratification in these hitherto largely undifferentiated societies" (Honigmann, 1972:244).

In southeastern Africa the building of the large Kariba Dam on the Zambesi River forced the dislocation and resettling of some fifty-seven thousand Tongan peoples, whose new way of life in the resettled areas included experimentation with cotton, livestock, and fishing (in the newly created lake behind the dam). Government programs involved special technologies ranging from pesticides and irrigation to tsetse fly control. Fishing bourgeoned in the lake for a time and then declined sharply as new predators, especially the tiger fish, took over the new habitat. Some of the Tongan peoples were economically successful, others were not, and it appeared that a new local elite was emerging. They were

familiar with the ways of the outside world. Either educated beyond primary school or with educated sons, they also had access to local transportation to carry their cotton to the nearest depot of the government marketing board. . . . Some of their number were sufficiently at ease with government officials to visit them in their offices in order to demand or otherwise arrange transport. . . . In Chipepo the innovators were prominent villagers with a history for initiating new enterprises. (SCUDDER and COLSON, 1972:63–64).

Modernization and Cultural Brokers

Although all human societies past and present have depended on interactions of various sorts with their human neighbors, a considerable number of the most important adaptive tasks in nonmodern societies have focused on relationships with the local *physical* environment. Hunting and gathering peoples have everywhere specialized in the expertise of finding and capturing animals, fishing, and gathering wild plants within their home range. Nomadic herdsmen have trained each succeeding generation in achieving high skills in the management of herds and in acquiring knowledge of grazing areas; and cultivators have had to be, above all else, experts in the preparation of plots, planting, tending crops, and management. Of course the present-day descendants of those hunting and gathering and cultivating peoples must still maintain a good deal of that kind of adaptive knowledge, but a new dimension has been added: dealing with the wider world.

With increasing delocalization, the most significant adaptive skill often comes to be bilingual, bicultural communication with other social worlds. The anthropologist John Bennett has discussed this in terms of microcosm-macrocosm relationships. The immediate world that people live in day to day can be thought of as their microcosm, linked by many kinds of economic and social transactions to provincial, state, national, and worldwide socioeconomic systems (the macrocosm). When a local community is dependent on the macrocosm for essential energy resources, cash, and other necessities, people in the local microcosms must learn to speak the dominant national language and to bargain with outside politicians and business operators, and they must often be able to communicate with the people in the macrocosm through writing. Literacy and "political" education become essential to adaptation, even though the people may still be spending much of their time in the same kinds of economic tasks that occupied them earlier. In many North American Inuit communities, for example,

hunting and trapping are still the economic mainstays, much as they were fifty years ago. But now each Inuit family is dependent on gasoline supplies for transportation, some individuals are directly involved in wage work for the national government, and a variety of governmental policies (e.g., welfare, family allowances, and old age pensions) require considerable red tape and paper work. Government agents in the form of police, health officials, and social welfare people come around frequently, and interactions are much more frequent than heretofore with the trading post and other commercial operations.

The heightened interaction between local microcosms and their wider worlds generally rests on the extensive bilingual and bicultural capabilities of *some* people in the local community who have special experience. These CULTURAL BROKERS are frequently individuals who have been out there in the wider macrocosm in wage labor or who happen to have been especially successful in school. Many successful cultural brokers got their bicultural training in military service.

Clyde Kluckhohn's sketch of "a Navajo politician" is an interesting example of a bicultural broker, illustrating the kinds of factors that may produce "social marginality" in such an individual. At the time Kluckhohn wrote his description, Bill had won a successful election campaign (not for himself, but for a friend) from which both Bill and his wife gained well-paid jobs.

In part, Bill's success in the field of power and politics must be attributed to a control of English unusual in a Navajo of his age and to the recognition by other Navajos that Bill understands whites and their ways, both skills deemed important in coping with white deviousness. . . . Bill likes people, loves to talk with everyone. He also likes to have people feel dependent upon him. And—let it be said candidly—he loves to manipulate people. . . . I have never known a Navajo of his age who was more deeply divided between the Navajo and white worlds. . . . He is known to some as a "progressive," as an acceptor and introducer of American foods, gadgets, and habits, but he publically laments the decline of Navajo customs among the younger generations. He insists that his English-speaking children speak some English to their children in the home, but he himself flaunts his classical (sometimes almost archaic) Navajo. (KLUCKHOHN, 1960:447–448)

Homo modernicus: Dimensions of the Contemporary Scene

It is significant that Bill's nickname among the Navajo was "Little School Boy." His mother died when he was less than two years old, and when his father remarried Bill was sent to be raised by other relatives. For some reason, he went to school at least five years—much longer than most Navajo before World War I. In addition to that boarding-school education, he also worked for a time for a White trader, improving his mastery of English and, more important, his understanding of White cultural ways.

This Navajo politician was the object of great ambivalence among his people: some distrusted him intensely, whereas others relied on him to handle important transactions in the wider world. It is not surprising that a man like "Little School Boy" became well known to anthropologists and often served as an informant and research assistant, although his antagonisms toward White people were generally close to the surface.

Paliau, a political leader among the Manus in the Admiralty Islands, is a striking example of an individual for whom the excitements, experience, and new knowledge acquired during World War II suggested possibilities for radical transformation of the local microcosm to fit in with the encroaching wider world.

During World War II Paliau was a policeman in Rabaul, New Guinea, which was held by the Japanese for a considerable time before Allied forces mounted the slow, costly counteroffensive. Some Australians considered Paliau a "war criminal" for serving under the Japanese, and after the war he was put in prison in Port Moresby, apparently in reprisal for political activities. When in 1946 he returned to his native area in the Admiralty Islands, he had a rich store of new information about the White people's world:

It was Paliau who had a program for action, an organized picture of change which involved genuine ethical ideals—he wanted all the people of the Admiralties to become one people, eschewing the narrow rivalries and hatreds between the different tribes and different villages, pooling their specialized skills and possessions. . . . By banding together as one people, there would be many of them, enough, if they used their resources wisely, to get good European goods and to live the way of life of the western world. (MEAD, 1956:190).

Margaret Mead has described how the political activist and cultural broker Paliau organized "The New Way" for the Manus people. The council structure, the committees, the school, and other features of "The New Way" were all part of the set of ideas that Paliau had put together during his years of working with the Japanese and the Australians. Unlike the Navajo "Little School Boy," Paliau had not been trained in any school; "instead, with help from his fellow police boys, he had taught himself to write and developed not the characterless printing or script of an unsuccessful school boy which most Manus used but a distinctive script and a real signature" (Mead, 1956:210).

One interesting feature of the Paliau movement of the Manus is that Paliau himself was not a native Manus but spoke a different language, as he came from the small island of Baluan, some thirty miles away. Thus, "He led a stranger people, whose spirit he admired extravagantly, whose landless fate he pitied far more than it deserved, whose vision of the world in which all children who were born lived, and no man's hand was turned against another . . . whom he must lead toward a limited earthly paradise to be realistically attained only by hard work and controlled behaviour" (Mead, 1956:210–211).

The point about cultural brokers that we are stressing here is that they are special persons who through some unique features of life history and temperament become unusually well-versed in information from *both* a local, usually non-European, microcosm *and* the broader social system. In some cases cultural brokers arrive from the outside, as school teachers, traders, or other representatives of the dominant social order. These brokers from the outside world become effective if they learn the local language and social patterns and mediate between local people and "the world out there." Whatever their origins, cultural brokers frequently have considerable economic and political power, which grows with each increase in delocalization.

Trying Out New Ideas: Who Are the Innovators?

A number of researchers have tried to answer the question: Which individuals in a community are most likely to adopt new ideas and practices first? Homer Barnett developed a general theory of inno-

485

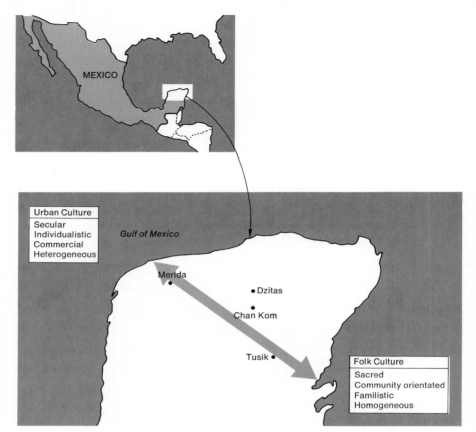

24.24 Redfield's folk-urban continuum theory. The urban end of the continuum is characterized by secular ways, individualism, commercialization, and heterogeneous culture patterns. His theory was based on research in the Yucatan peninsula.

vation based on the idea that readiness to try new things or to introduce cultural changes is most likely to appear among individuals who are marginal people or misfits or who are otherwise discontented: "When cultures meet, the majority of those who switch their allegiances are individuals with the least opportunity for full participation in the most valued activities of their own society" (Barnett, 1953:404).

A counter to this "marginal man" theory holds that, at least in economic matters, the people in a community who have the most material resources are likely to be the ones who are both able and willing to take the financial risks that innovations might require. A modification of this view is that the "middle class" is likely to be somewhat conservative about innovations even though they have the economic means.

In a study of modernization in the health-seeking behavior of Maya Indians in a Guatemalan town, Clyde Woods and his fellow researchers wanted to find out who used modern medical services (doctors, pharmacists, and nurses) rather than traditional folk healers. From interviewing and observations of forty families over the course of several months, Woods found that people quite often went to *both* traditional *and* modern medical practitioners in the course of an illness. Rather than putting all their faith and fortune in a particular type of healer, people might go first to the pharmacist or a minor lay curer (depending on the type of illness). Then, if the first line of medical aid didn't bring relief, they turned to another source, perhaps an M.D. Often the medical doctor was successful in curing, but there were occasions when people had to seek further for relief from illness with a visit to the local shaman, or perhaps they went back to some home remedy.

Woods and his colleague Theodore Graves ex-

486

amined the reasons for differences in degree of utilization of modern medical services and decided that a primary factor was people's general tendencies toward "innovativeness" in the adoption of new cultural practices. That factor, in turn, appeared to be dependent on the causal factors of *cash* and *exposure* to outside influences. Woods and Graves concluded that people often change their behavior first (when needs arise) and that changes in beliefs may come later (Woods and Graves, 1973).

The Folk-Urban Continuum

Since World War II, industrialization and other aspects of modernization have proceeded so rapidly that many of the formerly sharp contrasts between urban and rural scenes are being rapidly erased. Nonetheless, there are still interesting differences, and study of these has been a subject of anthropological concern for many years, even before the present period of very rapid social change. During the 1930s Robert Redfield and his associates at the University of Chicago conducted a number of community studies in the Yucatán Peninsula in Mexico and noted what they felt to be a gradual, unidirectional progression of changes associated with the "outreach" of urbanization. Redfield compared four communities—an isolated Indian village, a small town, a moderate-sized market center, and the city of Merida—and suggested that the trend involved changes toward: (1) greater cultural heterogeneity, (2) greater commercialism, (3) greater family disorganization, and (4) a shift away from a sacred orientation toward life as one moved closer to the city.

There has been a great deal of theoretical argument about the idea of the folk-urban continuum since Redfield first presented it. Many people have pointed out that although trends toward commercialization and secularism, for example, are often noted in patterns of modernization in rural areas, there are also instances in which sacredness (in the form of new religious movements) increases with modernization. Specific aspects of change in the shifts from rural toward urban probably take quite different forms depending on details of life style and ecology in a given region. However, it is interesting to note that some of the ideas presented by Redfield seem to be held by rural people as well.

Stephen Schensul set out to explore the question: What does the folk-urban continuum "look like" from the perspective of rural people? He went first to the Banyankole people in East Africa. He developed a game board (based on the idea of the SEMANTIC DIFFERENTIAL interview technique) on which people could respond to a set of statements about qualities of urban and rural life. Schensul asked respondents to place tokens representing "their village," "the market town," and "the city" on locations on the board that represented their view of the range of variation from, for example, "very religious" to "not religious," "much money" to "little money," and so on.

Rural villagers in Ankole (in Uganda) saw their home community as more hospitable, more peaceful, and less affluent than the city. They also regarded the village as a world in which "relatives are important." On the other hand, Schensul found that they tended to regard their village as *not more religious* than the town and city. It is also a bit surprising to learn that on the matter of "clean—dirty," Ankole people gave a cleaner rating to the city than to the village.

Schensul then took his "game board" to northern Minnesota, to farmers and villagers living in marginal economic circumstances in the cutover lands west of the Mesabi Iron Range. Most of these Minnesotans are descendants of Northern and Western Europeans. In many respects they expressed views similar to the Banyankole on the qualities of the

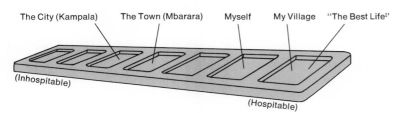

The City (Kampala)   The Town (Mbarara)   Myself   My Village   "The Best Life"

(Inhospitable)

(Hospitable)

24.25 The "semantic differential" board devised by Stephen Schensul to study people's cognitive definitions of "the city," "the town," and "our village" in Uganda and northern Minnesota. The lines point to the responses of the average Uganda villager in his sample.

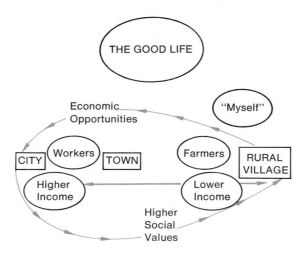

THE GOOD LIFE

Economic Opportunities

"Myself"

CITY — Workers — TOWN

Farmers — RURAL VILLAGE

Higher Income

Lower Income

Higher Social Values

24.26 The folk-urban continuum as seen by northern Minnesotans and by the Banyankole people in East Africa. They are a long way from the "good life."

city-town-village continuum. Basically, the city (Twin Cities) was seen as having large economic advantages; the village had more of the social values, including "peacefulness" and "hospitality." Neither city nor village was defined as "more religious."

Putting together all the different definitions and concepts about city, town, and village, Schensul could show a continuum of qualities separating urban and rural life into two distinct semantic realms (see Figure 24.26). Both Banyankole and northern Minnesotans are ambivalent about these two worlds, for they long for the economic advantages they perceive in urban life, but they also prize the moral, social qualities of their rural villages. In abstract "semantic space" the "good life," as defined by these people, can't be found at either end of the continuum. It's "off the board" (Schensul, 1969).

Summary: Processes of Delocalization

In spite of the many weaknesses and oversimplifications in the original "folk-urban continuum," the changes of the past thirty years since Redfield wrote his book would seem to bear out the more important of his generalizations, even as important exceptions

crop up to give us new insights into the varieties of human adaptations.

One point that now becomes clear is that long-run trends may turn around, reversing the seemingly irrepressible forces of delocalization. In some areas, for example among the Navajo people of the Southwest, there has been a resurgence of local organization and cooperative effort, with well-organized moves to reduce the economic and political power of outsiders. Attempts to reassert local autonomy seem to have much better chances of success in areas with some controllable natural resources.

Keeping in mind that long-term changes might easily turn out to look different from the short-run effects, the following processes appear quite frequently in modernization and delocalization:

1. There is a breakdown or simplification of family and community political organization as different individuals and groups compete for ties with the outside political and economic forces.

2. There is an integration or a SYNCRETIZATION of local and nonlocal belief systems and ceremonial practices, in order to adopt the social power of the

24.27 Modern air transport systems have had striking effects on the cultural and economic systems of previously remote peoples. (Bruno Barbey, Magnum)

24.28 Delocalization is especially visible in the spread of standardized commercial establishments throughout the world. Japan. (Tress, Magnum)

outside world without giving up everything identified with local traditional cultural ways. In many areas Christian religious practices are adopted but with an underlying maintenance of traditional deities, beliefs, and ceremonial practices.

3. In tightly organized societies, like those of the Pueblo Indians, many semi-isolated communities in central Mexico, and some of the island societies of the South Pacific, there is a tightening of controls vis-à-vis the wider world. After World War II, for example, the Zuñi community in New Mexico developed some interesting revivals of traditional ceremonies as a reaction to the disruptive influence of returning war veterans. Great effort was made to control and compartmentalize the impact of the returnees, though with varying success. As J. Adair and E. Vogt pointed out, the Zuñi reaction to these "winds of change" was quite different from the more open, flexible style of the Navajo peoples, whose returned veterans were considered in a more positive manner (Adair and Vogt, 1949).

4. Delocalization is socially less disruptive for those communities in which the basic subsistence economy remains viable, especially if that subsistence system can be partially diverted to a cash economy without serious disruption. In some areas the reindeer-herding economy of the Same seems to have provided just such an ideal transitional system, supporting the local people at a reasonable level even as they are drawn more and more into a cash-cropping style of husbandry. The same appears to hold for some of the coastal Same in Norway, whose fishing economies continue to provide them economic support. The opposite situation is apparent in the case of all the Plains Indians, whose lifeways were shattered beyond restoration by the total loss of the buffalo herds.

5. In recent times there has been a powerful new wave of delocalization affecting many areas. Tourism is now a significant and growing influence, socially and economically, in many areas. The effects of tourism are as yet largely unstudied, even though it is a major influence in many parts of the world.

Although tourists may be a potential source of economic gain for hinterland peoples, the usual practice is for Euro-American investors to reap the profits through control of lodgings, tours, and sales of "souvenirs." Preservation of the economic gains of tourism for the local populace seems to occur only in areas with strong local political organizations, as in some American Indian communities.

6. A second facet of recent delocalization is the rapid upsurge of interest in native handicrafts which has resulted in rising prices for handmade goods that were in earlier times ignored or even ridiculed. It is easy for armchair theorists to decry the "artificiality" of this new interest in traditional weaving, pottery, jewelry, and other products, but in many parts of the world the sales of such goods provide significant new economic possibilities for native producers.

7. We have barely touched on the myriad effects of delocalization. When we consider that many people distant from industrial centers are now exposed to hazardous amounts of airborne pollutants (e.g., strontium 90 in the food intake of Northern European Same) and that isolated peoples like the Bikinians are evacuated from island to island so that hydrogen bombs can be tested in the South Pacific, it is evident that the outreach from the industrialized world into the remaining semiautonomous regions of the world is rapidly intensifying.

City and Country: Pathways to Modernization

25

Population:
The Long Bomb

A million years ago, it is estimated, the human population on the face of the earth was perhaps 125,000 persons, and it required something like 230,000 years for that population to double to 250,000. The rate of increase was slow indeed.

In 1970 the estimated world population was over 3.5 billion persons, and it would take only 35 years to double.

Consider the equation:

$$\text{Population} \times \begin{matrix}\text{Consumption} \\ \text{per} \\ \text{person}\end{matrix} \times \begin{matrix}\text{Environmental} \\ \text{impact} \\ \text{of quantity} \\ \text{of goods} \\ \text{consumed}\end{matrix} = \begin{matrix}\text{Effects} \\ \text{on} \\ \text{environment}\end{matrix}$$

And let us also consider the ecological interrelations of population, industrial capital, agriculture, and pollution:

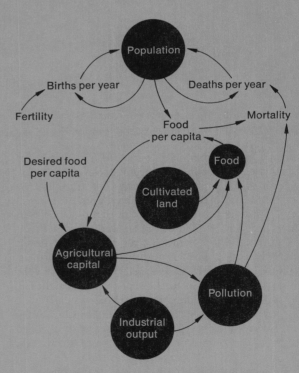

25.1 Feedback interconnections of agriculture, population, industrial output, and pollution in the theoretical model of the Club of Rome futurists. (Adapted from Meadows et al., 1972)

Both of these formulations show that population is a crucial variable in affecting cultural-environmental conditions, and it is one that we must pay careful attention to in trying to understand the evolutionary adaptations of human groups. We can begin with the questions: (1) How do human groups regulate (knowingly or unknowingly) their population growth? (2) Why did population grow so slowly throughout the long hunting-gathering phase of social evolution?

Population Dynamics in Hunting-Gathering Societies

Family organization, the processes of mate selection, and cultural regulations of sexual activity are among the crucial factors that affect population levels from the "input" side. Disease, wars, and other lethal forces affect population levels from the other end, through mortality.

It is not likely that the small-scale population groups of the Ice Ages had deliberate "population policies." On the other hand, the individual units (mated pairs and small family groups) may well have had reasons for the deliberate regulation of births. Among nomadic people one of the limitations on the desirability of births is the fact that babies are entirely dependent on others, mainly their mothers, for food and transportation for several years. It is common for infants to be nursed for at least two years, since mothers' milk is the most convenient and the best available food for infants. Babies have to be carried to food-gathering places and from one camp site to another. If babies were born every year, women in a hunting and gathering group would be burdened with the almost impossible task of carrying three or perhaps even four infants and children around. The disadvantages of frequent births are so great that, as the !Kung Bushmen comment, "A woman who gives birth like an animal to one offspring after another has a permanent backache" (Lee, 1972:332).

The modern Bushmen provide a clear example of the interaction between nomadism, women's work patterns, and "population policy." In his anthropological fieldwork, Richard Lee noted that gathering wild vegetable foods, moving camp sites, and visiting activities require that a typical Bushman mother carry each of her infants approximately 4,800 kilometers (2,880 miles) during the first two years of the child's existence, and "Over the four-year period of dependency a Bushman mother will carry her child a total distance of around 7,800 km (4,900 miles)." (Lee, 1972:331). We should add that when a Bushman group moves camp, each woman must also carry her own cooking utensils and other equipment, plus water supplies.

On the average, Bushman women bear their first children when they are about twenty years old, and after their first child they generally have more children "spaced three to five years apart until menopause occurs after age forty. Fertility appears to be

The Ancients Complain About Overpopulation

491

lower among the Bushmen than among other populations" (Lee, 1972:332). Lee and his co-workers found that among the nomadic groups there were no women with children closer in age than two years. Part of the birth control system for this birth spacing involves a post partum sex taboo for the first year of the baby's life. Other factors are apparently at work, however, for the resumption of sexual intercourse after the year's taboo does not result in regular two-year birth intervals, as we might expect.

Lee suggests that "long lactation suppresses ovulation in Bushman women" (Lee, 1972:340). He notes that the Bushmen lead active sex lives but that the continued frequent nursing of their babies apparently must directly suppress ovulation enough "to produce a four-year average birth interval." There is considerable debate in medical circles concerning the supposed relationship between nursing and susceptibility to pregnancy. Careful studies have demonstrated some such suppressive effects in populations in India and among the Ruwanda in Africa, whereas studies in other populations have not shown that ovulation is suppressed. Lee suggests that the Bushmen may be one population in which this suppressive effect of nursing is strong.

In those occasional cases when Bushman mothers do have babies two years or less after the birth of a child, there is a considerable possibility that the mother will not have sufficient milk to feed both, and the risks of mortality increase. In some cases, INFANTICIDE is the last resort for maintaining proper birth intervals.

A study by Patricia Townsend of a hunting-gathering population in New Guinea throws further light on this matter of population control in small-scale societies. She studied a community of 234 people in the Upper Sepik River region who make their living mainly from wild-growing sago palm plus some other wild plants and a few cultivated vegetable foods, a few pigs, some small game, fish, and insect larvae. Among the Sanio "subsistence is thus based almost entirely on wild food resources." However, the sago palm is so plentiful in the area that the people can live semipermanently in small hamlets consisting of a few nuclear families, and each hamlet can find all the food it needs within a radius of about a mile. Unlike the Bushmen, these people do not have to travel very much, so they do not have the same motivations as do Bushmen to maintain birth spacing. Townsend found that the population

was quite stable, although the average number of live births per woman was 5.3, and some women had given birth to as many as ten children. High rates of infant mortality contributed significantly to population control in this case, for the mortality rate among infants and children to age three was 43.2 percent.

Part of the high infant death rate was caused directly by the practice of infanticide. Anthropologist Townsend's careful inquiries of twenty-one women showed that "11 percent of all infants were killed at birth and 23 percent of infant and early childhood deaths are due to infanticide" (Townsend, 1971:19–24). The reason for the killing of infants is clear: if a baby is born too soon, while the previous child is still being nursed, then both children would face serious risks of malnutrition. The newborn baby is killed to save its older sibling from semistarvation.

In Sanio society cultural rules concerning sexual intercourse are intended to prevent the possibilities of frequent birth and the necessity for infanticide. Sexual intercourse between the parents of a child not ready for weaning is prohibited, so that the post partum sex taboo is approximately two years, twice as long as that among the Bushmen of the Kalahari. It is, of course, difficult to know how often this cultural rule is broken, but the fact that infanticide is fairly frequent suggests that the two-year rule is not taken completely seriously. The Sanio do have other contraceptive practices, including the use of a supposedly contraceptive ginger root, but its effectiveness is unknown.

Post partum sex taboos, infanticide, infant mortality from disease, and possibly other factors (such as maternal food taboos) have all played a part in variable degrees in maintaining the stability of hunter-gatherer populations. Many groups have undoubtedly died out from lowered birth rates and starvation in lean years. Among the Inuit in the harsh arctic environment, food shortages come at irregular intervals, and infanticide and starvation take their inevitable toll when the hunters can't find game. Some Australian aboriginal groups—for example, the people of Groote Eylandt—are reported to have had infant mortality rates as high as 60 percent, mostly from disease, so that infanticide has been almost unnecessary, nor has there been any birth control. The Bushmen, on the other hand, seem to have much lower infant mortality rates.

Homo modernicus: Dimensions of the Contemporary Scene

The Development of Agriculture and Population Dynamics

When the domestication of food crops and animals made possible the extraction of more calories per acre, the way was opened for significant population increases. But even without significant increases in food productivity, there may be an increase in population if women no longer have to carry their children from place to place as do nomadic foragers. This has happened in recent times among the Bushmen, some of whom have settled down in recent decades to plant crops of maize and sorghum and to raise a few animals. Lee reports that there is "some evidence of a lower birth interval—33 to 36 months—among the more sedentary Bushmen. It is possible that the availability of softer foods lessens the infant's dependence on breast milk and thus permits an earlier resumption of the mother's ovulatory cycles" (Lee, 1972:341). Lee suggests that "*Sedentarization alone may trigger population growth, since women may have children more frequently without any increase in work on their part and without reducing their ability to provide for each one*" (italics in the original; Lee, 1972:342).

The importance of sedentary life as a spur to population growth deserves careful attention, but we must note the example of the Sanio, who are relatively sedentary yet extremely interested in limiting their population. It is not just their sore backs that the women are interested in; they are also very much concerned with and motivated by the status of available food supplies for their children.

Whereas most hunting and gathering peoples have population densities of less than one person per square mile, horticulturalists with systems of extensive slash-and-burn cultivation can usually maintain population densities of at least five to ten persons per square mile, and in especially favored places much more than that. In some areas it appears that shifting cultivation has been carried on for many, many centuries, with fairly stabilized populations. On the other hand, in other areas the advent of cultivation tended to lead to ever-increasing population densities, ever-increasing settlement clusters, and ultimately city life and industrialization. In Europe the early inhabitants practiced slash-and-burn cultivation for centuries before the rise of the

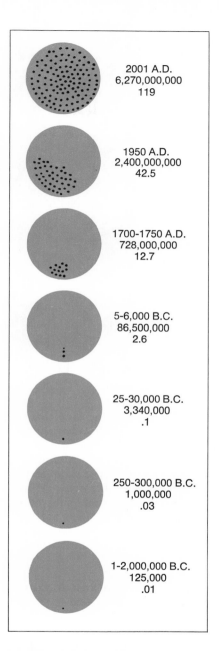

2001 A.D.
6,270,000,000
119

1950 A.D.
2,400,000,000
42.5

1700-1750 A.D.
728,000,000
12.7

5-6,000 B.C.
86,500,000
2.6

25-30,000 B.C.
3,340,000
.1

250-300,000 B.C.
1,000,000
.03

1-2,000,000 B.C.
125,000
.01

25.2 **Growth of human population during the past 2 million years of biocultural evolution. The dots signify average (estimated) population density per square mile, from one person per hundred square miles 2 million years ago to the predicted density of about 119 persons per habitable square mile in 2001 A.D.**

493

25.3 By the year 2000 our projected world population will be over 6 billion. (A. Devaney)

first Greek city-states and the glory that was Rome; and the Germanic tribes and other people north of the Alps maintained low population densities for centuries after the people in the core areas of the Roman Empire had developed more settled, sedentary living patterns, with intensive permanent cultivation of their fields. Permanent cultivation of fields was, of course, greatly aided by the use of large animals for pulling plows and other equipment, as well as by the development of methods of water control.

Population Growth and Agriculture: The Mesoamerican Case

Archaeologists have made very intensive studies of the growth of populations, the growth of agricultural systems, and other cultural events of prehistoric Mexico, especially in the areas around present-day Mexico City. Figure 25.4 shows a population curve for the Basin of Mexico in the centuries before the coming of the Spanish, and the dotted line is the population growth in the Teotihuacán Valley,

which was the site of a great prehistoric city. The graph shows that the population in the Teotihuacán Valley reached a peak between 600 and 700 A.D., and then the destruction of Teotihuacán City itself was followed by a sharp decline of population. The Valley did not again reach the levels of approximately 250 persons per square kilometer, although there was a considerable increase in population during the Aztec period up to 1519.

According to archaeologist William T. Sanders, the population density of the Teotihuacán Valley area rose from perhaps twenty-five persons per square kilometer in 100 B.C. to ten times that figure at its maximum in the seventh century A.D. (Sanders, 1972:108). What "caused" this marked population increase? There surely must have been some extensive changes in food production methods and capabilities.

In about 900 B.C., when the first evidences of settlement appear in the Teotihuacán Valley, there were a series of small hamlets and villages on the higher ground of Teotihuacán, based on a system of slash-and-burn cultivation with a fairly high yield.

494

Some time during the period 600–300 B.C., changes in settlement pattern took place in the form of two substantial villages at the edge of the alluvial plain. Sanders suggests, "it is probable that the appearance of these settlements is related to more intensive agricultural practices" (Sanders, 1972:112). As the population increased still further in the early phases of metropolitan Teotihuacán, there are evidences that irrigation systems were developed, though of a relatively simple kind. In some way the nascent city was gaining control of the entire population of the valley (perhaps fifteen thousand people) and was extending its political dominion into adjacent valleys. An estimated fifty-eight hundred hectares of the best land in the valley came under irrigation and hence was capable of supporting many times the population supportable by shifting slash-and-burn methods. It is likely that most of the area was still cultivated by the old techniques (which persist to this day in areas not far from the Basin of Mexico), but increasingly dense population concentrations were made possible by the gradual enlargement of *selected spots* of very intensive cultivation. The growth of a large city population gradually became possible, supported partly by the irrigated croplands, partly by the city dwellers' political control over areas of less intensive agriculture.

Later phases of still more intensive agricultural productivity in the Basin of Mexico were made possible through swamp reclamation, the growth of canal irrigation, and some terracing. Swamp reclamation brought about the construction of those famous artificial islands (*chinampas*)—protected by dikes and ditches and gradually built up to some ten thousand hectares of reclaimed land at the south end of the entire Basin. To this day, tourists flock to this area, known as Xochimilco, to ride the gaily colored boats, Venetian style, among the "floating gardens." It is estimated that the total population capacity produced by the "swamp reclamation in the Basin of Mexico . . . must have been well in excess of 250,000–300,000 people" (Sanders, 1972:116).

Many, many other fertile valleys of the Old World and the Americas show the same kind of population increase that we see charted in Figure 25.4. The older interpretation of these developments was that technological developments in food production made possible increased population growth, which continued up to the limits of food production. Then new methods were again developed that further increased food production and allowed the population again to expand, and so on. In this view, population expansion is the *result* of improved agricultural technology. This view has been sharply challenged, however.

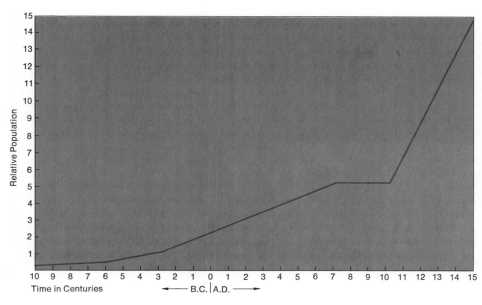

25.4 Population curve in the Basin of Central Mexico. The sharp rise after 1000 A.D. appears to correspond to a period of increasingly effective food production technology. (Reprinted by permission of MIT Press from W. Sanders, "Societal Evolution in Mesoamerica" in B. Spooner (ed.), *Population Growth, Anthropological Implications* (Cambridge, Mass.: MIT Press, 1972), p. 112.)

Population: The Long Bomb

Population Pressure Causes Agricultural Development?

Economist Esther Boserup has suggested that our common-sense view of the relationships between agricultural technology and population growth is backwards. She argues that population increase puts mounting pressure on agricultural development and that as people become seriously concerned with the specter of famine, these pressures lead to more intense cultivation, the elimination of extensive slash-and-burn agriculture in favor of continual cultivation, then multicropping and other methods that increase yields per acre. Boserup's argument, then, puts population growth *prior* to the development of improved agricultural production. This is in direct opposition to the famous Malthusian theory, according to which population growth results from and is dependent on the food production potential. She believes that the neo-Malthusian theories "are misleading, because they tend to neglect the evidence we have of growing populations which managed to change their methods of production in such a way as to preserve and improve the fertility of their land" (Boserup, 1965:22). Applying this perspective, one could suggest that hunting and gathering peoples in many areas where agriculture would be possible don't cultivate food crops because their population density is low enough so that *they don't need to;* and that food production was invented and improved by peoples who, for some reason, had developed settled ways of life and increasing populations and were *forced* to find new food sources. It is the horse (causal agent) of population pressure that pulls the cart of agricultural productivity and not the other way around.

From analysis of population changes and agricultural technologies in different portions of Middle America, William Sanders (1972) concluded that Boserup's argument about the importance of population pressure is sound for some areas under certain conditions, but not for others. For example, he notes that in Mexico's Tehuacán and Oaxaca valleys the people who moved into sedentary agriculture began to farm *intensively* in the richest alluvial areas long before there were any apparent population pressures on them. By Boserup's argument those people should have kept on with extensive slash-and-burn cultiva-

tion for a long, long time, until they were *forced* to change their food production methods. But that isn't what happened. On the other hand, the history of interrelations between agricultural production and population increase in the Basin of Mexico seems to fit with the Boserup theory. Overall, though, Sanders and many other archaeologists now argue that there are complex interactions between populations and agricultural methods that take different forms in different microenvironmental situations.

Rates of Population Growth During Neolithic Times

The appearance of the first cities in the Middle East occurred only about five or six thousand years after the earliest development of domesticated food production; so that from about 8000 B.C. to 4000 B.C. human lifeways in the Middle East changed from the hunting-gathering way of life practiced by perhaps 100,000 persons to a relatively densely populated, sedentary way of life, with the beginnings of the first urban sprawl. By 4000 B.C. there may have been somewhere between 500,000 and 1 million people in that area.

Many anthropologists and historians have viewed that growth as exceedingly rapid. And it is in relation to that of the ancient hunting-gathering peoples who maintained near-zero population growth rates. But how do the population growth rates in the Neolithic period of the Middle East compare with rates of population growth today? Our world population now has been increasing at around 2 percent per year, which, as we have noted above, gives us a population doubling time of only thirty-five years. Anthropologists R. Carneiro and D. Hilse have worked out a computation for estimating the population growth rate in the Middle East based on archaeological data. They suggest that the rate of growth during the Neolithic period in the Near East must have been somewhere in the neighborhood of .08 percent and .12 percent (Carneiro and Hilse, 1966). Looking at the rates of population increase in the Basin of Mexico area, where it appears that the population increased from perhaps 100,000 persons to a high of around 1.5 million in a mere two thousand years, we can, by using those same computations, suggest something like a .12 percent or .13

496

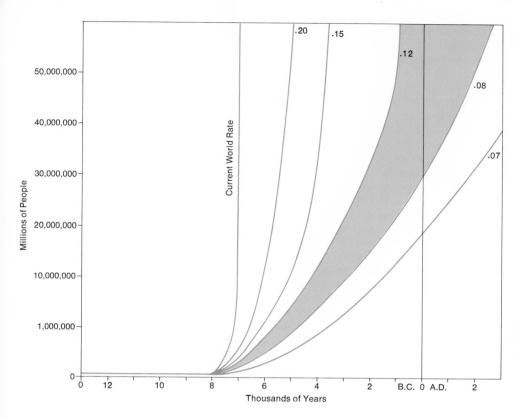

Millions of People

50,000,000

40,000,000

30,000,000

20,000,000

10,000,000

1,000,000

0

.20 .15 .12 .08 .07

Current World Rate

0   12   10   8   6   4   2   B.C. 0 A.D.   2

Thousands of Years

25.5 Rates of population growth in the Near East in Neolithic times. Calculations indicate the most likely rate to have been between .08 and .12 percent, far below the present world rate of nearly 2 percent.

percent population increase per year, again growth rates that seem very low compared to the fantastic 2 percent per year that we now have. The "population explosion" of the Neolithic revolution that brought about the first cities in the world was indeed modest compared to what is happening today.

Sex, Children, and Food Production

We have already discussed the idea that many hunting and gathering peoples probably live lives of relative affluence. The best available studies show that hunter-gatherers don't have to work nearly the number of hours per week that we moderns put in—and they maintain fairly good intakes of calories and proteins. The relative "affluence" of hunting-gathering peoples is evidenced in the fact that they seldom push their children to go out and do productive work. Hunter-gatherers' children fre-

quently spend a great deal of time just "messing around" and casually learning adult roles at an age when the younger generation in agricultural societies are busy watching animals, keeping birds and other scavengers away from crops, grinding grain and doing other heavy work. The more complex the agricultural process (until full-scale mechanization), the more likely that very small children will be involved directly in food production activities.

Food producers who need to grow only enough for their own nutritional needs do not necessarily have to press every child into active service all of the time. Most autonomous cultivators require some work of their children, often in connection with tending their domesticated animals, but production pressures on every family are not so great as to make child labor a necessity.

We think of children as being the direct responsibility of nuclear families and as their "helping hands." However, we must recall that with the rise of sedentary ways of life based on even moderately

497

intensive agriculture there has generally been a corresponding increase in the importance of unilineal kin groups, which are the corporate social groups that control lands, engage in political activities, and maintain their own religious activities. As we noted earlier, the growth of corporate kin groups is often accompanied by increased competition and group feuding. Now, if kin groups are fighting with one another, then they have some strong motivations for *increasing* their numbers over time to offset the growth in manpower of those other groups—we say *man*power because frequently it is an increase in males that is desired. This motivation applies especially to patrilineal societies, in which there is always the question of enough male heirs in individual family lines.

With the growth in cultural complexity that brought about multicommunity political centralization, the first city-states, and the rise of social stratification, there came even greater pressures for population increase—from the point of view of individual families, the corporate kin groups, *and the central government*. For peasant families the new problem that developed with the rise of political centralization was the matter of paying taxes.

Families that had previously managed well with modest plots of land found that they had to intensify cultivation in order to provide food to the continually growing numbers of people in the towns and cities. Add the factor of conscription in the army. With their older able-bodied sons gone to war now and again the agricultural kin groups and individual families had to press younger children, both male and female, into productive activities at earlier ages. Clearly parents who had an eye on the future often had reason to want more children as quickly as possible to help with the work.

Controls on Population Expansion: Disease, Famine, and Warfare

From the arguments we have just suggested, we can only wonder why there was not a serious population explosion fairly early in the Neolithic period. The most likely explanation for the continuing slow population growth is that the sedentary life and the domestication of plants and animals brought a very

considerable increase of disease. We have already discussed the health problems that sedentariness creates, especially from human wastes (pp. 427–428).

Compared to the population control mechanism of disease, the effects of increased warfare and occasional famines are probably rather negligible. However horrible the wars that raged across Europe and Asia in bygone times, they may have had as little effect on population increase as the massive slaughters of World War I, World War II, and other twentieth-century wars, which together have killed many tens of millions of people. These modern wars caused only a ripple in the curve of expanding population.

Both warfare and famine probably have had a significant impact on population control only when combined with the destructive effects of disease. (For example, the devastation of World War I included massive epidemics involving perhaps 30 million cases of typhus between 1917 and 1923, from which there were 3 million deaths in European Russia alone [Zinsser, 1967:160].) Ecologist Marston Bates has commented that "Through all of the period of complex culture, of civilization, while man flourished and increased so abundantly, disease was surely the chief agent of destruction, outrunning war and famine. Indeed, war and famine did not operate so much directly, as indirectly by favoring disease" (Bates, 1968:42).

Population Growth and the Rise of European Colonialism

From the birth of Christ to 1650 the world's population increased at an estimated rate of less than 0.1 percent per year. If disease was the major population control factor during the past six thousand years of sedentary human adaptations, then we could not expect much of a population explosion until modern science developed some curbs on infectious diseases. Significant changes in medical knowledge and public health practices did not occur much before the nineteenth century. Nevertheless, there was a potentially serious increase in rates of population growth *before* the nineteenth century. Somehow, from 1650 to 1850 the rate of population increase was multiplied fivefold! Mortality rates were still

Homo modernicus: Dimensions of the Contemporary Scene

> For each additional 1,000 people in California, an average of 238 acres of arable land (that is, land suitable for farming) has been covered by buildings and pavement . . . by 1960 some 3 million acres of California farmland, most of which was of high quality, had been converted to nonagricultural use. A projection to the year 2020 shows that 13 million acres—half of the state's arable land—will be lost to farming by then. . . . In addition, smog kills crops. If current trends continue, California eventually will not be able to feed herself, let alone export food as she does today. (EHRLICH et al., 1973:83)

extremely high, but people were having more children.

Many processes were at work in producing the population changes of the seventeenth and eighteenth centuries. One of the most important of these was the spread of European political and economic domination around the world through colonialism. At first contact, the Europeans' penetration into many parts of the world produced population decline, especially in the Americas, where the "White man's diseases" and forced labor recruitment reduced native populations drastically.

Curious things happened to the patterning of world population after the Europeans were fully established in the far-flung corners of their empires. The populations of Europe began to expand rapidly, even though there were not many medical breakthroughs to account for these changes. Overall, the standard of living in Europe was improving, and people were better able to feed themselves and to get rid of some of the worst of the filth they had been living in during the Middle Ages. The gradual improvement of economic conditions reflected two major forces: increased productivity and communication brought by new means of energy production, and the increased wealth derived from the exploitation of overseas colonies. Some new kinds of foods also played a role. For example, the introduction of the potato (from the Indians of the South American Andes) helped to increase European food supplies.

The curious thing is that in some colonial areas population also began to show considerable increase. By 1850 the world population had already topped 1 billion, and was increasing at the previously unheard of rate of over 0.6 percent per year. The marvels of medical science had not yet come to bear very much on the population centers of the world,

yet at that speed the mass of humanity in the world would double in just a little over a hundred years! By 1900, it is estimated, the population of the world was 1.6 billion persons.

A great deal has been written about the population-multiplying habits of peasant peoples. Historians, economists, demographers, and others frequently write as if the world's marginal rural peasants were bent on sinking the earth ship under the weight of reckless reproduction. We need to examine more carefully what factors during this particular period of time, after European expansion had taken place, encouraged so much population increase around the world. It does not seem reasonable to claim that standards of living were improved for most peoples outside of Europe and North America with the spread of Europeans. Whence, then, came the tendencies toward population expansion?

One factor that should not be overlooked is that wherever Europeans went they carried with them Christian religious ideals that favored uncontrolled population expansion. They denounced and prohibited infanticide, abortion, and post partum sex taboos, and clamped down on localized warfare and feuding. The Christian European *restriction* on polygamy also increased population growth, for it has been demonstrated that *polygynous* family organization tends to maintain somewhat *lower* birth rates than does monogamy.

A second and perhaps more decisive factor was the economic organization of European colonies. Because the "mother countries" extracted wealth—the products of the mines, plantations, and fields—the colonized peoples not only had to produce for their own subsistence but also had to meet the demands of their "protectors." The additional produc-

499

tion could somehow be wrested from the soil if all members of the family bent to work and if the family had extra hands—even little hands—to increase the intensity of their production efforts.

Population and Colonialism: The Javanese Example

Anthropologist Clifford Geertz has made a detailed analysis of agricultural practices, family structure, and population in Java during the colonial period. He notes that there were probably about 7 million people in Java in 1830 and that the figure rose to more than double that number by 1870. By 1900 there were some 28,400,000 persons: "an average annual increase of approximately 2 percent during seventy years" (Geertz, 1968:69). Geertz argues that there was no evidence of any "rising standard of living" to account for this increase in population, nor does it appear that any new public health and medical facilities affected mortality figures so dramatically. On the other hand, he points out the increased burden of taxation imposed upon the Javanese rice farmers by the Dutch colonial administration. Compared to the agricultural systems of many other areas of the world, the Javanese cultivation of rice was ideally suited to a never-ending intensification of hand labor in the rice paddies:

The practices have already been mentioned—pregermination, transplanting, more thorough land preparation, fastidious planting and weeding, razor blade harvesting . . . more exact regulation of terrace flooding, and the addition of more fields at the edges of volcanoes. The concentrative, inflatable quality of sawah [intensive rice cultivation], its labor-absorbing capacity, was an almost ideal (in an ecological, not a social, sense) complement to capital-intensive sugar growing. (Geertz, 1968:77–78)

Intensified labor demands do not necessarily lead to increases in children, particularly if the type of labor needed is not easily accomplished by the young and immature. However:

Java's main subsistence crop of irrigated rice is one of the most responsive of all to labor intensification. . . . This labor is mostly of the type that can be, and is, done by women and children throughout southeast Asia . . . we may thus suppose that in colonial Java, with high demand for labor and with land and crops still sufficiently responsive to labor intensification, a family's "demographic investment" in children would pay off. (White, 1973:231)

It is, of course, impossible at this late date to prove that individual Javanese families in the nineteenth century got busy producing more children because they all saw that they needed more hands to work for their European masters as well as to produce their own foods—but the fact is that the population increased extremely rapidly during the middle of the nineteenth century and that the increases seem to have been highest in exactly those regions where the colonial pressures of taxation and plantations were the greatest. The adaptive strategies of individuals, families, and communities were undoubtedly many-sided, and the increase in children to increase the labor power of the family was quite plausibly one part of their overall adjustment to the situation.

DDT, Public Health, and the Population Explosion: The Mauritius Case

Out in the Indian Ocean, some five hundred miles east of Madagascar, is an island about one tenth the size of New Jersey, which, in its isolated agony, exemplifies the twentieth-century population problem of the world. Mauritius was entirely uninhabited until the sixteenth century, when the Portugese accidentally landed there and found interesting species of animals, including the dodo bird and some large fruit-eating bats. The Dutch took over the island in 1598 and brought in a few slaves from Africa. Then in 1715 the French took over, brought in some settlers and some more slaves along with artisans from south India, and established a plantation system based on cotton, spices, sugar cane, and coffee. In 1810 the British captured the island and set about to really get going with sugar production.

In 1835 the population was slightly over 100,000, most of them slaves. By 1861 there were over 300,000 people. A large part of the increase was due to the migrants from India. In spite of their isolated location, there were frequent incursions of disease-producing microorganisms on the island. There were smallpox epidemics in 1742, 1754, 1756, 1758, 1770–1772, 1782–1783, and 1792–1793 and cholera epidemics in 1775, 1819–1820, 1854, 1856, 1859, and 1862, and influenza devastated the island several

Homo modernicus: Dimensions of the Contemporary Scene

times. Other diseases were also important, but malaria, another real killer, arrived in Mauritius in 1865. After that, periodically, malaria was a significant factor in keeping down population growth—the hard way.

From the figure of 310,000 people in 1861 the growth to an estimated population of 428,000 by 1946 was very slow, about 0.5 percent. The epidemics that swept the island so frequently in the nineteenth century and well into the twentieth century appear to have been the main factor in keeping down the rate of population growth, for neither famine nor warfare played much of a role. Malaria alone was probably the main cause of death.

DDT was introduced in 1948 and Mauritius became one of the showcase examples of new public health effectiveness. With typical British thoroughness the main malaria-bearing mosquitoes were practically eradicated by 1952: "The effect on population growth was dramatic. In one year the death rate fell by 32 percent. . . . The birth rate rose, though it is not clear how closely this is associated with the eradication of malaria. Between 1948 and 1958 population increased at the rate of 3 percent per annum" (Benedict, 1972:255).

The isolated island world of Mauritius can be looked at as a miniature of the entire globe. As economic conditions grew worse and worse in the 1950s, the populace had much reason to complain bitterly about lack of employment opportunities and the inadequacies of a government that could not provide for the large sector of poverty-stricken families. When birth control and family-planning organizations were set up on the island they were op-

posed by Muslim leaders and the Roman Catholic church on religious grounds, and "some Hindu leaders were claiming that birth control was a governmental device for limiting the Hindu population so that Christians might increase" (Benedict, 1972:266). Thus interethnic disputes mixed with religious ideas arose to frustrate attempts to control the runaway population increase. On the other hand, increasing numbers of individual families, disregarding the dictates of their churches and political leaders, showed interest in the possibilities that the size of their families might indeed be maintained within reasonable, supportable limits.

Some of the people of Mauritius have migrated to other lands. So the full pressures of their extraordinary population growth rate have not been concentrated completely on the island itself. As we view the growing desperateness of the economic and environmental situation of Mauritius, it is well for us to keep in mind that in the foreseeable future there are no practical possibilities for the migration of surplus population from our world island to some other less densely peopled land.

The Dampening Effect of Rising Standards of Living: A False Hope?

Some optimistic social thinkers and political planners like to point out evidence that shows that increased standards of living tend to produce declining birth rates. The evidence for this is extensive. In Europe and North America there have been marked

25.6 Advertising for birth control in India. (Cartier-Bresson, Magnum)

501

declines in children per family. Slightly more recently, the general effect of economic prosperity has become abundantly evident in Japan, where the availability of abortions and contraception has lowered the population increase rate to close to the zero point. The lesson is obvious: if we raise standards of living around the world, our population problems are solved. Unfortunately, trends in the world today are in the other direction, for the most part, for the so-called "developing nations" are not developing increased productivity and standards of living nearly so rapidly as their populations are increasing. The technological gap and per capita standard of living gap between the rich nations and the poor nations are widening rather than the reverse.

There is, however, another problem associated with raising standards of living, which we will take up in detail in Chapter 26. Suffice it to say here that increased standards of living go hand in hand with increased levels of pollution and consumption of nonrenewable resources. In spite of the fact that North Americans have a rather modest rate of population increase, the world can ill afford very much increase in their numbers—for each added *individual* raises the consumption levels drastically. It has been estimated that the drain per person on world resources caused by North American population increase is about *fifty times* the cost of added population in India. Because environmental pollution is so closely tied to industrialization we can probably use these same figures to suggest that each newborn North American is likely to pollute the environment fifty times as much as the corresponding individual in India.

The Matter of Population: A Summary

1. Human population increase has not proceeded in a steady, smooth curve. Instead, there was the long period of near-zero population growth during the Ice Ages, followed by a jump of growth *rate* associated with the development of food production. The rate leveled off until the new impetus to population growth during recent times, especially in the twentieth century.

2. As long as most human populations were migratory to some extent, *each family cluster* had strong motivations for *spacing* the number of offspring—because of the need for mothers to carry infants and very young children from place to place, plus the threat to infant nutrition if a new baby came along before it was time to wean the next older child.

3. Infanticide was probably an important means of population control in many earlier hunting-gathering populations, and other control methods were probably also used among some peoples.

4. The growth of social complexity, which involves the *consolidation* of decision making, means that kin groups and larger social units exert more and more control over individuals and their actions—including matters of family planning. As middle-range agricultural societies grew up, lineages and other territorially based groups came to exercise interests in "manpower," so that it is very likely that these social changes affected population "policies."

5. The major population control in the past two thousand and more years was probably disease, although at irregular intervals starvation and destructive war also played a part.

6. The rapid rise in birth rates during the past two centuries certainly reflects very complex causal factors, but the examples of Java and other areas of agricultural intensification, lend support to the idea that the taxing powers of and the commercial exploitation by European and North American economic interests have had the effect of inducing peasant families to have more children—as a rational survival mechanism.

7. Modern medical practices and public health measures, such as the eradication by DDT of mosquitoes in malarial areas, have played a major part in the growth of world population, especially since World War II, adding further impetus to a frighteningly high rate of population increase.

8. In terms of the world increase of population, the addition of each newcomer in affluent North America or in Europe costs much more in terms of both environmental pollution and the use of scarce resources than is the case with the addition of individuals in poor, destitute populations. Thus, simply from a position of environmental protection, the real dangers to the global environment appear to be from increases in the affluent sector of humankind.

Homo modernicus: Dimensions of the Contemporary Scene

The chronicle of cultural evolution has been an unfolding of continued increase in population, expansion of technology, and growth of social complexity. From where we stand today, in the midst of continued rapid growth, it sometimes appears that accelerated cultural evolution is to go on indefinitely, far beyond the reach of our current abilities of prediction.

In seeking some further underlying order, particularly in the continued growth of our technoeconomic systems, we should note carefully the role of energy utilization as a mainspring of change. In fact, the entire story from hunting and gathering to modern computer-age complexity of culture can be looked at as reflecting the control of energy sources. Nonhuman primates control only the energy stored in their bodies, fueled by the foods they eat. The same holds true for early hominids like *Australopithecus*. Humans, converting energy at about 20 percent efficiency, can produce daily averages per person of about one horsepower hour, or about 640 calories. For several hundreds of thousands of years humans have been able to add somewhat to their energy-conversion resources through the control of fire. Much later the domestication of animals for transport and other work increased the amounts of energy available to preindustrial peoples, but the total energy supplies in small-scale cultivating and animal husbandry societies is still much less than one horsepower hour per person per day.

The forces of the winds and the flowing waters have been major inorganic sources of energy for preindustrial peoples for a long time. People living on rivers have been able to utilize the downstream current for transporting goods (but the energy was good only in one direction), and the use of sails allowed seafarers to travel and trade over wide areas through the increased harnessing of the somewhat erratic energies of the winds. Ancient Egyptians designed and built ships that carried up to 150 tons, with an estimated speed of perhaps eight knots, requiring the equivalent of about eighty horsepower. Waterpower was used to grind grain, to run cloth-making machines, and to manufacture many other products.

Before the invention of the steam engine in the seventeenth century, most available types of usable energy were sharply limited in their location. Use of waterpower depended on specially favored locations on streams or seacoasts, for example. Harness-

Energy, Pollution, and the Limits to Growth

26

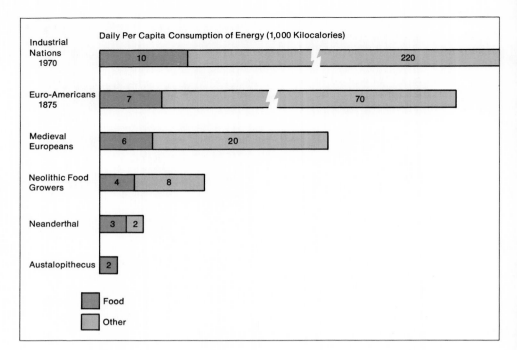

26.1 Daily per capita consumption of energy in different periods in human history. The amount expended for food production has not expanded greatly (per capita) but energy expenditure for other activities, especially transportation and the production of special goods, has expanded greatly.

ing animals to vehicles and other devices was considerably more versatile, but there are severe limitations on how much horsepower in the form of animals can be efficiently mobilized in a single unit.

The development of effective (if not very efficient) energy converters using wood and coal brought on vastly increased possibilities for manufacturing, rapid transportation, and other activities, which quickly led to large-scale social and political changes in nineteenth-century Europe and North America. The spreading influence of this control of energy around the world ushered in the era of

Table 26.1: Estimated Daily Consumption of Energy per Person

Historical Era	Kilocalories
Technological [*Homo technologicus*]	230,000
Industrial [nineteenth-century industrial society] (England circa 1875)	77,000
Advanced agricultural [preindustrial Europeans] (Northwest Europeans circa 1400 A.D.)	26,000
Early agricultural [Neolithic peoples] (Neolithic Farmers of Mesopotamia and Egypt circa 5000 B.C.)	12,000
Efficient hunting [*Homo erectus* and *Homo sapiens neanderthalensis*] (circa 100,000 years ago in Europe)	5,000
Early hominids of East Africa [*Homo erectus* and *Homo habilis*] (East Africa circa 1 million years ago)	2,000

Source: Adapted from COOK, 1971:136.

Homo modernicus: Dimensions of the Contemporary Scene

The idea of a steam engine was probably first dreamed up by the Alexandrian philosopher Hero, about two thousand years ago. He also devised a fountain in which the water was jetted up by steam or hot air. The use of a steam engine to do work was first developed in the seventeenth century for pumping water out of coal mines. The early steam engines were fairly crude until James Watt made some important design improvements on them in the early part of the eighteenth century.

greatly expanded commercial activity, spurred on in the nineteenth and twentieth centuries by the discovery of petroleum, leading to the modern era of gasoline-driven, diesel-driven, and rocket-fuel–driven industrialization. Table 26.1 provides a dramatic illustration of the effect of these recent changes in the energy-harnessing capabilities of humans by showing the amount of daily energy consumption per person through time. Note that an individual today uses three times as much energy (in the course of a day) as he would have used one hundred years ago and nineteen times as much as he would have used in the early Neolithic period.

Energy, Entropy, and Culture

"The disorder of the universe is always increasing."

This is one version of Newton's second law of thermodynamics, and it is the key to our understanding of our environment and what we do to it. Everywhere on the scene of human activity, as well as of all organic life, solar energy is temporarily captured, along with the various secondary or derived kinds of energies scattered through our earth's crust; and everyone and everything—humans, mollusks, potato plants, and blue-green algae—disperse

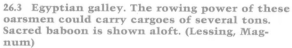

26.2 Windmill in Greece. (René Burri, Magnum)

26.3 Egyptian galley. The rowing power of these oarsmen could carry cargoes of several tons. Sacred baboon is shown aloft. (Lessing, Magnum)

505

energy in the process of maintaining themselves. This basic law of life and physical process is evident in the fact that we must eat much more than one pound of food in order to gain a pound. Green, leafy plants capture and make use of solar energy with an efficiency of about 1 percent. That is, a carrot or a potato plant that is "worth" a hundred calories must have used up the equivalent of about ten thousand calories of solar energy in order to encapsulate, temporarily, that bit of usable energy. The rabbit that comes along and eats the carrot is somewhat more efficient. It requires only six hundred to seven hundred calories of energy to add one hundred calories of organized energy to its body. But compared to those other living things, humans are prodigal abusers of energy.

However inefficient *Homo sapiens* might be as an energy-processing, biological organism, our real impact on the environment is in our cultural harnessing of power from those other plants and animals and from nonorganic sources of power. Newton's second law of thermodynamics tells us that, no matter what the source of energy and no matter how efficiently it is utilized, "power to do work" is dissipated irretrievably into the environment. We might feel that's not very serious when we consider the huge amounts of energy coming in daily from the sun. We are not at the moment running dangerously short of *total* available energy—even though we are annually getting deeper and deeper into an "energy crisis" in the short run because of our overdependence on fossil fuel and other nonrenewable sources.

Two main problems connected with the generation of energy in our modern technological-cultural systems are that (1) we increase the atmospheric heat load, and (2) we dissipate iron, copper, and other nonrenewable raw materials in connection with our high-powered production and consumption. Some attempts are being made to recycle our growingly scarce metals, yet daily our industrial system and our individual consumption patterns throw away nonrenewable resources in garbage dumps, in polluted rivers, lakes, and streams, and in other features of our increasingly man-made landscape. That too is ENTROPY—the gradual increase in disorder, the gradual decline in reusability through *deconcentration*. The problem of environmental pollution is not simply random acts of carelessness piled up over time but an absolutely intrinsic part of the latest phase of our cultural evolution.

26.4 This simple water pump requires human energy, but it can be kept operating even in times of severe fuel shortage. (Elliot Erwitt, Magnum)

The pollution is a direct product of industrial processes. The waste materials are just as much part of the system as are the floods of consumer products that spread out widely to consuming publics.

The lesson that ecologists are trying to convey—so simple, yet avoided by practically everybody—is that the natural resources of the earth, the climate and other physical features, our political-social systems of organization, and the industrial-technological processes we use to meet our needs make up a complex interrelated system—the parts are all

Homo modernicus: Dimensions of the Contemporary Scene

hooked together. What goes up must come down; what goes in must come out (e.g., waste products); and as biologist Barry Commoner argues it: "There is no such thing as a free lunch." In the following sections, then, we will look briefly at some of the main problems that current aspects of our human adaptation have created—for ourselves and for the biophysical world we inhabit.

In the Eye of the Beholder: Air Pollution

Recently we received a charming and excited letter from a student who was studying for a semester in Mexico. It was all "great, educational, much more real and relevant" than anything she had experienced back at the university in the United States. But, oh, the headaches she got every time she went into Mexico City—awful, unrelievable headaches. Then she realized what caused them—it was the smog, that pall of nitrogen oxide, carbon monoxide, hydrocarbons, ozone, sulpher oxide, and other pollutants discharged into the Mexico City air by the thousands and thousands of motor vehicles, the industrial plants, the incinerators, and other components of modern technology. Mexico City is not the worst of air-polluted cities, but it is especially striking there after one has experienced the fresh, sparkling atmosphere of the mountains of central Mexico.

Some years before concern about air pollution and general environmental deterioration became widespread in our society, Londoners got a bad scare that verged on disaster. Because of the unusual meteorological conditions that happened to coincide during one week of 1952, the usual smog over London was multiplied to such an extent that about four thousand people died from the direct effects of this air pollution. Usually it is not possible to identify "death from air pollution" clearly, for it results from the interaction of some kind of respiratory ailment (such as emphysema) with the damaging forces of pollutants.

Ecologist Paul Ehrlich and his associates sum up the effects of air pollution on individual health as follows:

Carbon monoxide combines with the pigment hemoglobin in our blood, displacing the oxygen that hemoglobin normally transports. When oxygen supply to the cells is reduced, the heart must work harder, as must the respiratory mechanism. These effects may produce a critical strain in people with heart and lung diseases. Spending eight hours in an atmosphere containing 80 parts per million (ppm) of carbon monoxide has the same effect as the loss of more than a pint of blood. When traffic is badly snarled, the carbon monoxide content of the air may approach 400 ppm. Symptoms of acute poisoning often experienced by people in traffic jams and on freeways include headache, loss of vision, decreased muscular coordination, nausea. (EHRLICH et al., 1973:117)

Much of the evidence concerning the health hazards of air pollution is "only statistical." That is, medical researchers have not yet demonstrated step by step how smog kills or injures people. The indirect evidence—in the form of correlations between levels of air pollution and deaths from lung cancer, increased infant mortality rates, and other health measures—is impressive. As of 1970, at least six different careful studies had been made of lung cancer rates in areas of air pollution as compared to "clean air" areas. One team of investigators studied the statistics on 178,783 White American males of fifty to sixty-nine years old in order to establish lung cancer death rates for U.S. cities as compared to those of rural areas. After adjusting their statistics to eliminate the effects of smoking habits and age differences, they established the following:

Urban areas: 52 per 100,000 population lung cancer deaths
Rural areas: 39 per 100,000 population lung cancer deaths

Petroleum was being utilized as an energy source for lamps by the ancient Greeks on the island of Sante in 400 B.C., Burmese drilled for oil in about A.D. 100, and it was used by scattered other peoples in ancient times. Natural gas, too, was utilized a thousand years before the birth of Christ, by the Chinese. (COTTRELL, 1955:93)

Early Users of Petroleum and Natural Gas

Energy, Pollution, and the Limits to Growth

Another team of researchers found that, although the difference between urban and rural lung cancer mortality rates for smokers was 110 to 80 per 100,000, among *nonsmokers* the rates were 36 to 11 per 100,000. Nonsmokers living in urban environments are *three times* as likely to die of lung cancer as are their nonsmoking country cousins. Another team of researchers in England found "a tenfold difference between the death rates for rural and urban areas." Another study of lung cancer and air pollution in eight northern European cities showed a correlation of .60 between degrees of air pollution and lung cancer mortality rates (Lave and Seskin, 1970:723–33).

The Greenhouse Effect: Air Pollution Number Two

Most of our concern about air pollution has thus far centered on that long and growing list of industrial cities and regions where there are now rapidly increasing concentrations of sulphates, particles of all kinds of waste products from asbestos to lead and other poisonous metals, ozone (O_3), and a variety of other materials. Except for those unfortunate rural residents who happen to be downwind from large industrial urban concentrations, we have generally considered our rural nonindustrialized areas to be safe from the specter of contaminated air. But all of the greatly increased manipulation of energy by humans may be threatening our globe with a much more widespread effect than simple contamination of the local metropolitan area.

Of grave concern are the effects of industrialization on the atmosphere—the mass of air (composed of gases, water vapor, and other materials) surrounding the earth—on which all life depends. One of the gases is carbon dioxide (CO_2), formed by respiration, decayed organic matter, and by the burning of fossil fuels such as coal, oil, and natural gas. Industrial activity has released into the atmosphere such large quantities of carbon dioxide that the total CO_2 content of the atmosphere has increased more than 12 percent since 1880 (Ehrlich et al., 1973:98). The atmosphere has also had to absorb the insult of many other kinds of waste from the activities of us earthlings. But what does it mean? What will it do?

The gases, water vapor, and other materials that make up the atmosphere serve as an invisible shield. It filters out the shortwave rays of solar radiation thereby protecting living creatures on earth. It also reflects back to earth the long wavelength radiation that would otherwise escape into space. Thus the maintenance of a reasonably steady temperature on the earth's surface is dependent on the atmosphere for trapping solar energy and for heat radiation—on both of which all life on earth depends.

This global climate system is referred to as "the greenhouse effect," because a greenhouse works on the same principles in regulating temperature. The glass or plastic shield allows solar radiation in and serves to retain the longwave (infrared) heat radiation emitted by the plants and soil within the greenhouse.

Any sizeable change in the composition of the earth's shield must have some effect. Unfortunately, at this time it is not possible to measure or predict exactly the effects of increasing carbon dioxide in the earth's atmosphere. The meteorological physics affecting climate on earth are complex indeed, and two quite opposite views have been advanced by scientists concerning the steady increase in carbon dioxide in our atmosphere.

Environmentalist Ritchie Calder suggests that the effect of increased carbon dioxide is an *increase* in overall temperatures. Calder notes that there has been a thinning of the northern polar ice sheet and changes in fish migration patterns in the North Atlantic, reflecting changed sea temperatures:

Glaciers are retreating either by melting or by breaking up, at coastal level, into icebergs. This, as has been pointed out, adds additional water to the ocean levels. It will, however, have other effects as well. Rivers which originate in glaciers or permanent snow fields will increase their flow. Vast amounts of water are at present retained (in the Himalayas, for example) by ice barriers, the melting of which would be like the breaking of massive dams. . . . it is scarcely necessary to remind people of what a few feet rise in the sea level . . . would do to our geography. Suffice it to say that it would be unwise to take a 99-year lease on coastal flats! (CALDER, 1968:139)

On the other hand, some experts read the statistics and find that the patterns are not all that clear. For example, the Ehrlichs and their associates believe that "Since the 1940s there appears to have

508

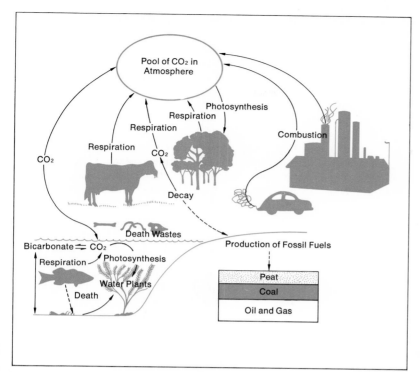

Pool of CO₂ in Atmosphere

Photosynthesis

Respiration

Respiration

Combustion

Respiration

CO₂

CO₂

Decay

Death Wastes

Bicarbonate ⇌ CO₂

Respiration

Photosynthesis

Production of Fossil Fuels

Water Plants

Peat

Death

Coal

Oil and Gas

26.5 The cycling of carbon (mainly in carbon dioxide) in the global ecological system. The solid arrows represent CO₂.

been a slight decline in the average temperature of the earth, in spite of a continued increase in the CO₂ content of the atmosphere'' (Ehrlich et al., 1973:199).

The effect of several massive volcanic eruptions in the nineteenth century, which released millions of tons of debris into the atmosphere, was apparently a significant *cooling* of the earth for a few years. This effect when compared with recent CO₂ pollution suggests that different *kinds* of pollutants in the atmosphere work in different directions and might offset one another. That might sound comforting, until we realize that probably the most serious threat to our human worldwide cultural system is from *uneven* profits and losses in heat exchanges through the atmosphere. Almost any change in climate is threatening to food production. The Ehrlichs and their associates note that ''any rapid change of climate in whatever direction is certain to decrease food supply. Should rapidly accelerating air pollution, a new volcanic incident, or civilization's heat production perturb climate enough to damage the

Northern Hemisphere's granaries, enormous famines would be inevitable'' (Ehrlich et al., 1973:200).

''We Have Met The Enemy and He Is Us.''—*Pogo*

''Water, Water Everywhere . . . ''

It only takes about three days to die of thirst, whereas the average human can go for weeks before he starves for lack of food. Water is probably our second most essential life support (if we count air as number one). Slow pollution of our precious water supplies had, of course, been proceeding without much comment from anybody for the past half century and more, but somehow it didn't frighten many people as long as water pollution seemed to be concentrated mostly in a few stinking creeks and rivers like the Hudson, the Rhine, and those backwaters down around South Chicago and Gary, Indiana. To most people it did not seem possible that large bodies of water like the Great Lakes or Long

509

Island Sound, for example, could ever become polluted to any significant degree.

Lake Erie is one of the more notable monuments of pollution in our modern industrialized culture. During the two hundred years and more that White people have lived on its shores, Lake Erie has provided an abundant catch of fish, a broad expanse for waterborne transport of goods and people, and beaches for summer recreation. Before 1900 the annual catch of sturgeon in Lake Erie was about 1 million pounds; a few years later, it was down to seventy-seven thousand pounds and declining. But of course we were a young nation before World War I, and nobody worried much about the disappearance of a few fish. One by one the other important food fish disappeared from the lake. The northern pike declined sharply in the 1920s. The cisco had once upon a time yielded 14 million pounds but declined rapidly during the 1930s; the yearly catch of cisco was about eight thousand pounds in the period 1960–1964, or *less than 1 percent* of what had once been a major industry.

Waterborne Health Hazards

North Americans are usually confident that their own tap water is perfectly safe to drink, whereas when we set foot in some other land, we search about for places to buy "pure water" in bottles. It is therefore surprising to find that a very considerable amount of our North American drinking water contains serious health hazards. In a recent study of over three thousand water samples from communities serving a total of 18 million people, it was found that 41 percent of these water systems failed to meet the 1962 Public Health Service drinking water standards in one way or another (Crossland and Brodine, 1973:11–24).

Down along the lower reaches of the Mississippi River, anyone raising a glass of water to his lips is exposing himself to a mixture of industrial pollutants and contamination from dead fish, plus the drainage from a lot of richly fertilized farmlands: "On a single day, each of 42 plants discharged at least one heavy metal to the river in amounts ranging upward from 5 pounds. The day's total included 3,700 pounds of lead from one plant, 71 pounds of cadmium from another, 396 pounds of copper from another, and 200 pounds of chromium from still another" (Crossland and Brodine, 1973:12).

The Limits to Growth

A group of scientists, humanists, industrialists, and politicians met in 1968 to study what they called "the predicament of mankind." The informal international group of "experts" is now known as the Club of Rome, and their first major study on the impending worldwide crisis has appeared under the title *The Limits to Growth* (Meadows et al., 1972). Their work is based on a series of computer simulations involving projected world resources of important metals, petroleum, natural gas; available lands for the growing of food; rates of population growth; and the best available estimates on the con-

26.6 Our deteriorating environment: water pollution. (Gilles Peress, Magnum)

Item: On June 15, 1973, the Environmental Protection Agency issued a statement that:

High concentrations of asbestos fibers have been discovered in the drinking water supply of Duluth and several communities on the Minnesota shore of Lake Superior.
The source of these fibers is believed to be the discharge of *taconite tailings* by Reserve Mining Company. . . . While there is no conclusive evidence to show that the present drinking water supply in this area is unfit for human consumption, the agency feels that prudence dictates that an alternative source of drinking water be found for very young children. (*Washington Post,* June 25, 1973)

What's wrong with a little bit of asbestos in the water anyhow? Well, for one thing there are plenty of studies that show a connection between asbestos breathed in by factory workers and their likelihood of incurring cancer of the lung, stomach, and colon. Apparently there are no studies as yet of the relationships between waterborne asbestos and disease, but the Environmental Protection Agency in issuing their report suggested that people might not want to wait and see the results before taking a few precautions. It's worth noting that Reserve Mining Company, as reported in the *Washington Post,* was dumping *daily* sixty-seven thousand tons of taconite tailings into relatively unpolluted Lake Superior. The Justice Department had already filed a suit in 1972, asking the company to discontinue this polluting of the lake.

tinuing increase in environmental pollution. Although the authors note that it is possible to change some of the trends, their study gives us a frighteningly pessimistic prediction of the future:

If the present growth trends in world population, industrialization, pollution, food production, and resource depletion continue unchanged, the limits to growth on this planet will be reached sometime within the next one hundred years. The most probable result will be rather sudden and uncontrollable decline in both population and industrial capacity. (MEADOWS et al., 1972:29)

This gloomy forecast tells what is likely to happen if *nothing* is done about any of the basic problems facing our world society. What is even more sobering is that the approaching world catastrophe predicted by the computer simulation does not change very much unless trends in *all* of the major factors— population, pollution, food production, and management of material and energy resources—are sharply altered. The Club of Rome people point out that even if we found vast amounts of minerals, metals, and other resources in unexplored parts of the world, it would not change the overall limits of our resources very much. This is because of the

Item: There are increasing reports of deaths among the beautiful whales of the Mediterranean. The whales washed up onto the beaches were not killed by any predator and were not suffering from disease, unless the modern civilized age of plastics be considered a "plague." Autopsies of the whales revealed that they had swallowed plastic garbage bags, thrown overboard from the ships that ply those ancient seas. From the point of view of the ships' crews and passengers, wrapping their garbage in plastic bags may seem to be a reasonable environmental precaution. Unfortunately, the whales encounter the often bright-colored bags and swallow them, but they are completely indigestible.

511

Energy, Pollution, and the Limits to Growth

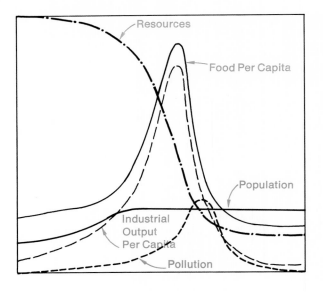

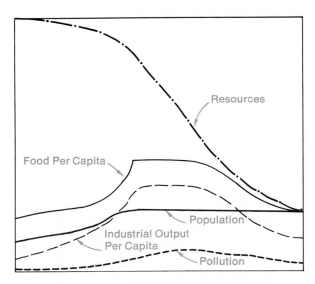

26.7 **Two computerized predictions about the future. In A, the first computation, a stabilized world population is assumed, but the continued growth of production, food per capita, and pollution, plus decline of scarce non-renewable resources, ends in catastrophic collapse a few decades after 2000 A.D. In situation B, both population and capital expenditure are stabilized. Pollution thus does not get out of hand, but diminishing resources produce some decline in food per capita and other goods. (Adapted from Meadows, et. al., 1972)**

rapid *exponential growth* in industrialization around the world. Each year the rates at which we are using scarce resources increase dramatically, and there is no sign of a slowdown. Table 26.2 shows the computer simulation predictions concerning some of our critical resources, including the prediction of how long these resources would last if we found that there are *five times* as much of these as calculated at present.

Humans found ways to use iron effectively a little less than four thousand years ago. Now the iron and steel industry is the backbone of our industrial system. Fortunately iron is very plentiful in the earth's crust, and even the most pessimistic estimate of our supplies of iron gives us at least ninety-three more years before this resource is exhausted. From Table 26.2 we note that one important industrial metal that is likely to become depleted soon is copper. If it turns out that our copper reserves are five times as plentiful as presently known, we still have only about forty-eight years left before that crucial industrial metal is essentially used up. Mercury is going to be used up even more rapidly. A glance at the statistics on aluminum indicates that aluminum beer cans are not going to be with us much longer and that we are going to have to find some other kind of material for our aircraft if these projections are correct.

Many people have accepted the idea that industrial growth and economic expansion are "good for the people and good for the country." Furthermore, they think that if it is a good thing that North Americans have experienced economic growth and hence a rising standard of living, then the same "progress" certainly would be desirable for the other peoples of the world.

If only the developing nations of Africa, Latin America, and Asia could catch up with the economic productivity of Europe and North America, we could avert all kinds of conflict and dangers of world war—it is often said. Unfortunately, all of the available economic statistics demonstrate quite clearly that the "developing nations" are *falling further behind* in the competition for scarce resources and industrial growth. The statistics are deceptively simple. The annual exponential growth rates of the wealthier nations are two or three times greater than those of the poorer nations. For example, although the estimated annual growth rate of gross national product per capita for the United

Homo modernicus: Dimensions of the Contemporary Scene

Table 26.2: Predicted Exhaustion of Some World Resources

Resource	Known Worldwide Reserves	Static[a] Index	Present[b] Projected Rate of Growth	Exponential[c] Index (Years until Total Depletion)	Total Depletion[d] Calculated from 5 Times Known Reserves
Natural gas	1.14×10^{15} cu ft	38 yrs.	4.7	22 yrs.	49 yrs.
Petroleum	455×10^9 bbls	31 yrs.	3.9	20 yrs.	50 yrs.
Tin	4.3×10^6 lg tons	17 yrs.	1.1	15 yrs.	61 yrs.
Iron	1×10^{11} tons	240 yrs.	1.8	93 yrs.	173 yrs.
Copper	308×10^6 tons	36 yrs.	4.6	21 yrs.	48 yrs.
Coal	5×10^{12} tons	2300 yrs.	4.1	111 yrs.	150 yrs.
Mercury	3.34×10^6 flasks	13 yrs.	2.6	13 yrs.	41 yrs.
Aluminum	1.17×10^9 tons	100 yrs.	6.4	31 yrs.	55 yrs.

[a]The number of years until exhaustion of the resource if our rate of consumption worldwide *does not increase.*
[b]Rate at which our consumption of this resource is *exponentially increasing* per year.
[c]Years until this resource is exhausted, calculated with exponential increase of consumption included.
[d]Years until this resource is exhausted if actual world reserves are five times those presently known.
Source: Adapted from MEADOWS et al., 1972:64–66.

States is about 3.4 percent and it is a whopping 9.9 percent for Japan and 5.8 percent for the USSR, the corresponding figure for India is only 1 percent and a minus 0.3 percent for Nigeria. Indonesia, with a population of 113 million people, shows an average annual growth rate per capita of only 0.8 percent. The generalization from these figures is that among the nations, the rich get richer and the poor get (relatively) poorer. This should come as no surprise to us. The steady economic growth of the richer nations has historically and until the present day depended on the exploitation of the resources and the labor of the rest of the world. Because the richer nations wield a great deal of economic and political power—both in the form of direct military power and in the financial manipulation of the world's monetary system—it is extremely difficult for the poorer nations to break out of the grip of economic marginality.

Richard N. Adams has analyzed the growing gap

26.8 **Modern agricultural technology depends on heavy expenditures of petroleum fuels to keep the system going. (Erich Hartmann, Magnum)**

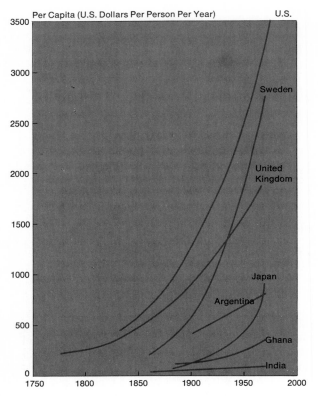

Per Capita (U.S. Dollars Per Person Per Year)

U.S.

Sweden

United
Kingdom

Japan

Argentina

Ghana

India

26.9 **Economic growth rates of the wealthier nations compared to developing nations. If these trends continue, as seems likely at this time, the rich will get richer and the poor get poorer. There is an ever-widening gap between the rich and poor nations.**

as a labor supply for his private use; or urban labor kept in a state of periodic unemployment . . . such that they never fully articulate their own controls in the system. . . . The obvious similarity between waste and marginal populations has been frequently noted in history. Marginal peoples have often been referred to by those in power as "human garbage" or "human trash." Aside from the folk usage, however, there are important analogies. I would suggest . . . that they . . . share the following features.

1. The rate of production of these "waste products" varies directly with both the rate of expansion and the technological level of the system.
2. Some waste and some marginals "decompose" rapidly and effectively reintegrate into the environment. Organic wastes particularly may do this. . . .
There is one absolutely crucial difference between marginals and waste: the former are alive and human, and can take positive action in their revindication. (ADAMS, 1974:50).

Adams's analysis, which shows a parallel between the material waste of industrialized society and the human waste in terms of the marginalizing of populations, points to the likelihood that both these processes will continue and become more marked unless countermeasures are developed by our mainline industrialized nations, the Euro-American powers.

Summary

In this chapter we have discussed the impact of human socially evolved energy systems as they affect our utilization of the environment and our future. The materials discussed suggest that we are on the brink of very large changes because the basis of human social organization—utilized energy—is in a state of disequilibrium and change.

1. As industrialization has accelerated during the past 150 years, more and more raw materials have been taken from the forests, the mines, the surface deposits of coal and iron, and other resource zones. At the same time, the spread of crop production and the spread of human populations and their migration to cities have further drastically modified features of the earth's crust, and industrial processes, with large amounts of waste products, have created serious problems of pollution.

between rich and poor nations in the current trends of industrial growth and pointed out that the general process of waste production in modern industrialized societies seems to apply as well to waste of people. His comments make clear that the marginalization and waste of people are a consequence of delocalization:

Marginality we have described as the process whereby some human beings have their major controls over operation in a particular system taken from them, so that their only autonomy of action does not directly articulate in any conflicting way with the dominant system. For example, there are cases of peasants with no lands who are totally dependent on landholders for their welfare, and whom the landholder then keeps

514

Homo modernicus: Dimensions of the Contemporary Scene

26.10 The debris of industrial society. (Bruce Davidson, Magnum)

26.11 Our deteriorating environment: visual pollution. (Deana H. Hoffman)

2. The high-energy, extensive environmental modification now common in our modern cultural systems uses up natural, nonrenewable resources at a rapid rate, and at this time there are only a few decades left for some important scarce resources.

3. The exponential increases in energy use by industrial nations produce extremely important changes in lifeways, particularly in the range of optional goods and services that become part of the cultural scene. It is also significant that the high-energy system can produce enough food for its membership with a labor investment of less than 10 percent of the population.

4. The basic source of energy, the sun, will certainly not be depleted for thousands of years. But the whole energy system of modern human societies will have to be changed dramatically in the near future, for petroleum and natural gas energy sources are only good for a few more decades and the prices of these sources will rise sharply in the final periods of depletion.

5. These matters of energy and energy sources seem remote from kinship networks, religious practices, song and dance, health care, and other social patterns. But they will inevitably have profound effects on the lifeways of people all over the world, for they will affect the Same's use of snowmobiles, the Miskitos' turtle hunting, the growth of industry in Saint Pascal, and the family life patterns of suburban North Americans.

6. The rapid deterioration of our environment suggests that, if left to individual choices in competing with one another for the scarce resources of the world, people may maximize short-run advantages and necessities at the expense of the future. The amazing growth and development of human societies have produced more kinds of problems than ever were dreamed of in most people's philosophies.

7. The forecasters of doom, as in the book *Limits to Growth*, agree that it need not turn out to be a catastrophe—the trends can be turned around. They can be turned around, though, only by quite drastic changes in everyone's lifeways. All this is part of human culture and society and, thus, part of the concerns of the science of anthropology.

Homo modernicus: Dimensions of the Contemporary Scene

Often the members of a society are highly sophisticated about the contingencies that constrain their actions, and there is certainly a great deal of conscious creativity involved in the history of the actions and inventions that help to shape the character (nature) of a particular society at a given point in time. On the other hand, the complex of interacting elements or forces that lead to or maintain that configuration are beyond the control of any individual, no matter how many resources he controls. From both the historical record and present-day observation, it would appear that most of the people, most of the time, accept at least the broad outlines of their life situations as given and develop strategies for maximizing their positions within these broader constraints.

Throughout history, however, there have been men and women who imagined alternatives, who thought about restructuring their societies in terms that they conceived of as better than current arrangements. Under some conditions there are many people in a society who come to feel that all is not well, and the groundwork is laid for movements of revolutionary social change or revitalization.

When people become so dissatisfied with their current situations that they are compelled to change them, there are a number of alternative courses of action that are open, and the type of action that is selected seems to be broadly patterned in relation to general sociocultural conditions. Thus, for example, messianic movements seem particularly likely to occur under some types of colonial situations, whereas peasant revolutions arise in ostensibly "postcolonial" circumstances. Also, while they may differ greatly in terms of the ideological content, movements of social change and revitalization often appear to have quite similar developmental sequences.

One striking difference among movements of deliberate social change is the extent to which they are given religious versus secular ideological structure. Many of the events or phenomena that we label as social change movements were conceived of by their participants as purely religious, often divinely inspired acts and are not intended to bring about social reform as an end in and of itself. On the other hand, many of the political revolutionary movements of the past one hundred years have been vociferously antireligious, completely rejecting at

Revitalization and Revolution: Creating New Lifeways

27

27.1 Alone in two environments: Hallway (Burk Uzzle, Magnum) Arctic (Burt Glinn, Magnum)

Homo modernicus: Dimensions of the Contemporary Scene

least established religious modes as a basis for re-organizing a social system. Still other movements fall between the two extremes, involving religious elements but not conceived of as wholly religious enterprises.

A second major dimension of variation among social movements is the extensiveness of the population that the movement seeks to encompass. The "Doomsday" groups, who recruit a small number of chosen people who will survive worldwide catastrophe and establish a new society on the ruins, represent one extreme. Their sweeping reforms are expected to become reality only after the vast majority of the population has been "wiped out." Many communal societies tend to be somewhat more generous in the scope of their intended beneficiaries, but they represent a withdrawal (at least in the short run) from the larger social scene into a more or less isolated environment in which an alternative to the current social organization is created. Oppressed minorities in many parts of the world have developed both secular and religious movements whose intended membership includes at least all of the members of that minority. And finally there are national and international revolutionary movements that intend to restructure society for everybody.

In the following sections we will discuss some of the actions that people have undertaken in their efforts to change their life situations through deliberate manipulation of themselves or their environments or both.

Messiahs, Prophesies, and Revitalization Movements

Some of the most far-reaching and swift-moving cultural transformations have been religious in nature, preached by MESSIAHS with new visions of better lives for the people. Anthony F. C. Wallace has studied a number of these social events, to which he gives the name REVITALIZATION MOVEMENTS: "to denote any conscious, organized effort by members of a society to construct a more satisfying culture. . . . It is attractive to speculate that all religions and religious productions, such as myths and rituals, come into existence as parts of the program or code of religious revitalization movements" (Wallace, 1966:30).

The Handsome Lake movement of the Iroquois Indians of New York State is an example of an effective and relatively enduring revitalization process. With the coming of White settlement, the Iroquois had suffered many losses and humiliations, particularly after they wound up on the wrong side—that is, the losing side—in the French and Indian Wars. Most of their lands were confiscated, and they were put on reservations, "slums in the wilderness," as Wallace calls them. By the end of the eighteenth century the Iroquois people were in the depths of poverty and despair. In 1799 a Seneca chief named Handsome Lake, "who had fallen upon evil days and become a drunkard" announced a new vision of a better way of life. "Heavenly messengers, he said, had told him that unless he and his fellows became new men, they were doomed to be destroyed in an apocalyptic world destruction. They must cease drinking, quarreling, and witchcraft, and henceforth lead pure and upright lives" (Wallace, 1966:31–32). Handsome Lake experienced a number of visions and received a set of instructions, according to which his people took on many of the White people's farming techniques, and men began to work in the fields, a job that had previously been defined as women's work. The code emphasized new, nuclear-family–oriented kinship relations, and as time went on the prophet added more and more details to this blueprint for revitalization.

From all reports, Handsome Lake's teachings were enormously successful in giving a new and vital force to the Iroquois way of life. There are still hundreds of his followers among the Iroquois in North America (in New York and Ontario for the most part), and the life history of the movement follows a set of stages very similar to those of many other prophetic cults and movements.

Comparing a considerable series of such cultural transformations, Wallace has identified the following steps in the progress of revitalization:

1. *Period of increased individual stresses, social disorganization, and cultural distortion.* The conditions bringing about revitalization movements are often caused by outside forces, especially increased oppression by colonialist powers or other outside social forces. Thus a great many small-scale societies, such as those of North American Indian groups, many peoples in European-dominated Africa, and other peoples of the Third World, have experienced or are experiencing conditions conducive to revitalization movements.

519

2. *Formulation of a code for revitalization.* Often the new code or "solution to the people's dilemmas" comes in the form of supernatural revelations in dreams or visions, announced by a prophet or messiah. Very often the visionary leader is a person who has suffered much from the deterioration of his people's way of life, and the visions from which he preaches often involve first and foremost his own reform and salvation.

3. *Communication and preaching of the word.* The first job of a revitalization movement is to gain converts, through promises of spiritual salvation, honor and fame, and solutions to the basic problems the people are facing. Sometimes the message of the movement includes the threat that people who do not reform themselves and accept the new ideology are likely to be in great peril.

4. *Organization of the movement.* With growth in membership through conversions, revitalization programs begin to differentiate: a set of disciples, the "true believers," take on the job of administration (including economic management) while the prophet goes on with his preaching. The mass of followers who give social and economic support to the movement makes up a third subgroup within the order.

5. *Adaptation to social realities.* Revitalization movements are always looked on with a good deal of suspicion by many people in the wider social system, especially those people of the "establishment" who may stand to lose much if the movement succeeds in its intentions. There may be revisions in order to attract more converts, and there are all kinds of adjustments that can be made in trying to further the adaptive success of the new organization.

6. *Cultural transformation of the society.* In the case of successful revitalization movements, such as the Handsome Lake religion of the Iroquois, the whole life style of a people is changed, new technology may be developed, and new kinds of social relations and social organization not foreseen in the original message come into being. The Palian movement among the Manus (see pp 485–486) is an excellent example of a successful revitalization movement with a continuing output of new cultural ideas: new suggestions about schooling, new modes of behavior between the sexes, and other cultural changes.

7. *Routinization and stabilization of organization.* In the early period movements operate on the emotional and social energies generated by charismatic leaders. After a while, though, as the movement succeeds to some extent and goes on with its work, charisma wears out, and the emotional fervor of the followers inevitably dims. By this time either the movement is ended or it maintains its forward motion through organization, with officers, lines of command, budgets, and other trappings of bureaucracy. By this time, however revolutionary the movement was in the first place, it very easily becomes conservative in its basic characteristics. For it now has a stake in the maintenance of at least some aspects of the status quo. If the movement remains a small, "deviant" group within a larger society, it will in some way come to terms with the facts of life by carving an isolated social niche that it can occupy and maintain for the loyal followership.

Methodism: A Successful Revitalization Movement

From the perspective of the mid-1970s, the Methodist Church seems a far cry from visionary, emotion-charged revitalization. In its beginnings, however, Methodism was heady stuff indeed and had its origin in the personal religious experience of John Wesley. That was back in the early 1700s, when England was in a period of social disorganization and increasing "cultural distortion" brought on by the opening rounds of the Industrial Revolution. In 1735 John Wesley went to Georgia as a minister of the Church of England to preach to the settlers and to carry out missionary work among the Indians. He was strictly "high church" and very intellectual about it. He did the best he could, but the people in Georgia were not all that interested in his brand of religion. He returned to England "thoroughly discouraged and sick at heart." There he met a Moravian preacher "who urged upon him the need of purging away his intellectualism and accepting a simple faith." At a prayer meeting in Aldersgate Street John Wesley experienced a sudden spiritual awakening, and he felt "that his sins had been taken away from him and that he was saved from the law of sin and death." Here is Preserved Smith's description of John Wesley's early Methodist preaching:

This style of preaching, maudlin and ecstatic as it appeared to the cultivated, did fearful execution upon the poor and ignorant to whom it was primarily addressed. John Wesley recorded in his diary, with satisfaction, the violent effects of his sermons, effects which he esteemed as signs of God's approving intervention. During the years 1739 to 1743 he reported that his preaching had caused 234 cases of hysteria, manifested in convulsive tearings, trembling, crying, groans, tears, and occasionally much more serious symptoms. Eighty-five of his hearers, he reported, had "dropped as dead"; two had developed psychogenic blindness, fourteen had been made temporarily insane, and nine had been driven into incurable madness. (SMITH, 1930:465–466).

John Wesley's partner, George Whitefield, developed the idea of preaching in the open air—soon Whitefield and Wesley were preaching to crowds of ten thousand to twenty thousand. There was a lot of opposition but plenty of success. Wesley was a good organizer and held frequent classes of a dozen or so persons who met to confess their sins and share their religious experiences. So the group developed a cadre of lay preachers. Meanwhile, Whitefield took the movement to America, where it caught on quickly. By 1784, when the dust had cleared away from the turmoil and struggle of the American Revolution, there were already fifteen thousand Methodists in the States. The movement at that point decided to become completely independent of the Anglican Church and adopted the name Methodist Episcopal Church. By 1844 they had increased to a million or more converts.

The adaptational phase of Methodism is well illustrated by the way that the slavery issue interacted with the history of the new religion. The Methodists had been against slavery in 1800. But in 1846 there was a split between the northern and southern conferences, and in 1856 the northern branch of Methodism took the position that slavery in any form was a sin against God and humanity. Southerners were not nearly so sure of how to define the spiritual meaning of slavery and could not bring themselves to condemn it. By that time what had begun as a revitalization movement was a well-organized and nonrevolutionary part of the North American social fabric. The emotion-packed preaching styles of Wesley, Whitefield, and other early Methodists had given way to the straightforward church service that is still familiar in modern North American communities. By 1945 the Methodist organization had grown to over 8 million members, the largest of the Protestant groups in North America, and held immense economic assets, including the ownership of several large colleges and universities.

As a social movement the Methodists did not seek to overthrow the government or to bring about massive transformation of the economic system. Their goals were aimed at reshaping the lives of individuals and "saving their souls" in relation to a spiritual hereafter. Certainly for thousands of those people who were converted to Methodism in those early days, the effect was a cultural transformation for them and their families, though in most instances this did not mean that whole communities completely changed their style of living. This illustrates, then, one basic dimension among social movements: some are particularly oriented toward individuals, whereas others are aimed at modifications of "the whole system." Revitalization movements today in North America and elsewhere run this same gamut.

The "Cargo Cults" of Melanesia

A particularly fascinating and many-sided cluster of social movements has sprung up in New Guinea and the nearby islands of Melanesia. Collectively, these many different movements have all been labeled CARGO CULTS because a common theme crops up over and over again—the idea that through some supernatural means ships or planes will arrive with stores of material goods for the people—the stuff of a new way of life. Sometimes these goods are seen as already belonging to the people, but the White people have kept them from being delivered to the rightful owners. In some cases the ships bearing the cargo are also to include the people's ancestors, the remembered dead, brought back to life to enjoy the dawn of the millennium. The idea of "the cargo" and its association with supernatural deliverance from the domination of a White people's economy and political system identifies the cargo cults of Melanesia as "millenarian movements," because they prophesy a significant transformation of life on earth through some kind of supernatural agency that is coming soon and the new life will be enjoyed by

521

the faithful, while the nonbelievers will disappear from the scene.

The various cargo cults in the Madang and Morobe districts of New Guinea can serve as examples because they share many characteristics with cults all over Melanesia. A cargo movement that had originated in another area came into these districts in the 1930s and intensified in 1939–1940 in a movement that merged a traditional ritual and myth about the two brothers Kilibob and Manup with the biblical myth about the fate of Ham and his Black descendants, "so that Kilibob-Shem-Japheth became the ancestor of the Whites and had the Cargo, whereas the descendants of Ham-Manup did not" (Worsley, 1968:212).

The people prayed to their ancestors for cargo. They quit planting and killed off their pigs. Followers of the new myth were encouraged to learn English, but they were deeply suspicious of the missionaries who had kept from them the true secrets of the Bible. In 1940 one prophet set himself up as king of the entire Madang area, and his cult spread rapidly. Another man, who claimed to communicate directly with God by wireless, claimed that he was the apostle Paul.

There were a series of other movements as well. In the Morobe district the people built cargo houses, ritually consecrated by the pouring of blood of sacrificed pigs on the doors. But it didn't bring the cargo. A variety of other tactics were adopted by the people, all with the intent that a cargo would arrive if they did the right thing. Some of the people felt that "the root of the trouble was sin. Sin must be rooted out by public confessions and public punishment. But after the confessions had been made and the sinners punished, still the Cargo failed to arrive" (Worsley, 1968:213–214).

World War II came and went. A new leader arose, a man named Yali who had been a sergeant major during the war and had returned home with high prestige. He had visited Australia and seen the complexities of the Whites' way of life, but to the cargo cult leaders the story was transformed into his death, his visit to God in heaven, and the promise from God that his people would receive the cargo.

Yali was a reluctant figurehead. At first he attacked the cargo ideas and apparently showed great reservations about taking on the responsibilities of leadership. Gradually, however, he became more disillusioned with the Christian missionaries and

with the Europeans, especially when he learned that the Europeans believed in evolution; "the Europeans, then, really believed in descent from animals, the old totemic religion of his own people. He felt cheated . . . and turned once more toward the religion of his ancestors" (Worsley, 1968:217)

Some of the new ideas that he introduced into the movement included increasingly antimissionary views as well as other activities that threatened the established European dominance in the area. Finally, in 1950 Yali was arrested on trumped-up charges and sentenced to prison. This particular cargo cult thereafter lost its momentum, though Yali returned to the Madang area from jail in 1955.

A number of social theorists have noted the supernatural and "magical" flavor of the cargo cults and use this to suggest that the Melanesians are relatively irrational and otherworldly in their world view. Anthropologist Peter Worsley points out, though, that the Melanesians were acting completely rationally within the world as they knew it and defined it. Before the Europeans came, and especially before World War II, most of these people had had no contact with the mighty engines of destruction and other technology that suddenly appeared on their shores. Those massive warships and squadrons of airplanes only reinforced their beliefs in spirit beings and what we would label "magical" ways of doing things. They, after all, had not had the experience of gradual technological evolution over decades and generations from simple industrial machines to the complex technology Europeans had achieved by 1940. Like Rip Van Winkle they had to compress a lot of new information into some kind of explanation in a great hurry. They did it with clear logic—by regarding all that fantastic gear of the Europeans as magically transported and produced.

The florescence of cargo cults among Melanesians developed in the face of very serious cultural distortion and social disorganization of their lifeways. Many of the people had experienced serious economic pressures from the new Europeanized way of life, for they had been dragged into labor on the copra plantations and were already dependent on the highly unstable world copra market. A second factor of instability in the area was contributed by the history that first brought German and then Dutch colonialists, then the Japanese expansion, followed during the war by the Americans, the British, and the Australians. In addition confusion was

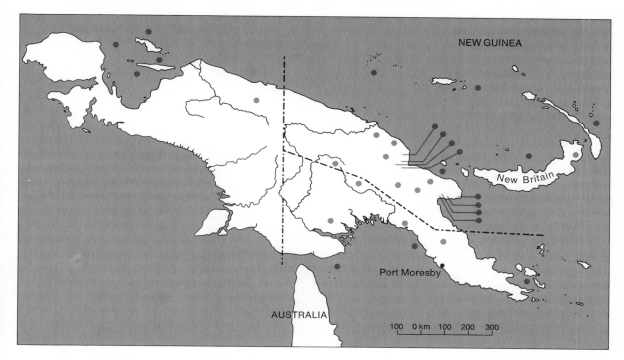

27.2 **Cargo cult movements have sprung up in a number of different locations in Melanesia in response to changes brought by increasing European penetration of the social and economic fabric.**

engendered by the multiple missionaries in the area, including German Lutherans, the London Missionary Society, Presbyterians, Roman Catholics, Seventh Day Adventists, Wesleyan Methodists, and others. It is not surprising that this mixture of different messages about the Christian religion, often coupled with crassly materialistic economic domination over local populations, led to efforts to construct a more satisfying culture.

Messiahs and Prophets

Before the Christian revitalization movement two thousand years ago, there had been a whole series of prophets who foretold again and again the miraculous coming of a new order. The Book of Daniel, probably composed about 165 B.C. during the Maccabean revolt, prophesied that Israel would over-

throw its enemies and rule the world for all eternity. Under Roman domination in the first two centuries after Christ, the Semitic peoples suffered much, and correspondingly there were a variety of individuals who announced blueprints for the removal of oppression and the coming of a millennium.

Fifteen hundred years before the earliest Jewish prophesies, an Egyptian, Ipuwer, wrote of the calamities that had befallen the land, of the plagues, of fathers and sons hating each other, of rising crime rates, and of crocodiles gorging on the flesh and blood of people who committed suicide. "Great and small say: 'I wish I might die,'" but Ipuwer assured his listeners that a messiah was coming, "bringing with him coolness to the land." There were many other messianic messages in early Egyptian writing.

In Europe 1660 was a big year for prophesies. Many Christians and Cabalists had been predicting that a messiah would appear in 1648. In 1650 there appeared a book, *The Sounding of the Last Trumpet: Severall Visions, Declaring the Universal Overturning and Rooting Out of All Earthly Powers in England. With Many Other Things Foretold, Which Shall Come to Passe in This Year, 1650.* Because 1648

523

hadn't worked out very well, a number of Christians in England and Jews throughout Europe decided that 1666 was the promised date.

As predicted, a messiah appeared. He was Sabbathai Zvi of Smyrna, son of a poultry seller. As Wilson Wallis describes it:

Sabbathai had made rapid progress in his study of the *Cabala* and at the age of eighteen was a rabbi. . . . Daily his virtue grew and his fame spread. His beauty likewise increased daily. From his body came a pleasant perfume which physicians pronounced a natural exhalation. He preached, called himself Son of David, and uttered the ineffable name *Jahweh* (WALLIS, 1943:40–41).

Sabbathai made various pilgrimages and had a strong following when he went to Jerusalem and again proclaimed himself the messiah. His fame spread. Returning to his home town in 1665, he was met with a tremendous ovation by the people of Smyrna. "Worshipers shouted exultantly, 'Long live our King, our Anointed One!' Women, young girls, and children fell into trances and, in the language of the *Sohar*, declared Sabbathai the true savior" (Wallis, 1943:41). People got ready for an exodus to the Holy Land and ordinary work of the day was suspended. The word of the new messiah spread quickly throughout Europe, and many Christians believed the message along with the Jews.

Sabbathai's downfall came quickly. He was denounced to Turkish authorities and imprisoned. Quick-thinking Sabbathai declared himself a Muhammadan and promised to advocate the abolition of Judaism.

That didn't stop the Sabbathai movement, however. His followers claimed that it was an impostor who had gone over to the Turks and that their messiah had gone to heaven and soon would return to get on with the job of creating the new millennium for the Jewish people. His disciples continued to preach the millennium, and several new messiah candidates appeared, including a lad who claimed to be the son of Sabbathai, born of a posthumous union—his deity-father reincarnated. Sabbathaianist sects of various sorts continued well into the eighteenth century and later.

The list of messianic cults, large and small, is enormous, and not at all confined to any one people or area of the world. On an average per century, perhaps, the Jews have had more messiahs than their oppressors, the Christians, because on balance the Jews were the more vulnerable and the more frequent recipients of religious persecution and cultural disdain. "The hope that springs eternal" was revived again and again in different quarters, as now one visionary, then another, proclaimed the news of an imminent coming of the messiah or gave out the even gladder news that he himself was the promised redeemer of his people.

There is no sign that they are less believed now than they ever were. Some self-proclaimed "Christs" do, it is true, get sent to mental institutions. The psychologist Milton Rokeach (1964) made a thorough-going study of the belief systems and psychological characteristics of "three Christs at Ypsilanti"—at a Michigan mental hospital. The likelihood of new messiahs' being sent to mental hospitals or to jail or, on the other hand, roaming freely about converting people to their faith and preaching the message of a new millennium seems to be a matter of accident and who happens to hear them first. It may also depend to a considerable extent on the general social competence of the prophets. Some of them probably sound a little queer and get put away quickly before they can gain a following.

Rebellions and Revolutions: Armed Social Change

Some people chafing under the domination of alien rulers, the oppression of landlords and tax collectors, or other types of sufferings have turned to religious revitalization movements; other prophets have led movements for social change with secular blueprints of action. Often large-scale movements for change include a variety of different sectors, some religiously oriented, others completely nonreligious. In the Russian Revolution, for example, the upheaval was so vast that there was room for all kinds of different views of intended outcomes, at least until the Bolshevik group gained control of the movement.

Study of the more notable peasant uprisings and revolutions during the twentieth century should lead one to be cautious concerning generalizations about these significant social events. Although there may be certain common threads in the development and structure of violent social upheavals, the ecological contexts are quite varied and have powerful

Homo modernicus: Dimensions of the Contemporary Scene

A Messiah for the 1970s

One of the most successful new messiahs is the guru Maharaj Ji, from India, who announces himself as the Perfect Master and king of kings. By 1973 his following supposedly numbered some 6 million people around the world, with forty thousand to fifty thousand in the United States. It is widely reported that he has palaces in various parts of the world, donated by the faithful.

The faithful, at least in the United States, are to be found especially in Divine Light living groups (*ashrams*), where religious services (*satsang*) are held. The teachings of Maharaj Ji involve "The Knowledge." Some of The Knowledge is spread in the *Divine Times*, the rapidly growing newspaper of the movement published in Denver, Colorado.

A typical issue of the *Divine Times* includes news of the guru's travels and pictures of his loyal followers; recipes that follow the vegetarian outlook of the movement; notes on health, child raising, and other items of interest; and a sort of "want ad" section that includes items like these:

Divine Services—Atlanta: Anyone interested in working as a painter, carpenter, plumber, electrician, or window cleaner for Guru Maharaj Ji through Divine Services, please come or contact . . .

Three birds with one stone: outdoor exercise, propagation of The Knowledge, community recycling, brought to you by the Grace of Our Lord through jumbling. You'll have to try it to believe it. Contact your local real life Divine Sales store.

Guru Maharaj Ji, who was sixteen years old in 1974, seems to have achieved the ultimate of simplicity in his message. "The Knowledge" does not involve any complex scriptures but is basically meditation on the four concepts—the "light of God," the "sweet nectar of living water," the "word of God which is the ultimate existing in everything," and its "vibration which is the collective harmonies of the universe." Peace is one of his major messages, and the ritual of the movement includes singing, prayers and incantations, and speeches by the disciples.

The movement was founded in India in 1960 by the guru's father, who passed on the title of "the Perfect Master" to the present guru when he was but eight years old.

525

Revitalization and Revolution: Creating New Lifeways

27.4 The end of colonialist rule in Indonesia. (Cartier-Bresson, Magnum)

effects on what finally happens. The establishment of Communist China, for example, took a course very different from patterns in the Russian Revolution, and again the development of Castro's Cuba, compared to the working out of the Mexican Revolution, represents a fairly different historical cultural process.

One of the first points to be made about revolutions is that they do not always arise from clearly stated ideologies or social philosophies. In the Mexi-

can Revolution, for example, discontent with the government of the dictator Porfirio Díaz developed separately and for different reasons in various parts of Mexico after 1900. In the south, the land squeeze on peasants from the haciendas, along with the other economic policies of the haciendas, was a major fomenter of discontent, which became organized by the popular leader, Emiliano Zapata. Zapata himself was a small-scale landowner, or *ranchero*.

27.5 Flags, songs, and public speeches are part of the communication process in a social movement. Fidel Castro. (Romano Cagnoni, Magnum)

Whereas the peasants under Zapata were fighting for land to improve the quality of their small-scale subsistence agriculture, the insurrectionists from northern Mexico were cowboys and other foot-loose adventurers under the banner of the legendary Pancho Villa. The original challenge to the established Mexico City government was issued by the liberal landowner Francisco Madero, who assumed the provisional presidency of Mexico in 1910 and sought to institute orderly elections and a constitutional government. He didn't last long. As the Mexican Revolution grew more complex and many-sided throughout the period from 1910 to 1920, more and more blood was shed, disorder intensified, and a variety of leaders had their days of glory and disappeared rapidly, many of them through assassination.

In the end, because the various different revolutionary generals had to seek public support and try to win followers, they gradually developed some social philosophy, which, in time, became the complex of laws, reforms, and slogans of the PRI, the Party of the Institutional Revolution, which has held power to this day in postrevolutionary Mexico. Thus the ideological and social outcomes of the Mexican social revolution were the work of a "committee" and have taken different forms with the varying fortunes of different factions within the single dominant political party.

Revolution in China

Unlike the Mexican Revolution, with its lack of ideological underpinnings, in the early phases at least, the decades of revolutionary upheavals in China that finally ended with the Communist victory in 1949 were very strongly influenced by Marxist and other revolutionary teachings. Perhaps the organization of so vast a population—about 600 million people by 1950—could not have been achieved without the cement of a powerful and elaborate revolutionary message.

The old imperial government of China had finally fallen apart in 1911, more from internal decay and interference by European powers than from organized revolution. The political groups that gradually rose to power in the new Republic of China were strongly influenced by Communist support from Moscow. The supposedly Communist-oriented political organization, the Kuo Min Tang, had received direct aid from the Soviets beginning in 1923 and had consolidated their hold over the Chinese government in 1927 under the leadership of the famed Chiang Kai-shek.

At first, the Communist Party in China was allied with the Kuo Min Tang, but there was a falling out with Chiang's organization in the late 1920s, especially after Kuo Min Tang troops put down a worker's uprising in Shanghai, massacring thousands of Communists. After the disastrous losses in Shanghai, the Communists adopted a new strategy, in which they played down their involvement in the industrializing cities and set out to consolidate a base of support in the peasant hinterlands. This "retreat into the backlands" was a strategy devised by the new Communist leader, Mao Tse-tung, a student who had been one of the founders of the Party. His background as a son of rich peasants in an interior region (Hunan) may have been a factor in his decision to shift attention to the peasant interior. The famous "Long March" of the Communists started in 1934, when Chiang Kai-shek's armies drove them from areas in South Central China, from which they moved some six thousand miles to establish their base of operations far to the northwest, in the Shensi area.

The new policies of Mao were rapidly successful in winning support among peasant populations. Their tactics were based on establishing village cooperatives, in which wealthier peasants were not eliminated but progressive taxes were instituted in order to bring about more egalitarian economic and social conditions. The areas of main Communist strength had a predominantly landowning peasantry, much different from the prevailing peonage and haciendas in prerevolutionary Mexico.

In summarizing some of the main writing and research on the Chinese Communist Revolution, Eric Wolf noted that the success of the Communists was probably strongly influenced by the Japanese invasion of China in the late 1930s: "Without warfare as a catalyst, it is unlikely that the Communist-led coalition with the peasantry could have scored the notable success that it did" (Wolf, 1969:154).

Even though they were poorly armed, the Red Army forces were able to mount successful campaigns against the Japanese forces, at the same time consolidating their organization of peasant villages over wider and wider areas. The contrast between the corruption within Chiang Kai-shek's KMT gov-

527

27.6 The "Long March" of Mao's Communist Chinese in the years from 1934 to 1936. In their base in the north they eventually grew strong enough to overthrow the Chiang Kai-shek government and set up the present Chinese state.

ernment and the austere, well-organized governance by Mao's Communists was also a factor in causing large-scale desertion by KMT troops into the Red Army.

The Communists who took control of China in 1949, driving Chiang Kai-shek into ignominious refuge on Taiwan, were led by people who were for the most part sons and daughters of the tiny pre-revolutionary economic elite of China: "All of them had higher educations, and most of them had studied abroad. . . . The majority were alienated intellectuals, men and women whose Western educations isolated them from the main currents of Chinese society" (North, 1965; quoted in Wolf, 1969:150).

The old order in China had fallen apart from the inside, to a large extent because of commercial and military pressures from Europe plus the pressures of a rapidly expanding population that was no longer able to feed itself under the traditional agrarian economy. Thus both the Chinese and the Mexican revolutions were triggered by the obsolescence of preindustrial political and economic systems. In

Mexico land reform emerged as a major issue among the Mexican revolutionaries, but in many areas they did not get around to large-scale redistribution of the hacienda fields until many years after the revolution. In China, on the other hand, land reform as such was not a major issue in quite the same way, but more general reform of the social-economic system gained the support of masses of peasants.

One other major contrast stands out between the Mexican and Chinese revolutions: in Mexico the old order crumbled to make way for a capitalistic private enterprise system, whereas the Chinese went from an agrarian state to a communist structure, after the chaotic interlude of the short-lived Republic.

The qualities that make some twentieth-century national revolutions seem different from the revitalization movements of earlier centuries probably reflect differences in technological levels—especially in means of communication—that make it possible to unite large numbers of frustrated people under the banners of revolutionary action. At the same

528

27.7 One of the major figures of the Russian Revolution, Leon Trotsky, is now half-forgotten. (Robert Capa, Magnum)

time, the age of widespread transformations in the name of religious movements seems to have given way to a period in which the ideologies of social transformation are more often secular.

Although social revolutions in Russia, China, and elsewhere are still in process, it is possible to regard them as now being "routinized" in terms of Wallace's outline of stages. The Russian Revolution, particularly, has become quite "established" and less visionary in language and political action.

Even though they claim to be basically nonreligious and quite "rational" in aims and ideology, it is extremely interesting to note the extent to which these social transformations have the same emotional elements as the more clearly supernatural revitalization movements. They tend after a while, to convert early leaders into supernatural "saints"—as witnessed in the ritual significance of Lenin's tomb in Moscow, the adulation of Marx, and the special and growing reverence addressed to Mao Tse-tung in China. Also, the recent history of communist movements shows the same patterns of fis-

sion, faction, and redefinition as we see in the history of Christianity. Like Catholicism, the core of communism appeared to hold a steady, monolithic unity, until special adaptive demands in different areas brought about the splitting off of various new forms. We now have different styles of communist belief and practice in China, the USSR, Cuba, and other areas, with the strong likelihood that there will be more splinters and redefinitions until some new prophet with a new form of revitalization movement comes along.

Social Movements Without Revolution

In recent years there has been a significant increase in revitalization movements in North America. The Black Power movement, for example, came into being in the 1960s and spread rapidly throughout our social system, forcing changes in the policies of educational institutions, raising the consciousness of cultural identity of Black people, setting in motion a whole series of related movements among other ethnic groups, who now use slogans of "Brown Power," "Red Power," and so on.

Anthropologists Luther Gerlach and Virginia Hine have studied the characteristics of such movements and find that they have certain main features in common. These researchers compared the Black Power movement, Pentecostalism, and more recently the "ecology movement" in order to identify common elements. Some of the essential features of successful movements, according to Gerlach and Hine, include the following:

1. They consist of a cell-like, nonhierarchical structure, in which there is *no single central leader* or "headquarters" and no single clearly defined constitution and ideology. Rather, they are a series of independent, small-scale organizations, which recognize loose ties to a general common cause or idea. Usually there is a good deal of communication among the groups, particularly in the form of "traveling evangelists," who spread the ideals of the movement and carry local news of social and political activities from community to community. Occasionally the independent cells come together or cooperate in some especially important action: various Black Power groups have temporarily coalesced around significant political issues, and the many

529

27.8 The Black Panthers are one branch of the complex, multifaceted Black Power movement. (Charles Harbutt, Magnum)

different varieties of peace groups of the late 1960s occasionally joined forces in massed protest marches or other temporary coalitions. Although many of their supporters bemoaned the fact that the various peace coalitions usually "fell apart" because of internal differences, Gerlach and Hine argue that the looseness of these organizations and the independence of the various units or segments are actually a strength instead of a weakness. As they express it, "The idea that each cell should contribute in its own way, doing its own thing without cumbersome bureaucratic controls, puts a premium on innovation, initiative, and entrepreneurship. This provides the maximum opportunity for personal involvement" (Gerlach and Hine, 1973:169).

2. Social movements usually have simple and *flexible ideological messages*, in which there is "something for everybody." The various minority movements all have slogans that are extremely general and attractive, with room for local interpretation of details. To some people, the slogans refer to "better jobs and better pay"; in other communities the main focus of meaning can be in housing and education. Ideologies, and their embodi-

ment in slogans, songs, wall murals, and other forms, practically always offer some appeal to the self-worth of individuals and hold out promise of future benefits.

3. In social movements there is a *commitment process* by which new recruits experience some dramatic personal change of situation that emotionally binds them to their new status as movement members. Some sort of "bridge-burning" event that cuts individuals off from easily backsliding into their previous, uncommitted status is also frequently found. In religious movements such a process takes the form of "conversion," whereas among political groups these experiences are often referred to as "radicalization." Bridge burning can take the form of a change of residence or a public performance in an event (like a protest march) that marks one as a full participant. The many different forms of initiation rites in both modern and nonmodern societies are generally emotion-charged and publicly staged commitment procedures.

4. The recruitment of new members often is most effective when it is carried out in personalized encounters among friends and relatives. This form of recruitment through "personal networks" is especially notable in the rapid spread of Pentacostalism around the world.

5. *Opposition* to a social movement generally enhances its salience for people and generates heightened commitment. During the height of the peace marches and other protests against the Vietnam war, large numbers of people were apparently recruited into the movement by their reactions to the behavior of police and other forms of opposition. Gerlach and Hine mention a participant in the October 1967 Pentagon confrontation who said that the experience of opposition in that situation "made believers of sympathizers, activists of pacifists" (Gerlach and Hine, 1973:184).

The Health Food Movement: A Bourgeoning Social Action

During the 1970s there has been a rapid spread of interest in health foods, organic gardening, and vegetarianism in a manner that seems to fit quite closely with some of the main ideas expressed by Gerlach and Hine. The movement is diffuse and segmented, with no overall central organization. The basic ideology of the movement is based on a deep

530

suspicion of the processed foods in the supermarket, along with a wide range of beliefs about the health-giving qualities of particular foods and the dangers of chemical fertilizers, preservatives, and other adulterants.

Some segments of the health food movement take their ideological cues from the vegetarian philosophies of India and the Far East, whereas others are based on the teachings and research of Adelle Davis, Ralph Nader, Euell Gibbons, and other North American writers. The movement derives some of its following from a "back to the land" trend, whereas other adherents are most imbued with an environmentalist-ecological ethic.

The process of commitment to vegetarianism or other forms of health food adherence can be very thorough and emotionally convincing. It seems to be psychologically easier if individuals can join vegetarian cooperative dining groups or communes. Further social support can be derived from immersion in the growing literature of the movement, which includes dozens of paperbacks, magazines, pamphlets, and other materials.

Anthropologist Randy Kandel has described features of the health food movement in a New England city, where she found a "cell-like, nonhierarchical structure" with units that included macrobiotic communes; the "Tree of Life" profit-sharing vegetarian restaurant; a natural food restaurant and bakery operated by volunteer workers; "The Grecian Health Resort" (a raw-food–eating institute and guest house in a large mansion), and other active groups. In addition, there were several health food stores and other suppliers, as well as some small religious sects with health food interests:

There is considerable communication among various cult groups, yet they retain their independence both ideologically and organizationally. Occasionally small groups splinter off from the established cults, creating yet other cells of the movement. Outside the social network of the "joiners" are the "independents," adherents to the movement who are usually tied into the network through communications media. (KANDEL and PELTO, 1973:31)

Red Power: The Indian Social Movement

As long as most North American Indian people remained isolated on reservations, there was little prospect that a pan-Indian political and social movement could develop much momentum. Now, however, there are thousands of Indians in Chicago, San Francisco, Los Angeles, Denver, and other major cities. The interaction among different Indian groups in cities, in relation to their communications with reservation populations, has sparked a growingly active movement with all the characteristics outlined above.

The book *Custer Died for Your Sins*, by Vine Deloria, Jr. (who is a Standing Rock Sioux and former executive director of the National Congress of American Indians), is a widely read statement of the movement's ideology. For many, a major step in commitment was taken in 1969 when:

a contingent of American Indians, led by Adam Nordwall, a Chippewa from Minnesota, and Richard Oakes, a Mohawk from New York, landed on Alcatraz Island in San Francisco Bay and claimed the 13-acre rock "by right of discovery." . . . Since there are Federal treaties

27.9 **The pan-Indian movement of Red Power is rapidly gaining followers. (Charles Gatewood, Magnum)**

Revitalization and Revolution: Creating New Lifeways

giving some tribes the right to abandoned Federal property within a tribe's original territory, the Indians of the Bay area felt that they could lay claim to the island (DELORIA, 1971:235–236)

Since that first headlined take-over of Alcatraz, similar defiant acts at Wounded Knee, South Dakota (1973), and at the Bureau of Indian Affairs in Washington (1972) have further elaborated on the ideology and emotional expression of various facets of the Red Power movement. These actions serve the organizational purpose of giving concrete form to the abstract ideas expressed by Deloria and other Indian writers and speakers.

From the Gerlach and Hine point of view the many different tribal identities are an ideal form of "segmental organization"—maintaining cohesion in dozens of relatively small, face-to-face groups, which occasionally unite in intertribal actions that, to a growing degree, express the common interests of Indian people cutting across tribal boundaries. Intertribal powwows and other celebrations give further emotional impetus to the movement.

Communal Societies: Stemming the Tide of Delocalization

The most pervasive direction of change in the world today is the seemingly inexorable delocalization of all aspects of cultural life. The direction is away from "neighborhood control" and toward loss of autonomy in every aspect of decision making as the daily affairs of practically everyone become ever more thoroughly articulated to the "one world" of commerce, politics, and electronic communications.

Communal societies are small-scale attempts to turn around the trends of delocalization. One could even say that they are local efforts to preserve small islands of organization against the universal tide of "social entropy" (if we can thus bend the meaning of Newton's second law).

More than anything else, communal societies try to take control back into their own hands—growing their own food, maintaining their own energy sources, and devising their own cultural norms and creeds. These attempts at reestablishing local control are quite varied: not all communes establish their own energy systems, and they are quite varied in their degree of interest in home-grown foods. Above all, however, they seek shields against the homogenizing forces of mainstream mass cultures.

For more than two thousand years there have always been some followers of Judeo-Christian philosophies who have interpreted the religious writings as calling for a socialistic organization of society. The esoteric sect known to us as the Essenes are the earliest communist society of which we have a clear record. The sect, composed wholly of males, existed from about 200 B.C. to 200 A.D., recruiting new members by adopting male children. Although they did not live in permanent, separate villages, they maintained a rigid communism of property and emphasized the virtues of a nonmaterialistic, ascetic life style.

During the eleventh and twelfth centuries heretical sects established communes, and by the end of the fifteenth century there were perhaps as many as 150,000 men and women living in communities in which the way of life was based, as closely as possible, on the rules of conduct laid out in the Sermon on the Mount. But it was the Protestant Reformation of the sixteenth century that provided the most powerful impetus for the establishment of communal religious societies. Although Luther himself began with very revolutionary ideas, he fairly quickly built up an authoritarian state religion in which democratic sects, such as the Anabaptists, were severely persecuted. Nonetheless, the social and ideological ferment of the Reformation period provided the milieu for religious movements in which ideas about religious reform were coupled with concerns about social reform.

Nineteenth-Century Communes in North America

One of the most interesting of the reformist groups are the Hutterites, an Anabaptist group established in 1528. Persecuted in Europe for their social and religious beliefs, members of the sect migrated to North America in the latter part of the nineteenth century; here they became one of the most successful of the then-current communal societies. In 1874 a journalist, Charles Nordhoff, set off to study the communal societies of the United States and found that there were more than seventy-two communes, the majority of which were founded

27.10 An interracial commune. (Dennis Stock, Magnum)

as religious communities. Nordhoff's research was motivated by his belief that communistic rural societies might provide an outlet for the growing dissatisfaction of the industrial workers, acting as a kind of safety valve for the security of the capitalists. He wrote, "Aside from systematized emigration to unsettled or thinly peopled regions . . . the other outlets for the mass of dissatisfied hand-laborers lie through co-operative or communistic efforts" (Nordhoff, 1875:17). Despite the decided ideological position with which he approached the subject, his "eye-witness" accounts of life in Shaker, Rappist, Zoarite, and Amana communities are relatively unbiased and invaluable sources of information.

The utopian communes of the nineteenth century were based on common ownership of all property and rigid egalitarianism, at least with respect to material life style and work requirements. For the majority of them, common ownership was a basic tenet of the new communities' raison d'être. For example, the Shakers accepted common ownership as one of the five basic principles of the Pentecostal church, from which they drew their inspiration. Those groups that were founded on the ideas of two French socialists, Saint-Simon and Fourier, also stressed the basic importance of a common "social fund." On the other hand, some groups that had not been explicitly socialistic in their initial philosophy reorganized their communities on a communal basis as a means of solving the problems of their older and poorer members. For example, the followers of George Rapp, a German Lutheran preacher who was fined and jailed for his heretical beliefs, immigrated to the United States in 1805 in order to set up a community in which they could worship without persecution. When they organized as the Harmony Society they found that many of their members "were too old or too poor to maintain themselves, [so] the Society resolved to adopt communism. The members agreed to place all their possessions in a common fund, to adopt a uniform and simple style of dress and of house, and to labour for the good of the whole body" (Holloway, 1951:90). Similarly, the Zoarites, who established a religious community in Ohio in 1817, did not originally intend to establish a communal society but quickly found it was very much to their advantage to do so.

533

The communes that Nordhoff visited were philosophically committed to producing, as far as possible, everything that the community members consumed. They were heavily involved in agriculture, as well as the production of clothing, furniture, and other necessities. In addition, most communes undertook some manufacturing activities, which were intended to give the community money for inevitable purchases. The Shakers were famous throughout the country as producers of superior garden seed and furniture, Amana was well known for its woolen goods, and Oneida developed a large industry based on the manufacture of silk twist and steel traps.

Although most of the communes began with very slim economic resources, some of them became quite successful financially. Some communities were able to attract wealthy converts who contributed their private fortunes to the common fund, but their growth has been attributed mainly to effective economic management. For example, the Oneida commune, which began with very little capital, was worth more than $600,000 when it was disbanded years later.

The nineteenth-century communes varied in their degree of democracy of organization and management. At one extreme was the system in operation at Icaria, in which the president was elected for a single year and was "simply an executive officer to do the will of the majority, which [was] expressed or ascertained every Saturday night" (Nordhoff, 1966:393). One member of the commune reported that "The president could not sell a bushel of corn without instructions from the meeting of the people." On the other hand, several of the communes (including those of the Shakers, the Rappists, and the Amana groups) had relatively greater centralized authority, and the community leaders, who were often selected with the aid of spiritual consultation, had a great deal of autonomy in decision making. It is interesting to note that in several of the communities in which authority was heavily vested in the hands of a few "elders" or "trustees," women were given equal opportunity with men to hold the important offices. Both the Shaker and the Oneida communes were strongly egalitarian with regard to sex and sought to maintain a balance of men and women in administrative positions. The historical roots of such practices lie, perhaps, in the philosophies of many heretical Christian sects. As Holloway comments about seventeenth- and eighteenth-century sects, "The perfect equality of men and women as servants of God was almost always acknowledged in the heretical sects: women often exerted as much influence in their leadership as well as in their membership, as men" (Holloway, 1951:54).

On the other hand, with the exception of admin-

27.11 Amish farmers built this barn in a day to illustrate the effectiveness of cooperative work. (UPI photo)

534

Homo modernicus: Dimensions of the Contemporary Scene

istrative jobs, which, in some communes, were shared by both men and women, the division of jobs into men's work and women's work was generally quite sharply drawn. The women had major responsibility for child care, kitchen work, and food storage, and the men were responsible for farm work and manufacturing. However, the more progressive communes, such as Oneida, made some effort to break down the traditional role structure. For example, in Oneida girls as well as boys were taught a variety of skills, including machinist's work. (However, we know of no case in which men were assigned duties in the realm of cooking or child care in the nineteenth-century utopian communities.)

Many of the communes Nordhoff visited were inspired by religious ideology; in contrast to the guiding spirit of Chinese communism, as epitomized in the expression "Serve the People," the majority of the nineteenth-century utopian communities were dedicated to serving God. Ritual observances played an important part in daily activities and reinforced community solidarity. In Amana, for example, there were community services three mornings a week and every evening. The Shakers developed some unique rituals, which have even served as inspiration for contemporary artistic expression. At the time Nordhoff observed them (in 1874) their rituals were highly structured:

After the singing of a hymn, the elder usually makes a brief address . . . followed by the eldress; and thereupon the ranks are broken, and a dozen of the brethren and sisters, forming a separate square on the floor, begin a lively hymn tune, in which all the rest join, marching around the room to a quick step, the women following the men, and all often clapping their hands. . . .

In their marching and dancing they hold their hands before them, and make a motion as of gathering something to themselves: this is called gathering a blessing. . . .

All the movements are performed with much precision and in exact order; their tunes are usually in quick time and the singers keep time admirably. (NORDHOFF, 1966:143–144)

Contrasting with the religious communes were groups like Robert Owen's New Harmony and Brook Farm, which were inspired by the philosophies of Saint-Simon and Fourier. The Oneida community (whose unusual form of group marriage is described in Chapter 14) represented an interesting amalgam of religious and nonreligious socialist philosophy. Hymn singing, faith healing, and other spiritual activities were a regular part of life. At the same time, the emphasis on the perfectability of individuals and on human interactions, rather than on human relationships with God, represents a point of view that has inspired nonreligious communes down to present times.

The New Communalists

There is today a worldwide trend toward the establishment of small communal groups as "dropouts" from industrialized mass-culture ways of living. Although many social reformers view this trend disapprovingly as "the ultimate cop-out," the more eloquent advocates of the movement suggest that communes are not passive escapism but serious and determined efforts to create more satisfying alternative life styles in order to effect radical social change by means of these communal experiments. In part the justification is spiritual: "We cannot change the world until we change ourselves."

One of the main problems that face many of the new communes is finding effective ways of translating their ideological commitments into the organization of communal life. Some communes develop very structured ideas, like Twin Oaks in Virginia, based on a *Walden Two* (B. F. Skinner) approach. More often, however, they are "antiorganization" in their philosophies and do not want to create the kind of "organizational charter" that helps Hutterite and other rigidly structured communes to operate smoothly.

Many of the life histories of communal societies document a continuing search for economic activities that can provide a measure of cash income without incurring complex dependence on the wider macrocosm. The Bruderhof, with their successful colonies in Pennsylvania, New York, and Connecticut, maintain their economy on a thriving toy-manufacturing business. Twin Oaks got into printing and hammock making. Earlier they had tried making building blocks, just as in the fictional commune Walden Two. The building-block business was not economically successful, nor were their efforts at calf raising. The hammock business is doing well, but meanwhile Twin Oaks gets along on an income derived largely from some of the mem-

535

Revitalization and Revolution: Creating New Lifeways

bers who are wage earners outside the community.

At the other end of the country, the loosely organized commune High Ridge Farm in Oregon gets its income from welfare payments, some child support money from an absentee father, and a wide variety of odd jobs, including office work in the city on an occasional basis. The lesson from High Ridge is that it helps if a few of the members are skilled in some easily salable occupation. (One of them is a CPA.)

At Twin Oaks members have worked out a system of labor that is designed to be highly egalitarian. Members take turns working on the commune and in the city (where money earned is contributed to the group), and all work is calculated in terms of a quota and labor credit system: "The credits assigned each job varied from week to week. The more popular decreased in value; the less popular increased . . . the system ensured that everyone did the same amount of work and prevented a skilled elite from monopolizing jobs that could be learned and performed by anyone" (Houriet, 1971:300–301).

At High Ridge Farm egalitarianism takes a much different form. The ethic there is that people should work only when they feel like it. The only scheduled work is making the evening meal—the one planned meal of the day. "Without the aid of committees, chairmen, quotas, policy or timeclocks, the household chores eventually got done, just as they get done in any other American household—except that the eleven adults and six children of the farm are not a family in the traditional sense" (Houriet, 1971:64).

Robert Houriet's description of a variety of "intentional communities" from Vermont to California and back again gives a fair indication of the variety of communal structures that have been tried out. Many of them last only a few months, some endure. It would, of course, be unwarranted to label the ones that fold up as "failures."

Rosabeth M. Kanter made a careful analysis of successful communes of the nineteenth century and then applied her analysis to the new wave of communal societies beginning in the 1960s. In the nineteenth-century communes she found that the groups most likely to succeed (to endure) were the ones that had strong means of *commitment*, by which individuals affirmed their allegiance to the collective group. Ceremonial and ideological means of com-

munal identification were an aid to longevity, and homogeneity of ethnic or religious background was also important. Most of these mechanisms of solidarity and commitment are lacking in contemporary North American communal groups. Finally, Kanter noted that "success" is indeed a very complex concept, for it might be that even very temporary communal societies have quite beneficial results, so temporariness is not at all a clear measure of their effectiveness (Kanter, 1972).

Summary: On Revitalization and Social Movements

Millions of people, in practically all parts of the world, have found reason to complain about the shape of their lives, and not a few of them have, from time to time, set up some sort of movement of protest or reform to change things. In areas with powerful social stratification and real oppression any larger reforms of "the system" have tended toward revolution, and a major share of the world's population has experienced bloody revolution in the twentieth century.

Short of revolution, many people have joined movements of revitalization and reform, seeking to bring about permanent changes in themselves and their surroundings. Often changes in one's spiritual relationships to the supernaturals are seen as a way to make a better life—in varieties of Christian and non-Christian revival movements. The movements themselves tend to have striking similarities in beginnings, development, and routinization. Some major worldwide religious groups—perhaps all of them—had their beginnings in what were at first localized, often extremist, revitalizations.

Political, secular revitalization may take a somewhat different form from religious movements, especially because it generally aims at changes in the established social system rather than a reshuffling of individual beliefs and behavior. It is more likely to be greeted by swift opposition from political powers, although political powers don't always distinguish between secular and sacred revitalization efforts.

Movements take their shapes from differences in the social and physical environments in which they arise. But there is a good deal of ideational leeway,

536

537

Revitalization and Revolution: Creating New Lifeways

because some of the more effective and influential movements have arisen from the visions and sudden revelations of individual prophets—some of whom weren't all that well attuned to ecological realities.

The short-run origins of revitalization movements may have a good deal of "ideational causation"—in the long-run they have their successes in relation to their fit with environmental and economic realities.

Homo modernicus: Dimensions of the Contemporary Scene

Why Anthropology?

28

This last chapter will be a somewhat personal view of what this profession is all about, in relation to our lives, our students, and the people that anthropologists study. The whole business of anthropology, so deeply involved in the fabric of people's lifeways, probably always has a personalized, emotional aspect, even when its practitioners become quite scientific in their information-gathering style. Our view is that to be scientific is to be more human —because it can lead us to be more honest and truthful about people's lives, closer to verifiable, factual information that does poetic justice to other views besides that of the writer.

Times change, and so do the issues. A large part of the anthropological profession has always felt that the production of valid information about the lifeways of various peoples is a useful enterprise in and of itself, especially as these data are used to develop a general understanding of human behavior and social life. In earlier times anthropologists helped to dispel the notion that all Indians were bloodthirsty savages lusting for the scalps of White settlers. Ethnographic reporting demolished the idea that there were peoples in the world without religion or morals. And anthropologists have worked to provide the data and the argument to demonstrate that different "races," ethnic groups, and cultural systems are on a par in their morality, their logic, and their right to a fair place on this globe. For example, Franz Boas was a major leader in campaigns against racism and cultural ethnocentrism during the period from 1910 to 1940.

The general spirit of anthropology during the 1920s and 1930s was an affirmation of the powerful substance of native cultures, in opposition to what was felt to be the "spurious" nature of culture in industrialized societies. For people imbued with that version of the anthropological ethic, it was not immediately necessary to go out and work for the betterment of individual peoples. The bigger task was in spreading the message of cultural relativism in the universities, among people who would soon take their place as the legislators and executors of "The Establishment."

The tendency to identify non-Western cultural ways with "the good life" was expressed by Edward Sapir in his well-known paper "Culture, Genuine and Spurious." Sapir reflected on the "genuineness" of life experiences in Indian communities and other small traditional societies. He made clear what was

28.1 After the Vicos potato harvest, a cooperative work group of men, women, and children sort potatoes by size and quality for market. (Paul Doughty)

539

probably a majority opinion of anthropologists at the time he was writing (in the 1920s) that our industrialized way of life is "spurious":

The great cultural fallacy of industrialism, as developed up to the present time, is that in harnessing machines to our uses it has not known how to avoid the harnessing of the majority of mankind to its machines. The telephone girl who lends her capacities, during the greater part of the living day, to the manipulation of a technical routine that has an eventually high efficiency value but that answers to no spiritual needs of her own is an appalling sacrifice to civilization. As a solution of the problem of culture she is a failure. . . . The American Indian who solves the economic problem with salmon-spear and rabbit-snare operates on a relatively low level of civilization, but he represents an incomparably higher solution than our telephone girl of the questions that culture has to ask of economics. . . . The Indian's salmon-spearing is a culturally higher type of activity than that of the telephone girl or mill hand simply because there is normally no sense of spiritual frustration during its prosecution, no feeling of subservience to tyrannous yet largely inchoate demands, because it works in naturally with all the rest of the Indian's activities instead of standing out as a desert patch of merely economic effort in the whole of life. (SAPIR, 1924:411–412)

During World War II many anthropologists went to work for the war effort, convinced that the cause of Euro-American democracy was a just one in the face of Nazi and Japanese military expansionism. Thus, for the first time on a massive scale, anthropologists directly and unblushingly bent their research and scientific writing to the furtherance of practical, applied ends. By the war's end a number of people had quite inflated ideas of the future prospects for applied anthropology, and the Society for Applied Anthropology blossomed into a major establishment in its own right.

We should set the record straight by pointing out that some North American anthropologists, and a very considerable portion of British and European anthropologists, throughout the nineteenth and early twentieth centuries, were paid by their governments to produce information for use in the governing and managing of native peoples conquered by the military contingents of the colonialist nations. Some British anthropologists, for instance, worked for the Colonial Office, generating information about peoples of Africa who were newly subjugated wards of colonialism. The anthropologists who were in these activities claimed to be developing information that would enable their governments to be humane and reasonable in governance, instead of heavy-handed and arbitrary. In some cases the effects of this anthropological research may have been benign, but it serves no purpose to deny that a part of our profession worked on behalf of colonial administration.

Anthropology, Politics, and Ethics

Before the late 1950s anthropologists were not much concerned about the possibilities of subversion of anthropological data for antihumane, military, and other nonscientific purposes. (One exception to this is an incident at the end of World War I, when Franz Boas denounced some anthropologists for complicity in spying, suggesting that this would backfire on the entire anthropological enterprise.) By the middle 1960s, however, a major scandal had developed that graphically demonstrated the problem of social science data gathering and international politics and diplomacy. Project Camelot, sponsored by the U.S. Department of Defense, had been launched in Chile as part of a general plan to develop data for counterinsurgency measures in various parts of the world. Anthropologists and sociologists were involved in collecting data for this plan, but the implications of the research became clear to some Chileans, and strong protests were voiced. President Johnson quickly dropped the project.

Since the days of Project Camelot and the Vietnam war, anthropological research in potentially sensitive areas has come under serious questioning by many scholars. The problem is that even the most innocent research, if carried out in thoroughgoing ethnographic fashion, can provide information about leadership, social structure, and other data of usefulness and interest to military people or others promoting their own special interests. Some safeguards are clearly necessary in order to render the data neutral and innocuous, if there is danger that they could be wrongly used.

In 1970 the American Anthropological Association adopted a new code of ethics that set out the responsibilities of field researchers with regard to the

Homo modernicus: Dimensions of the Contemporary Scene

people they study, to students, to the discipline, to financial sponsors of research, and to governments, both one's own and the ones within whose domains the research takes place. From the anthropologist's point of view the prime responsibility is to the people among whom research is carried out:

1. The need for anonymity. The first requirement for protecting the rights of research subjects is through the maintenance of *anonymity.* Nowadays most anthropological writers use pseudonyms for particular individuals, and a growing number of ethnographic reports use pseudonyms for communities as well. (Plainville and Yankee City were among the early and famous disguised names.) In some cases individual privacy is protected even further by changing some identifying details about individuals.

One problem with pseudonyms is that often many people in the communities that anthropologists study are attracted by the prospect that their town and their own identities will appear in print. Sometimes their cooperation with the anthropologist is motivated by the likelihood of published fame, and some people will feel that the protective cloak of anonymity has deprived them of their right to public notice in this otherwise impersonal world.

On the other hand, it goes without saying that anthropologists are morally obliged to protect completely the confidentiality of personal information about individuals. This has become especially important in recent times as anthropologists have worked with drug addicts, inner-city gangs, and other types of people whose personal activities would be of interest to the police and other agencies.

2. Open covenants, openly arrived at. Generally field workers have intended that the people they work with have a clear view of the nature of their research. Many peoples of the world are now fairly well informed about what it means when the anthropologist says he intends to "write a book about them." Most people regard that as a compliment rather than a threat, especially after the fieldworker has established his or her trustworthiness. The code of ethics of the association requires that anthropologists make sure that the people in the research communities understand what they intend to do with the data—and that they will do nothing that could bring harm to the community.

3. No secret agreements, no secret reports. Another part of the code of ethics is that there will be no production of secret information for anybody. Any research report *must* be available in the public domain rather than locked up in the secret files of some agency or corporation. From time to time the Department of Defense and other agencies have asked anthropologists to produce secret information, and, for the most part, researchers have strongly resisted any kind of clandestine research, especially if sponsorship came from politico-military channels.

4. A fair return. Ethical standards also require that fieldworkers not exploit people for their own private gain. Often the anthropologist receives many hours of time from informants, in addition to the value of the information itself. The information about local behavior is usually defined as a "free good" by most people. That is, once a person has established a certain minimal trust relationship, the conveying of locally relevant information is not usually seen as a directly financial transaction. On the other hand, many anthropologists do pay some of their informants for their time, especially in the form of gifts and food.

Most anthropologists spend fairly large amounts of time and resources in maintaining reciprocal relationships with their research communities. The most common items of exchange in these relationships are transportation and minor medical care. The example of John Middleton's health clinic among the Lugbara peoples goes somewhat beyond the usual in this respect:

Lugbara were always sick, with malaria, dysentery, sores, yaws, wounds of many kinds. . . . The local government doctor . . . supplied me with a few simple drugs. . . . Every day people would come to me to ask for medicine. All I could do was give aspirin and to dress the more dreadful looking sores and cuts brought to me. . . . I set aside an hour each morning to give what help I could. This meant that from seven until eight each day I would help, as best I could, several dozen people. (MIDDLETON, 1970:22–23)

The ethics of the complex exchange relationship of fieldwork require that researchers be prepared to use considerable amounts of their financial resources, skills, and information for the benefit of the people who supply them with data in the long hours and days of the fieldwork enterprise. Recently, some anthropologists have felt that the profits from the sale of ethnographic books should be shared with the people who provided the information, and this is likely to become a common practice.

541

Another significant service that many anthropologists give to their research communities is basic current information. P. Doughty reports: "I did this often in Huaylas, Peru, sharing historical findings, census results and other general data with the community. They then took the information and translated it into plans and projects . . . for which they subsequently obtained funding" (Doughty, personal communication).

Another aspect of a "fair return" involves sharing data with social scientists in the host country and aiding in the research training of their students. Too often, our critics say, North American anthropologists go into research sites with their own students, ignoring the fact that the host country often has very slim facilities for training their students. Anthropological research projects, especially training programs, should be designed to include the support and training of students from the host country. At the same time, sharing data with the social scientists of the host country often facilitates the goals of those scientists and helps build an international community of scholars.

The Search for Cultural Identity: One Role for Anthropology

Early in the nineteenth century a number of groups in Europe were awakening to the need for establishing their cultural identities and histories through collecting oral history, linguistic materials, and general cultural lore. In Finland, for example, the rise of cultural nationalism was spurred by the discovery and recording of the *Kalevala* sagas (see pp. 398–399) along with a rich body of other Finnish folklore. The ethnographers Mattias Alexanteri Castrén and Andreas Sjögren embarked on extensive fieldwork among the Same, Karelians, and Finno-Ugric groups in Siberia to study the origins and affinities of the Finnic-speaking peoples. This early anthropological work was an important factor in laying the foundations for what later became the culturally and politically independent Finnish nation.

Anthropological data on cultural histories, oral traditions, land tenure and inheritance, and other sectors of culture have provided important information for the people of the newly independent nations of Africa, for cultural revitalization in some American Indian groups, and for other cultural minorities. Through the magazine *El Grito*, anthropologist Octavio Romano V. has been active in producing literature and other materials for the Chicano movement. Leaders of many other North American movements make use of anthropological materials to give their people an appreciation and understanding of their own cultural backgrounds.

In Mexico the many rich and varied archaeological sites, such as Tula, Teotihuacán, Monte Albán, and Bonampak, have provided a major ingredient in the development of the contemporary Mexican national self-image. The role of archaeological materials in providing tangible embodiment to people's cultural identities has also been of great importance in South America and many parts of the Mediterranean. For the casual tourist the main attractions are perhaps the monumental architecture and exciting works of art. But for people whose historical and literary pasts are embodied in the archaeological sites, the continuing ethnohistorical and ecological research provides an ever-expanding vista of a cultural past that had been obliterated by the expansion of Western European commerce and technology.

Among the Baganda people of East Africa there is an individual who is recognized as "the authority" on aspects of Baganda custom and tradition. As the "unofficial anthropologist" for his people, Michael Nsimbi is charged with providing the answer to all the minutiae of cultural detail that come up in court disputes, problems of land tenure, and other arguments (Robbins, personal communication). Of course many peoples in the world are not as acutely conscious of their cultural traditions as are the Baganda; the psychological meaning of cultural knowledge is very much a matter of degree.

In many parts of the world ethnic identity is growing as a principle around which people organize their psychic and social alignments. The example of the Kiowa Indian people in San Francisco, studying their own traditional cultural background, is duplicated in many other places. Often the ethnographic writings of anthropologists are the "handbooks" studied by people seeking a firmer hold on a cultural identity. J. A. Paredes has described the awakening of Indian pride and identity among Creek peoples in Alabama—in which the anthropologist has helped the people to write their history and promotional materials (Paredes, 1974).

Applied Anthropology: The Experiment at Vicos, Peru

In the postwar years almost no one in the profession was as thoroughly devoted to the idea of applied anthropology as Allan Holmberg and his colleagues at Cornell University. When he heard that the feudalistic hacienda of Vicos, Peru, was up for lease in 1952, he convinced Cornell University to take up the lease in partnership with the Peruvian Indian Institute. In an unprecedented anthropological experiment the researchers, backed by the university, became the controllers of a hacienda with its subserviant population of 2,250 Indian people. During the ensuing ten years Holmberg and his colleagues put into effect a program of applied change that is to this date without parallel. The anthropologists made several key assumptions:

1. That the aspirations of the people of Vicos could not be achieved unless their economic base was significantly improved.
2. That however long they had been in complete subservience to hacienda masters, the Vicos Indians could be induced to take the initiative in working for economic and social improvements.
3. That the structure of social change in the community must be worked out by the people themselves, with the outsiders, the anthropologists, simply facilitating whatever the people decided to do.

28.2 The scattered houses of the people set against the twenty-thousand-foot peaks of the Cordillera Blanca, Vicos. (Paul Doughty)

543

4. That such changes would be considered "good" by the local people and would not bring retribution from the wider community.

In this overtly action-oriented program the anthropologists introduced new kinds of potatoes to the community of Vicos, as well as other agricultural improvements. The changes, however, were introduced gradually, allowing the people to decide on their own priorities. Step by step the Vicosiños embarked on agricultural improvements, as they worked out the problems of decision making in the community and reorganized the political and economic structure of the estate. Over time there were significant improvements in the economic situation in Vicos, particularly in potato production, and the people took on more and more projects of self-improvement, including building a school, promoting some public health measures, and other programs suggested and explained by the anthropologists in long-term "seminars" with the people of Vicos. At the end of ten years the Vicosiños were able to buy their own lease and finally obtain their freedom from outside control, after centuries of subservience under oppressive landlords. As benign as this seemed, the project had dangerous political implications nationally because it was the first thorough, if small, attempt at land reform ever undertaken in modern Peru.

This lesson in self-determination was not lost on some of the neighboring peoples, and there were some violent confrontations at other haciendas when Indian peoples sought to take over control of their own economic situation, as they felt the Vicos people had done. In 1960 three serfs were killed in a battle at Huapra, one of the neighboring haciendas, when peasants sought to take control of the lands. The situation of the peasants in the highlands of Peru has since changed dramatically with land reforms introduced by more recent Peruvian governments. Two of the Peruvian anthropologists who had been Allan Holmberg's associates have since been in high positions in the Peruvian government, especially concerned with matters of rural land reform. These are not the first anthropologically trained people to achieve high political office. The leader of Kenya's native revolt, Jomo Kenyatta, was trained in anthropology and frequently used this background in political matters. Similarly, Manuel Gamio, trained in anthropology under Franz Boas, became a leader in the Mexican revolutionary government after 1920.

El Barrio: Action Research in the City

In 1969 Stephen Schensul and his associates began anthropological research in a Chicano community in West Side Chicago. They were part of a community mental health program and originally felt themselves to be providing useful information to the medical people in the community. They felt that the psychiatrists and other workers in the medical establishment could substantially improve their services for Chicano patients if they had a fuller understanding of Chicano cultural patterns and life styles. This is, of course, the almost universal attitude justifying applied anthropological research for service institutions.

It is also part of the experience of applied anthropologists that they often have serious difficulties in communicating with administrators and other personnel associated with mainstream institutions. Schensul and his group of researchers were no exception in this regard. Gradually they felt they were being eased out of the discussion of mental health concerns, as their research data were deemed not particularly relevant to the daily work of the psychiatric staff. At the same time the anthropologists were developing closer ties with community activists, especially with a group of young men who were bent on developing strong Chicano community programs and building up local leadership for social change. In the summer of 1969 there were some community events in which the anthropologists participated. These included protest demonstrations aimed at influencing the policies downtown at City Hall.

Over the next two years, the researchers became more and more involved with the Chicano community leaders and less concerned with the ongoing activities of the mental health program. One day, in response to the challenge of an establishment-sponsored mental health training program, the Chicanos decided to draft their own grant proposal for training mental health workers. The proposal was greatly strengthened by the availability of anthropological data, and the anthropologists had a major role in writing the grant proposal. The Chicano mental health training program was funded in 1972, and the group quickly followed up with a drug action proposal, which also received substantial government funding.

With these developments the Chicano activitists were in a situation of relative affluence with government-funded programs, and the anthropologists were deeply involved in a new role—writing grant proposals and actively participating in the planning sessions of the organizations in El Barrio. The researchers had positions on the planning boards and councils of several Mexican-American programs, all operating from the newly organized Chicano Community Center. This involvement was several steps further along the way toward activism than is usually found in applied anthropology.

The perspective developed by Schensul and his group is based on the idea that the research facilities of the anthropologists should be at the disposal of the community organizations, to further their aims of community development. However, the research capabilities of the group cannot be easily utilized by the community unless the anthropologists stay in day-to-day contact with the activities in El Barrio. Thus the researchers work very closely with local people in all phases of community operations. Furthermore, several people from the neighborhood have joined the research staff, for part of their policy is to help train members of the community to carry out their *own* anthropological research. The research style, then, of this group of "action anthropologists" is intended to facilitate the direct use of anthropological data by the people of the community.

The role of the anthropologists in the Vicos and El Barrio examples, is, in part, that of a special kind of cultural broker along the lines discussed above (pp. 484–485). As cultural brokers, the anthropologists brought in information from the outside world (the macrocosm) and worked with the local people in translating the ideas in terms of the local conditions. We should note that the cultural broker does not act as an "expert" but more as an information carrier. Communications from the local microcosm, especially to state federal agencies, form the other side of the brokerage activity.

In Miami anthropologists have been playing an increasingly important role as cultural brokers between medical institutions and the large minority populations of the city, especially the Spanish-speaking Cubans. Professor Hazel Weidman has been concerned about the large gap between "modern" medical systems and the health concerns and beliefs of the people served by these systems. To bridge this gap, her Health Ecology Project is explicitly geared to the use of anthropologists as brokers between the medical establishment and the Cuban, Puerto Rican, Bahamian, Haitian, and southern Black populations in the city. A main task of applied anthropologists in this program is to provide articulation and translation between folk medical concepts like *susto* (Cuban), "blacking out" (Bahamian), and *la congestion* (Haitian) and the medical beliefs and practices of physicians and other health workers involved with the city's ethnic minorities (Weidman, 1973). In one sense this applied anthropological role can be regarded as a special kind of "consumer advocacy."

The Wider Uses of Anthropology

Socially concerned anthropologists sometimes turn to examples of applied research for validation of the discipline. Truly credible and unambiguous examples of applied anthropology are rather few, however, and even the best cases raise debate over the short term and long-term ethics of the applications. Very few projects in applied anthropology have had the favorable opportunities for success enjoyed by Vicos and El Barrio.

We feel that anthropologists should take these successful cases seriously and should seek to expand the range of applied work. But avoiding entrapment in the demands and expectations of the sponsors of research is often a tricky business; and what does one do in communities in which small *nonrepresentative* groups of "local leaders" have taken over the scene for their own aggrandizement? In a fair number of instances it is extremely difficult to work cooperatively with "the community" because the most visible, vocal leaders are not trusted by the people they claim to represent. Who does the applied anthropologist work with in a factionally split community?

The justification for anthropology as a discipline would be slim indeed if it rested on the currently available instances of applied research! We can hope

545

that there will be a rapid expansion of occasions for the practical application of anthropological data and insights, but that also depends on attitudes and responses of people in government, in agencies, and in local communities—they aren't necessarily eager to enter into communication with anthropologists.

Beyond the moderate promises of a future applied anthropology, we feel that the justification of the subject matter and activities of anthropology rests much more firmly on that somewhat vaguer but nonetheless substantial contribution by which anthropology "holds up a mirror to humanity." The cross-cultural emphasis in our discipline is constantly presenting human behavior as a *wide range of variation* with a great variety of alternative life styles, so that people, in their problem-solving, need not be stuck with a narrow view of the adaptive capabilities and possibilities of humankind.

In an age when the foundations of our own societies are being thoroughly challenged, it is more important than ever for the protagonists in the argument to have available the best information on the different ways in which human groups have met the challenges of adapting to some of the life situations that confront us all. For instance, when some people seriously question the rationality and viability of the monogamous nuclear family (considered "natural" by most North Americans), it is extremely useful to consider the available information about family structures with different characteristics—to see where they have developed and why.

Various forms of communal and cooperative social organization are being explored by serious people for whom the available social data about other similar experiments in community organization are vital for anticipating and understanding possible outcomes. The same holds for people experimenting and theorizing about child training and socialization. So many seemingly minor details of human behavior are in for change and reevaluation in these times that *all* available information about the varieties of adaptive patterns will be of continuing importance as alternative models for what can be done.

Careful anthropological research can provide us with critically important information about how biosocial systems "really work" and what happens when they are rapidly changed. For example, the fieldwork in Brazil by Daniel Gross and Barbara Underwood documents in detail the nutritional consequences of the shift from subsistence farming to sisal production (see pp. 433–434). Similarly, Marvin Harris, Richard Franke, and others have studied the ways in which the "Green Revolution" (introduction of high-productivity seeds in Third World countries) has had unforeseen, negative consequences (see, for example, Franke, 1974). And the varied, unforeseen, and often negative effects of new technologies have been documented for many areas of the world (see, for example, Bernard and Pelto, 1972).

But the past is of no use to us unless it tells us about the future. The moment we say this, we realize that our entire store of learned reactions and ideas *is the past* and that we are constantly using our past experiences to frame reactions and actions for the future. People seeking their cultural identities in literary sources are only substituting books for grandparents—the processing of wisdom is qualitatively the same. Even if anthropological study has not achieved these ideals, the main intention of this branch of study has been to provide a sufficient background so that future actions can be wise instead of foolish, open to alternatives rather than narrow-minded.

Anthropology does not hold up a mirror for humankind in order to amuse and entertain with examples of the bizarre, the weird, and the unbelievable. The mirror—of anthropological data—is held up so that we may see ourselves in fullest perspective of our adaptive capacities. The mirror shows that humans have an almost unbelievably wide range of adaptive capability; we have hardly touched the expanded possibilities of consciousness and social organization yet open to *Homo sapiens*. If, as suggested by the current arguments about the "limits to growth," our social systems must soon adapt to situations without ever-expanding horizons, ever-expanding populations, and ever-expanding economies, then the repertoires of human societies already have in storage some of the cultural information for adjusting our economies and our behavior to those eventualities.

546

Glossary

Aboriginal. Indigenous or native; pertaining to the original inhabitants of a region, country, or continent.

Abstraction. An idea or expression considered apart from particular objects or events (e.g., the general idea of "table" considered apart from any one particular table).

Adaptation$_1$. The process of genetic (heritable) modification of features of organisms that contributes to the survival chances of that population of organisms.

Adaptation$_2$. The process of nongenetic modification of behavior or physical functioning that contributes to the survival chances of an organism or group of organisms.

Adaptive flexibility. The quality of an organism or a population that permits relatively rapid modification in structure and/or behavior in response to environmental changes.

Adaptive radiation. A relatively rapid increase in the number of varieties and species of an animal in a favorable environment.

Affinal. Related by marriage.

Age grade. A culturally recognized stage of the life cycle in terms of which people are grouped into organizations (e.g. "the young warriors").

Age set. A group whose members' assigned roles are determined by the socially designated age category to which they belong; typically part of an age organization composed of several such grades.

Aggression. (in humans) The causing of, or intending to cause, harm to other persons or things.

Agnate. A kinsman whose connection is exclusively through males; one related by descent through the male line.

Alleles. Alternative forms of a gene that can occupy a particular locus on a chromosome (e.g., genes in ABO blood series).

Altruistic suicide. Taking one's own life in order to bring some supposed benefit to one's survivors.

Androgen. Any of the hormones having to do with the development and operation of male properties and powers in vertebrate animals.

Animism. Belief in spirits and other supernatural beings (E. B. Tylor's minimal definition of religion).

Anomic suicide. Taking of one's life because of feelings of unrelatedness to society or feelings of worthlessness.

Anthropoid. Pertaining to the suborder of primates that includes monkeys, apes, and humans.

Arboreal. Adapted to living in trees (in contrast to terrestrial).

Archaeology. The study of historic or prehistoric peoples, based principally on artifacts and other material remains of their cultures.

Artifact. Any human-made material object.

Association. A social group formed on the basis of shared interests and/or attributes.

Assortative mating. Prevalence of nonrandom mating between phenotypically similar individuals (positive assortative mating) or between dissimilar individuals (negative assortative mating).

Asymmetrical. Lacking symmetry; uneven, unbalanced, or unequal.

Atheism. Philosophical view that denies the existence of gods or other supernatural beings.

Australopithecus. Category of fossil hominids of the Pliocene and early Pleistocene, thought to be ancestral to modern *Homo sapiens.*

Autonomous. Independent, self-sufficient.

Autosome. Any chromosome except a sex chromosome (there are 22 pairs of autosomes in humans).

B

Band. A small, territorially based social group most of whose members are related.

Barrio. A ward or other segment of a community or town in Mexico and other parts of Latin America. More generally, "subcommunity."

Bifurcate. To divide or fork into two separate branches.

Bilateral descent. A system for reckoning descent in which relationships of an individual are traced through both parents.

Bilocal residence. Culture pattern in which a married couple may establish residence with either the bride's or the groom's kin.

Binary code. Any system of communication constructed of paired alternative units (e.g., the 0/1 system in electronic computers).

Biocultural evolution. In humans, the modification, over time, of interrelated genetic (bodily) features *and* accumulated cultural patterns and artifacts.

Bipedalism. Locomotion on two legs (as in humans, birds, etc.).

Blood brotherhood. A tie of ritual allegiance between two unrelated individuals, establishing a kinship-like bond (see *Bratstvo*).

Body language. Any communication of emotional or other information by use of gestures or other body movements.

Bourgeoisie. People of the middle class; (in radical socialism) people with private property interests.

Brachiation. Locomotion by swinging arm over arm in trees (typical of gibbons).

Bride price. (or **Bride wealth**) Goods, usually property or money, given by a prospective husband and his kinsmen to the family of the bride.

Bride service. Labor or other services rendered to a woman's kinsmen by her husband before or after marriage.

Bull roarer. A flat board that makes a loud whirring noise when twirled at the end of a string.

C

Cantometrics. System of notation and classification for cross-cultural study of music.

Cargo cult. Any of a number of social movements in Melanesia in which members seek to receive large amounts of factory-produced material goods through supernatural means.

Cargo system. A system of essentially voluntary religious service, often interrelated with holding of civil offices, widespread in Latin American communities.

Carnivorous. Reliant mainly on meat-eating.

Cash crops. Crops raised for marketing outside the local community, especially for "international trade."

Caste. An hereditary, endogamous group usually identified with a specific occupation; typically one of several such groups, all of which are ranked hierarchically in terms of social position.

Caucasian, Caucasoid. So-called "White race".

Cenozoic. Geological era ("Age of Mammals") lasting from approximately 70 million years ago to the present.

Cereal. Any grass-yielding grain used as food; e.g., wheat, barley, rice, etc.

Charisma. An aura of magnetism or extraordinary power radiated by a person.

Chauvinism. Exaggerated expression of belief in purported superiority of one's group or social category, as in "male chauvinism." (Originally meant superpatriotism or nationalism.)

Chromosome. Structure in nucleus of a cell containing the genetic (hereditary) materials transmitted from one generation to the next.

Cicatrization. Scar tissue produced by incising the skin to make decorative or symbolically significant patterns.

City. Large and nucleated population center with some occupational specialization and complex organization. (In many modern nations "city" is a designated administrative category.)

Clan. A descent group whose members claim descent from a remote common ancestor, often a mythical figure; sometimes used to refer to a residential kin group composed of a core of unilineally related persons and their wives or husbands.

548

Class. A social stratum composed of persons sharing basically similar economic, social, and other cultural characteristics; one of several such strata within a ranked system.

Clientship. State of dependency through asymmetrical ties to individual or group with economic and social power.

Cline. Distribution (as on surface of a map) of variations in frequencies of a thing or quality (e.g., in clinal maps of blood-group frequencies).

Cognition. Knowledge, or a way of perceiving and thinking about reality.

Collateral. Referring to relationship through non-direct or horizontal links, as in the instance of one's "uncles," "aunts," and "cousins."

Colonialism. System of economic and political dominance and exploitation of one population by another; pertains to nations.

Commercialism. Pervasive presence of cash transactions of material goods in a social system (contrasted with barter or subsistence economy).

Communalist. A person or a quality supporting or participating in a system of group-owned rather than individually owned economic resources.

Commune. A local community with group-owned and controlled economic resources (e.g., a *kibbutz* in Israel).

Communication. Any act or event having some influence or potential influence on the behavior of another organism.

Compadrazgo. The Spanish term for the institution of ritual co-parenthood.

Conjugal. Pertaining to marriage or marital relations.

Consanguinity. Pertaining to kinship based on common descent; of the same "blood".

Corporate. Pertaining to a group of individuals whose organization and actions are continuous and independent of the existence of individual members.

Cross-cousins. The offspring of siblings of unlike sex; i.e., the child of ego's father's sister or of ego's mother's brother.

Cult. An organized group of people (usually few in number) with special religious beliefs and rituals that differentiate them from the rest of their society (see Cargo cult).

Cultural broker. Individual who acts as an intermediary between two different cultural groups.

Cultural diffusion. Process whereby cultural items or complexes are spread from one society to another.

Cultural evolution. The gradual change of cultural forms, usually tending toward greater complexity and elaboration.

Cultural relativism. The idea or postulate that cultural items and cultural systems must each be judged and evaluated in their own terms so that *cross-culturally* there are no "superior" or "inferior" cultures.

Culture. The systematic patterns of explicit and implicit concepts (ideas) for behavior settings (environments) learned and used by individuals and groups in adapting to their environments.

Culture area. A geographical region in which the cultures tend to be similar in a number of significant aspects.

Culture pool. The total of all ideas, beliefs, and other concepts in a particular community or population.

Culture, personal. The learned ideas, beliefs, and other concepts of an individual, whether or not shared with other members of his/her society.

Culture, public. The shared and mutually agreed on ideas, standards, rules, traditions, beliefs, and other concepts characteristic of a community.

Cuneiform. Writing system invented in the Near East in fourth millenium B.C. (usually wedge-shaped impressions on clay tablets).

Curandera, curandero. A folk curer or healer in Spanish-speaking communities.

D

Deductive, deduction. Research or reasoning from general theory or principles to more concrete results or conclusions.

Deep structure. Underlying fundamental system of relationships in a language system.

Deleterious. Injurious.

Delocalization. Pertaining to increased dependency on outside energy and other resources in any community or region; a general aspect of increased modernization.

Design features. Characteristics of a system that influence its effectiveness and flexibility.

Diachronic. Pertaining to events or phenomena as they change through time.

Dialect. Any subvariety of a language, characteristic of a locality, specialized occupational group, or other subgroup within the total range of a particular language.

Dialectical materialist theory. The social theory of Karl Marx and others according to which social change and evolution are caused by the conflicts and contradictions that arise as different social classes of people pursue their economic interests in a social system.

Dialectology. The study of the distributions and other characteristics of dialects.

Diffusion. The transmission of a culture trait from one group to another in the absence of face-to-face contact.

549

Discreteness. Quality of a meaningful unit of sound being sharply contrasted with other such units, rather than gradually; used in reference to communications systems.

Displacement. The capability of referring to information not immediately present in that time and place; used in reference to communications systems.

Divination. Foretelling future events or obtaining other information (e.g., diagnosis of disease) through supernatural means, including "reading" of palms, bones, flights of geese, entrails of animals, etc.

DNA (Deoxyribonucleic acid). The complex molecule in cell nuclei that carries the essential genetic code from one generation to the next.

Domestication. Creation of a dependency relationship between humans and other organisms (animals or plants) leading to genetic and behavioral modification of those organisms and systematic utilization of them by humans.

Dominance (genetic). The quality of an allele that allows it to determine the phenotypic outcome in an organism in the presence of other (recessive) alleles.

Double descent. The coexistence in a single society of patrilateral and matrilateral systems for tracing descent.

Dromedary. The single-humped camel of Arabia and North Africa.

Dryopithecus. Genus of Miocene fossil hominoids believed by some researchers to be ancestral to both humans and the great apes.

Duality of patterning. A quality of the human language system whereby transmission and comprehension of information depend on regularities in individual sounds *and* (simultaneously) in the clusters of the sounds.

Dyad. Any interacting pair in a system (e.g., married couple, paired chromosomes, pitcher-catcher, etc.)

E

Ecclesiastical religion. Religious system characterized by complex theology, organized and trained body of priests, and other features.

Ecological system. The complex interrelationships of any population with the environment.

Ecology. The study of the systems of interrelationship between organisms and their environments.

Ego. The "I" in kinship analysis; the hypothetical person used as the point of reference in diagramming relations; also, in psychology, the rational, planning sector of an individual personality.

Egoistic. Pertaining to the pursuit of individual self-interests.

Empirical. Based on verifiable evidence or experience.

Enculturation. The processes by which a person gradually learns and assimilates the patterns of cultural behavior expected in a particular society.

Endogamy. The custom or rule requiring or encouraging a person to marry within some particular social group to which he or she belongs.

Entropy. A measure of the dispersion, or unavailability, of energy in a thermodynamic system.

Environment. The physical, geographic, biological, and social context or setting within which an organism or population lives.

Enzyme. Any protein that functions as a catalyst in the breakdown or synthesis of the constituents of living organisms.

Eocene. The geological epoch lasting from approximately 55 million to 34 million years ago.

Estrogen. A hormone having an effect on the estrous cycle and other female sex processes and characteristics in mammals.

Eta. The Japanese term for the members of low caste groups in Japanese society.

Ethnic. Pertaining to the distinctive social, cultural, linguistic, and physical attributes of a particular group.

Ethnocentrism. Pertaining to attitudes concerning the inherent superiority of one's own culture and people as compared with others.

Ethnography. That aspect of cultural and social anthropology devoted to the objective, first-hand description of particular cultures.

Ethnology. Theoretical analysis and interpretation based on ethnographic data.

Ethnomusicology. The anthropological study of music; particularly the study of the music of nonliterate peoples, with emphasis upon the place of music in cultural context.

Etiology. The study of the causes of diseases.

Eutrophication (ecology). "Overfertilization," especially of bodies of water, causing production of algae and gradual depletion of oxygen.

Evolution. Descent with modification.

Exogamy. The socially enforced requirement that a person marry outside the culturally defined group to which he or she belongs.

Explicit. Open; unambiguous; with no disguised meaning.

Exploitation. Use of resources, especially someone else's resources, for one's own gain or satisfaction.

Exponential growth. Growth or increase at an ever-increasing rate.

Expressive culture. Patterns of behavior which include or give substance to emotions, motivations,

550

and other personality characteristics of people (e.g. art, music, games, etc.).

Extended family. Family group consisting of two or more related marital units; often a married pair and their married sons or daughters.

F

Family, conjugal-natal. A social group composed of spouses and their offspring.

Fertile Crescent. The arc of especially productive lands extending from Egypt and the eastern Mediterranean coastal area through Syria to the Tigris-Euphrates delta.

Feud. Bitter, long-lasting, generally overt hostilities between two groups within a society.

Feudal. Pertaining to or like the social and economic system in Europe during the Middle Ages, based on the holding of lands in fief.

Field dependence. Quality of mental functioning of an individual that interferes with effective discrimination of a figure or form because of confusion with the "field" or background (as in a picture).

Fieldwork. Research carried out in the natural habitat or location of the people, animals, or other phenomena to be studied. Characteristic of anthropology, geology, and other natural sciences.

Fixed-action sequence. Connected series of behaviors of an animal thought to be genetically inborn (e.g., nest-building activities of some species of birds).

Folk-urban continuum. Hypothesized progression of cultural-social forms characteristic of the evolution from small-scale isolated societies to modern city lifeways.

Food chain. The sequence of organisms feeding on other organisms in a given ecological system (e.g., the series: vegetation—insects—trout—human).

Founder effect. Pertaining to changes in genetic makeup in populations brought about when the founders of a new population (e.g., migrants) are an aberrant or skewed sample of a larger parent population.

Frequency interpretation. The ability of humans and other animals to learn from experience through remembering (approximately) the positive effects of advantageous choices, and avoiding the negative effects of wrong choices.

G

Game. Any activity that has a set of rules and involves some sort of contest (of skill, chance, or strategy) played for amusement.

Gene. Basic unit of hereditary material, composed of DNA. Each human sex cell is estimated to contain somewhere between 10,000 and 1,000,000 genes.

Genealogy. A record or account of the ancestry of a person or kin group.

Gene flow. Changes of gene frequencies in populations through migration or through intermating of members of different populations.

Generalized reciprocity. Exchange system in which individuals distribute food or other goods and services to other members without expectation of direct, equivalent return.

Genetic. Of, pertaining to, or produced by genes; pertaining to developmental origins.

Genetic drift. Process whereby a descendant population has somewhat different gene frequencies than the parent population because of sampling error (e.g., differential fertility of the members in the population). "Founder effect" or "boatload effect" is an example also.

Genetic mutation. A "mistake" or alteration in genetic material (DNA), caused by radiation, heat, chemicals, or other factors.

Genotype. The genetic makeup of an individual derived from the union of parental sex cells (contrasted with phenotype).

Genus (pl. genera). One or more closely related species; a category at the less abstract end of general biological taxonomy.

Glaciation. The spread of glacial ice over large areas of land (e.g., Europe, North America) during long periods of cold climate on earth.

Godparent. Person selected to serve as ritual sponsor of an individual in baptism, confirmation, or other rite of passage, and who generally has lifelong ritual relationship to the sponsored individual and to the parents.

Greenhouse effect. Hypothesized effect of increased carbon dioxide in the atmosphere; believed to cause slowly rising temperatures on earth.

Grimm's Law. Principle of systematic correspondences in phonetic changes as related languages are modified through time. (First stated by Jacob Grimm, 1822).

Group marriage. Conjugal unit in which marital relationships are shared among several males and several females.

H

Hallucinogen. Any chemical or drug whose prominent effect on normal individuals is eliciting optical or auditory hallucinations, depersonalization, perceptual disturbances, and disturbances of thought processes.

Handaxe. General purpose stone tool, especially in early and middle Pleistocene time; often almond-shaped, probably not hafted, hence not truly an axe, believed used for cutting and skinning animals.

Hardy-Weinberg formula. Mathematical expression of the proportions of various genotypes in a stable population.

Hectare. Widely used metric measure of land surface; 10,000 square meters (approx. 2.47 acres).

Heredity. Transmission of physical and behavioral characteristics from one generation to the next.

Heterogeneity. Having diversity of qualities; differentiated (as opposed to homogeneous).

Heterosis. Hybrid vigor. Increased vigor or growth in offspring of crossbred plants and animals.

Heterozygous. Having two different alleles (two different forms of a gene) at corresponding loci on homologous chromosomes (contrasts with homozygous).

Hierarchy. Organization on the basis of ranked groups of unequal status.

Hieroglyphics. Writing system in ancient Egypt and elsewhere involving complex combinations of pictures and symbols (literally: sacred inscriptions).

Holistic. Pertaining to attempts to describe phenomena, cultural systems, social systems, etc., as whole systems, rather than piecemeal.

Holocene. Geologically recent (post-glacial) epoch.

Hominid, hominidae. Pertaining to the family within the order Primates to which humans and our closest fossil ancestors are assigned (as distinguished from the apes).

Hominoid, hominoidea. Pertaining to superfamily of the order Primates that includes both humans and the apes.

Homo erectus. Fossil hominids from the Pleistocene, exemplified by materials from Java, Peking, East Africa and other locations. Thought to be direct ancestor of *Homo sapiens*.

Homo habilis. Designation for skeletal remains of several hominid individuals found in East Africa (believed by some to be a species of *Australopithecus*).

Homo sapiens. Species to which modern humans belong. Many researchers also consider Neanderthal to be of this same species but a different "race" or subspecies.

Homogeneity. Opposite of heterogeneity (see above).

Homozygous, homozygosity. Pertaining to the condition of having identical genes (same allele) on both homologous chromosomes (contrasts with heterozygous).

Hormone. Physiological substance secreted by one organ of the body having effects on other organs; a chemical messenger in an organism.

Horticultural society. Group whose predominant subsistence economy is horticulture (even if supplemented by hunting, fishing, etc.).

Horticulture. In anthropology, the cultivation of plants without the use of draft animals, irrigation, or heavy equipment.

Household. A group of people living together in a single domicile, sharing food and other resources, whether or not consanguineally related.

Hunting-gathering society. Group of people whose predominant subsistence economy is hunting animal foods and gathering of nondomesticated vegetable foods. Subsistence economy based wholly on nondomesticated food sources.

Hunting magic. Magical practices especially designed to improve chances of success in hunting.

Hybridization. Cross-breeding of heterogeneous types and species in plant and animal populations.

Hypoglycemia. Low levels of glucose in circulating blood; deficiency in blood sugar level.

Hypothesis. A proposition; any statement tentatively set forth as a "target" to be tested through empirical research.

I

Ideograph. A nonphonetic symbol drawn, carved, or painted, that represents an object or an idea in the language of its user.

Ideology. General social philosophy or set of principles affecting various aspects of behavior or hoped for future changes in a social group or individual (e.g., "revolutionary ideology").

Imitation. Copying the attitudes and behavior of other individuals.

Implicit. Opposite of explicit (see above).

Inbreeding. Mating within a population that increases the frequency of homozygosity (e.g., any mating among consanguineally related individuals).

Incest. Sexual relations with kinsmen with whom such relations are prohibited by custom or law.

Indigenous. Aboriginal or native; pertaining to the original inhabitants of a region, country, or continent.

Inductive (research). Reasoning or research proceeding from observation of concrete particulars to more abstract generalizations; opposite of deductive.

Industrialism. Economic system characterized by large-scale use of harnessed energy for the production of factory-made goods and services (including transportation).

Industrialization. Conversion of low-energy production system or agricultural society into greater emphasis on factory production using steam and fossil-fuel (or other) high-energy systems.

Industrial Revolution. Period in Europe and North America (especially nineteenth century) characterized by rapid conversion to high-energy, factory-centered production of goods and services (also the same process at later periods in other areas.)

Infanticide. The killing of infants; in some non-modern societies a population-control measure.

Innovators. Persons in a social group who invent, advocate, or otherwise promote new cultural forms and techniques.

Instinct. Species-specific behavior of any animal that is transmitted genetically from one generation to the next.

Intensive agriculture. Food production system with use of draft animals, irrigation, fertilizers, heavy equipment and/or other complex techniques, generally with relatively continuous occupation and utilization of cultivable lands.

I.Q. (intelligence quotient). Individual performance as measured by I.Q. tests. Thought by some researchers to be an estimate of the individual's capacity to perform in certain categories of activity (e.g., music I.Q. test).

Itinerant. Traveling about; going about from place to place.

K

Kalahari. A desert region in Southwest Africa, largely in Botswana.

Key informant. Any person in a community who assumes a role of relating and explaining aspects of local cultural forms to an anthropologist or other field researcher.

Kibbutz. Type of communal (generally agricultural) community in Israel.

Kindred. An "ego-focused" group of bilaterally related kinsmen.

Kinesics. The study of bodily movement.

Kinship. Relationship between any two or more individuals based on consanguinal or affinal (in-law) ties.

L

Lactation. Production of milk by any female animal for feeding its young.

Lamarckian inheritance. The idea or belief in inheritance of acquired characteristics (e.g., inheritance of short tails by offspring of parent mice with tails chopped off). Largely discredited.

Language. Any abstract code system used for complex communications (e.g., computer language, morse code, etc.).

Language family. Group of related languages thought descended from a common ancestral form.

Lapp. (see Same).

Law. A social norm usually sanctioned by the threat of physical coercion by persons whose right to the exercise is socially legitimized.

Legend. A story, usually of some length orally transmitted through the generations and purportedly of historical accuracy, though unverifiable (e.g., the legend of Hiawatha).

Lemur. Nocturnal, arboreal prosimian primate; several species on the island of Madagascar.

Levirate. Custom whereby a widow marries her deceased husband's brother; "brother-in-law" marriage.

Lexicon. The vocabulary of a particular language; the total inventory of morphemes in a given language.

Lifeway. The cultural patterns of a people.

Lineage. A group of kinsmen who share unilateral descent from a common known ancestor; such a group usually spans at least three generations.

Linguistics. The study of language systems.

Litigation. Pertaining to a contest at law; a lawsuit.

M

Macrocosm. In anthropology, any larger (regional, national, or international) social system of which a local community is a part (contrasts with microcosm).

Magic. Beliefs and practices seeking to control events through compulsive formulae thought to have influence supernatural world.

Maladaptive. Having consequences detrimental to an individual or group.

Manioc. Cassava; a tropical plant cultivated for its tuberous roots, which yield a nutritious starch.

Marginality, (social, cultural). State of being in ambiguous or indefinite relationship to particular group or organization (e.g., a person of ethnically or denominationally mixed parentage).

Marginal person theory. Set of propositions concerning the special roles of "marginal persons" in bringing about social change and cultural innovations.

Marketplace. Any publically assigned location, often an open square in a town, where regular market days are held for sale or exchange of goods; also the abstract concept of the social-and-economic network in which prices are thought established through "supply and demand" principles.

553

Marriage. A socially approved (usually ritually celebrated) sexual and economic union between individuals that is presumed to be more or less permanent and marks obligations and rights of spouses (and their children) in relation to their society.

Marsupial. Category of mammals in which the young are carried in pouches on the mother's abdomen (e.g., kangaroos).

Materialism. Theoretical system founded on the assumption that material conditions of life plus economic relations determine other aspects of social and cultural systems.

Matriarchy. A society ruled by females; no actual known historical cases, but widely believed as legends, e.g., of the Amazons.

Matriclan; matrilineal clan. Usually several descent groups with a tradition of relationship based on the belief that they are all descended through the female line from a common ancestress.

Matrifocal family. Family organization with woman head of household, with husband-father either absent or subordinate.

Matrilateral. Pertaining to kin on the "mother's side".

Matrilineage. A lineage based upon descent traced exclusively through females.

Matrilocal or Uxorilocal. Pertaining to residence of the husband and wife within or near the household of the parents of the wife.

Meiosis. The process of cell division that produces sex cells (ova and spermata) in animals.

Melanesia. A major cultural and geographic area in the South and Southwest Pacific, including the Solomon Islands, the New Hebrides, New Caledonia, the Bismarck Archipelago, the Admiralty and Fiji Islands, and New Guinea.

Melanin. Granules of brown and black pigment present in the skin, hair, and other parts of various animals; the major factor in affecting the "white" to dark brown (black) skin color in humans.

Mesolithic. "Middle Stone Age." Cultural period after the Ice Ages and lasting until the Neolithic period (length varies in different geographic locales).

Mesozoic. Geological era characterized by dominance of reptiles; "Age of Dinosaurs" (in popular thought); approximately 225 million to 70 million years ago.

Messiah. A prophesized deliverer or savior of a people; usually associated with millenarian movements.

Microcosm, (social). Local small group considered as part of, or related to a regional, national, or supranational "macrocosm."

Microenvironment, microenvironmental niche. The specific environmental conditions of a small subgroup such as a household (e.g., relations to other households, nearness of water, fields, game, etc.).

Midewiwin. Religious, shamanistic society among the Ojibwa (Chippewa) peoples particularly concerned with curing.

Millenarian. Pertaining to a prophesied millenium.

Miocene. Geologic epoch about 25 to 15 million years ago; period of proliferation of hominoids.

Mitosis. Process of cell division that results in identical "daughter cells," replicas of original cell.

Model, (science). Any representation—whether physical, pictorial, mathematical, or verbal imagery—used to give embodiment to a complex of theoretical relationships as an aid to research and synthesis.

Modernization. Process of relatively rapid change in any human society generally tending toward greater dependency on goods, services, and energy from other areas; loss of autonomy; usually increase in cash and commercial sectors of economy; growing articulation to industrialized societies.

Moiety. Half; the social group formed when a community is divided into halves on the basis of their kinship affiliations.

Money. Anything customarily used as a medium of exchange and standard of value.

Monogamy. Marriage with but one person at a time.

Monogenism. Belief that all humans are descended from a common ancestor and hence are of a single species (contrasts with polygenism).

Monotheism. The belief in or worship of a single god.

Monozygous twins. The offspring of a single fertilized ovum; hence "identical twins".

Morpheme. One or more phonemes having a unitary meaning.

Morphology. In linguistics, the aspect of grammar concerned with the patterns of word formation, including inflection, derivation, and composition.

Mothering. Caring for and nurturance of an infant, as by a mother.

Multicentric. Many centered.

Mutation. (see genetic mutation).

Myth. Tale or narrative referring to a past time that reflects on, and gives explanation for, some aspects of peoples' behavior and social identity (e.g., "the myth of White supremacy").

N

Natural selection (genetic). Process of interaction between organisms and their environments whereby some individuals with less well adapted characteristics are successively eliminated in favor of individuals with better adapted qualities.

Neanderthal. Fossils considered by many researchers to be *Homo sapiens neanderthalensis* (hence of the same species as modern humans); prevalent in parts of Europe, Africa and Asia from 100,000, to 20,000 years ago.

Neo-Darwinism. Pertaining to the theory of biological evolution developed by Charles Darwin, modified in the light of modern genetics.

Neoevolutionary. Referring to contemporary unilinear evolutionary theory.

Neolithic (age). Literally "New Stone Age"; beginning in the Near East about 11,000 years ago; characterized by domestication of plants and animals for food.

Neolithic revolution. Period of relatively rapid increase of settled populations and food production capacity following from development of plant and animal domestication (somewhat a misnomer).

Nuclear family. The family group composed of one set of parents and their children, and no other relatives.

Nucleotide. Single unit of deoxyribonucleic acid (DNA) or of ribonucleic acid (RNA) of which genes and chromosomes are composed.

O

Occiput. The back of the skull.

Oligocene. Geologic epoch beginning about 40 million years ago, lasting until about 25 million years ago.

Omnivore. Animal using both plants and animals for food; neither carnivore nor herbivore.

Overt culture. Cultural patterns consciously and openly known and practiced by any group (contrasts with covert culture).

P

Paddy. A rice field.

Paleontology. Scientific study of living things and their evolution as read from fossil remains.

Paleospecies. Species differing from other related species because it is identifiable with an earlier time period and does not overlap with more recent species.

Paralinguistic behavior. Pertaining to activity occurring with or parallel to spoken language; includes body language, pauses, intonation, facial expression, etc.

Parallel cousins. The children of one's father's brother or of a mother's sister; cousins whose related parents are of like sex.

Parasitic. Dependent upon another for nourishment and shelter.

Pastoralism. A subsistence technology centered about the herding and husbandry of domesticated animals.

Patination. Encrustation, color change, or other modification of surface of an object because of use and exposure.

Patriarchy. Absolute rule by the males of a society or group.

Patriclan. A clan based upon descent traced exclusively through males.

Patrilateral. Pertaining to kin traced through an individual's father's side.

Patrilineage. A group of kinsmen related exclusively through the male (agnatic) line to a common known male ancestor.

Patrilocal or virilocal. Pertaining to the establishment of postnuptial residence with or near the kinsmen of the husband.

Peasants. Communities of food-producing people who are parts of nation-states, supplying food needs of an urban sector, but who are culturally distinct and produce most of their own food locally.

Pebble tool. One of the earliest forms of human tools; a pebble only slightly modified by breaking off a few flakes to produce an edge.

Peonage. Form of serflike servitude of agricultural peoples in Latin America; status of much of the Mexican population before the Mexican Revolution.

Personal culture. Beliefs, values, traditions, and other ideas and concepts held by an individual learned in the process of adapting to his or her environment.

Peyote. A variety of cactus (*Lophophora williamsii*) ingested to induce visions as part of a religious ritual.

Phenotype. The observable manifestation of genetic endowment in an individual (contrasts with genotype).

Phone. A speech sound.

Phoneme. A minimal unit of spoken sound, a change in which produces an alternation of meaning in the utterance.

Phonemics. Pertaining to the study of phonemes.

Phonetics. The scientific study of speech sounds.

Phonology. The study of speech sounds with emphasis upon the rules governing their sequence and upon the theoretical analysis of sound changes.

Phratry. Two or more clans united by an often mythical belief that they share a remote common ancestor.

Physical anthropology. The branch of anthropology that studies human evolution and physical variation.

Pictograph. Any picture intended to describe or depict a situation or record an event; a writing system consisting of such pictures.

555

Pleistocene. Geological epoch generally considered the Ice Age, beginning about 3,000,000 years ago, continuing to about 10,000 years ago.

Pliocene. Geological epoch immediately preceding the pleistocene.

Pollution. Any modification of water, air, landscape, or other environmental feature in a manner that poses health hazards for the organisms regularly inhabiting that environment (e.g., addition of DDT into an area).

Polyandry. A form of marriage in which a woman has more than one husband at a time.

Polygamy. The practice of having more than one spouse at a time.

Polygenism. Belief that humans are descended from several different ancestors; hence, that humans are several species instead of one.

Polygyny. A form of polygamy in which a man has two or more wives at the same time.

Polynesia. An area of the Central Pacific that falls within a triangle formed by Hawaii, Easter Island, and New Zealand (literally: many islands).

Polyphony. The quality of a musical composition having two or more voices or parts, each with an independent melody but all harmonizing.

Polytheism. A religion that entails belief in more than one god.

Population. Any identifiable group of animals tending to intermate more frequently among themselves than with individuals in other groups.

Possession. A state in which a person is believed to be "possessed" or inhabited by some supernatural being.

Potassium-argon dating. Method of assigning age to a specimen through measurement of relative amounts of radioactive potassium and argon.

Potlatch. Ceremonial, often competitive, gift giving among the Indians of the northwest Pacific coast.

Potsherd. A broken pottery fragment.

Power elite. Any minority group of individuals in a society who control major resources and can effectively monopolize political decision making.

Powwow. Any of a variety of celebrations of North American Indian peoples that includes characteristic dancing around a musical group consisting of drummers and singers. Can also include speeches, political activities, and other events.

Prayer. A devout petition to any object of worship, usually to a supernatural being.

Predatory. Habitually preying upon other animals.

Probability inference. Judgement from observation concerning the likelihood of an event or outcome; e.g., estimate of experienced person concerning the likelihood of rain tomorrow.

Progenitor. A biologically related ancestor; a forefather.

Progesterone. Corpus luteum hormone regulating the menstrual cycle and related female features.

Projection. The expression, often unconscious, of inner psychological states, emotions, motives in some overt, nonpragmatic form (e.g., projection of one's happiness by playing lilting, lively music). Also, the same process manifested in one's assessment of the psychological state of another person.

Proletarian. Pertaining to membership in a property-less class.

Property. The socially regulated collection of rights and privileges concerning use and control of material and nonmaterial things.

Prophecy. Prediction of some important coming event, especially if supernaturally inspired.

Propitiate. To appease or conciliate.

Prosimian. A suborder of the primates that includes lemurs, tarsiers, and tree shrews.

Proto- (as in proto-science, proto-human). Prefix meaning "earliest" or "not yet fully developed."

Proto-Indo-European. The ancient language from which the modern Indo-European languages are descended.

Proxemics. The study of patterns of spatial relationships in animal (including human) interaction.

Psychosis. An extreme behavior disorder marked by relatively fixed patterns of maladaptive attitudes and responses.

Public culture. Cultural patterns publicly acknowledged as "agreed on" or representing the consensus in any society.

Pueblo. A village composed of compound dwellings constructed of clay (adobe) bricks, or stones characteristic of the Indians of the U.S. Southwest and Mexico.

Purdah. Cultural practices having to do with seclusion of women, especially in Muslim societies.

R

Race. A term of disputed scientific utility, used to designate a population whose members' inherited physical appearance tends to manifest their distinctive genetic heritage.

Radicalization. Process of making more radical or revolutionary by proselytizing.

Radiocarbon dating. Method of assigning age to specimens through measurement of radioactive carbon. Generally useful for materials not older than 60,000 years.

Ramapithecus. Genus of fossil primates known from East Africa and Asia and thought by some researchers to be ancestral to *Homo sapiens*; dating from the Miocene epoch.

Rank. Pertaining to the position of a person or a number of persons within a graded social hierarchy.

Recessive allele. Allele whose genetic expression is inhibited by presence of a dominant allele (see dominance, genetic).

Redundancy. Excess of information beyond minimum necessary for communication (e.g., extra letters in "through").

Reify. To treat or regard an abstraction or idea as a concrete thing.

Reinforcement. Pertaining to the environmental effects on an individual. When an individual acts, the effects are "rewarding" or "punishing," hence either "positively" or "negatively" reinforcing one's behavior.

Religion. Any set of attitudes, beliefs, or practices pertaining to supernatural forces.

Revitalization movement. Any social doctrine or organized effort to change a social and cultural system to increase the satisfaction levels of the members.

Revitalize. To give new life.

Revolution. A process of social change that is relatively rapid, resulting in large-scale changes in relations of economic and political power in a society; especially the overthrow of a power elite.

Ritual. An established ceremonial procedure.

Role. The behavior culturally defined as appropriate to a particular status or position, such as that of father.

Routinization. Establishing of more fixed and predictable modes of day-to-day operation in any social institution or individual behavior.

S

Sabbat. Supernatural meeting or celebration at which witches are said to consort with devils and other supernatural creatures.

Sacerdotal. Pertaining to the priestly activities of a religious functionary.

Sacrifice. The propitiatory offering of plant, animal, or human life, or of some other valued thing, to a supernatural being.

Saga. An oral narrative, usually thought to be historical, of a person or group.

Saltation. Discontinuous variation; emergence of new type of organism through a large change; a "genetic leap."

Sanction. A reaction operating to induce conformity to a culturally defined standard of behavior; may be either negative or positive.

Sawah. System of intensive wet-rice cultivation in Java.

Scarification. See Cicatrization.

Science. Accumulation of knowledge through interrelated empirical observation, theory-building, and hypothesis-testing.

Secularism. Pertaining to the mundane, natural world, as opposed to concern with the sacred, supernatural world.

Sedentary. Pertaining to human groups that remain more or less permanently settled; not migratory.

Segmentary. A descent group in which internal divisions result in the frequent emergence of new and separate descent groups.

Semantic differential. Method of interviewing people about concepts by means of graded continuum of opposed attributes (e.g., rich—poor; healthy—unhealthy).

Semantic universals. Features of language structure that are thought to be pan-human.

Serfdom. State of servitude to landlords or other powerholders in an agricultural system; characteristic of peasants in prerevolutionary Russia and other parts of the world.

Sexual dimorphism. Differences in shape and size between males and females in any population.

Shaman. A person who is assumed to have direct contact with supernatural powers for curing, foretelling, and other purposes.

Shamanism. System of curing and dealing with other problems by shamans.

Sib. A unilateral descent group, often synonymous with clan.

Sibling. One of two or more children of the same parents.

Silent barter. Exchange between persons who do not directly encounter one another but leave goods anonymously for other party to accept or reject.

Slash-and-burn. see Swidden.

Smelt. To fuse or melt ore to separate the metal.

Social Darwinism. Application of the ideas of "survival of the fittest" to assessment of a social system, implying that the rich and successful are the "fittest" and the poor deserve what they get.

Social race. Population socially identified as having a different physical appearance (hence presumed genetically different) from another such social category.

Socialization. The early stages of the learning process during which the young child internalizes the behaviors required of him by society.

Society. A generally large group of people who share a common culture and a sense of common identity; also, the system of interpersonal and intergroup

557

relationships among the members of such a group.

Sociolinguistics. Study of the interrelations of social data and language use.

Sorcery. The use of supernatural power for aggressive purposes.

Sororal polygyny. The simultaneous marriage of two or more sisters to one husband.

Sororate. A practice whereby a woman marries the husband of her deceased sister.

Species (genetics). Population of actually or potentially interbreeding organisms, believed to be genetically isolated from other organisms.

Spiritualist. Individual, often a cult leader, who is believed to communicate with supernaturals; especially one thought to communicate with departed dead on behalf of others.

Squatter settlement. Group of households settled illegally on government or other "owned" lands. Especially groups on outskirts of rapidly growing cities in Latin America, Africa, and Asia.

State. A heterogenous society controlled by a centralized political government with system of laws, police, and other administration.

Status. The position of an individual in relation to others within a society.

Stigmatize. To give negative social identification to a person, group, or type of behavior.

Stone age. The cultural period before development of widespread metal use in tool-making; ended in different times in various parts of the world.

Stratification, social. Condition when part of a society controls significant portions of the means of economic production so that the rest of the society is in a disadvantaged relationship to economic resources.

Stress. Psychological or physiological strain conditions sufficient that the body must (or should) respond with defensive measures including altered heartbeat, breathing, sweating, and other changes.

Subculture. A significantly distinctive but nonautonomous sector of a larger culture; often based on differences in ethnic identity, class or caste, and/or upon geographical separation.

Subjective culture. Concepts and ideas reflecting psychological states and emotions of individuals and groups.

Subsistence crop. Food crop grown for consumption by the grower rather than for sale (contrasts with cash crop).

Suburb. Area on the outskirts of an urban concentration; often applied to residential areas at a distance from "downtown" commercial zones.

Supernatural. That which cannot presently be explained as resulting from natural causes.

Superstition, Usually pejorative term referring to magical beliefs.

Surface structure. The apparent superficial features of language (contrast with deep structure.)

Survival advantage. Effect of a behavior or quality in increasing the likelihood of an animal living longer and producing more offspring.

Swaddling. Tight wrapping of infants in cloth or other restraining materials, usually for many hours each day (includes use of cradleboard).

Swidden. Crop-growing system that involves cutting down and burning forest vegetation for garden plots, which are abandoned after a few years because of declining fertility.

Syllabary. Writing system in which each symbol stands for a cluster of sounds (syllable) rather than a single sound unit as in alphabetic writing.

Symbiosis. The mutually beneficial living together of dissimilar organisms.

Synchronic. Concerned with events within a limited time period, usually ignoring historical processes.

Syncretism. The fusion of two distinct systems of belief and practice.

Syntax. The study of how words and significant features of intonation are arranged in phrases or sentences and of how sentences relate to each other.

T

Taxonomy. The systematic classification of things according to scientific principles.

Technology. The tools, techniques, and ideas used by any group to produce food and other goods and services to satisfy their needs.

Territoriality. Pertaining to the tendencies of animals to inhabit and "lay claim to" demarcated locales or territories.

Theocracy. Government by those persons who are in charge of the religious system; opposite of "separation of church and state".

Tonowi. A political and economic leader or "big man" among the Kapauku of New Guinea.

Tool. Any physical object manufactured or modified to achieve some practical purpose.

Tool kit. An individual's or group's total inventory of tools.

Totem. An object, often an animal, plant, or place, ritually related to a particular social group.

Tradition. Any element or item, especially of ritual behavior, of fairly long standing in the culture of an individual or group (e.g., our family has a tradition of eating chicken every Sunday).

Transformational grammar. Grammatical analysis focusing on deep structure of a language.

Transhumance. The regular movement of livestock in response to seasonal shifts in the availability of pasturage.

Trephination. Surgical cutting of holes in the skull for medical purposes.

Typological thinking. Thinking in stereotypes instead of recognizing the arbitrariness of descriptive categories.

U

Unilineal descent. The tracing of descent through kinsmen of one sex only; i.e., a line of descent traced exclusively through males or through females.

Untouchable. An English term for certain members of Hindu society who are categorized as outside the formal structure of the caste system.

Urbanization. The tendency, now world-wide, for larger percentages of populations to seek habitation in urban areas; hence, growth of urban populations relative to rural populations.

Use rights or Usufruct. Property rights granted to individuals or groups as long as they make productive use of the property; if they abandon the property, the rights lapse.

Uxorilocal or matrilocal. The practice of establishing postnuptial residence in or near the domicile of the wife's family.

V

Village. Any small, usually clustered settlement of households, generally with little commercialization or other specialized activities.

Village exogamy. Social rule or tendency for individuals to seek marital partners from outside their own villages (contrasts with village endogamy).

Virilocal or patrilocal. Pertaining to the practice of establishing postnuptial residence in or near the household of the husband's family.

Vocal channel. Having to do with the mouth and throat.

Voodoo. The American vernacular for a system of religious beliefs and practices brought to the Americas, principally to the Circum-Caribbean region, by West Africans from Dahomey. Vodun, vodu, or vodou, in the language of Haiti.

W

Wampum. Any of several different kinds of shell money among Indians of the eastern United States.

Wattle. Stakes or rods interwoven with twigs or tree branches.

Wealth. Ownership and control of scarce material goods.

Witchcraft. Ability or practice of harming, influencing, or helping other persons through magical means (sometimes specially restricted to inadvertent abilities.)

Z

Zinjanthropus boisei. East African fossil now thought to belong to the genus *Australopithecus*.

References Cited

A

Aberle, D. F., 1961, "Matrilineal Descent in Cross-Cultural Perspective," in D. M. Schneider and K. Gough (eds.), *Matrilineal Kinship.* U. of California, Berkeley and Los Angeles, pp. 625–727.

Ackernecht, E. H., 1965, *History and Geography of the World's Most Important Diseases.* Hafner, New York.

Adair, J., and E. Vogt, 1949, "Navajo and Zuñi Veterans: A Study of Contrasting Modes of Culture Change," *American Anthropologist,* **51,** 547–561.

Adams, M., and J. V. Neil, 1967, "Children of Incest," *Pediatrics,* **40,** 55–62.

Adams, R. McC., 1960, "The Origin of Cities," *Scientific American,* **203,** 153–168.

———, **1966,** *The Evolution of Urban Society: Early Mesopotamia to Prehispanic Mexico.* Aldine, Chicago.

Adams, R. N., 1974, "Harnessing Technological Development," in J. Poggie and R. Lynch (eds.), *Rethinking Modernization.* Greenwood Press, Westport.

Alland, A., 1970, *Adaptation in Cultural Evolution: An Approach to Medical Anthropology.* Columbia U.P., New York.

———, **1971,** *Human Diversity.* Columbia U.P., New York.

Aquinas, St. T., *ca.* 1250, in J. S. Slotkin (ed.), 1965, *Readings in Early Anthropology.* Aldine, Chicago, pp.24–28.

B

Barnett, H. G., 1953, *Innovation: The Basis of Cultural Change.* McGraw-Hill, New York.

Barnicot, N. A., 1964, "Taxonomy and Variation in Modern Man," in A. Montagu (ed.), *The Concept of Race.* Free Press, New York, pp. 180–227.

Barry, H., M. K. Bacon, and I. L. Child, 1957, "A Cross-Cultural Survey of Some Sex Differences in Socialization," *Journal of Abnormal and Social Psychology,* **55,** 327–332.

———, **I. L. Child, and M. K. Bacon, 1959,** "Relation of Child Training to Subsistence Economy," *American Anthropologist,* **61,** 51–63.

Bates, M., 1955, "Role of War, Famine, and Disease in Controlling Population," in L. B. Young (ed.), 1968, *Population in Perspective.* Oxford U.P., New York, pp. 30–49.

Beattie, J., 1965, *Understanding an African Kingdom: Bunyoro.* Holt, Rinehart and Winston, New York.

Benedict, B., 1972, "Controlling Population Growth in Mauritius," in H. R. Bernard and P. J. Pelto (eds.), *Technology and Social Change.* Macmillan, Inc., New York, pp. 245–276.

Benedict, R. F., 1934, *Patterns of Culture.* New American Library, New York.

———, **1940,** *Race: Science and Politics.* Viking, New York.

Bennett, J. W., 1944, "The Development of Ethnological Theories as Illustrated by Studies of the Plains Sun Dance," *American Anthropologist,* **46,** 162–181.

———, **1967,** *Hutterian Brethren.* Stanford University Press, Stanford.

Berlin, B., and P. Kay, 1969, *Basic Color Terms.* U. of California, Berkeley and Los Angeles.

Bernard, H. R., and P. J. Pelto (eds.), 1972, *Technology and Social Change.* Macmillan, Inc., New York.

Beveridge, W. I. B., 1957, *The Art of Scientific Investigation.* Vintage, New York.

Birdsell, J., 1972, *Human Evolution.* Macmillan, Inc., New York.

Birdwhistell, R. L., 1970, *Kinesics and Context: Essays on Body Motion Communication.* U. of Pennsylvania, Philadelphia.

Blom, J. P., and J. J. Gumperz, 1972, "Social Meaning in Linguistic Structures: Code-Switching in Norway," in J. J. Gumperz and D. Hymes (eds.) *Directions in Sociolinguistics.* Holt, Rinehart and Winston, New York, pp. 407–434.

Blumenbach, J. F., 1775, *The Anthropological Treatises of Johann Friedrich Blumenbach.* T. Bendyshe (ed.), 1865, Longman, Green, Longman, Roberts, and Green, London.

Bogoras, W., 1904–1909, "The Jessup North Pacific Expedition," in F. Boas (ed.), *The Chuckchee,* vol. 7, A.M.N.H., New York.

Bohannan, P., and G. Dalton (eds.), 1962, *Markets in Africa.* Northwestern U.P., Evanston, Ill.

Bolinger, D., 1968, *Aspects of Language.* Harcourt Brace and Jovanovich, New York.

Bolton, R. L., 1972, *Aggression in Qolla Society.* Unpublished Ph.D. dissertation, Cornell U., Ithaca.

Boserup, E., 1965, *The Conditions of Agricultural Growth: The Economics of Agrarian Change under Population Pressure.* Aldine, Chicago.

Brace, C. L., 1964, "The Fate of the 'Classic' Neanderthals: A Consideration of Hominid Catastrophism," *Current Anthropology,* **5,** 3–46.

Braidwood, R. J., 1960, "The Agricultural Revolution," *Scientific American,* **203,** 131–148.

Bregenzer, J. M., 1967, *The Pronoun of Address: A Cross-Cultural Study.* Unpublished M.A. dissertation, U. of Minnesota, Minneapolis.

Bronfenbrenner, U., 1970, *Two Worlds of Childhood: U.S. and U.S.S.R.* Russell Sage Foundation, New York.

Bruner, E. M., 1973, "Kin and Non-Kin," in A. Southall (ed.), *Urban Anthropology: Cross-Cultural Studies of Urbanization.* Oxford U.P., New York, pp. 373–391.

Buettner-Janusch, J., 1966, *Origins of Man: Physical Anthropology.* Wiley, New York.

———, **1973,** *Physical Anthropology: A Perspective.* Wiley, New York.

Buffon, L., et. al., 1791, in J. S. Slotkin (ed.), 1965, *Readings in Early Anthropology.* Aldine, Chicago, pp. 182–186.

Burlung, R., 1970, *Man's Many Voices: Language in Its Cultural Context.* Holt, Rinehart and Winston, New York.

Burton, R. V., and J. W. M. Whiting, 1961, "The Absent Father and Cross-Sex Identity," *Merrill-Palmer Quarterly of Behavior and Development,* **7,** 85–95.

Butterworth, D. S., 1970, "A Study of the Urbanization Process Among Mixtec Migrants from Tilantongo to Mexico City," in W. Mangin (ed.), *Peasants in Cities: Readings in the Anthropology of Urbanization.* Houghton Mifflin, Boston, pp. 98–113.

C

Calder, R., 1968, *Man and the Cosmos: The Nature of Science Today.* Pall Mall: London.

Calhoun, J. B., 1962, "A Behavioral Sink,'" in E. L. Bliss (ed.), *Roots of Behavior.* Harper & Row, New York.

Cambel, H., and R. Braidwood, 1970, "An Early Farming Village in Turkey," *Scientific American,* **222,** 50–56.

Campbell, B. G., 1966, *Human Evolution: An Introduction to Man's Adaptations.* Aldine, Chicago.

Carneiro, R., 1970, "A Theory of the Origin of the State," *Science,* **169,** 733–738.

———, **and D. F. Hilse, 1966,** "On Determining the Probable Rate of Population Growth During the Neolithic," *American Anthropologist,* **68,** 177–181.

Casagrande, J. B., 1960, *In the Company of Man.* Harper & Row, New York.

Chagnon, N. A., 1968, *Yanomamö: The Fierce People.* Holt, Rinehart and Winston, New York.

Chard, C. S., 1969, *Man in Prehistory.* McGraw-Hill, New York.

Child, I. L., and L. Siroto, 1965, "Bakwele and American Esthetic Evaluations Compared," *Ethnology,* **4,** 349–360.

Childe, V. G., 1946, *What Happened in History.* Pelican, New York.

———, **1951,** *Man Makes Himself.* Mentor, New York.

Chomsky, N., 1968, *Language and Mind.* Harcourt Brace Jovanovich, New York.

Cicero, n.d., in R. Benedict, 1940, *Race: Science and Politics.* Viking, New York, p. 7.

561

Clark, J. G. D., 1962, *Prehistoric Europe: The Economic Basis.* Stanford U.P., Stanford.

Coe, M. D., 1966, *The Maya.* Praeger, New York.

Cohen, R., 1967, *The Kanuri of Bornu.* Holt, Rinehart and Winston, New York.

Colson, E., 1954, "The Intensive Study of Small Sample Communities," in R. Spencer (ed.), *Method and Perspective in Anthropology.* U. of Minnesota, Minneapolis, pp. 43–59.

———, **1954,** "Ancestral Spirits and Social Structure Among the Plateau Tonga," *International Archives of Ethnography,* **47,** 21–68.

Commoner, B., 1971, *The Closing Circle: Nature, Man, and Technology.* Knopf, New York.

Cook, E. F., 1971, "Flow of Energy in an Industrial Society," *Scientific American,* **225,** 134–142.

Coon, C. S., 1939, *The Races of Europe.* Macmillan, Inc., New York.

Cottrell, W. F., 1955, *Energy and Society: The Relation Between Energy, Social Change, and Economic Development.* McGraw-Hill, New York.

Cowper, W., 1781, "Retirement," in H. S. Milford (ed.), 1926, *The Poetical Works of William Cowper* (3rd ed.). Oxford U.P., London.

Crossland, J., and V. Brodine, 1973, "Drinking Water," *Environment,* April 1973, 11–19.

D

Dalton, G., 1965, "Primitive Money," *American Anthropologist,* **67,** 44–65.

Darwin, C., 1872, *The Expression of the Emotions in Man and Animals.* John Murray, London.

———, **1927,** *The Origin of the Species by Means of Natural Selection, or, the Preservation of Favored Races in the Struggle for Life.* Macmillan, Inc., New York.

Davenport, W., 1959, "Non-Unilineal Descent and Descent Groups," *American Anthropologist,* **61,** 557–572.

Davis, K., 1967, "Population Policy: Will Current Programs Succeed?" *Science,* **158,** 730–739.

Deevy, E. S., 1960, "The Human Population," *Scientific American,* **203,** 194–204.

De Havenon, A. L., 1970, "The Quantification and Analysis of Family Authority Structure," mimeo.

D'Hertefelt, M., 1965, "The Rwanda of Rwanda," in J. L. Gibbs (ed.), *Peoples of Africa.* Holt, Rinehart and Winston, New York, pp. 403–440.

Deloria, V., 1971, *Custer Died for Your Sins.* Collier Macmillan Publishers, London.

Deng, F. M., 1972, *The Dinka of the Sudan.* Holt, Rinehart and Winston, New York.

Dentan, R., 1968, *The Semai: A Non-Violent People of Malaya.* Holt, Rinehart and Winston, New York.

De Patot, T., 1710, in J. S. Slotkin (ed.), 1965, *Readings in Early Anthropology,* Aldine, Chicago, pp. 191–192.

De Saussure, F., 1916, *Cours de Linguistique Generale.* Payot, Paris.

DeVore, I. (ed.), 1965, *Primate Behavior: Field Studies of Monkeys and Apes.* Holt, Rinehart and Winston, New York.

———, **and S. L. Washburn, 1963,** "Baboon Ecology and Human Evolution," in F. C. Howell and F. Bourliere (eds.), *African Ecology and Human Evolution.* Aldine, Chicago, pp. 335–367.

DeVos, G., and H. Wagatsuma (eds.), 1967, *Japan's Invisible Race: Caste in Culture and Personality.* U. of California, Berkeley and Los Angeles.

Dobzhansky, T., 1955, *Evolution, Genetics, and Man.* Wiley, New York.

———, **1962,** *Mankind Evolving: The Evolution of the Human Species.* Yale U.P., New Haven.

Doughty, Paul, 1970, "Behind the Back of the City: 'Provincial' Life in Lima, Peru," in W. Mangin (ed.), *Peasants in Cities: Readings in the Anthropology of Urbanization.* Houghton Mifflin, Boston, pp. 30–46.

Dozier, E. P., 1970, *The Pueblo Indians of North America.* Holt, Rinehart and Winston, New York.

Drucker, P., 1965, *Cultures of the North Pacific Coast.* Chandler, San Francisco.

Dubois, C., 1944, *The People of Alor: A Social Psychological Study of an East Indian Island.* U. of Minnesota, Minneapolis.

Dubos, R., 1959, *Mirage of Health: Utopias, Progress, and Biological Change.* Harper & Row, New York.

Durkheim, E., 1971, "The Elementary Forms of the Religious Life," in W. A. Lessa and E. Z. Vogt (eds.), *Reader in Comparative Religion* (3rd ed.). Harper & Row, New York, pp. 66–76.

Durrell, G., 1966, *Two in the Bush.* Viking, New York.

E

Edgerton, R. B., 1971, *The Individual in Cultural Adaptation.* U. of California, Berkeley and Los Angeles.

Ehrlich, P., et. al., 1973, *Human Ecology: Problems and Solutions.* W. H. Freeman, San Francisco.

Ekvall, R. B., 1968, *Fields on the Hoof: Nexus of Tibetan Nomadic Pastoralism.* Holt, Rinehart and Winston, New York.

Ember, C. R., 1971, "Warfare and Unilineal Descent," Paper presented at the 70th Annual Meeting of the American Anthropological Association, New York.

———, **and M. Ember, 1971,** "The Conditions Favoring Matrilocal versus Patrilocal Residence," *American Anthropologist,* **73,** 571–594.

Engels, F., 1891, *The Origin of the Family, Private Property, and the State in Light of the Researches of Lewis Henry Morgan.* Charles Kerr, Chicago.

Erasmus, C. J., 1961, *Man Takes Control: Cultural Development and American Aid.* U. of Minnesota, Minneapolis.

F

Fei-tzu, Han, *ca. 500* **B.C.,** in G. Hardin, (ed.), 1969, *Population, Evolution, and Birth Control: A Collage of Controversial Ideas.* W. H. Freeman, San Francisco, p. 18.

Fischer, A., 1970, "Field Work in Five Cultures," in P. Golde (ed.), *Women in the Field: Anthropological Experiences.* Aldine, Chicago, pp. 267–289.

Flannery, K., 1965, "The Ecology of Early Food Production in Mesopotamia," *Science,* **147,** 1247–1255.

———, **1972,** "The Origins of the Village as a Settlement Type in Mesoamerica and the Near East: A Comparative Study," in P. Ucko, et. al., (eds.), 1972, *Man, Settlement and Urbanism.* Schenkman, Cambridge, pp. 23–53.

Forde, C. D., 1937, *Habitat, Economy, and Society: A Geographical Introduction to Ethnology* (2nd ed.). Dutton, New York.

Fortes, M., 1960, "Oedipus and Job in West African Religion," in C. Leslie (ed.), *Anthropology of Folk Religion.* Vintage, New York, pp. 5–49.

Foster, G. M., 1965, "Peasant Society and the Image of Limited Good," *American Anthropologist,* **67,** 293–315.

———, **1967,** *Tzintzuntzan: Mexican Peasants in a Changing World.* Little, Brown, Boston.

Foulks, E., 1972, *The Arctic Hysterias of the North Alaskan Eskimo.* American Anthropological Association, Washington, D.C.

Franke, R. W., 1974, "The Ecology Bomb," *Reviews in Anthropology,* **1,** 157–165.

Freedman, J., 1971, "The Crowd—Maybe Not So Maddening After All," *Psychology Today,* **5,** 58–61.

———, **1972,** "Crowding and Human Aggressiveness," *Journal of Experimental Social Psychology,* **8,** 528–548.

Freilich, M. (ed.), 1970, *Marginal Natives: Anthropologists at Work.* Harper & Row, New York.

Freud, S., 1913, *Totem and Taboo.* Hogarth, London.

Fried, M. H., 1967, *Evolution of Political Society: An Essay in Political Anthropology.* Random House, New York.

———, **et. al. (eds.), 1968,** *War: The Anthropology of Armed Conflict and Aggression.* Natural History, Garden City.

G

Gardner, P., 1966, "Symmetric Respect and Memorate Knowledge: The Structure and Ecology of Individualistic Culture," *Southwestern Journal of Anthropology,* **22,** 389–415.

Gardner, R. A., and B. Gardner, 1969, "Teaching Sign Language to a Chimpanzee," *Science,* **165,** 664–672.

Geertz, C., 1960, *The Religion of Java.* Free Press, New York.

———, **1963,** *Agricultural Involution: The Process of Ecological Change in Indonesia.* U. of California, Berkeley and Los Angeles.

Gerlach, L. P., and V. H. Hine, 1970, *People, Power, Change: Movements of Social Transformation.* Bobbs-Merrill, Indianapolis.

———, **1973,** *Lifeway Leap: The Dynamics of Change in America.* U. of Minnesota, Minneapolis.

Gibbs, J. L. (ed.), 1965, *Peoples of Africa.* Holt, Rinehart and Winston, New York.

Golde, P. (ed.), 1970, *Women in the Field: Anthropological Experiences.* Aldine, Chicago.

Goodall, J. van L., 1964, "Tool Using and Aimed Throwing in a Community of Free-living Chimpanzees," *Nature,* **201,** 1264–1266.

———, **1965,** "Chimpanzees on the Gombe Stream Reserve," in I. A. DeVore (ed.), *Primate Behavior.* Holt, Rinehart and Winston, New York, pp. 425–473.

———, **1971,** *In the Shadow of Man.* Houghton Mifflin, Boston.

Goodenough, W. H., 1955, "A Problem in Malayo-Polynesian Social Organization," *American Anthropologist,* **57,** 71–83.

———, **(ed.), 1964,** *Explorations in Cultural Anthropology: Essays in Honor of George Peter Murdock.* McGraw-Hill, New York.

———, **1971,** *Culture, Language, and Society,* Module 7. Addison-Wesley, Reading.

Gough, E. K., 1959, "The Nayars and the Definition of Marriage," *Journal of the Royal Anthropological Institute,* **89,** 23–34.

———, **1959,** "Criterion of Caste Ranking in South India," *Man in India,* **39,** 115–126.

Gould, R. A., 1968, "Chipping Stones in the Outback," *Natural History,* **77,** 42–49.

Graburn, N. (ed.), 1971, *Readings in Kinship and Social Structure.* Harper & Row, New York.

Graves, T. D., 1970, "The Personal Adjustment of Navajo Indian Migrants to Denver, Colorado," *American Anthropologist,* **72,** 35–54.

Green, E. L. (ed.), 1973, *In Search of Man: Readings in Archaeology.* Little, Brown, Boston.

Greenberg, J. H., 1963, "Some Universals of Grammar with Particular Reference to the Order of

563

Meaningful Elements," in J. H. Greenberg (ed.), 1966, *Universals of Language*. MIT, Cambridge, pp. 73–113.

———, **1966,** *Universals of Language*. MIT, Cambridge.

Griffitt, W., 1969, "Environmental Effects on Interpersonal Affective Behavior: Ambient Effective Temperature and Attraction," *Journal of Personality and Social Psychology,* **15,** 240–244.

Gross, D. R., 1970, "Sisal and Social Structure in Northeastern Brazil," Ph.D. dissertation, Columbia U., New York.

———, **and B. Underwood, 1969,** "Technological Change and Caloric Costs on Northeastern Brazilian Sisal Plantations," Paper presented at the Annual Meeting of the American Association for the Advancement of Science, Boston.

——— **and** ———, **1971,** "Technological Change and Caloric Costs: Sisal Agriculture in Northeastern Brazil," *American Anthropologist,* **73,** 725–740.

Gudschinsky, S., 1967, *How to Learn an Unwritten Language*. Holt, Rinehart and Winston, New York.

Gulick, J., 1963, "Images of an Arab City," *Journal of the American Institute of Planners,* **29,** 179–198.

Gumperz, J. J., and D. Hymes (eds.), 1964, *The Ethnography of Communication*, American Anthropologist Special Publication **66,** Part 2, No. 6.

——— **and** ——— **(eds.), 1972,** *Directions in Sociolinguistics*. Holt, Rinehart and Winston, New York.

Gusinde, M., 1931, in R. Naroll, 1962, *Data Quality Control—A New Research Technique*. Free Press, New York.

H

Hall, R. A., 1966, *Pidgin and Creole Languages*. Cornell U.P., Ithaca.

Hallowell, A. I., 1936, "Psychic Stresses and Culture Patterns," *American Journal of Psychiatry,* **92,** 1291–1310.

Halpern, J., and B. Halpern, 1972, *A Serbian Village in Historical Perspective*. Holt, Rinehart and Winston, New York.

Hammel, E., 1968, *Alternative Social Structures and Ritual Relations in the Balkans*. Prentice-Hall, Englewood Cliffs.

Haralambos, M., 1970, "Soul Music and Blues: Their Meaning and Relevance in Northern United States Black Ghettos," in N. E. Whitten and J. F. Szwed (eds.), *Afro-American Anthropology: Contemporary Perspectives*. Free Press, New York, pp. 367–383.

Hardin, G. (ed.), 1969, *Population, Evolution, and Birth Control: A Collage of Controversial Ideas*. W. H. Freeman, San Francisco.

Harding, T. G., 1967, *Voyagers of the Vitiaz Strait*. Washington U.P., Seattle.

Harlan, J. R., 1967, "A Wild Wheat Harvest in Turkey," *Archaeology,* **20,** 197–201.

Harner, M. J., 1968, "The Sound of Rushing Water," *Natural History,* **77,** 28–33.

———, **1970,** "Population Pressure and the Social Evolution of Agriculturalists," *Southwestern Journal of Anthropology,* **26,** 67–86.

——— **(ed.), 1973,** *Hallucinogens and Shamanism*. Oxford U.P., London.

———, **n.d.,** personal communication.

Harris, M., 1966, "The Cultural Ecology of India's Sacred Cattle," *Current Anthropology,* **7,** 51–66.

———, **1968,** *The Rise of Anthropological Theory*. Crowell, New York.

———, **1970,** "Referential Ambiguity in the Calculus of Brazilian Racial Identity," *Southwestern Journal of Anthropology,* **26,** 1–14.

———, **1971,** *Culture, Man, and Nature: An Introduction to General Anthropology*. Crowell, New York.

Harrison, G. A., et.al., 1964, *Human Biology: An Introduction to Human Evolution, Variation, and Growth*. Oxford U.P., New York.

Haviland, W. A., 1967, "Stature at Tikal, Guatemala: Implications for Ancient Maya Demography and Social Organization," *American Antiquity,* **32,** 316–325.

Heath, F. G., 1972, "Origins of the Binary Code," *Scientific American,* **227,** 76–83.

Heider, K., 1970, *The Dugum Dani*. Aldine, Chicago.

Helbaek, H., 1959, "Domestication of Food Plants in the Old World," *Science,* **130,** 365–372.

Helm, J., 1966, *Pioneers of American Anthropology: The Uses of Biography*. American Ethnological Society Monograph 43.

Herodotus, n.d., in G. Rawlinson (trans.), 1945, *The History of Herodotus*. Dutton, New York.

Hiebert, P. G., 1971, *Konduru: Structure and Integration in a Hindu Village*. U. of Minnesota, Minneapolis.

Higgs, E. S. (ed.), 1972, *Papers in Economic Prehistory*. Cambridge U.P., Cambridge.

Hirsch, J., 1970, "Behavior—Genetic Analysis and Its Biosocial Consequences," *Seminars in Psychiatry,* **2,** 89–105.

———, **1972,** "Genetics and Competence: Do Heritability Indices Predict Educability?" in J. McVicker Hunt (ed.), *Human Intelligence*. Dutton, New York, pp. 7–29.

Hockett, C., 1958, *A Course in Modern Linguistics*. Macmillan, Inc., New York.

———, **1960,** "The Origin of Speech," *Scientific American,* **203,** 88–96.

564

———, **and R. Ascher, 1963,** "The Human Revolution," *Current Anthropology,* **5,** 135–168.

Hoebel, E. A., 1972, *Anthropology: The Study of Man.* McGraw Hill, New York.

Hoijer, H., 1951, "Cultural Implications of Some Navajo Linguistic Categories," *Language,* **27,** 111–120.

Hollingshead, A. B., and F. C. Redlich, 1953, "Social Stratification and Psychiatric Disorders," *American Sociological Review,* **18,** 163–169.

———, **1958,** *Social Class and Mental Illness.* Wiley, New York.

Holloway, M., 1951, *Heavens on Earth: Utopian Communities in America 1680–1880.* Turnstile Press, London.

Holmberg, A., 1960, *Nomads of the Long Bow: The Sirionó of Eastern Bolivia.* U. of Chicago, Chicago.

Honigmann, J. J., 1970, "Field Work in Two Northern Canadian Communities," in M. Freilich (ed.), *Marginal Natives: Anthropologists at Work,* Harper & Row, New York, pp. 39–72.

———, **1972,** "Housing for New Arctic Towns," in H. R. Bernard and P. J. Pelto (eds.), *Technology and Social Change.* Macmillan, Inc., New York, pp. 227–244.

Houriet, R., 1971 *Getting Back Together.* Avon, New York.

Howell, F. C., 1952, "Pleistocene Glacial Ecology and the Evolution of 'Classical Neandertal' Man," *Southwestern Journal of Anthropology,* **8,** 377–410.

———, **1962,** "Potassium-Argon Dating at Olduvai Gorge," *Current Anthropology,* **3,** 306–308.

———, **1970,** *Early Man.* Time-Life, New York.

Howells, W. W., 1960, "The Distribution of Man," *Scientific American,* **203,** 112–120.

Hulse, F., 1963, *The Human Species: An Introduction to Physical Anthropology.* Random House, New York.

Hutt, C., 1972, *Males and Females.* Penguin, Baltimore.

J

Jacobson, D., 1973, *Itinerant Townsmen: Friendship and Social Order in Urban Uganda.* Cummings, Menlo Park.

Jensen, A., 1969, "How Much Can We Boost I.Q. and Scholastic Achievement?" *Harvard Educational Review,* **29,** 1–123.

Jiménez Moreno, W., et al., 1965, *Historia de México* (2nd ed.). Editorial Porrua, S.A., Mexico.

Jochelson, W., 1926, "Yukaghir Picture Writing and Loveletters," in M. Mead and R. Bunzel (eds.), 1960, *The Golden Age of American Anthropology.* Braziler, New York, pp. 331–339.

Johnson, A. W., 1972, "Individuality and Experimentation in Traditional Agriculture," *Human Ecology,* **1,** 149–159.

Johnson, F. E., 1973, *Micro-Evolution of Human Populations.* Prentice-Hall, Englewood Cliffs.

Jolly, A., 1972, *The Evolution of Primate Behavior.* Macmillan, Inc., New York.

K

Kalevala, Land of Heros **(anon., n.d.); 1907 (rev. ed.).** Dutton, New York.

Kandel, R., and G. H. Pelto, 1973, "Vegetarianism and Health Food Use Among Young Adults in Southern New England," Paper presented at the 72nd Annual Meeting of the American Anthropological Association, New Orleans.

Kanter, R. M., 1972, *Commitment and Community: Communes and Utopias in Sociological Perspective.* Harvard U.P., Cambridge.

Kaplan, B., and T. Plaut, 1956, *Personality in a Communal Society.* U. of Kansas, Lawrence.

Keiser, L., 1969, *The Vice Lords: Warriors of the Streets.* Holt, Rinehart and Winston, New York.

Kephart, W. M., 1972, "Experimental Family Organization: An Historico-Cultural Report on the Oneida Community," in M. Gordon (ed.), *The Nuclear Family in Crisis: The Search for an Alternative.* Harper & Row, New York, pp. 59–77.

Klima, G., 1970, *The Barabaig: East African Cattle-Herders.* Holt, Rinehart and Winston, New York.

Klineberg, O., 1935, *Negro Intelligence and Selective Migration.* Columbia U.P., New York.

Kluckhohn, C., 1960, "A Navajo Politician," in J. B. Casagrande (ed.), *In the Company of Man.* Harper & Row, New York, pp. 440–465.

Kortland, A., 1962, "Chimpanzees in the Wild," *Scientific American,* **206,** 128–134.

Kranz, G., 1968, "Brain Size and Hunting Ability in Earliest Man," *Current Anthropology,* **9,** 450–451.

Kroeber, A. L., 1917, "The Superorganic," *American Anthropologist,* **19,** 163–213.

———, **1948,** *Anthropology.* Harcourt Brace Jovanovich, New York.

———, **1952,** *The Nature of Culture.* U. of Chicago, Chicago.

———, **and C. Kluckhohn, 1952,** *Culture: A Critical View of Concepts and Definitions.* Anthropological Papers, Peabody Museum No. 47.

Krutz, G., 1973, "Compartmentalization as a Factor in Urban Adjustment: The Kiowa Case," in J. Waddell and O. M. Watson, eds., *American Indian Urbanization.* Purdue Research Foundation, West Lafayette, Ind., pp. 101–116.

Kummer, H., 1971, *Primate Societies: Group Techniques on Ecological Adaptation.* Aldine, Chicago.

L

Labov, W., 1969, "The Logic of Non-Standard English," in F. Williams (ed.), *Language and Poverty*. Georgetown Monograph Series in Languages and Linguistics, pp. 153–189.

———, **1972,** "On the Mechanism of Linguistic Change," in J. J. Gumperz and D. Hymes (eds.), *Directions in Sociolinguistics*. Holt, Rinehart and Winston, New York, pp. 512–537.

Lambert, W. W., et. al., 1959, "Some Correlates of Beliefs in the Malevolence and Benevolence of Supernatural Beings: A Cross-Societal Study," *Journal of Abnormal and Social Psychology*, **58,** 162–169.

Landes, R., 1937, "The Ojibwa of Canada," in M. Mead (ed.), *Cooperation and Competition Among Primitive Peoples*. McGraw-Hill, New York, pp. 87–126.

———, **1968,** *Ojibwa Religion and the Midewiwin*. U. of Wisconsin, Madison.

Lanning, E. P., 1967, *Peru Before the Incas*. Prentice-Hall, Englewood Cliffs.

Larson, L., 1973, "Archaeological Indications of Social Stratification at the Etowah Site, Georgia," in E. L. Green (ed.), *In Search of Man: Readings in Archaeology*. Little, Brown, Boston, pp. 269–282.

Laughlin, W. S., 1968, "Hunting: An Integrative Biobehavior System and Its Evolutionary Importance," in R. B. Lee and I. DeVore (eds.), *Man the Hunter*. Aldine, Chicago, pp. 304–320.

Lave, L., and E. Seskin, 1970, "Air Pollution and Human Health," *Science*, **169,** 723–733.

Leacock, E., 1971, *The Culture of Poverty: A Critique*. Simon and Schuster, New York.

Leakey, L. S. B., 1961, "A New Lower Pliocene Fossil Primate from Kenya," *Annals of the Magazine of Natural History*, **14,** 689–696.

Leakey, M. D., 1966, "A Review of the Oldowan Culture from Olduvai Gorge, Tanzania," *Nature*, 462–466.

Leakey, R. E., 1969, "Early *Homo sapiens* Remains from the Omo River Region of Southwest Ethiopia," *Nature*, **222,** 1132–1138.

———, **et. al., 1970,** "New Hominid Remains and Early Artifacts from Northern Kenya," *Nature*, **226,** 223–230.

Lebeuf, A., 1971, "The Role of Women in the Political Organization of African Societies," in D. Paulme (ed.), *Women of Tropical Africa*, U. of California, Berkeley and Los Angeles, pp. 93–119.

Lee, R. B., 1966, "!Kung Bushman Subsistence: An Input-Output Analysis," in A. P. Vayda (ed.), 1969, *Environment and Cultural Behavior: Ecological Studies in Cultural Anthropology*. Natural History, New York, pp. 47–79.

———, **1968,** "What Hunters Do for a Living, or, How to Make Out on Scarce Resources," in R. B. Lee and I. DeVore (eds.), *Man the Hunter*. Aldine, Chicago, pp. 30–48.

———, **1972,** "The Intensification of Social Life Among the !Kung Bushmen," in B. Spooner (ed.), *Population Growth: Anthropological Implications*. MIT, Cambridge, pp. 343–350.

———, **1972,** "Population Growth and the Beginnings of Sedentary Life Among the !Kung Bushmen," in B. Spooner (ed.), *Population Growth: Anthropological Implications*. MIT, Cambridge, pp. 329–342.

———, **and I. DeVore (eds.), 1968,** *Man the Hunter*. Aldine, Chicago.

Leeds, A., and A. P. Vayda (eds.), 1965, *Man, Culture, and Animals: The Role of Animals in Human Ecological Adjustments*. Publication No. 78 of the American Association for the Advancement of Science, Washington, D.C.

Lenneberg, E. H., 1967, *Biological Foundations of Language*. Wiley, New York.

Leslie, C. (ed.), 1960, *Anthropology of Folk Religion*. Vintage, New York.

Lessa, W. A., 1966, *Ulithi: A Micronesian Design for Living*. Holt, Rinehart and Winston, New York.

———, **and E. Z. Vogt (eds.), 1958,** *Reader in Comparative Religion*. Row, Peterson, Evanston.

Lévi-Strauss, C., 1963, *Structural Anthropology*. Basic Books, New York.

LeVine, R., and D. Campbell, 1971, *Ethnocentrism: Theories of Conflict, Ethnic Attitudes, and Group Behavior*. Wiley, New York.

———, **and B. LeVine, 1963,** "Nyansongo: A Gusii Community in Kenya," in B. B. Whiting (ed.), *Six Cultures: Studies of Child Rearing*. Wiley, New York, pp. 15–202.

Lewis, O., 1951, *Life in a Mexican Village: Tepoztlán Restudied*. Illinois U.P., Urbana.

———, **1960,** *Tepoztlán: Village in Mexico*. Holt, Rinehart and Winston, New York.

———, **1966,** *La Vida: A Puerto Rican Family in the Culture of Poverty—San Juan and New York*. Random House, New York.

———, **1970,** *Anthropological Essays*. Random House, New York.

Lieberman, P. H., et al., 1969, "Vocal Tract Limitations on the Vowel Repertoires of Rhesus Monkeys and Other Non-human Primates," *Science*, **164,** 1185–1187.

———, **1973,** "On the Evolution of Language: A Unified View," *International Journal of Cognitive Psychology*, **2,** 59–94.

Liebow, E., 1967, *Tally's Corner: A Study of Negro Street-Corner Men*. Little, Brown, Boston.

566

Little, K., 1965, *West African Urbanization: A Study of Voluntary Associations in Social Change.* Cambridge U.P., Cambridge.

Lomax, A., 1968, *Folk Song Style and Culture.* American Association for the Advancement of Science, Washington, D.C.

Lorenz, K., 1963, *On Aggression.* Harcourt Brace Jovanovich, New York.

Loudon, J. B., 1960, "Psychogenic Disorder and Social Conflict Among the Zulu," in M. K. Opler (ed.), *Culture and Mental Health.* Macmillan, Inc., New York, pp. 351–369.

Lowie, R. H., 1924, *Primitive Religion.* Liveright, New York.

——— , **1935,** *The Crow Indians.* Rinehart, New York.

——— , **1954,** *Indians of the Plains.* Natural History, Garden City.

——— , **1961,** *Primitive Society.* Harper & Row, New York.

Lyashchenko, P. I., 1949, *History of the National Economy of Russia to the 1917 Revolution.* Macmillan, Inc., New York.

M

MacNeish, R., 1964, "Ancient Mesoamerican Civilization," *Science,* **143,** 531–537.

——— , **1964,** "The Origin of New World Civilization," *Scientific American,* **211,** 29–37.

Malinowski, B., 1931, "Culture," *Encyclopaedia of the Social Sciences,* **2,** 621–646. Macmillan, Inc., New York.

——— , **1954,** *Magic, Science, and Religion and Other Essays.* Doubleday, Garden City.

——— , **1961,** *Argonauts of the Western Pacific: An Account of Native Enterprise and Adventure in the Archipelagoes of Melanesian New Guinea.* Dutton, New York.

Mangelsdorf, P. C, et. al., 1964, "Domestication of Corn," *Science,* **143,** 538–545.

Marshall, G., 1970, "In a World of Women: Field Work in a Yoruba Community," in P. Golde (ed.), *Women in the Field: Anthropological Experiences.* Aldine, Chicago, pp. 167–191.

Marshall, L., 1965, "The !Kung Bushmen of the Kalahari Desert," in J. L. Gibbs (ed.), *Peoples of Africa.* Holt, Rinehart and Winston, New York, pp. 241–278.

Martin, P., and H. E. Wright (eds.), 1967, *Pleistocene Extinctions: The Search for a Cause.* Yale U.P., New Haven.

Marx, K., and F. Engels, 1888, *Communist Manifesto.* Reeves, London.

Mead, M., 1935, *Sex and Temperament in Three Primitive Societies.* Norton, New York.

——— , **1949,** *Male and Female: A Study of the Sexes in the Changing World.* Morrow, New York.

——— , **1956,** *New Lives for Old: Cultural Transformation—Manus 1928–1953.* Morrow, New York.

——— , **and R. Bunzel (eds.), 1960,** *The Golden Age of American Anthropology.* Braziller, New York.

Meadows, D. H., et. al., 1972, *The Limits to Growth.* New American Library, New York.

Meek, C. K., 1946, in M. H. Fried, 1967, *Evolution of Political Society: An Essay in Political Anthropology.* Random House, New York, pp. 201–202.

Meggitt, M. J., 1962, *Desert People.* U. of Chicago, Chicago.

Meighan, C. W., 1966, *Archaeology: An Introduction.* Chandler, San Francisco.

Meillassoux, C., 1968, *Urbanization of an African Community.* U. of Washington, Seattle.

Mellaart, J., 1964, "A Neolithic City in Turkey," *Scientific American,* **210,** 94–105.

——— , **1965,** *Earliest Civilization of the Near East.* McGraw-Hill, New York.

Middleton, J., 1960, *Lugbara Religion.* Oxford U.P., London.

——— , **1965,** *The Lugbara of Uganda.* Holt, Rinehart and Winston, New York.

——— , **1970,** *The Study of the Lugbara: Expectation and Paradox in Anthropological Research.* Holt, Rinehart and Winston, New York.

——— , **(ed.), 1970,** *From Child to Adult: Studies in the Anthropology of Education.* Natural History, Garden City.

Millon, R., 1970, "Teotihuacán: Completion of Map of Giant Ancient City in the Valley of Mexico," *Science,* **170,** 1077–1082.

Minturn, L., and J. T. Hitchcock, 1966, *The Rajputs of Khalapur, India.* Wiley, New York.

——— , **and W. W. Lambert, 1964,** *Mothers of Six Cultures: Antecedents of Child Rearing.* Wiley, New York.

Miracle, M., 1965, "The Copperbelt—Trading and Marketing," in P. Bohannan and G. Dalton (eds.), *Markets in Africa.* Doubleday, Garden City, pp. 285–332.

Monboddo, J. B., 1773, in J. S. Slotkin (ed.), 1965, *Readings in Early Anthropology.* Aldine, Chicago, pp. 206–208.

Money, J., and A. A. Ehrhardt, 1972, *Man and Woman, Boy and Girl.* Johns Hopkins U.P., Baltimore.

Montagu, M. F. A. (ed.), 1964, *The Concept of Race.* Free Press, New York.

——— , **(ed.), 1968,** *Man and Aggression.* Oxford U.P., New York.

Moore, S. F., 1963, "Oblique and Asymmetrical

Cross-Cousin Marriage and Crow-Omaha Terminology," *American Anthropologist*, **65**, 296–311.

Morgan, L. H., 1877, *Ancient Society*. Holt, Rinehart and Winston, New York.

Murdock, G. P., 1949, *Social Structure*. Macmillan, Inc., New York.

———, **1957,** "World Ethnographic Sample," *American Anthropologist*, **59**, 664–687.

———, **1967,** *Ethnographic Atlas*. U. of Pittsburgh, Pittsburgh.

———, **1968,** "The Current Status of the World's Hunting and Gathering Peoples," in R. B. Lee and I. DeVore (eds.), *Man the Hunter*. Aldine, Chicago, pp. 13–20.

Murphy, R. F., and J. H. Steward, 1956, "Tappers and Trappers: Parallel Process in Acculturation," *Economic Development and Cultural Change*, **4**, 335–355.

N

Nadel, S. F., 1940, "The Kede: A Riverian State in Northern Nigeria," in E. E. Evans-Pritchard and M. Fortes (eds.), *African Political Systems*. Oxford U.P., London, pp. 165–195.

———, **1952,** "Witchcraft in Four African Societies: An Essay in Comparison," *American Anthropologist*, **54**, 18–29.

Naroll, R., 1962, *Data Quality Control—A New Research Technique*. Free Press, New York.

———, **and R. Cohen (eds.), 1970,** *A Handbook of Method in Cultural Anthropology*. Natural History, Garden City.

Nelson, R. K., 1969, *Hunters of the Northern Ice*. U. of Chicago, Chicago.

Newman, P. L., 1964, "'Wild Man' Behavior in a New Guinea Highlands Community," *American Anthropologist*, **66**, 1–19.

———, **1964,** "Religious Belief and Ritual in a New Guinea Society," *American Anthropologist*, **66**, 257–272.

———, **1965,** *Knowing the Gururumba*. Holt, Rinehart and Winston, New York.

Nickul, K., 1948, *The Skolt Lapp Community Suenjelsyd During the Year 1938*. Hugo Gebers Forlag, Stockholm.

Nietschmann, B., 1972, "Hunting and Fishing Focus Among the Miskito Indians, Eastern Nicaragua," *Human Ecology*, **1**, 41–67.

———, **1973,** *Between Land and Water*. Seminar, New York.

Nordhoff, C., 1875, *The Communistic Societies of the United States*. Harper & Row, New York.

North, R., 1965, in E. Wolf, 1969, *Peasant Wars of the Twentieth Century*. Harper & Row, New York, pp. 150–151.

O

Otterbein, K. F., 1970, *The Evolution of a War: A Cross-Cultural Study*. HRAF, New Haven.

P

Paredes, A. J., 1974, "The Emergence of Contemporary Eastern Creek Indian Identity," in T. K. Fitzgerald (ed.), *Social and Cultural Identity*. U. of Georgia, Athens, pp. 63–80.

Parker, S., 1962, "The Wiitiko Psychosis in the Context of Ojibwa Personality and Culture," *American Anthropologist*, **62**, 620.

———, **and R. Kleiner, 1966,** *Mental Illness in the Urban Negro Community*. Free Press, New York.

Paul, B. D., 1969, *Health, Culture, and Community: Case Studies of Public Reactions to Health Programs*. Russell Sage Foundation, New York.

Paulme, D. (ed.), 1971, *Women of Tropical Africa*. U. of California, Berkeley and Los Angeles.

Paulson, R. E., 1973, *Women's Suffrage and Prohibition: A Comparative Study of Equality and Social Control*. Scott, Foresman, Glenview.

Pearson, K., 1972, in J. Hunt (ed.), *Human Intelligence*. Dutton, New York, cited by J. Hirsch, p. 12.

Pelto, P. J., 1962, *Individualism in Skolt Lapp Society*. Kansatieteellinen Arkisto Monograph 16, Helsinki.

———, **1970,** *Anthropological Research: The Structure of Inquiry*. Harper & Row, New York.

———, **1973,** *The Snowmobile Revolution: Technology and Social Change in the Arctic*. Cummings, Menlo Park.

Pettigrew, T. F., 1964, *A Profile of the Negro American*. Van Nostrand, New York.

Pfeiffer, J. E., 1969, *The Emergence of Man*. Harper & Row, New York.

Piddock, S., 1965, "The Potlatch System of the Southern Kwakiutl: A New Perspective," *Southwestern Journal of Anthropology*, **21**, 244–264.

Pilbeam, D., 1972, *The Ascent of Man*. Macmillan, Inc., New York.

Plato, 1968 (new ed.), *The Republic*. Basic Books, New York.

Pospisil, L., 1958, *Kapauku Papuans and Their Law*. Yale U. Publications in Anthropology, No. 54.

———, **1963,** *The Kapauku Papuans*. Holt, Rinehart and Winston, New York.

Powdermaker, H., 1966, *Stranger and Friend: The Way of an Anthropologist*. Norton, New York.

R

Radin, P., 1927, *Primitive Man as Philosopher*. Appleton-Century-Crofts, New York.

———, **1956,** *The Trickster: A Study in American Indian Mythology*. Bell, New York.

568

Rappaport, R. A., 1967, "Ritual Regulation of Environmental Relations Among a New Guinea People," *Ethnology,* **6,** 17–30.

————, **1968,** *Pigs for the Ancestors: Ritual in the Ecology of a New Guinea People.* Yale U.P., New Haven.

Read, K., 1965, *The High Valley.* Scribner, New York.

Redfield, R., 1942, *The Folk Culture of Yucatan.* U. of Chicago, Chicago.

————, **1960,** *The Little Community and Peasant Society and Culture.* U. of Chicago, Chicago.

Reiner, P., and B. Reiner, 1973, "Earliest Radiocarbon Dates for Domesticated Animals," *Science,* **179,** 235–239.

Reynolds, V., 1967, *The Apes.* Dutton, New York.

————, **and F. Reynolds, 1965,** "The Chimpanzees of the Budongo Forest," in I. DeVore (ed.), *Primate Behavior: Field Studies of Monkeys and Apes.* Holt, Rinehart and Winston, New York, pp. 368–424.

Ribeiro, D., 1968, *The Civilizational Process.* Smithsonian Institute Press, Washington, D.C.

Robbins, M. C., 1966, "House Types and Settlement Patterns: An Application of Ethnology to Archaeological Interpretation," *Minnesota Archaeologist,* **28,** 1–25.

————, **P. J. Pelto, and B. R. DeWalt, 1972,** "Climate and Behavior: A Biocultural Study," *Journal of Cross-Cultural Psychology,* **3,** 331–344.

Roberts, J. M., 1965, "Oaths, Autonomic Ordeals, and Power," in L. Nader (ed.), *The Ethnography of Law.* American Anthropologist Special Publication **67,** no. 6, part 2, 186–212.

————, **M. J. Arth, and R. R. Bush, 1959,** "Games in Culture," *American Anthropologist,* **61,** 597–605.

————, **and B. Sutton-Smith, 1962,** "Child Training and Game Involvement," *Ethnology,* **1,** 166–185.

Rohner, R. P., 1970, "Parental Rejection, Food Deprivation, and Personality Development: Tests of Alternative Hypotheses," *Ethnology,* **9,** 414–427.

Rohrl, V. J., 1970, "A Nutritional Factor in Windigo Psychosis," *American Anthropologist,* **72,** 97–101.

Rosner, M., 1967, "Women in the Kibbutz," *Asian and African Studies,* **3,** 35–68.

Rowe, W., 1973, "Caste, Kinship, and Association in Urban India," in A. W. Southall, *Urban Anthropology: Cross-Cultural Studies of Urbanization.* Oxford U.P., New York, pp. 211–249.

S

Sahlins, M., 1957, "Land Use and the Extended Family in Moala, Fiji," *American Anthropologist,* **59,** 449–462.

————, **1958,** *Social Stratification in Polynesia.* U. of Washington, Seattle.

————, **and E. R. Service (eds.), 1960,** *Evolution and Culture.* U. of Michigan, Ann Arbor.

St. Paul Pioneer Press: "Heat Explodes Hate," August 16, 1965.

Samarin, W. J., 1967, *Field Linguistics: A Guide to Linguistic Field Work.* Holt, Rinehart and Winston, New York.

Sanday, P., 1968, "The 'Psychological Reality' of American-English Kinship Terms: An Information-Processing Approach," *American Anthropologist,* **70,** 508–523.

Sanders, W. T., 1972, "Population, Agricultural History, and Societal Evolution in Mesoamerica," in B. Spooner (ed.), *Population Growth: Anthropological Implications.* MIT, Cambridge, pp. 101–153.

————, **and B. J. Price, 1968,** *Mesoamerica: The Evolution of a Civilization.* Random House, New York.

Santayana, G., 1896, *The Sense of Beauty.* Scribner, New York.

Sapir, E., 1924, "Culture, Genuine and Spurious," *American Journal of Sociology,* **29,** 401–429.

Sargent, F., 1963, "Tropical Neurasthenia: Giant or Windmill?" *Environmental Physiology and Psychology in Arid Conditions.* UNESCO, Paris.

Sauer, C., 1969, *Seeds, Spades, Hearths, and Herds* (2nd ed.). MIT, Cambridge.

Schaller, G. B., 1964, *The Year of the Gorilla.* U. of Chicago, Chicago.

————, **1965,** "The Behavior of the Mountain Gorilla," in I. DeVore (ed.), *Primate Behavior.* Holt, Rinehart and Winston, New York, 324–367.

Schensul, S. L., 1969, *Marginal Rural Peoples: Behavior and Cognitive Models Among Northern Minnesotans and Western Ugandans.* Unpublished Ph.D. dissertation, U. of Minnesota, Minneapolis.

Schlegel, A., 1972, *Male Dominance and Female Autonomy.* HRAF, New Haven.

Schneider, D. M., and E. K. Gough (eds.), 1961, *Matrilineal Kinship.* U. of California, Berkeley and Los Angeles.

Schwab, W., 1970, "Comparative Field Techniques in Urban Research in Africa," in M. Freilich (ed.), *Marginal Natives: Anthropologists at Work.* Harper & Row, New York, pp. 73–121.

Scrimshaw, N., and C. Tejada, 1970, "Pathology of Living Indians as Seen in Guatemala," in T. D. Stewart (ed.), *Handbook of Middle American Indians,* Vol. 9. U. of Texas Press, Austin, pp. 257–289.

Scudder, T., and E. F. Colson, 1972, "The Kariba Dam Project: Resettlement and Local Initiative," in H. R. Bernard and P. J. Pelto (eds.), *Technology and Social Change.* Macmillan, Inc., New York, pp. 39–70.

Service, E. R., 1962, *Primitive Social Organization:*

569

An Evolutionary Perspective. Random House, New York.

Sherwood, J. J., and M. Nataupsky, 1968, "Predicting the Conclusions of Negro-White Intelligence Research from Biographical Characteristics of the Investigator," *Journal of Personality and Social Psychology,* **8,** part 1, 53–58.

Shryock, R. H., 1960, *Medicine and Society in America, 1660–1860.* Cornell U.P., Ithaca.

Sigerist, H. E., 1943, *Civilization and Disease.* U. of Chicago, Chicago.

Simič, A., 1973, *The Peasant Urbanites: A Study of Rural-Urban Mobility in Serbia.* Seminar, New York.

Simmons, L. W., 1942, *Sun Chief.* Yale U.P., New Haven.

Simons, E., 1972, *Primate Evolution: An Introduction to Man's Place in Nature.* Macmillan, Inc., New York.

Slotkin, J. S. (ed.), 1965, *Readings in Early Anthropology.* Aldine, Chicago.

Smith, P., 1930, *A History of Modern Culture.* Holt, Rinehart and Winston, New York.

Solecki, R. S., "Prehistory in Shanidar Valley, Northern Iraq," *Science,* **139,** 179–193.

Soustelle, J., 1970, *Daily Life of the Aztecs.* Stanford U.P., Stanford.

Southwick, C. H. (ed.), 1963, *Primate Social Behavior: An Enduring Problem—Selected Readings.* Princeton U.P., Princeton.

Spencer, B., and F. J. Gillen, 1927, *The Arunta: A Study of a Stone Age People.* Macmillan, Inc., New York.

Spencer, P., 1965, *The Samburu: A Study of Gerontocracy in a Nomadic Tribe.* U. of California, Berkeley and Los Angeles.

Sperry, R. W., 1972, "Mental Unity Following Surgical Disconnections of the Cerebral Hemispheres," in S. L. Washburn and P. Dolhinow (eds.), *Perspectives on Human Evolution.* Holt, Rinehart and Winston, New York, pp. 395–420.

Spindler, G. D. (ed.), 1970, *Being an Anthropologist: Fieldwork in Eleven Cultures.* Holt, Rinehart and Winston, New York.

———, **and L. Spindler, 1958,** 'ale and Female Adaptations in Culture Change," *American Anthropologist,* **60,** 217–233.

Spiro, M., 1956, *Kibbutz: Venture in Utopia.* Harvard U.P., Cambridge.

———, **1958,** *Children of the Kibbutz.* Harvard U.P., Cambridge.

———, **and R. G. D'Andrade, 1958,** "A Cross-Cultural Study of Some Supernatural Beliefs," *American Anthropologist,* **60,** 456–466.

Spooner, B. (ed.), 1972, *Population Growth: An-thropological Implications.* MIT, Cambridge.

Spuhler, J. N. (ed.), 1959, *The Evolution of Man's Capacity for Culture.* Wayne State U.P., Detroit.

Stands-in-Timber, J., and M. Liberty, 1967, *Cheyenne Memories.* Yale U.P., New Haven.

Stephens, W. N., 1963, *The Family in Cross-Cultural Perspective.* Holt, Rinehart and Winston, New York.

Steward, J. H., 1936, "The Economic and Social Basis of Primitive Bands," in R. Lowie (ed.), *Essays in Anthropology Presented to A. L. Kroeber.* U. of California, Berkeley, pp. 331–350.

———, **1938,** *Basin-Plateau Aboriginal Socio-Political Groups.* Bureau of American Ethnology, Bulletin 120.

———, **1955,** *Theory of Culture Change: The Methodology of Multilinear Evolution.* U. of Illinois, Urbana.

———, **1968,** "Causal Factors and Processes in the Evolution of Pre-Farming Societies," in R. B. Lee and I. DeVore (eds.), *Man the Hunter,* Aldine, Chicago, pp. 321–334.

Stocking, G. W., 1968, *Race, Culture, and Evolution: Essays in the History of Anthropology.* Free Press, New York.

Suttles, G., 1968, *The Social Order of the Slum: Ethnicity and Territory in the Inner City.* U. of Chicago, Chicago.

Suttles, W., 1968, "Coping with Abundance: Subsistence on the Northwest Coast," in R. B. Lee and I. DeVore (eds.), *Man the Hunter.* Aldine, Chicago, pp. 56–68.

T

Talmon, Y., 1965, *Family and Community in the Kibbutz.* Harvard U.P., Cambridge.

Tax, S., 1955, "From Lafitau to Radcliffe-Brown: A Short History of the Study of Social Organization," in F. Eggan (ed.), *Social Anthropology of North American Tribes* (2nd ed.), U. of Chicago, Chicago, pp. 445–481.

Teleki, G., 1973, *The Predatory Behavior of Wild Chimpanzees.* Bucknell, Lewisburg.

Tertullian, ca. 200 A.D., in G. Hardin (ed.), 1969, *Population, Evolution, and Birth Control: A Collage of Controversial Ideas.* W. H. Freeman, San Francisco, p. 18.

Thomas, E. M., 1959, *The Harmless People.* Knopf, New York.

Tiger, L., 1969, *Men in Groups.* Random House, New York.

Titiev, M., 1958, "The Religion of the Hopi Indians," in W. A. Lessa and E. Z. Vogt (eds.), *Reader in Comparative Religion.* Row, Peterson, Evanston, pp. 532–539.

570

References Cited

Townsend, P., 1971, "New Guinea Sago Gatherers," *Ecology of Food and Nutrition*, November 1971, 19–24.

Tuden, A., and L. Plotnicov (eds.), 1970, *Social Stratification in Africa.* Free Press, New York.

Turgot, A., 1750, in J. S. Slotkin (ed.), 1965, *Readings in Early Anthropology*, Aldine, Chicago, pp. 358–363.

Turnbull, C., 1962, *The Forest People.* Doubleday, Garden City.

————, **1965,** *The Mbuti Pygmies: An Ethnographic Survey.* Anthropological Papers of the American Museum of Natural History, **50,** part 3. New York.

————, **1968,** "The Importance of Flux in Two Hunting Societies," in R. B. Lee and I. DeVore (eds.), *Man the Hunter.* Aldine, Chicago, pp. 132–137.

Tylor, E. B., 1891, *Primitive Culture: Researches into the Development of Mythology, Philosophy, Religion, Language, Art, and Custom* (2 vols.). John Murray, London.

U

Ullman, S., 1966, "Semantic Universals," in J. Greenberg (ed.), *Universals of Language.* MIT, Cambridge, pp. 217–262.

United Press International Wire Service Bulletin, New Guinea, 1970.

V

Vaillant, G. C., 1962, *Aztecs of Mexico: Origin, Rise and Fall of the Aztec Nation.* Pelican, New York.

Valentine, C. A., 1961, *Masks and Men in a Melanesian Society.* U. of Kansas, Lawrence.

————, **et. al., 1969,** "Culture and Poverty: Critique and Counter-Proposals," *Current Anthropology*, **10,** 181–201.

Van Gennep, A., 1960, *The Rites of Passage.* U. of Chicago, Chicago.

Vayda, A. P., 1968, "Hypotheses About the Function of War," in M. Fried, et. al. (eds.), *War: The Anthropology of Armed Conflict and Aggression.* Natural History, New York, pp. 85–91.

W

Walker, M., 1963, *The Nature of Scientific Thought.* Prentice-Hall, Englewood Cliffs.

Wallace, A. F. C., 1956, "Revitalization Movements," *American Anthropologist*, **58,** 264–281.

————, **1961,** "Mental Illness, Biology and Culture," in F. Hsu (ed.), *Psychological Anthropology.* Dorsey, Homewood, pp. 255–295.

————, **1961,** *Culture and Personality.* Random House, New York.

————, **1966,** *Religion: An Anthropological View.* Random House, New York.

Wallis, W., 1943, *Messiahs: Their Role in Civilization.* American Council on Public Affairs, Washington, D.C.

Warner, W. L., M. Meeker, and K. Eells, 1960, *Social Class in America.* Harper & Row, New York.

Washburn, S. L., and V. Avis, 1958, "Evolution of Human Behavior," in A. Roe and G. G. Simpson (eds.), *Behavior and Evolution.* Yale U.P., New Haven, pp. 421–436.

————, **1960,** "Tools and Human Behavior," *Scientific American*, **203,** 62–75.

————, **(ed.), 1961,** *Social Life of Early Man.* Viking Fund Publications in Anthropology, No. 31.

Washington Post, May 25, 1973 (article on Taconite tailing pollution in Lake Superior.)

Watson, J. D., 1968, *The Double Helix.* New American Library, New York.

Weidman, H., 1973, "Implications of the Culture-Broker Concept for the Delivery of Health Care," Paper presented at the Annual Meeting of the Southern Anthropological Society, Wrightsville Beach, N.C.

Wells, C., 1964, *Bones, Bodies, and Disease.* Praeger, New York.

White, A. D., 1955, *A History of the Warfare of Science with Theology in Christendom.* Braziller, New York (first published 1895).

White, B., 1971, "Demand for Labor and Population Growth in Colonial Java," in *Human Ecology*, **1,** 217–236.

White, L. A., 1943, "Energy and the Evolution of a Culture," *American Anthropologist*, **45,** 335–356.

————, **1959,** *The Evolution of Culture.* McGraw-Hill, New York.

Whiting, B. B. (ed.), 1963, *Six Cultures: Studies of Child Rearing.* Wiley, New York.

Whiting, J. W. M., 1969, "Effects of Climate on Certain Cultural Practices," in W. H. Goodenough (ed.), *Explorations in Cultural Anthropology.* McGraw-Hill, New York, pp. 511–544.

————, **and I. L. Child, 1953,** *Child Training and Personality: A Cross-Cultural Study.* Yale U.P., New Haven.

Whitten, N. E., 1970, in M. Freilich (ed.), *Marginal Natives: Anthropologists at Work.* Harper & Row, New York, pp. 339–402.

————, **and J. F. Szwed (eds.), 1970,** *Afro-American Anthropology: Contemporary Perspectives.* Free Press, New York.

Whorf, B., 1941, "The Relation of Habitual Thought and Behavior to Language," in L. Spier, et. al. (eds.), *Language, Culture, and Personality.* Sapir Memorial

571

Publication Fund, Menasha, Wisconsin, pp. 75–93.

Wissler, C., 1960, "The Social Life of the Blackfoot Indians," in M. Mead and R. Bunzel (eds.), *The Golden Age of American Anthropology,* Braziller, New York, pp. 344–361.

Wittfogel, K., 1957, *Oriental Despotism: A Comparative Study of Total Power.* Yale U.P., New Haven.

Wolf, E. R., 1966, *Peasants.* Prentice-Hall, Englewood Cliffs.

———, **1969,** *Peasant Wars of the Twentieth Century.* Harper & Row, New York.

Wollstonecraft, M., 1792 (reprinted 1967), *A Vindication of the Rights of Women.* Norton, New York, p. 39.

Woodburn, J., 1968, "An Introduction to Hadza Ecology," in R. B. Lee and I. DeVore (eds.), *Man the Hunter.* Aldine, Chicago, pp. 49–55.

Woods, C., and T. Graves, 1973, *The Process of Medical Change in a Highlands Guatemalan Town.* U. of California, Los Angeles.

Worsley, P., 1968, *The Trumpet Shall Sound: A Study of 'Cargo' Cults in Melanesia.* Schocken, New York.

Wright, G. A., 1971, "Origins of Food Production in Southwestern Asia: A Survey of Ideas," *Current Anthropology,* **12,** 447–477.

Y

Yang, M. C., 1945, *A Chinese Village: Taitou, Shantung Province.* Columbia U.P., New York.

Yengoyan, A., 1970, in M. Freilich (ed.), *Marginal Natives: Anthropologists at Work.* Harper & Row, New York, pp. 403–439.

Young, L. B. (ed.), 1968, *Population in Perspective.* Oxford U.P., New York.

Z

Zeuner, F. E., 1963, *A History of Domesticated Animals.* Harper & Row, New York.

Zinsser, H., 1967, *Rats, Lice and History.* Bantam, New York.

572

References Cited

573

579